TRUTH IS TRICKIEST

The Case for Ambiguity in the Exeter Book Riddles

Truth Is Trickiest

*The Case for Ambiguity
in the Exeter Book Riddles*

JENNIFER NEVILLE

UNIVERSITY OF TORONTO PRESS
Toronto Buffalo London

© University of Toronto Press 2024
Toronto Buffalo London
utorontopress.com

ISBN 978-1-4875-5252-7 (cloth)   ISBN 978-1-4875-5255-8 (EPUB)
                                    ISBN 978-1-4875-5257-2 (PDF)

Library and Archives Canada Cataloguing in Publication

Title: Truth is trickiest : the case for ambiguity in the Exeter Book riddles / Jennifer Neville.
Names: Neville, Jennifer, 1968– author.
Description: Includes bibliographical references and index.
Identifiers: Canadiana (print) 20240316908 | Canadiana (ebook) 20240316932 | ISBN 9781487552527 (cloth) | ISBN 9781487552572 (PDF) | ISBN 9781487552558 (EPUB)
Subjects: LCSH: Exeter book. | LCSH: Riddles, English (Old) – History and criticism. | LCSH: English poetry – Old English, ca. 450–1100 – History and criticism. | LCSH: Riddles, Latin – England – History and criticism. | LCSH: Riddles, English (Old) – Themes, motives. | LCSH: Riddles in literature.
Classification: LCC PR1764 .N48 2024 | DDC 829/.1009 – dc23

Cover design: Val Cooke
Cover images: (front) William of Normandy at an open-air feast with his nobles and his half-brother Bishop Odo of Bayeux who is saying grace. Bayeux Tapestry. Art Collection 3 / Alamy Stock Photo; (background) Interior Gallery/Shutterstock.com

We wish to acknowledge the land on which the University of Toronto Press operates. This land is the traditional territory of the Wendat, the Anishnaabeg, the Haudenosaunee, the Métis, and the Mississaugas of the Credit First Nation.

This book has been published with the help of a grant from the Federation for the Humanities and Social Sciences, through the Awards to Scholarly Publications Program, using funds provided by the Social Sciences and Humanities Research Council of Canada.

University of Toronto Press acknowledges the financial support of the Government of Canada, the Canada Council for the Arts, and the Ontario Arts Council, an agency of the Government of Ontario, for its publishing activities.

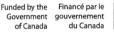

Contents

Preface   vii

Acknowledgments   ix

Abbreviations   xi

Riddle Titles   xiii

1 Introduction: *Soð bið Swicolast* "Truth Is Trickiest"   3
2 The Joy of Limits: The Heroic Idiom as "Code"   23
3 Muddying the Waters: The Heroic Idiom as Camouflage and Disguise   61
4 Dark Tracks through the Heroic Idiom: Aporia, Irony, and Paradox   105
5 Domestic Practices: Manufacturing and Implements   150
6 The Strange Game of Sex: Asexual Reproduction and Gratuitous Sex   188
7 Not Concluding but Continuing   243

Appendix: The Argument over Solutions   253

Bibliography   299

Index of Solutions   351

Index   363

Preface

In Exeter Cathedral there is a manuscript (Exeter, Cathedral Library, MS 3501) that was written in the tenth century by one careful, well-trained scribe. It contains some of the most beloved and well-known poems in Old English, but its rationale, meaning, and purpose are a puzzle. It seems fitting, then, that it should end with a collection of unsolved riddles.

This book sets out to take the Exeter Book riddles as seriously as the scribe of the Exeter Book did. They are not amusing trifles inserted in leftover spaces; they are a collection of texts presented just as carefully as Cynewulf's *Christ II*, the hagiographical *Guthlac A* and *B*, and the more famous elegiac masterpieces, *The Wanderer* and *The Seafarer*. They are extraordinarily demanding. We cannot simply follow their flow of syllables to a given destination. Like other riddles, they require us to inspect, dissect, interpret, reinterpret, and then respond – but unlike other riddles, at the end of that process, they offer no guarantee of resolution, no way to validate any response, other than to start again with another round of inspection, dissection, and interpretation. This absence of solutions, I argue, is not simply an accident of manuscript transmission; rather, it is a defining characteristic of these texts and a key to understanding their place in the Exeter Book. These riddles have clear connections with vernacular traditions of folk riddling, and they undoubtedly arose from the Anglo-Latin tradition of education, but they are not simply jokes, and they are not texts for teaching the young and inexperienced. They call for the skill of an expert, a reader or listener who already understands hagiography, the allegorical techniques of the *Physiologus*, the encyclopedic tradition, poetic themes of exile and heroism, runic encryption, and complex theological issues.

In what follows, I approach the riddles through their use of enigmatic tropes: obscure, often metaphorical, and deceptively familiar ways of presenting their subjects. For example, many of the riddles refer to a *þegn* "servant" and a *hlaford* "lord." An audience familiar with Old English poetry will be aware of the value-laden relationship between a "servant" and a "lord," but an audience familiar with riddles will also be aware of the implement trope: the presentation of a tool and its user as a servant and a lord (or *vice versa*). Yet neither awareness grants an easy, certain solution, for these riddles are deliberately inconsistent in their use of figurative language. As one riddle proclaims, *Soð is æghwylc / þara þe ymb þas wiht wordum becneð* "everything indicated about this creature with words is true," but in every case the seeker after truth must recognize and then doubt what has been recognized, much as the successful cracker of one riddle's runic code must start again when faced with another. Knowing a trope is as dangerous as not knowing it, and so *Soð bið swicolost* "truth is trickiest": a response to a text will not be arrived at quickly, and it may be swept away by another as soon as it has been formulated.

Join in the game ... if you dare.

Acknowledgments

This book has had a very long gestation period, and so its debts run very deep. The seed came from an MA dissertation at the University of Toronto, patiently supervised by David Townsend, more than thirty years ago. A lot of other things happened between then and now. I owe a huge debt of gratitude to colleagues and students of Royal Holloway, University of London, who have heard me muttering about this project for two decades. Peregrine Horden, Robert Hampson, Catherine Nall, Ruth Kennedy, and Doug Cowie have pruned and nourished it, reading drafts and providing invaluable advice; their generosity in reading material so completely outside their own areas of specialization has not only taught me how to communicate but also revived my faith in the academy. Members of the MA in Medieval Studies and the Old English Reading Group strengthened and refined my ideas, often by offering competing views, as have numerous audiences at conferences and seminars.

I am grateful, almost every day, for being a member of the Department of English at Royal Holloway – a place largely unknown to the world, but idyllic in so many ways. In particular, I am grateful that the department generously and graciously provided periods of research leave, without which the book would have died in the ground. I am also grateful for a matching leave grant from the Arts and Humanities Research Council in 2007, which allowed the roots to grow into a strong foundation.

Colleagues from outside Royal Holloway have also been important. Megan Cavell (Birmingham University), Michael Bintley (Birkbeck, University of London), and David Clark (formerly at University of Leicester) have listened, read, and generously given from their own research. Clare Lees (now at the Institute of English Studies), Jane Roberts (emerita at King's College London), and Elaine Treharne (now at Stanford University) have been my heroines, my role models, my supporters, and key movers and shakers – both of my field as a whole and of me personally at crucial moments. *A scæl gelæred smið, swa he gelicost mæg, be bisne wyrcan butan he bet cunne* "an educated smith must always work according to his exemplar as closely as he can, unless he knows how to do better."[1] I do not yet know how to do better. My erstwhile student, Pirkko Koppinen, who has probably taught me more than I have ever taught her, watched me start, stop, forget, remember, restart, and restart this project again. She has been unwavering in her support, and she has saved me from more infelicities than I care to admit. Any philosophical sophistication that might be found here can be traced back to her.

My sister, Kat Kavanagh, was the final midwife, forcing me to bear down and finish the long gestation. I cannot thank her enough for the sacrifice of her time and positivity. The anonymous readers for the University of Toronto Press offered invaluable criticism of the highest quality; my gratitude for their professionalism and generosity is profound.

Finally, I owe an unrepayable debt to my husband, Carlos Pittol, for always saying yes to yet another conference (and yet another book purchase), for always believing that my work was the most important thing at that particular moment, and for believing that this project would, eventually, be finished. Here it is.

---

1 N.R. Ker, "A supplement to *Catalogue of Manuscripts Containing Anglo-Saxon*," ASE 5 (1976): 127.

Abbreviations

ANQ	*American Notes and Queries*
Archiv	*Archiv für das Studium der neueren Sprachen und Literaturen*
ASE	*Anglo-Saxon England*
ASPR	The Anglo-Saxon Poetic Records; see individual volumes edited by George Phillip Krapp and Elliot van Kirk Elliot Dobbie.
BAR	British Archaeological Reports
Bosworth-Toller	Bosworth, Joseph, and T. Northcote Toller. *An Anglo-Saxon Dictionary*. Rev. and enlarged addenda by A. Campbell. 3 vols. 1972; Oxford: Clarendon Press, 1898–1921.
Clark-Hall	Clark Hall, J.R. *A Concise Anglo-Saxon Dictionary*. 4th ed. Supplement by Herbert T. Merritt. Medieval Academy Reprints for Teaching 14. 1894; Toronto: University of Toronto Press, 1960.
DOE	*The Dictionary of Old English: A to H Online*. Ed. Angus Cameron, Ashley Crandell Amos, Antonette diPaolo Healey, et al. Toronto: Dictionary of Old English Project, 2016.
DOE Corpus	*The Dictionary of Old English Corpus on CD-ROM*. Toronto: Pontifical Institute of Mediaeval Studies for the Dictionary of Old English Project, 2009.
EETS	Early English Text Society
ES	*English Studies*
JEGP	*Journal of English and Germanic Philology*
Krapp and Dobbie	Krapp, George Philip, and Elliott Van Kirk Dobbie, eds. *The Exeter Book*. ASPR 3. New York: Columbia University Press, 1936.

LSE	*Leeds Studies in English*
MÆ	*Medium Ævum*
MLN	*Modern Language Notes*
MLR	*Modern Language Review*
MLQ	*Modern Language Quarterly*
MP	*Modern Philology*
N&Q	*Notes & Queries*
Neophil	*Neophilologus*
NIV	*The Holy Bible: New International Version.* London: Hodder and Stoughton, 1973.
NM	*Neuphilologische Mitteilungen*
OED	*Oxford English Dictionary Online.* 3rd ed. Oxford: Oxford University Press, 2013.
Pinsker and Ziegler	Pinsker, Hans, and Waltraud Ziegler, eds and trans. *Die altenglischen Rätsel des Exeterbuchs: Text mit deutscher Übersetzung und Kommentar.* Anglistische Forschungen 183. Heidelberg, Germany: Carl Winter, 1985.
PMLA	*Publications of the Modern Language Association*
PQ	*Philological Quarterly*
RES	*Review of English Studies*
SN	*Studia Neophilologica*
SP	*Studies in Philology*
Vulgate	*Biblia sacra iuxta vulgatam versionem.* 5th ed. Ed. Robert Weber and Roger Gryson. Stuttgart: Deutsche Bibelgesellschaft, 2007.

Riddle Titles

Throughout the discussion that follows, I identify the riddles by titles rather than by their disputed solutions. These titles are derived from quotations from the texts themselves. For convenience of reference, I list the titles that I have adopted here, along with their ASPR numbers and the Old English text from which they are derived, but please see the Introduction for a fuller explanation of my practice.

ASPR Number	Riddle Title	Old English Source
1	Glorious I Thunder	þrymful þunie
2	Under Waves' Pressure	under yþa geþræc
3	No Escape	nah hwyrftweges
1–3 as one riddle	Glorious Servant	þrymful þeow
2–3 as one riddle	Ocean's Bottom	garseces grund
4	Periodically Busy	þragbysig
5	Lone Dweller	anhaga
6	I Burn the Living	cwice bærne
7	Travelling Spirit	ferende gæst
8	Old Evening Poet	eald æfensceop
9	They Gave Me up for Dead	mec deadne ofgeafun
10	Nose in Confinement	neb on nearwe
11	Dark-Stained	hasofag
12	I Travel on Foot	fotum ic fere
13	Ten Brothers and Sisters	x gebroþor ond sweostor
14	Weapon-Warrior	wæpen wiga
15	White Neck	hals hwit
16	Fight against Wave	wiþ wæge winnan
17	Protector	mundbora
18	Large Belly	wide wombe
19	Bright-Headed	heafodbeorht
20	Cursed among Weapons	wæpnum awyrged
21	Downward Nose	neb niþerweard
22	Peace-Horses	fridhengestas
23	Wob	agof

xiv Riddle Titles

ASPR Number	Riddle Title	Old English Source
24	Six Letters	siex stafas
25	Useful to Neighbours	neahbuendum nyt
26	Famous Name	nama mære
27	Binder and Scourger	bindere ond swingere
28	Hardest and Sharpest	heardestan ond scearpestan
29	Air-Vessel	lyftfæt
30a	Flame-Busy A	legbysig
30b	Flame-Busy B	ligbysig
31	Eager to Go	feþegeorn
32	Grind against Grit	grindan wið greote
33	Terrible Laughter	gryrelic hleahtor
34	Feeds Cattle	feoh fedeð
35	Hopeful Garment	hyhtlic gewæd
36	Man Woman Horse	monn wiif hors
36.1–7	Six Heads	siex heafdu
36.8–13	Travel Flood-Ways	for flodwegas
37	Belly Behind	womb on hindan
38	Greedy for Youth-Mirth	geoguðmyrþe grædig
39	Most Wretched of All	earmost ealra
40	Circle of the Earth	ymbhwyrft
40–41 as one riddle	Circle Renewed	ymbhwyft edniwu
41	Mother of Many Races	moddor monigra cynna
42	Two Proud Ones	heanmode twa
43	Guest in the Enclosures	giest in geardum
44	Hanging Head	hangellan heafde
45	Boneless	banleas
46	A Man Sat at Wine	wer sæt æt wine
47	Moth	moðñe
48	Ring without Tongue	hring butan tungan
49	Earth-Fast	eardfæst
50	Bright Warrior	torht wiga
51	Four Creatures	wuhte feower
52	Captives	ræpingas
53	Towering Tree	beam hlifian
54	In a Corner	wincsele
55	Wolf-Head-Tree	wulfheafedtreo
56	Turning Wood	holt hweorfende
57	Abounding in Song	sanges rope
58	One-Footed	anfetu
59	Golden Ring	hring gylden
60	Mouthless by Sand	be sonde muðlease
61	Head Stuck In	heafod sticade
62	Strong Going In/Out	(h)ingonges strong

Riddle Titles xv

ASPR Number	Riddle Title	Old English Source
63	Shining with Gold	glæd mid golde
64	Joy and Ice	wynn ond is
65	I Was Alive	cwico wæs ic
66	Bigger than the Earth	mare þonne middangeard
67	Word-Spell	wordgaldor
68	Creature Went Away	wiht on weg feran
69	Wonder on the Way	wundor on wege
68–9 as one riddle	Water Turned to Bone	wæter wearð to bane
70	Cunningly Made	orþoncum geworht
70a	Sings through Its Sides	singeð þurh sidan
70b	Tall and Beautiful	heah ond hleotorht
71	Clothed in Red	reade bewæfed
72	Boundary-Paths	mearcpaþas
73	Brain-Locker	brægnloca
74	Grey-Haired Queen	feaxhar cwene
75	Swift on a Track	swift on swaþe
75–6 as one riddle	Swift and Sitting	swift ond sittende
76	Woman Sitting Alone	ides sittende ane
76–7 as one riddle	Footless Woman	ides feþeleas
77	Footless	feþeleas
78	Cunning Thing in Waves	orþonc yþum
79	Noble's Possession and Desire	æþelinges æht ond willa
79–80 as one riddle	Noble's Shoulder-Companion	æþelinges eaxlgestealla
80	Warrior's Companion	fyrdrinces gefara
81	Puff-Breasted	byledbreost
82	Swallows Grit	greate swilgeð
83	Old Ancestry	frod fromcynn
84	Mother of Many	modor monigra
85	My Hall Is Not Silent	nis min sele swige
86	Twelve Hundred Heads	xii hund heafda
87	Barked, Wavered	beorcade wancode
88	Brotherless	broþorleas
89	The Creature Had a Belly	se wiht wombe hæfde
90	Wolf	lupus
91	Forged by Hammer	homere geþuren
92	Brown Ones' Boast	brunra beot
93	Younger Brother	gingra broþor
94	Higher than Heaven	hyrre þonne heafon
95	Hide My Track	swaþe mine bemiþe

TRUTH IS TRICKIEST

The Case for Ambiguity in the Exeter Book Riddles

Chapter One

Introduction: *Soð bið Swicolast* "Truth Is Trickiest"[1]

The Exeter Book riddles are strange, non-normative, and disruptive of accepted divisions and orders. They speak the unspeakable, they revel in incongruity and paradox, and they turn the world upside down. Although you might think that you can settle things back into their assigned places and orientations by solving them properly, the truth is that the things that you have found – the solutions – are not resolved. They are not quite what you thought they were. They are not the same things that they were before you solved the riddles. And neither are you.

While all riddles invite us to explore the ways in which we view the world, the Exeter Book riddles add a crucial twist to the genre that has far-reaching consequences. That is, unlike modern riddles and the Anglo-Latin tradition from which they spring, the Exeter Book riddles do not come with solutions. To generations of scholars, that reality has represented an absence to be filled and an error to be corrected, but what if the absence is not an error? In this book I argue that the absence of solutions reveals something important about the nature of the Exeter Book riddles. The continuing stream of proposals for new solutions is not a failure to meet the challenge posed by the Old English collection but rather a clue to their essential nature. What the Exeter Book riddles demand is not final answers but an ongoing, open-ended debate.

Take, for example, this riddle:

Ic sceal þragbysig   þegne minum,
hringum hæfted,   hyran georne,
min bed brecan,   breahtme cyþan

---

[1] I adopt this translation from Richard Marsden, *The Cambridge Old English Reader*, 2nd ed. (Cambridge: Cambridge University Press, 2015), 344. See further discussion below.

4   Truth Is Trickiest

>   þæt me halswriþan   hlaford sealde.
> 5   Oft mec slæpwerigne   secg oðþe meowle
>   gretan eode;   ic him gromheortum
>   winterceald oncweþe. Wearm lim
>   gebundenne bæg   hwilum bersteð;
>   se þeah biþ on þonce   þegne minum,
> 10 medwisum men,   me þæt sylfe,
>   þær wiht wite,   ond wordum min
>   on sped mæge   spel gesecgan. (*Periodically Busy*, R.4)[2]

(Periodically busy, confined in rings, I must eagerly obey my servant, break my bed, and announce loudly that the lord gave me a neck-collar. Often a man or woman went to greet me, sleepy and weary, and I, winter-cold, reply to those grim-hearted ones. Sometimes a warm limb bursts through the bound ring; that, however, is agreeable to my servant, a foolish man, and to myself – if I were to know anything, and could tell my story successfully in words.)

I have previously done my best to solve this riddle, but what is important for this discussion is that "Sun" is not *the* solution but *a* solution, one of more than a dozen valiant attempts provoked by this puzzling text, which include bell, millstone, necromancy, flail, lock, hand mill, pen, phallus, bucket, guard-dog, devil, plough-team, sword, and city gate.[3] The argument will certainly continue, for I have not yet found anyone who admits to being convinced by my solution. The effort to propose and defend future solutions will elicit further research and ingenuity; the text will continue to teach us about early medieval England and about ourselves.

Conversely, take this riddle:

> Wundor wearð on wege: wæter wearð to bane. (*Wonder on the Way*, R.69)

(A wonder happened on the way: water turned to bone.)

For over a hundred years, scholars have solved this short riddle as "ice," with hardly any argument at all. Yet, Adam Roberts, a colleague

---

2   Citations from the riddles are taken from *The Exeter Anthology of OE Poetry: An Edition of Exeter Dean and Chapter MS 3501*, ed. Bernard J. Muir, 2nd rev. ed., 2 vols (Exeter: University of Exeter Press, 2000). All translations are my own unless otherwise specified. For explanation of the riddle-titles, see discussion below.
3   Jennifer Neville, "Sorting Out the Rings: Astronomical Tropes in *Þragbysig* (R.4)," in *Riddles at Work in the Early Medieval Tradition: Words, Ideas, Interactions*, ed. Megan Cavell and Jennifer Neville, Medieval Literature and Culture 32 (Manchester: Manchester University Press, 2020). For the history of previous solutions, see the appendix, "The Argument over Solutions," below.

of mine, recently solved it differently, suggesting that the "wonder" here is not the change of state undergone by water at low temperatures but rather the growth of young bones nourished by the presence of calcium in "water," which metonymically denotes another liquid: milk.[4] Both processes are every-day, taken-for-granted miracles; both solutions provoke prospective riddle-solvers to reconsider aspects of the world that they might otherwise overlook. Of course, people in early medieval England would never have proposed "milk" as a solution since they were unaware of the role of calcium in bone production. On the other hand, people in early medieval England might have proposed other things of which we now, living in very different circumstances, are completely unaware, too. The absence of solutions means that the text remains pregnant with unforeseeable possibilities.

These two cases begin to illustrate what we have gained from the absence of solutions. Accepting this absence as an essential quality of these texts, however, means that we may not have fully understood them. It means that, despite their indisputable connections both to folklore riddles and the Anglo-Latin riddling tradition, the Exeter Book riddles are a different kind of text, with a different purpose. Hints of that purpose can be glimpsed by thinking about the manuscript context in which these riddles have been preserved. While modern readers have struggled to perceive a clear purpose for the contents of the Exeter Book and its ultimate intention remains inscrutable, strong arguments have been advanced against the idea that it is simply a miscellany, a random collection of poems.[5] Neither does it look like a classroom text, for it lacks instructional glosses and annotations.[6] Instead, its contents suggest a wider didactic mission, with its selection of varied genres supporting an intellectual and cultural context often associated with the Benedictine Reform.[7] The Exeter Book looks like a book that rewards a meditative

---

4 *The Riddles of The Hobbit* (Basingstoke: Palgrave Macmillan, 2013), 51–2.
5 For a review of past views and support for the manuscript being thoughtfully and purposefully arranged, see Muir, *Exeter Anthology*, 16–25. See also Eric Weiskott, "The Exeter Book and the Idea of a Poem," *ES* 100 (2019): 599.
6 John D. Niles, *God's Exiles and English Verse: On the Exeter Anthology of Old English Poetry* (Exeter: University of Exeter Press, 2019), 35.
7 Mechthild Gretsch attributes "the immense increase in flexibility and sophistication in the use of the vernacular which occurred between Alfred and Ælfric" to the work of educators like Æthelwold, who trained their students through rigorous exegesis of Aldhelm's hermeneutic style. *The Intellectual Foundations of the English Benedictine Reform* (Cambridge: Cambridge University Press, 1999), 426. See also the discussion of the Exeter Book in the context of the Benedictine reform in Niles, *God's Exiles*, 40–61.

and contemplative style of reading,[8] a book that invites individuals to consider their own integration into Christian faith and their role in society,[9] a book "concerned with the transmission of knowledge,"[10] a book that calls its readers to be "avid decipherer[s] of … verbal and spiritual mysteries."[11] Within that manuscript context, a collection of riddles might be expected to do more than test its readers' memories of riddles that they have heard before. While a collection with solutions might provide "practice in the interpretation of ambiguous texts,"[12] a collection *without* solutions does more. It challenges its readers to engage in "active, evaluative discernment of shifting perspectives" and a deeper level of epistemological questioning.[13] The Exeter Book riddles lead us not only to accept "that the Other occasionally evades one's grasp"[14] but also to embrace a process of interpretation that does not require resolution.

My starting point for this argument and the source for my title come from another Old English poem, *Maxims II*.[15] There, following a series of statements about the superlative coldness of winter, the superlative swiftness of the wind, the superlative loudness of thunder, and the superlative power of Christ, we are told that *Soð bið swicolast* "truth is most treacherous" (10a) – or, in the less alarming translation I have adopted for my title, "trickiest." This statement would be startling in most contexts, but after seemingly inarguable statements about seasons and the essential qualities of the world, this labelling of truth as not merely "deceitful," "false," or "treacherous" but "*most* treacherous" has led many scholars to presume that the scribe made a mistake in copying out this poem.[16] Although other suggestions have been made, the most concise explanation is that the "c" in *swicolast* should have been a "t"; emending that "c" to a "t" results in

---

8   Hugh Magennis, *Images of Community in Old English Poetry* (Cambridge: Cambridge University Press, 1996), 10.
9   Gunhild Zimmerman, *The Four Old English Poetic Manuscripts: Texts, Contexts, and Historical Background* (Heidelberg: Universitätsverlag C. Winter, 1995), 25.
10 Jan-Peer Hartmann, "The Structure of the Exeter Book: A Reading Based on Medieval Topics," *LSE*, n.s., 47 (2016): 60.
11 Niles, *God's Exiles*, 30.
12 Brian McFadden, "Raiding, Reform, and Reaction: Wondrous Creatures in the Exeter Book Riddles," *Texas Studies in Literature and Language* 50 (2008): 329.
13 Britt Mize, "Enigmatic Knowing and the Vercelli Book," in *Riddles at Work in the Early Medieval Tradition: Words, Ideas, Interactions*, ed. Megan Cavell and Jennifer Neville, Manchester Medieval Literature and Culture 32 (Manchester: Manchester University Press, 2020), 254.
14 McFadden, 341.
15 The poem is contained in British Library Cotton Tiberius B.i, which can be viewed online here: http://www.bl.uk/manuscripts/Viewer.aspx?ref=cotton_ms_tiberius_b_i_f115r. All Old English poetry other than the riddles and *Beowulf* is cited from ASPR.
16 For these translations, see Bosworth-Toller *s.v. swicolast*.

a much less troubling reading: *soð bið switolast* "truth is clearest." Over time that interpretation has been challenged, however, and most editors have now restored *swicolast* to its place in the poem.[17] Whatever the original poet may have intended, restoring the scribe's text forces modern readers to ponder the same questions faced by early medieval readers of the manuscript: how and why is truth the trickiest thing? The text as we have it stops us in our tracks and demands that we consider how to approach this statement. Should we consider it seriously, as a philosophical issue? Should we approach it sceptically, as a potential error? Or is our understanding of the statement incomplete? Alfred Bammesberger, for example, suggests that it is our understanding of *soð* rather than *swicolast* that needs adjusting. If *soð* is taken in a legal sense, as "justice" or "judgement," then it is easier to accept that judgment is difficult or tricky.[18]

Yet even with a careful reappraisal of *soð* it is still not entirely comfortable to think that judgment is the trickiest thing. Considering that possibility requires us to think again about our fundamental assumptions about the world. That may be a heavy burden for the single letter "c" to bear, but it would be worse to underestimate this text than to overestimate it,[19] especially given the difficulty that modern readers have experienced in understanding the unfamiliar genres associated with Wisdom Literature.[20] Maxims may be self-evident statements of what everybody knows,[21] but what everybody knows is not always a simple matter for assent. Sometimes a statement of what everybody

---

17 For a summary of the debate, starting in 1876 with Henry Sweet's influential emendation of the text, see Leonard Neidorf, "*Maxims II*, Line 10: Truth and Textual Criticism," *SN* 91 (2019): 241–2; Neidorf supports the emendation on the basis of the uncontroversial statements about the natural world with which the line is juxtaposed (244). Important discussions in favour of retaining the manuscript reading include J. K. Bollard, "The Cotton Maxims," *Neophil* 57 (1973): 185; Fred Robinson, "Understanding an Old English Wisdom Verse: Maxims II, lines 10ff," in *The Wisdom of Poetry: Essays in Early English Literature in Honor of Morton W. Bloomfield*, ed. Larry Dean Benson and Siegfried Wenzel (Kalamazoo: Medieval Institute Publications, Western Michigan University, 1982); and E. G. Stanley, "The Gnomes of Cotton MS Tiberius B.I," *N&Q* 62 (2015): 190–9.
18 Alfred Bammesberger, "*Maxims II*, Line 10a: *Soð bið swicolost*, and the Meaning of Old English *Soð*," *N&Q* 67 (2020): 166–8.
19 "I have chosen to retain the MS. reading rather than run the risk of eliminating what could well be an insight into a very elusive subject" (Bollard, "Cotton Maxims," 185).
20 Paul Cavill, *Maxims in Old English Poetry* (Cambridge: Brewer, 1999), 156–7. Note also the important studies to which Cavill refers: T.A. Shippey, *Poems of Wisdom and Learning in Old English* (Cambridge: Brewer, 1976) and Elaine Tuttle Hansen, *The Solomon Complex: Reading Wisdom in Old English Poetry* (Toronto: University of Toronto Press, 1988).
21 See *OED*, s.v. maxim.

knows can be a challenge to look at the world again. Despite what we might have expected, the text that has survived to confront us today tells us that we need to consider the possibility that truth is trickiest.

Just as modern readers have expected self-evident truths from *Maxims II*, so they have expected something simple from the Exeter Book riddles: single, correct solutions. That expectation is based on our contemporary understanding of the riddle-genre, which tells us that riddles are questions with answers.[22] That expectation has determined most readers' experience of these texts, for modern editions and translations always present the riddles of the Exeter Book with solutions, usually as a numbered list following the texts, but sometimes as titles.[23] These contemporary editing

---

22 See, for example, the definition of "riddle" in the *OED*: "A question or statement intentionally phrased to require ingenuity in ascertaining its answer or meaning, frequently used as a game or pastime; an enigma; a conundrum." Cf. also important discussions in Archer Taylor, "The Varieties of Riddles," in *Philologica: The Malone Anniversary Studies*, ed. Thomas Austin Kirby and Henry Bosley Woolf (Baltimore: Johns Hopkins Press, 1949), 3; Elli Köngäs Maranda, "Structure des énigmes," *L'Homme*, 9 (1969): 5–48; W.J. Pepicello and T.A. Green, *The Language of Riddles: New Perspectives* (Columbus: Ohio State University Press, 1984), 88; John D. Niles, *Old English Enigmatic Poems and the Play of the Texts* (Turnhout: Brepols, 2006), 12; Patrick J. Murphy, *Unriddling the Exeter Riddles* (University Park: Pennsylvania State University Press, 2011), 22.

23 Editions, like those by Krapp and Dobbie, Williamson, Pinsker and Ziegler, Muir, and Orchard, list a range of past solutions in their notes but usually select one as correct. See *The Exeter Book*, ed. George Philip Krapp and Elliott Van Kirk Dobbie, ASPR 3 (New York: Columbia University Press, 1936); *The Old English Riddles of the Exeter Book*, ed. Craig Williamson (Chapel Hill: University of North Carolina Press, 1977); *Die altenglischen Rätsel des Exeterbuchs: Text mit deutscher Übersetzung und Kommentar*, ed. and trans. Hans Pinsker and Waltraud Ziegler, Anglistische Forschungen 183 (Heidelberg: Carl Winter, 1985); *Exeter Anthology*, ed. Muir; *The Old English and Anglo-Latin Riddle Tradition*, ed. and trans. Andy Orchard, Dumbarton Oaks Medieval Library 69 (Cambridge, MA: Harvard University Press, 2021). The same is true of many earlier editions; see, for example, *The Riddles of the Exeter Book*, ed. Frederick Tupper Jr (London: Ginn, 1910); *Die altenglischen Rätsel (Die Rätsel des Exeterbuchs)*, ed. Moritz Trautmann (Heidelberg: Carl Winter, 1915); *The Exeter Book, Part 2: Poems 9–22*, ed. and trans. W.S. Mackie, EETS, o.s., 194 (London: Humphry Milford and Oxford University Press, 1934). Public-facing editions and translations usually supply a list of single solutions at the end; see, for example, *Anglo-Saxon Riddles*, trans. John Porter (Hockwold-cum-Wilton: Anglo-Saxon Books, 1995); *Old English Riddles from the Exeter Book*, trans. Michael Alexander, 2nd ed. (London: Anvil Press, 2007); *Old English Poems and Riddles*, trans. Chris McCully (Manchester: Carcanet, 2008); *The Word Exchange: Anglo-Saxon Poems in Translation*, ed. Greg Delanty and Michael Matto, foreword by Seamus Heaney (New York: W.W. Norton, 2011). For titles given before the text, see, for example, Kevin Crossley-Holland, trans., *The Exeter Riddle Book* (London: Folio Society, 1978), who provides solutions as illustrations before each text, and Marsden, *Cambridge Old English Reader*, 360–4, who entitles each text with a single, modern English solution.

practices do not, however, match up with the way in which the riddles have come down to us. The creator of the tenth-century Exeter Book, who carefully organized pre-existing materials,[24] seems not to have shared our modern view that riddles should always be accompanied by authoritative answers. Other early medieval people also seem to have lacked our modern expectations. For example, the exemplar(s) from which the Exeter Book riddles were copied may also have lacked solutions. Whether or not this is true is unknowable, but either option is significant: if the exemplar(s) lacked solutions, the Exeter Book's omission signals agreement with previous authors and scribes that solutions should not be provided; if the exemplar(s) provided solutions, their absence in the Exeter Book signals that a choice was made to omit them. Perhaps most telling, however, is that no early medieval editor, corrector, or reader thought it necessary to supply what would be a glaring omission for a modern reader – and, indeed, for the early medieval readers of most other riddle collections. Even if early collections of Latin riddles did begin circulating without solutions, as Whitman suggests, most surviving manuscripts do include solutions now, whether as integral features of the original plan for the texts or as "accretions" added by copyists and readers.[25] In contrast, while there are runic letters in the margins of the Exeter Book that seem to point towards solutions, there are at most six of these in a collection that currently contains over ninety riddles.[26] And even if runic clues were provided for every riddle, hints are not the same as solutions. In the Exeter Book, as Bilbo Baggins says, "Answers were to be guessed not given."[27]

---

24 Bernard J. Muir, "Issues for Editors of Anglo-Saxon Poetry in Manuscript Form," in *Inside Old English: Essays in Honour of Bruce Mitchell*, ed. John Walmsley (Oxford: Blackwell, 2006), 188. Muir also offers an overview of the practices that led to the creation of the manuscript in the introduction to his edition (*Exeter Anthology*, 1–41); note especially his statement that "the anthologist who compiled the present collection drew his material from other collections available to him and arranged it in a meaningful manner ... If this manipulation of the material was not carried out during the preparation of the present manuscript (DandC MS 3501), then it is to be attributed to the anthologist of its exemplar(s)" (7).
25 F.H. Whitman, "Aenigmata Tatwini," *NM* 88 (1987): 8–9; for further discussion see Andy Orchard, "Enigma Variations: The Anglo-Saxon Riddle-Tradition," in *Latin Learning and English Lore: Studies in Anglo-Saxon Literature for Michael Lapidge*, ed. Katherine O'Brien O'Keeffe and Andy Orchard, 2 vols. (Toronto: University of Toronto Press, 2005), 1: 285–6.
26 The runic letters added in the margins next to the Exeter Book riddles may or may not be medieval; see photographs and discussion in Williamson, 51–62. It is usually assumed that the scribe originally included one hundred riddles, but damage to the manuscript has reduced the extant number.
27 J.R.R. Tolkien, *The Hobbit*, 5th ed. (London: HarperCollins, 1995), 97.

The way in which the manuscript has survived to confront us today thus supports the argument that final answers are not the ultimate goal of the Exeter Book riddles. After all, if the purpose of these texts were simply to lead audiences to the satisfaction of a solved puzzle, they would be much more likely to succeed if they were accompanied by correct solutions, for the omission of solutions means that the riddling process can end in failure. Such a result is inconceivable in the riddle-scenarios studied by folklore specialists, since the power-dynamic between riddler and riddlee and the resulting social tension depend upon the riddler's ability to confirm, deny, or supply the solution.[28] Although it is easy to imagine a scribe miscopying a "t" as a "c" by accident, we can assume that those responsible for creating the Exeter Book did not omit the solutions for almost one hundred riddles by accident, and, although we cannot know what they intended, we may guess that they did not deliberately create texts whose goal was liable to failure.

Yet, at the same time, the Exeter Book riddles signal their participation in a literary, monastic tradition:

> A riddle or enigma signifies through obscure likenesses or representations (*imagines*), the interpretation of which depends on a system of correspondences within the cultural encyclopedia. [...] The knowledge of these tropes was taken for granted as a fundamental part of literacy, reading, and interpretation, and in the context of monastic life, proficiency in decoding tropes, figures, and allegory was an index to one's capacity for wisdom and spiritual insight.[29]

Although this book does not address them in much detail,[30] the Latin riddle collections of Symphosius, Aldhelm, Bern, Lorsch, Tatwine, Eusebius,

---

28 See, for example, the overview of a Finnish riddling competition in Annikki Kaivola-Bregenhøj, "The Riddle: Form and Performance," *Humanities* 7 (2018): article 49, 11–12.

29 Martin Irvine, *The Making of Textual Culture: "Grammatica" and Literary Theory, 350–1100* (Cambridge: Cambridge University Press, 1994), 438–9.

30 For the relationship between the Exeter Book riddles and the Anglo-Latin riddles, see Dieter Bitterli's full-length study, *Say What I am Called: The Old English Riddles of the Exeter Book and the Anglo-Latin Riddle Tradition* (Toronto: University of Toronto Press, 2009). For recent studies that productively analyse the Exeter Book riddles in the context of their Latin tradition see, for example, Matthew Aiello, "Books in Battle: The Violent Poetics of Misdirection in Old English *Riddle 53*," *RES* 71 (2020): 207–28 and Amy W. Clark, "Familiar Distances: Beating the Bounds of Early English Identity" (PhD diss., University of California, Berkeley, 2020), 33–88. Earlier studies were dominated by the more limited idea of the Old English riddles as translations of Latin texts; see, for example, Frederick Tupper Jr., "Originals and Analogues of the Exeter Book Riddles," *Modern Language Notes* 18 (1903): 97–106.

and Boniface constitute an ever-present context for the Exeter Book riddles.[31] It is not simply that some of the Exeter Book riddles are translations of Latin riddles, or that some address similar topics, but rather that they assume an audience conversant with that "cultural encyclopedia" and, indeed, with the Latin riddling tradition itself.[32] However, they often assume familiarity with that tradition only to ambush the expectations that come with it. Readers of the Exeter collection quickly learn that what they have seen before is not a reliable guide to solving the next riddle. Even within the collection itself, the sequence of texts prevents confidence in any developing competence. For example, in the small subset of the collection that deploys runic letters as part of the riddling challenge, successfully solving one rune-puzzle provides little advantage in solving the next, assuming, of course, that modern scholars have solved these puzzles correctly. That is, while the technique necessary for dealing with the runes in *Bright-Headed* (R.19) is to use each rune as a letter and then to reverse the letter order to make four words, following this technique when facing *Six Letters* (R.24) would lead to frustration, for in this latter case the riddlee needs to unscramble the runic letters to create one word. Likewise, in *Two Proud Ones* (R.42), the riddlee is faced not with runic letters but their names; these names need to be converted to letters and then unscrambled to create two words. Finally, in *Joy and Ice* (R.64), the runic letters spell out only the first two letters of each word; the riddlee then needs to complete the words. Thus attempting to use a previously successful technique leads to failure in successive riddles. In addition, for *Bright-Headed* (R.19), at least, cracking the runic code is only the beginning of the process of arriving at a solution.[33]

---

31 A recent scholarly edition of Symphosius can be found in *Symphosius, The Aenigmata: An Introduction, Text and Commentary*, ed. T. J. Leary (London: Bloomsbury, 2014). Scholarly editions of the others can be found in *Variae Collectiones Aenigmatum Merovingicae Aetatis*, ed. Fr. Glorie, 2 vols, CCSL, 133 and 133A (Turnholt: Brepols, 1968). For Aldhelm, see 1: 377–540. For the Bern Riddles, see 2: 547–610. For the Lorsch Riddles, see 1: 347–58. For Tatwine, see 1: 167–208. For Eusebius, see 1: 211–71. For Boniface, see 1: 273–343. The early medieval English riddling tradition as a whole can be conveniently surveyed with facing-page translations in Orchard's *Old English and Anglo-Latin Riddle Tradition*. Many of these texts (with translations and commentaries) can also be found on http://theriddleages.com.

32 Murphy, *Unriddling*, 11. Cf. also Anita R. Riedinger's argument that these texts rely on an audience familiar with traditional formulae in "The Formulaic Style in the Old English Riddles," *SN* 75 (2003): 30–43.

33 See discussion in chapter 2 below. Cf. also the interpretation of *Bright-Headed* (R.19) and *Joy and Ice* (R.64) in Williamson, *Old English Riddles*, 186–92 and 325–30 and of *Bright-Headed* in Mark Griffith, "Riddle 19 of the *Exeter Book*: SNAC, an Old English Acronym," *N&Q* 39 (1992): 15–16.

An audience conversant with the Latin riddling tradition – and, indeed, with Old English poetry more generally – would also be familiar with a large body of tropes. By "trope" I mean both "a particular manner or mode" and, more particularly, a "turning" of a word or phrase's meaning away from its literal sense.[34] As cognitive linguists have shown, such "turning" is not exclusively a characteristic of literary language; conceptual metaphors in particular are essential to the understanding of complex or abstract ideas in all forms of communication.[35] Nevertheless, tropes lie at the heart of the Exeter Book riddles, and so, when we as modern readers read these texts, we must make recourse to manners and modes from over a thousand years ago. Over the years scholars have come to understand many of them well. For example, most modern readers of Old English poetry are familiar with the heroic idiom, a trope which pervades almost every poem to the point that it can be identified as a constituent of the poetic form as much as the alliterative long line.[36] Other tropes are less familiar to modern readers, in part because those tropes are mostly restricted to the riddles themselves, but we have nevertheless learned to read them. In this study, for example, I discuss the implement trope, the trope of manufacturing, and the trope of reproduction, among others. In the focus of past scholarship on solutions, however, these tropes have been treated as if they were (or should be) transparent and as if they ultimately conveyed nothing more than solutions. The riddles' lack of resolution, however, means that these tropes are not, in fact, transparent. Initially, at least, and, in some cases, perpetually, audiences are not able to see through these tropes, and the tropes themselves thus become visible and available for scrutiny in a way that language rarely does for both modern and early medieval audiences. The potentially interminable process of interpretation caused by the absence of authoritative solutions eventually leads audiences of the riddles to unlearn those familiar manners and modes, with the result that the

---

34 *OED*, s.v. trope. The first part of this definition comes close to some definitions of "discourse." See, for example the definition in Chris Baldick, *The Concise Oxford Dictionary of Literary Terms* (Oxford: Oxford University Press, 1990), 59: discourse denotes "any coherent body of statements that produces a self-confirming account of reality by defining an object of attention and generating concepts with which to analyse it" (59). For further discussion of "discourse," see chapter 4 below. For a different and equally valid definition of "trope" see Niles, *God's Exiles*, 156–9.
35 See George Lakoff and Mark Johnson, *Metaphors We Live By*, with a new afterword (1980; Chicago and London: University of Chicago Press, 2003).
36 The heroic idiom, and its definitive role in Old English poetry, will be discussed at length in chapter 2 ("The Joy of Limits") below.

Introduction 13

tropes, rather than the solutions, can become the focus of our attention[37] and what everybody knows becomes alien, challenging, and queer.

The Exeter Book riddles, like the gnomic statements in *Maxims II*, are thus not quite what we expected. Just as the series of inarguable truths in *Maxims II* leads to serious and disturbing questions, so these riddles lead us ultimately not to single solutions but rather to an open-ended process, an ongoing debate, and *things* that cross boundaries, ruffle feathers, and challenge expectations.[38] Even if we do manage to achieve the "inner click" that marks an elegant, satisfying answer,[39] the riddle has led us to imagine things that not only metamorphose from one identity to another while we attempt to solve them but also retain lingering questions afterward. Importantly, those questions always include, "What is it?" Even if one solution commands assent for over a century, another elegant, satisfying answer is still possible; the question remains open. A key argument for this book is that multiple solutions, however long they persist, are the motivation for, not the consequence of, having no solutions in the manuscript.

The absence of authoritative solutions changes everything. We cannot simply say "I give up; what is it?" and so we cannot circumvent the interpretative process. Even more important, because we cannot vanquish lingering doubts by comparing our best guess against an authoritative answer, the Exeter Book riddles make concluding difficult. We may think that we have found a good solution that satisfies exacting criteria,[40] but we can always think again – and again and again and again. The ongoing interpretation that is facilitated by lingering doubt encourages me to consider significances beyond what we might normally ascribe to such short texts and to a genre that is usually viewed

---

37 Cf. Matthew Aiello, "Books in Battle: The Violent Poetics of Misdirection in Old English *Riddle 53*," *RES* 71 (2020): 207–28.
38 The Exeter Book riddles have already provided productive sites of investigation for scholars working with Thing Theory. See, for example, James Paz, *Nonhuman Voices in Anglo-Saxon Literature* (Manchester: Manchester University Press, 2017), who offers an excellent summary and overview of Thing Theory on 3–6 and explores the riddles on 59–97.
39 I adopt the ideas of "elegance" and the "inner click" from Niles, *Old English Enigmatic Poems*, 12. Niles derives the latter from Leo Spitzer, *Linguistics and Literary History* (Princeton, NJ: Princeton University Press, 1948), 7.
40 For example, "A solution is 'correct' if it accounts for all the elements in the text (both positive clues and deliberate obfuscations) and if the solution corresponds to some reality known to have been within the grasp of an Anglo-Saxon riddler." Alger N. Doane, "Three Old English Implement Riddles: Reconsiderations of Numbers 4, 49, and 73," *MP* 84 (1987): 244. Cf. also the criteria in Niles, *Old English Enigmatic Poems*, 29–31 and the long exploration of "unriddling" in Murphy, *Unriddling*, 27–77.

as humorous and not serious.[41] Sometimes I may go too far. Some of the interpretations that I propose in this book might seem ridiculous, but being ridiculously wrong sometimes strikes me as an appropriate response to these texts, which so often confront us with ridiculous scenarios and require us to wonder how they can possibly be true.

Craig Williamson links this quality of the riddles to "negative capability,"[42] John Keats' idea of being able to linger "in uncertainties, mysteries, doubts, without any irritable reaching after fact and reason."[43] James Paz draws upon Thing Theory to argue that "the unsolved thing forces the human reader to hover over a threshold" and "start to wonder."[44] Both these approaches have influenced my thinking, but the frustrating, iterative process of trying to resolve clues with no guarantee of a resolution also reminds me of "disidentification," a term that comes from queer theorists like Judith Butler and José Esteban Muñoz. Disidentification refers to the rhetorical practice of adopting the language of universalizing and exclusionary power but recycling, scrambling, and redeploying it in subversive ways that say what normally cannot be said and give a voice to those who normally cannot speak:[45]

> Disidentification is a performative mode of tactical recognition that various minoritarian subjects employ in an effort to resist the oppressive and normalizing discourse of dominant ideology. Disidentification resists the interpellating call of ideology that fixes a subject within the state power apparatus. It is a reformatting of self within the social, a third term that resists the binary of identification and counteridentification. Counteridentification often, through the very routinized workings of its denouncement of dominant discourse, reinstates that same discourse.[46]

---

41 See, for example, Niles, *God's Exiles*, 168: "humour ... is inherent in riddling as a genre." For an analysis of humour and riddles in a folklore context, see Annikki Kaivola-Bregenhøj, "Riddles and Humour," *Folklore* 69 (2017): 195–210. For discussion of humour in the Exeter Book riddles, see especially Jonathan Wilcox, "Humour and the *Exeter Book* Riddles: Incongruity in *Febegeorn* (R.31)," in *Riddles at Work in the Early Medieval Tradition: Words, Ideas, Interactions*, ed. Megan Cavell and Jennifer Neville, Manchester Medieval Literature and Culture 32 (Manchester: Manchester University Press, 2020), 128–45.
42 Williamson, *Old English Riddles*, 26–7.
43 *The Letters of John Keats 1814–1821*, 3 vols, ed. Hyder Edward Rollins (Cambridge: Cambridge University Press, 1958), I, 193.
44 Paz, *Nonhuman Voices*, 81.
45 Judith Butler, *Bodies That Matter: On the Discursive Limits of "Sex"* (New York: Routledge, 1993), and José Esteban Muñoz, *Disidentifications: Queers of Color and the Performance of Politics*, Cultural Studies of the Americas 2 (Minneapolis: University of Minnesota Press, 1999).
46 José Esteban Muñoz, "'The White to Be Angry': Vaginal Davis's Terrorist Drag," *Social Text* 52–3 (1997): 83.

Like a "minoritarian subject," a riddle-subject reformats itself: a sword presents itself as a reluctantly celibate retainer.[47] In the same way, a riddle-object resists the "normalizing discourse of dominant ideology": the accepted hierarchical structure is reversed when two noble warriors are bound and controlled by a slave.[48] A riddle thus presents something comparable with "a third term," a strange and sometimes paradoxical image, a monster that confounds expectations set by "the state power apparatus."

What comes next with most riddles, however, is resolution of the "binary of identification and counteridentification." Successfully solving a riddle replaces the initially perplexing, misrecognized image with one that reinstates the dominant cultural discourse:

> When at last we have got to the bottom of something which seemed to us strange and unintelligible, when we have managed to accommodate it within our linguistically ordered world, then everything falls into place, just as it does with a difficult chess problem, where only the solution renders the necessity of the absurd setup intelligible, down to the very last piece of the board.[49]

Over the past 150 years scholars have assiduously pursued this goal of making everything fall neatly into place. A good example is the effort that scholars have expended to justify the presence of the double-entendre riddles in the Exeter Book. What we know about the early Middle Ages suggests that such open depictions of (apparently) sexual acts should never have been included in a monastic production, and so scholars have interpreted the texts as a reinstatement of the expected prohibition: counteridentification thus gives way to identification.[50] Yet the Exeter Book riddles resist "the interpellating call of ideology"; it is not easy to reinstate the "dominant discourse" at the end of the process. Sometimes a comfortable reassertion of what everyone knows

---

47 For discussion of *Cursed among Weapons* (R.20), see chapters 2, 4, and 6, below. Throughout this study, I refer to the topics of first-person riddles as "riddle-subjects" and that of third-person riddles as "riddle-objects." The distinction between subjects and objects is usefully complicated by Thing-theory; see discussion in Paz, *Nonhuman Voices*, 9–13.
48 For discussion of *Captives* (R.52), see chapter 4, below.
49 Hans Georg Gadamer, "Rhetoric, Hermeneutics, and the Critique of Ideology: Metacritical Comments on Truth and Method," in *The Hermeneutics Reader: Texts of the German Tradition from the Enlightenment to the Present*, ed. Kurt Mueller-Vollmer (New York: Continuum, 1985; repr. 1994), 284.
50 See discussion in chapter 6, below.

to be true remains out of reach simply because solutions remain unfound[51] or because the solutions remain vigorously contested.[52] Even when an elegant solution has been found, however, some of the Exeter Book riddles continue to disturb and intrigue, stimulating ongoing debate across generations of scholars.[53] Despite scholarly efforts, a residue of queerness remains. Perhaps such unease is characteristic of riddles in general,[54] but in the Exeter Book it persists longer than it might have done because of the absence of solutions in the manuscript. In most riddling situations, "success in untangling the true meaning of the riddle-sentence from the knots of verbal deceit depends upon the confirmation of the solution by the riddle-poser."[55] In the case of the Exeter Book, since the riddler has declined to supply that confirmation, we can never be truly certain that we have correctly interpreted what the words mean. We can only engage in the debate.

When I claim that the Exeter Book riddles are queer – not just about sex but about everything – I am conscious that everything is queer these days[56] and that medieval scholars always claim that their pet texts anticipate innovative modern developments.[57] This book is not about queer theory, but, having struggled over many years to articulate the delightful strangeness, the frustratingly enjoyable tickling of the brain that accompanies an encounter with these texts, I found in the quotation from Muñoz above useful echoes of what I have been trying to say, particularly about the tension between identification and counteridentification. The Exeter Book riddles' queerness, their resistance to

---

51 Although good arguments have been made, I do not believe that fully satisfying solutions have yet been offered for *Hardest and Sharpest* (R.28) and *Most Wretched of All* (R.39), for example. For past solutions for these and other riddles, see the appendix, below.
52 A good example is *Periodically Busy* (R.4), discussed above.
53 A good example is *I Travel on Foot* (R.12), whose story of a dark-haired Welsh woman's night-time activities has inspired horror, fascination, and many, many scholarly discussions. See discussion in chapter 6, below.
54 See, for example, Dan Pagis, "Toward a Theory of the Literary Riddle," in *Untying the Knot: On Riddles and Other Enigmatic Modes*, ed. Galit Hasan-Rokem and David Shulman (Oxford: Oxford University Press, 1981), 98.
55 Dan Ben-Amos, "Solutions to Riddles," *Journal of American Folklore* 89 (1976): 249.
56 Karen Tongson, "Queer Fundamentalism," *Social Text* 32 (2014): 117–23.
57 See, for example, Paul Strohm, *Theory and the Premodern Text* (Minneapolis: University of Minnesota Press, 2000), 160; Anna Wilson, "Fan Fiction and Premodern Literature: Methods and Definitions," *Transformative Works and Cultures* 36 (2021): paragraph 1.2, https://journal.transformativeworks.org/index.php/twc/article/view/2037; Erica Weaver, "Premodern and Postcritical: Medieval Enigmata and the Hermeneutic Style," *New Literary History* 50 (2019): 45.

resolution, is what continues to drive scholars to propose further interpretations even when solutions have commanded assent for decades, and it is ultimately what makes them attractive to readers of all kinds. Despite our best efforts, uncertainty persists. That uncertainty sends us back again and again to ponder the questions that, in other riddling traditions, are "empty and of no importance" once a solution has been reached.[58] The "symptomatic reading" that the Exeter Book riddles demand in their call to *Saga hwæt ic hatte* "say what I am called" proves impossible to complete: even though we know that the language of the riddle is deceptive and superficial, even though it explicitly requires "detection and interpretation by an interpreter,"[59] in the end we cannot dispense with the misrecognized or disidentified image, because it can always lead us to yet another solution.

In response to these qualities, this book calls for a change in the way we approach the Exeter Book riddles. Rather than propose and defend one solution that negates and triumphs over all others, this book argues that we should explore and embrace the range of solutions that a medieval audience might have proposed, which may include far-fetched answers, too. An important tactic in my reading of the riddles is thus the creation of series of solutions; in the course of this book, I will solve and re-solve some riddles again and again. At the same time, debate remains just as important as openness.[60] The riddles call us to challenge the solutions of the *inflatos ... sofos* "proud wise ones" of the past[61] and to be challenged in our turn.

The discussion of the Exeter Book collection's play with expectations begins in chapter 2, "The Joy of Limits: The Heroic Idiom as 'Code,'" which focuses on the riddles' use of the trope of the heroic idiom to describe components of the heroic world. For the texts in this chapter, the familiar, limited arena of Old English heroic poetry serves as a boundary or set of limits within which riddlees can interpret ambiguous

---

58 Annikki Kaivola-Bregenhøj, *Riddles: Perspectives on the Use, Function and Change in a Folklore Genre*, trans. Susan Sinisalo (Helsinki: Finnish Literature Society, 2001), 19. Cf. Northrop Frye: puzzles "are to be solved and annihilated." *Anatomy of Criticism* (Princeton: Princeton University Press, 1957), 88.
59 Stephen Best and Sharon Marcus, "Surface Reading: An Introduction," *Representations* 108 (2009): 1.
60 Adam Davis argues that conflict between riddler and riddlee is central to riddles; see "Agon and Gnomon: Forms and Functions of the Anglo-Saxon Riddles," in *De Gustibus: Essays for Alain Renoir*, ed. John Miles Foley, J. Chris Womack, and Whitney A. Womack, Albert Bates Lord Studies in Oral Tradition 11 (New York: Garland, 1992), 110–50.
61 Aldhelm, Enigma 100 (*Creatura* "Creation"), line 83.

descriptions, and thus it is a code not only for behaviour but for content. That is, like most Old English poems, many of the Exeter Book riddles present actors, objects, ethics, and activities associated with a military elite. Unlike most other Old English poems, however, the riddles demand that their audiences become critically aware of the presence of that code. That awareness is necessary, because, although many of the riddles use the heroic idiom as a metaphor, the riddles explored in this chapter do not. The bending thing in *Wob* (R.23), which shoots things that kill people, really is a bending thing that shoots things that kill people (probably a *boga* "bow"), and the thing in *Cursed among Weapons* (R.20), which bears treasure, receives the praise of rulers, and kills the living, really is a thing that bears treasure, receives the praise of rulers, and kills the living (probably a *sweord* "sword"). The texts discussed in this chapter, although scattered throughout the collection, provide the baseline for my argument, for their presence means that any riddle in the collection could simply be what it says it is: a literal (even if ambiguous) description of an object from the poetic world of heroic action. As a result, any aspiring riddle-solver must always keep the literal, surface meaning of the texts in mind. In fact, the absence of authoritative solutions in the manuscript means that even a clever, metaphorical solution does not eliminate the legitimacy of a literal interpretation of the riddle. That uncertainty subjects the heroic idiom itself to an intense scrutiny not always required for the interpretation of other Old English poems.

Chapter 3, "Muddying the Waters: The Heroic Idiom as Camouflage and Disguise," turns to riddles whose surfaces are not what they seem: riddles that use the familiar language of the heroic idiom either to obscure the object with a smokescreen of irrelevant heroic attributes or to change its appearance with a metaphorical disguise. In so doing, these texts destroy any confidence we might have developed when reading the riddles discussed in the previous chapter, for we cannot take their descriptions literally. *Terrible Laughter* (R.33), *One-Footed* (R.58), and *Turning Wood* (R.56), for example, use heroic language to present objects (perhaps *is* "ice," a **rad-rod* "well-beam," and a *web-beam* "loom" or *turnus* "pole-lathe") that lie outside the world of battle. To propose solutions for these riddles, we need to ignore the associations raised by the heroic idiom, and yet, as always, the residue of that language remains, both colouring our perception of the riddle-objects and calling our attention to the multiple possible meanings of the heroic idiom itself. The pressing need to evaluate *how* heroic language is being used leads me to consider multiple interpretations of texts like *Towering Tree* (R.53) and, especially, *Protector* (R.17). Instead of developing confidence in our ability to interpret language as we engage with successive riddles, we become increasingly suspicious of apparently familiar surfaces, with the result that even an elegant solution does not terminate the process of interpretation.

That suspicion leads to inquiries beyond the identities of objects and into interrogations of the cultural values that surround them. Chapter 4, "Dark Tracks through the Heroic Idiom: Aporia, Irony, and Paradox," thus pursues the queerness that persists even after good solutions have been found, for sometimes solving a riddle only raises more questions, questions that are uncomfortable and troubling. In this chapter, I wonder whether *Fight against Wave* (R.16), a riddle whose solution (*ancor* "anchor") has never been doubted, shows the limitations of heroic action, whether *Cursed among Weapons* (R.20), almost always solved as *sweord* "sword," subjects heroic culture to searching questions about its value, and whether *Four Creatures* (R.51), a text that probably portrays a scribe writing a text, makes a joke of scribal self-importance. In these readings I am reaching out doubtfully for hints of irony that I may not be competent to discern, but my unease, my sense of lingering queerness, suggests that even short texts like *Captives* (R.52) and, especially, *Lone Dweller* (R.5) can raise important questions about early medieval English culture. To read these texts, audiences – then and now – must scrutinize what is normally assumed and unspoken: the discourse that defines value.

The scrutiny invited by persisting unease continues in chapter 5, "Domestic Practices: Manufacturing and Implements," which considers how the riddles raise questions about violence and social hierarchy. The creation of a book in *Famous Name* (R.26) provides a model of the trope of manufacturing, which usually contains four key components – violence, sympathy, ingenuity, and value – and sets out a narrative that, even as it gives a voice to the victim, justifies suffering as necessary and productive. That narrative can be found in several riddles, but it is not always a comfortable story of human triumph. Thus in *Lone Dweller* (R.5) the expected justification of a valuable product (whatever it might be) does not arrive, and suffering ends only in destruction: violence fails to create value. In other riddles, even when the expected value is created, violence brings with it unwelcome consequences. Things bite back and take revenge on their makers; for example, in *Binder and Scourger* (R.27) the product of manufacturing (usually accepted to be *medu* "mead") strips human beings of their agency and will. What everybody knows is that suffering leads to beauty and that glory is attained in battle, but here there is a cycle of violence begetting violence without any hope of profit. Similarly, another trope, the implement trope, draws attention to another unquestionable good of early medieval society: stable hierarchies. Although the riddles that figure the relationship between a user and a tool in terms of the relationship between a lord and a servant do not appear to question the essential rightness of hierarchies, they narrate reversible reciprocities that elsewhere would seem dangerously provocative. It is, of course, natural that *fyr* "fire" should be kept safely under control, but it is radical to propose that servants should moderate the pride of the noble elite – or it would be, if *Bright Warrior* (R.50) were not a riddle, and if the implement trope were not a trope. That we cannot simply look through such tropes to replace the disidentified image with one that suits "the interpellating call of ideology that fixes a subject within the state power apparatus"[62] is illustrated by *Earth-Fast* (R.49), a riddle from which an inner click has yet to be coaxed. Its ability to evade resolution comes in part from its deceptive use of familiar tropes: if my proposed solution of *hyf ond beo* "hive and bee" is correct, the expectations created by the implement and literacy tropes are red herrings designed to deceive competent riddlees who think they know how to play the game. The Exeter Book riddles teach their readers to be suspicious of what they think they know, and they remain full of significance regardless of whether the riddle has been solved or not. And, of course, both past and future solutions remain targets for debate.

Chapter 6, "The Strange Game of Sex: Asexual Reproduction and Gratuitous Sex," brings the arguments of the book to a head. Looking first at the nine riddles that use the trope of reproduction, I note that this metaphor denotes natural production (as opposed to human manufacturing) without reference to sex: water gives birth to ice and the earth gives birth to metal without a preceding act of coitus. Conversely, the trope of sex, a metaphor that can denote a wide range of activities, almost always omits reference to offspring. In fact, the trope of sex confounds modern scholarly expectations again and again, so the bulk of this chapter is taken up with investigating past symptomatic readings and peering obsessively at the surfaces of the fifteen riddles that make use of it. I show that "sex" in these riddles occurs (in most cases) not only without offspring but also without either shame or pleasure; its essential quality is hard work; and it is associated mainly with the upper classes. In the end I grapple with the endlessly fascinating question of why these startlingly frank texts exist here, in a manuscript created within an institution that strictly restricted the practice of sex and forbade the representation of it. While I do not pretend to know the manuscript-creator's intentions, I contend that the sexual riddles amplify the effect achieved by all the Exeter Book riddles: they stop readers in their

---

62 Muñoz, "'White to Be Angry,'" 83.

tracks; they challenge us to evaluate our way of evaluating things; they demand that we remain open to multiple ways of reading.

One thing that has stopped me in my tracks is the apparently simple matter of how to refer to these texts. As my discussion thus far should indicate, the Exeter Book riddles cannot be entitled by their solutions, since those solutions are – not only properly but essentially – subject to ongoing debate. Starting a discussion of a riddle with its solution misrepresents the game that the scribe set before us. However, the tradition of referring to each riddle by number, although helpful for thinking about sequences and relationships between riddles, suffers from two major problems: first, numbers are not memorable enough to allow a reader to recall quickly which text is under consideration, and, second, different editors and translators number the riddles in different ways, with the result that ASPR's 95 is Grein's 89, Assmann's 95, Thorpe's 30, Trautmann's 93, Tupper's 95, Wyatt's 93, Mackie's 94, Baum's 67, Williamson's 91, Muir's 94, and Orchard's 91. In such circumstances, it will be a rare reader indeed who can pinpoint a riddle-text without having a copy to consult. In 2019, therefore, I proposed that the riddles should be identified instead by titles, and I created a list of titles derived from memorable words within the riddle-texts themselves.[63] In 2020 Megan Cavell and I trialled using my titles in the essay collection that we edited together, *Riddles at Work in the Early Medieval Tradition*. We were happy with the result, but such changes are always disruptive, and I have continued to revise and experiment with my original list of titles to make them more memorable and easier to use. In this current book I refer to each riddle according to a revised list of titles, along with frequent references to the traditional numbers from ASPR in brackets to aid readers trying to locate these texts in editions and past scholarship.

The big change from my previous lists is that these titles are now translations into modern English of a lightly revised list of memorable words from the riddle texts. Each title aims to be a partial answer to the question "What am I?" or "What is it?" The best ones are translations of unique nouns, adjectives, or noun phrases that directly describe the riddle-subject or object. For example, the title for ASPR's riddle 11 is *Dark-Stained*, a translation of the word *hasofag*;[64] this word describes the riddle-subject and does not appear anywhere else in the corpus of

---

[63] Jennifer Neville, "A Modest Proposal: Titles for the *Exeter Book* Riddles," *Medium Ævum* 88 (2019): 116–23.
[64] For analysis of this difficult word, see C.P. Biggam, *Grey in Old English: An Interdisciplinary Semantic Study* (London: Runetree, 1998), 281–7.

Old English poetry. Similarly, *Periodically Busy* is a translation of *þragbysig*, another unique word in the corpus and thus my choice for the text previously known as riddle 2 or 4.[65] Where it has not been possible to find a noun, adjective, or noun-phrase that directly describes the riddle-subject or -object and is distinct enough to be memorable, I have chosen a word or phrase that seems key to proposed solutions, if possible from early in the text. Thus, for example, *They Gave Me Up for Dead* (R.9) may serve to remind a reader of the story narrated by the text. Unfortunately, it has not always been possible to find distinctive enough phrases at the beginnings of texts. For example, the opening of *Younger Brother* (R.93) is too badly damaged to supply a memorable identifier, but recalling the story of the woeful speaker replaced by its younger brother should help a reader to identify the text under consideration. I do not expect to have entitled every one of the riddles definitively, but I hope that this system helps readers to distinguish the texts being discussed without having to resort always to solutions that should be contested rather than accepted before interpretation has begun.

A record of those contests can be found at the end of this book, in the appendix entitled "The Argument over Solutions." In it I list all the past solutions to the riddles that I have been able to find. This appendix is not simply a reference tool, however; it is a visualization of the ongoing process of interpretation inspired by these texts, a representation of the history of riddle-solving as if it were one long argument – which is the correct response to them. *Soð bið swicolast* "truth is trickiest," and the Exeter Book riddles challenge their readers to think the unthinkable, question what cannot be questioned, and contribute to the ongoing debate. Now it is your turn to join in the process. *Ic gecende be ðam ðe ic cuðe; se ðe bet cunne, gecyðe his mare* "I have made known what I know; let the one who knows better reveal his greater [knowledge]."[66] Go on. I dare you.

---

65 For an argument for this meaning of this word, see Neville, "Sorting Out the Rings," 24, 35.
66 This is the final sentence of *Gerefa*, in Cambridge, Corpus Christi College, MS 383, fol. 69r, which can be viewed at Parker Library on the Web (https://parker.stanford.edu/parker/catalog/mv34oty8592) or in *Die Gesetze der Angelsachsen*, ed. Felix Liebermann, 3 vols (Halle: Niemeyer, 1903–1916), 3: 245.

Chapter Two

The Joy of Limits: The Heroic Idiom as "Code"

Introduction: The Heroic Idiom as a Starting Point

The heroic idiom is the language used to depict an idealized, archaic warrior culture: the world of generous warlords, loyal thegns (that is, military retainers), cunningly wrought equipment, and great acts of courage.[1] Old English poetry presents that world as the *soð* "truth" that everybody knows; the heroic idiom conveys the "interpellating call of ideology" that commands assent from its audiences.[2] It is difficult to overstate the importance of the heroic idiom to Old English poetry, for it constitutes its basic fabric; indeed, it is not much of an exaggeration to say that in the Old English poetic tradition the heroic idiom denotes not only heroic culture but also poetry itself.[3] The near equivalence of the poetic with the heroic can be observed in the special diction that marks poetry and identifies it as distinct from prose, much of which pertains specifically to battle, its personnel, and its equipment.[4] In poetry, for example, people of all kinds, including women, can be described as

---

1 I have adopted the term "heroic idiom" from Pirkko Koppinen, "*Swa þa Stafas Becnaþ*: Ciphers of the Heroic Idiom in the Exeter Book Riddles, *Beowulf*, *Judith*, and *Andreas*" (PhD diss., Royal Holloway, University of London, 2009), 94–8.
2 José Esteban Muñoz, "'The White to Be Angry': Vaginal Davis's Terrorist Drag," *Social Text* 52–3 (1997): 83.
3 Cf discussion in Ursula Schaefer, "From an Aesthetic Point of View: Receptional Aspects of Old English Poetry," in *De Gustibus: Essays for Alain Renoir*, ed. John Miles Foley, J. Chris Womack, and Whitney A. Womack, Albert Bates Lord Studies in Oral Tradition 11 (New York: Garland, 1992), 526, 533.
4 See the useful list of poetic words in M.S. Griffith, "Poetic Language and the *Paris Psalter*: The Decay of the Old English Tradition," *ASE* 20 (1991): 183 and the discussion in Dennis Cronan, "Poetic Words, Conservatism and the Dating of Old English Poetry," *ASE* 33 (2004): 23–50. Cf. Koppinen's discussion of the heroic idiom as an "aesthetic code" ("*Swa þa Stafas Becnaþ*," 95).

hæleþa "heroes" or "fighters";[5] in prose, even Alfred the Great cannot be so described.

To solve or even simply to read riddles written within the heroic idiom, we, like earlier audiences, must be able to recognize that idiom. Such recognition is often straightforward, even if the heroic idiom is presented elliptically or ornamented with rhetorical tropes such as prosopopoeia. In fact, many of the riddles in the Exeter Book deploy the heroic idiom in the same way as other Old English poems, and they corroborate what we find there regarding the loyalty owed by a thegn to his lord, the love of expensive, beautiful equipment, the ever-present likelihood of battle, and the need for courage. In the context of this heroic world, it is unsurprising to find riddles describing martial equipment: martial equipment is the natural subject for martial language. Thus most critics agree that the Exeter Book riddles include swords, bows, spears, horns, battering rams, and mail coats.[6]

The status of the heroic idiom as basis and starting point for audiences of these riddles is the key point of this chapter. The heroic idiom is the dominant mode or manner through which almost all the riddles, not only the ones selected for discussion in this chapter, are presented: it is a kind of master trope within which the other riddling tropes operate.[7] Anyone attempting to read these texts, whether to solve them or to analyse them in other ways, must first deal with the heroic idiom, deciding whether to interpret it as denotative, ornamental, metaphorical, allegorical, or a combination of these (and other) possibilities. Whether a native speaker of Old English steeped in the heroic tradition, a scholar of early medieval English literature and culture, or a modern reader unfamiliar with other Old English poems and approaching the text in translation for the first time, any interpreter of the Exeter Book riddles must develop a keen awareness of the heroic idiom and the ways in which it may be used. This "keen awareness" is not simply the "competence" gained by any reader interpreting a text, however.[8] As I argue throughout my discussion, the Exeter Book collection frustrates

---

5 See, for example, *Christ and Satan* 581b; *Christ I* 266b and 372b; *The Phoenix* 135b.
6 These are the most generally accepted solutions for *Weapon-Warrior* (R.14), *Cursed among Weapons* (R.20), *Wob* (R.23), *Hopeful Garment* (R.35), *Towering Tree* (R.53), *Clothed in Red* (R.71), *Brain-Locker* (R.73), and *Warrior's Companion* (R.80). Further solutions can be found in the appendix.
7 Cf. Kenneth Burke, *A Grammar of Motives* (New York: Prentice Hall, 1945), Appendix D, 503–17. For Burke the master tropes are metaphor, metonymy, synecdoche, and irony.
8 Cf. Umberto Eco, *The Role of the Reader: Explorations in the Semiotics of Texts* (Bloomington: Indiana University Press, 1979), 7–8.

its audiences' growing competence. The more riddles we read, the less certain we can be about what we think we know. Thus developing a keen awareness of the heroic idiom ultimately leads to scrutiny of the central fabric of Old English poetry, the heroic idiom itself. This self-consciousness is significant and unusual. Other texts in Old English display few signs of subjecting the heroic idiom to such scrutiny. In fact, it has been argued that ascribing such self-consciousness to Old English poetry is anachronistic – an imposition of a detached modern view.[9] The riddles, however, require precisely that self-conscious scrutiny that we should not expect, for example, in *The Battle of Maldon*, a poem that celebrates its characters' identification with the "normalizing discourse of dominant ideology."[10]

In this chapter, I begin to explore how the Exeter Book riddles use the heroic idiom. In some of these texts, the heroic idiom seems to function as a context that is so clearly demarcated, so fully familiar,[11] that it *almost* becomes a code, a set of "already defined meanings" that are "univocally related to signifiers."[12] Such a code is particularly useful when the text itself contains things that simply cannot be known, where the manuscript is damaged, for example, or things that might not be known, such as the meaning of runic letters. However, while the heroic idiom reduces ambiguity in some texts, it does not do so in all. As we shall see towards the end of this chapter (and in more detail in the following chapters), the riddles disappoint expectations of univocal signifiers more often than not. Yet they do not always do so. My study thus begins with texts that require their audiences to take the heroic idiom literally. These texts may seem less interesting than those with startling metaphors and opaque clues, but they are a crucial component of the challenge posed by the Exeter collection as a whole: the fact that some texts *must* be taken literally means that any other *could* be. All aspects of the heroic idiom – all the actors, items, and ethics that in other Old

---

9 T.A. Shippey, "'Grim Wordplay': Folly and Wisdom in Anglo-Saxon Humor," in *Humour in Anglo-Saxon Literature*, ed. Jonathan Wilcox (Cambridge: Brewer, 2000), 34.

10 Muñoz, "'The White to Be Angry,'" 83. Cf., for example, the overview of the comitatus-ideal in Paul Battles, "'Contending Throng' Scenes and the *Comitatus* Ideal in Old English Poetry, With Special Attention to *The Battle of Maldon* 122a," *SN* 83 (2011): 42–5 and the argument against those who see the poem as critical in George Clark, "The Battle of Maldon: A Heroic Poem," *Speculum* 43 (1968): 52–71.

11 For a full exploration of the idea of a familiar language in Old English poetry, see Elizabeth M. Tyler, *Old English Poetics: The Aesthetics of the Familiar in Anglo-Saxon England* (Cambridge: Boydell and Brewer, 2006).

12 Jonathan Culler, *Structuralist Poetics: Structuralism, Linguistics and the Study of Literature* (London: Routledge and Kegan Paul, 1975), 20.

English texts appear self-evident and thus may pass by unquestioned and unnoticed – are liable to scrutiny in the riddles.

The Heroic Idiom Encapsulated: *Weapon-Warrior* (R.14)

Weapon-Warrior (R.14), unanimously solved as *horn* "horn," can be seen as a microcosm of heroic culture.[13] Although the text contains only nineteen lines, its use of the heroic idiom allows whole vistas of experience to be assumed behind its elliptical, yet nevertheless unambiguous, references:

> Ic wæs wæpen wiga.　Nu mec wlonc þeceð
> geong hagostealdmon　golde ond sylfore,
> woum wirbogum.　Hwilum weras cyssað;
> hwilum ic to hilde　hleoþre bonne
> 5 wilgehleþan;　hwilum wycg byreþ
> mec ofer mearce;　hwilum merehengest
> fereð ofer flodas　frætwum beorhtne;
> hwilum mægða sum　minne gefylleð
> bosm beaghroden;　hwilum ic on bordum sceal,
> 10 heard, heafodleas,　behlyþed licgan,
> hwilum hongige　hyrstum frætwed,
> wlitig on wage　þær weras drincað,
> freolic fyrdsceorp;　hwilum folcwigan
> on wicge wegað,　þonne ic winde sceal
> 15 sincfag swelgan　of sumes bosme;
> hwilum ic gereordum　rincas laðige
> wlonce to wine;　hwilum wraþum sceal
> stefne minre　forstolen hreddan,
> flyman feondsceaþan.　Frige hwæt ic hatte. (*Weapon-Warrior*)

(I was a warrior's weapon.[14] Now a proud young warrior covers me in gold and silver, with intricate interlace. Sometimes men kiss [me]; sometimes I summon willing companions to battle with my song; sometimes a horse

---

13 Cf. Elinor Teele, who describes this text as a simple example of using the heroic setting as "convenient shorthand" in "The Heroic Tradition in the Old English Riddles" (PhD diss., University of Cambridge, 2004), 38. For an overview of the poetic art used to convey this microcosm, see Megan Cavell, "Sounding the Horn in Exeter Book Riddle 14," *Explicator* 72 (2014): 324–7.

14 The line may also be construed – as most editors do – as "I was a weaponed warrior" without altering the argument here; see discussion in Williamson, *Old English Riddles*, 171 and Muir, *Exeter Anthology*, 2: 617.

bears me over the boundary; sometimes a sea-steed carries [me], bright with trappings, over the currents; sometimes a maiden adorned with rings fills my bosom; sometimes, hard and headless, I characteristically[15] lie despoiled on tables;[16] sometimes, shining, adorned with treasures, I hang on the wall where men drink – a noble piece of military equipment. Sometimes warriors carry me on a horse; then I, adorned with treasure, swallow the wind from a man's bosom. Sometimes I summon proud warriors to wine with my voice; sometimes with my call I recover from enemies what had been stolen and put robbers to flight. Find out what I am called.)

It is notable that, from the very first line, every aspect of this object pertains to heroic culture: even the origin of the manufactured object, the animal who originally bears the horn, is a fighter, in contrast to the pacific trees who unwillingly become a weapon in *Towering Tree* (R.53) or a warrior in *The Dream of the Rood*.[17] Even if we cannot solve the riddle, we can hardly fail to recognize the world in which this object appears. In fact, the horn here is even more comprehensively indexical of heroic culture than its usual representative, the sword, for the horn signals not only battle but also the peaceful, social events of the mead hall.[18] Thus, following the initial militaristic presentation of the object's origin, we see, in very quick succession, skilled craftsmanship, men gathering for war,

---

15 I have somewhat awkwardly translated *sceal* here as "characteristically" rather than "must," because the riddle, like a maxim, describes the essential nature of the object rather than its moral (or other) obligations. This understanding of *sceal* applies to all three of its appearances in *Weapon-Warrior*, but I have simply used the present tense in the other two. See discussion of *sceal* in Paul Cavill, *Maxims in Old English Poetry* (Cambridge: Brewer, 1999), 45–50.

16 9b–10 may also be translated, "sometimes, hard and headless, I lie deprived of embroidered [covers]"; cf. A.J. Wyatt, ed., *Old English Riddles* (Boston: D.C. Heath, 1912), 74. For discussion see Williamson, *Old English Riddles*, 172 and Muir, *Exeter Anthology*, 2: 618.

17 For discussion of this shared motif, see, for example, Margaret Schlauch, "*The Dream of the Rood* as Prosopopoeia," in *Essential Articles for the Study of Old English Poetry*, ed. Jess B. Bessinger Jr and Stanley J. Kahrl (Hamden, CT: Archon, 1968), 428–41 and Peter Orton, "The Technique of Object-Personification in *The Dream of the Rood* and a Comparison with the Old English Riddles," *LSE*, ns, 11 (1980): 1–18. Note also Edward B. Irving's discussion of "draftee riddles": "Heroic Experience in the Old English Riddles," in *Old English Shorter Poems: Basic Readings*, ed. Katherine O'Brien O'Keeffe (New York: Garland, 1994), 206–9. These are further discussed in Teele, "Heroic Tradition," 77–86.

18 An "index" is a sign that "interrelates with its semiotic object through some actual or physical or imagined causal connection." Floyd Merrell, "Charles Saunders Peirce's Concept of the Sign," in *The Routledge Companion to Semiotics and Linguistics*, ed. Paul Cobley (London and New York: Routledge, 2001), 31. In this case, the horn represents heroic culture through its actual participation in many of the activities associated with heroic culture.

28 Truth Is Trickiest

travel on horseback, travel by sea, a woman serving drink, a decorated wall, a call to wine, and successful defence of the home against thieves.

These images each last only one to two lines, but the heroic idiom allows a reader to expand them to encompass much fuller scenarios, which are described at length in other poems. Perhaps most important are the multiple references to adornment and treasure – eight in all. These are insistent if brief reminders of the lavish descriptions of noble equipment in, for example, *Waldere*:

> Standeð me her on eaxelum   Ælfheres laf,
> god and geapneb,   golde geweorðod,
> ealles unscende   æðelinges reaf
> to habbanne,   þonne hand wereð
> feorhhord feondum. (*Waldere* B 18–22a)

(Ælfhere's heirloom sits here on my shoulders: splendid, fine-meshed, and made precious with gold, [it is] entirely unscathed, armour for a prince to have, when hand protects life-hoard against enemies.)

Similar passages occur in *Beowulf, The Battle of Maldon,* and *Genesis A*.[19] Such equipment is more than functional, as it marks both the people bearing it and the verse describing it as elite. Yet even this understanding of treasure's meaning underestimates the importance of treasure in the heroic idiom. Treasure is not only a sign of wealth and power; it also signifies reward for loyalty, gratitude for previous service, future obligations, good fortune, and, ultimately, approval from God.[20] Its presence indicates individuals enjoying a society in a state of health, strength, and security. In short, its presence signifies happiness.[21] The bliss imagined of the long-dead occupants of a ruined Roman city (Bath or a place like it)[22] is an extreme but representative example:

> ... þær iu beorn monig
> glædmod ond goldbeorht   gleoma gefrætwed,

---

19 See, for example, the description of Beowulf's equipment for his expedition against Grendel's mother (*Beowulf* 1441b–54); the attention awarded to Byrhtnoth's sword despite his imminent death (*Maldon* 160–7a); the threat intimated by the unsheathing of swords (*Genesis A* 1991b–3a).

20 For gold as a sign of approval from God, see especially John Tanke, "Beowulf, Gold-Luck, and God's Will," *SP* 99 (2002): 356–79: "Gold-luck ... expresses, without explaining or justifying, the will of God" (379).

21 Cf. Pat Belanoff, "The Fall(?) of the Old English Female Poetic Image," *PMLA* 104 (1989): 822.

22 Muir summarizes the scholarly debate over the identity of the ruins and the genre of the poem (*Exeter Anthology*, 2: 699). For recent discussions of the poem, see, for

>   wlonc ond wingal   wighyrstum scan;
> 35 seah on sinc, on sylfor,   on searogimmas,
>   on ead, on æht,   on eorcanstan,
>   on þas beorhtan burg   bradan rices. (*The Ruin* 32b–7)

> (Long ago many a man – joyous and alight with gold, adorned with gleaming things, proud and merry with wine – shone there in war-trappings. He gazed on treasure, on silver, on intricately wrought gems, on riches, on possessions, on precious stones, [and] on a shining city in a broad kingdom.)

Although the wine is undoubtedly a contributory factor, treasure here emphatically constitutes the good life. In other texts, even the exceptions prove the rule. In *Beowulf*'s "Lament of the Last Survivor," for example, a man possesses an immense hoard of treasure and nevertheless dies in despair (2247–66). This ironic reversal of the usual causal relationship between treasure and joy does not destroy their normal equivalence, however, for the Last Survivor's treasure still signifies a society in a state of health, strength, and security, but in the long-lost past, not the present.

The bliss experienced by the previous inhabitants of a Roman city, although perhaps hyperbolic, matches the mood of *Weapon-Warrior* (R.14). Every aspect of the heroic idiom in the riddle pertains to pleasure and happiness. After the treasure of lines 1b to 3a, in line 3b we find kissing. The clues of the first two lines suggest an object rather than a person, so a listener or reader can recognize this kissing not as an intimate, affectionate act but rather as a metaphor, possibly the pleasant touch of drink to lips, but – given the immediately following line and a half, which explicitly describe the horn's song – more likely the cause of the horn's musical call. In either case, the kiss brings pleasant connotations. Although drinking can be either positive or negative in Old English poetry, in the heroic context, at least, it forms an important part of an idyllic social scene.[23] Music enjoys exclusively positive connotations; indeed, the same word, *dream*, seems to mean both music and joy.[24] In

---

example, Lawrence Beaston, "The Ruin and the Brevity of Human Life," *Neophil* 95 (2011): 477–89; Joshua Davies, *Visions and Ruins: Cultural Memory and the Untimely Middle Ages* Manchester Medieval Literature and Culture 19 (Manchester: Manchester University Press, 2018), 18–64; Brian Cook, "The Ruin: An Old English Mnemonic?" *Neophil* 105 (2021): 123–36.

23 See discussion in Hugh Magennis, *Images of Community in Old English Poetry* (Cambridge: Cambridge University Press, 1996), 35–59, and Magennis, *Anglo-Saxon Appetites: Food and Drink and their Consumption in Old English and Related Literature* (Dublin: Four Courts, 1999), 21–8.

24 See *DOE*, s.v. *dream*; see also the fuller discussion in Anya Adair, "Dream, Bliss, and the Shaping of Emotional Meaning in *Beowulf*," *JEGP* 121 (2022): 68–71.

this case, the music is a call to war, but it brings with it dear companions and the joys of a communal life, not dire expectations of death.

These companions are followed by journeys on horseback (5b–6a). Such journeys may not immediately signify heroic joy to the modern mind, but riding fine horses in Old English poetry is an elite pastime, a sign of wealth, joy, and peace. In part, of course, this is because horses themselves are treasure: Hrothgar gratefully presents not only weapons but also horses to Beowulf, and Beowulf loyally passes all but one of these on to Higelac and Hygd.[25] Possessing treasure, as we have seen, is positive, but *The Riming Poem* indicates that the experience of riding in itself could bring pleasure:

> Secgas mec segon,   symbel ne alegon,
> feohgiefe gefegon;   frætwed wægon
> wicg ofer wongum   wennan gongum,
> lisse mid longum   leoma getongum. (*Riming Poem* 5–8)

(Men recognized me, never denied me feasts, and exulted in rich gifts. Ornamented horses bore me over the fields in journeys of joy – in pleasure from the long strides of their limbs.)[26]

Thus horses, like treasure and feasting, both signify and cause joy. In addition, *The Rune Poem* confirms that the right kind of horse can improve one's appearances:

> ᛖ [eh] byþ for eorlum   æþelinga wyn,
> hors hofum wlanc,   ðær him hæleþ ymbe
> welege on wicgum,   wrixlaþ spræce … (*Rune Poem* 55–7)

(The steed, the horse proud in his hooves, is the joy of princes in front of noblemen, where warriors wealthy in horses exchange reports about him.)

The word *wicg*, used here in the *Rune Poem*, in *Weapon-Warrior* (R.14), and also in *Warrior's Companion* (R.80), another riddle usually interpreted as

---

25 See also my fuller discussion of horses in *Beowulf* in "Hrothgar's Horses: Feral or Thoroughbred?" *ASE* 35 (2007): 131–58.
26 This translation is speculative, but the inclusion of riding horses as part of idyllic joy is not in doubt. I retain the manuscript reading *getongum* rather than ASPR's *gehongum* here. Cf. O.D. Macrae-Gibson, ed. and trans., *The Old English Riming Poem* (Cambridge: Brewer, 1983), 31: "Men's eyes beheld me, happy in their gift of life; feasts never failed, and long-striding horses in fair harness carried them in sweet and joyous course over the land".

describing the *horn* in heroic culture, marks the horse as special, a sign of status, for this word appears predominantly in elite, heroic contexts.[27] Its presence not only reinforces the activation of the heroic idiom but indicates what such a horse is: an ostentatiously expensive possession, possibly the product of controlled breeding.[28] What is more specifically notable here, however, is the connection between the proud horse and reputation. The prince standing before other noblemen, whose status is measured in the possession of horses, is also measured – favourably – by the possession of his *wlanc* "proud" horse. He experiences joy because of what these wealthy men say about it. That is, the prince's standing is improved by possession of this treasure.

The remaining signs of the joyful heroic world in *Weapon-Warrior* (R.14) may be addressed more briefly. Travel by ship (6b–7) recalls the daring adventures of warriors like Beowulf, Higelac, and Scyld Scefing, who crossed the sea to achieve glory.[29] Although these journeys do not always lead to joy – Higelac's ended in his death – here riding the *merehengest* "sea-stallion, ship" (6b) is at worst neutral, and, given the context and the elevation granted by the poetic kenning, it seems likely that the connotations of this travel are positive.[30] The following image of the woman (8–9b) is similarly positive. Although often underestimated by modern readers,[31] the figure of the woman adorned with treasure

---

27 *Wicg* "horse" (as opposed to the insect, [*ear*]*wicga*) appears thirty-five times in the DOE corpus of Old English, twenty of which are in poetry: *Andreas* 1095b, *Elene* 1195b, *Gifts of Men* 70a, *Riming Poem* 7a, *Weapon-Warrior* (R.14. 5b), *Peace-Horses* (R.22. 2b, 9b, and 21b), *Warrior's Companion* (R.80. 7b), *Beowulf* 234b, 286b, 315a, 1045a, 1400a, 2174b, *Maldon* 240b, *Rune Poem* 57a and 85b, *Solomon and Saturn I* 155b, *Seasons for Fasting* 147a. Clark-Hall describes the word *wicg* as "very rare in prose," but it does appear four times in glosses, twice in law codes referring to a title, four times in charters referring to place-names or geographical descriptions, once in the *Martyrology* referring to a title, and seven times in the Anglo-Saxon Chronicle referring to a place-name and a title (these seven occurrences represent two terms, which are repeated in the A, C, and D manuscripts; the E manuscript has the place-name only).
28 Neville, "Hrothgar's Horses," 140–3.
29 This idea of crossing the sea may also have had a much deeper mythological significance for early medieval English people; see Nicholas Howe, *Migration and Mythmaking in Anglo-Saxon England* (New Haven: Yale University Press, 1989).
30 This passage could also refer to international trade, whence gold and silver came, but heroic literature does not usually acknowledge trade (as opposed to inheritance or looting) as a source of treasure.
31 Wealhtheow, the most fully developed image of this figure, has been characterized as pathetic and powerless by many scholars. See Alain Renoir, "A Reading Context for *The Wife's Lament*," in *Anglo-Saxon Poetry: Essays in Appreciation*, ed. Lewis E. Nicholson and Dolores Warwick Frese (Notre Dame: Notre Dame University Press, 1975), 229–30; Helen Damico, *Beowulf's Wealhtheow and the Valkyrie Tradition*

and serving drink constitutes an important aspect of heroic culture, implicated in the creation of the joyful, secure social spaces where gift-exchange and thus loyalty transpire. In the heroic idiom these social spaces are invariably represented as the mead hall, the central place of joy. Here the mead hall itself is not explicitly named, yet the heroic idiom can easily supply it: decorated with treasure, the wall surrounding the place *þær weras drincað* "where men drink" (12b) can hardly be anything else.[32]

There are, however, essential items missing from this microcosm of the heroic world: wounds, death, funerals, defeat, exile, feud, loss, and sorrow. The riddle depicts a utopia, and it is only at its very end that we find the possibility of a threat to the apparently unmitigated joy of heroic life. This threat comes from *wraþum* and *feondsceapan* "enemies" and "harmful foes" (17b, 19a). Yet even these foes are easily dismissed, simply by the sound of the horn; they pose no real threat to the heroic world. Presumably this is how we should imagine Hrothgar's Heorot before Grendel arrived: a place of song, loyal companions, fine horses, adventurous travel, peaceful social gatherings, excellent equipment, and a confident ability to defend the home from external threats. *Beowulf*, however, never presents such an unadulterated description of peace, pleasure, and joy; in that poem, as in many Old English poems, joy is characteristically mixed and endures for only a short time.[33] Even the incomparable glory of the unfallen angels in the Old English *Genesis A* lasts less than ten lines.[34]

Weapon-Warrior (R.14) thus provides an unusual example of how the heroic idiom can encapsulate all things good about life – secular, elite, male, early medieval English life, at least – without qualification. Although the uncharacteristic positivity of this text is notable, the point of this discussion is not so much to contest the usual view of Old English

---

(Madison: University of Wisconsin Press, 1984), 127; Edward B. Irving Jr., *Rereading Beowulf* (Philadelphia: University of Pennsylvania Press, 1989), 74; Gillian R. Overing, *Language, Sign, and Gender in Beowulf* (Carbondale: Southern Illinois University Press, 1990), 90–101; Michael J. Enright, *Lady with a Mead Cup: Ritual, Prophecy, and Lordship in the European Warband from La Tène to the Viking Age* (Dublin: Four Courts Press, 1996), 24; Shari Horner, *The Discourse of Enclosure: Representing Women in Old English Literature* (Albany: State University of New York Press, 2001), 77–81; Teele, "Heroic Tradition," 127–9. I disagree; see Jennifer Neville, "Women," in *Reading the Lord of the Rings*, ed. Robert Eaglestone (London: Continuum, 2005), 101–10.

32 For an overview of this important and much discussed setting, see Kathryn Hume, "The Concept of the Hall in Old English Poetry," *ASE* 3 (1974): 63–74.
33 See, for example, *The Wanderer* 108–10, *The Seafarer* 66b–71, and *The Riming Poem* 30–7 and 55–8.
34 See *Genesis A* 12b–21 and *Genesis B* 252–8.

poetry as gloomy and fatalistic[35] as to demonstrate how riddles may use the heroic idiom in a straightforward, direct way to describe heroic life without poetic periphrasis, disguise, or irony. With the exception of the vague description of the original animal in the first line and the immediately explained metaphor of "kissing" in 3b, the text comprises a series of literal descriptions of the object in various contexts,[36] all immediately recognizable within the heroic idiom. In fact, despite the unmistakably riddling closing formula, *Weapon-Warrior* is so straightforward that it may be fairly asked whether it makes any attempt at dissimulation at all.[37]

For modern audiences this riddle may serve as a kind of elementary test of our competence in reading the heroic idiom. For an early medieval English audience, made up of people who may have actually used such horns and were much more familiar with literature containing them, it may be assumed that solving this riddle would pose little challenge. In fact, if the game initiated by *Weapon-Warrior* were merely to guess its solution, it could be terminated by its fourth line. Reading to the end does more than simply reinforce a solution, however; it provides a very selective overview of heroic culture as a whole, a rose-tinted microcosm whose absences contrast strongly with heroic culture as presented in other texts. The riddle does not instruct its audience to do anything further with its description of heroic culture. Nevertheless, its presence among other enigmatic texts encourages a more than superficial reading: solving a riddle requires close attention to details, which may need to be pondered, twisted, or read in more than one way. In *Weapon-Warrior* such close attention probably results in the same solution as a superficial reading, but in the process the values and aspirations of heroic culture itself are subject to scrutiny. Given the production and reception of the Exeter Book within ecclesiastical institutions,[38] its early medieval audiences, at least, may have noticed other things missing from this idyllic view of life:

---

35 This is the view presented in *The Norton Anthology of English Literature*, ed. M.H. Abrams, 7th ed., 2 vols (New York: W.W. Norton, 2000), 1: 5. Cf., however, Jean I. Young, "*Glaed waes ic gliwum*: Ungloomy Aspects of Old English Poetry," in *The Early Cultures of North-West Europe: H.M. Chadwick Memorial Studies*, ed. Cyril Fox and Bruce Dickins (Cambridge: Cambridge University Press, 1950), 273–87, and see discussion in Jonathan Wilcox, "Introduction," in *Humour in Anglo-Saxon Literature*, 1 and, in the same volume, Shari Horner, "'Why Do You Speak So Much Foolishness?' Gender, Humor, and Discourse in Ælfric's *Lives of Saints*," 127.
36 Cf. Teele's reading of Riddle 14 as a "functional riddle" ("Heroic Tradition," 36–9).
37 Cf. Teele, who characterizes it as a riddle with "superficial engagement" with the heroic world ("Heroic Tradition," 36).
38 Many critics have attempted to interpret the Exeter Book in the context of the Benedictine reform, for example. See Gunhild Zimmerman, *The Four Old English Poetic*

not only feud, exile, and death but also God, prayer, and heaven. Much attention has been devoted to understanding how a monastic audience might receive the double-entendre riddles or the pre-Christian world of *Beowulf*,[39] but it is worth considering the same kind of question here, unanswerable as it may be. There is no hint in *Weapon-Warrior* that this purely secular, heroic world is anything other than ideal: it is heaven on earth. Such a view is unthinkable in the context of *Christ, Guthlac, The Wanderer, Vainglory,* and other poems in the Exeter Book, yet the riddle provides no judgement on that view. We cannot know what individuals in early medieval England might have thought about it, but we can perhaps assume that, having looked hard at it, they *did* think about it. Arriving at a solution, whether at line 4 or later, does not necessarily end the processes initiated by the riddle. The audiences of *Weapon-Warrior*, then and now, must evaluate the heroic world that it celebrates.

Such processes may also have led to further, less obvious solutions, even if modern scholars have seen no need for them. An early medieval audience, too, may simply have shouted (or mentally exulted), *"Horn!"* and moved on to the next riddle. Yet even then the processes initiated by *Weapon-Warrior* do not entirely cease, for the experience of reading this riddle has an impact upon the reading of other riddles. Any audience attempting to interpret other texts in the collection must keep in mind the possibility that their statements are simply what they say: even a text adorned with *hapax legomena*, kennings, and other poetic compounds from the heroic idiom may need to be taken literally.

Manuscripts: Texts, Contexts, and Historical Background (Heidelberg: Universitätsverlag C. Winter, 1995), 90–182; Melanie Heyworth, "*Be rihtre æwe*: Legislating and Regulating Marital Morality in Late Anglo-Saxon England" (PhD diss., University of Sydney, 2005), 150–60, with particular attention to the riddles' ability to contribute to moral regulation at 160–75; John D. Niles, *God's Exiles and English Verse: On the Exeter Anthology of Old English Poetry* (Exeter: University of Exeter Press, 2019), 40–61. Magennis discusses this context for Old English poetry more generally in his *Images of Community*, 3–15.

39 For reception of the double-entendre riddles, see chapter 6, below. Discussion of the reception of *Beowulf* is vast, but see, for example, Margaret E. Goldsmith, "The Christian Perspective in Beowulf," in *An Anthology of Beowulf Criticism* (Notre Dame and London: University of Notre Dame Press, 1963), 373–86; Patrick Wormald, "Bede, *Beowulf*, and the Conversion of the Anglo-Saxon Aristocracy," in *Bede and Anglo-Saxon England: Papers in Honour of the 1300th Anniversary of the Birth of Bede,* ed. Robert T. Farrell (Oxford: British Archaeological Reports, 1978), 32–95; Edward B. Irving Jr, "The Nature of Christianity in *Beowulf*," *ASE* 13 (1984): 7–21; Fred C. Robinson, *Beowulf and the Appositive Style* (Knoxville: University of Tennessee Press, 1985), 29–59; Peter Orton, "Burning Idols, Burning Bridges: Bede, Conversion and *Beowulf*," *LSE* 36 (2005): 5–46.

Reading Literally

Although *Weapon-Warrior* describes the heroic world at some length, other riddles invoke the elite military world, with its connotations of violence, glory, loyalty, courage, elitism, wealth, and social joys, with very few words: making reference to objects, attitudes, places, and actions that have become associated with each other allows speakers, writers, listeners, and readers to require only a few of these to distinguish a very extensive and complex variety of human actions from the rest of human experience.[40] An audience that recognizes the trope of the heroic idiom can quickly narrow the range of possible answers. For example, even modern readers may not need the encrypted solution in the first line to solve *Wob* (R.23) as a *boga* "bow":

> Agof[41] is min noma   eft onhwyrfed.
> Ic eom wrætlic wiht   on gewin sceapen.
> Þonne ic onbuge,   me of bosme fareð
> ætren onga.   Ic beom eallgearo
> 5 þæt ic me þæt feorhbealo   feor aswape.
> Siþþan me se waldend,   se me þæt wite gescop,
> leoþo forlæteð,   ic beo lengre þonne ær,
> oþþæt ic spæte,   spilde geblonden,
> ealfelo attor   þæt ic ær geap.
> 10 Ne togongeð þæs   gumena hwylcum,
> ænigum eaþe   þæt ic þær ymb sprice,
> gif hine hrineð   þæt me of hrife fleogeð,
> þæt þone mandrinc   mægne geceapaþ,
> full ferfæste[42]   feore sine.
> 15 Nelle ic unbunden   ænigum hyran
> nymþe searosæled.   Saga hwæt ic hatte. (*Wob*)

(*Wob* is my name turned backwards. I am an amazing creature shaped in struggle. When I bend, a poison sting moves out of my belly. I am prepared

---

40 Cf. John P. Hermann, *Allegories of War: Language and Violence in Old English Poetry* (Ann Arbor: University of Michigan Press, 1989), 39.
41 This is the manuscript reading. Most editors emend to "agob," which, when reversed, spells *boga* "bow". See discussion in Muir, *Exeter Anthology*, 2: 625.
42 Instead of the manuscript's *full wer fæste* or Muir's *fullwerod fæste*, I follow here Williamson's reading, which is supported by Pinsker and Ziegler. For discussion see Williamson, *Old English Riddles*, 81 and 206–7; Pinsker and Ziegler, 46–7; and Muir, *Exeter Anthology*, 2: 626.

to sweep that deadly thing far away. After my ruler, the one who shaped that torment for me, releases my limb, I am longer than I was before, until I spit out the dire poison, blended with destruction, that I swallowed earlier. What I speak of here does not happen to any man lightly, if what flies from my belly touches him, so that he pays for that evil drink with his strength, for that dangerous cup with his own life. Unbound I will not obey anyone, unless cleverly fettered. Say what I am called.)

Even leaving aside the apparently misspelled reversed revelation of the solution in the first line, this riddle is remarkably explicit. It not only locates this weapon squarely within its usual context (*on gewin* "in conflict or struggle");[43] it also describes the action of the bow (taking in and expelling a deadly sting) and the effect of its use (death), albeit in elliptical language. The metaphors used to describe this process – bending of the bow as torment, length of the bow as limb, shooting as spitting, centre of the bow as belly, arrow-head as poison, injury as loss of strength – require little mental strain, with one exception: the portrayal of death as a drink that must be paid for with one's life.[44] Additional clues may be found in a pun: the repeated use of the verb *scieppan* "to make" at 2b and 6b may draw attention to the bow's changing *shape* as it is used. In this context, providing the solution, even backwards, in the first line may have seemed too easy and thus led the Exeter Book scribe (or a previous scribe) to attempt to slow down the process by adding the twist of a misspelling.[45] The usual pattern in the Anglo-Latin riddling tradition is thus reversed: rather than the text expanding upon or mystifying its title,[46] the initially unfathomable nonsense word of the "solution" is de-mystified by the terms supplied by the text. Overall, however, *Wob* requires its audience to take its language fairly literally: the bending thing that shoots deadly missiles and only works when bound is, in fact, a bending thing that shoots deadly missiles and only works when bound – a weapon located logically in the military context of *gewin* "struggle." Of course, as with *Weapon-Warrior* (R.14), the process of looking hard at this

---

43 Cf., however, Stanley, "Heroic Aspects," who suggests that *on gewin sceapen* might mean "destined to strife" (208).
44 The "cup of death" motif is discussed in Carleton Brown, "*Poculum Mortis* in Old English," *Speculum* 15 (1940): 389–99. See also discussion in Hugh Magennis, "The Cup as Symbol and Metaphor in Old English Literature," *Speculum*, 60 (1985): 522–30.
45 Wyatt suggests this (*Old English Riddles*, 81). Williamson, however, argues that the substitution was not arbitrary but an attempt to correct archaic spelling (*Old English Riddles*, 204–5).
46 Cf. Nicholas Howe, "Aldhelm's *Enigmata* and Isidorian Etymology," *ASE* 14 (1985): 57.

text can raise plenty of interesting ideas even after a solution is found,[47] but for the purposes of this chapter, the key thing to note is the need to take much of the language here literally.

The beginning of *Cursed among Weapons* (R.20) is similarly explicit about its terms of reference and thus readily gives away a solution:

> Ic eom wunderlicu wiht, on gewin sceapen,
> frean minum leof, fægre gegyrwed.
> Byrne is min bleofag, swylce beorht seomað
> wir ymb þone wælgim þe me waldend geaf,
> 5 se me widgalum wisað hwilum
> sylfum to sace. Þonne ic sinc wege
> þurh hlutterne dæg, hondweorc smiþa,
> gold ofer geardas. Oft ic gæstberend
> cwelle compwæpnum... (*Cursed among Weapons* 1–9a)

(I am a remarkable creature, shaped in struggle, dear to my lord, beautifully adorned. My mail-coat is decorated, and bright filigree also twines around the death-jewel that my ruler gave to me – he who sometimes guides me to battle. Then throughout the clear day I wear treasure, the handwork of smiths, and gold around the courts. I often kill the living with battle-weapons.)

Conflict, military equipment, treasure, battle, the courts surrounding the mead-hall, and death by weapons activate an audience's expectations of the heroic idiom once again. In such a context, the question of what kind of object kills people is very likely to yield *sweord* "sword" as a first answer.[48] Few alternatives have ever been proposed, yet another twenty-six lines of verse follow, and previously there were more: although we cannot know how much text has been lost, it is agreed that a folio is missing after the last remaining word of *Cursed among Weapons*.[49] This folio may have contained little more than a closing formula, or it may have contained further development of an object already explored at considerable length: with thirty-five surviving lines, *Cursed among Weapons* is longer than all but three of the Exeter Book riddles.

---

47 See, for example, my discussion in chapter 5 below.
48 For discussion of some of these solutions, see chapter 4, below; the full list of alternatives can be found in the appendix, below.
49 Muir, *Exeter Anthology*, 1: 300: "The outer sheet of the fourteenth gathering has been lost, so that there is a folio wanting ... after the present folio." See also discussion in Williamson, *Old English Riddles*, 198–9.

Regardless, these first eight and a half lines share with *Wob* (R.23) their direct use of the heroic idiom to describe heroic culture. The rest of the riddle, in contrast, uses this idiom differently, as a metaphorical disguise: the sword presents itself as if it were a human warrior. In fact, the use of the heroic idiom as a disguise occurs in the first eight and a half lines, too, for the mail-coat referred to in line 3a is probably a scabbard rather than a metal tunic. I shall discuss the use of the heroic idiom as a disguise in the following chapter, but it is worth noting the unevenness in its use here. In *Cursed among Weapons*, an audience must manage this switching of uses from one line to the next; sometimes it must read the heroic idiom metaphorically, and sometimes it must accept it at face value. Nevertheless, in the first eight and a half lines, at least, *gewin* "struggle" is (at least in part) armed struggle, *gegyrwed* "adorned" refers to metal ornament, *sinc* "treasure" is treasure, and *sæcc* "battle" is military battle.[50]

The Value of a Code: Filling in Physical Gaps

Being able to rely upon the heroic idiom can be not only helpful but essential to reading a text. *Clothed in Red* (R.71) provides a good example of how knowledge of a well-established trope like the heroic idiom can lead to a satisfying solution even when the text is partly missing. The first half of the text, although unaffected by physical damage, does not appear to refer to the heroic idiom and so grants only a vague sense of the riddle-subject's value and manufacturing:

> Ic eom rices æht, reade bewæfed,
> stið ond steapwong. Staþol wæs iu þa
> wyrta wlitetorhtra; nu eom wraþra laf,
> fyres ond feole, fæste genearwad,
> wire geweorþad. (*Clothed in Red* 1–5a)

(I am the possession of a powerful man, clothed in red, stiff and high-cheeked. Previously my place was one of beautiful plants; now I am the leavings of enemies, of fire and file, firmly confined and honoured with metal ornament.)

---

50 The *gewin* "struggle" may refer to the manufacturing process as well as armed conflict. Elsewhere, "struggle," "ornament," "treasure," and "battle" have different referents. For struggle, for example, see discussion of *Four Creatures* (R.51) in chapter 4 below; for treasure, see *Mundbora* (R.17) in chapter 3 below; for battle see *Fight against Wave* (R.16) in chapter 3 below.

This is something owned by the rich, surrounded by something red, almost certainly made of metal because left behind by fire and file, and probably valuable. Beyond these points, little is certain. *Steapwong* "high-cheeked" does not help me, at least, to visualize the object, if indeed modern scholars have interpreted this half-line correctly.[51] In contrast, although badly damaged and thus fragmentary, the second half of the riddle locates this object securely within heroic culture:

>   Wepeð hwilum
> for minum gripe   se þe gold wigeð,
> þonne ic yþan sceal   [. . . . . . .]fe,
> hringum gehyrsted.   me [.]i[. . . .
> . .]go[.]dryhtne   min[. . . . . . .
> . . . .] wlite bete. (*Clothed in Red* 5b–10)[52]

(He who wears gold sometimes weeps because of my grip, when I must destroy [… life?], adorned with rings. Me [?...] my (gold)-lord [?...] improve [his] appearance.)

Although precisely what is happening at the end of this mutilated text is unknowable, we can fill in a surprising number of gaps if we recognize the heroic idiom.[53] For example, the heroic idiom provides an immediate set of connotations for *se þe gold wigeð* "the one who wears gold" (6b): he is at the very least a proven warrior, or, more likely, a lord who leads warriors into battle and rewards their courage with weapons of great value, probably identical with the *dryhten* "lord," probably a *golddrihten* "gold-lord," who appears three lines later (9a). The word *go[ld]drihten* is actually generated by the heroic idiom itself. The word is a modern guess, built from two surviving letters and a gap for two letters in front of the surviving word *dryhtne*; *golddrihten* does not appear anywhere in the surviving corpus of Old English poetry.[54] However, an analogous term, *goldwine* "gold-friend," referring to the lord who gives gifts of gold in return for a

---

51 See discussion in Williamson, *Old English Riddles*, 341, and Muir, *Exeter Anthology*, 2: 711–12.
52 For the arrangement of this fragmentary text, see discussions in Krapp and Dobbie, 370; Williamson, *Old English Riddles*, 342; Muir, *Exeter Anthology*, 2: 712.
53 Cf. Umberto Eco, *A Theory of Semiotics* (Bloomington: Indiana University Press, 1976), 135–6.
54 See Muir, *Exeter Anthology*, 2: 712, who follows the suggestions in *The Exeter Book, Part II: Poems IX–XXXII*, ed. and trans. William S. Mackie, EETS, o.s. 194 (London: Humphry Milford and Oxford University Press, 1934), 208.

thegn's loyalty, appears nine times.[55] Modern readers' knowledge of the heroic idiom has thus led to the restoration (or possibly to the creation) of a word that contributes to the understanding and solving of the riddle.

The heroic idiom can also supply further information. In answer to the question of who or what would make a lord weep, it seems likely that the *gripe* "grip" (6a) is the "bite" or wound made by a sword, the weapon almost exclusively associated with the military elite. Other texts confirm that such a sword may be *hringum gehyrsted* "adorned with rings" (8a), like the speaker in this text.[56] *Beowulf* confirms that carrying such a sword *wlite bete* "improves (one's) appearance" (10): when the hero first arrives in Denmark, the coast-guard notes that perceptions of a warrior's worth may derive solely from the weapons he bears (*Beowulf* 249b–51), and, later, the boat-guard was more valued in Hrothgar's court after Beowulf's gift of a sword to him (1900–3a). Using the heroic idiom, we can solve the riddle: it is a *sweord* "sword," the traditional weapon of the elite warrior in heroic culture.

It is important to note, of course, that what is plausible is not the only possibility. For example, although the reference to the *gripe* "grip" renders the identification of the riddle-object as a "sword" attractive, there are other things that "bite." Swords do "grip" in *Beowulf* 1566b and 1765a and in *Waldere B* 13a, but elsewhere spears (*Genesis A* 2063b–4, *Andreas* 187a), fire (*Elene* 1302a, *Solomon and Saturn I* 48a, *Juliana* 391a), stones (*Solomon and Saturn I* 76a), and the sea (*Genesis A* 1381b) impose this inescapably fatal attack.[57] In addition, although a sword may be appropriately described as being "adorned with rings," the phrase may not refer to the speaker: it may refer instead to the one who wears gold or perhaps to another object destroyed by the speaker, hidden within the holes in the manuscript: elsewhere mail-coats, ships, helmets, and halls are described as being adorned with rings.[58] The heroic idiom cannot reduce this shattered text to a set of truly univocal signifiers.

---

55 *Elene* 201a, *Judith*, 22a, *The Wanderer* 22b and 35b, and *Beowulf* 1171a, 1476a, 1602a, 2419a, and 2584a.

56 Cf. *Beowulf* 672b (*hyrsted sweord* "adorned sword"), 1521b, 1564b, 2037a (*hringmæl* "ring-mailed one," referring to a sword), and *Genesis A* 1992b (*hringmæled sweord* "ring-mailed sword"). See also discussion in Hilda Ellis Davidson, *The Sword in Anglo-Saxon England: Its Archaeology and Literature*, corrected reprint (1962; Woodbridge, Suffolk: Boydell, 1994), 71–7.

57 These examples are restricted to metaphorical "gripping"; people, monsters, and devils can also grip literally, i.e., with fingers.

58 Mail coats: *Beowulf* 322b, 1245b, 1889b, 2615b, 2754b; *Maldon* 145a. Ships: *Beowulf* 1131a, 1897b, 1862a; *Elene* 248b. Helmet: *Beowulf* 1503b. Halls: *Beowulf* 2010a, 2840a, 3053a.

Nevertheless, an audience facing *Clothed in Red*, even in its current fragmentary state, may use the heroic idiom as a code to fill in enough of its gaps to arrive at a solution. Yet even in this apparently satisfactory interpretation what seem like plausible assumptions must be tested as the text proceeds, and that process of testing puts the heroic idiom itself under examination. In this case, for example, solving this riddle requires an audience to think about the gender stereotypes pertaining to the heroic idiom. According to modern critical views, at least, the one who weeps and wears gold *ought* to be a woman, for women are famously identified as being *hringum gehrodene* "adorned with rings" (*Judith* 37a),[59] and mourning has been identified as the particular attribute of women.[60] Mourning is not, however, an exclusively feminine role in the heroic idiom; Hrothgar, for example, weeps when the hero departs (*Beowulf* 1872b). Although the *Beowulf* poet does not state that this behaviour is inappropriate for men, modern scholars have interpreted such male weeping in a very negative light.[61] This view of male weeping influences the interpretation of *Clothed in Red*, with the result that modern gender-stereotypes may even over-write the grammar of the Old English text: Davidson, for example, surmises that the "'bearer of gold' is presumably a woman, who weeps because she is bereaved by the action of the sword."[62] Yet the masculine gender of *se þe* "the one who" (6b) indicates that the mourner here is male.[63]

---

59 Cf. also Mary in *Christ I* (292a), Wealhtheow (614a, 623b, 640b, 1163b), Modthryth (1948a), Freawaru (2025a), and Hygd (2175b–6) in *Beowulf*, and the proverbial queen in *Maxims I* (126b).

60 See, for example, Alain Renoir, "A Reading Context for *The Wife's Lament*," in *Anglo-Saxon Poetry: Essays in Appreciation for John C. McGalliard*, ed. Lewis E. Nicholson and Dolores Warwick Frese (Notre Dame: Notre Dame University Press, 1975), 224–41; Joyce Hill, "'Þæt wæs geomuru ides!' A Female Stereotype Examined," in *New Readings on Women in Old English Literature*, ed. Helen Damico and Alexandra Hennessey Olsen (Bloomington: Indiana University Press, 1990), 242; Jane Chance, "The Structural Unity of Beowulf: The Problem of Grendel's Mother," in *New Readings on Women*, 251; Shari Horner, *The Discourse of Enclosure: Representing Women in Old English Literature* (Albany: State University of New York Press, 2001), 82.

61 See, for example, Mary Dockray-Miller's reading of this scene in "*Beowulf*'s Tears of Fatherhood," *Exemplaria* 10 (1998): 1–28. Cf., however, the very different reading of Hrothgar in Harriet Soper, "Reading the Exeter Book Riddles as Life-Writing," *RES* 68 (2017): 841–64 and the critical analysis of how modern readings can distort the depiction of weeping men in Robin Norris, "Sad Men in *Beowulf*," in *Dating Beowulf: Studies in Intimacy*, ed. Daniel C. Remein and Erica Weaver (Manchester: Manchester University Press, 2020), 210–26.

62 Davidson, *Sword*, 155.

63 Cf. the careful analysis of the significance of assigning masculine pronouns to Grendel's mother in Renée Rebecca Trilling, "Beyond Abjection: The Problem with Grendel's Mother Again," *Parergon* 24 (2007): 14–16.

Despite the physical gaps and ambiguities, the place of the riddle's speaker within heroic culture seems almost unquestionable, and thus almost all the solutions proposed for *Clothed in Red* are weapons: while *wæpen* "weapon," *hand-seax* "dagger," *helm* "helmet," and *scield* "shield" have all received support, "cupping glass" has not.[64] The apparent certainty of the riddle's context, however, is only apparent. It derives from the heroic idiom, which is brought to our attention – activated, as it were – by a remarkably small number of words (*gripe* "grip, bite, wound," *gold* "gold," *yþan* "destroy," *hringum gehyrsted* "adorned with rings," *go(ld)dryhten* "gold-lord") whose significance derives mainly from their collocation rather than their membership in a marked vocabulary.[65] Individually these words provide little certainty. Found together, however, these words direct the audience to interpret the text within the dictates of the heroic idiom, the world in which gold-friends, violence, and, significantly, ring-adorned swords appear.

Once activated, the heroic idiom allows an audience to fill in an amazing number of gaps, to the point that this process of interpretation seems almost capable of creating a "whole" text, one without holes; it may even create a narrative, although there is no real foundation for it. Such a narrative might run as follows. A man wearing gold weeps because of a wound – perhaps a metonym or litotes for death – caused by a sword. Who is this man? Almost all elite warriors in the heroic idiom wear gold, but, given the value placed on courage in the face of death, most do not weep for their own wounds or deaths: despite being wounded, for example, Byrhtnoth laughs triumphantly as he fights the Vikings (*Maldon* 146–7).[66] Nevertheless, although warriors do not weep for their own wounds – within the heroic idiom, at least – certain men do weep for the wounds and deaths of others. The man weeping here may therefore be interpreted as a lord mourning the death of his thegns in battle, destroyed by ring-adorned swords: for example, in *Beowulf* Hrothgar mourns the death of his thegns, even if the text does not say that he weeps at this particular point (*Beowulf* 130–1, 146b–9a, 1306b–9). The emphasis on gold and thus the role of the gift-giving lord renders this interpretation most likely, but the heroic idiom also allows the possibility that this man is a father mourning his sons.[67]

---

64 See the appendix, below, for the list of these solutions and the scholars who proposed them.
65 Clark-Hall does not mark any of these words as "poetic"; Griffith includes only *hyrstan* in his list of poetic words in Old English ("Poetic Language," 184).
66 For discussion of this laughter, see John D. Niles, "Byrhtnoth's Laughter and the Poetics of Gesture," in *Humour in Anglo-Saxon Literature*, 11–32.
67 An unnamed father and Hrethel mourn their sons in *Beowulf* 2444–71. Fathers also mourn their sons in Old Icelandic literature; see summary in Cathy Jorgensen

Meanwhile (or at another time), and probably elsewhere, a sword's ornamentation and innate value raise the profile and prestige of its owner. The story now begins to appear complete enough to *be* a story, rather than simply a description. In fact, it could easily be inserted into another, equally fragmentary narrative: *Waldere*. There, too, a precious, value-laden sword destroys a lord's thegns. From that story we could fill in the name of the lord, some of the thegns, and even the sword itself: "Mimming," the famous sword forged by Weland (*Waldere A* 2–3).

Such a solution is built on almost nothing – on physical and semantic absences, on gaps in the text. It cannot be proven, and its specificity seems out of place in context: the Exeter Book riddles refer to types, not individuals.[68] Indeed, the story that I have created is generic enough that it could equally be superimposed upon a story in *Beowulf*, the hypothetical story in which the hero anticipates sword-deaths inspired by the sight of a ring-adorned sword. Beowulf predicts that, after Hrothgar's attempt to create peace between the Danes and Heathobards with a royal marriage, a guest in Ingeld's courts may see a warrior *frætwum hremig* "rejoicing in treasure" (*Beowulf* 2054a), one whose appearance has been improved with the guest's own father's looted sword. The sight of that treasure will initiate another *billes bite* "blade's bite" (*Beowulf* 2060a) that results in death, a failed peace-treaty, an ongoing conflict, and a lord suffering from *cearwælmum* "surging sorrows" (*Beowulf* 2066a). Similar connections could be made between my narrative and *Beowulf*'s Finnsburg episode, for there, too, *hildeleoman* "battle-lights, swords" (*Beowulf* 1143b), and the *laðbite* "hate-bites, wounds" (1122a) caused by them, lead men on both sides (as well as one woman, Hildeburh) to *sorge* "sorrow" (1149b). My point, however, is not to offer Mimming or any other particular sword as the solution to *Clothed in Red* but rather to demonstrate how an audience can derive the heroic idiom from knowledge of other texts and use it to insert what is not there into a text – not simply a solution, but a whole world. In fact, the riddle's audience *must* use the heroic idiom, must supply this world, to read this text and, indeed, most Old English poetry.

Itnyre, "The Emotional Universe of Medieval Icelandic Fathers and Sons," in *Medieval Family Roles: A Book of Essays*, ed. Cathy Jorgensen Itnyre (New York: Garland, 1996), 173–96.

68 "A common accessibility to possible solutions seems a necessary pre-requisite to the riddling game" (Williamson, *Old English Riddles*, 193).

Relying on the Code: Restoring the Fabric

The heroic idiom may allow an audience not only to read, not only to fill in missing letters, but even to rewrite the text preserved by the Exeter Book scribe. *Brain-Locker* (R.73) is usually solved as *gar* "spear" or, better, *æsc* "ash," a word that designates both the "spear" and the tree commonly used to make spears, but it has also been solved as *ramm* "ram." At the beginning of this text, we observe the transformation of the tree destined to become a wooden object:

> Ic on wonge aweox,   wunode þær mec feddon
> hruse ond heofonwolcn,   oþþæt me onhwyrfdon
> gearum frodne,   þa me grome wurdon,
> of þære gecynde   þe ic ær cwic beheold,
> 5 onwendan mine wisan,   wegedon mec of earde,
> gedydon þæt ic sceolde   wiþ gesceape minum
> on bonan willan   bugan hwilum. (*Brain-Locker* 1–7)

(I grew up on a plain, dwelt where earth and the sky's clouds fed me, until those who became hostile to me changed me, old in years, from the nature that I previously had when alive. They changed my ways, moved me from the land, forced me sometimes to bend against my shape, according to a killer's desire.)

At this point, the holes that mar many of the riddles at the end of the manuscript render the next fourteen and a half lines of this text a lacework of editorial guesses:

> Nu eom mines frean   folme bysigo[d
> ....]dlan dæl,   gif his ellen deag,
> 10 oþþe æfter dome [.]ri[......
> ....]ian   mæ[r]þa fremman,
> wyrcan w[..............
> ....]ec on þeode   utan we[.....
> ....]ipe
> 15 ond to wrohtstæp[e...........
> ....]eorp,   eaxle gegyrde,
> wo[..................]
> ond swiora smæl,   sidan fealwe
> [.......]   þonne mec heaþosigel
> 20 scir bescineð   ond mec [.....]
> fægre feormað.... (*Brain-Locker* 8–21a)

(Now I am employed in my lord's hand, [?] share, if his courage prevails, or after glory [?] perform famous deeds, work [?], among the people outside [?], and as an injury [?], (dark?), shoulders bound [?] and a small neck, yellow sides [?] when the bright battle-sun shines on me and [?] kindly feeds me ...)

We can be certain of almost nothing here; even the number of lines and division of half-lines are guesses.[69] It is thus unsurprising that, although many scholars have tentatively proposed individual letters and words to fill in some of these gaps, few have been bold enough to attempt to create a narrative out of this part of the text.[70] Yet even so the presence of the heroic idiom, with its references to *ellen* "courage" (9b), *dome* "glory" (10a), and *mærþa fremman* "performing famous deeds" (11b), is unmistakable, and so, as with *Clothed in Red* (R.71), we may use the heroic idiom to fill in the physical holes on folio 126, at least in broad strokes: we may assume that the *heaþosigel* "battle-sun" (19b) shines down on a battlefield, where a brave warrior uses a weapon with a *swiora smæl* "narrow neck" (18a), some kind of *eaxle* "shoulders" (16b) with bindings, and *fealwe* "yellow?" (18b) sides.[71] These assumptions are apparently confirmed by the less fragmentary conclusion of the riddle:

>   ...ond on fyrd wigeð
>   cræfte on hæfte.   Cuð is wide
>   þæt ic þristra sum   þeofes cræfte
>   under brægnlocan   [* * *]
> 25 hwilum eawunga   eþelfæsten
>   forðweard brece,   þæt ær frið hæfde.
>   Feringe from,   he fus þonan
>   wendeð of þam wicum.   Wiga se þe mine
>   siþas cunne,   saga hwæt ic hatte. (*Brain-Locker* 21b–9)

(... and carries [me] with skill in the army, in bondage. It is widely known that I, one of the bold ones, with a thief's skill, [?do something?] into/under the brain-locker; sometimes, advancing, I openly break into the

---

69 See Muir for discussion of past attempts at emendation and justification for spacing (*Exeter Anthology*, 2: 714–15).
70 Franz Dietrich fills in all the gaps; see "Die Rätsel des Exeterbuchs: Würdigung, Lösung und Herstellung," *Zeitschrift für deutsches Altertum* 11 (1859): 481–2, but cf. the more conservative texts in Muir (*Exeter Anthology*, 1: 365–6) and Williamson (*Old English Riddles*, 114), both of which follow the arrangement in Mackie, 210–14.
71 The meaning of *fealu* is a riddle in itself: see Jennifer Neville, "Hrothgar's Horses: Feral or Thoroughbred?" *ASE* 35 (2007): 145–52 (and references therein). Here, however, *fealu* may simply remind that the object is made of wood.

home-fortress that previously had peace. Bold and prompt in departure, it turns from there, out of the settlements. Warrior who knows my journeys, say what I am called.)

The military nature of the activity in the fragmentary part of the text seems fully confirmed by these concluding lines, and, in turn, the certainty of this military context has encouraged editors to emend the manuscript reading *hrægnlocan* (24a), whose meaning is unknown, to *brægnlocan* "brain-locker, skull."[72] This emendation makes sense: having been carried to war, a spear, like others of its kind (*pristra* "bold ones", 23a) may enter a skull. Although the action itself is unknown – at least a half-line, including the verb in question, is missing at line 24[73] – the immediately following description of the object breaking into a fortification may be a metaphorical description of the same act. Breaking into a skull may be metaphorically described as breaching a fortress, which *ær frið hæfde* "previously had peace" (26b). In turn, this understanding makes sense of the following line and a half: the unidentified *he* is the *gæst* "spirit, life, soul" of the breached skull, which is now obliged to depart this mortal life, and the *wic* "dwellings" (28a) become a metaphorical description of the body itself.[74] Anyone familiar with the heroic idiom, whether a literal *wiga* "warrior" (28b) or simply a riddlee struggling against the challenge of the text, knows the ways of such a common weapon and can thus say the object's name, *æsc* "ash-spear," as the riddle demands.

Yet even a *gar-berend* "spear-bearer" could be wrong, for the wooden weapon described here could also be a *boga* "bow."[75] This solution suits the age of the tree better, for a spear is made out of a tree that is not *gearum frod* "old in years" (3a), while a bow is normally carved out of the heart-wood of a larger tree.[76] It also suits the tree's transformation better: a spear remains straight, but a bow characteristically must *wiþ gesceape*

---

72 Muir summarizes previous scholarship (*Exeter Anthology*, 2: 715). Cf. Williamson, *Old English Riddles*, 346–7. Pinsker and Ziegler emend to *under hærnflotan* "zwischen die Schiffe" (306).
73 Williamson suggests it might have been *gebugan*, to alliterate with *brægnlocan* (*Old English Riddles*, 347).
74 See Williamson, *Old English Riddles*, 348, for further discussion of this description of the body and comparison with *Christ II* 766–70.
75 Alger N. Doane, "Three Old English Implement Riddles: Reconsiderations of Numbers 4, 49, and 73," *MP* 84 (1987): 256–7.
76 Doane, 256, citing Adolph Shane, *Archery Tackle: How to Make It and How to Use It* (1990; Azle, TX: Bois d'Arc Press, 1936), 17.

minum ... bugan "bend against its shape" (6b–7). Conversely, while a bow may shoot an arrow (*þristra sum* "one of the bold ones") *under brægnlocan* "under a brain-chest," it does not itself *eþelfæsten ... brece* "break into a home-fortress," as seems to be the case here. Whether we accept *æsc* "spear" or *boga* "bow," however, it is worrying that the "inner click" for this riddle derives from the emendation of *hrægnlocan* to *brægnlocan*. The emendation *makes* sense; it *creates* a meaning. Any reading of any text must do this, but, in the riddle-game, at least, changing the question is not normally an acceptable strategy for supporting a solution: "The doctoring of legitimate Old English passages to bolster one's solution is not a sound editorial practice."[77] The question, of course, is how to decide what is legitimate. The debate over the practice of editing Old English poetic texts is too complex to do justice to it here,[78] but it is crucially important: if the Exeter Book scribe did not accurately convey the subtle clues that constitute the game of a riddle, should we attempt to "fix" the errors?

It matters in this case, for if it were not for the clue of the emended *brægnlocan* "brain-box, skull," breaking into a fortress could be taken literally, as an additional activity carried out by the speaker, who might then be better identified as another *ramm* "battering ram," despite the probable absence of battering rams from early medieval England, the concern over the object's *swiora smæl* "small neck" (18a), and the fact that a battering ram probably could not be wielded by a singular user, as this object apparently is (*eom mines frean folm bysigo[d]* "I am employed in my lord's hand" 8).[79] The *he* who boldly leaves the settlements is less easy to identify in the context of breaking into a literal fortification, too, although it could be the *frið* "peace" previously enjoyed there, which conceivably would depart with the entry of the invading army. *Frið* is a masculine noun and so could be a "he."[80] Without *brægnlocan*, no satisfying explanation for these lines has been found, and, given the

---

77 Williamson, *Old English Riddles*, 342.
78 For a sobering discussion of scribal inaccuracy and intervention, see Douglas Moffat, "Anglo-Saxon Scribes and Old English Verse," *Speculum* 67 (1992): 805–27. The issue of editing Old English texts is discussed in detail in the essays collected in *The Editing of Old English*, ed. D.G. Scragg and Paul E. Szarmach (Cambridge: Brewer, 1994). For discussion of the Exeter scribe's practice in particular, see Bernard J. Muir, "Issues for Editors of Anglo-Saxon Poetry in Manuscript Form," in *Inside Old English: Essays in Honour of Bruce Mitchell*, ed. John Walmsley (Oxford: Blackwell, 2006), 181–202.
79 Williamson rejects "battering ram" for the final two reasons (*Old English Riddles*, 345).
80 Niles, drawing upon Trautmann in opposition to Tupper, argues that we should be alert to the significance of grammatical gender in the riddles (*Enigmatic Poems*, 103–10, especially 104n6). But cf. Muir, referring to *Wob* (R.23), line 7: "Anglo-Saxon authors do not always practise strict observance of gender agreement" (*Exeter Anthology*, 2: 625).

damage to the manuscript, we probably cannot hope to make any better sense than *æsc* "spear" or *boga* "bow" from the existing text.

Literal with Complications: Runes and Metaphors

The same kind of scaffolding can be used to solve *Bright-Headed* (R.19), even if the audience lacks sufficient knowledge of runic letters to decode them:

   Ic on siþe seah   .ᛗ ᚱ ᚠ
   ᚾ· hygewloncne,   heafodbeorhtne,
   swiftne ofer sælwong   swiþe þrægan.
   Hæfde him on hrycge   hildeþryþe
5   .ᛏ ᚠ ᚾ.   nægledne rad
   .ᚠ ᚷ ᛗ ᛈ.   Widlast ferede
   rynestrong on rade   rofne .ᚻ ᚠ
   ᚹ ᚠ ᚠ ᚾ.   For wæs þy beorhtre,
   swylcra siþfæt.   Saga hwæt hit[81] hatte. (*Bright-Headed*)[82]

(I saw a [?] on a journey: proud-minded, bright-headed, and swift, it ran vigorously over a plain. On its back it had battle-power. A [?] rode the nailed one. A widely travelling [?], strong in his running, bore a bold [?] on an expedition. The going, the journey of those ones, was the brighter. Say what it is called.)

An audience that cannot read the runic letters in this text might provide a translation like the one offered above: a text as full of gaps as *Clothed in Red* (R.71). Those gaps draw attention to what is present in the texts; we must identify and then work with what is there. These become cues, words such as *hildeþryþ* "battle-power" (4b) and *rof* "bold" (7b), that activate the heroic idiom and thus place the riddle-subject into a familiar, limited context. In this case, knowing *Beowulf* may not be enough to fill in the gaps, but we nevertheless see hints of the horse and ship that figure prominently in most scholars' interpretations of the text. For example, the first encrypted

---

81 Here I follow the emendation of the manuscript's *ic* suggested by Muir, *Exeter Anthology*, 2: 622–3, and Williamson, *Old English Riddles*, 192, but see also discussion below. For a defence of the manuscript reading on other grounds, see Victoria Symons, *Runes and Roman Letters in Anglo-Saxon Manuscripts* (Berlin: Walter de Gruyter, 2016), 62.
82 Muir substitutes Latin letters for the runes in his edition, but given their importance to my discussion, I have included them in my citation of the text; see Williamson, *Old English Riddles*, 78.

entity is described as *hygewlonc* "proud-minded" (2a). Although men and women, too, can be *wlonc* in Old English poetry,[83] "pride" is a distinguishing attribute of elite horses,[84] which characteristically would be *heafodbeorht* "bright-headed" (2b) like this object, that is, shining with ornaments attached to the bridles, like the horses with *fætedhleore* "gold-adorned faces" that Beowulf receives from Hrothgar (*Beowulf* 1036a).[85] A *nægled* "nailed" (5b) thing could be any kind of treasure – *nægled* treasure appears in the *Husband's Message* (35a) and *Beowulf* (2023b) – but a moving nailed thing is likely to be a ship: *nægledbord* refers to ships in *Genesis A* (1418b and 1433b) and *One-Footed* (R.58. 5a). With these hints of "horse" and "ship," and, given the repeated references to a journey (*siþe* 1a, *rad* 7a, *for* 8b, *siþfæt* 9a), an audience that knows the heroic idiom might hazard *brimhengest* "sea-horse, ship" even without attempting to tackle the runes.[86]

Audiences able to interpret the runic letters proceed differently, of course, but may arrive, eventually, at the same solution. Such audiences must first supply the names of the runes to complete the alliteration and metre of the lines in which they appear to recognize and read the poem as a poem. They then transform the names into letters, reverse the order of the letters, and form the letters into words:

I saw a sun-riding-god-hail [S-R-O-H→ *hors* "horse"] on a journey: proud-minded, bright-headed, and swift, it ran vigorously over a plain. On its

---

83   For a detailed discussion of this word in Old and Middle English, see Michael von Rüden, *Wlanc und Derivate im Alt- und Mittelenglischen: Eine wortgeschichtliche Studie* (Frankfurt: Peter Lang, 1978). The word is particularly significant in the double-entendre riddles; see discussion in chapter 6, below.

84   See discussion of horses in *Weapon-Warrior* (R.14) and the *Riming Poem* above, as well as discussion of the horses in *Warrior's Companion* (R.80) in chapter 3, below.

85   For discussion of the archaeological evidence for this aspect of early medieval English horses, see Chris Fern, "The Archaeological Evidence for Equestrianism in Early Anglo-Saxon England, c.450–700," in *Just Skin and Bones? New Perspectives on Human-Animal Relations in the Historical Past*, ed. Aleksander Pluskowski (Oxford: Archaeopress, 2005), 43–71.

86   "Sea-horse" is a common kenning for ship in poetry. For example, *brimhengest* appears in *Andreas* 513b and the *Rune Poem* 47a and 66a. Other variations include: *sæhengest* (*Andreas* 488a), *fearoðhengest* (*Elene* 226b), *wæghenest* (*Elene* 236b, *Guthlac B* 1329a), *sundhengest* (*Christ II* 852b and 862b), and *merehengest* (*Weapon-Warrior*, R.14. 6b, *Meters of Boethius* 26. 25a). Niles solves *Joy and Ice* (R.64) as "ship" and discusses some of these kennings (*Enigmatic Poems*, 142, 147), but for *Bright-Headed* (R.19) he prefers *snac(c)* (105n8), the solution proposed in Mark Griffith, "Riddle 19 of the Exeter Book: SNAC, an Old English Acronym," *N&Q* 39 (1992): 15–16. Note that *Grinds against Grit* (R.32) and *Man Woman Horse* (R.36), also solved as ships, are of a very different character: they are not heroic sailing vessels but barges, with language consistent with their different status.

back it had battle-power. A need-god-man [N-O-M → *mon* "man"] rode the nailed one. A widely travelling oak-gift-horse-joy [A-G-E-W *wega* "warrior"], strong in his running, bore a bold torch-god-wealth-god-oak-hail [C-O-F-O-A-H → *haofoc* "hawk"] on an expedition. The going, the journey of those ones, was the brighter. Say what it is called.[87]

Deciphering the runes does not answer the riddle, for decisions need to be made about literal as opposed to metaphorical meaning. Does this text simply encode an image of a man riding a horse with a hawk on his arm?[88] I do not think so.[89] Although a horse may wear equipment made with rivets, the animal itself seems unlikely to be described as *nægled* "nailed," and *rynestrong* "strong in running" is an odd way to describe a warrior. Thus this horse is a ship – perhaps bearing a decorated figurehead (*heafodbeorht* "bright-headed") and carrying armed forces (*hildeþryþe* "battle-power") – and the warrior who is *rynestrong* "strong in its running" and carries the "hawk" is the sea,[90] or possibly, the wind.[91] Williamson interprets the hawk as the ship's sail, but the bold thing borne by the broad sea may be the ship as a whole, which, like the craft sailed by Beowulf and Andreas, is *fugole gelicost* "most like a bird" (*Beowulf* 218b, *Andreas* 497b). Despite this metaphorical turn, the heroic idiom remains, and parts of it can still be taken literally: whether literal or metaphorical, the horse participates in the sphere demarcated by the heroic idiom. This remains true even if one proceeds further to interpret the runic clusters as an acronym that spells out *SNAC*, a word for a fast warship.[92]

We should proceed a little further still. Given the care that the Exeter Book scribe took, especially when transcribing runic texts, we should not

---

87 The interpretation of the runes here follows that in Williamson, *Old English Riddles*, 186–91.
88 See, for example, discussions in Erika von Erhardt-Siebold, "The Old English Hunt Riddles," *PMLA* 63 (1948): 3–6; Paull F. Baum, *Anglo-Saxon Riddles of the Exeter Book* (Durham, NC: Duke University Press, 1963), 54. For other proponents of this view, see the appendix, below.
89 I follow here the argument in Williamson, *Old English Riddles*, 186–92.
90 Perhaps *wiga* "warrior" is an oblique reference to *garsecg*, a poetic word for the sea that may literally mean "spear man." For discussion of *garsecg*, see R.L.M. Derolez, "'– and that Difficult Word, *Garsecg*' (Gummere)," *MLQ* 7 (1946): 445–52.
91 Cf. Aldhlem's Enigma 2 (*De vento*) in which the wind is characterized by its strength and travelling.
92 Griffith, "Riddle 19". Cf., however, the different reading in Symons, *Runes and Roman Letters*, 57–64.

emend away the apparently erroneous pronoun at the end of the riddle too quickly. *Bright-Headed* seems to begin as an "I saw a creature" riddle[93] and thus creates the expectation that the solution will be the thing that the narrator saw, but the final line of the text is not *Saga hwæt **hit** hatte* "say what **it** is called," as I have presented and translated it above, but rather *Saga hwæt **ic** hatte* "say what **I** am called" (9b). Although most editors have rejected this manuscript reading,[94] it is possible to make sense of it even without resorting to the idea of the "mock riddle," a joke drawing attention to the figure of the riddler and riddling process itself.[95] Having recognized the heroic idiom, decoded the runes, and worked out the metaphor, no audience is likely to be satisfied with "me, the riddler" as a solution, but that final line should nevertheless be taken seriously. It requires an audience to go beyond the discovery of the *brimhengest* "seahorse, ship" to ask: what kind of thing would see that ship travelling across the sea? There are many potential answers to that question, but there are two that seem most relevant to the final clue in the text: *for wæs þy beorhtre* "the journey was the brighter" (8b). At first glance, there is no explanation for the increased brightness of the journey, but Empodocles' classical explanation of vision as "extramission," the sending of a beam of light from the eye to an object,[96] provides a way of making the opening "I saw" formula into a meaningful clue. Whose glance falls upon the ship sailing on the sea not only like but with a gleam of light? It could be a *fyr-torr* "lighthouse,"[97] but probably it is simply the *sunne* "sun."[98]

---

93 Cf. *Ten Brothers and Sisters* (R.13), *Air-Vessel* (R.29), *Grinds against Grit* (R.32), *Feeds Cattle* (R.34), *Man Woman Horse* (R.36), *Belly Behind* (R.37), *Greedy for Youth-Mirth* (R.38), *Two Proud Ones* (R.42), and *Four Creatures* (R.51), among others.
94 In addition to Williamson, *Old English* Riddles, 192, see, for example, Wyatt, *Old English Riddles*, 78, Krapp and Dobbie, 331, and Muir, *Exeter Anthology*, 2: 622–3.
95 Jonathan Wilcox, "Mock-Riddles in Old English: Exeter Riddles 86 and 19," *SP* 93 (1996): 180–7.
96 For discussion of the persistence of this ancient idea in contemporary children and adults, see Gerald A. Winer and Jane E. Cottrell, "The Odd Belief That Rays Exit the Eye during Vision," in *Thinking and Seeing: Visual Metacognition in Adults and Children*, ed. Daniel T. Levin (Cambridge, MA: MIT Press, 2004), 97–119.
97 The remains of a Roman lighthouse still exist near Dover, Kent. Aldhelm also writes about one; see his Enigma 92 (*Farus Editissima* "Loftiest Lighthouse").
98 I am grateful to Jane Roberts for this latter suggestion (personal communication, 10 January 2022).

Noise in the Code

Bright-Headed (R.19) is not a simple text. It demands multiple interpretive processes. Those processes, however, are still contained by the heroic idiom: while it may not deliver meanings "univocally related to signifiers,"[99] the heroic idiom still exercises a limiting function that allows audiences safely to ignore the wide world beyond the experience of warriors. Given the successes gained by working with the heroic idiom in *Bright-Headed* (R.19), *Cursed among Weapons* (R.20), *Clothed in Red* (R.71), and *Brain-Locker* (R.73), it is thus unsurprising that most scholars interpret *Towering Tree* (R.53) as a weapon of war, a *ramm* "battering ram":[100]

    Ic seah on bearwe   beam hlifian,
    tanum torhtne.   Þæt treow wæs on wynne,
    wudu weaxende.   Wæter hine ond eorþe
    feddan fægre,   oþþæt he frod dagum
5 on oþrum wearð   aglachade
    deope gedolgod,   dumb in bendum,
    wriþen ofer wunda,   wonnum hyrstum
    foran gefrætwed.   Nu he fæcnum weg
    þurh his heafdes mægen   hildegieste
10 oþrum rymeð.   Oft hy an yst strudon
    hord ætgædre;   hræd wæs ond unlæt
    se æftera,   gif se ærra fær
    genamnan in nearowe   neþan moste. (*Towering Tree*)

(I saw a tree bright in its branches tower up in a grove. That tree, the growing wood, was in joy. Water and earth fed it beautifully, until, old in days, it experienced another state, one of misery: [it was] deeply wounded, voiceless in bonds, wrapped over its wounds, adorned in front with dark ornaments. Now through the power of its head it opens a deceitful way[101] for another battle-guest. Often they plundered the hoard together in the tempest. The follower was prompt and unwearied, if the leader was allowed to risk danger[102] in a narrow place for his companion.)

---

99 Culler, *Structuralist Poetics*, 20.
100 The following discussion of *Towering Tree* is based on that in Jennifer Neville, "The Exeter Book Riddles' Precarious Insights into Wooden Artefacts," in *Trees and Timber in the Anglo-Saxon World*, ed. Michael D.J. Bintley and Michael G. Shapland (Oxford: Oxford University Press, 2013), 130–2.
101 It is possible, however, to read this line differently; see the discussion in chapter 3, below.
102 There is an accent on *fær* in the manuscript. That accent may simply help to identify a short word, or it may indicate a long vowel. Kenneth Sisam argues that

Much here is blissfully clear. The text does not suffer from manuscript damage. It does not require prior knowledge of runic letters or techniques for decoding them. The transformation from tree to wooden object in the first six lines is unambiguous,[103] and the presence of the heroic idiom in the last five and a half lines is similarly unambiguous: although only *hildegiest* "battle-guest" (9b) appears to be specifically poetic,[104] *mægen* "power, army" (9a), *strudon* "plunder" (10b), *hord* "hoard" (11a), *hræd* "ready, prompt" (11b), and *neþan* "venture, dare, risk" (13b) together create the familiar context of military courage for glittering rewards. As we have seen, audiences of the Exeter Book have ample precedent for taking the battle-guest, hoard, and danger literally and thus solving the riddle literally. Yet somehow this interpretation does not feel quite right. It lacks elegance; it does not lead to an inner click. Such judgement is, of course, subjective, but it is possible to articulate more precise arguments against the battering ram solution, based on the reassuring solidity of material culture. The early medieval English may not have used battering rams at all, much less *oft* "often" (10b).[105] Even if they did use them, or even if they had merely read about them, an apparently singular man (*se æftera* "the following one" 12a) cannot wield a ram on his own; a ram requires a team. It is also puzzling that the path of the ram is described as *facnum* "deceitful, vile, worthless" (8b), for the path of a battering ram, far from being a tool of

---

"the acute accent had so many values in Old English writings that its failure as a distinctive mark of length was inevitable." See *Studies in the History of Old English Literature* (Oxford: Clarendon, 1953), 191. In contrast, Williamson argues that the scribe "is usually careful to [mark the long vowel with an accent] when a confusion in meaning would occur without it" (*Old English Riddles*, 298–9). Muir notes contradictory evidence but concludes that, since the scribe "usually plac[ed accents] on etymologically long vowels," the reading here is *fǣr*, "danger" (*Exeter Anthology*, 1: 27). Wilcox argues that the scribe's inconsistency allows for the accent to be disregarded here; see Jonathan Wilcox, "New Solutions to the Old English Riddles: Riddles 17 and 53," *PQ* 69 (1990): 407n41. Given the ambiguity, I interpret *fær* as "danger" here but as "journey" in my discussion in chapter 3, below.

103 Cf. *Dream of the Rood*. See F.H. Whitman, "Significant Motifs in Riddle 53," *MÆ* 46 (1977): 2–5. Wilcox also compares other riddles in his "New Solutions," 398–9.

104 Not only is *hildegiest* a *hapax legomenon*, but its initial element, *hild-*, appears only in poetry. See Clark-Hall, *s.v. hild* and Griffith, "Poetic Language," 184.

105 Fortification of settlements across Europe was rare: see Guy Halsall, *Warfare and Society in the Barbarian West, 450–900* (New York: Routledge, 2003), 215–27. Some early medieval writers, however, knew about battering rams from textual sources; Aldhelm, for example, mentions them in his Enigma 86 (*Aries* "Ram"). See May Lansfield Keller, *The Anglo-Saxon Weapon Names* (Heidelberg: Winter, 1906), 66–7; Williamson, *Old English Riddles*, 297; see also discussion in Wilcox, "New Solutions," 398.

treacherous or inglorious warfare, is a central feature of the most obvious of military assaults.[106]

Perhaps we should be looking for some other weapon. *Gar* "spear" fares better, as it is made of wood, was ubiquitous in early medieval English warfare, and was easily handled by a single man. We might object, as Doane does with regard to a similar phrase in *Brain-Locker* (R.73), that the trees used to make spears are not *frod dagum* "old in days" (4b),[107] but the *fæcnum wæg* "deceitful way" (8b) also poses a problem for this solution; spears, like rams, are open, obvious, and respectably heroic.[108] Another alternative is to borrow Doane's solution for *Brain-Locker*: *boga* "bow."[109] This solution, although not proposed elsewhere for *Towering Tree*, possesses several advantages: for example, bows are made out of the heartwood of an old tree, and the references to bonds and tying link up satisfyingly with the stringing of a bow.[110] An arrow's path may well be considered *fæcnum* "deceitful" (8b),[111] and the *yst* "tempest" (10b) could indicate a hail of arrows through which a hoard, perhaps the booty stripped from the slain, is plundered. However, it is more difficult to match other details in the latter part of the riddle with the shooting of a bow. What part of a bow is the *heafdes* "head" (9a) that provides the power to launch the arrow, the *hildegieste* "battle-guest" (9b)? If the arrow is the *hræd ond unlæt* "prompt and unwearied" (11b) second member of the team, in what sense does the bow *fær / genamnan in nearowe neþan* "risk danger in a narrow place for its companion" (12b–13)?

There are similarly difficult problems with solving the riddle as a whole as *flan* "arrow." Once again, arrows are not made from trees that are *frod dagum* "old in days" (4b). The arrowhead could be the *heafdes mægen* "power of the head" (9a) that opens a *fæcnum wæg* "deceitful

---

106 Whitman, "Significant Motifs," 1; Wilcox, "New Solutions," 399.
107 Doane, 256.
108 Possession of a spear was a sign of free status according to early medieval English laws; see Michael J. Swanton, *The Spearheads of the Anglo-Saxon Settlements* (Leeds: Royal Archaeological Institute, 1973), 3. Cf., however, the discussion of the complex archaeological evidence for status in Heinrich Härke, "Early Anglo–Saxon Social Structure," in *The Anglo–Saxons from the Migration Period to the Eighth Century: An Ethnographic Perspective*, ed. John Hines (Woodbridge: Boydell, 1997), 142–6.
109 Doane, 254–7.
110 Cf. the description of the *boga* "bow" in *Wob* (R.23), discussed above.
111 The Homeric idea of bows as effective but "decidedly unsporting" may have been shared by early medieval writers; see Edward B. Irving, "Heroic Experience in the Old English Riddles," in *Old English Shorter Poems: Basic Readings*, ed. Katherine O'Brien O'Keeffe (New York: Garland, 1994). Cf. also J. Manley, "The Archer and the Army in the Late Saxon Period," *Anglo-Saxon Studies in Archaeology and History* 4 (1985): 231.

path" (8b), perhaps through the air, or perhaps into a victim's body, but, if so, it is not clear who the *hildegieste* "battle-guest" (9b) for whom this path is opened might be. "Battle-guest" seems an unlikely designation for an arrow-shaft as opposed to an arrowhead, and it seems similarly unlikely that an arrow-shaft would be described as an *æftera* "follower" (12a) who is *hræd on unlæt* "prompt and unwearied" (11b) if the former, the arrowhead, ventures into a narrow place (the wound?). Other than the problem of the type of wood involved, this interpretation of *Towering Tree* as a *flan* "arrow" is possible, but the description of the shaft's speed being contingent upon the head's venturing into the wound seems unnecessarily awkward. Perhaps an archer could see it more clearly.

Or perhaps we need to situate this text just outside the literal battlefield, in the margins of the heroic world. Wilcox proposes that *Towering Tree* conceals not a weapon but a *gealga* "gallows": a tree that, having been cut down and bound with rope (*deope gedolgod, dumb in bendum* "deeply wounded, voiceless in bonds" 6), uses the power of its head (*heafdes mægen* 9a) to open up the *weg* "way" (8b) to the narrowness of hell (*nearowe* 13a) for the *fæcnum* "deceitful" (8b) man who previously plundered the hoard (10b-11a); meanwhile, his accomplice escapes the same fate by being *hræd ond unlæt* "prompt and not negligent" (11b).[112] This solution possesses significant advantages over *ramm* "battering ram" and *gar* "spear," particularly in its explanation for the otherwise inexplicable deceit indicated by *fæcnum* "treacherous, deceitful" (8b), which Wilcox interprets as standing in apposition to the thief about to be hanged, the *hildegieste* "battle-guest" (9b), rather than describing the *weg* "way" (8b). It also benefits from the substantial surviving evidence for early medieval English gallows; we may doubt the existence of battering rams in the period, but we cannot miss the many appearances of the gallows in law codes, literary texts, and manuscript illustrations.[113] The metaphorical description of death as a journey into the narrowness of hell is attractive, as is the interpretation of the final two and a half lines as an example of wry "gallows humour": a thief who has observed his companion being hanged does not wait around idly for the same fate.

Yet I have some problems with this interpretation. For example, it is unclear why the gallows would have *wonnum hyrstum* "dark ornaments" (7b) fixed to its front.[114] More important, however, is the way

---

112 Wilcox, "New Solutions," 398–400.
113 Wilcox, "New Solutions," 401–2; see also Niles, *Old English Enigmatic Poems*, 73–4. Gallows are also mentioned in literary texts; see, for example, *Beowulf* 2444–9.
114 Most of the solutions for *Towering Tree* do not adequately account for the *wonnum hyrstum*, but see my discussion in chapter 3, below.

56 Truth Is Trickiest

in which Wilcox deals with the relationship between the singular object described at the beginning of the riddle and the plural actors mentioned near the end. Wilcox translates these lines as follows:

> … Now it clears a way
> for the wicked one, the battle-guest
> through the power of its head. Often they had violently plundered
> a hoard together; the second one
> was quick and not negligent, if the first had to venture on a journey
> from his companion into confinement.[115]

My translation differs in several details, three of which are significant:

> Now through the power of its head it opens a deceitful way for another battle-guest. Often they plundered the hoard together in the tempest. The follower was prompt and unwearied, if the leader was allowed to risk danger in a narrow place for his companion.[116]

The first significant difference lies in Wilcox's omission of the word *oþrum* (10a) from his discussion and translation. I understand the change from the singular *he* "it" (8b) to plural *hy* "they" (10b) as the simple addition of an *oþrum* "other one" (10a) to the initial wooden object, with two actors henceforth working together as they *strudon / hord ætgædre* "plundered the hoard together" (10b–11a). *Oþer* generally refers to "one of two" or "the second one,"[117] and the text appears to confirm this sense of two individuals by later labelling them *se ærra* "the first one" and *se æftera* "the following one" (12). By omitting *oþrum*, Wilcox excludes the initial wooden object from the pair of actors described in the last three and a half lines and thus finds not two but three entities in this text: the gallows itself, a thief who is hanged, and a second thief who escapes. Wilcox admits that the second thief is an "as yet unclear accomplice,"[118] but, if we include *oþrum*, we can explain the change from singular to plural without having to find more than

---

115 Wilcox, "New Solutions," 401. A similar translation of the first sentence also appears on 399.
116 For a different translation, see discussion of *Towering Tree* in chapter 3 below.
117 See Clark-Hall, B-T, and the glossary of *A Guide to Old English*, ed. Bruce Mitchell and Fred C. Robinson, 8th ed. (Oxford: Blackwell, 2012), s.v. *oþer*. Cf. Alistair Campbell, *Old English Grammar* (1959; Oxford: Clarendon, 1983), §692 (on ordinal numbers).
118 Wilcox, "New Solutions," 400.

the tree-object and one accomplice in the plundering of the hoard, and without understanding the plundering to have taken in a previous past ("they *had* plundered").[119]

The second significant difference lies in our interpretation of the final word of the riddle, the modal verb *moste* (13b). In his discussion, Wilcox suggests that "the former [thief] is made to venture on a journey,"[120] but, although it can convey compulsion, *motan* primarily indicates conditional ability – permission or opportunity.[121] That is, the text seems to indicate that the second thief's activity depends upon the first thief being *permitted* to venture "into danger" or "on a journey."[122] Granting a thief permission to be hanged or to go to hell seems incongruous. Such incongruity might create humour, which is consistent with Wilcox's reading of "comic cynicism,"[123] but, along with doubt over the omission of *oþrum*, it might also create enough unease to disqualify *gealga* "gallows" as an acceptable solution.

This second difference is also significant in another way. There is no grammatical reason why *moste* cannot be translated in exactly the way Wilcox has done.[124] He has chosen to read compulsion into *moste* because of the enforced nature of an execution; once on the gallows, there is no question of needing permission to go on the journey. His solution, *gealga* "gallows," determines how the natural ambiguity of the modal verb should be resolved. The same applies to a third difference in our

---

119 Although he does not discuss this particular case, Bruce Mitchell argues that a simple past tense in a sequence of simple past tenses cannot have a pluperfect meaning unless there is a grammatical or contextual hint (for example, an adverb such as *ær* "before"). See his "Linguistic Facts and the Interpretation of Old English Poetry," in *On Old English: Selected Papers* (Oxford: Basil Blackwell, 1988), 159–67.
120 Wilcox, "New Solutions," 400.
121 The idea of permission appears first in the lists of definitions provided in Clark-Hall and B-T; it is the only definition provided in the glossary of Mitchell and Robinson's *Guide to Old English*. Cf. also T. A. Shippey's argument for the distinction between permission and obligation in *Maldon*: "one modal verb is after all [not] about as good as another" ("'Grim Wordplay,'" 46). See also the discussion in Bruce Mitchell, *Old English Syntax*, 2 vols (Oxford: Clarendon, 1985), 1: 424–5.
122 For the distinction between "danger" and "journey," see discussion of the accent mark on *fær*, above.
123 Wilcox, "New Solutions," 400. For further discussion of incongruity in humour, see idem, "Introduction," in *Humour in Anglo-Saxon Literature*, 4–5 and Hugh Magennis, "A Funny Thing Happened on the Way to Heaven: Humorous Incongruity in Old English Saints' Lives," in *Humour in Anglo-Saxon England*, 137–8 (see especially the references in note 1).
124 See Clark-Hall, s.v. *motan.

translations: I read *fæcnum* as referring to the *weg* "way" (8b),[125] but, having chosen the solution *gealga* "gallows," Wilcox logically identifies the *hildegieste* "battle-guest" as a thief, who may appropriately be described as *fæcne* "deceitful, treacherous," unlike the path of a *ramm* "battering ram," which is nothing if not overt. If we do not accept Wilcox's solution, we need to account for the negative connotations of the *fæcnum weg* "treacherous way" (8b) or *fæcnum ... / hildegiest / oþrum* "other treacherous battle-guest" (8b–10a) in some other way.

It may be that the key to the "inner click" still remains hidden in the ground (or uncatalogued in a museum's warehouse), awaiting a lucky archeological discovery. With our incomplete knowledge of early medieval material culture, we might not recognize the object described here even if we saw it: it is worth remembering that currently obscure objects may once have been obvious.[126] Although it may seem disappointing to leave *Towering Tree* here without a fully satisfying solution, that disappointment derives from inappropriate expectations of these texts. In fact, the failure to find a single "inner click" ensures rather the success of the text in inspiring an interpretive process that is not terminated too soon. *Towering Tree*, after all, has already led us to ponder the military equipment and legal system of early medieval England. It may also have inspired early medieval readers to analyse the tropes by which they narrated their physical and social worlds. Such analysis is only possible, however, if an audience either initially fails to solve the riddle *or* fails to be satisfied even if it has arrived at an elegant solution. Too often we have been satisfied with solutions and thus left the riddles' enigmatic potential unexplored. Yet there are other possibilities, too. Perhaps we do not require additional knowledge but rather a different approach. We will return to *Towering Tree* again.

Conclusions

The assumption underlying the "battering ram" solution for *Towering Tree* (R.53), as well as the other four solutions proposed above, is that the language of the heroic idiom literally describes the limited range

---

[125] Whitman argues that *fæcnum* must be taken with *weg*, because "it is rare to find an adjective and a noun separated to such an extent in this order; where similar separations occur the noun is usually given first." This argument seems plausible, but he provides no evidence to back up the claim ("Significant Motifs," 1). Neither Williamson nor Muir comment on *fæcnum*.

[126] Cf. Niles, *Enigmatic Poems*, 111.

of actions, personnel, and equipment that pertain to the heroic world. Although the text contains plenty of metaphors – a tree manufactured into an object does not literally suffer *wunda* "wounds" and a battle is not literally an *yst* "storm" – these readings approach the *hildegieste* "battle-guest" (9b) and *hord* "hoard" (11a) as literal referents within the heroic idiom. Given the riddle genre's intimate connection with metaphor, modern audiences' insistence on a literal reading of this text may seem odd, but it is justified by the texts discussed in this chapter – by the successful literal interpretation of the heroic idiom in *Weapon-Warrior* (R.14), *Bright-Headed* (R.19), *Wob* (R.23), *Clothed in Red* (R.71), and the first part of *Cursed among Weapons* (R.20). These riddles use "straight," that is, non-turning, more or less literal, descriptions to refer to heroic culture. Other riddles may, too. However, *Towering Tree* may not. How can we tell?

We cannot. And so the riddles' audiences, whether early medieval or modern, must always start by reading the heroic idiom literally. For an audience that knows the dominant trope of the Old English poetic tradition, the limits created by the heroic idiom offer a considerable advantage for even a rudimentary grasp of the trope can be enough to facilitate elegant solutions; more extensive knowledge of Old English poetry can create coherent narratives even in riddles that are fragmentary due to manuscript damage or potentially undeciphered runic clues.[127] As we have seen in *Towering Tree*, however, it is not always possible to know whether these limits are in play or being played with. In such cases, the use of the heroic idiom itself must be evaluated. It cannot be taken for granted. Thus recognition of the heroic idiom, the familiar, pervasive trope that defines Old English poetry, opens up not a flap on an advent calendar but a large can of worms: it delivers not a flat, single reward but a complex, intertwined mass of shifting possibilities.The presence of the heroic idiom in the riddles signals the initiation of a game that may or may not continue past a literal decoding of poetic language.

The Exeter Book riddles not only allow but demand self-conscious scrutiny of the dominant trope of Old English poetry and perhaps also of its dominant ideologies. If we are to *saga hwæt hit hatte* "say what [a riddle-subject] is called," we must attend carefully to what the text says and what it fails to say. Thus we may ponder the relationship between

---

127 Cf. discussion of "literary competence" as an appeal to norms in Jonathan Culler, *The Pursuit of Signs: Semiotics, Literature, Deconstruction* (London: Routledge and Kegan Paul, 1981), 50–1.

tears and masculinity in *Clothed in Red* (R.71) and note that *Weapon-Warrior* (R.14) does not acknowledge that the heroic world can be threatened from both within and without; in later chapters, I will look further at the riddles' capacity for social commentary. What is most important here is that the literal cannot simply be discarded. At the same time, finding a response to the literal surface does not mark the end of the interpretive process; the quest for a solution may yield multiple re-solutions, a series of competing responses. The absence of solutions in the manuscript means that this series could continue indefinitely, for there can always be another re-solution and the authority of none can be guaranteed. The list of past solutions that I have compiled in the appendix conveys some of that potential.

In this chapter, the potentially limitless play of signification has been constrained within the limits of a (mostly) literal understanding of the heroic idiom. As *Towering Tree* shows, however, those limits are not always reliable. Chapter 3 examines how the riddles joyfully ignore those limits and instead use the heroic idiom to camouflage or disguise riddle-subjects.

Chapter Three

Muddying the Waters: The Heroic Idiom as Camouflage and Disguise

Introduction

The previous chapter discussed riddles in which the familiar heroic idiom generates elegant solutions when interpreted literally: the gold-adorned weapon in the courts of *Cursed among Weapons* (R.20) is a *sweord* "sword," and the bent and bound killer of *Wob* (R.23) is a *boga* "bow." What is familiar, however, does not always reveal. Although Old English heroic poetry has been characterized as having "an extensive and easily expanded vocabulary which was never used in other contexts,"[1] this chapter addresses riddles that present the usual personnel, actions, and equipment of the heroic idiom in incongruous combination with other personnel, actions, and equipment. In these riddles the familiar vocabulary of the heroic idiom *is* used in other contexts, namely agriculture and the natural world, either as camouflage or as disguise.

The riddles in the first part of this chapter use the heroic idiom as camouflage, its familiar language obscuring the identity of the riddle-objects and causing them to blend into what is effectively an ornamental smoke-screen. Unlike the objects discussed in the previous chapter, these exist outside the heroic world; they are not swords, bows, horns, or ships, nor do they claim to be, unlike those discussed later in this chapter. Since at least some of the imagery used to describe them does come from the heroic world, however, their identity becomes blurred. These riddles use the poetic resources of the heroic idiom to camouflage objects that have been identified by riddle-solvers as well-sweeps,

---

1 Dennis Cronan, "Poetic Meanings in the Old English Poetic Vocabulary," *ES* 5 (2003): 418.

ice, and looms.² Their solutions can still, of course, be challenged. Even safe bets, however, retain traces of their disguise: the camouflage is not completely wiped away. Riddle-subjects and -objects remain hybrid, strange creatures that cross the line between animate and inanimate, and so the practical, inanimate tool that lifts water from a well is a loyal servant, the solidified form of water threatens hostility, and the peaceful act of weaving takes place among battle and torture.

The riddles in the rest of this chapter use the heroic idiom not as a smokescreen but as a disguise or mask. The distinction between these two approaches is rather fine, but, for the discussion here, I have tried to isolate texts that rely exclusively on the heroic idiom to furnish a (mostly) consistent but illusory identity. Solving the riddle requires an audience not only to reject the literal meaning of the heroic idiom but also to interpret it as a system of metaphors. For example, the apparently human *geselda* "retainer" in *Warrior's Companion* (R.80) may be interpreted as a personification of a horn;[3] interpreting that metaphorical companion not only furnishes the solution but also allows the various activities described in the text to be re-interpreted. As a result we have riddles whose subjects pretend to be weapons or warriors but are probably non-martial objects, for example, the sun, an inkhorn, and a bee-hive.[4]

As in the previous chapter, familiarity with the heroic idiom is a necessary starting point: audiences must first recognize heroic culture with its key figures, equipment, ethics, and activities, as well as the poetic techniques through which early medieval English poets conveyed that culture. Yet such recognition is only a starting point, and this time it is a false start. In these riddles the characteristic language of the Old English poetic tradition is exploited and extended to become a method through which the presentation of riddle-subjects and riddle-objects is made poetic but general and frustratingly unspecific. This familiar poetic language does not work as it does in the texts considered in the previous chapter. It neither conveys information nor serves as a convenient

---

2 *Rad-rod* "well-sweep," a beam or rod used in lifting water from a well, is the most common solution for *One-Footed* (R.58). *Is* "ice" or *is-beorg* "iceberg" is usually accepted as the solution for *Terrible Laughter* (R.33). *Web-beam* "loom" is the most common solution for *Turning Wood* (R.56), but *turnus* "pole-lathe" may be a better one; see discussion, below. For other solutions to these texts, see the appendix.

3 *Horn* "horn" is accepted as the solution by most commentators (see the appendix for details), but see also the discussion below for another possibility.

4 These are the most generally accepted solutions for *I Burn the Living* (R.6), *Brotherless* (R.88), and *Protector* (R.17).

short-hand; rather, it defers comprehension and transforms the familiar into the unfamiliar. We see ordinary things through new eyes. Things are not all that we come to see, however. When we cannot look through the obscuring language, we become aware of the language itself, and so the familiar language of the heroic idiom itself becomes a focus of attention, for we must observe *how* it has been deployed if we are to respond to the riddles' demand to say what they are called.

Reading Camouflage in *One-Footed* (R.58) and *Turning Wood* (R.56)

One-Footed (R.58) begins by announcing that its subject performs heroic deeds despite some significant disadvantages.

> Ic wat anfete   ellen dreogan
> wiht on wonge.   Wide ne fereð,
> ne fela rideð,   ne fleogan mæg
> þurh scirne dæg,   ne hie scip fereð,
> 5 naca nægledbord;   nyt bið hwæþre
> hyre mondryhtne   monegum tidum.
> Hafað hefigne steort,   heafod lytel,
> tungan lange,   toð nænigne,
> isernes dæl;   eorðgræf pæþeð.
> 10 Wætan ne swelgeþ   ne wiht iteþ,
> foþres ne gitsað,   fereð oft swa þeah
> lagoflod on lyfte;   life ne gielpeð,
> hlafordes gifum,   hyreð swa þeana
> þeodne sinum.   Þry sind in naman
> 15 ryhte runstafas,   þara is Rad forma. (*One-Footed*, R.58)

> (I know a one-footed creature that performs deeds of courage on the field. It does not travel widely or ride much, nor can it fly through the bright day, nor does a ship, a vessel made of nailed wood, carry it. It is nevertheless useful to its lord on many occasions. It has a heavy tail, a small head, a long tongue, no teeth, and a piece of iron. It makes a path over a hole in the earth. It neither swallows water nor eats anything nor craves food, but even so it often carries water into the air. It does not boast of life [or its] lord's gifts, but even so it obeys its own lord. Correctly there are three rune-letters in its name, of which ᚱ ["Riding"] is first.)

The creature's single foot may be enough to make an audience wary of taking *ellen* "deeds of courage" (1b) literally, but, if not, the following list of negations and strange characteristics locate the riddle-subject far

64   Truth Is Trickiest

outside the heroic idiom activated in the first line. The three references to the "lord" (*mondryht* 6a, *hlaford* 13a, and *þeoden* 14a) repeatedly reinstate the connection to the heroic world, but they hardly constitute a serious attempt at obfuscation in themselves, and in the context of lifting water into the air (11b–12a), it is clear that this riddle-subject is not one of the usual heroic characters or items of equipment.[5] Lifting water, however, is a specific enough context to allow most commentators to see through the camouflage and identify the riddle-subject as a **rad-rod* "well-sweep":[6] the long beam fixed in a fulcrum that facilitates the raising of a bucket from the bottom of a well. The bucket dangles from its *tungan lange* "long tongue" (8a), which is attached to the comparatively *heafod lytel* "small head" (7b) of the sweep, while, on the other end of the sweep, its *hefigne steort* "heavy tail" (7a) counterbalances the weight of the upcoming water. In this obviously inappropriate description of lifting water as *ellen*, the heroic idiom is used to generalize the activity and thus make it ambiguous. Yet this camouflage does not merely obscure the *One-Footed*; it also approves it, effectively raising the idea of *nytt* "useful service" to the level of heroic action. In this case, the incongruity of this apparent equivalence does not seem to be ironic, as such equivalency may be elsewhere,[7] but it could be. The possibility requires pause, and that pause can lead to further questions, as we shall see in later chapters.

Turning Wood (R.56) also describes an object that stands outside the heroic sphere, despite its references to struggle, wounds, arrows, and the lord in the mead hall:

```
   Ic wæs þær inne    þær ic ane geseah
   winnende wiht    wido bennegean,
   holt hweorfende;    heaþoglemma feng,
   deopra dolga.    Daroþas wæron
5  weo þære wihte,    ond se wudu searwum
   fæste gebunden.    Hyre fota wæs
   biidfæst oþer;    oþer bisgo dreag,
   leolc on lyfte,    hwilum londe neah.
   Treow wæs getenge    þam þær torhtan stod
```

---

5   In fact, the relationship between the object and its "lord" is an example of the Implement Trope, which will be discussed in detail in chapter 5, below.
6   For this particular interpretation of the runic clue, see Niles, *Enigmatic Poems*, 89–92.
7   See discussion in chapter 4, below.

10 leafum bihongen.   Ic lafe geseah
minum hlaforde,   þær hæleð druncon,
þara flana geweorc   on flet beran. (*Turning Wood*)

(I was inside, where I saw a single labouring creature, a turning timber, wound a wooden thing. It received battle-gashes, deep wounds. Spears and that wooden thing securely bound with skill were [the cause of] harm to the creature. One of its feet was fixed; the other took part in labour: it flew up into the air and sometimes near the land. A tree hung about with leaves was near to it, where that splendid thing stood. I saw the leavings, the work of the arrows, carried onto the floor to my lord, where the warriors drank.)

This text requires an audience to look beyond the heroic idiom to find a context that will allow its heroic language to be understood. The riddle provides few clues to this non-heroic context, yet these are enough to reveal that, despite wounds and weapons reminiscent of Byrhtnoth's last stand against the Vikings,[8] no literal battle transpires here: the action takes place *inne* "indoors" (1a); the wounds derive not from metal weapons but from a manufactured wooden object (*wudu searwum / fæste gebunden* "a wooden thing securely bound with skill" 5b–6a); the creature in question is not a dynamic warrior, as might have been supposed of a *winnende wiht* "striving creature" (2a) but rather a *biidfæst* "stationary" thing (7a) with a part that moves up and down (*leolc on lyfte, hwilum londe neah* "it flew up into the air and sometimes near the land," 8). In this indoor setting, we know that the *heaþoglemma* "battle-gashes" (3b) cannot be what they say they are; we may also assume that the *treow* (9a) is not actually a tree, and thus the *leaf* (10a) are not actually leaves. These phrases are usually interpreted as obscuring the process of weaving.[9] Thus the struggling creature camouflages the moving parts of the *web-beam* "loom"; the spear camouflages the

---

8 See, for example, *The Battle of Maldon* 130–51.
9 See Erika von Erhardt-Siebold, "The Old English Loom Riddles," in *Philologica: The Malone Anniversary Studies*, ed. Thomas Austin Kirby and Henry Bosley Woolf (Baltimore: Johns Hopkins Press, 1949), 9–17, and Megan Cavell, *Weaving Words and Binding Bodies: The Poetics of Human Experience in Old English Literature* (Toronto: University of Toronto Press, 2016), 27–47. Further information about weaving can be found in Maren Clegg Hyer and Gale Owen-Crocker, "Woven Works: Making and Using Textiles," in *The Material Culture of Daily Living in the Anglo-Saxon World*, ed. Maren Clegg Hyer and Gale R. Owen-Crocker (Exeter: University of Exeter Press, 2011), 166–72.

shuttle; wounds camouflage the penetration of the shuttle between the threads of the warp; leaves hanging on a tree camouflage the distaff hung with flax or wool; and the corpse riven by arrows (*flana geweorc* "the work of arrows" 12a), a victim of heroic struggle brought before the lord of a mead hall (*minum hlaforde, þær hæleð druncon* "to my lord, where the warriors drank" 11), camouflages the product of the loom. That is, the *laf* "leavings" (10b) of this "battle" are woven garments,[10] perhaps very fine ones, fit for the lord of the mead hall, although the lord and the place where men drink may be metaphors for a different context, too.[11]

Yet the heroic idiom could be camouflaging other non-heroic domestic objects, too, for *Turning Wood* may be interpreted as disguising a *turnus* "pole-lathe."[12] Most modern readers do not agree,[13] but the barrier to accepting the pole-lathe solution may be our own ignorance of the craft of wood-working, an ignorance that people in early medieval England would not have shared.[14] Some knowledge can be gained from watching videos on the internet, listening to practitioners, and reading

---

10 For discussion of the key term, *laf*, see Phyllis Portnoy, *The Remnant: Essays on a Theme in Old English Verse* (London: Runetree Press, 2005).

11 For example, *minum hlaforde* "my lord" could be part of the implement trope (see chapter 5, below), while the place where men drink could be the church. Cf. Elinor Teele, "The Heroic Tradition in the Old English Riddles" (PhD diss., University of Cambridge, 2004), 147.

12 I have been unable to find an Old English term for "pole-lathe." The Old English term for a turner's workshop, glossing the Latin *tornatorium*, is *þyrel-hus* (see Thomas Wright and R.P. Wülker, *Anglo-Saxon and Old English Vocabularies*, 2 vols, 2nd ed. (London: Trübner, 1884), 1: col. 185), so the Old English term for "pole-lathe" may also have incorporated the root *þyrel* "hole, perforation." **Þyrel-tol* "turning tool" is my best guess, but I will use the confirmed Latin term, *turnus*.

13 "Pole-lathe" was first mentioned by Franz Dietrich, but he preferred "loom" as the solution; see "Die Räthsel des Exeterbuch: Verfasser, Weitere Losungen," *Zeitschrift für Deutsches Alterthum* 7 (1865): 238–9, note 7. "Pole-lathe" is accepted by Pinsker and Ziegler, 277. Tupper, however, rejects this solution "unhesitatingly" (*Riddles of the Exeter Book*, 192), and all other scholars have followed until very recently; Cavell, for example, now agrees that "pole-lathe" may be a good solution; see her note on *The Riddle Ages*, https://theriddleages.com/riddles/post/commentary-for-exeter-riddle-56/).

14 While museums and poetry tend to focus on metal, the use of wood was ubiquitous. See J.M. Coles, S.V.E. Heal and B.J. Orme, "The Use and Character of Wood in Prehistoric Britain and Ireland," *Proceedings of the Prehistoric Society* 44 (1978): 1–45.

archaeological reports, however,[15] and even such limited knowledge can support the view that the heroic idiom camouflages a pole-lathe here. Like the *web-beam*, a key characteristic of the pole-lathe is its dynamic motion: it is a wooden tool that is characteristically *winnende* "labouring" (2a) and *hweorfend* "turning" (3a). To make a wooden cup or bowl, a block of wood (*wido* 2b) is fixed with a shaft or spindle (a mandrel) to the turning arm of the pole-lathe. The *daropas* "darts" (4b) are the woodworker's tools, the gouges and chisels that create deep wounds in the face of the block, the *wudu searwum fæste / gebunden* "wooden thing securely bound with skill" (5b–6a), and carve out its interior. The force of the essential turning motion derives ultimately from the woodworker's foot, which presses rhythmically upon a treadle. The treadle is attached to cord, which is wound around the arm of the lathe and then attached to a pole, which is often a young, springy tree, but may also be a flexible pole fixed in place.[16] One *fot* (6b) of this pole is securely *biidfæst* "fixed" (7a) to the ground; the other moves up and down: *bisgo dreag, / leolc on lyfte, hwilum londe neah* "takes part in labour, flies up into the air [and] sometimes near the land" (7b–8). The tree standing nearby may thus, surprisingly, be a literal tree, *leafum bihongen* "hung with leaves" (10a) as trees often are, although they are less often *inne* "inside" (1a), as the *Turning Wood* is said to be. It is also possible that the feet have nothing to do with the lathe. They may be the feet of the wood-turner, one of which stays planted on the ground while the other moves up and down to provide the driving force for the treadle; in this reading, the human operator becomes a part of the marvellous riddle-object.[17] The wood left behind after the turning process, the *lafe* "leavings" (10b), are appropriately brought to the lord *on flet* "in the hall" (12b), the place

---

15   For example, Ben and Lois Orford, "How to Turn a Bowl on the Pole Lathe with Ben Orford," five parts at https://youtu.be/pNtyo7IyOAQ?si=MktI2L913eh RxNR5, https://youtu.be/AJUC2b1QXBI?si=D-OcIRl627a24Osh, https://youtu.be/jKUZtCheu-w?si=mHZnop-OkoE6bTXV, https://youtu.be/LZsv_yETRSo?si=a-11ji4mcFSjdYON, and https://youtu.be/5NhZXu94mSM?si=nE4RY_Xpj1Uqa5hy; Carole A. Morris, "Anglo-Saxon Lathe-Turning: Tools, Techniques, Products," paper given at the *Woodlands, Trees, and Timber in the Anglo-Saxon World*, 14 November 2009; Carol A. Morris, *Craft, Industry and Everyday Life: Wood and Woodworking in Anglo-Scandinavian and Medieval York* (York: Council for British Archaeology for the York Archaeological Trust, 2000), 2116–36.

16   A diagram is supplied in Roland Williamson and Ben Levick, "Woodworking," *Regia Anglorum* website, https://regia.org/research/life/woodwork.htm.

17   I am indebted to Sharif Adams, a pole lathe bowl turner, for this interpretation (personal communication, 22 December 2021).

þær hæleð druncon "where warriors drink" (11b). The Sutton Hoo burial contains the remains of some high-quality drinking vessels produced using just this technique.[18]

In some ways *turnus* "pole-lathe" seems a better solution for *Turning Wood* than *web-beam* "loom"; the language of "turning" and the opposition between the *fot* on the ground and the *fot* flying up in the air seem very apt for a pole-lathe but only approximately apt for a loom – particularly the vertical looms used in the early medieval period, both of whose two feet needed to remain on the ground.[19] On the other hand, the leaves on the nearby, indoor tree are better explained by the process of weaving. Another, more elegant solution may still remain undiscovered.

The main point here is not to arrive at a final solution, however, but to consider the use of the heroic idiom. As mentioned earlier, *Turning Wood* provides just enough information to reveal that its battle-wounds are not derived from a real battle. That information, however, is overwhelmed in detail and in interest by the language of the heroic idiom. The context that would allow us conclusively to identify the object is thus camouflaged; it is difficult to determine whether that context is wood-working, weaving, or perhaps something else entirely. An audience that has successfully negotiated the texts in the previous chapter thus finds here that the familiar heroic idiom cannot be relied upon to lead to a solution; rather, that language obscures (perhaps permanently) the identity of the riddle-object. Even if we choose "loom" or "lathe" and convince ourselves that the riddle is solved, the riddle-object remains slightly strange, slightly queer, a hybrid creature that incorporates the human agent into itself along with the world of battle.

---

18 See, for example, Angela Care Evans, *The Sutton Hoo Ship Burial*, rev. ed. (1986; London: British Museum, 1994), 64–9.

19 Cavell, *Weaving Words*, 30 offers two possible explanations for the otherwise inexplicable feet. Following Erhardt-Siebold, "Old English Loom Riddles," 15, and Williamson, *Old English Riddles*, 307, she interprets the "feet" as the two rows of warp threads, one of which moves while the other stays in place. Alternatively, following Maren Clegg Hyer's argument in *The Encyclopedia of Medieval Dress and Textiles*, ed. Gale R. Owen-Crocker, Elizabeth Coatsworth, and Maria Hayward (Leiden: Brill, 2012), 456, Cavell posits that the feet may indicate the loom posts and horizontal heddle rods (*Weaving Words*, 30). In my view, neither convincingly matches the description in the riddle. Against the former, I would argue that loom weights are not fixed to the ground; against the latter, two posts and a heddle rod add up to more than two feet.

Although the surface content of *Turning Wood* derives mostly from the heroic idiom, other riddles use it more sparingly. For example, the heroic idiom features in only one small part of *Terrible Laughter* (R.33):

Wiht cwom æfter wege   wrætlicu liþan,
cymlic from ceole   cleopode to londe,
hlinsade hlude –   hleahtor wæs gryrelic,
egesful on earde.   Ecge wæron scearpe;
5 wæs hio hetegrim,   hilde to sæne,
biter beadoweorca;   bordweallas grof,
heardhiþende.   Heterune bond,
sægde searocræftig   ymb hyre sylfre gesceaft:
"Is min modor   mægða cynnes
10 þæs deorestan,   þæt is dohtor min
eacen uploden,   swa þæt is ældum cuþ,
firum on folce,   þæt seo on foldan sceal
on ealra londa gehwam   lissum stondan." (*Terrible Laughter*)

(A magnificent creature came sailing on the wave. The beautiful one called to the land from her throat [and] resounded loudly. Her laughter was terrible, fearsome on the earth; her edges were sharp. She was grim with hate, [yet] slow in battle. Bitter in battle-work, hard-ravaging, she carved the shield-walls. She [kept] bound a hateful secret. The cunning one spoke about her own nature: "My mother is of the most precious race of women – she who is [also] my daughter, pregnant, grown up; likewise it is known to men, to people among the nation, that she exists gracefully on the earth, in every land.")

There is much of interest in this text,[20] but for the present discussion it is most important to note that the heroic idiom is limited to lines 4b–7a and thus contributes only one approach out of three to the riddle-subject. The poet draws upon poetic resources beyond the heroic idiom, including the Latin riddle-tradition, in which the paradox of water being both the mother and daughter of ice receives attention.[21]

---

20 See, for example, the discussions in Amy W. Clark, "Familiar Distances: Beating the Bounds of Early English Identity" (PhD diss., University of California, Berkeley, 2020), 80–1; Corinne Dale, "(Re)viewing the Warrior Woman: Reading the Old English 'Iceberg' Riddle from an Ecofeminist Perspective," *Neophil* 103 (2019): 435–49; and Thomas Klein, William F. Klein, and David Delehanty, "Resolving Exeter Book Riddles 74 and 33: Stormy Allomorphs of Water," *Quidditas* 35 (2014): 29–47.
21 See Williamson, *Old English Riddles*, 238, who also cites previous discussions.

The few lines that do employ the heroic idiom provide an example of how this trope may succinctly summon up the world of battle and provide a vivid metaphor to camouflage an aspect of human experience that does not, in fact, have any connection with swords, treasure, or loyal warriors. Thus the ominous approach of the ice (whether an iceberg or ice floe) towards the ship becomes a paradoxically slow flurry of blades (*ecge* 4b) against a defensive shield-wall (*bordweallas* 6b). The result is that what otherwise might have been seen as the impersonal indifference of the natural world becomes the willed act of a hostile, treacherous enemy (*hetegrim*, *searocræftig* 5a, 8a). Here the metaphorical equivalent of the human defence that often proves successful in real battles offers no resistance whatsoever: the *bordweallas* of the ship prove no match for the grinding ice. There is no possibility of victory in this fight; the natural world measures the elite world of heroic action and responds with *hleahtor... gryrelic* "horrible laughter" (3b). If the heroic idiom conveys the best that Old English poetry can imagine for the human race,[22] here it is clear that this best is not nearly good enough.[23]

Other riddles weave metaphors from the heroic idiom into their descriptions in parallel ways, with the same potential for continuing interpretation and evaluation. For example, *No Escape* (R.3) describes the storm as a rampaging warrior beyond the understanding and control of human beings;[24] *White Neck* (R.15) describes a female animal (whether a *fox* "fox," *il* "hedgehog," *il* "porcupine," *brocc* "badger," *weosule* "weasel," or some other animal) as a reluctant but successful defender;[25] *Peace-Horses* (R.22) describes what may be the revolution of Ursa Major through the northern sky as warriors with elite horses sailing a ship

---

22 Cf. Jennifer Neville, "Redeeming Beowulf: The Heroic Idiom as Marker of Quality in Old English Poetry," in *Narration and Hero: Recounting the Deeds of Heroes in Literature and Art of the Early Medieval Period*, ed. Victor Millet and Heike Sahm (Berlin: De Gruyter, 2014), 60–1.

23 Cf. Jennifer Neville, *Representations of the Natural World in Old English Poetry* (Cambridge: Cambridge University Press, 1999), 52.

24 For a recent discussion of this riddle alongside the preceding two "storm" riddles, see James Paz, "Mind, Mood, and Meteorology in Þrymful Þeow (R. 1–3)," in *Riddles at Work in the Early Medieval Tradition: Words, Ideas, Interactions*, ed. Megan Cavell and Jennifer Neville, Manchester Medieval Literature and Culture 32 (Manchester: Manchester University Press, 2020), 193–209.

25 For relatively recent discussions see Dieter Bitterli, "Exeter Book Riddle 15: Some Points for the Porcupine," *Anglia* 120 (2002): 461–87; Marijane Osborn, "Vixen as Hero: Solving Exeter Book Riddle 15," in *The Hero Recovered: Essays on Medieval Heroism in Honor of George Clark*, ed. Robin Waugh and James Weldon (Kalamazoo, MI: Medieval Institute, 2010), 173–87; Megan Cavell, "The Igil and Exeter Book Riddle 15," *N&Q* 64 (2017): 206–10.

across the sea;[26] *Air-Vessel* (R.29) imagines the sun and moon as warriors contending over territory (the sky) and booty (light);[27] and *Younger Brother* (R.93) briefly identifies the stag on which an antler grows as its lord.[28] In all these cases, the heroic idiom only partially obscures the object, and the partial nature of this camouflage allows an audience to recognize the heroic idiom as camouflage and thus to identify the weapons, warriors, horses, and deeds of courage as poetic descriptions rather than literal components of the heroic world. However, solving the clues – for example, recognizing the *is* "ice" camouflaged by the heroic idiom in *Terrible Laughter* – does not shut down the interpretive process. Not only does *Terrible Laughter* move on to a different way of looking at its subject after line 7, but the transferral of the heroic idiom to the realm of the natural world also invites a critical evaluation of human endeavour: these obscuring metaphors often warrant scrutiny in themselves. For example, the use of the heroic idiom as camouflage in *Turning Wood* creates the opportunity for thought-provoking comparisons between the arts of weaving and violence, as Megan Cavell's studies have shown.[29] Those reflections remain potent even if different solutions are preferred; indeed, the pursuit of competing solutions may be the best way to lead an audience to pause and scrutinize what might otherwise seem familiar, obvious, and right: the heroic idiom itself.

Seeing through Camouflage in *Towering Tree* (R.53)

In the previous chapter, I argued that interpreting the heroic idiom literally in *Towering Tree* (R.53) leads to rather unconvincing solutions. The examples of *Terrible Laughter* (R.33), *Turning Wood* (R.56), and *One-Footed* (R.58) suggest a different approach might fare better, especially since the heroic idiom in *Towering Tree* appears only in a self-contained section of the text, just as it does in *Terrible Laughter*. Perhaps the battle described by this text camouflages a wooden contraption that is not a

---

26 Patrick J. Murphy, *Unriddling the Exeter Riddles* (University Park: Pennsylvania State University Press, 2011), 111–23.
27 For discussion, see Murphy, *Unriddling*, 123–39.
28 For discussion, see Dieter Bitterli, *Say What I Am Called: The Old English Riddles of the Exeter Book and the Anglo-Latin Riddle Tradition* (Toronto: University of Toronto Press, 2009), 157–63.
29 Cavell, *Weaving Words*, 27–47; Cavell, "Looming Danger and Dangerous Looms: Violence and Weaving in Exeter Book Riddle 56," *LSE* 42 (2011): 29–42; Cavell, "Seeing Red: Visuality, Violence, and the Making of Textiles in Early Medieval Enigmatic Poetry," *Medieval Feminist Forum* 57 (2021): 17–48.

weapon at all, something which, like *One-Footed*, has a moving wooden part. The result of this action is the "destruction" of a collection of some valuable material (the *hord* "hoard") in the midst of some kind of commotion (the *yst* "tempest"). What is it?

It could be a flail. In the 21st-century world of combine harvesters and urban dwelling, few readers will have seen a flail, but the jointed, wooden tool used to separate grain from straw was a well-known object in early medieval England,[30] and there are two other riddles that may also address it.[31] Let us scrutinize *Towering Tree* again with *perscel* "flail" in mind.

> Ic seah on bearwe   beam hlifian,
> tanum torhtne.   Þæt treow wæs on wynne,
> wudu weaxende.   Wæter hine ond eorþe
> feddan fægre,   oþþæt he frod dagum
> 5 on oþrum wearð   aglachade
> deope gedolgod,   dumb in bendum,
> wriþen ofer wunda,   wonnum hyrstum
> foran gefrætwed.   Nu he fæcnum weg
> þurh his heafdes mægen   hildegieste
> 10 oþrum rymeð.   Oft hy an yst strudon
> hord ætgædre;   hræd wæs ond unlæt
> se æftera,   gif se ærra fær
> genamnan in nearowe   neþan moste. (*Towering Tree*)

(I saw a tree bright in its branches, towering up in a grove. That tree, the growing wood, was joyful. Water and earth fed it beautifully, until, old in days, it experienced a different state, one of misery: [it was] deeply wounded, voiceless in bonds, its wounds tied over, adorned in front with dark ornaments. Now through the power of its head it opens a deceitful road for another battle-guest. Often they plundered the hoard together in the tempest. The follower was prompt and unwearied, if the leader was allowed to risk danger in a narrow place for his companion.)

---

30 See discussion of threshing in Debby Banham and Rosamond Faith, *Anglo-Saxon Farms and Farming* (Oxford: Oxford University Press, 2014), 64–5 and in Peter Fowler, *Farming in the First Millennium AD: British Agriculture between Julius Caesar and William the Conqueror* (Cambridge: Cambridge University Press, 2002), 171.

31 For an interpretation of *Periodically Busy* (R.4) as a flail, see Dorothy Hartley, *Lost Country Life* (New York: Pantheon Books, 1979), 184. I accept Trautmann's "flail" as a solution for *Captives* (R.52); see discussion in Williamson, *Old English Riddles*, 295–7 and chapter 4, below.

As before, most of the riddle, from lines 1 to 8a, tells us that the object is made out of wood, which is subject to the tortures involved in the manufacturing process.³² However, if this wooden object is a flail, we can interpret that process a bit more specifically than before. Once its wood is cut into the correct size and shape, the handle of the flail, *dumb in bendum* "unspeaking in bonds" (6b), is attached to the swingle or swipple, the swinging part of the flail, with a cord, rope, or chain tied through the hole or "wound" at its end (*wriþen ofer wunda* 7a). *Nu* "now" that the two parts are connected, the handle clears a *fæcnum weg* "treacherous path" (8b) for its accompanying *hildegieste* "battle-guest" (9b) through the momentum created by its swinging "head" (*heafdes mægen* "power of its head" 9a). This "treacherous path" is the first problem with the flail-solution, but it could represent the potentially dangerous momentum of the swingle, which in the course of threshing passes close to the wielder's head.³³ A swinging swingle may indeed be a *hildegieste* "enemy" to a person wielding it unskilfully. If all goes well, however, the two together may *strudon / hord ætgædre* "ravage the hoard together" (10b–11a) – that is, separate the "treasure," the grain, from the straw with violent blows.³⁴ The following swingle (*se æftera*) moves very quickly (*hræd*) and without hesitation (*unlæt*) after the handle (*se ærra*). This description seems very apt to a flail, but it is difficult to see how a flail might operate *in nearowe* "in a narrow place." Translating the last line and a half differently may help: perhaps we should read *gif se ærra fær / genamnan in nearowe neþan moste* "if the first was permitted to venture on a journey (while) in the narrowness of its companion."³⁵ Perhaps the riddle specifies that the great speed of the swingle is dependent upon being tied to the narrow opening (*nearowe*) at the end of its companion (*genamnan*, taken as a genitive), the handle.

---

32 For further discussion of manufacturing in the riddles, see chapter 5, below.
33 Cf. Walter Needham, *A Book of Country Things*, recorded by Barrows Mussey (Brattleboro, VT: Stephen Greene, 1965), 31–2: "You just keep your ears folded back and don't hit yourself in the head, and you're all right."
34 I am tempted here to attempt to read a "wheat-and-chaff hermeneutics" into the text, but Newman's rejection of Robertsonian "either/or" exegesis must surely be as appropriate to the Exeter Book riddles as it is to later medieval literature. See Barbara Newman, *Medieval Crossover: Reading the Secular against the Sacred* (Notre Dame, IN: University of Notre Dame Press, 2013).
35 Cf., however, my reading of *fær* as "danger" in chapter 2, above. Trautmann takes *fær* as "journey," although in support of a different solution (*besma* "broom"); see *Die altenglischen Rätsel* (Heidelberg: Carl Winter, 1915), 32, 111–12.

This dependency is certainly true of a flail, but I am not ready to wager money on this solution, especially since it does not clearly explain what the *wonnum hyrstum / foran* "dark ornaments in front" (7b–8a) are. Nevertheless, the aptness of the conditional speed of *se æftera* is tempting. This solution also provides one additional point of interest: the use of the heroic idiom to describe a flail anticipates the flail's development into a weapon commonly used from the thirteenth to fifteenth centuries. Perhaps the flail was already recognized as a potential weapon even in the early medieval period, and perhaps the riddle represents a musing on the phenomenon of beating ploughshares into swords. Early medieval England was, of course, subject more to war than to peace.

Or perhaps we need yet another perspective. I gained one from Carole A. Morris's description of her experience and knowledge of early medieval wood-turning.[36] Her attempts to reproduce the castoffs, waste, and finished products found in the ground in York presented me with an image of a pole-lathe that I could not have imagined before and that can be tested against *Towering Tree*, too. As before, lines 1–8a describe the creation of a wooden object, the painful transformation from happy, living tree to wounded, bound implement of power. If the object in question is a pole-lathe, the *wonnum hyrstum* "dark ornaments" (7b) at last receive an explanation, for they may represent the metal centre points, the only parts of a pole-lathe that could not be made of wood, which serve as the pivots on which a block of wood is turned. The *heafdes mægen* "power of the head" (9a) consequently refers to the mandrel, which acts as the drive-shaft, directing the force from the foot-treadle to the block of wood and holding the wooden block firmly in place during the turning process. The *hildegieste / oþrum* "other battle-guest" (9b–10a), the turner's gouge, carves out the core of the block to make a cup or bowl. The risk of cutting too far, of ruining the unfinished vessel, might explain why this process is called a *fæcnum wæg* "treacherous way" (8b). The immobilizing mandrel and sharp gouge together remove the core of the block of wood, its heart or *hord* "hoard" (11a), in an *yst* "storm" (10b), a shower of shavings and water,[37] but the gouge, *se æftera* "the following one" (12b), can only be *hræd ... ond unlæt* "prompt and unwearied" (11b) if the mandrel, *se ærra* "the first one" (12b), is *fær / genamnan in nearowe neþan moste*

---

36 See Morris, *Craft, Industry and Everyday Life*, 2116–39. The discussion that follows is heavily indebted to this work.
37 Carole A. Morris, personal communication (2011).

"permitted to venture on a journey into [or risk danger in] a narrow place for its companion" (12b–13).[38] In other words, the gouge can only work effectively if the mandrel is securely fixed into the core of the unfinished vessel.[39]

Without a visual demonstration of the process, this interpretation of the riddle's elliptical description may appear rather vague (unless the reader has already observed a working reconstruction of an early medieval pole-lathe, of course).[40] Nevertheless, although my own knowledge and experience is only second-hand, testing that knowledge and experience against the riddle suggests that it *can* be interpreted as a pole-lathe, but it is also possible that some other wooden implement lies hidden here. With our incomplete knowledge of early medieval material culture, we might not recognize the object described here even if we saw it. Archaeological research into the material culture of the period may yet unearth new possibilities, but, since the only thing that is certain about this object is that it is made of wood, and since wooden artefacts rarely survive in the archaeological record,[41] we may remain forever uncertain, even if the object itself was very common and thus familiar to contemporary audiences.[42]

The essentially enigmatic nature of *Towering Tree* thus remains: the manuscript presents no limit or point of termination to the process of interpreting it, and so we can rest no more securely with *turnus* "pole-lathe" as a solution than we can with *perscel* "flail." We cannot see *through* this riddle to discover facts about the material culture of early medieval England, other than the facts that pertain equally well to battering rams, spears, bows, arrows, gallows, flails, and pole-lathes. There may be further possibilities, too, for it is possible to interpret the

---

38 Both translations of *fær*, with or without an accent, seem potentially meaningful for this solution.
39 Morris notes that the mandrel can be fixed so tightly to the turned cup or bowl that it can be difficult to remove (*Craft, Industry and Everyday Life*, 2128).
40 It is possible to observe such a reconstruction in use at Jarrow Hall, near Newcastle. There are also videos on YouTube by craftsmen such as Sharif Adams, How to Turn a Wooden Bowl on a Pole Lathe, https://youtu.be/aKU-2ZUE8lA?si=9tuZh7dxX0SfL4KF.
41 The problem is not simply one of survival but of recording. The guidelines published by Historic England provide an overview of the issues; see "Waterlogged Wood: Guidelines on the Recording, Sampling, Conservation and Curation of Waterlogged Wood" (1 April 2010), https://content.historicengland.org.uk/images-books/publications/waterlogged-wood/waterlogged-wood.pdf/.
42 Cf. David Hill, "Riddle 8: A Problem of Identification or a Problem of Translation," *Medieval Life* 11 (1999): 22–3.

heroic idiom in still other ways.[43] The familiar but unhelpful heroic idiom is easy to recognize but not always so easy to read. The riddles thus require their audiences to scrutinize language and ideas that might have been passed over quickly in other texts.

Disguise: The Heroic Idiom as a System of Metaphors

As is well known, the tropes and ideas that make up the heroic idiom are widespread. Outside the Exeter Book riddles Old English poetry uses the heroic idiom to describe not only heroic culture but also other things, most famously spiritual matters, in which the heroic idiom glorifies what might superficially appear to be unheroic people, activities, and contexts. The transferral of military language to spiritual activity is not, of course, unique or original to Old English poetry, but it is an important feature of it.[44] Here the transferral of military language to spiritual activity may stand as a model for the use of the heroic idiom as disguise. For example, the poetic language of warriors and battle is applied to praise Christian evangelism in *Andreas*:[45]

---

43 See F.H. Whitman, "Significant Motifs in Riddle 53," *MÆ* 46 (1977): 1–11 and the development of his spiritual interpretation in Jennifer Neville, "The *Exeter Book Riddles*' Precarious Insights into Wooden Artefacts," in *Trees and Timber in the Anglo-Saxon World*, ed. Michael D.J. Bintley and Michael G. Shapland (Oxford: Oxford University Press, 2013), 122–43. Cf. also Matthew Aiello, "Books in Battle: The Violent Poetics of Misdirection in Old English *Riddle 53*," *RES* 71 (2020): 207–28.

44 There were patristic models for the use of military imagery for saints, for example; for a brief discussion see Stanley B. Greenfield and Daniel G. Calder, *A New Critical History of Old English Literature* (New York: New York University Press, 1986), 158. For one discussion (among many) of this transferral in Old English poetry, see, for example, Joyce Hill, "The Soldier of Christ in Old English Prose and Poetry," *LSE* 12 (1981), 57–80.

45 Discussion of *Andreas* has previously been dominated by the question of its relationship with *Beowulf*; see, for example, the discussion in Anita R. Riedinger, "The Formulaic Relationship between *Beowulf* and *Andreas*," in *Heroic Poetry in the Anglo-Saxon Period: Studies in Honor of Jess B. Bessinger Jr.*, ed. Helen Damico and John Leyerle (Kalamazoo, MI: Medieval Institute, 1993), 283–312; *Andreas: An Edition*, ed. Richard North and Michael D.J. Bintley (Liverpool: Liverpool University Press, 2016), 62–81. For my purposes what is more important is *Andreas*' relationship to the heroic idiom in general. I do not do justice to the complexity of that relationship here, but for discussion of some major features of the poem's use of heroic language, see Edward B. Irving Jr, "A Reading of *Andreas*: The Poem as Poem," *ASE* 12 (1983): 215–37; Daniel G. Calder, "Figurative Language and its Contexts in *Andreas*: A Study in Medieval Expressionism," in *Modes of Interpretation in Old English Literature: Essays in Honour of Stanley B. Greenfield*, ed. Phyllis Rugg Brown, Georgia Ronan Crampton, and Fred C. Robinson (Toronto: University of Toronto Press, 1986), 115–36; Andy Orchard, "The Originality of *Andreas*," in *Old English Philology: Studies in Honour of R.D. Fulk*, ed. Leonard Neidorf, Rafael J. Pascual, and Tom Shippey, Anglo-Saxon Studies 31 (Cambridge: Brewer, 2016), 331–52.

> Hwæt! We gefrunan   on fyrndagum
> twelfe under tunglum   tireadige hæleð,
> þeodnes þegnas.   No hira þrym alæg
> campræedenne   þonne cumbol hneotan,
> 5 syððan hie gedældon,   swa him Dryhten sylf,
> heofona heahcyning,   hlyt getæhte.
> Þæt wæron mære   men ofer eorðan,
> frome folctogan   ond fyrdhwate,
> rofe rincas,   þonne rond ond hand
> 10 on herefelda   helm ealgodon,
> on meotudwange. (*Andreas* 1–11a)

(Listen! We have heard of twelve victory-blessed heroes in days long past, thegns of the prince under the stars. Their power in warfare did not weaken when banners clashed, after they parted [from each other], just as the lord himself, the high-king of the heavens, assigned them their lot. They were men famous across the world – leaders bold and keen for war, strong warriors when shield and hand defended the helmet on battlefields and plains of war.)

This introduction to the story of Andrew's conversion of the cannibalistic Mermedonians could easily be rewritten as a riddle (presented here in condensed form): "Who are the twelve glorious warriors whose power in warfare did not weaken after the high-king of heaven separated them? They were famously bold when shield and hand defended the helmet on the battlefield. Say what they are called." Every detail in this "riddle" points to the heroic idiom, and thus a list of famous military leaders might be expected. An audience alert to the significance of the number twelve, however, might suspect that the text describes not famous warriors from the secular tradition but rather the twelve apostles of Christ, who accepted death passively in the course of their struggles to spread the gospel to unbelievers.

Andreas, of course, is not a riddle – its next half-line explicitly names Matthew, and the following text describes how he spread the gospel amongst the Jews – yet even in this case an audience must know that Matthew did not spread the gospel on a literal battlefield, with a literal shield and helmet, in order to understand what the battle, war-skill, and equipment described here are.[46] The heroic idiom completely

---

46 The shield and helmet here are probably those of Ephesians 6: 14–17. The schema established there does not cover all the items in this passage (the *cumbol*, for example), but it has been argued that we should not expect specific correspondences; see John P. Hermann, *Allegories of War: Language and Violence in Old English Poetry* (Ann Arbor, MI: University of Michigan Press, 1989), 37. Cf. also W.F. Bolton, *Alcuin and Beowulf: An Eighth-Century View* (London: Edward Arnold, 1979), 40.

enfolds the non-heroic content; the traditional narrative of warriors, lords, battle, and equipment becomes a system of metaphors for a different kind of personnel, activity, location, and material culture while at the same time ascribing to it a similar ethic and an equally high value and prestige.[47]

Like the Exeter Book riddles, *Andreas* does not explain *how* it is to be interpreted, but its explicit reference to Matthew ensures that reinterpretation does take place. In the Exeter Book riddles the direction to interpret and reinterpret comes first from recognition of the riddle-genre itself.[48] Such recognition comes in part from the presentation of the riddles as a collection, but, as we saw in the previous chapter, some riddles explicitly signal their genre through initial or concluding formula such as *Frige hwæt ic hatte* "find out what I am called" (Weapon-Warrior, R.14. 19b).[49] Other riddles lack such explicit direction and cue their readers to interpret further in other ways. Chief among such cues is incongruity. *I Burn the Living* (R.6), for example, does not provoke interpretive processes with a riddlic formula, but, even if it were not part of a riddle collection, the incongruity attending its heroic action would probably inspire an audience to reinterpret it:

> Mec gesette soð   sigora waldend
> Crist to compe.   Oft ic cwice bærne
> unrimu cyn   eorþan getenge,
> næte mid niþe,   swa ic him no hrine,
> 5 þonne mec min frea   feohtan hateþ.
> Hwilum ic monigra   mod arete,
> hwilum ic frefre   þa ic ær winne on
> feorran swiþe;   hi þæs felað þeah,

---

47 Cf. the fuller discussion in Hermann, *Allegories of War*, 37–52. Another notable example is *Juliana*, also contained in the Exeter Book. Lines 382–409a describe spiritual conflict in terms of fortresses, arrow, combat, and courage; for discussion see Hermann, *Allegories of War*, 43–4.

48 Cf. Susanne Kries, "*Fela í rúnum eða í skáldskap*: Anglo-Saxon and Scandinavian Approaches to Riddles and Poetic Disguises," in *Riddles, Knights and Cross-Dressing Saints: Essays on Medieval English Language and Literature*, ed. Thomas Honegger (Bern: Peter Lang, 2004), 149–50, 159–60. For classification of the Exeter Book riddles by opening formulae, see Ann Harleman Stewart, "Old English Riddle 47 as Stylistic Parody," *Papers in Language and Literature* 11 (1975): 230.

49 See Andy Orchard, "Enigma Variations: The Anglo-Saxon Riddle-Tradition," in *Latin Learning and English Lore: Studies in Anglo-Saxon Literature for Michael Lapidge*, ed. Katherine O'Brien O'Keeffe and Andy Orchard, 2 vols (Toronto: University of Toronto Press, 2005), 1: 289–90.

swylce þæs oþres,   þonne ic eft hyra
10 ofer deop gedreag   drohtað bete. (*I Burn the Living*)

(Christ, the true ruler of victories, ordained me for battle. I often burn the living, oppressing the countless races of the earth. I afflict [them] with destruction when my lord commands me to fight, although I do not touch them. Sometimes I gladden the minds of many; sometimes I comfort those against whom I previously strove fiercely from afar. Nevertheless they feel the former as well as the latter, when I again improve their condition over the deep tumult.)

Warriors are rarely found comforting their former enemies, although such action is imaginable.[50] Battle without contact, however, stops a literal reading of the heroic idiom in its tracks; in a real battle, even projectiles like arrows *hrine* "touch" their victims, as they do in *Wob* (R.23.12a), for example. The denial of contact thus requires an audience to reinterpret the speaker here as something beyond the limits of heroic culture, like the camouflaged objects discussed earlier in this chapter. Unlike in *Turning Wood* or *One-Footed*, however, in *I Burn the Living* the change in appearance is (almost) complete; there are no leafy trees or water lifted up in the air to identify a scenario partially obscured by the poeticizing language. Here, then, the heroic idiom is not merely camouflage but disguise: it is a (mostly) consistent system of metaphors whose individual, apparently military elements may all be translated into non-military referents.

How to interpret the heroic idiom, of course, remains open. The first line and a half of the riddle, for example, might encourage us to interpret the familiar heroic idiom in a familiar way, in terms of spiritual battle: the warrior ordained for battle by Christ could be an evangelist like Andrew or any Christian beset by temptation. Modern readers generally do not read the text in this way, however. Instead, they interpret its language in terms of wisdom literature, whose key tenet is the divinely ordered nature of creation.[51] In this interpretive context,

---

50 Thomas D. Hill argues that this combination of roles is based on Macrobius' description of Apollo as god of healing and plague. "Killer and Healer: Late Classical Analogues for the Old English Sun Riddle," *PQ* 90 (2011): 387–94.
51 For definitions of "wisdom literature" in relation to Old English poetry, see M.W. Bloomfield, "The Notion of Wisdom," in *The Role of the Poet in Early Societies*, ed. M.W. Bloomfield and C.W. Dunn (Cambridge: Brewer, 1989), 106–19; Bloomfield, "Wisdom Genres and Types of Literature," also in *The Role of the Poet*, 120–49; Elaine Tuttle Hansen, *The Solomon Complex: Reading Wisdom in Old English Poetry* (Toronto: University of Toronto Press, 1988), 10–11.

the warrior "ordained by God" is not a human being but rather a central object within the divinely ordered creation: the *sunne* "sun," which burns, torments, gladdens, and comforts human beings from far off.[52] No matter how this riddle is approached, however, its subject is no ordinary thegn, and ultimately no aspect of the heroic idiom in *I Burn the Living* can be interpreted literally. Audiences must re-read the familiar language of warriors and conflict to discover how to understand it.

Although fragmentary at both its beginning and end due to manuscript damage, *Brotherless* (R.88) also presents a recognizable heroic narrative without riddlic opening or closing tags. If it were not for its place within a riddle-collection, an audience could – initially, at least – interpret the text as a lyric, comparable with *The Wanderer*, about a young man who spent his youth adventurously with his heroic brother until both were tragically exiled by usurping younger kin:

    Ic weox þær ic s[. . . . .
    . . . .] ond sumor   mi[. . . . . . .
    . . . .] me   wæs min ti[. .
    . . . .
5 sto]d ic on staðol[e . . . .
    . . . . . .]um geong,   swa [. . . . .
    . . . .] seþeana
    oft geond [. . . . . o]fgeaf,
    ac ic uplong stod,   þær ic [. . . . . .]
10 ond min broþor;   begen wæron hearde.
    Eard wæs þy weorðra   þe wit on stodan,
    hyrstum þy hyrra.   Ful oft unc holt wrugon,
    wudubeama helm   wonnum nihtum
    scildon wið scurum;   unc gescop meotud.
15 Nu unc mæran twam   magas uncre
    sculon æfter cuman,   eard oðþringan
    gingran broþor.   Eom ic gumcynnes
    anga ofer eorþan;   is min [innaþ] blæc

---

52 This solution is universally accepted, in part because of the support granted by the "S" runes that both precede and follow this text. The former is often interpreted as indicating the solution of the previous riddle, *Lone Dweller* (R.5); for images of these runes see *The Exeter Book of Old English Poetry*, ed. Raymond W. Chambers, Max Förster, and Robin Flower (London: Percy Lund, 1933), fols 102v and 103r, Williamson, *Old English Riddles*, 52, or Bernard J. Muir, *The Exeter DVD*, fols 102v and 103r. For discussion of these marginal runes, see Williamson, *Old English Riddles*, 151, and my brief discussion in chapter 1.

wonn ond wundorlic.   Ic on wuda stonde
20 bordes on ende.   Nis min broþor her,
ac ic sceal broþorleas   bordes on ende
staþol weardian,   stondan fæste;
ne wat hwær min broþor   on wera æhtum
eorþan sceata   eardian sceal,
25 se me ær be healfe   heah eardade.
Wit wæron gesome   sæcce to fremmanne;
næfre uncer awþer   his ellen cyðde,
swa wit þære beadwe   begen ne onþungan.
Nu mec unsceafta   innan slitað,
30 wyrdaþ mec be wombe;   ic gewendan ne mæg.
Æt þam spore findeð   sped se þe se[. .
. . . .]   sawle rædes. (*Brotherless*, R.88)[53]

(I grew where I [stood?] ... and summer ... my ... me ...was mine ... I [stood?] at the place ... young as ...yet often through ... gave up, but I stood upright where I ... and my brother; we both were hardy. The land on which we two stood was more worthy and illustrious because of [our? its? us?] ornaments. Very often the forest, the shelter of trees, covered us in dark nights [and] shielded [us] from showers. The creator shaped us. Now our two greater kinsmen, our younger brothers, will inevitably[54] come after us [and] seize the land. I am the only one of [my] kind on the earth; my inside is black – dark and wondrous. I stand on wood, at the end of a board. My brother is not here; instead, brotherless, I must guard the place, stand firm at the end of the board. I do not know where my brother, the tall one who previously dwelt by my side, must inhabit the expanse of the earth among the possessions of men. We two were together in order to perform battle; never did either of us make known his courage unless both of us prospered in the battle. Now monsters slice my innards, injure me in the belly; I cannot escape. The one who [seeks] ... counsel for the soul ... will find prosperity on that track.)

Hiding in the forest by night may not be traditional heroic behaviour, but audiences familiar with the heroic idiom can easily observe here

---

53 See Muir, *Exeter Anthology*, 2: 725–6 for discussion of the damage to the manuscript and the history of proposed emendations.
54 As mentioned previously, I translate *sceal* as indicating an action that is "characteristic" or "natural" rather than morally binding or compelled; see discussion of *sceal* in Paul Cavill, *Maxims in Old English Poetry* (Cambridge: Brewer, 1999), 45–50.

the value placed on gaining glory in battle, standing firm, and maintaining loyalty as well as the transience of security, even within families. Such audiences can also recognize the speaker's elegiac lament for better times in the midst of present torment, for, like the Wanderer, this speaker steadfastly faces a future of isolation with no hope of improvement (*ic gewendan ne mæg* "I cannot escape" 30b).[55] That is, *Brotherless*, like *Beowulf*, celebrates the values of heroic culture even as it acknowledges its limits.[56] Whatever *ræd* "wisdom, advice, counsel" (32) might have been found at the damaged end of the riddle, there is apparently no hope for the riddle-subject itself.

Indeed, at the end of the riddle we learn that this unfortunate warrior suffers a fate worse than that of the Wanderer, for he stands helpless on a board, impaled by *unsceafta* monsters (29a). Such an outlandish scenario is not impossible in a heroic tale, but by this point the riddle has already disrupted any potential audience-identification with its speaker, for halfway through the text we are invited to contemplate the young warrior's *wonn ond wunderlic* "dark and wondrous" innards (18b–19a).[57] However moving the heroic story of the exiled brother may be, reference to his wondrous, dark innards marks the story as different from a typical heroic narrative, and thus audiences interpret the story not as a tragic lyric but as the biography of a *heortes horn* "stag's antler," previously one of a pair that grew up tall on a stag's head and served it well in battle until inevitably shed according to the seasonal cycle, to be replaced in the spring by a new, larger set (the *mæran twam magas* "two greater kinsmen" 15). Although damage to the manuscript makes the end of the text elliptical, in the context of a *spore* "track" (31a) that brings *ræd* "advice, wisdom" (32), it is reasonable to surmise that the fallen antler standing on the table or desk has been made into a container for ink, a tool for

---

55 Cf. *The Wanderer* 15–16: *Ne mæg werig mod wyrde wiðstondan, / ne se hreo hyge helpe gefremman* "the weary heart cannot withstand its fate, nor can the troubled mind provide any help."
56 Cf. Peter S. Baker, *Honour, Exchange, and Violence in Beowulf* (Cambridge: Boydell and Brewer, 2013), 238.
57 Some of this incongruity is based upon an emendation which is debatable (cf. argument for a different emendation in Krapp and Dobbie, 377). The manuscript reading of lines 18b–19a (*is min bæc / wonn ond wunderlic* "my back is dark and wondrous") has been rejected as unmetrical (see discussion in Williamson, *Old English Riddles*, 381–2 and Muir, *Exeter Anthology*, 2: 726), but, even if it were to be retained, it, too, would disrupt the image of a human warrior and create incongruity; human backs are rarely described as "dark and wondrous."

the technology of literacy.[58] The elegiac mood may not entirely disappear, but recognition of the non-heroic, inanimate object distances the audience from the story and the social issues it raises, whether that audience views the human drama as trivialized or the inanimate inkpot as made worthy of human sympathy.[59] That is, to solve the riddle an audience must step back from the heroic idiom, the trope through which Old English poetry typically expresses both joy and sorrow. Recognizing the heroic idiom as a disguise draws attention to the trope itself: although it is natural, traditional, and perhaps even inevitable in Old English poetry to ascribe value to courage and loyalty, here these values belong to something outside heroic culture – an inanimate object that cannot be courageous, express loyalty, or mourn loss. The Exeter Book riddles thus offer an opportunity to think about heroism that is not natural, traditional, or inevitable, and to look again at what is normally assumed.

Being Suspicious of the Familiar: Unrecognizing *Warrior's Companion* (R.80)

Warrior's Companion (R.80) also makes the heroic idiom something to question rather than something to affirm. Its metaphorical disguise thus reveals more (and perhaps less) than material culture:

> Ic eom æþelinges   eaxlgestealla,
> fyrdrinces gefara,   frean minum leof,
> cyninges geselda.   Cwen mec hwilum
> hwitloccedu   hond on legeð,
> 5   eorles dohtor,   þeah hio æþelu sy.
> Hæbbe me on bosme   þæt on bearwe geweox.
> Hwilum ic on wloncum   wicge ride
> herges on ende;   heard is min tunge.

---

58 The physical torment by the *unsceaftas* is usually taken to represent the manufacturing process; for further discussion of torment and manufacturing, see chapter 5, below. The "tracks," with their beneficial qualities, participate in the trope of writing that can be observed in many riddles (see, for example, *Four Creatures* (R.51); the emendation of line 18b (discussed above) relies upon this understanding of the antler's relation to writing. It is notable, however, that no interest is expressed in literacy itself here; cf. also *Younger Brother* (R.93), which includes the physical process of writing but not the magic of literacy.

59 *A Feast of Creatures: Anglo-Saxon Riddle-Songs*, trans. Craig Williamson (Philadelphia: University of Pennsylvania Press, 1982), 43–6.

Oft ic woðboran   wordleana sum
10 agyfe æfter giedde.   Good is min wise
ond ic sylfa salo.   Saga hwæt ic hatte.[60] (*Warrior's Companion*)

(Dear to my lord, I am the close companion of a prince, the comrade of an army-warrior, the retainer of a king. Sometimes a fair-haired queen, an earl's daughter, lays her hand on me, although she is noble. I have in my bosom what grew in a grove. Sometimes, in the front line of an army, I ride a proud steed. My tongue is firm. After a song I often give rewards to a poet for his words. My character is good, and I myself am dark. Say what I am called.)

In quick succession here we may observe the affection of a lord for his thegn,[61] the comradeship of the *comitatus*, the noblewoman's place in the hall, riding proud horses, and an additional pleasure: poetry. It hardly needs to be said, given the list of worldly joys that makes up the bulk of the riddle, but *Warrior's Companion* explicitly proclaims its positive status: *good is min wise* "my character is good" (10b). Although translated as "character" here, *wise* usefully encapsulates a wide range of connotations relevant to the actions described in the riddle, including the noble, society-preserving *custom* of loyalty, the essential social organization represented by the *way* of the woman in the hall, the expensive, status-building *fashion* of riding well-bred horses, and even the pleasing *melody* of a well-wrought poem worthy of reward.[62] This is unambiguously the good life, represented by a single indexical sign, the subject of the riddle.

This subject participates in this heroic world as if "he" were a human being, a warrior who acts as well as being acted upon. Thus he is not simply carried by a proud steed; rather, he rides one, and at the head of the army, too – a fitting place for the *æþelinges eaxlgestealla* "prince's close companion" (1). He rewards poets with gifts. He even receives

---

[60] Williamson considers the single line that precedes this text, *Ic eom æþelinges æht ond willa* "I am a prince's possession and joy," to be part of the riddle, even though the scribe sets it out as a separate riddle (*Old English Riddles*, 111). I have followed Muir in keeping the two texts separate (see *Exeter Anthology*, 1: 368). The line's presence or absence does not have an impact upon my discussion of *Warrior's Companion*.

[61] This apparently warm relationship between lord and thegn also functions as part of the implement trope, which can be observed in many of the Exeter Book riddles. For discussion, see chapter 5, below.

[62] See B-T, *s.v. wise*; definitions include: "way, manner, mode, fashion, state, condition, disposition." Clark-Hall adds "habit, custom, and melody."

the advances of a noble woman, despite the restraint demanded by her high rank (æpelu 5b): such a lady presumably would not lay her hands on a warrior in polite company. Her (apparently) desiring hand moves the riddle into another sphere, that of the double entendre,[63] and the apparent lack of propriety on the part of the emphatically noble woman[64] provides the first clue that what we have here is not, in fact, a human warrior. The next line confirms the need to reinterpret the "warrior," for having "what grew in the grove" in its bosom suggests that *Warrior's Companion* is a container of some kind.

Most scholars interpret this container as a *horn* "horn" and describe *Warrior's Companion* as the "companion piece" of *Weapon-Warrior* (R.14).[65] Like *Weapon-Warrior*, it apparently describes two different uses of an animal horn: first as a drinking vessel in the familiar world of the *meduheall* "mead-hall," kept close by noblemen and handled publicly by noblewomen; second as a musical instrument, carried on horseback to war; and finally once again as a drinking vessel, conveying the reward of drink to a successful poet. Yet other objects from heroic culture have also been proposed: falcon, hawk, spear, sword, and scabbard,[66] and even unsolved the riddle expresses cultural truths for affirmation or evaluation. The expectation of a certain type of behaviour from a noblewoman, for example, functions as proscriptive moral regulation: the riddle provides a positive role model and a standard of behaviour for its audience.[67] This is not, however, the threatened heroic culture of *Beowulf*, but rather the rose-tinted heroic culture of *Weapon-Warrior* (R.14), that impossible heaven on earth that does not exist in

---

63 For discussion of the double entendre, see chapter 6, below.
64 The words used to describe her – *cwen, hwitloccedu, eorles dohtor, æpelu* – all pertain to nobility. See *DOE* s.v.v. *cwen* ("woman; noblewoman, lady; queen, female ruler, wife or consort of a king"), *eorl* ("nobleman"), *æpele* ("noble, famous, glorious, holy, splendid, magnificent"). For the associations of *hwitloccede* "fair-haired, blonde" with nobility, see David A. E. Pelteret, *Slavery in Early Mediaeval England from the Reign of Alfred until the Twelfth Century* (Woodbridge: Boydell, 1995), 51–3; Debby Banham, "Anglo-Saxon Attitudes: In Search of the Origins of English Racism," *European Review of History* 1 (1994): 151–2. For discussion of class in relation to ethnicity, see N.J. Higham, *An English Empire: Bede and the Early Saxon Kings* (Manchester: Manchester University Press, 1995), 226–40.
65 See, for example, Tupper, *Riddles of the Exeter Book*, 227, and Williamson, *Old English Riddles*, 360. For discussion of *Weapon-Warrior*, see chapter 2, above.
66 See the appendix, below, for details.
67 Cf. Melanie Heyworth, "Perceptions of Marriage in *Exeter Book Riddles* 20 and 61," *SN* 79 (2007): 171–84.

other Old English poems except in the lost past:[68] a world where there are warriors without war, queens without feuds, and drinking without drunkenness.

Even modern readers can recognize the heroic warrior as a disguise for an inanimate container, but it is possible that the heroic idiom is also working as camouflage here, too, obscuring the context in which the riddle-subject acts. *Horn* functions so admirably as an index of the idiom that it is all too easy to fill in the scene in the hall, even though the text does not actually supply some crucial parts of it, and even though some of the clues may not quite fit. Most critics believe that *Warrior's Companion* describes drinking in the hall, but the act of drinking does not appear in this text: unlike *Weapon-Warrior*, *Warrior's Companion* does not reside in the place *þær weras drincað* "where men drink" (*Weapon-Warrior* 12b), and, unlike other riddles about drinking, *Warrior's Companion* is not kissed.[69] Despite the absence of such tropes for drinking, most readers assume that the riddle-subject is a container for an alcoholic beverage, because it apparently depicts life in the hall as *Weapon-Warrior* does, and because it contains *on bosme þæt on bearwe geweox* "in its bosom what grew in a grove" (6). The barley and grapes from which beer and wine are made do not grown in shady groves, and so to interpret this clue critics have looked to *Binder and Scourger* (R.27), in which the raw material for mead, nectar, is *brungen of bearwum ond of burghleoþum, / of denum ond of dunum* "brought from groves and from mountain slopes, from valleys and from hills" (2–3a). At first glance these two passages seem to refer to the same substance, but in fact growing in a grove is not the same as being brought from a grove, and it should be noted that the substance in *Binder and Scourger* is also brought from mountains, valleys, and hills, too. What grows in a grove is a tree.[70]

---

68 See, for example, *Seafarer* 80b–88a, *The Ruin* 32b–41, and *The Riming Poem* 1–42 (for lost past) and 43–69 (for sorrowful present).

69 See, for example, *Shining with Gold* (R.63): *Hwilum mec on cofan cysseð muþe / tillic esne* "sometimes a good servant kisses me on the mouth" (4-5a). This text is usually solved as *glæs-fæt* "glass beaker." Cf. also Aldhelm's Enigma 80 (*Calix vitreus* "Glass Goblet"). The absence of "kissing" is also significant for the other role played by *horn* in *Weapon-Warrior*, for the references to kissing in that text pertain not to drinking but to the playing of a musical instrument. *Warrior's Companion* contains no clues that can be confidently linked to a musical instrument, with the possible exception of *heard is min tunge* "my tongue (voice?) is hard (loud?)" or perhaps "my tongue (wooden mouthpiece?) is hard" (8b), although I have been unable to find any evidence for the use of such mouthpieces.

70 Within the Exeter Book riddles alone, groves are explicitly said to be the source of trees and wood in *Glorious I Thunder* (R.1. 8b–9a), *Downward Nose* (R.21. 7a),

If the substance contained by *Warrior's Companion* is wood, neither "horn" nor any of the other previous solutions constitutes a satisfactory response to the text, and, once this doubt arises, other questions may follow. For example, the colour of individual horns varies considerably, ranging from white to beige to brown to black, but generally a horn is a "light creamy colour, sometimes streaked with white, brown or black patches";[71] a riddle-solver could justifiably object that *salo* "dark" (11a) is not an accurate description of horns in general, and particularly not of the ones used for drinking, which could be ornamented with silver fittings.[72] Perhaps modern audiences, although capable of recognizing the warrior as a metaphorical disguise for a container, have been too quick to believe in the camouflaging façade of the heroic idiom. An early medieval audience, especially one which ascribed nobility, bravery, glory, and victory to spiritual as well as – or even in preference to – physical warfare,[73] may have been more suspicious. As E.G. Stanley states, "because [dark] does not make sense there is good reason for doubting that 'horn' is the correct solution, though widely accepted."[74]

In fact, the solution *rod* "cross" makes good sense of a surprising number of *Warrior's Companion*'s clues. The original cross was indeed a very close *eaxlgestealla* "shoulder-companion" (1a) of Christ, who is often referred to as *æþeling* "prince" (1a), *frea* "lord" (2b), and *cyning* "king" (3a), most famously in *The Dream of the Rood*.[75] A crucifix could be carried or worn by a bishop or priest, who might be imagined as a *fyrdrinc* "warrior" (2a) of

---

Flame-Busy (R.30. 4a), and *Towering Tree* (R.53. 1a). Cf. also *Genesis A* 902a, 1480a, 2554b–2555a, 2841b, *Phoenix* 122, *Wife's Lament* 27b, *Beowulf* 1363b–1364a, *Judgement Day II* 1–2, among others.

71 See, for example, the samples for sale at Abbeyhorn.co.uk. The quotation can be found on Abbeyhorn's "Sources of Horn" page: http://www.abbeyhorn.co.uk/index/sources-of-horn_41.htm.

72 For the fittings on the Taplow drinking horns, see Leslie Webster, *Anglo-Saxon Art: A New History* (London: British Museum, 2012), 58 and 63; for those on the Sutton Hoo drinking horns, see Evans, *Sutton Hoo Ship Burial*, 65.

73 Cf. Jocelyn Wogan-Browne, "The Hero in Christian Reception: Ælfric and Heroic Poetry," in *Old English Literature: Critical Essays*, ed. R. M. Liuzza (New Haven: Yale University Press, 2002), 225–8 and Shari Horner, "'Why Do You Speak So Much Foolishness?' Gender, Humor, and Discourse in Ælfric's Lives of Saints," in *Humour in Anglo-Saxon Literature*, ed. Jonathan Wilcox (Cambridge: Brewer, 2000), 134.

74 "Exeter Book *Riddles*, II: The Significant but Often Misleading Opening Word," *N&Q* 64 (2017): 363.

75 See, for example, *Dream of the Rood* 58a (*æþeling* "prince"), 33b (*frea* "lord"), and 44b (*cyning* "king").

Christ,[76] and such an image of the cross might also contain a fragment of the original one as a relic.[77] A reliquary might quite properly be touched, as an act of reverence, by a noble lady, and *þæt on bearwe geweox* "what grew in the grove" (6b) would then refer to the tree from which the cross was made, now held in the reliquary's *bosom* "bosom" (6a). A reliquary's *wise* "character" would certainly be *good* "good" (10b), and it could easily be carried on a horse.[78] Other clues may appear less appropriate to a reliquary, however. Although not impossible, it seems slightly forced to interpret *Oft ic woðboran wordleana sum / agyfe æfter giedde* "after a song I often give to a poet rewards for his words" (9–10a) as the relic's response to a penitent's verse prayer. A reliquary could be *salo* "dark," but it need not be. Indeed, it could be made of ivory, and, like a drinking horn, adorned with precious metals and gems. Also uncertain is the "hard tongue," although it could be a latch or binding holding the reliquary shut.[79]

What value, then, does *rod* "cross" have as a response to *Warrior's Companion*? It demonstrates the need to approach the heroic idiom with more suspicion than modern readers normally do. Although the Exeter Book riddles sometimes portray heroic culture, they also play with it – stretch it, distort it, and apply it to unsuitable scenarios. Their audiences need to be suspicious of the familiar.

---

76 Cf. Ælfric's presentation of Saint Martin, for example, as a solider; see discussion in Marcia A. Dalbey, "The Good Shepherd and the Soldier of God: Old English Homilies on St. Martin of Tours," *NM* 85 (1984): 422–34.

77 For an early medieval English pectoral reliquary cross made of ivory, see Paul Williamson, *Medieval Ivory Carvings: Early Christian to Romanesque* (London: Victoria and Albert Museum, 2010), 248–53. Such pectoral reliquary crosses may have been more common in Byzantium; Elizabeth Coatsworth mentions two in "The Robed Christ in Pre-Conquest Sculptures of the Crucifixion," *ASE* 29 (2000): 155–6. Larger, non-pectoral reliquary crosses were probably more common; see, for example, the Victoria and Albert Museum reliquary cross described in Williamson, *Medieval Ivory Carvings*, 238–41, which still held a finger-bone when examined in 1926 and apparently had previously held a collection of relics.

78 Relics were used regularly in seasonal processions as well as in times of need and were collected by kings and other laymen; Asser reports that Alfred, for example, always carried relics with him. See *Asser's Life of King Alfred, Together with the Annals of Saint Neots Erroneously Ascribed to Asser*, ed. William Henry Stevenson, with an introductory article by Dorothy Whitelock (Oxford: Clarendon, 1959), 90 (§104). See also discussions in, for example, Max Förster, *Zur Geschichte des Reliquienkultes in Altengland*, Sitzungsberichte der Bayerischen Akademie der Wissenschaften, Philosophisch-historische Abteilung 8 (Munich: Verlag der Bayerischen Akademie der Wissenschaften, 1943), 4–10, D.W. Rollason, *Saints and Relics in Anglo-Saxon England* (Oxford: Blackwell, 1989), and Julia Smith, "Portable Christianity: Relics in the Medieval West (c.700–1200)," Raleigh Lecture in History for 2010, *Proceedings of the British Academy* 181 (2012): 143–67.

79 I am grateful to Pirkko Koppinen for this suggestion (personal communication, March 2007).

A Case Study in Ambiguity: A Close Reading of *Protector* (R.17)

This requirement is even more evident in *Protector* (R.17). This text provides little indication that the heroic idiom should be taken anything other than literally, yet the generally accepted military solutions have never provided a convincing "click."

    Ic eom mundbora   minre heorde,
    eodorwirum fæst,   innan gefylled
    dryhtgestreona.   Dægtidum oft
    spæte sperebrogan;   sped biþ þy mare
5   fylle minre.   Frea þæt bihealdeð,
    hu me of hrife fleogað   hyldepilas.
    Hwilum ic sweartum   swelgan onginne
    brunum beadowæpnum,   bitrum ordum,
    eglum attorsperum.   Is min innað til,
10 wombhord wlitig,   wloncum deore;
    men gemunan   þæt me þurh muþ fareð. (*Protector*)

(Secure with enclosing wires and filled inside with noble treasures, I am the protector of my herd. During the day I often spit out spear-terror: because of that the success of my contents is greater. [My] lord observes how battle-darts fly out of my belly. Sometimes I begin to swallow swarthy, dark battle-weapons, sharp points, painful poison-spears. My inner womb-hoard is excellent, radiant, and precious to the powerful. Men remember what comes through my mouth.)

The text contains few obvious stumbling blocks: unlike *Brain-Locker* (R.73), it contains no unfathomable words in need of emendation;[80] unlike *Clothed in Red* (R.71) and *Brotherless* (R.88), it does not suffer from manuscript damage; unlike *Towering Tree* (R.53), its syntax poses no special difficulties. Despite these advantages, *Protector* has previously resisted a confident scholarly consensus, not only because modern audiences lack knowledge of early medieval material culture, but because the text provides few cues to direct the process of interpretation. While *Protector* contains recognizably metaphorical and non-heroic elements, it never fully disqualifies a literal reading of the heroic idiom, and so we cannot tell which parts of the text are metaphorical and which are

---

80 *Protector* does contain three *hapax legomena*, but they are easily understood; see discussion below and Wilcox, "New Solutions," 397.

90 Truth Is Trickiest

not. Ultimately the problem is that the riddle never reveals whether the heroic idiom is a disguise or not.[81] This problem probably afflicted early medieval audiences, too.

We – modern audiences, at least – locate this riddle, like other texts examined in this chapter, within the heroic world because of its references to weapons, a lord, and treasure. The process of locating it there is both initiated and discouraged in the very first half-line: *Ic eom mundbora* "I am a protector."[82] *Protector* is a word applied almost exclusively to people, to the kings and lords who stand at the centre of heroic societies and to the Christian God, saints, and bishops who often appear in the stance of heroic defender in Old English literature.[83] With our cumulative knowledge of the Exeter Book collection, we can note the likelihood that this protecting person is not, in fact, a person but an object or animal, since anthropomorphism is a prominent feature of the riddle genre,[84] and there are, in fact, very few riddles in the Exeter Book whose solutions are generally agreed to refer to people.[85] Even

---

81 Cf. Williamson, *Old English Riddles*, 181.
82 Cf. discussion in Wilcox, "New Solutions," 394.
83 The only exception is *Beowulf*'s dragon, which is described as the *mundbora* of its treasure (2779b). The other sixty-three instances of *mundbora* are all people, not abstractions ("protection") or inanimate objects. See discussion of *mundbora* in Stefan Brink, *Lord and Lady – Bryti and Deigja: Some Historical and Etymological Aspects of Family, Patronage and Slavery in Early Scandinavia and Anglo-Saxon England* (London: Viking Society for Northern Research, University College, London, 2008), 13. The cognate word in Old High German also refers to a person; see D.H. Green, *The Carolingian Lord: Semantic Studies on Four Old High German Words: Balder, Frô, Truhtin, Hêrro* (Cambridge: Cambridge University Press, 1965), 197. Cf. also *eodor* "enclosure," *helm* "cover," and *hleo* "shelter," which in poetry can be used metaphorically to refer to kings who protect their people. Even in poetry, however, these words can be used literally; *eodor* "enclosure," for example, refers to buildings in *Wanderer* 77b and *Beowulf* 1037a.
84 A little more than half of the Exeter Book riddles (fifty of the ninety-five entries listed in ASPR) make use of anthropomorphism, particularly in those texts – including *Protector* – that present the first-person voice of the riddle-subject. For discussion of anthropomorphism as a key element of the *Riddles*, see, for example, Williamson, *Old English Riddles*, 26, and Murphy, *Unriddling*, 29–31.
85 The exceptions are *A Man Sat at Wine* (R.46) and *Twelve Hundred Heads* (R.86), almost unanimously solved as Lot and his Family and One-Eyed Garlic-Seller respectively. Of course, this generalization does not preclude the possibility that other riddles in the collection have been or will be solved as human beings; the Exeter Book collection resists attempts to formulate safe generalizations about it. For example, *Hide My Track* (R.95) has been solved as a "prostitute" (Kevin S. Kiernan, "'Cwene': The Old Profession of Exeter Riddle 95," *MP* 72 (1975): 384–9), and *Bright-Headed* (R.19) and *Joy and Ice* (R.64) are sometimes interpreted as hunters with horses and hawks.

an experienced riddle-solver, however, must wait for further information to determine whether the *mundbora* is a person, animal, or object. The second half-line is not helpful in this regard, as it states that the protectee is a *heord*. Literally this should mean "herd" or "flock," neither of which fit in the heroic context initiated by *mundbora*,[86] but two puns on *heord* are possible, either of which might bring the topic back into the heroic context: we can, for example, read *heord* as wordplay on *hord* "hoard, treasure-trove" or *hired* "household, body of men."[87] Conversely, *heord* could simply be a metaphor for a group of human beings or for the abstract idea of "custody."[88] At the end of the first line, therefore, we cannot tell whether the heroic world is the correct domain in which to find the solution. It is possible that the heroism suggested by *mundbora* is a metaphor or even a false clue, and that the riddle will lead to a veiled discussion of animal husbandry, with *heord* pointing towards the solution. It is equally possible that *heord* is a metaphor or false clue, and that the puns point the way to a solution derived from the heroic world.

Moving on to the next lines provides some help, for the riddle-subject reveals that it is *eodorwirum fæst, innan gefylled / dryhtgestreona* "secure with enclosing wires (and) filled inside with noble treasures" (2–3a). These lines are unique in the riddle, as they describe a physical characteristic – being enclosed with wires and filled with treasure – that can be attributed to the riddle-subject itself as opposed to objects associated with it. This characteristic probably eliminates the answer "shepherd" and any other to do with people or animals from consideration. Yet within these first two and a half lines of the riddle, there are four words that are potential metaphors. We may be reasonably certain that *mundbora* "protector" is a metaphor for some type of object that offers some kind of protection, rather than a person who physically, socially, or spiritually shields other people. We may also entertain reasonable convictions regarding *heord* "herd": strictly speaking this word indicates animals, but even without assuming a pun it could be metaphor for a collection of objects or people. However, while *eodorwirum* "surrounding wires" may eliminate some of the ambiguity of *mundbora*, it is possible that it, too, is a metaphor for a kind of enclosure, rather than actual

---

86 Cf. Stanley, "Heroic Aspects," 204.
87 "*Heord* in the sense of *grex* or *familia* is very common." Tupper, *Riddles of the Exeter Book*, 107, citing C. W. M. Grein, *Sprachschatz der angelsächsischen Dichter*, 2 vols (Cassell: Georg H. Wigand, 1861–4), 2: 68.
88 See *DOE, s.v. heord*.

wires. In any case, *wir* normally indicates ornamental metalwork rather than merely metal drawn out to a thread.[89] Similarly, *dryhtgestreona* "noble treasures" could be glittering swords, helmets, buckles, and jewellery – trappings of the heroic elite like those dug up at Sutton Hoo – but they could also be a metaphor for any kind of valuable object, abstract virtues, or even human beings.[90]

Metaphor is famously important to riddles.[91] Some riddles may be no more than a single metaphor; some contain a series of seemingly incompatible metaphors. Metaphor is so essential that a riddle without one at its centre hardly seems a riddle at all. Metaphor need not be consistently present, however: a riddle may be exclusively metaphorical; it may contain a combination of metaphorical and literal description; or it may weave different metaphors together. As we have already seen, the Exeter Book riddle collection maintains no consistency in this regard, and the collection thus provides no guidelines by which to identify what is metaphorical and what is literal in *Protector*. Yet, as we have seen in *I Burn the Living* (R.6) and *Warrior's Companion* (R.80), other riddles do signal the presence of metaphor with incongruity. *Protector*, in contrast, seems to provide no obvious clues to establish the level of its use of metaphor. This coyness may not be unexpected in the first two and a half lines, but the riddle maintains a similar level of ambiguity throughout.

For example, the next few lines contain at least five potential metaphors:

> Dægtidum oft
> spæte sperebrogan;   sped biþ þy mare
> fylle minre.   Frea þæt bihealdeð,
> hu me of hrife fleogað   hyldepilas.
> Hwilum ic sweartum   swelgan onginne

---

89 See, for example, *Andreas* 302b, *Elene* 1263a, *Weapon-Warrior* (R.14. 3a), *Cursed among Weapons* (R.20. 4a and 32a), *Famous Name* (R26. 14b), *Circle of the Earth* (R.40. 47b), *Abounding in Song* (R.71. 5a), and *Beowulf* 1031a and 2413a. *Ruin* 20a may be an exception, but even here the reference may be to ornamentation rather than attachment. The same may be true of *Elene* 1134a, which refers to the nails of the crucifixion as *wira*, since these nails are precious relics rather than building materials.

90 Cf. *Andreas* 362a: *heahgestreon* "noble treasure" refers to the saint and Christ on board a ship. Cf. also *Phoenix* 255a: *woruldgestreon* "worldly treasure" refers to fruits of the earth, whereas elsewhere it refers quite obviously to money.

91 This is asserted by Aristotle and many others: see, for example, discussions in Tupper, *Riddles of the Exeter Book*, xii–xiv, Williamson, *Old English Riddles*, 26, and Murphy, *Unriddling*, 30–1.

brunum beadowæpnum,   bitrum ordum,
eglum attorsperum. (*Protector* 3b–9a)

(During the day I often spit out spear-terror; because of that the success of my contents is greater. [My] lord observes how battle-darts fly out of my belly. Sometimes I begin to swallow swarthy, dark battle-weapons, sharp points, painful poison-spears.)

As *eodorwirum* probably specifies an inanimate object, we may guess that its *hrife* "belly" is metaphorical. Such a belly can only *spæte* "spit" (4a) metaphorically; it can perhaps "expel" or "pour out," like the *boga* "bow" in *Wob* (R.23).[92] We may also assume that *swelgan* "swallow" (7b) is a metaphorical description of the act of taking in. The *frea* "lord" (5b) who observes this action may also be a metaphor for the "owner" or "user" of an object.[93] Unfortunately, the riddle provides no other indication of the relationships existing between *ic* "I," the subject of the riddle, the *heord* "herd / hoard / household," and the *frea* "lord / owner / user." In the midst of these four likely metaphors are the "spears," which are described in comparatively extensive detail. Many scholars have interpreted them literally; some have interpreted them metaphorically. Some have given up and declared the riddle unsolved.[94]

Ultimately, the only thing that is certain in *Protector* is the presence of the heroic idiom: within only eleven lines, the riddle contains five words for weapons: *sperebrogan* "spear-terror" (4a), *hyldepilas* "war-darts" (6b), *beadowæpnum* "battle-weapons" (8a), *ordum* "points" (8b), and *attorsperum* "poison-spears" (9a). Yet in this case, evident fact is not enough to solve the riddle, for we must decide how to interpret the heroic idiom. That is, we must decide whether the objects described really are spears, some other kind of weapon, things that look like spears,[95] or things that hurt or cause damage.[96] If the spears are taken literally, the act of spitting them out may simply indicate the shooting of an arrow or other projectile. However, the fact that three of these five terms for weapons

---

92 See discussion in chapter 2, above.
93 See discussion of the implement trope in chapter 5, below.
94 See, for example, Williamson, *Old English Riddles*, 181.
95 The fox, badger, hedgehog, porcupine, or weasel in *White Neck* (R.15) bears *beadowæpen* "battle-weapons" (3a) and walks on *ordnum* "points" (5b).
96 In the past one might have thought here of "elf-shot" – viruses and bacteria imagined as invisible spears – but see Alaric Hall's rejection of the "elf-shot conspiracy" in his *Elves in Anglo-Saxon England: Matters of Belief, Health, Gender and Identity*, Anglo-Saxon Studies 8 (Cambridge: Boydell, 2007), 96–118.

(*sperebrogan*, *hyldepilas*, and *attorsperum*) are *hapax legomena* – unique, poetic compounds – may point towards a special, non-literal meaning. In addition, it may be significant that the other imagery in the riddle is generally agreed to be metaphorical. The "body" described in this riddle, with its *muþ* "mouth" (11b), *innan* "inside" (2b), *hrife* "belly" (6a), *innað* "innards" (9b), and *womb* "womb" (10a), seems to refer to an inanimate container with an opening rather than a living creature.[97] Yet the metaphorical nature of one image does not guarantee the metaphorical nature of another; a metaphorical mouth could swallow literal spears.[98]

Deciding whether the "spears" are metaphorical or not is the key to solving the riddle, but closer scrutiny yields still further ambiguity. For example, the relationship between the individual statements in the text is unclear. Is success guaranteed by the *Protector* being full of "treasure" or full of "spears"? Does the "lord" see the darts going in as well as going out? In addition, the attitude held towards the object as a whole is equivocal: the "treasure" that it contains seems positive, but the "spears" that it ejects are terrifying, painful, and poisonous. It is also difficult to know whether the time-scale of actions mentioned is significant or not. *Dægtid* "day-time" (3b) is needed for alliteration, so it may be a line-filler rather than a restriction on time of action, and *hwilum* "at times, on some occasion, sometimes" (7a) could mean that these actions occur regularly or only occasionally.[99] Likewise, it is unclear whether the sequence of events is significant. First "spears" are spat out; then "spears" are swallowed. This is the reverse of the usual chronology of firing a weapon or loading a quiver; normally a container must first "swallow" what it later "spits" out. Finally, the riddle gives no explanation of the relationship between the spears, the treasure, and the *innað* "innards." Dark and bright reside together in the riddle-subject's womb, but there seems to be a strong contrast between the darkness and poison going in (7–9a) and the goodness, excellence, brightness, and value of what is inside: *Is min innað til, / wombhord wlitig, wloncum deore* "My inner womb-hoard is excellent, radiant, and precious to the

---

97 Cf. the mouths in *Large Belly* (R.18), usually interpreted as a *win-crog* "wine-jug," *Shining with Gold* (R.63), usually interpreted as a *glæs-fæt* "glass beaker," and *Beowulf* 724a, where *recedes muþ* "hall's mouth" refers to Heorot's doorway.
98 Indeed, Wilcox interprets the contrast between metaphorical and literal imagery as part of the riddle's artistry; he solves the riddle as *cocer* "quiver" ("New Solutions," 397).
99 DOE, s.v. *hwilum*.

powerful" (9b–10). Although other readers have thought differently, the "spears" and "treasure" seem to be two different things.

This brings us, still baffled, to the end of the riddle, which, instead of demanding an answer, seems to assure us that the subject of the riddle (or, at least, something connected with the subject) is generally known: *men gemunan þæt me þurh muþ fareð* "men remember what comes through my mouth" (11). Yet here again there is a great deal of ambiguity. Mouths speak as well as spit, so it is possible that this sentence means "men remember what I say." If this is true, the object described here is not only personified for the purpose of the riddle but actually has a voice. This voice could still be metaphorical, however, for the riddle could describe an object inscribed with a message; the usual way of describing an inscribed object in riddles is to describe it speaking, usually silently.[100] If what travels through the subject's mouth is not metaphorical, however, it is presumably a reference to the spears spat out earlier. Of course, either weapons or treasure could be described as memorable. We are not told *why* men remember what comes from this mouth – whether it is because this object is dangerous or precious (or both). The final clue, then, resolves nothing.

Perhaps it is not so surprising, then, that previous solutions have not easily won support. These include *ballista* "ballista," a siege engine that hurls projectiles, *cocer* "quiver," *burg* "fortress," *smiððe* "forge," *ofen* "oven," and *blæchorn* "inkwell." The first, *ballista*, is among the most commonly accepted, even though, like the battering ram sometimes seen as the solution to *Towering Tree* (R.53, solved in the last chapter as *þerscel* "flail" among other things) and *Brain-Locker* (R.73, probably *æsc* "ash-spear"), it is by no means clear that early medieval English audiences would have known what such a thing was.[101] Nevertheless, considering *ballista* as a solution is worthwhile, for it reveals one extreme response to the essential question of what is metaphorical and what is not in *Protector*, for to solve it as "ballista" is to reject metaphor: the "spears" are projectile weapons, and what men remember is simply the devastating fire-power that this instrument of war possesses. Yet even in such a literal reading, the "mouth," "womb," and "spitting" are metaphorical, anthropomorphized characteristics of the inanimate weapon; an audience must identify the literal within the metaphorical.

---

100 See, for example, discussion in Marie Nelson, "The Paradox of Silent Speech in the Exeter Book Riddles," *Neophil* 62 (1978): 609–15.
101 See discussion in Williamson, *Old English Riddles*, 180.

The same process of distinction is required if the preferred solution is *burg* "fortress" or *smiðiðe* "forge," and a similar one for *cocer* "quiver," although in this latter case the "spears" are actually arrows.

To solve *Protector* as *ofen* "oven" or as *blæchorn* "inkwell" requires that the "spears" be taken metaphorically, as sparks or pens. Although fewer scholars have been enthusiastic about these solutions, they possess an important advantage over the more popular, military solutions: they make a contrast between the precious, shining treasure and the dark, poisonous weapons. Despite Tupper's assertions, I am not convinced that the darts of a *ballista* inspired "that joyous pride of the Anglo-Saxons in their war-weapons,"[102] and, despite Wilcox's persuasive argument, I can find no indication that early medieval English poets expected arrows to be *wlitig* "radiant, beautiful."[103] Of course, ultimately, all three of us are guessing how early medieval English people felt about weapons, and riddles often disguise objects by describing them in unusual ways: we have already learned that all is fair in the Exeter Book riddle collection. Yet if we solve *Protector* as *ballista*, quiver, bow, fortress, or forge, the weapons are not disguised by unusual presentation; they are presented explicitly as "spears." It is difficult to justify an argument for riddling disguise here, unless, of course, they are disguised by not being disguised. This may actually be the case: perhaps the game is to hide the solution by placing it where we will not look for it, right in front of our noses. Conversely, perhaps they are *not* spears.

There is a previously unremarked incongruity that suggests that these are not ordinary "spears," so let us look carefully at them again.

> Dægtidum oft
> spæte sperebrogan;   sped biþ þy mare
> fylle minre.   Frea þæt bihealdeð,
> hu me of hrife fleogað   hyldepilas.
> Hwilum ic sweartum   swelgan onginne

---

102   Tupper, *Riddles of the Exeter Book*, 106.
103   Wilcox interprets the treasure as the arrows in a quiver but admits that, while weapons are often viewed as treasures, these hoards "rarely explicitly include bows and arrows" ("New Solutions," 406n27). In my search of Old English poetry in the *DOE Electronic Corpus*, *flan* and *stræle* generally appear without visual description, ornamentation, and elaboration, although *stræle* are *biter* "bitter, sharp" three times (*Christ II* 765b, *Beowulf* 1746a, *Paris Psalter* 77.11), *stedeheard* "firm" once (*Judith* 223a), and *strang* "strong" once (*Paris Psalter* 76. 14 line 31a). Interestingly, while arrows are not associated with treasure or light-imagery, spears can be; see discussion, below.

brunum beadowæpnum, bitrum ordum,
eglum attorsperum. (*Protector* 3b–9a)

(During the day I often spit out spear-terror: because of that the success of my contents is greater. [My] lord observes how battle-darts fly out of my belly. Sometimes I begin to swallow swarthy, dark battle-weapons, sharp points, painful poison-spears.)

Unlike most of the other elements of the riddle, these "spears" receive considerable attention. They fill, fly, and bring success, are spat, watched, and swallowed, and are *biter* "sharp" (8b) and *egle* "painful" (9a). Of these characteristics, only the idea of filling a container seems inappropriate to a literal interpretation of spears, unless, of course, the container is a *ballista* or *cocer* "quiver." Yet the spears have yet another attribute: they are *sweart* "dark" (7a). Why would a spear be *sweart*? Searching the *DOE* Electronic Old English Corpus reveals that this is not a usual way of describing spears. Spears (*gar, spere, æsc, franca*) normally appear without modification, but occasionally they can be *scearpe* "sharp," *blodig* "bloody," *giellende* "yelling," *hlude* "loud," *feolhearde* "file-hardened," *gegrundene* "sharpened," *superne* "of a southern make," *wac* "slender," *goldwreken* "clothed in gold," or *golde fah* "marked with gold."[104] They may even *lixan* "flash."[105] Thus far, at least, I have not found any dark ones. This inconspicuous word thus may be an indication that we should not be looking for ordinary spears. Previous critics have not noted this admittedly small incongruity, perhaps in part because they have focused upon *brun*.

Brun (8a) is yet another attribute of the "spears" in *Protector*. Like many terms for colour in Old English, its meaning has been disputed. In this particular case, we must choose whether to interpret *brun* as "brown, dark" or "shiny."[106] "Shiny," "glittering," or "gleaming" suits

---

104 What is notable here is the limited instances of adjectival modification. *Scearpe*: Paris Psalter 54.20 line 66b, Ælfric's *Admonitio ad filium spiritualem* (for text see H.W. Norman, ed., *The Anglo-Saxon Version of the Hexameron of St. Basil, or, Be Godes Six Daga Weorcum and the Saxon Remains of St. Basil's Admonitio ad filium spiritualem*, 2nd ed. (London: J.R. Smith, 1849), chapter 2, p. 36). *Blodig*: Beowulf 2440b, Maldon 154b. *Giellende*: Widsiþ 128a, For a Sudden Stitch 9b. *Hlude*: Genesis A 1982b. *Feolhearde*: Maldon 108b. *Gegrundene*: Maldon 109a. *Superne*: Maldon 134b. *Wac*: Maldon 43b. *Goldwreken*: The Will of Wulfsige (SS 1537; for text see number 27 in *Anglo-Saxon Wills*, ed. and trans. Dorothy Whitelock [Cambridge: Cambridge University Press, 1930], 74). *Golde fah*: Maxims II 22a. *Gafeluc* "spear" only appears in prose, but it, too, appears without modification.
105 Elene 23b, 125b.
106 See *DOE*, s.v. *brun*. Williamson glosses *brun* as "brown, gleaming" (*Old English Riddles*, 414).

the heroic idiom and, as we have seen, spears, and thus scholars and translators have "traditionally" taken the appearance of *brun*, in poetry at least, as referring to the reflectivity of elite swords, knives, and helmets.[107] Carole Biggam, however, demolishes the evidence for shininess in her analysis of *græg*, another colour lexeme that has been interpreted as meaning "shiny," and suggests that shininess has been inappropriately been applied to *brun*, too.[108] Even if we assume that *brun* can mean "shiny" in the context of weaponry, however, we are faced with a circular argument for it here. "Shiny" is only appropriate if we assume that the riddle describes metallic weapons; if the riddle does not describe metallic weapons, *brun* is even less likely to mean "shiny." We do, however, have a reason to break out of this circular argument and diverge from the interpretation of *brunum beadowæpnum* as "gleaming battle-weapons," for, as we have already discussed, these same "spears" are unambiguously described as *sweart* "dark" in the previous line. The "traditional" misunderstanding of *brun* has led us to overlook the significance of *sweart* here. If we abandon the possibility of "shininess,"

---

107 In *Beowulf*, see, for example, the translations and glosses to *brunecg* (1546a), *brun* (2578a), and *brunfagne* (2615a) in *Klaeber's Beowulf*, 4th ed., ed. R.D. Fulk, Robert E. Bjork, and John D. Niles (Toronto: University of Toronto Press, 2008), 358; *Beowulf: A Dual-Language Edition*, ed. and trans. Howell D. Chickering (Garden City, NY: Anchor Press/Doubleday, 1977), 139, 205, and 207; *Beowulf with the Finnsburg Fragment*, ed. C.L. Wrenn and W.F. Bolton, 5th ed. (Exeter: University of Exeter Press, 1996), 226; *Beowulf: An Edition with Relevant Shorter Texts*, ed. Bruce Mitchell and Fred C. Robinson (Oxford: Blackwell, 1998), 249. "Traditionally" is how the *DOE* designates these interpretations; it is not clear whether the implication is that these interpretations are widespread but incorrect. The belief that *brun* and other Old English colour terms indicates "shininess" is based on a small number of often-cited studies, the most influential of which are William E. Mead, "Color in Old English Poetry," *PMLA* 14 (1899): 169–206; L.D. Lerner, "Colour Words in Anglo-Saxon," *MLR* 46 (1951): 247; and Nigel F. Barley, "Old English Colour Classification: Where do Matters Stand?" *ASE* 3 (1974): 24. See, however, further discussion, below.

108 See *Grey in Old English: An Interdisciplinary Semantic Study* (London: Runetree, 1998), 80–4; *Blue in Old English: An Interdisciplinary Semantic Study* (Amsterdam: Rodopi, 1997), 52–63. I have previously rejected the sense of reflectivity in another ambiguous word, *fealu* – in the context of horses at least (see Neville, "Hrothgar's Horses," 145–53). Nevertheless, the idea of "shininess" in these Old English colour-words remains firmly fixed in many scholars' minds, as Biggam notes: "a single mention of shininess in articles on Old English colour [i.e. William Mead's 1899 article] constitutes a highly contagious disease" (*Blue*, 63). Wilcox mentions it, for example ("New Solutions," 396), and, in 2006, audiences to oral versions of my paper on "Hrothgar's Horses" were unwilling to surrender it.

we are more likely to notice that spears are neither *brun* "dark" nor *sweart* "swarthy" in Old English literature. The fact that their darkness is repeated twice suggests that we should think further about "spears" rather than spears, about metaphors rather than literal weapons. This is true even if we were to retain the "traditional" *brun* "gleaming" spears here, for we would still have to explain why they are *sweart* "swarthy."

There is, in fact, a metaphorical interpretation of these dark "spears" which has recently gained favour, although it has taken decades to enter into the conversation among English-speaking scholars. According to this interpretation, the "spears" are bees, and the solution of the riddle is **beo-hyf* "bee-hive."[109] Working through the clues with this solution in mind provides several "inner clicks." For example, the hive is a protector of its *heord* "herd" (1b), which, according to this reading, does refer to a collection of livestock. The literal meaning of "herd" thus turns out to be important, as it is a clue that may turn the audience away from the disguise of the heroic world; even so, the word play on *hired* "household" and *hord* "hoard, treasure" remain meaningful, for a hive does contain both a community (the colony) and a treasure (the honey). With reference to bees the first temporal element in the riddle represents a clue rather than a filler for alliteration as we might have thought, for sting-bearing bees fly from the hive only *dægtidum* "by day," and the sequence of events, with the bees first leaving and then returning to their hive, is logical and natural. The rather vague statement about being more successful or lucky when filled is now meaningful, whether it refers to "spears" (bees) or "treasure" (honey), for the

---

109 This solution was first proposed by Peter Bierbaumer and Elke Wannagat, "Ein neuer Lösungsvorschlag für ein altenglisches Rätsel (Krapp-Dobbie 17)," *Anglia* 99 (1981): 379–82. Ten years later, Wim Tigges claimed to arrive at the same solution independently and proposed **beo-hyf* as the unattested Old English word: "Signs and Solutions: A Semiotic Approach to the Exeter Book Riddles," in *This Noble Craft: Proceedings of the Xth Research Symposium of the Dutch and Belgian University Teachers of Old and Middle English and Historical Linguistics, Utrecht, 19–20 January, 1989*, ed. Erik Kooper (Amsterdam: Rodopi, 1991), 59–82. Another proposed Old English term for the bee-hive is *beo-leap*: see Marijane Osborn, "'Skep' (*Beinenkorb* [sic], *beoleap*) as a Culture-Specific Solution to Exeter Book Riddle 17," *ANQ* 18 (2005): 7–18. **Beo-lester*, of Celtic origin, has also been suggested; see W. Sayers, "Exeter Book Riddle 17 and the L-Rune: British **lester* 'vessel, oat-straw hive'?" *ANQ* 19 (2006): 4–8. It should be noted that these last two solutions attempt to relate to the two runic letters that precede *Protector*. Williamson argues that these runic letters were not contributed by the main scribe (*Old English Riddles*, 182). Their authority is thus doubtful, but see Murphy's argument for *leo ond beo* as a response to them in *Unriddling*, 157–73.

colony can only survive, particularly through the winter, if numbers are plentiful and sufficient honey has been stored. The "lord," as it turns out, is not really part of the implement trope at all; he is the bee-keeper, the owner who watches over it, sees the "spears" flying in and out of the hive's "belly," and has the right to extract "tribute" (honey) from it, just as a lord might do from human beings living on his land.[110] Finally, now that we are thinking about bees, we may recall that Aldhelm made the link between bees and spears in his own riddle on the bee.[111]

This solution also makes good sense out of the other temporal element in the riddle. *Hwilum* "at times" (7a) refers to specific times, and the action from 5b–9a describes an important process in a bee-keeper's (and a bee's) career: swarming.[112] Before the invention of the modern hive, which allows expansion and harvesting without harm to the colony,[113] a bee-keeper who did not wish to destroy his colony had to watch his hive closely, for to harvest its honey he had to wait until the colony grew too large for the structure provided for it and swarmed, that is, flew away in search of a new site. A bee-keeper placed a new, larger hive nearby in hope that it would stay under his control. Thus here we may understand the emphasis on "the lord" *seeing* the darts flying in and out. The bee-keeper watches for the bees to swarm, first to leave the old hive (*me of hrife fleogað hyldepilas* "battle-darts fly out of my belly") and then to enter the new hive (*ic swelgan onginne* "I begin to swallow"). This process may explain the apparently large numbers involved, which might otherwise seem overstated for the steady trickle of normal bee-life.

---

110 Cf. the Old English bee charm, in which the bee-keeper exhorts the bees to *Beo ge swa gemindige mines godes, / swa bið manna gehwilc metes and eþeles* "be as mindful of my property as is every man of food and his homeland" (11–12). James B. Spamer notes that this creates a hierarchical, social relationship between the bee-keeper and the bees; see "The Old English Bee Charm: An Explication," *Journal of Indo-European Studies* 6 (1978): 289.

111 Marijane Osborn, "Anglo-Saxon Tame Bees: Some Evidence for Beekeeping from Riddles and Charms," *NM* 107 (2006): 278. For text see Enigma 20 (*Apis*), in Aldhelm, *Aldhelmi Opera*, ed. Rudolf Ewhald, Monumenta Germaniae Historica, Auctores Antiquissimi 15 (Berlin: Weidmann, 1919), 106.

112 The following information about hives and swarming derives from Spamer, "The Old English Bee Charm, 280–2. Osborn's more recent article on bee-keeping derives much of its information from this same source ("Anglo-Saxon Tame Bees," 278–81).

113 Osborn notes that this invention was patented in 1852 ("Anglo-Saxon Tame Bees," 280).

Even this solution, however, does not answer all my questions. Perhaps the biggest problem lies in the *eodorwirum* "protective wires," for this does not seem an obvious or metaphorical way of describing a structure made of straw and wattled mud.[114] There is no problem, however, with the treasure: it can easily be interpreted as honey, a *dryhtgestreaona* "treasure suitable for nobles" (3a) in the form of mead but also precious as the most potent sweetener available before discovery of the New World. Wilcox rejects the bee-hive solution because it "leaves out" the honey,[115] but, while the riddle does leave out the idea of sweetness, it certainly does not fail to describe the treasure, which is *til* "good, excellent" (9b), *wlitig* "beautiful, radiant" (10a), and *deor* "expensive, valuable" (10b).[116] Finally, the bee-hive solutions allows the last line of the riddle to be read in two, equally satisfying ways: men remember and value the honey itself, and, with a touch of grim humour that seems appropriate for the conclusion of a riddle, men remember a swarm of enraged bees coming out of a hive.

This solution might occur more readily to people in early medieval England, who did not have supermarkets and artificial sweeteners and so were probably more familiar with these processes than modern audiences.[117] Even with this familiarity, however, *Protector* obscures as much by vagueness (camouflage) as by metaphor (disguise), and thus even for early medieval audiences **beo-hyf* might have been a hard-won solution. In fact, familiarity, particularly familiarity with the heroic idiom, could have proven a disadvantage. The language of spears, lords, and treasure probably would have summoned up a world of images for early medieval audiences even more quickly than it does for us now, but this clearly recognizable and easily imagined world obscures rather than reveals.

It is interesting to note that a learned, clerical audience approaching this riddle would probably possess no advantage over a secular one, for *Protector* does not refer to the qualities with which bees were traditionally associated in literary works: industry, wisdom,

---

114 Williamson discusses the problems with this half-line in more detail (*Old English Riddles*, 182–3). Osborn sees no incongruity, however, and suggests that the "wires" are "a vegetative binding material such as de-thorned bramble" ("Anglo-Saxon Tame Bees," 277). Cf. also discussion in Sayers, "Exeter Book Riddle 17," 5.
115 "New Solutions," 396.
116 Sayers notes also that beeswax might be an additional element of the treasure contained within the hive ("Exeter Book Riddle 17," 6).
117 Spamer argues that there was "a fairly sophisticated knowledge of apiculture among the Anglo-Saxons" ("Old English Bee Charm," 280).

chastity, social order, and the sweetness laboriously derived from divine scripture.[118] Yet an audience familiar with such associations might have continued the interpretive process beyond the "elegant" solution *beo-hyf* "bee-hive," as a few scholars have done. For example, drawing upon the meanings associated with bees and honey by patristic writers, Gregory Laing has suggested that *Protector* represents the bee-hive as a figure for the mind, which can hold and spit forth both mellifluous and poisonous words,[119] while Patrick Murphy has argued that the riddle indicates a specific bee-hive, the one described in Samson's mysterious riddle to the Philistines: "Out of the eater came what is eaten, and out of the strong came what is sweet" (Judges 14: 14).[120] In many ways, it would be very satisfying if *Protector* were in fact a difficult riddle about another very famous – and notoriously difficult – riddle.

It cannot be proven that early medieval audiences read *Protector* in any of these ways, but it also cannot be proven that they did not. Individual scholars may feel that allegorical interpretations of the riddles are inappropriate,[121] but, since we do not have a Delilah to bring the process to an end, there is no way to rule out such interpretations.[122] There is no preface at the beginning of the riddle-collection indicating that these texts pertain to objects from the physical world, just as there is

---

118 See the discussion in Augustine Casiday, "St Aldhelm's Bees (*De uirginitate prosa* cc. IV–VI): Some Observations on a Literary Tradition," *ASE* 33 (2004): 1–22.

119 Gregory L. Laing, "Exeter Book Riddle 17: A Possible Solution," paper given at the International Congress on Medieval Studies, 6 May 2006. Marijane Osborn draws attention to another Old English poem that makes explicit reference to this connection ("Anglo-Saxon Tame Bees," 274): Homiletic Fragment 1 describes the duplicitous orator as one who masks malicious thoughts with sweet words *swa ða beon berað buta ætsomne / arlicne anleofan, ond ætterne tægel / hafað on hindan, hunig on muðe* ... "just as bees carry both together – have honourable nourishment, honey in the mouth, and a poisonous tail behind" (*Homiletic Fragment I* 19–21). *Mundbora* substitutes the visual image of shining treasure for the gustatory idea of sweetness, however.

120 Patrick J. Murphy, "*Leo ond beo*: Exeter Book Riddle 17 as Samson's Lion," *ES* 88 (2007): 371–87; Murphy, *Unriddling*, 160–73. The biblical riddle refers to a hive in the carcass of the lion that Samson killed with his bare hands.

121 Peter Kitson, for example, considers "*Physiologus*-type moralizing" to be alien to "Old English riddle-poetry"; see "Swans and Geese in Old English Riddles," *Anglo-Saxon Studies in Archaeology and History* 7 (1994): 82n11. Cf. also Tigges, "Signs and Solutions," 66, and Osborn, "'Skep,'" 13, both of whom argue for the riddles' essential focus on material culture.

122 Samson's audience was given seven days in which to solve the riddle. In fact the one who gave away the authoritative solution was not Delilah but his unnamed first wife; see Judges 14: 15–18.

no instruction to penetrate their literal surfaces to see allegorical truths, and, while most of the riddles do seem to focus on physical objects, at least one, *Guest in the Enclosures* (R.43), is universally accepted by modern scholars as an allegory of the journey of the *gæst ond lic-hama* "soul and body." Every single text, in fact, can be an exception to prove whatever rule we might wish to observe about the collection. The resulting openness to multiple approaches is a characteristic to which I shall return throughout my discussion.

Conclusions

Protector (R.17), whether successfully solved as **beo-hyf* "bee-hive" or not, is important to my discussion in this chapter because of the ambiguity surrounding its representation of heroic culture. While *Turning Wood* (R.56) helpfully dislocates its "battle" of "spears" to an indoor setting, the "spears" of *Protector* look almost real. The same problem arises in *Towering Tree* (R.53): although many modern readers assume that the text deploys the heroic idiom literally to represent a weapon of war and thus solve it as *ramm* "battering ram," it is also possible to interpret its presentation of heroic culture metaphorically and solve it as *þerscel* "flail," *turnus* "pole-lathe," or, indeed, other objects.[123] In pondering such riddles, it is easy to forget that the ones discussed in the previous chapter required an audience to take the heroic idiom literally. Having learned in that chapter that things may be what they seem, in this chapter we learn instead that they may not be, and, as *Protector* demonstrates, it is not easy to tell when they are and when they are not. Of course, the absence of solutions in the manuscript remains the bottom-line guarantee of uncertainty, and even elegant solutions are always open to further challenges: the thing in question remains in question. Even if we do achieve the satisfaction of an "inner click," however, and even if scholars achieve a complete consensus about a solution, the identity of riddle-subjects and riddle-objects remains partly overshadowed by alternatives – by memories and echoes of rejected solutions. In the end we cannot fully resolve the "binary of

---

123 See Neville, "Precarious Insights." Since that publication there has been a new interpretation of the text as a description of a *boc and feðer* "book and quill-pen." See Matthew Aiello, "Books in Battle: The Violent Poetics of Misdirection in Old English Riddle 53," *RES* 71 (2020): 207–28.

identification and counteridentification."[124] False identities become part of new identities, the pole-lathe becomes more than simply a tool for making wooden bowls, and we see it with new, wondering eyes. Indeed, for me *Towering Tree* (R.53) flickers from one identity to another – now ram, now gallows, now flail, now pole-lathe, now cross – rather like the vision of the cross in *The Dream of the Rood*, whose appearance to the dreamers conveys both its reality as a wooden instrument of torture and its reality as an ornamental symbol of the triumph of Jesus Christ over sin and death:

> Geseah ic þæt fuse beacen
> wendan wædum ond bleom;   hwilum hit wæs mid wætan bestemed,
> beswyled mid swates gange,   hwilum mid since gegyrwed.
> *(Dream of the Rood* 21b–3)

(I saw that eager beacon change in its clothes and colours; sometimes it was drenched with water, soaked with the flow of blood, [and] sometimes [it was] adorned with treasure.)

The cross in *The Dream of the Rood* must be both those apparently incompatible things; even as the poem emphatically declares, *Ne wæs ðær huru fracodes gealga* "indeed that was not the gallows of a criminal" (10b), it narrates the cross' story of being the gallows on which criminals were executed. In the same way, as a result of the interpretative process, the (possibly) non-military objects that have been camouflaged and disguised by the familiar language of the heroic idiom become something unfamiliar and strange, a "third term" that does not belong to the heroic idiom and yet cannot be fully extricated from it, even if a riddlee does choose a solution.[125] We have to think about war to think about pole-lathes (and other things). The object comes into focus clouded with values, violence, and danger – if it comes into focus at all. Thus, as we shall see in the next chapter, the work to be done does not end with the identification of objects. The riddles provide a site where not only things but also values are held up for review and questioning.

---

124 José Esteban Muñoz, "'The White to Be Angry': Vaginal Davis's Terrorist Drag," *Social Text* 52–3 (1997): 83.
125 See chapter 1 above for discussion of the "third term" in Muñoz, "'The White to Be Angry,'" 83.

Chapter Four

Dark Tracks through the Heroic Idiom: Aporia, Irony, and Paradox

Introduction

An aporia is an irresolvable inner contradiction. Irony is a state of affairs that seems deliberately contrary to what might be expected. Paradox is an apparently absurd or self-contradictory statement.[1] As the previous chapters have shown, all three of these constitute the bread and butter of the Exeter Book riddles: among other wonders, their readers encounter voiceless speech, posthumous strength, monstrous bodies, and impossible family structures.[2] Solving a riddle could eliminate that absurdity, contrariness, and contradiction, but the Exeter Book riddles should never be considered fully solved. This is not only because the absence of solutions in the manuscript means that no solution can ever be fully certain, but also because, even when we possess elegant, uncontested solutions, some strangeness remains. That strangeness, like the strangeness that initially elicits the drive to solve the riddles, demands that the reader or listener continue to engage with the process of interpretation, even if a satisfactory solution has already been found.

An ongoing process of interpretation allows the possibility of new solutions, but, as we have already observed, finding solutions is not the only kind of interpretation that can be instigated by these texts. Just as reading

---

1 See *Oxford Dictionaries*, en-oxforddictionaries.com, *s.v.* aporia; *OED*, *s.v.* irony, definition 3 and *s.v.* paradox, definition 2a. For a much fuller and more precise exploration of these tropes, see Elise Louviot, *Direct Speech in Beowulf and Other Old English Poems* (Cambridge: Brewer, 2016), 223–50. Louviot raises important questions about the way in which modern scholars identify irony in Old English texts.
2 For voiceless speech, see, for example, *Golden Ring* (R.59); for posthumous strength, see *Greedy for Youth-Mirth* (R.38); for a monstrous body, see *Man Woman Horse* (R.36); for an impossible family, see *A Man Sat at Wine* (R.46).

Weapon-Warrior (R.14) may lead to the assertion that the heroic life is heaven on earth, with all the attendant questions and suspicions that follow on from such an assertion,[3] so other riddles in the collection can give rise to questions that are not answered by solutions. Some of these questions concern heroic culture itself. That is, sometimes the riddles' use of the heroic idiom seems to be ironic. On the surface, making a claim for irony in the heroic idiom requires no justification, for irony, especially expressed through litotes, is a characteristic feature of Old English poetry.[4] At the same time, however, Old English poetry is usually interpreted as taking itself very seriously, and, within it, the heroic idiom generally marks weighty, important matters that are accorded the most value in early medieval English culture. The wry humour that distinguishes the elite warrior and elite poetry does not undercut the values of heroic culture or its elite status. With their focus on the trivial, the riddles may appear to be a special case, but in fact their focus is only apparently trivial. In this chapter I argue that some of the riddles are exceptional for the explicit critical distance they maintain from the trope of the heroic idiom, a distance which may even result in parody.

The exceptional nature of this critical distance needs to be stressed, for it is not a feature of most Old English literature. Although *The Battle of Maldon* lucidly illustrates that the wages of heroism are death, and although critics debate whether Byrhtnoth's *ofermod* is a virtue or a vice,[5] the poem unquestionably celebrates the strength, loyalty, resolve, skill, equipment, and actions of warriors participating in battle. The potentially competing values of Christianity, explicitly present in the form of Byrhtnoth's prayer, do not replace, undermine, or supplement those of the heroic idiom, even though there is evidence to indicate that the values of heroic culture were modified outside of poetic texts. In penitential literature, for example, killing by a lord's command or in a public war occasions penance, not praise, even if that penance is reduced to days rather than years as for murder or vengeance.[6] Even *Beowulf*,

---

3 See chapter 2, above.
4 Roberta Frank, "The Incomparable Wryness of Old English Poetry," in *Inside Old English: Essays in Honour of Bruce Mitchell*, ed. John Walmsley (Oxford: Blackwell, 2006), 59–73.
5 J.R.R. Tolkien, for example, argues that it is a vice; see "The Homecoming of Beorhtnoth Beorhthelm's Son," *Essays and Studies*, n.s., 6 (1953): 1–18. Against this view, see, for example, T.A. Shippey, "Boar and Badger: An Old English Heroic Antithesis?" *LSE*, n.s., 16 (1985): 220–39. The issue continues to be debated; for an overview of past scholarship and yet another argument about it, see John Halbrooks, "Byrhtnoth's Great-Hearted Mirth, or, Praise and Blame in *The Battle of Maldon*," *PQ* 82 (2003): 235–55.
6 See, for example, *The Canons of Theodore*, IV: *De Occisione Hominum*. For text, see *Paenitentiale Umbrense*, ed. Michael D. Elliot, http://individual.utoronto.ca/

which has been interpreted as a criticism of heroic culture,[7] does not advocate values outside of that culture.[8] The most telling evidence of the enduring value ascribed to heroic culture, however, is the fact that the heroic idiom is appropriated in Old English poetry to distinguish Christianity's elite: for example, God in *Genesis A* is represented as both a powerful hero and a generous lord;[9] Christ in *The Dream of the Rood* is represented as a strong warrior;[10] and Abraham in *Genesis A* is represented as performing heroic action.[11] In all these cases, the value ascribed to heroic culture seems unquestioned. Heroic culture itself represents value.[12]

There are, however, a few Old English riddles that may be interpreted as playing with the heroic idiom's grave seriousness and presenting heroic culture ironically. Not everyone has seen these riddles as ironic; the irony that I identify in these texts is subtle and disputable. Most modern readers of *Lone Dweller* (R.5), for example, solve it as *scield* "shield" and see in it a moving elegy for the courageous warrior, a

---

michaelelliot/manuscripts/texts/transcriptions/pthu.pdf, or *Die Canones Theodori Cantuariensis und ihre Überlieferungsformen*, ed. P. Finsterwalder (Weimar: H. Bölhaus, 1929), 294–5. For translation see John T. McNeill and Helena M. Gamer, *Medieval Handbooks of Penance: A Translation of the Principal Libri Poenitentiales and Selections from Related Documents* (New York: Columbia University Press, 1938), 187.

7 See, for example, David Clark, "Relaunching the Hero: The Case of Scyld and Beowulf Re-Opened," *Neophil* 90 (2006): 621–42 and Clark, *Between Medieval Men: Male Friendship and Desire in Early Medieval English Literature* (Oxford: Oxford University Press, 2009), 130–52.

8 See John M. Hill, *The Anglo-Saxon Warrior Ethic: Reconstructing Lordship in Early English Literature* (Gainesville: University Press of Florida, 2000), 15: "I see no alternative presented to heroic institutions in *Beowulf*."

9 See especially *Genesis A* 49–64; for discussion, see, for example, Peter J. Lucas, "Loyalty and Obedience in the Old English *Genesis* and the Interpolation of *Genesis B* into *Genesis A*," *Neophil* 76 (1992): 121–35, who also summarizes previous discussions of this theme. For a more recent discussion, situating this theme in the context of land tenure, see Scott Thompson Smith, "Faith and Forfeiture in the Old English *Genesis A*," *Modern Philology* 111 (2014): 593–615.

10 See especially *Dream of the Rood* 33b–42a; for the classic discussion, see Carol Jean Wolf, "Christ as Hero in *The Dream of the Rood*," *NM* 71 (1970): 202–10.

11 See especially *Genesis A* 2045–2095. For discussion, see, for example, Andy Orchard, "Conspicuous Heroism: Abraham, Prudentius, and the Old English Verse Genesis," in *The Poems of MS Junius 11: Basic Readings*, ed. R.M. Liuzza, Basic Readings in Anglo-Saxon England 8 (New York: Routledge, 2002), 119–36.

12 See Jennifer Neville, "Redeeming Beowulf: The Heroic Idiom as Marker of Quality in Old English Poetry," in *Narration and Hero: Recounting the Deeds of Heroes in Literature and Art of the Early Medieval Period*, ed. Victor Millet and Heike Sahm (Berlin: De Gruyter, 2014), 45–69

serious deployment of the heroic idiom that validates all its usual values.[13] The riddles, however, allow multiple readings, some built upon each other, some in conflict with each other: it is not necessary for every audience to interpret a riddle in the same way.[14] Indeed, it is probably impossible. Yet, while the absence of authoritative solutions means that many different solutions and many different approaches are possible if not inevitable, every attempt to interpret these riddles requires their audiences to scrutinize the heroic idiom contained in them and to determine whether it is to be taken at face value, as camouflage, as disguise, or even as parody. To make such distinctions, an audience needs to be aware of the heroic idiom as a trope. Solving the Exeter Book riddles is consequently a very literary game, one that requires reflection on other riddles but also a second or even a third look at the text at hand. It is that second or third look that allows these texts to be a site where the accepted and the valued can be reviewed and questioned.

To read the Exeter Book riddles early medieval English audiences thus had to observe the strictures and limitations of the heroic idiom and think about the way they thought about things. Such reflection can be risky. Indeed, Irving suggests that the potential for "criticism" in the riddles would be "dangerous" in "serious" literature.[15] Riddles, however, seem to enjoy a licence to play and even to speak the unspeakable because of their apparently trivial nature.[16] The Exeter collection exploits that licence to the full. This is particularly noticeable in the riddles' approach to sex, as we shall see below in chapter 6, but this chapter focuses on the "dark tracks" running through the bright, shining ideals of heroic culture itself: the moments of aporia, irony, paradox, and parody within the heroic idiom.[17]

---

13 See, for example, *Old English Riddles*, ed. F.H. Whitman (Ottawa: Canadian Federation for the Humanities, 1982), 47. Cf., however, Irving, who notes that *Lone Dweller* runs the "risk of challenging the fundamental values of heroic behavior" ("Heroic Experience," 201).

14 Cf. Tiffany Beechy, "Wisdom and the Poetics of Laughter in the Old English Dialogues of Solomon and Saturn," *JEGP* 116 (2017): 145.

15 Irving, "Heroic Experience," 201. See, however, Shippey, who suggests that Old English heroic poetry in general possesses an "emotional maturity" that allows something like the interpretive distance that I find in the riddles ("Boar and Badger," 235).

16 Cf. Eleanor Cook, *Enigmas and Riddles in Literature* (Cambridge: Cambridge University Press, 2006), 127. For a detailed discussion of speaking the unspeakable in a variety of contexts, see Victoria Blud, *The Unspeakable, Gender and Sexuality in Medieval Literature 1000–1400* (Cambridge: Boydell and Brewer, 2017), 1–19.

17 The "dark tracks" (*swearte ... lastas*) appear in *Four Creatures* (R.51), discussed below.

Embodying the Anchor

Fight against Wave (R.16) is a riddle with one, elegant, undisputed solution:

> Oft ic sceal wiþ wæge winnan   ond wiþ winde feohtan,
> somod wið þam sæcce [fremman],   þonne ic secan gewite
> eorþan yþum þeaht;   me biþ se eþel fremde.
> Ic beom strong þæs gewinnes,   gif ic stille weorþe;
> 5 gif me þæs tosæleð,   hi beoð swiþran þonne ic,
> ond mec slitende   sona flymað,
> willað oþfergan   þæt ic friþian sceal.
> Ic him þæt forstonde   gif min steort þolað
> ond mec stiþne wiþ   stanas moton
> 10 fæste gehabban.   Frige hwæt ic hatte. (*Fight against Wave*)

(Often I must struggle against wave and fight against wind – perform battle against them both – when I go to seek the earth covered by waves. That homeland is alien to me. If I become still, I will be strong in that struggle. If that [stillness] eludes me, they will be stronger than I, and by tearing me they will put me to flight. They wish to take away what I should protect. I can withhold that from them if my tail endures, and if stones are allowed to hold me firmly, stiff against them. Find out what I am called.)

The inanimate *ancor* "anchor" here describes its activity using six words, which, although they also have general meanings that are ultimately more appropriate to the situation in question, are commonly used to depict the world of battle: *winnan* "to fight, strive, make war," *feohtan* "to fight, combat, contend, struggle," *sæcce* "strife, conflict," *gewin* "conflict, battle, strife, hostility, war," *flieman* "to put to flight," and *forstandan* "to defend, protect, oppose."[18] Despite the unusual setting beneath the sea and the absence of both a loyalty-inspiring lord and a supporting band of fellow-warriors, the text presents a figure easily recognized within the heroic idiom: the brave warrior who, although outnumbered by implacable foes, resolutely fights to defend *þæt ic friþian sceal* "what I should protect" (7b).

In a real battle, what must be protected could be the lord himself or the *eþel* "homeland," but in this case both lord and homeland seem far away. This distance, of course, is not only physical, for the idea of the stalwart warrior doing battle here is camouflage for the non-human,

---

18 See *DOE* and B-T.

inanimate, unthinking resistance of the *ancor* "anchor" to the force of waves and wind. The text makes no attempt to create a complete disguise out of the heroic idiom; despite the number of words pertaining to battle that it contains, the riddle clearly and precisely locates its battle not in the world of heroic action but under the sea, with resistance offered not by hand, sword, and shield but by the speaker's *steort* "tail."[19] It thus apparently gives its solution away rather easily.

Most modern critics have not felt impelled to consider the text further. With a unanimous consensus on the solution, the acts of textual emendation and noting parallels with Latin analogues generally complete the interpretive process, and there seems to be little expectation that there could be much more to say once the "inner click" has been found.[20] Admittedly, the text asks its audience merely to *frige hwæt ic hatte* "find out what I am called" (10b); it does not explicitly demand its audience to reconsider prevailing views of heroic action or anything else. Since other riddles have inspired interpretation without even the instruction to solve them, however, the absence of explicit direction here need not deter further enquiry.[21] As far as I know, however, only one critic has done so. Jember interprets *Fight against Wave* not only as an *ancor* but also as a figure of the soul.[22] The idea of the soul resisting

---

19 This "tail" probably refers to one of the (usually paired) pointed arms attached to the shank of the anchor, which were designed to grip the sea-floor. For discussion of anchorage, see Seán McGrail, *Ancient Boats in North-West Europe: The Archaeology of Water Transport to AD 1500* (London: Routledge, 1987), 251–7.

20 Williamson is normally very thorough, but in this case he discusses only the question of a Latin source and textual emendations (*Old English Riddles*, 178–9); Tupper's earlier analysis also discusses these points and includes references to the use of anchors in other texts (*Riddles of the Exeter Book*, 104–5). Irving notes the paradox of the anchor's heroic stillness ("Heroic Experience," 202) but makes no further comment about it. Niles notes only that *ancor* is grammatically masculine and thus suited to the warrior-figure created by the riddle; see John D. Niles, *Old English Enigmatic Poems and the Play of the Texts* (Turnhout: Brepols, 2006), 105. Dieter Bitterli mentions the text in passing but offers no extended analysis of it; see *Say What I am Called: The Old English Riddles of the Exeter Book and the Anglo-Latin Riddle Tradition* (Toronto: University of Toronto Press, 2009), 18, 101, 166. Patrick Murphy only notes it as not being connected to the runes found after it in the manuscript; see *Unriddling the Exeter Riddles* (University Park: Pennsylvania State University Press, 2011), 157.

21 Less than fifty per cent of the riddles have such an instruction; see discussion in Susanne Kries, "*Fela í rúnum eða í skáldskap*: Anglo-Saxon and Scandinavian Approaches to Riddles and Poetic Disguises," in *Riddles, Knights and Cross-Dressing Saints: Essays on Medieval English Language and Literature*, ed. Thomas Honegger (Bern: Peter Lang, 2004), 149.

22 Gregory K. Jember, "Literal and Metaphorical: Clues to Reading the Old English Riddles," *Studies in English Literature* [n.v.] (English and Japanese Issues) (1988): 47–56.

the buffeting of the forces in the world, held firm by the rock of the church, has merit; indeed, a very similar metaphor can be found at the conclusion of *Christ II*, where the journey of the soul through life is compared to that of a ship struggling through stormy waters until it comes at last to a place where it can rest *ancrum fæste* "secure in its anchors" (863b). However, such a solution does not immediately make sense out of all the clues in the riddle. For example, Jember does not explain what a soul must defend. Yet the attention that Jember pays to the moral quality of the riddle's action is certainly not redundant; even the usual solution, the physical anchor, can be seen as a symbol of hope and perseverance in the face of adversity.[23] It is therefore useful to follow Jember's lead and ponder the text in the context of the embattled sinner, even if his solution does not inspire total confidence.

Doing so might yield *lic-hama* "life-house, body" as a more apt solution than *gast* "soul,"[24] for it is the body that holds the soul, and the soul is a good candidate for the treasure that demonic forces seek to wrest away.[25] Thus we may interpret the wind as a metaphor for physical desires, demonic forces,[26] or the sinful thoughts warned against in *Juliana*, which explicitly figures such thoughts as stormy winds:

> Forþon ic, leof werod,   læran wille,
> æfremmende,   þæt ge eower hus
> gefæstnige,   þy læs hit ferblædum
> windas toweorpan.   Weal sceal þy trumra
> strong wiþstondan   storma scurum,
> leahtra gehygdum. (*Juliana* 647–52a)

(Therefore, dear company, you who carry out the law, I wish to teach you so that you might make fast your house, lest the winds throw it down with

---

23 Cf. Hebrews 6:19. In her discussion of Symphosius' *Enigma* 61 (*Anchora*), Manuela Bergamin refers to a series of patristic sources that interpret the anchor as a symbol of hope; see *Aenigmata Symposii: La Fondazione dell'Enigmistica come Genere Poetico*, ed. Manuela Bergamin (Florence: Edizioni del Galluzzo per la Fondazione Ezio Franceschini, 2005), 160.

24 Niles argues that the riddle demands a masculine noun as a solution (*Old English Enigmatic Poems*, 105), and so I use *gast* "spirit, life, soul" rather than the feminine noun, *sawol* "soul."

25 Cf. *Dark-Stained* (R.11), which refers to the soul as the *horda deorast* "most precious of hoards" (9b).

26 G.V. Smithers cites Cyprian's *De Mortalitate* as one of many potential sources for the metaphor of the "storms of the world": "The Meaning of *The Seafarer* and *The Wanderer* (cont)," *Medium Ævum* 28 (1959): 2.

sudden blasts. The wall must be the firmer – strong [enough] to withstand the showers of storms, the thoughts of sins.)

Similarly, in *Fight against Wave*'s paradoxically *eþel fremde* "alien homeland" (3b) we may recognize a reference to the earthly life of spiritual exile in a world which is *yþum þeaht* "covered with waves" (3a) – an unenlightened, unspiritual world inhabited by *sundbuend* "sea-dwellers" (*Christ I* 73a).[27] Strictly speaking the plural *stanas* "stones" (9b) here may not be equated with the singular rock upon which Christ built the Church (Matthew 16:18), or the single rock upon which the wise builder laid his foundations (Matthew 7:24–7), but, of course, these biblical rocks are metaphors, too, whose import is relevant to the problem of instability raised in the riddle. Thus these stabilizing entities can be linked with faith or the many virtues that can be gripped as solid rocks in the face of the world's storms. More puzzling is the *steort* (8b); a body does not have an obviously relevant "tail" (in this context, at least), but it may perhaps be interpreted as a good ending or death: a body has not truly triumphed over demonic or worldly forces until it has reached the "tail" or end of its life.[28]

A body, unlike a soul, may fight both literal and allegorical waves, like the Seafarer, whose *heortan geþohtas* "heart's thoughts" impel him to seek out the *sealtyþa gelac* "tumult of the salty waves" (*Seafarer* 34a, 35a) or the Wanderer, who must *hreran mid hondum hrimcealde sæ* "stir with his hands the ice-cold sea" (*Wanderer* 4). Just as the Wanderer and Seafarer's physical experience of hardship on the sea may be interpreted as both real and allegorical,[29] so the sea-imagery in *Fight against Wave* may similarly convey a multiple significance. The *lic-hama* solution also makes sense of the last three lines of the riddle, for the stillness that brings victory for a body may be recognized as the physical posture of prayer.[30] Nevertheless, the

---

27 Cf. the metaphorical use of seafaring in *Exodus* 105b–6a, 133a, 223a, 331b, etc.
28 I am grateful to Patricia Gillies for this suggestion (personal communication, 2006). Cf. *OED*, *s.v.* "tail," definition 4b: "the terminal or concluding part of … a period of time." The earliest occurrence of this use of the word comes from *Piers Plowman* (1377). Unfortunately there is no record of *steort* being used in this way in Old English; the *Mapping Metaphor* project lists only "promontory/headland/cape" as a metaphorical meaning of *steort* (http://mappingmetaphor.arts.gla.ac.uk).
29 Juan Camilo Conde Silvestre, "The Semiotics of Allegory in Early Medieval Hermeneutics and the Interpretation of *The Seafarer*," *Atlantis* 16 (1994): 88.
30 Cf. the later morality play, *Mankind*, in which the "everyman" figure tries to pray but is distracted by the devil calling his attention to his physical needs (552–60). For text see *Everyman and Mankind*, ed. Douglas Bruster and Eric Rasmussen (London: Methuen, 2009).

portrayal of the body as a heroic champion protecting the soul is not easily reconciled with the usual Christian approach to the body, for Christianity traditionally views the body with suspicion if not loathing,[31] as an enemy, not a defender. This incongruity may simply invalidate *lic-hama* as a solution, but, as we shall see, in the Exeter Book riddles persisting strangeness is not unique to *Fight against Wave*, or even to the representation of the relationship between the soul and body; *Guest in the Enclosures* (R.43), for example, may also present a rather unorthodox view of the relationship.[32] As has been noted many times before, the Exeter Book riddles do not simply portray things; they require their audiences to look differently at things. *Fight against Wave* may thus challenge its audiences to look differently at the relationship between soul and body.

An Aporia in Action

Yet the same kind of reasoning may also lead to a different solution, one that refers not to the general, abstract idea of the body but rather to a particular type of body. The one who *sceal wiþ wæge winnan* "must struggle against a wave" may be an *ancor* "anchorite," a religious recluse.[33] All options remain, of course, open, but the word-play is attractive: a pun on "anchor" and "anchorite" may be the best solution. Even so, the story of the *lic-hama* "body" remains relevant; indeed, in many respects the story of the anchorite is exactly the same as that of the *lic-hama*. Surrounded by the *eþel fremde* "alien homeland" (3b) of the secular world, the anchorite can only withstand the waves and winds of sinful thought and demonic temptation if he or she achieves the stillness of prayer. In this telling of the story, the plural *stanas* (9b) lead to a more specific meaning: the *stanas* "stones" may constitute the stone walls of a recluse's

---

31 This negative view is succinctly expressed, for example, in *The Vision of the Monk of Wenlock*, where the monk returning to his body after his vision of heaven and hell regards his body with disgust. For text see "An Old English Translation of a Letter from Wynfrith to Eadburga (A.D. 716–17) in Cotton MS Otho C," ed. Kenneth Sisam, in his *Studies in the History of Old English Literature* (Oxford: Clarendon, 1953), 199–224 (§16). Cf. also the angry diatribe aimed at the body in *Soul and Body II* 17–96.

32 See discussion in Jennifer Neville, "Pondering the Soul's Journey in Exeter Book Riddle 43," in *The World of Travellers: Exploration and Imagination*, ed. Kees Dekker, Karin E. Olsen, and Tette Hofstra, Germania Latina 7 (Leuven: Peeters, 2009), 147–62.

33 For discussion of anchorites, see Tom Licence, *Hermits and Recluses in English Society 950–1200* (Oxford: Oxford University Press, 2011). Guthlac is an early medieval English example; for a recent discussion of him, see Lisa M.C. Weston, "Guthlac Betwixt and Between: Literacy, Cross-Temporal Affiliation, and an Anglo-Saxon Anchorite," *Journal of Medieval Religious Cultures* 42 (2016): 1–27.

cell, which provide a safe haven in a stormy world.[34] That is, the *stanas* may be a synecdoche rather than a metaphor. Like the *lic-hama*, the anchorite needs the *stanas* to stabilize him- or herself until the "tail-end" of life, so that *þæt ... friþian sceal* "what he or she must protect" (7b) is not taken away. In this case, what must be protected might still be the soul, but it could also be rewards stored up in heaven.[35]

It is worth noting that the anchor – and, indeed, the body – do not disappear with these additional readings; the physical object gains significance, just as the sailor, sea, and sea-birds do in *The Seafarer*. Thus the important issue for my reading of this text is not which solution is correct, since *ancor* "anchor," *lic-hama* "body," and *ancor* "anchorite" all participate in the same complex of ideas. What is important is the continuation of pondering itself. Solving this riddle, whether as *ancor* "anchor," *lic-hama* "body," or *ancor* "anchorite," creates series of metaphors, or mini-riddles, each of which can lead to its own "inner click," but only if the audience takes the time to tease out the text's significance.[36]

Such interpretations for the elements of *Fight against Wave* are neither exotic nor anachronistic. Yet should we initiate this process? The attempt to continue the interpretive process is worthwhile, even if it does not prove "successful" in the sense of yielding superior or even equally satisfactory solutions. It is not necessary to re(-)solve *Fight against Wave* as *lic-hama* "body" or *ancor* "anchorite" to observe the potential for a spiritual interpretation of holding fast to "rocks" (values, virtues, spiritual laws) in the midst of "storms" (upheavals, troubles, temptations), but to see these additional meanings it is necessary to continue the interpretive process beyond the "inner click" that occurs upon discovering the *ancor* "anchor." If we do continue this process, however, we

---

34 Although anchoritic spirituality became more prevalent in the twelfth century, it was not a new phenomenon. See Tom License, "Evidence of Recluses in Eleventh-Century England," *ASE* 36 (2007): 221–34. Ælfric, for example, complains about a recluse maintained by a nobleman named Sigefyrth (License, 225). Licence presents evidence for eight recluses in eleventh century England.

35 Cf Luke 12:33: *facite vobis sacculos qui non veterescunt thesaurum non deficientem in caelis quo fur non adpropiat neque tinea corrumpit* (Vulgate) "provide purses for yourselves that will not wear out, a treasure in heaven that will not be exhausted, where no thief comes near and no moth destroys" (NIV).

36 Other paths of interpretation are possible, too. I have focused on waves, wind, and stones, but the architectural elements in *Juliana* might lead to different ways of approaching the idea of the body in *Wiþ Wæge Winnan*, too. For discussion of the soul as fortress, for example, see James F. Doubleday, "The Allegory of the Soul as Fortress in Old English Poetry," *Anglia* 88 (1970): 503–8; cf. also the wider exploration in Michael J. Bintley, *Settlements and Strongholds: Texts and Landscapes in Early Medieval England* (Turnhout: Brepols, 2020), 157–86.

can find more than the traditional symbolism of the anchor as hope. We can find in *Fight against Wave* something strange to ponder, for, whether we interpret the heroic idiom in it as a system of metaphors for nautical or spiritual reality, it jars against the expectations created by the heroic idiom itself, for stasis is not a usual way of depicting heroic action.

The emphasis on inaction should not be overlooked as something inevitable to the subject matter, for it is absent from Symphosius' Riddle 61 (*Anchora* "anchor"), sometimes seen as a source for *Fight against Wave*:[37]

> Mucro mihi geminus ferro coniungitur uno.
> Cum vento luctor, cum gurgite pugno profundo.
> Scrutor aquas medias, ipsas quoque mordeo terras.[38]

(My twinned [end] is joined into one iron point. I wrestle with the wind. I fight with the deep sea. I scrutinise the intervening waters. I also bite the lands themselves.)

Although Symphosius' anchor undoubtedly performs the same immobilizing function found in *Fight against Wave*, it does so with a series of verbs (*luctor* "wrestle," *pugno* "fight," *scrutor* "view," *mordeo* "bite") that give no sign that the aim of this struggle is stillness. In fact, Symphosius' *anchora* disguises its stillness as military action.[39]

In contrast, what we find in *Fight against Wave* is not simply, as in the opening of *Andreas*,[40] the appropriation of the heroic idiom to reinterpret Christian virtue as military *action*, but a valuation of *inaction* itself. The cross in *The Dream of the Rood*, whose lord's command forces it *not* to act, constitutes a similarly striking figure: its heroism comes from *not* performing the expected heroism. In fact, in this riddle the heroic idiom does not so much conceal the subject as become transformed by it, so that the familiar heroic idiom, like the *epel* "homeland," becomes *fremde* "strange, alien."[41] As a result, instead of the commonplace process of

---

37   See, for example, Tupper, *Riddles of the Exeter Book*, 104–5. Williamson compares the two poems but finds little specific in common between them (*Old English Riddles*, 178).
38   Text is taken from *Symphosius, The Aenigmata: An Introduction, Text and Commentary*, ed. T.J. Leary (London: Bloomsbury, 2014), 47. I have silently added capitals to the opening of sentences.
39   Cf. discussion in Bergamin, *Aenigmata Symposii*, 159–60, and Leary, *Symphosius, The Aenigmata*, 173–4.
40   See discussion in chapter 3, above.
41   Cf. the idea of "defamiliarisation" in Victor Shklovsky, "Art as Technique," in *Russian Formalist Criticism: Four Essays*, trans. and introduction by Lee T. Lemon and Marion J. Reis (Lincoln: University of Nebraska Press, 1965), 12–13.

spiritual resistance being redefined as action, here heroic action, usually characterized by forward motion,[42] is redefined as passive stasis without, it should be noted, any explicit reference to the spiritual realm. Although this strange, alien form of heroism does not undercut normal heroic action, it does mark a space for heroism outside of the usual heroic scenario.

Such heroism is an almost unimaginable paradox, an aporia, for there is no language (other than in dreams) to describe it adequately, especially in Old English poetry whose poetic resources derive in great part from the vocabulary of military action. *Fight against Wave* thus necessarily uses the language of action but predicates success upon the cessation of action: *ic beom strong þæs gewinnes, gif ic stille weorþe* "I am strong in that struggle, if I become still" (4). Strength, even in an allegorical battle against vices or devils, can normally be measured only through action; even a defensive victory requires movement. For this warrior, however, success requires perfect stillness, perhaps of the kind advocated in Psalm 46:10: *Vacate, et videte quoniam ego sum Deus* "Be still and know that I am God."[43] The comparison is instructive, for, like *Fight against Wave*, Psalm 46 describes a world of movement and chaos – war, earthquakes, and floods threaten on all sides – in opposition to which stands the inscrutable, negative power of God, which stops wars and destroys weapons, and which can be known only in stillness.[44] Yet *Fight against Wave* does not mention God in opposition to the world of struggle and movement. The text does not instruct its audience to connect its imagery with any Christian doctrine. The paradoxical heroism described by this text thus disturbs the heroic idiom in which it is expressed; as in *Weapon-Warrior* (R.14), pondering *Fight against Wave* beyond its solution reveals an absence that demands further exploration, a gap that must be bridged, a blind spot in the heroic idiom. That aporia raises productive questions. Who, for example, gives permission for the *stanas* "stones, rocks" to hold against the anchor?[45] If early medieval

---

42 See, for example, *Battle of Maldon* 246b–7: *ic heonon nelle / fleon fotes trym, ac wille furðor gan* "I will not flee a foot's pace from here; instead I will advance further."

43 Psalm 45:11 (Vulgate), Psalm 46:10 (NIV). See also the Old English prose version in the *Paris Psalter*: *Geæmetgiað eow nu, and gesioð þæt ic eom ana God* "Be still now and see that I alone am God." For text see *Old English Psalms*, ed. and trans. Patrick P. O'Neill, Dumbarton Oaks Medieval Library 42 (Cambridge, MA: Harvard University Press, 2016).

44 For analyses of the often-neglected topic of stasis, see the studies in *Stasis in the Medieval West?: Questioning Change and Continuity*, ed. Michael J. Bintley, Martin Locker, Victoria Symons, and Mary Wellesley (New York: Palgrave Macmillan, 2017).

45 To ask this question we must translate *moton* as "are allowed." It is possible to translate the verb as "be obliged," but this meaning seems less likely here (cf. B-T, s.v. motan). See also discussion of its use in *Towering Tree* (R.53) in chapter 3, above.

English audiences noticed that gap, they need not have searched far to find material to fill it – the psalms were the best known texts among both clerical and lay audiences[46] – but to do so they must have pondered the text longer than most modern audiences have, long enough to find the place where the heroic idiom fails to contain this strange, alternative heroism. Modern readers' puzzlement over the placement of such apparently trivial texts in the product of a learned scriptorium may derive from our too rapid reading habits.

Dark Looks at the Sword: *Cursed among Weapons* **(R.20)**

Fight against Wave is not the only riddle whose use of the heroic idiom as a disguise can lead us to contemplate ideas that cannot readily be articulated within the heroic idiom, which, as we have seen, constitutes the core of Old English poetry. In fact, in *Cursed among Weapons* (R.20), a long but incomplete text usually solved as *sweord* "sword,"[47] the depiction of heroic culture has often been viewed as ambivalent.[48] We have already looked at *Cursed among Weapons* in chapter 2, where its first eight lines serve as an example of the heroic idiom (more or

---

46 Helen Appleton and Francis Leneghan, "The Psalms in Anglo-Saxon and Anglo-Norman England," *ES* 98 (2017): 1–4.
47 There has been some debate over the solution, but most relate to swords in some way. For example, Lawrence K. Shook argues that the solution is *heoruswealwe* "sword-sparrow," a kenning for a hawk; see "Old English Riddle No. 29: *Heoruswealwe*," in *Franciplegius: Medieval and Linguistic Studies in Honor of Francis Peabody Magoun Jr.*, ed. Jess B. Bessinger Jr and Robert P. Creed (New York: New York University Press, 1965), 194–204. Marie Nelson extends this reading and interprets the *heoruswealwe* as a metaphor for the monk; see "Old English Riddle 18 (20): A Description of Ambivalence," *Neophil* 66 (1982): 292. Other critics argue over whether the riddle refers to a sword described as a phallus (Williamson, *Old English Riddles*, 195), or to a phallus described as a sword (Donald Kay, "Riddle 20: A Revaluation," *Tennessee Studies in Literature* 13 [1968]: 133–9), or to a warrior described as a sword-phallus (John Tanke, "The Bachelor-Warrior of Exeter Book Riddle 20," *PQ* 79 [2000]: 409–27). More recently scholars have opted for *wæpen*, which can mean both "sword" and "penis"; see Ruth Wehlau, *"The Riddle of Creation": Metaphor Structures in Old English Poetry* (New York: Peter Lang, 1997), 112–13; Niles, *Old English Enigmatic Texts*, 137–9; Murphy, *Unriddling*, 208–9. Another alternative is *secg*, meaning both "sword" and "man"; see *The Old English and Anglo-Latin Riddle Tradition*, ed. and trans. Andy Orchard, Dumbarton Oaks Medieval Library 69 (Washington, D.C.: Harvard University Press, 2021), 752.
48 See, for example, Nelson, "Old English Riddle 18 (20)"; Irving, "Heroic Experience," 205–6; Tanke, "Bachelor-Warrior"; Melanie Heyworth, "Perceptions of Marriage in Exeter Book Riddles 20 and 61," *SN* 79 (2007): 171–84.

less) straightforwardly describing the material culture of heroic society. Even within these eight lines, however, starting at line 3, we can observe a less straightforward, metaphorical description of an object disguised as a human warrior who loyally serves his lord.[49] Initially, at least, the metaphor is as positive as the literal object, but half-way through the surviving text the positive values accruing to treasure and heroic action are abruptly juxtaposed with some of the negative features of heroic culture so markedly absent from *Weapon-Warrior* (R.14):

> Byrne is min bleofag, swylce beorht seomað
> wir ymb þone wælgim þe me waldend geaf,
> 5 se me widgalum wisað hwilum
> sylfum to sace. Þonne ic sinc wege
> þurh hlutterne dæg, hondweorc smiþa,
> gold ofer geardas. Oft ic gæstberend
> cwelle compwæpnum. Cyning mec gyrweð
> 10 since ond seolfre ond mec on sele weorþað;
> ne wyrneð wordlofes, wisan mæneð
> mine for mengo, þær hy meodu drincað,
> healdeð mec on heaþore, hwilum læteð eft
> radwerigne on gerum sceacan,
> 15 orlegfromne. Oft ic oþrum scod
> frecne æt his freonde; fah eom ic wide. … (*Cursed among Weapons* 3–16)

(My mail-coat is marked with colour, and bright interlace hangs around the slaughter-jewel that the ruler gave to me – the one who sometimes guides me, a wandering one, to battle. Then I carry gold, treasure, smiths' craftsmanship out of the enclosures during the bright day. I often kill life-bearers with battle-weapons. The king adorns me with treasure and silver and honours me in the hall. He does not hold back words of praise; he praises my ways before the multitude, where they drink mead. He [sometimes] holds me in confinement, sometimes again allows me, weary of riding, to hasten unfettered, bold in battle. I often fiercely harm another near his friend. I am gleaming everywhere.)

Although modern readers may not embrace the violence described here, our responses probably do not match those of *Cursed among Weapons*'s original audience. I have thus tried to translate the text according to

---

49 This is an example of the implement trope, in which the relationship between object and user is described as that between lord and thegn or lord and servant; see further discussion in chapter 5, below.

the positive value that the heroic idiom normally marks in Old English poetry rather than according to my own view of violence. Within the heroic idiom, killing *gæstberend* "life-bearers" (8b) and harming *frecne* "fiercely" (16a) are virtues congruent with the treasures and praise received from the king. Such activity is *fag* "marked" (from *bleo-fag* in 3a) as glory; colours, treasure, and praise are signs of the warrior's success. Even killing a man *æt his freonde* "near his friend" (16a) may contribute glory to the warrior who, perhaps, takes credit for overcoming two opponents at once. As we shall see, this is not the only way of interpreting this line, but, if we subscribe to the values of the heroic idiom, we may read the second occurrence of *fah* near the end of this passage (16b) as I have translated it above, simply as a restatement of the warrior-sword's reputation for heroic action: the sword is not only "gleaming" but "marked" by its excellence.[50]

As we strain our "ears" to hear what early medieval English audiences might have said about the *sweord* in *Cursed among Weapons*, it is worth thinking again about the heroic idiom not only as a trope but as a discourse. As a discourse, the heroic idiom constrains what can and cannot be said. Above all it ascribes value to certain actors, items, and actions as opposed to others.[51] Thus in Old English poetry value is expressed through the heroic idiom. Indeed, it is difficult to think of positive qualities in Old English poetry described without reference to treasure, strength in battle, courage, generosity, loyalty, and nobility; these are all key elements of heroic culture, although not, of course, restricted to it. This is not to say that the people in early medieval England did not value anything outside of heroic culture, only that, within poetry, at least, value tends to be marked by the presence of the heroic idiom. In this context, there seems little room for questions about the sword; an early medieval English audience responding to *Cursed among Weapons* surely would view it in terms of positive value. As Shippey notes in a different context, "The idea of an Anglo-Saxon poet somehow detached from his own tradition and commenting on its failings is an unlikely anachronism."[52] Theorists of discourse agree: discourse constrains what can be thought, and it is only our position outside the

---

50 See *DOE* s.v. *fah*, definition 2: "particoloured, variegated; discoloured, stained, marked; bright, shining, gleaming, adorned." Cf. also the brief discussion in C.P. Biggam, *Grey in Old English: An Interdisciplinary Semantic Study*, Costerus n.s. 110 (London: Runetree, 1998), 287.
51 Cf. Michel Foucault, *The Archaeology of Knowledge and the Discourse on Language*, trans. A. M. Sheridan Smith (New York: Pantheon, 1972), 216.
52 Shippey, "Boar and Badger," 233.

discourses dominant in early medieval England that allows us to question the sword's value.[53]

Yet, while we can interpret *fah* in positive terms, it is not so easy to validate the next half line, for the sword is not only *fah* but *awyrged*:

> fah eom ic wide,
> wæpnum awyrged. (*Cursed among Weapons* 16b–17a)

(I am *fah* [gleaming? marked for excellence?] everywhere, cursed among weapons.)

With the appearance of *awyrged* in the riddle, any modern unease with the slaughter, killing, and hostility seems less unfounded, less anachronistic, and here, too, as in *Weapon-Warrior* (R.14), there are some notable absences. There is, in fact, no mention of glory, victory, former insults to be avenged, or, indeed, any enemies at all; even the target of violence harmed by the sword is *æt his freonde* "near his friend" (16a) not his enemy. An audience that lives within or even merely knows the heroic idiom can, of course, easily supply these missing elements, but the gap between approbation and damnation for the sword remains. As far as I can tell, the *sweord* has not done anything wrong according to the traditions of the heroic idiom – quite the contrary. Nevertheless it is *awyrged* "cursed." This one word may change everything. For example, instead of *æt his freond* (16a) indicating a heroic battle against difficult odds (as suggested above), it may be interpreted as a betrayal of friendship.[54] In the same way, *fah* can be retranslated, retrospectively, as "hostile."[55] The

---

53 "The effect of discursive practices is to make it virtually impossible to think outside of them; to be outside of them is, by definition, to be mad." Derek Hook, "Discourse, Knowledge, Materiality, History: Foucault and Discourse Analysis," *Theory and Psychology* 11 (2001): 522.

54 Re-reading this line after reaching the end of the riddle, with its reference to other types of relationships, may raise the possibility of reading *freond* as "lover," too, as in *Wife's Lament* 33b. I am grateful to Megan Cavell for this suggestion (personal communication, April 2019).

55 See *DOE* s.v. *fah*, definition 1: "hostile, in a state of enmity." The *DOE* notes that "in some instances a deliberate ambiguity [i.e., between the senses of shining/marked and hostile] may have been intended." See also further discussion of *fah*, definition 1, below, and Filip Missuno, "Glowing Paradoxes and Glimmers of Doom: A Re-evaluation of the Meaning of Old English *fāh* in Poetic Contexts," *Neophil* 99 (2015): 125–42. Most translators interpret *fah* negatively; see, for example, William S. Mackie, ed. and transl., *The Exeter Book, Part II: Poems IX–XXXII*, EETS, os 194 (London: Humphrey Milford and Oxford University Press, 1934), 111 ("hated"); Kevin Crossley-Holland, trans., *The Exeter Riddle Book* (London: Folio Society, 1978), 39 ("reviled"); John Porter, trans., *Anglo-Saxon Riddles* (Hockwold-cum-Wilton: Anglo-Saxon Books, 1995), 37 ("hated").

abrupt change from positive to negative at line 17a has provoked a sense of unease among modern readers, a feeling that some kind of explanation is necessary. Thus Holthausen suggests that a line is missing after *wide* (16b),[56] and Trautmann suggests emending the text.[57] Most critics stop short of changing the text and instead imagine an explanatory scenario: Irving elliptically notes that "something sinister is suggested" by the line;[58] Nelson explores the potential difficulties of having a hawk indoors;[59] and Tupper and Williamson mention the "table catastrophe" that can occur when drinking while armed and refer to the laws banning the drawing of swords in the mead-hall.[60]

If we take *Cursed among Weapons* at its word, it seems reasonable to read *fah* as "hostile" in the context of being *awyrged* "damned" in the immediately following half-line, rather than "gleaming" as I translated it above. Yet how far back should this retrospective adjustment go? Should *all* the preceding lines be re-evaluated? Should the killing of *gæstberend* "life-bearers" (8b) be considered a sin? Should the possession of treasure, eagerness for battle, and the praise of the king be rejected? An audience appreciative of glittering gold and brave action may view violence and death not only as a price that must sometimes be paid for what is ultimately worthwhile but also as goods in themselves.[61] An audience for whom treasure and glory in battle are vanity may not. Both kinds of audience, however, must deal with the gap between the apparent ascription of value at the beginning of the riddle with the apparent denial of value that is marked by *awyrged* "damned" (17a).[62]

Cursed among Weapons does not explain the relationship between what appear to be positive heroic values and the condemnation that follows them. This reticence leaves audiences of the riddle wavering between (at least) two powerful discourses that would circumscribe the significance of the sword itself and tell us how to interpret this text. The heroic idiom

---

56 Ferdinand Holthausen, "Zu altenglischen Denkmälern," *Englische Studien* 51 (1917): 185.
57 He suggests an emendment to *wordum awyrged* "cursed by words" or *wæpnum awyrded* "injured by weapons." For the former, see Moritz Trautmann, ed., *Die altenglischen Rätsel* (Heidelberg: Carl Winter, 1915), 82. For the latter, see Trautmann, "Zu meiner Ausgabe der altenglischen Rätsel," *Anglia* 42 (1918): 130.
58 "Heroic Experience," 211n14.
59 "Old English Riddle 18 (20)," 299n13.
60 Tupper, *Riddles of the Exeter Book*, 113; Williamson, *Old English Riddles*, 196. Tupper also connects this view of the sword with Psalm 144:10.
61 See, for example, Hill, *Anglo-Saxon Warrior Ethic* and Peter S. Baker, *Honour, Exchange, and Violence in Beowulf* (Cambridge: Boydell and Brewer, 2013).
62 This "contradictory ethical space" is explored in a different way by Tanke, "Bachelor-Warrior," 420.

would ascribe a high, positive value to the sword and its activities, while Christian spirituality would ascribe them no value at all or, at least, no value in and of themselves. Although the Christian Church certainly did value military action for its own purposes, it never considered violence itself a virtue but rather a sin to be expiated by penance.[63] Modern audiences may or may not subscribe to either heroic culture or Christianity, but early medieval English audiences probably subscribed to both, especially since the heroic idiom supplied the language for spiritual struggle. Yet *Cursed among Weapons* seems to ascribe a negative value to the trope used to convey value without appealing to Christianity, the other main arbiter of value that Old English literature had at its disposal, which might have supplied a less positive view of violence. Like the paradoxical valuation of stasis in *Fight against Wave*, this rejection of heroic values seems remarkable. In *Cursed among Weapons*, it is not that flawed human beings have failed to live up to heroic values, for the sword speaking as a human thegn claims to have served loyally and received ample rewards; nor is it that these values are limited in comparison with Christianity's values, for these latter values are not present for comparison. It may be going too far to assert that "the audience was expected to be seduced by, and then reject, heroic codes of conduct,"[64] but at the end of line 17a we have reached another aporia: if weapons, treasure, and *wordlof* "praise" (11a) do not mark value, what do they mean? Being a riddle, of course, *Cursed among Weapons* never explicitly says what it means. The question may be important, perhaps more important than the solution. Before that question can be fully explored, however, the game changes.

Up unto line 17b, *Cursed among Weapons* is a thoroughly masculine text, concerned only with male activities and roles. The next ten lines remain focused on masculine concerns, but they also hint at a world beyond the values of the heroic idiom:

>   Ic me wenan ne þearf
> þæt me bearn wræce   on bonan feore,
> gif me gromra hwylc   guþe genægeð;
> 20 ne weorþeð sio mægburg   gemicledu
>   eaforan minum   þe ic æfter woc,

---

63   The contradiction in this position did not go unnoticed; Frantzen notes that, in Francia, at least, nobles rebelled when the church imposed penance for violence undertaken during "just wars." See Allen Frantzen, *The Literature of Penance in Anglo-Saxon England* (New Brunswick, NJ: Rutgers University Press, 1983), 112.

64   Elinor Teele, "The Heroic Tradition in the Old English Riddles" (PhD diss., University of Cambridge, 2004), 65.

> nymþe ic hlafordleas hweorfan mote
> from þam healdende þe me hringas geaf.
> Me bið forð witod, gif ic frean hyre,
> 25 guþe fremme, swa ic gien dyde
> minum þeodne on þonc, þæt ic þolian sceal
> bearngestreona. (*Cursed among Weapons* 17b-27a)

> (I need not hope for a son to avenge me on the life of my killer, if some enemy attacks me with war. The family will not be increased with my descendants, those whom I engendered after me, unless I, lordless, am permitted to turn away from the ruler who gave me rings. Henceforth, if I obey my lord [and] perform battle as I hitherto did in gratitude to my lord, it will be ordained that I must do without the begetting of children.)

Nothing has changed: the all-male community continues with its usual activities, including battles, vengeance, gift-giving, and loyal service. Yet everything has changed. Even though there is no woman here, the male-only activities that fill the first half of the text are now redefined by the absence of children. The ability to engage in battle – previously a glorious opportunity to earn treasure and the lord's praise in the meadhall – now seems undercut by the absence of a son to avenge death in war: while the riddle-subject seems to have craved only individual glory up to this point, now it reflects on the descendants that it cannot have without giving up its relationship with its lord. The importance of this situation is emphasized by being presented twice in an almost chiastic pattern: I will have no offspring unless I leave my lord (20–3); if I stay with my lord, I will have no offspring (24–7a).[65] At the very least, the value of what has previously seemed to be the highest and best state of earthly life has been defined as incomplete. At worst, the heroic lifestyle is emptied of value. In this context, it almost does not matter whether we read this text through the discourse of heroism or Christianity. What matters is that participation in those activities denies the riddle-subject children.

And then, at last, in line 27b a woman enters the text:

> Ic wiþ bryde ne mot
> hæmed habban, ac me þæs hyhtplegan
> geno wyrneð, se mec geara on
> bende legde; forþon ic brucan sceal
> on hagostealde hæleþa gestreona. (*Cursed among Weapons* 27b–31)

---

[65] Young men might leave a lord's service in order to marry; see Guy Halsall, *Warfare and Society in the Barbarian West 450–900* (London: Routledge, 2003), 49–50.

(I am not permitted to have sex with a woman; rather, the one who years ago placed me in bonds refuses me that joyful play. Therefore I must enjoy the treasures of warriors in celibacy.)

This *bryd* "woman" may simply be the biological complement needed to create children that the speaker must "do without," especially since she appears immediately after the *bearngestreona* "begetting of children" (27a) in the previous half-line. These four and a half lines do not simply reiterate the desire for children, however, for they introduce yet another absence: the act of intercourse itself, a pleasurable activity that is replaced by the enjoyment of treasure. Like participation in battle, the enjoyment of treasure in the first half of the text seems complete in itself; the riddle-subject wears gems, gold, and silver that, like the lord's praise, indicate his successful status. When juxtaposed with *hæmed* "sex" (28a), however, even the *hæleþa gestreona* "treasures of warriors" (31b) pale. This positive perspective on sex is important, and I shall consider it in more detail in chapter 6. Here, however, what is key is its value relative to the joys offered by elite heroic society. That value seems to be at least equal to the celibate enjoyment of treasure. Indeed, the emphasis placed on the pleasure of sex – it is not merely *hæmed* "sex" (28a) but *hyhtplega* "joyful play" (28b) – hints that what is banned here might even have a superior value.

Strictly speaking, no woman has actually entered the text yet, since lines 27b-31 refer to a woman who is *not* there, a woman who is denied. In line 32, however, a woman does appear. Yet this woman arrives neither for the begetting of children nor the enjoyment of intercourse:

Oft ic wirum dol wife abelge
wonie hyre willan; heo me wom spreceð,
floceð hyre folmum, firenaþ mec wordum,
ungod gæleð. Ic ne gyme þæs
compes ... (*Cursed among Weapons* 32–6)

(Often, foolish among my ornaments, I anger a woman [and] curtail her desires. She speaks insults to me, claps her hands, reviles me with words, chants evil. I do not heed this battle ...)

The text breaks off at this point due to the loss of a leaf in the manuscript,[66] so it is impossible to understand this exchange fully. What we have left,

---

66 Max Förster, "General Description of the Manuscript," in *The Exeter Book of Old English Poetry*, with introductory chapters ed. Raymond W. Chambers, Max Förster,

however, suggests that we are about to change tack again. We may speculate that the woman is jealous of the sword,[67] or that she resents its celibacy,[68] or that she attacks its power,[69] or that she accuses it of raping her,[70] or that she has lost her husband to its violence.[71] Given the fragmentary nature of the text, it is impossible to be certain, but the probable meaning of the clapping as a sign of grief makes the last seem most likely.[72]

Previous scholars have taken these lines as a continuation of the sword's life-story. Up to this point the object has been speaking as if it did have the power to kill, beget children, enjoy treasure, and feel deprivation; it might seem unsurprising, therefore, to find the sword shrugging off or repenting of the woman's accusations as if it were a human warrior.[73] Yet, although the sword still speaks in its own voice at the end of what is left of the text, here it admits that it is *dol wirum* "foolish among its ornaments" (32a). As we have known all along, it is an inanimate object without a voice, unlike the woman who *spreceð* "speaks" (33b), *firenaþ* "reviles" (34b), and *gæleð* "chants" (35a). Therefore it is not that the sword refuses to respond to the woman's cries but rather that it cannot. A sword cannot repent, make amends, or defend itself, just as it cannot beget children, and so, as an inanimate object, it inevitably *ne gyme[ð] þæs compes* "does not heed that battle" (35b). This reality is, of course, obvious: inanimate objects cannot heed. Up to this point in the text,

---

and Robin Flower (London: Bradford, Percy Hund, Humphries for the Dean and Chapter of Exeter Cathedral, 1933), 59; Williamson, *Old English Riddles*, 198–9. For an overview of losses from the Exeter Book, see John C. Pope, "Palaeography and Poetry: Some Solved and Unsolved Problems of the Exeter Book," in *Medieval Scribes, Manuscripts and Libraries: Essays Presented to N. R. Ker*, ed. M.B. Parkes and Andrew G. Watson (London: Scolar, 1978), 25–65.

67 Kevin Crossley-Holland, trans., *The Exeter Book Riddles*, rev. ed. (1993; London: Enitharmon, 2008), 93.
68 Nina Rulon-Miller, "Sexual Humor and Fettered Desire in Exeter Book Riddle 12," in *Humour in Anglo-Saxon Literature*, ed. Jonathan Wilcox (Cambridge: Brewer, 2000), 111–12.
69 Wim Tigges, "Snakes and Ladders: Ambiguity and Coherence in the Exeter Book Riddles and Maxims," in *Companion to Old English Poetry*, ed. Henk Aertsen and Rolf H. Bremmer Jr (Amsterdam: V.U. University Press, 1994), 102.
70 Tanke, "Bachelor-Warrior," 419.
71 Heyworth, "Perceptions of Marriage," 176–7. Murphy summarizes this argument but concludes that "the darkness of riddling is not best explained by storytelling of this kind" (*Unriddling*, 214).
72 Tauno F. Mustanoja, "The Unnamed Woman's Song of Mourning over Beowulf and the Tradition of Ritual Lamentation," *NM* 68 (1967): 1–27; Heyworth, "Perceptions of Marriage," 153–79.
73 Heyworth, "Perceptions of Marriage," 176.

however, we might have expected it to do so, for we have been listening to that inanimate object boast of its heroic successes and lament its enforced chastity for over thirty lines. The question over the value of heroic culture, the aporia lying between its approbation and its damnation, and the revaluing of it in comparison with the production of children and the pleasure of sex – all these have taken place without any questioning of the sword's agency. Although scholars have not always noticed, however, this is the point at which the text breaks open its own anthropomorphic disguise. Here the metaphor announces itself as a metaphor.

Because of the damage to the manuscript, we cannot tell what other surprises *Cursed among Weapons* might have held in store for us. What we do have, however, has already subjected the heroic idiom to an uncomfortable level of scrutiny, with the result that neither the sword nor the young warrior that it impersonates escape without questions about their value. Above all the text reminds us that, however familiar the literary world of the heroic elite might be, it is not complete. It may not even be best. And at this point, at its current end, *Cursed among Weapons* requires us to take another step back and recognize its riddling technique of anthropomorphism for what it is: a trope. It thus makes both its discourse and its practice visible, and it demands that its audiences adopt a critical distance sufficient to recognize them, too.

Irony and the Mock Heroic: *Four Creatures* (R.51)

In *Cursed among Weapons* the riddle-subject claims that it engages in a range of heroic activities and is excluded from marriage and the procreation of children only by its lord's prohibition; then it admits that it is actually an inanimate object that cannot even defend itself from a woman's verbal attack. *Cursed among Weapons* thus ends (in its current state) by confirming that its opening statements are ironic. Most modern critics agree that irony is a major feature of Old English poetry,[74] and yet, for all its pervasiveness, it is impossible to prove that it exists in any particular case. Indeed, Elise Louviot argues strongly against using the term "irony" for Old English poetry at all, even for cases in which there is "a subtle and deliberate use of phrases in seemingly inappropriate contexts to spark reflection."[75] It is consequently important

---

74 See the many examples listed in Frank, "Incomparable Wryness." For an extended discussion of irony in *Beowulf*, see Tom Clark, *A Case for Irony in Beowulf, With Particular Reference to its Epithets* (Bern: Peter Lang, 2003).
75 Louviot, *Direct Speech*, 250. Cf., however, the argument in Eric Weiskott, "An Oxymoron in *Beowulf*," *ANQ* 29 (2016): 51–2.

to acknowledge both the importance and the subjectivity involved in identifying irony. Choosing to read a text ironically can transform a tragic epic into "an extended alcoholic joke"[76] and a great, heroic king into an emasculated figure worthy of derision.[77] We must be cautious; we must choose appropriately. The basis for such choice, however, once careful analysis of text and context has been done, is ultimately the reader's own sense of the "elegance" or "rightness" of an interpretation. Yet, if Shippey is correct in his assessment of the sense of humour expressed in these texts, early medieval English poets would not have wanted it any other way. Shippey argues that, alongside valuing grim amusement in the face of one's own pain, early medieval English humour "turns on recognizing the enormous differences of meaning between barely perceptible or imperceptible differences of sound."[78] With their challenges to discernment the riddles are both the obvious place for such humour and the hardest place in which to identify it, for when we cannot identify with certainty what an object is, we can hardly determine whether it is presented ironically. For example, only if we accept Wilcox's solution of *gealga* "gallows" for *Towering Tree* (R.53) can we perceive its final lines as gallows-humour; if *se ærra* "the first one" is not a hanged thief but the handle of a flail, his partner's consequent quickness is not amusing.[79] Even when there is general agreement upon a riddle's solution, there may be differences in the perception of its seriousness. For example, while Irving sees *Brotherless* (R.88) as comical, most other readers have not seen the joke in an antler's need for its brother "to be a completely fulfilled individual."[80]

Although I agree with Irving that the transferral of heroic value from the animate to the inanimate world is potentially comical, in the case of *Brotherless*, at least, the social issues raised by the riddle do not disappear or lose their significance once a solution has been found. The

---

76 Raymond P. Tripp Jr, "Humor, Wordplay, and Semantic Resonance in *Beowulf*," in *Humour in Anglo-Saxon Literature*, ed. Jonathan Wilcox (Cambridge: Brewer, 2000), 60.
77 Although other critics have also seen Hrothgar as pathetic, Mary Dockray-Miller's reading of the text stands out for its extensive reliance on irony. See "*Beowulf*'s Tears of Fatherhood," *Exemplaria* 10 (1998): 1–28.
78 T.A. Shippey, "'Grim Wordplay': Folly and Wisdom in Anglo-Saxon Humor," in *Humour in Anglo-Saxon Literature*, 45.
79 See discussion in chapter 3, above. The spiritual solution for *Towering Tree* (R.53), suggested by F.H. Whitman in his "Significant Motifs in Riddle 53," *MÆ* 46 (1977): 1–11, does not allow much room for irony, either.
80 Irving, "Heroic Experience," 209. For discussion of *Brotherless* (R.88), see chapter 3, above.

incongruity of the trivial, inanimate object juxtaposed with heroic elegy does not undercut the values of loyalty and courage espoused by the heroic idiom. The idiom retains its status as a marker of value and, even in the context of incongruity and humour, irony does not necessarily undercut heroic culture itself. This seems to be true even when the heroic idiom appears to be emptied of significance, as in *Four Creatures* (R.51):

> Ic seah wrætlice   wuhte feower
> samed siþian;   swearte wæran lastas,
> swaþu swiþe blacu.   Swift wæs on fore,
> fuglum framra;   fleag on lyfte,
> 5   deaf under yþe.   Dreag unstille
> winnende wiga,   se him wegas tæcneþ
> ofer fæted gold   feower eallum. (*Four Creatures*)

(I saw four creatures travel strangely together; their tracks were dark, their footprints extremely black. A swift thing, bolder than birds, was on a journey; it flew aloft and dove under the wave. He suffered restlessly – that striving warrior who showed the ways over the gold ornamentation to all four of them.)

The flight of the quill-pen *on lyfte* "aloft, in the air" (4b), the ink imagined as a body of water (represented as an *yþ* "wave" 5a), the dark tracks (2b–3a), and the *wegas* "ways, paths" (6b) are common features of riddles pertaining to writing.[81] Indeed, the combination of these elements constitutes another trope, the trope of literacy. Yet in the midst of this scriptorium context, a *winnende wiga* "striving warrior" (6a) appears. This warrior is notably lacking in heroic equipment, companions, attitude, and action, even more so than the *ancor* "anchor" in *Fight against Wave*. He may represent no more than another instance of the camouflage or generalization of the heroic idiom, like that found in *One-Footed* (R.58), in which the **rad-rod* "well-beam" *ellen dreogan* "performed deeds of courage" (1b),[82] but two other interpretations are possible.[83]

The first is that the riddle appropriates the value associated with the heroic idiom for what might otherwise have been thought of as the

---

81 Williamson discusses the motifs of the three fingers, feather-pen, and black tracks, which also appear in Anglo-Latin enigmata (*Old English Riddles*, 293–4).
82 See chapter 3, above.
83 The following discussion of *Four Creatures* follows that in Jennifer Neville, "Redeeming Beowulf," 55–9.

unheroic act of writing: although stationary, solitary, and devoid of danger (unlike the *ancor* in *Fight against Wave*, R.16), writing is exalted as an activity equivalent to glorious warfare, and thus appropriately associated with *fæted gold* "gold ornamentation" in the last line.[84] The value associated with the heroic idiom is thus ascribed to the world of writing.[85] Underlying this transferral of value is the idea of the scribe, the *winnende wiga* "striving warrior," as a *miles Christi* doing battle against the devil through the labour of copying sacred texts,[86] and there is evidence elsewhere that suggests that some scribes were indeed seen as fighting for God in this way.[87] Yet, while this understanding is possible, the text provides little to ensure that this connection is made. Hermann has argued that "only minimal development" of the idea of the "ancient strife" against the devil is necessary to activate it in a text,[88] but I am not sure that even that minimal level is achieved here, for there is no mention of conflict itself, demonic enemies, or even the spiritual value of the words in the manuscript. The results of this labour remain *lastas* "tracks" (2b); they are not even words, much less blows against the devil, and the warrior's labour is limited to "showing the ways" (*wegas tæcneþ* 6b) to his fingers and pen. The difference between this scenario and that in *Solomon and Saturn I* is striking, for in the latter text the letters of the *Pater Noster*

---

84 Treasure can be an icon of moral worth in the context of the heroic idiom; see Elizabeth M. Tyler, *Old English Poetics: The Aesthetics of the Familiar in Anglo-Saxon England* (Cambridge: Boydell and Brewer, 2006), 13; cf. Ernst Leisi, "Gold und Manneswert im *Beowulf*," *Anglia* 71 (1952–3): 259–73.

85 See, for example, the argument for the physical and intellectual labour of writing in Clare A. Lees, "Basil Bunting, *Briggflatts*, Lindisfarne, and Anglo-Saxon Interlace," in *Anglo-Saxon Culture and the Modern Imagination*, ed. David Clark and Nicholas Perkins (Cambridge: Brewer, 2010), 126.

86 Teele, 92. An alternate interpretation of the riddle sees the "warrior" as a priest performing mass; see Scott Gwara, and Barbara L. Bolt, "A 'Double Solution' for Exeter Book Riddle 51, 'Pen and Three Fingers,'" *N&Q* 54 (2007): 16–19. Although I like this possibility of another solution, the problems I raise below regarding the language applied to the "warrior" are even more disturbing if the figure here is imagined as a priest in front of his flock.

87 See, for example, Cassiodorus' *Institutiones* 1.30: *Felix intentio, laudanda sedulitas, manu hominibus praedicare, digitis linguas aperire, salutem mortalibus tacitum dare, et contra diaboli subreptiones illicitas calamo atramentoque pugnare* "it is a happy effort, a painstaking to be praised, to preach to men with the hand, to open tongues with the fingers, to give health to mortals silently, and to fight against the unlawful thefts of the devil with pen and ink." Text is taken from *Cassiodori Senatoris Institutiones*, ed. R.A.B. Mynors (1937; Oxford: Clarendon Press, 1963).

88 John P. Hermann, *Allegories of War: Language and Violence in Old English Poetry* (Ann Arbor: University of Michigan Press, 1989), 39.

themselves become warriors who attack the devil in explicitly physical ways. For example,

↑ T hine teswað   and hine on ða tungan sticað,
wræsteð him ðæt woddor   and him ða wongan brieceð.
(*Solomon and Saturn I* 94–5)

(T hurts him [the devil] and stabs him in the tongue; he twists his throat and breaks his jaws.)

Although it lacks the elevated equipment commonly found in the heroic idiom, *Solomon and Saturn I* certainly values its violence, which it uses as a metaphor for spiritual "action."[89] The scribe in *Four Creatures* may similarly be waging war against the devil, but, if he is, the audience must supply the war.

The "warrior-scribe" here thus seems incongruous. As a warrior he should fight battles of some kind, resist metaphorical or literal enemies, and, of course, *dreogan ellen* "perform deeds of courage" (*One-Footed* 1b), but here he merely gives directions and *dreag unstille* "suffer[s] restlessly." This half-line is awkward to translate, for it does not seem appropriate either to the disguising heroic idiom or to the literal action of writing. The situation would be simpler if the verb, *dreag*, were transitive, for a warrior-scribe could, for example, "perform [deeds of courage]" or "endure [struggle]" or "carry out [his lord's command]" or "experience [battle]" or "enjoy [victory]." All of these would be suitable activities for both literal and spiritual warriors.[90] Without an object for *dreag*, however, the warrior-scribe may only "act," "be busy," "suffer," or, perhaps, "wander."[91] Although "act" and "be busy" are reasonable, if vague, possibilities for a scribe or warrior, neither should "wander"; and, if the import is "suffer," the cause and import of the suffering is unexplained. In my translation I assume that it refers to the stiff back, shoulder, neck, arm, and fingers caused by long hours of writing,[92] but such suffering, however real, is not equivalent to the life-threatening wounds endured by a *wiga* "warrior."

---

89 For discussion of the anthropomorphism of the letters in this poem, see *The Old English Dialogues of Solomon and Saturn*, ed. Daniel Anlezark (Cambridge: Boydell and Brewer, 2009), 28–31.
90 See *DOE* s.v. *dreogan*.
91 See *DOE* s.v. *dreogan*, but for "wander" see Clark-Hall s.v. *dreogan*.
92 See the colophons discussed in Richard Gameson, *The Scribe Speaks? Colophons in Early English Manuscripts* (Cambridge: Department of Anglo-Saxon, Norse and Celtic, 2001), 41.

Similarly uncomfortable connotations encompass the word *unstille*: although the word may simply mean "moving," neither a scribe nor a warrior should be "uneasy" or "restless" but rather *anræd* "resolute," whether for glory in battle or faith in God's word.[93] The phrase is less troubling if we interpret the *winnende wiga* not as the scribe but rather as his hand (or arm), as some modern readers do.[94] The motion of the hand across the page does supply a suitable image of restless wandering. It does not, however, supply a suitable analogy for military conflict. With a little effort, a scribe writing a book may be labelled a *wiga* "warrior" because of the possible connection to the idea of the *miles Christi* fighting an invisible, spiritual battle, but a hand or arm moving across a manuscript page, although making sense of the idea of "wandering," requires a much larger effort to justify being labelled a "warrior." It is possible – we can take "hand" as a synecdoche for the scribe[95] and then proceed to make the connection with the *miles Christi* – but the process seems over-extended, tenuous, and perhaps a bit ridiculous. In fact, it begins to remind me of Alexander Pope's belaboured comparison of Belinda's preparations with those of Homeric epic in Canto 1 of *The Rape of the Lock*.[96] It is certainly possible to make the comparison, and it is not unmeaningful, but it seems to have been pushed a little too far.[97]

Overall, then, in *Four Creatures* the heroic idiom may not elevate the scribe's work to the level of heroic champion so much as over-inflate it. Whether the text describes a "wandering" hand or an "acting" scribe, this motion in itself does not constitute heroic performance, and dressing it in the heroic idiom, without the concurrent justification of

---

93 *Unstille* could be taken as an adjective modifying the *wiga* "warrior" in the following line (6a), but I follow Williamson in interpreting it as an adverb (*Old English Riddles*, 457), even though I cannot find another instance of it being used adverbially (B-T does not list one, either).
94 Williamson, *Old English Riddles*, 294.
95 Anderson argues, for example, that the *cuþe folme* referred to in *Beowulf* 1303a is a synecdoche for Æschere: J.J. Anderson, "The 'Cuþe Folme' in *Beowulf*, Line 1303a," *Neophil* 67 (1983): 126–30. Cf. also the rather different view of hands in John M. Hill, "The Sacrificial Synecdoche of Hands, Heads, and Arms in Anglo-Saxon Heroic Story," in *Naked before God: Uncovering the Body in Anglo-Saxon England*, ed. Benjamin C. Withers and Jonathan Wilcox, Medieval European Studies 3 (Morgantown: West Virginia University Press, 2003), 116–37.
96 Alexander Pope, "The Rape of the Lock," 1.121–148, in *Alexander Pope: Selected Poetry*, ed. Pat Rogers (Oxford: Oxford University Press, 1996), 36–7.
97 *Andreas* may be another example of a poet deliberately pushing the application of the heroic idiom too far for the purposes of humour. See discussion in *Andreas: An Edition*, ed. Richard North and Michael Bintley (Liverpool: Liverpool University Press, 2016), 64–81.

an encoded spiritual meaning, makes it seem potentially ridiculous. It is, once again, impossible to prove that an early medieval English audience would have seen irony here,[98] but, as mentioned earlier, the humour in these texts seems often to have turned on subtlety so fine that the majority do not perceive it.[99] Certainly modern critics struggle to perceive it, as can be observed, for example, in their debates over interpreting Unferth in *Beowulf*. There is no question that there is irony involved in the conversation between Unferth and the hero, but where it begins and ends is disputed: is Unferth a respected official challenging an arrogant young man, or is he a craven coward, representative of the failed Danish court, whose drunken jibes are easily rebutted by a flawless hero? Critics have made convincing arguments on both sides.[100] With *Four Creatures*, the brevity of the text means there is much less evidence to consider, but the incongruity of the abrupt, unsupported application of the heroic idiom to the scribe suggests to me, at least, that there may be irony here.[101]

It would be unwise, of course, to put much weight on such slight evidence (if a feeling of incongruity can be considered evidence at all), but the possibility of irony in this trivial context may be worth a little further exploration. Using the heroic idiom to make a joke in this way requires a consciousness of the resources of the poetic tradition itself: to make such a joke, a poet must be conscious of the usual appropriation of the heroic idiom, whether in Old English poetry more generally as a metaphor for spiritual conflict, or in the riddles more specifically as a disguise for other things; and such a poet must also be conscious

---

98 For the difficulty of detecting incongruity, see Jonathan Wilcox, "Introduction," in *Humour in Anglo-Saxon Literature*, 5.
99 See Shippey, "'Grim Wordplay,'" 42–4 for examples from *Durham Proverbs, Wulf and Eadwacer*, and *Deor*.
100 See, for example, Michael J. Enright, "The Warband Context of the Unferth Episode," *Speculum* 73 (1998): 297–337, Roberta Frank, "'Mere' and 'Sund': Two Sea-Changes in *Beowulf*," in *Modes of Interpretation: Essays in Honour of Stanley B. Greenfield*, ed. Phyllis Rugg Brown, Georgia Ronan Crampton, and Fred C. Robinson (Toronto: University of Toronto Press, 1986), 160–2; Carol J. Clover, "The Germanic Context of the Unferþ Episode," *Speculum* 55 (1980): 444–68; E.L. Risden, "Heroic Humor in *Beowulf*," in *Humour in Anglo-Saxon Literature*, 73; Leonard Neidorf, "Unferth's Ambiguity and the Trivialization of Germanic Legend," *Neophil* 101 (2017): 439–54; Neidorf, "On Beowulf and the Nibelungenlied: Counselors, Queens, and Characterization," *Neohelicon* 47 (2020): 657–65.
101 Bitterli disagrees and strongly defends the heroism of scribal activity at some length (*Say What I am Called*, 148–50). I am not convinced, however, that the quill here is "equally militant" (149).

of scribes' feelings of self-importance.[102] It is worth noting, however, that, as in *Brotherless* (R.88), the irony here, if any, is not aimed at heroic culture: the values usually espoused within the heroic idiom are not undercut or questioned in any way, even if the poetic technique of appropriating the heroic idiom to discuss other spheres of human experience may be.[103] Ultimately, of course, it is also possible that the poet used *winnende wiga* simply because it was a handy half-line with alliteration on *w*, but the risk of reading too much into this text is finely balanced by the risk of reading too little into it and missing the joke.

"Heroic" Subjection in *Captives* (R.52)

Irony is probably more defensible in *Captives* (R.52):

Ic seah ræpingas   in ræced fergan
under hrof sales   hearde twegen
þa wæron genamnan,   nearwum bendum
gefeterade   fæste togædre;
5   þara oþrum wæs   an getenge
wonfah wale,   seo weold hyra
bega siþe   bendum fæstra. (*Captives*)

(I saw two brave captives brought into the hall, under the roof of the building; they were companions,[104] fettered firmly together with tight bonds.

---

102 Laurence K. Shook advocates "the whimsicality that ought to attach to the relationship between a scribe and his pens" in his interpretation of *Protector* (R.17), *Large Belly* (R.18), *Earth-Fast* (R.49), and *Abounding in Song* (R.57); he mentions but does not discuss *Four Creatures* (R.51) as one of the "riddles relating to the Anglo-Saxon scriptorium." "Riddles Relating to the Anglo-Saxon Scriptorium," in *Essays in Honour of Anton Charles Pegis*, ed. J. Reginald O'Donnell (Toronto: Pontifical Institute of Mediaeval Studies, 1974), 227.

103 Cf., however, Teele, who argues that riddles about the scriptorium present secular heroic concepts and traditional diction "in order to discredit their values by riddlic appropriation" (112).

104 *Genamnan* "companions" is an emendation of the manuscript's *genamne*. Williamson summarizes the scholarly debate over this emendation and adopts a different one, *genumne*, which eliminates the "companions" and leads to the translation, "which were seized (held) by tight bonds" (*Old English Riddles*, 296). It may be significant that the only other recorded instance of *genamnan* "companion" occurs in the immediately following riddle, *Towering Tree* (R.53). The difference between the two readings, however, is slight. *Genumne* leads to a reduced emphasis on the relationship between the two captives and a correspondingly increased emphasis on their bound state, but the key elements of the riddle remain the same: two captives bound together.

One of the two was near to a dark-hued Welsh-woman, who controlled the journey of both of them, fast in bonds.)

Here we seem to see two *hearde* "fierce, brave" warriors who have been taken captive in war, led into the hall bound with ropes. Although we do not observe such captivity in *Beowulf* or *The Battle of Maldon*, this fate is readily imaginable within heroic culture and so not an inappropriate subject to be narrated within the heroic idiom. Bede, for example, tells a story about a man named Imma, a nobleman who was enslaved in war.[105] We could begin to formulate a gnomic sentiment to accompany the riddle's narrative – a statement about the transience of fortune, perhaps, or how low the mighty may fall, perhaps even with learned references to Boethius' *De consolatione Philosophiae*. We could even see in the last line, with its reference to bondage and a journey, a hint of the Theme of Exile.[106]

As far as I know, no modern reader has responded to *Captives* in this way, probably because such a response makes no attempt to offer a solution.[107] Yet it is primarily our identification of the text as a riddle, because of its initial *Ic seah* "I saw" formula[108] and its place in a riddle collection, that instigates the interpretation of the heroic idiom as a disguise, for, unlike *Brotherless* (R.88), there is no blatant incongruity here, at least not for modern readers. If it were not for the perceived need to solve the riddle, modern readers might not have noticed anything strange in the portrayal of these two warriors fallen upon hard times. An early medieval English audience, more aware of its own expectations of class, ethnicity, and gender, however, might have been more alert to the presence of irony. From this (admittedly reconstructed and assumed) point of view, the pity that we might have felt for these brave companions is ultimately cut short by the incongruity of their subjection to a member of the lowest and most subservient class in society: not merely a Welsh slave, but a female Welsh

---

105 See 4.22 in *Bede's Ecclesiastical History of the English People*, ed. Bertram Colgrave and R.A.B. Mynors, rev. ed. (Oxford: Clarendon, 1991), 400–4.
106 See Stanley B. Greenfield "The Formulaic Expression of the Theme of 'Exile' in Anglo-Saxon Poetry," *Speculum* 30 (1955): 200–6.
107 See, however, Lindy Brady's analysis of the Welsh trade in cattle and slaves that lies behind the imagery of bondage in this text: "The 'Dark Welsh' as Slaves and Slave Traders in Exeter Book Riddles 52 and 72," *ES* 95 (2014): 248–50.
108 Of the seventy-seven riddles she deems "classifiable" according to their opening formulae, Ann Harleman Stewart identifies twenty-one as being of this type of "third-person eyewitness account." See "Old English Riddle 47 as Stylistic Parody," *Papers on Language and Literature* 11 (1975): 230.

slave.[109] Despite her lowly status, she can single-handedly control them both at the same time.[110] Such subjection would be unthinkable for the kind of human beings who ordinarily would be described as *hearde … genamnan* "brave companions" (2b, 3a); members of the warrior-elite should never sink so low. Thus, in his story of Imma, Bede makes it clear that a nobleman captured in war would normally be killed rather than enslaved; Imma escapes this fate by lying about his status.[111] What the Welsh slave controls must therefore be something else: perhaps a *besma* "broom," a *geoc oxena* "yoke of oxen," another *perscel* "flail," or *twa stoppa* "two buckets" (used for carrying water from a well).

The problem with deciding between these solutions is that, once the heroic idiom stops infusing meaning into this text by limiting its vocabulary to specific contexts, the riddle quickly becomes an empty shell. For example, outside the heroic idiom the *ræced* (1b) or *sele* (2a) could be any kind of "building," not the exalted mead-hall where noble warriors should be,[112] while the *siþ* upon which the "companions" are sent could be any kind of "motion," not an "expedition" or "enterprise" undertaken by warriors.[113] Ultimately there is little within the text to make one of the four solutions mentioned above absolutely superior to the others, although some seem a bit less plausible. For example, it seems odd to describe a broom as *two* things joined together; a handle and a collection of bristles, strictly speaking, add up to more than two "companions." Similarly, it seems doubtful that a female slave would control a yoke of

---

109 The designation "Welsh" indicates ethnicity or status or both, but in either case it is generally interpreted as pejorative, at least by the tenth century. See David A.E. Pelteret, *Slavery in Early Mediaeval England from the Reign of Alfred until the Twelfth Century* (Woodbridge: Boydell, 1995), 322; Rulon-Miller, "Sexual Humor," 115; Debbie Banham, "Anglo-Saxon Attitudes: In Search of the Origins of English Racism," *European Review of History* 1 (1994): 143–56; Brady, "The 'Dark Welsh.'"
110 For further discussion of the *ræpingas* as either war captives or criminals, see Megan Cavell, *Weaving Words and Binding Bodies: The Poetics of Human Experience in Old English Literature* (Toronto: University of Toronto Press, 2016), 164–7.
111 Note, however, that this is not the case in the version of the story retold by Ælfric; see his *Hortatorius Sermo de Efficacia Sanctae Missae*, §21.143 in *Ælfric's Catholic Homilies, The Second Series: Text*, ed. Malcolm Godden, EETS, s.s. 5 (London: Oxford University Press, 1979), 204. See also discussion in Pelteret, *Anglo-Saxon Slavery*, 63.
112 *Sæl* (or *sele*) is a specifically poetic word, not used in prose (see designation in Clark-Hall and Griffith, "Poetic Language," 183–5; Cronan, "Poetic Words," does not discuss it). Clark-Hall, Cronan, and Griffith do not identify *ræced* (or *reced*) as a specifically poetic word, but I cannot find any instance of its use in prose in the *DOE* Corpus, either as a simplex or in compounds. *Captives* (R.52) has thus used words for building most likely to be associated with the heroic world, presumably to create a suitable environment for the "brave companions."
113 For definitions of *sele*, *ræced*, and *siþ*, see B-T and Clark-Hall.

oxen, as this task seems to be associated with groups of males.[114] The movement of the flail, with the handle and swingle[115] travelling back and forth together on swinging journeys as the corn is threshed, is an attractive option, especially since the text specifies that *þara oþrum wæs an getenge* "one of the two was touching" (5) the Welsh slave, as opposed to both of them, and especially since the repeated reference to a building fits well with the usual practice of threshing indoors.[116] However, illustrations of threshing from early medieval England suggest that it was men, not women, who performed this task.[117] Buckets might be sent on a journey down a well, but probably not while chained together; they could, however, be tied together afterwards, to facilitate carrying.

Another possible scenario, not suggested before, is that of weaving. Weaving is a process that takes place indoors, under a *hrof* "roof" (2a), and it is one that naturally invites images of binding.[118] It is also an activity that, unlike ploughing and threshing, is associated specifically with women. The *ræpingas* could, therefore, be loom-weights: *hearde* "hard," doughnut-shaped objects made of stone or clay that are tied to bunches of warp-threads in an upright loom.[119] As the weaver

---

114 The ploughman and oxherd in *Ælfric's Colloquium* seem to be male, for example; for text see *Ælfric's Colloquy*, ed. G.N. Garmonsway (Exeter: University of Exeter Press, 1991), 20–1. The depiction of ploughing in Cotton Julius A. vi presents an all-male team accompanying the oxen; see reproduction in David Hill, "Prelude: Agriculture through the Year," in *The Material Culture of Daily Living in the Anglo-Saxon World*, ed. Maren Clegg Hyer and Gale R. Owen-Crocker (Exeter: University of Exeter Press, 2011), 10.
115 This is the top section of the flail, the part that swings. See discussion in Hill, "Prelude," 20 and in chapter 3, above.
116 Hill, "Prelude," 17–18.
117 Hill, "Prelude," 18, provides a reproduction of the illustration for December in Cotton Julius A. vi and assumes that *Captives* describes a flail. As he notes, the calendar depicts two men using flails (19), but *Captives*, unlike the translation from Crossley-Holland that Hill uses, specifies a *female* Welsh slave. Evidence from the early twentieth century seems to restrict threshing to men, too; see Fowler, *Farming*, 169. It is worth acknowledging, however, that the record of female activity at this time is very incomplete. For discussion of the patchiness of the record even for noble Carolingian women, see Julia M. H. Smith, "Gender and Ideology in the Early Middle Ages," *Studies in Church History* 34 (1998): 51–73. Our knowledge of what female slaves did and did not do is even less comprehensive.
118 Indeed, Cavell, *Weaving Words* explores this connection in exhaustive detail. For a brief overview of the weaving process and its equipment, with a useful diagram, see 29–32. For more detail, see Gale Owen-Crocker, rev. ed., *Dress in Anglo-Saxon England* (1986; Cambridge: Boydell, 2004), 286–91.
119 See illustration in Owen-Crocker, *Dress in Anglo-Saxon England*, colour plate F and discussion on 275.

passes her shuttle through the gap (the "shed") between the warp-threads, she controls the *siþ* "journey" of the paired loom-weights forward and backward by moving the heddle bar, resulting in one of the pair (*þara oþrum…an* 5) being temporarily closer to the weaver. The repeated reference to binding in this short, seven-line text – *ræpingas* "captives" (1a), *nearwum bendum* "tight bonds" (3b), *gefeterade fæste* "fettered firmly" (4a), *bendum fæstra* "fast in bonds" (7b) – makes this solution attractive, but it could justly be objected that a collection of loom-weights involves many more than the *twegen* "two" components mentioned here.[120]

Ultimately, however, my objections could be surmounted, and any of these solutions could be defended, as could a potentially endless series of others: finding the correct solution would be satisfying but ultimately is not my primary concern. Rather, what is important for this discussion is that, regardless of which solution is chosen, audiences follow the same process of reading and then re-reading the heroic idiom, moving from what appears to be a recognizably specific scenario compatible with heroic culture to a vague and thus only imperfectly recognizable one that seems to derive from a non-heroic, domestic context.

It is important to step back from the position that I have posited here. We should not, of course, fail to note its racism and its misogyny.[121] What is more important, however, is the fact that without that chauvinism, without the reference to the *wonfah wale*, there is no incongruity to mark the heroic idiom as ironic. Once the heroic idiom has been marked as ironic, however, it is possible to understand that the *hearde … genamnan* "brave companions" (2b, 3a) are not, in fact, brave, and that their "companionship" is merely an unexplained physical connection, not a relationship of noble loyalty. In the process, the value that usually accompanies the heroic idiom disappears, and thus once again, as in *Cursed among Weapons* (R.20), we are left with the question of what the heroic idiom means when it does not mark value.

---

120 For an in-depth discussion of loom-weights, see Christina Petty, "Warp Weighted Looms, Then and Now: Anglo-Saxon and Viking Archaeological Evidence and Modern Practitioners" (PhD diss., University of Manchester, 2014), 38–54.

121 Cf. John W. Tanke's discussion of the figure of the denigrated "Welsh slave" in *I Travel on Foot* (R.12): "*Wonfeax Wale*: Ideology and Figuration in the Sexual Riddles of the Exeter Book," in *Class and Gender in Early English Literature: Intersections*, ed. Britton J. Harwood and Gillian R. Overing (Bloomington: Indiana University Press, 1994).

Lone Dweller (R.5)

This question becomes more urgent when we turn to *Lone Dweller* (R.5). The hero of this poem stoically endures another fate likely to befall those who seek glory in battle: injuries.[122]

> Ic eom anhaga   iserne wund,
> bille gebennad,   beadoweorca sæd,
> ecgum werig.   Oft ic wig seo,
> frecne feohtan.   Frofre ne wene,
> 5 þæt mec geoc cyme   guðgewinnes,
> ær ic mid ældum   eal forwurðe,
> ac mec hnossiað   homera lafe,
> heardecg heoroscearp,   ondweorc smiþa,
> bitað in burgum;   ic abidan sceal
> 10 laþran gemotes.   Næfre læcecynn
> on folcstede   findan meahte,
> þara þe mid wyrtum   wunde gehælde,
> ac me ecga dolg   eacen weorðað
> þurh deaðslege   dagum ond nihtum. (*Lone Dweller*)

(I am a lone dweller, wounded by iron, injured by blade, sated with battle-work, weary of swords. I often see a dangerous battle fought. I do not expect comfort – that rescue from war-struggle will come to me before I entirely perish among men. Instead, the leavings of hammers, the handiwork of smiths, hard-edged and battle sharp, will bite me within the fortifications. I must await a more unpleasant meeting. In the settlement I could never find [one of] the race of doctors, [one of those] who might heal [my] wounds with herbs. Instead day and night the scars from swords become greater with [every] deadly stroke.)

In many ways, the description of the battle-survivor here represents the other side of the coin that possesses the greatest currency in heroic

---

122 For discussions of such injuries in medieval culture, see *Wounds and Wound Repair in Medieval Culture*, ed. Larissa Tracey and Kelly DeVries (Leiden: Brill, 2015). Note, in particular, discussions of later medieval battle wounds by Robert C. Woosnam-Savage and Kelly DeVries, "Battle Trauma in Medieval Warfare: Wounds, Weapons and Armour" and M.R. Geldof, "'And Describe the Shapes of the Dead': Making Sense of the Archaeology of Armed Violence", as well as the discussion of early medieval medical treatment of wounds in Debby Banham and Christine Voth, "The Diagnosis and Treatment of Wounds in the Old English Medical Collections: Anglo-Saxon Surgery?"

poetry like *Beowulf* and *The Battle of Maldon*. In these poems wars may be lost or won, and men may live or die, but there is always the possibility of success, whether through glorious victory or glorious defeat. In *Lone Dweller*, in contrast, the battle is over, and its outcome is of no consequence. Whether or not the past battle was a success, the present contains not glory but pain and despair. Thus we see the walking wounded, the battered veteran, whose future encompasses no hope, only more of the same until the inevitable final destruction.

This grim view of the ordinary warrior's life has received comment before.[123] At the same time, however, even modern readers have understood that the tragedy here is not to be taken too seriously, for this, too, is no ordinary warrior, even if the incongruity is less blatant than in *I Burn the Living* (R.6).[124] At least two characteristics of this "warrior" alert audiences to the fact that the image of the human warrior is a disguise. First, this *anhaga* "lone dweller" paradoxically has not left society behind, for he exists in the *folcstede* "settlement" (11a), within the *burgum* "fortifications" (9a),[125] *mid ældum* "among men" (6a). Second, the ability of this "warrior" to survive repeated wounds from swords is super-human; real warriors do not survive even one *deaðslege* "deadly blow" (14a), much less the repeated ones experienced and anticipated here.[126]

Because of these incongruities, modern readers agree that this tragic image of the beleaguered warrior is ironic: our pity is aroused inappropriately for an inanimate object that can neither feel pain nor derive anycomfort from our sympathy. Most modern readers, however, interpret this "warrior" as a metonym for the real warrior; that is, just as the fallen antler in *Brotherless* (R.88) stands for a human warrior, so the sword-hacked *scield* "shield" stands for the sword-hacked warrior, and thus the pity does have an appropriate target, even if it is partly deflected by the intervening figure of the shield. As with all solutions, "shield" makes sense out of the riddle's otherwise incongruous list of attributes: a shield does go to battle, where it "survives" even though it is endlessly bitten by swords. As an inanimate object

---

123 See especially Irving, "Heroic Experience," 205, and Teele, "Heroic Tradition," 56.
124 See discussion in chapter 3, above.
125 The word *burg* can indicate a very wide range of structures, from ditch enclosure to city; for discussion see, for example, Simon Draper, "The Significance of Old English *Burh* in Anglo-Saxon England," *Anglo-Saxon Studies in Archaeology and History* 15 (2008): 240–53; Nicole Guenther Discenza, *Inhabited Spaces: Anglo-Saxon Constructions of Place* (Toronto: University of Toronto Press, 2017), 194–8; Bintley, *Settlements*, 119–55.
126 For a brief overview of the burial of battle victims, see Andrew J. Reynolds, *Anglo-Saxon Deviant Burial Customs* (Oxford: Oxford University Press, 2009), 40–4.

made of wood, it is beyond a doctor's help, and thus the damage incurred by contact with swords will grow greater with every encounter until the accumulated damage renders it useless. At this point it will face a *laþran gemotes* "more unpleasant meeting" (10a), in which it will *eal forwurðe* "entirely perish" (6b), perhaps by being thrown into a fire, for *mid ældum* "among men" (6a) may also be translated as "among flames."

Most modern readers of the riddles are content with this solution. Indeed, "shield" allows for the continuing process of interpretation that I advocate throughout this discussion, since the juxtaposition of the inanimate object and the warrior that both disguises it and is represented by it may provoke contemplation and even question of the value of heroic culture. Yet there are three remaining incongruities which suggest that the irony permeates more deeply.[127] First, *anhaga* "lone dweller" is not an especially apt title for a shield; although a warrior carries only one at a time, he deploys a shield only in the company of other shields, and it seems likely that shields out of use were stored in groups, too: when Beowulf arrives in Denmark, he and his men are asked to leave their shields and spears together before they approach Hrothgar's throne (*Beowulf* 397–8),[128] and when the Danes go to sleep after their celebratory feast, they set their shields in a row over their heads (*Beowulf* 1242–3). Second, when in use, a shield should encounter battle on a battlefield, not *in burgum* "within the fortifications" (9a). Third, and perhaps most important, such battles should occur during the day, not *dagum ond nihtum* "by day and by night" (14b), for early medieval English warriors, unlike Tolkien's, sensibly fought only from sunrise to sunset.[129] This is not to say that a shield would never find itself in use in single combat, or inside the fortifications, or at a nocturnal raid, but rather that these are not the circumstances that define a shield's normal use. Thus, as in *Protector* (R.17), the heroic idiom may here disguise an object from outside heroic culture.

---

127 Some of my arguments here are anticipated by Trautmann, *Die altenglischen Rätsel*, 69 and Pinsker and Ziegler, 155–6.
128 For the placement of these shields inside the hall, see Larry J. Swain, "Of Hands, Halls, and Heroes: Grendel's Hand, Hrothgar's Power, and the Problem of *Stapol* in *Beowulf*," *Anglia* 134 (2016): 268.
129 See, for example, *The Anglo-Saxon Chronicle A*, s.a. 871: *onfeohtende wæron oþ niht* "they were fighting until night"; for text see *The Anglo-Saxon Chronicle: Vol. 3, MS A*, ed. Janet M. Bately (Cambridge: Brewer, 1986), 48. Cf. also the more extended statement in *Brunanburh* 13b–15. In contrast, the fictional Battle of Helm's Deep takes place after midnight (J.R.R. Tolkien, *The Lord of the Rings* [London: HarperCollins, 1991], 520).

In 1915, Trautmann proposed that the object represented here is not a heroic shield but rather a homely *onheaw* "chopping block": the stump or block of wood used as the platform on which segments of wood are split into useable chunks (for example, for firewood). Most modern audiences do not agree;[130] Bernard Muir for example, rejects this solution as "unlikely."[131] It is worth considering what criteria might have led to this judgement, however, because domestic objects are accepted as solutions to other riddles from the Exeter Book collection;[132] the mundane subject matter in itself does not disqualify this solution. Nonetheless, Muir, like others, presumably rejects *onheaw* "chopping block" because he perceives incongruity between the seriousness of the riddle's heroic themes and the mundanity of the object. Here we return to the problem of irony and humour, both of which are difficult to perceive in any written text. Even today, writing informally to friends with whom we share a language, cultural context, and personal experiences, we often feel the need to flag statements that are to be taken ironically. Old English poetry, coming to us in a language we do not fully understand, using poetic conventions that we perceive only with great effort, and addressed to unknowable audiences, unfortunately contains no icons to guide our reading. This is a serious enough issue in *Beowulf*, which, despite its ambiguity, can probably be considered a serious poem,[133] but the Old English riddles compound this problem in two ways. First, they are, almost by definition, deliberately misleading, so that their words cannot always be taken at face value. Second, because of the playfulness of the collection as a whole, sometimes their words must be taken at face value.[134] In these circumstances, it is impossible to be certain how to interpret incongruity. Muir and others consider the incongruity of a "heroic" chopping block to mean that this solution is incorrect, but humour may be another explanation.

This riddle, like *Four Creatures* (R.51), may be a joke.[135] This possibility cannot be ruled out, for scanning through the collection as a whole reveals a wide range of tones, from the sombre to the

---

130 Notable exceptions include Pinsker and Ziegler, 155, Tigges, "Snakes and Ladders," 100, and Stanley, "Heroic Aspects," 206.
131 Muir, *Exeter Anthology*, 2: 656.
132 See, for example, *Downward Nose* (R.21), *Feeds Cattle* (R.34), *Boneless* (R.45), and *In a Corner* (R.54).
133 See, however, Tripp, "Humor, Wordplay, and Semantic Resonance."
134 For further examples, see discussion in chapter 2, above.
135 For discussion of the similarities and differences between riddles and jokes, see Elliott Oring, *Jokes and Their Relations* (Lexington: University Press of Kentucky, 1992), 1–6.

light-hearted: *Glorious I Thunder* (R.1), *Under Waves' Pressure* (R.2), and *No Escape* (R.3), for example, whether taken as one text or three, seem very serious, while *Twelve Hundred Heads* (R.86) seems designed to provoke laughter.[136] Perhaps, then, the "warrior" here experiences not battles but "battles"; perhaps the elevated language, particularly that pertaining to the "swords" that damage "him," over-inflates the import of this scenario. Perhaps, rather than the laudable fortitude of *The Battle of Maldon*'s doomed warriors, we should be thinking once again of the ridiculous bellicosity of *The Rape of the Lock*'s small-minded aristocrats.

"Mock-heroic" is not a term commonly associated with Old English poetry,[137] yet there are reasons for identifying it here, in addition to the questions attending the traditional solution for *Lone Dweller*. First, irony is a necessary element even of the *scield* "shield" solution. Although the riddle-subject claims a place for itself within the battles where human warriors prove their courage against high-status weapons, a shield performs no action itself. It is utterly passive and helpless. Further justification for the possibility of irony arises because, as mentioned earlier, the *scield* solution leaves the riddle with three incongruities: the singularity of the *anhaga* "lone dweller," its location, and the timing of the "battles." The *onheaw* "chopping block" removes two of the problems. Unlike a *scield*, which is unlikely to be used unless other shields are being used in the immediate vicinity, a stump or log used

---

136 For discussion of *Twelve Hundred Heads* as a "mock-riddle," see Jonathan Wilcox, "Mock-Riddles in Old English: Exeter Riddles 86 and 19," *SP* 93 (1996): 180–7. Although Hans Pinsker rejects the link to Symphosius that provides the solution accepted here and by most scholars, he, too, considers the riddle an outrageous joke; see "Ein verschollenes altenglisches Rätsel?," in *A Yearbook of Studies in English Language and Literature*, ed. Siegfried Korninger (Vienna: Braumuller, 1981), 53–9.

137 The main exception to this generalisation may be *Andreas*, which has previously been described as mock-heroic; see discussions in Edward B. Irving Jr., "A Reading of *Andreas*: The Poem as Poem," *ASE* 12 (1983): 229; Ivan Herbison, "Generic Adaptation in *Andreas*," in *Essays on Anglo-Saxon and Related Themes in Memory of Lynne Grundy*, ed. Jane Roberts and Janet Nelson, King's College London Medieval Studies 17 (London: King's College London, Centre for Late Antique and Medieval Studies, 2000), 181–211; Jonathan Wilcox, "Eating People Is Wrong: Funny Style in *Andreas* and Its Analogues," in *Anglo-Saxon Styles*, ed. Catherine E. Karkov and George Hardin Brown (Albany: State University of New York Press, 2003), 201–22; *Andreas: An Edition*, ed. Richard North and Michael Bintley (Liverpool: Liverpool University Press, 2016), 64–81. *Judith* has also been seen to contain some elements of the mock heroic; see Hugh Magennis, "A Funny Thing Happened on the Way to Heaven: Humorous Incongruity in Old English Saints' Lives," in *Humour in Anglo-Saxon Literature*, ed. Jonathan Wilcox (Cambridge: Brewer, 2000), 138; Ivan Herbison, "Heroism and Comic Subversion in the Old English *Judith*," *ES* 91 (2010): 1–25.

as a platform for chopping wood characteristically stands alone in a cleared space, and so can appropriately be described as an *anhaga* "lone dweller." Like a wooden shield, a chopping block receives incurable wounds from blades (in this case, axes) until chopped up for firewood itself and thrown into the fire; unlike a shield, however, a chopping block may plausibly experience these blows within the *burgum* "fortifications" (9a), close to where firewood is required for heat and cooking. *Onheaw* "chopping block" thus seems to match up with the clues of the riddle better than *scield* "shield," even if its ordinary, domestic status does not match up with the text's tone.

There is, however, still one incongruity that is not addressed by *onheaw* "chopping block," and that is the inadvisability of chopping wood both *dagum ond nihtum* "day and night" (14b).[138] In fact, in a time before electricity, any activity requiring sharp objects would be risky at night,[139] but the riddle is emphatic that blades – *iserne* "iron (blade)" (1b), *bille* "blade" (2a), *ecgum* "swords" (3a), *homera lafe* "remnants of hammers (swords)" (7b), *hondweorc smiþa* "hand-work of smiths" (8b), *ecga* "swords" (13a) – are involved here. We could dispose of the problem simply by rejecting the specificity of *dagum ond nihtum* and interpreting it as having a generalized meaning such as "repeatedly" or "continuously."[140] The phrase, *dagum ond nihtum*, occurs only two other times in the *DOE* Electronic Corpus, however, and in both these cases the context seems to require the meaning "twenty-four hours per day," for in one case it refers to the pillar of cloud that leads the Israelites by day and by night, and in the other it refers to the soul's unceasing reflection on divine and earthly matters (in contrast to the body's cessation of activity at night).[141] The phrase appears much more frequently in the singular, as *dæges ond nihtes*: 150 times in total, with twelve instances in poetry. This formulation might make a generalized meaning such as "always" more plausible, but even in these cases the literal idea of activity that takes place both in daylight and in the darkness of night

---

138 Ferdinand Holthausen anticipates this objection and thus prefers "shield." See "Zu den altenglischen Rätseln," *Anglia Beiblatt* 30 (1919): 50–5. As mentioned earlier, battles, too, tend to be restricted to daylight hours.
139 We are largely unconscious of the limitations of darkness in the twenty-first century, but ours is a recent freedom; see discussion in A. Roger Ekirch, *At Day's Close: A History of Nighttime* (London: Weidenfeld and Nicolson, 2005).
140 This is how Pinsker and Ziegler interpret the half-line ("ständig," 156).
141 See *Exodus* 97b and *Meters of Boethius* 20.213b. Excluding instances that refer to a count of days and nights ("many," "seven," "forty," etc.), the phrase is rare in prose, too, and in all cases the meaning requires the inclusion of nocturnal hours rather than a general meaning of "continuously."

seems relevant.[142] Another option is to take *dagum ond nihtum* simply as exaggeration – part of the over-inflated, hyper-heroic description that renders the mundane *onheaw* "chopping block" equivalent to elite warriors fighting battles against enemies bearing the best equipment imaginable.

If, however, we accept this clue at face value, we have a problem, for wielding a blade of any kind at night is a somewhat risky and thus unlikely business. Activities that are less hazardous are more likely to happen indoors, however, where artificial light can be provided even after the sun has set. Sayers has argued that the object in question is a whetstone,[143] a solution that possesses several advantages over *scield* "shield" and *onheaw* "chopping block": it is possible to sharpen a blade safely even under low lighting, and the large number of references to blades is fully appropriate. *Anfilt* "anvil" is another possibility: another singular object surrounded by bladed weapons, whose use in the presence of fire would allow for activity both day and night, and whose name (*anfilt*) might find an echoic clue in the text's first line (*anhaga*).[144] A small objection might be that neither a whetstone nor an anvil suffers noticeable damage from ordinary use; the *dolg* "wounds" (13a) that lead to their ultimate destruction accumulate slowly, over years of use, but both anvil and whetstone satisfy the text's requirements better than the more popular shield solution. Nevertheless, particularly because of the text's reference to herbs, I prefer to think of this heroic, long-suffering object as an implement in the kitchen: a cutting board for vegetables (a **mete-bord*).[145] There is no archaeological evidence for such an object in early medieval England, but the text itself explains why this should be: a cutting board is consumable, a useful but unremarkable object to be recycled for fuel when damaged beyond use. Cutting board, like chopping block, brings the "battle" described in the text inside the *burgum* "fortifications," and it renders the temptation to consider this text in terms of the mock-heroic even stronger, for the glorious work of smiths, the emphatically sharp and dangerous "swords," are reduced to women's

---

142 I list only the instances in poetic texts here, as they are most relevant for thinking about poetic formulae: *Genesis A* 2351b, *Christ and Satan* 497a, *Homiletic Fragment I* 33b, *Elene* 198b, *Guthlac* 610b, *Phoenix* 147a and 478a, *Beowulf* 2269a, *Paris Psalter* 54.8, *Exhortation to Christian Living* 68a and 76b, *Lord's Prayer II* 107b, *A Prayer* 63a.
143 William Sayers, "Exeter Book Riddle No. 5: Whetstone?," *NM* 97 (1996): 387–92.
144 I am grateful to Jane Roberts for suggesting this solution (personal communication, 23 November 2018).
145 See brief discussion in Tigges, "Snakes and Ladders," 100.

tools,[146] and the battle itself represents the rather mundane business of chopping up food, including herbs like the *wyrtum* mentioned here (12a). Of course, such herbs, even if regularly applied to the board's wounds, would not promote healing.

Once again, however, having posited irony and humour in *Lone Dweller*, we are left with the serious question of discourse. If the heroic idiom is the discourse of value in Old English poetry, does an ironic use of it reject its value? In fact *Lone Dweller*, unlike *Four Creatures* (R.51) and *Captives* (R.52), can be, and has been, read as a rejection of the gloriousness of heroic culture.[147] This reading of *Lone Dweller* is open to the same criticism levelled at modern responses to *Beowulf* and *The Battle of Maldon*, however: although within them there is a recognition of the tragedy that may accompany heroic culture, there is no trace of an alternative to it. Thus the object in *Lone Dweller*, whatever it is, anticipates its "death" as sad but inevitable. From my point of view, then, heroic values and the idiom through which they are conveyed are not rejected in these texts.

And it is still possible that this wonderful little text is not funny at all. Although the combination of herbs and knives is satisfying, other work for blades might be closer to the interests of those making the manuscript: the work of the stylus on a writing tablet.[148] That is, *Lone Dweller* might be describing the "damage" done to the wax surface of a writing tablet, parallel to what Aldhelm describes in his Enigma 32 (*Pugillares* "Writing Tablets"): *Nunc ferri stimulus faciem proscindit amoenam* "Now a spur of iron ploughs my pleasant face" (4).[149] Although Aldhelm's text acknowledges the spiritual benefit of such writing – *semen segiti de caelo ducitur almum / quod largos generat millena fruge maniplos* "the nourishing seed of the field, which generates abundant sheaves with

---

146 Such knives are the most common find in graves, accompanying men, women, and children. See, for example, Gale R. Owen-Crocker, "'Seldom ... Does the Deadly Spear Rest for Long': Weapons and Armour," in *The Material Culture of Daily Living in the Anglo-Saxon World*, ed. Maren Clegg Hyer and Gale R. Owen-Crocker (Exeter: Exeter University Press, 2011), 202–3.
147 Teele, 106–15.
148 For a description of writing tablets as well as the remaining archaeological evidence for them, see Victoria Symons, *Runes and Roman Letters in Anglo-Saxon Manuscripts* (Berlin: Walter de Gruyter, 2016), 75–7. Note especially the evidence of the Blythburgh Tablet (British Museum no. 1902, 3–15, I), also briefly discussed in R.I. Page, *An Introduction to English Runes*, 2nd ed. (1973; Woodbridge: Boydell, 1999), 217.
149 Aldhelm, *Enigmata ex diversis rerum creaturis composite,* in *Aldhelmi Opera*, ed. Rudolf Ehwald, Monumenta Germaniae Historica, Auctores Antiquissimi, 15 (Berlin: Weidmann, 1919), 111.

thousand-fold fruit, is brought from heaven" (6–7) – his riddle-subject, like the speaker in *Lone Dweller*, nevertheless laments the suffering inflicted upon it by "weapons": *Heu! Tam sancta seges diris extinguitur armis* "Alas! Such a sacred field is destroyed by fearful weapons" (8). In Aldhelm's text, that "field" probably represents the wax surface, whose letters are inscribed and then destroyed when the tablet is re-used, but the scoring sustained by the Blythburgh tablet indicates that the underlying surface itself could also feel the point of a "sword."[150] The Blythburgh tablet is made of whalebone, not wood, but the Springmount Bog Tablets, another rare surviving example of this ephemeral artefact of writing, are made of wood.[151] In fact the material does not matter, for, unlike Aldhelm's Writing Tablets, *Lone Dweller* does not specify the material from which it is made. Finally, although it seems likely that most early medieval English writing took place during daylight hours, Cynewulf suggests that some might have taken place by night: his colophon to *Elene* refers to him wielding his *wordcræft* (1237a) during *nihtes nearwe* "the confines of night" (1239a).[152]

Although it could be argued that a writing tablet, like a shield, is not really an *anhaga* "lone dweller," there is a good fit between the actions described in *Lone Dweller* and the life-story of the writing tablet, doomed to suffer repeated scoring by sharp, metal styli until thrown away. Yet it is unsurprising that this solution has not been suggested for *Lone Dweller* before, for the fatal violence that dominates this text would seem to have no place at all in the scriptorium, except, perhaps, in the context of spiritual battle against the devil. Indeed, here we have all the battle-imagery that was lacking in *Four Creatures* (R.51). Reading *Lone Dweller* in this spiritual context also raises the possibility of yet another solution. As mentioned earlier, one of the problems to be addressed by any interpreter of the text is the incongruity of wielding a blade of some kind at night. One way of responding to this incongruity is to remove the object from the physical world and translate its terms into metaphors for spiritual truths. Jember thus solves the riddle as *scyld* "guilt" and sees the text as "an early version of the tradition of the 'pang of conscience.'"[153] No one, as far as I know, has seriously considered this as a possible solution. Indeed, his reading makes no

---

150 See plates and discussion in Symons, *Runes and Roman Letters*, 101–2; cf. 217.
151 See discussion in Symons, *Runes and Roman Letters*, 75–6.
152 It is, of course, possible that Cynewulf refers here to the mental labour of composition rather than the toil of writing.
153 Gregory K. Jember, "An Interpretive Translation of the Exeter Riddles" (PhD diss., University of Denver, 1975), 74.

attempt to account for most of the details of the text, and it seems illogical that "guilt" should be attacked, even by metaphysical weapons. Yet it is possible to provide a plausible, spiritual interpretation and resolve *Lone Dweller* as *sawol* "soul."[154] Like the *onheaw* "chopping block," the soul is an *anhaga* "lone dweller,"[155] isolated from other spiritual beings in its prison of flesh, where it is attacked by temptations (the weapons of the devil) and constantly faces spiritual battles. Such battles end only at death, at which point the soul can expect a *laþran gemotes* "more unpleasant meeting" (10a) – the experience of judgement, purgatory, or hell. It is noteworthy that there is no hope of salvation here. A soul could not, of course, expect healing from a human doctor with herbs, but it should think to turn to a confessor or to the great *hælend* "healer," Christ himself.[156] This soul seems unaware of the possibility of salvation, and thus its wounds, which penetrate *dagum ond nihtum* "day and night," as wounds from an earthly battle cannot do, become ever greater. A more precise solution thus may be *fæge sawol* "damned soul." Again, it is unlikely that a modern reader would prefer *fæge sawol* "damned soul" over secular solutions like *scield* "shield," *onheaw* "chopping block," *hwet-stan* "whetstone," *anfilt* "anvil," or **metebord* "cutting board."[157] Yet it is worth keeping in mind that an early

---

154 I have chosen *sawol* instead of *gast* because of the "S" rune in the margin.
155 Cf. the *anfloga* "lone flier" in *The Seafarer* (62b), which many scholars have interpreted as a metaphor for the mind or soul.
156 Cf. Judgement Day II, where Christ is called the *uplicum læce* "heavenly doctor" (46b); for discussion see Hermann, *Allegories of War*, 46. The idea of the confessor as physician is a commonplace; see, for example, John T. McNeill and Helena M. Gamer, *Medieval Handbooks of Penance: A Translation of the Principal Libri Poenitentiales and Selections from Related Documents* (1990; New York: Columbia University Press, 1938), 7. The idea of Christ as Physician is based on Matthew 9:12 and runs, for example, through many of the sermons of Augustine of Hippo: see *Saint Augustin: Sermon on the Mount, Harmony of the Gospels, Homilies on the Gospels*, trans. William Findlay, S.D.F. Salmond, and R.G. MacMullen, ed. Philip Schaff (New York: Christian Literature, 1888). Near the end of his influential *Carmen de Virginitate* Aldhelm characterizes *Tristitia* as a despairing soul rejecting Christ the physician; see *Aldhelmi Opera*, ed. Rudolf Ehwald, Monumenta Germaniae Historica, Auctores Antiquissimi, 15 (Berlin: Weidmann, 1919), 461 (l. 2660); for translation see *Aldhelm: The Poetic Works*, trans. Michael Lapidge and James L. Rosier, with an appendix by Neil Wright (Cambridge: Brewer, 1985), 161. See also the discussion of Christ as compassionate physician in later medieval texts in Virginia Lagnum, "'The Wounded Surgeon': Devotion, Compassion and Metaphor in Medieval England," in *Wounds and Wound Repair in Medieval Culture*, ed. Larissa Tracey and Kelly DeVries (Leiden: Brill, 2015), 269–90.
157 Teele, for example, rejects the possibility that *Lone Dweller* might refer to the wounds of sin ("Heroic Tradition," 70).

medieval English audience, particularly a monkish audience in the context of the Benedictine Reform, might be inclined always to read texts, especially enigmatic, difficult texts, within the flexible, productive confines of spiritual allegory.[158]

Lone Dweller thus requires more from its audience than a clear-sighted recognition of the limitations of heroic culture. More even than the elliptical *Beowulf*, it demands that its presentation of heroic culture be scrutinized, weighed, and interpreted. What is most interesting to me, therefore, is the possibility that in reading *Lone Dweller* audiences might have stepped back from the heroic idiom and recognized it *as* a trope – not merely a poetic *koine* or way of saying things that were true, but a set of constructed values that could be isolated, scrutinized, and parodied, even if they could not ultimately be rejected.

Conclusions

Unlike the *Bestiary*, but like the sacred text of the Bible, the riddles do not provide instructions. They also do not supply quotation marks to indicate when a "battle" is not a meeting of soldiers with spears and swords but rather a metaphor for a different kind of conflict, such as that of the *ancor* "anchor" against the waves or the *ancor* "anchorite" against temptations in *Fight against Wave* (R.16). Thus in any one riddle, the heroic idiom may be literal, decorative, deceptive, ironic, or allegorical, and, as we have seen, the grounds for identifying this use are frequently difficult to justify. As a result, audiences, whether early medieval or later, must pay close attention to the heroic idiom and become aware of it as something that is neither neutral nor natural.

The heroic idiom encompasses a set of values that modern audiences should be able to observe as neither neutral nor natural, even if scholars who work on Old English poetry for a long time (I include myself) may forget that. It would, of course, be entirely understandable if early medieval English audiences did, too – or rather, if they were unconscious of the fact that the heroic idiom does not inevitably depict worth and success. Theorists of discourse, in fact, posit that it is not possible to speak of things outside of existing discursive formations.[159] Thus Old English poetry does not speak of or value networking, social mobility,

---

158 "Reform culture is marked by a particular interest in language and in its manipulation as a means of creating difference." Catherine Cubitt, "Review Article: The Tenth-Century Benedictine Reform in England," *Early Medieval Europe* 6 (1997): 89.
159 See, for example, Foucault, *Archaeology of Knowledge*, 44–9.

nationalism, or female emancipation, even if we, working within our own discursive formations, can identify elements within it that remind us of these things.[160]

Yet the riddles seem to be a place where it is not only possible but important to observe discourses and the limits that they impose. Thus *Fight against Wave* has at its centre the awkward task of construing stasis and passivity as valuable within the heroic idiom. Similarly, to solve *Lone Dweller* (R.5), whether as *scield* "shield," *onheaw* "chopping block," *hwet-stan* "whetstone," *anfilt* "anvil," **mete-bord* "cutting board," *pugillares* "writing tablet," or *fæge sawol* "damned soul," an audience, then or now, has to recognize the heroic idiom as *a* way of describing the world rather than *the* way of describing the world – as a constrained, artificial entity, not a natural rendering of the truth. To solve the riddles, or even simply to read them, we have to recognize the frames of reference through which value is determined in Old English poetry *as* frames of reference rather than as value itself.

Not all Old English texts demonstrate visible edges of the discourse contained within the heroic idiom, and I am keenly aware of Shippey's point, cited earlier in this chapter, that it would be anachronistic to expect people in early medieval England to be detached from their own traditions.[161] I would like to argue, however, that the riddles are a special case, not only, as previous critics have suggested, because of their content and levity, but also because they require their audiences to be aware of the tropes and discourses that depict and define their world.

---

160 For example, we could interpret *Dark-Stained* (R.11) as *cumbol* "battle-standard" rather than the more usual *win* "wine" and see in it a commentary on nationalistic pride, but it seems unlikely that an early medieval English audience would do so.
161 It may be condescending, however, to deny early medieval readers the consciousness that post-modern readers claim to have. After all, 21st century Westerners who live within the discourse of capitalism are often unconscious of the assumptions and actions that are governed by it, but they are still able to appreciate, for example, the *Dilbert* comic strip, which daily ridicules office life. Those living in early medieval England may similarly have been conscious of the assumptions within which they lived, even without a miraculous foreknowledge of Foucault.

Chapter Five

Domestic Practices: Manufacturing and Implements

Introduction: Domestic Practice

One of the things that modern readers of the Exeter Book riddles have valued from very early on is that these texts address subject matters not contained in other early medieval texts, and the riddles thus contribute precious knowledge about early medieval English culture.[1] Without *In a Corner* (R.54), for example, we would know little about wooden objects like the *cyrn* "churn," which does not appear in heroic literature, law codes, or religious treatises and rarely leaves archaeological traces.[2] Without *Useful to Neighbours* (R.25), we would possess little evidence for appreciation of the *cipe* "onion" in early medieval England. Without *Hanging Head* (R.44), we could not have guessed that early medieval English audiences enjoyed jokes based on the phallic action of a *cæg* "key" in a lock. The riddles thus provide hints of the much wider culture that once surrounded the tiny religious and political elite that bequeathed to us most of the period's remains. Perhaps most tantalizing of these hints are those regarding attitudes towards slaves and women's sexual desires.[3]

---

1 See, for example: *The Riddles of the Exeter Book*, ed. Frederick Tupper Jr (London: Ginn, 1910), lxxxvi–lxxxvii; C.W. Kennedy, *The Earliest English Poetry: A Critical Survey of the Poetry Written before the Norman Conquest with Illustrative Examples* (London: Oxford University Press, 1943), 134; John D. Niles, *Old English Enigmatic Poems and the Play of the Text* (Turnhout: Brepols, 2006), 52–3. Elsewhere, despite their ambiguity and literary nature, the riddles are used as a source of information on early medieval material culture; see, for example, David Hill, "Anglo-Saxon Mechanics. 1. blæstbel(i)g-the Bellows. 2. ston mid stel-the Strikealight," *Medieval Life* 13 (2000): 9–13. Further examples will be discussed below.
2 For what (and how) we can know about early medieval English churns, see David Hill, "*Cyrn*: The Anglo-Saxon Butter Churn," *Medieval Life* 15 (2001): 19–20.
3 Discussion of these topics can be found in chapter 4, above, and chapter 6, below.

Given the rarity of this kind of information, it is unsurprising that modern commentators sometimes overlook the fact that these topics do not come to us as helpful explanations of the everyday, domestic world. Thus archaeological articles cite the riddles to explain the workings of material objects found in the ground.[4] Such use of the riddles is justifiable but risky. As Thing-theory teaches us, these are *things*, not objects; they do not simply throw themselves open before our senses but rather exceed our attempts to name them,[5] and, as I have already discussed, the absence of solutions in the manuscript removes any chance of certainty. In addition, and most importantly for the purposes of this chapter, these texts necessarily organize, arrange, select, adapt, slant, and assign value and meaning to the aspects of that world that they represent. Once again, the Exeter collection embeds its descriptions of everyday objects in riddling tropes. The riddles thus enable us not so much to identify everyday objects as to scrutinize the manners and modes by which early medieval English people approached their everyday life.

Although I draw upon and adopt here some of the ideas and terminology from De Certeau's *The Practice of Everyday Life*, it is important to note that De Certeau seeks to map out the "practices" and "tactics" that people adopt to work outside or against the ideologies that dominate their lives.[6] We no longer have access to the actual practices of everyday life in early medieval England, only the tropes used to convey them. Nevertheless, in this chapter I am concerned with what could be called minor tropes: manners and modes operating within or beneath the dominant tropes of the heroic idiom, which I discussed in the previous three chapters, and Christianity, the controlling ideology of the time. The tropes addressed in this chapter thus share the sense of ephemerality

---

4 For example, David Hill presents *Downward Nose* (R.21), with a "literal" translation, as a "detailed description of the plough and of its action" in "*Sulh*: The Anglo-Saxon Plough c. 1000 A.D.," *Landscape History* 22 (2000): 9. Although he notes the ambiguity in the text, Peter Fowler also uses this "always quoted" text to illustrate the early medieval English plough (or ard): *Farming in the First Millennium AD: British Agriculture between Julius Caesar and William the Conqueror* (Cambridge: Cambridge University Press, 2002), 193–4. Earlier scholars were less circumspect; see, for example, the confident conclusions derived from *Downward Nose* in B. Colgrave, "Some Notes on *Riddle 21*," MLR 32 (1937): 281–3. For a fuller discussion of the problem of interpreting *Downward Nose*, see Jennifer Neville, "The *Exeter Book Riddles*' Precarious Insights into Wooden Artefacts," in *Trees and Timber in the Anglo-Saxon World*, ed. Michael D.J. Bintley and Michael G. Shapland (Oxford: Oxford University Press), 122–43.
5 Paz, 9, 80–1.
6 Michel de Certeau, *The Practice of Everyday Life*, trans. Steven Rendall (Berkeley: University of California Press, 1984).

and triviality ascribed to "practices" and "tactics" by De Certeau. Yet even apparently trivial riddles about everyday topics can be seen to participate in much larger, social issues, and so, as De Certeau notes, we can begin to see "other interests and desires that are neither determined nor captured by the systems in which they develop."[7] In the discussion that follows, I shall argue that the trope of manufacturing, which glorifies human ingenuity, power, and control, also circles around and critically assesses the issue of violence, and that the use of the implement trope constitutes a potentially subversive meditation on the hierarchal nature of society. These are weighty issues, especially considering that the texts involved seem merely to describe ordinary, everyday objects. However, if we avoid the view that riddles are no more than puzzles "to be solved and annihilated,"[8] these apparently trivial texts can reveal a great deal more than we might have expected: a thoughtful questioning and perhaps some unease regarding the central pillars of society.

The Trope of Manufacturing: The Glory of Violence

Many riddles in the Exeter Book describe the creation of manufactured goods in some detail; over the course of reading the collection, the multi-stepped processes that transform raw materials into human possessions become recognizable as a trope, a mode that modern readers learn to recognize, and that early medieval audiences either already knew or learned by reading the collection. This trope contains four key components, although not all of them appear in every text. First, the process of manufacturing is represented as violence: the subject of the riddle undergoes mutilation.[9] Second, sympathy is generated for the apparently sentient being that suffers excruciating torments: for example, a tree grows joyfully before being brutally felled (*Towering Tree*, R.53), a *winnende* "struggling" wooden artefact is painfully pierced by arrows (*Turning Wood*, R.56), and even metal suffers wounds (*Forged by Hammer*, R.91). The emotive language surrounding these objects derives from the common riddling technique of prosopopoeia, but the pathos

---

7 De Certeau, xviii.
8 Northrop Frye, *Anatomy of Criticism: Four Essays* (Princeton, NJ: Princeton University Press, 1957), 88.
9 My ideas regarding the representation of manufacturing as violence in the riddles have been influenced by Alice Jorgensen, "The Exeter Book Riddles and the Unmaking of the World," paper given to the Leeds International Medieval Congress, 9 July 2008. Jorgensen's discussion drew upon Elaine Scarry, *The Body in Pain: The Making and Unmaking of the World* (Oxford: Oxford University Press, 1985).

creates not only the humorous incongruity that inspires a potential riddle-solver to interpret and reinterpret the literal words but also a discordant contrast with the third recognizable part of this trope: the celebration of human labour and ingenuity, the *eorles ingeþonc* "man's intention" and *swiþre hond* "right hand," which together create a *wundres dæl* "portion of wonder" (*Mouthless by Sand*, R.60. 13a, 12b, 10b).[10] This labour and ingenuity lead to the fourth key component of the trope: the final product's usefulness or beauty – its value. Ultimately, the trope of manufacturing asserts not only human mastery over the natural world but also the value that comes out of suffering.[11]

The riddles present this trope of manufacturing, with its four key components of violence, sympathy, ingenuity, and value, in different ways and with varying levels of detail and completeness. The first half of *Famous Name* (R.26), for example, dwells especially on human ingenuity:

    Mec feonda sum   feore besnyþede,
    woruldstrenga binom,   wætte siþþan,
    dyfde on wætre,   dyde eft þonan,
    sette on sunnan,   þær ic swiþe beleas
5 herum þam þe ic hæfde.   Heard mec siþþan
    snað seaxses ecg,   sindrum begrunden;
    fingras feoldan,   ond mec fugles wyn
    geondsprengde speddropum,   spyrede geneahhe[12]
    ofer brunne brerd,   beamtelge swealg,
10 streames dæle,   stop eft on mec,
    siþade sweartlast.   Mec siþþan wrah
    hæleð hleobordum,   hyde beþenede,
    gierede mec mid golde;   forþon me gliwedon
    wrætlic weorc smiþa,   wire bifongen.
15 Nu þa gereno   ond se reada telg
    ond þa wuldorgesteald   wide mære

---

10 Cf. Fred C. Robinson's discussion of the pleasure and comfort granted by artistic control over the natural world in *Beowulf and the Appositive Style* (Knoxville: University of Tennessee Press, 1985), 72 and Megan Cavell, *Weaving Words and Binding Bodies: The Poetics of Human Experience in Old English Literature* (Toronto: University of Toronto Press, 2016), 91.

11 See further the discussion of the riddles' presentation of the world of suffering in Corinne Dale, *The Natural World in the Exeter Book Riddles* (Woodbridge: Boydell and Brewer, 2017), 57–86.

12 I have adopted Williamson's punctuation here; see *The Old English Riddles of the Exeter Book* (Chapel Hill: University of North Carolina Press, 1977), 83.

dryhtfolca helm,   nales dol wite.
Gif min bearn wera   brucan willað,
hy beoð þy gesundran   ond þy sigefæstran ... (*Famous Name* 1–19)

(An enemy robbed me of my life, deprived me of physical strength, then wet me, immersed me in water, did it again, then set [me] in the sun, where I completely lost the hair that I had. Afterwards the edge of the knife – hard, ground with ashes – cut me; fingers folded [me] and the bird's joy sprinkled me with useful drops, frequently made tracks over the brown rim; it swallowed wood-dye, a portion of the stream, stepped again on me, and, dark-tracked, wandered on. Afterwards a man covered me with protecting boards, spread a hide [over me], adorned me with gold; therefore the wondrous work of smiths glistens on me, hung about with interlace. Now the ornaments and the red dye and the glorious treasure widely celebrate the protector of the lordly people – let not the fool find fault.[13] If the sons of men wish to use me, they will be healthier and firmer in glory as a result ...)

There is some sympathy for the victim here, but it is quickly overshadowed by the detailed exposition of the craftsmen's activities. In turn, in the latter part of the riddle (18–26a), this exposition is overtaken by an exultant catalogue of the benefits accrued as a result of the craftsmen's art (only the first two lines of this catalogue are cited here). There is little debate over the solution to this riddle (it is generally accepted to be some kind of religious book, probably a *Cristes boc* "Gospel book"), but, even if the solution were unknown, the value added to natural material by human labour would be evident. The riddle asserts the human craftsman's ability to triumph over the natural world, to the great benefit of humanity and perhaps even of God (15–17a), despite the potential resistance that a creature, presented as being in opposition to *feonda sum* "an enemy" (1a) and possessing *woruldstrenga* "physical strength" (2a), might have offered.

Hardest and Sharpest (R.28), although lacking the long catalogue of benefits in *Famous Name*, also illustrates the trope of manufacturing in its documentation of the value that derives from torment:

Biþ foldan dæl   fægre gegierwed
mid þy heardestan   ond mid þy scearpestan
ond mid þy grymmestan   gumena gestreona,

---

13 My translation follows the discussion in Williamson, *Old English Riddles*, 215, which in turn follows that in William S. Mackie, "Notes on the Text of the 'Exeter Book'," *MLR* 21 (1926): 300.

corfen, sworfen,   cyrred, þyrred,
5 bunden, wunden,   blæced, wæced,
   frætwed, geatwed,   feorran læded
   to durum dryhta.   Dream bið in innan
   cwicra wihta: clengeð, lengeð,
   þær þær ær lifgende   longe hwile
10 wilna bruceð   ond no wiht spriceð,
   ond þonne æfter deaþe   deman onginneð,
   meldan mislice.   Micel is to hycganne
   wisfæstum menn,   hwæt seo wiht sy. (*Hardest and Sharpest*)

(There is a portion of the earth beautifully adorned with the hardest and with the sharpest and with the grimmest treasure of men. [It is] cut, ground down, changed, dried, bound, wounded, bleached, thinned, ornamented, adorned, led from afar to the doors of men. The joy/music of living creatures is inside [it], [which] clings and remains there, where previously, [while] living, for a long time it enjoys pleasures and does not speak at all, and then after death it begins to declare and speak differently. It is much for a wise man to think what this creature is.)

As the long list of entries in the appendix testifies, this riddle continues to evade scholars' efforts to pin it down to an elegant solution, but it is still possible to recognize its use of the trope of manufacturing, especially when juxtaposed with *Famous Name* (R.26). Thus, whatever the object in question might be, we can observe the painful process of mutilation (4–6a), what might be sympathy for the previously living creature (7b–10), and the celebration of human craftsmanship, which results in the object's miraculous ability to speak (11–12a), as well as the beauty of the final product (1–3).

Familiarity with the trope of manufacturing allows us to identify it even when a text does not include all four of its usual elements. For example, *Forged by Hammer* (R.91), usually solved as *cæg* "key," frames its arguably double-entendre action with brief references to its violent creation and its connection with value: the acts of hammering, wounding, and filing of its head (1–2) enable it to guard its lord's hoard.[14] Similarly, although it does not explicitly describe the process, *I Travel on Foot* (R.12) narrates the story of a vigorous living creature that *foldan slite* "slits the earth" (1b) being transformed into something that *dryhtum þeowige* "serves the lordly multitude" (15b).[15] In both riddles our

---

14 For other solutions and further discussion, see chapter 6, below.
15 The creature is usually interpreted as an *oxa* "ox" and the product *leðer* "leather." This riddle will receive further attention in chapter 6, below.

attention is mostly consumed by the double-entendre game, but it is clear that an object has been manufactured. In fact, it is possible to observe the trope of manufacturing even when the text insists that what it is describing is not relevant:

> Mec se wæta wong, wundrum freorig,
> of his innaþe ærist cende.
> Ne wat ic mec beworhtne wulle flysum,
> hærum þurh heahcræft, hygeþoncum min.
> 5 Wundene me ne beoð wefle, ne ic wearp hafu,
> ne þurh þreata geþræcu þræd me ne hlimmeð,
> ne æt me hrutende hrisil scriþeð,
> ne mec ohwonan sceal am cnyssan.
> Wyrmas mec ne awæfan wyrda cræftum,
> 10 þa þe geolo godwebb geatwum frætwað.
> Wile mec mon hwæþre seþeah wide ofer eorþan
> hatan for hæleþum hyhtlic gewæde.
> Saga soðcwidum, searoþoncum gleaw,
> wordum wisfæst, hwæt þis gewæde sy. (*Hopeful Garment*, R.35)

(The cold, wet field begat me wondrously from its innards. In my mind's thoughts I know that I have not been made from woolly fleece, from hairs through elevated craft. No woof is wound in me, nor do I have a warp, nor does a thread resound in me through a crowd of throngs, nor does the whizzing shuttle glide through me, nor does the reed strike me anywhere. The worms that adorn yellow, fine cloth with ornaments did not weave me by the crafts of fates. Nevertheless, widely throughout the earth one would call me a desirable garment for men. You [who are] skilful in cunning thoughts and securely wise in words, say in truthful speech what this clothing might be.)

The text describes the process of manufacturing a woven object in some detail, but only in the negative: however this wondrously begotten creature was transformed into a garment, it was *not* on a loom.[16] Today, with so many synthetic materials derived from petroleum products (i.e. wondrously begotten from the earth's innards), there are many desirable garments that could satisfy the conditions of *Hopeful Garment*. In early medieval England, in contrast, there were fewer materials that

---

16 Cf., however, discussion in Benjamin Weber, "The Isidorian Context of Aldhelm's 'Lorica' and Exeter Riddle 35," *Neophil* 96 (2012): 457–66: the riddle is about weaving because byrnies are described as woven.

came out of the ground, and so, even if we did not possess the probable source of the Old English text, Aldhelm's helpfully entitled Enigma 33 (*Lorica* "Mail-Coat"), *Hopeful Garment* probably would still have been unanimously solved as *byrne* "mail coat."[17] This solution, however, is of less interest for my purposes than the fact that neither the mail coat nor its making is actually presented here.

Also absent is the mail coat's context, the world of war expressed by the heroic idiom. This absence is striking not only because the heroic idiom is usually ubiquitous in Old English poetry, but also because there is a traditional connection between weaving and battle imagery: one of the tools used in weaving, the batten or reed, can be referred to as a "weaving sword" or *spatha*.[18] In *Turning Wood* (R.56), for example, which is usually solved as *web-beam* "loom," the weaving process includes *heaþoglemma* "battle-wounds" (3b) and *daroþas* "darts" (4a).[19] In *Hopeful Garment*, in contrast, the only hint of the heroic idiom is the word *hæleþ* (12a), which occurs so often in Old English poetry outside its literal place on the battlefield that it has become generalized to mean "man" rather than "warrior," and so this sly clue, which replaces the more explicit reference to weapons in the Latin analogue, may be easily missed. Klein argues that battle is brought back into the text through the suggestive sounds of lines 6–8,[20] but otherwise *Hopeful Garment* seems to have been thoroughly purged of any suggestion of battle.

Hopeful Garment, then, works by carefully avoiding one trope, the heroic idiom, which would have revealed the identifying context for this *gewæde* "garment" (14b), and prominently presenting another, the trope of manufacturing. This trope is more than prominently presented,

---

17 For Aldhelm's riddles, see *Aenigmata Aldhelmi*, in *Collectiones Variae Aenigmatum Merovingicae Aetatis*, ed. Fr. Glorie, CCSL 133 (Turnholt: Brepols, 1968), 377–540; *Lorica* is on 471.

18 The weaving sword is briefly mentioned in Erika von Erhardt-Siebold, "The Old English Loom Riddles," in *Philologica: The Malone Anniversary Studies*, ed. Thomas Austin Kirby and Henry Bosley Woolf (Baltimore: Johns Hopkins Press, 1949), 12; Gale R. Owen-Crocker, *Dress in Anglo-Saxon England*, rev. ed. (Cambridge: Brewer, 2004), 276, and also, in another context, in Joshua Holo, "Genizah Letter from Rhodes Evidently concerning the Byzantine Reconquest of Crete," *Journal of Near Eastern Studies* 59 (2000): 7n26. For discussion of the relation between weaving and war, see Megan Cavell, "Looming Danger and Dangerous Looms: Violence and Weaving in Exeter Book Riddle 56," *LSE* 42 (2011): 29–42; and Jill Frederick, "The Weft of War in the Exeter Book Riddles," in *Textiles, Text, Intertext: Essays in Honour of Gale R. Owen-Crocker*, ed. Maren Clegg Hyer and Jill Frederick (Woodbridge: Boydell, 2016), 130–52.

19 For further discussion of *Turning Wood* (R.56), see chapter 3, above.

20 Thomas Klein, "The Old English Translation of Aldhelm's Riddle *Lorica*," *RES*, n.s., 48 (1997): 348–9.

however. Because the text denies every aspect of the particular content of that trope – the raw materials, the processes, the tools, the products – all that it actually contains is, in fact, the idea of manufacturing itself. That is, the trope of manufacturing, which I have derived from the text's hints of violence, the multi-stepped process of production, and the value created by that process, becomes a surrogate for description of the object.

Hopeful Garment thus provides a good example of how tropes become visible during the interpretative process: this text requires its reader to recognize both present and absent tropes as well as attend to its specific details, which provide images of weaving that are explicitly stated to be irrelevant. Yet the expectations created by recognition of a trope can also be disappointed. Thus, for example, the catalogue of woes suffered by the subject of *Lone Dweller* (R.5) might, at first, suggest the trope of manufacturing:

> Ic eom anhaga   iserne wund,
> bille gebennad,   beadoweorca sæd,
> ecgum werig.   Oft ic wig seo,
> frecne feohtan.   Frofre ne wene,
> 5 þæt me geoc cyme   guðgewinnes,
> ær ic mid ældum   eal forwurðe,
> ac mec hnossiað   homera lafe,
> heardecg heoroscearp,   hondweorc smiþa,
> bitað in burgum;   ic abidan sceal
> 10 laþran gemotes.   Næfre læcecynn
> on folcstede   findan meahte,
> þara þe mid wyrtum   wunde gehælde,
> ac me ecga dolg   eacen weorðað
> þurh deaðslege   dagum ond nihtum. (*Lone Dweller*, R.5)

(I am a lone dweller, wounded by iron, injured by blade, sated with battle-work, weary of swords. I often see a dangerous battle fought. I do not expect comfort – that rescue from war-struggle will come to me before I entirely perish among men [*or*: in flames]. Instead, the leavings of hammers, the handiwork of smiths, hard-edged and battle sharp, will bite me within the fortifications. I must await a more unpleasant meeting. In the settlement I could never find [one of] the race of doctors, [one of those] who might heal [my] wounds with herbs. Instead day and night the scars from swords become greater with [every] deadly stroke.)

The opening of this riddle is not so different from the hammering, wounding, and filing at the beginning of *Forged by Hammer* (R.91), but in this case the violence leads not to ingeniously achieved and admired value but rather to complete destruction. Thus the suffering of the embattled object receives no compensation: no beauty or utility results from this violence. It is interesting to note that *Lone Dweller* collapses the distinction that Scarry makes between tools and weapons: "what we call a 'weapon' when it acts on a sentient surface we call a 'tool' when it acts on a non-sentient surface."[21] Although the *Lone Dweller* is "non-sentient," an object rather than a body, it is nevertheless acted upon by weapons, not tools, and so it remains strongly implicated with the human warrior that constitutes its disguise. This entanglement of the disguising metaphor and its supposed referent may help to explain the affective power of this riddle.[22]

I have already discussed other aspects of this riddle (including its solution) in the previous chapter,[23] but at this point what interests me is the way in which the trope of manufacturing creates the expectation of value from violence. In *Lone Dweller* that expectation is disappointed. Such thwarting of expectation is, of course, a traditional riddling strategy,[24] but in this case it may also point to a subtle disquiet with the way in which the trope of manufacturing situates violence as a good. Although we may shrug off the suffering of the animal whose skin constitutes the gorgeous *Cristes boc* "Gospel book" because of the overwhelming benefits that result from its sacrifice, we cannot do so with the creature in *Lone Dweller*, because no benefits result. Unlike other Old English poems, such as *The Battle of Maldon*, *Lone Dweller* does not present violence as glory.[25] Ultimately, of course, the absence of benefits results because what we have here is not the trope of manufacturing at all. This disquiet, however, is not unique to *Lone Dweller*. Other riddles can also be seen to voice uneasiness with the link between violence and value that the trope of manufacturing asserts. In fact, the riddles may be seen to question or perhaps even criticize the sanctioned and glorified violence that prevails widely within Old English poetry in general.

---

21 Scarry, *Body in Pain*, 173.
22 See especially the discussion in Edward B. Irving Jr, "Heroic Experience in the Old English Riddles," in *Old English Shorter Poems: Basic Readings*, ed. Katherine O'Brien O'Keeffe (New York: Garland, 1994), 199–201.
23 See chapter 4, above.
24 See, for example, W.J. Pepicello. and T.A. Green, *The Language of Riddles: New Perspectives* (Columbus: Ohio State University Press, 1984), 84. Note, however, Patrick J. Murphy's contention that apparently paradoxical statements were conventional and thus transparent: *Unriddling the Exeter Riddles* (University Park: Pennsylvania State University Press, 2011), 10.
25 Cf. Irving, "Heroic Experience," 200–1.

Manufactured Things Bite Back: Vengeance for Violence[26]

Lone Dweller (R.5) raises questions about heroic action because of the apparent lack of value or purpose to the violence that fills its lines: despite what the trope of manufacturing might lead us to expect, violence here leads to oblivion, not value. In other riddles, even when the trope of manufacturing delivers on its promise of beauty or utility, violence also leads to another worrying outcome: revenge, the continuation and escalation of violence. The beauty and utility created by human labour comes at a price that is paid not only by the suffering subject but also by its human creators, for the concentrated application of human ingenuity results in objects that are dangerous to human beings. In an ironic twist, the raw materials that have been forcibly taken from the natural world, mutilated, and subjected to human domination acquire something like the dangerous power of the natural world demonstrated, for example, in *No Escape* (R.3), in which the storm devastates a ship *gæsta fulne* "full of souls" (30b), and *Terrible Laughter* (R.33), in which the terrible laughter of the *is* "ice" promises deadly battle for a ship.[27] Thus the transformation from peaceful, happy creature to dangerous antagonist could be interpreted as the natural world biting back. Yet the subjects of these riddles belong to the human world; it is human ingenuity, not nature, that makes them into *things* and gives them the power to enact revenge upon their own makers.

In some of these cases, the objects in question may be interpreted as weapons. Thus, for example, *Wob* (R.23), unanimously solved as *boga* "bow," makes a direct link between the imposition of violence upon it and its resulting ability to deal out violence in return. Although it refers to its manufacturing in the barest possible way – *ic eom wrætlic wiht on gewin sceapen* "I am an amazing creature shaped in struggle" (2) – human cruelty continues after its creation, and, indeed, continually "shapes" the riddle-subject: its ruler shaped torture for it (*se waldend ... me þæt wite gescop* 6). This violence is necessary – *Nelle ic unbunden ænigum hyran* "Unbound I will not obey anyone" (15) – yet it inevitably leads to more violence, which, as the text drily notes, *Ne togongeð þæs gumena hwylcum, / ænigum eaþe* "does not happen lightly to a man, to anyone" (10–11a), for it results in death.

---

26 This heading echoes Edward Tenner, *Why Things Bite Back: Technology and the Revenge of Unintended Consequences* (New York: Knopf, 1996).
27 Cf. discussion of the antagonistic natural world in Jennifer Neville, *Representations of the Natural World in Old English Poetry* (Cambridge: Cambridge University Press, 1999), 19–52.

Towering Tree (R.53) is also frequently solved as a weapon: the *ramm* "battering ram." I interpret it differently,[28] but here I wish to draw attention to the turning point: after the initial period of natural peace has been shattered by the painful process of manufacturing, *nu* "now" (8b) the riddle-subject engages in a battle through *heafdes mægen* "the power of its head" (9a) and *strudon / hord* "ravage[s] the hoard" (10b–11a). *Brain-Locker* (R.73), also discussed in detail earlier in this study[29] and also usually solved as a weapon of some kind (for example, *æsc* "spear," *ramm* "ram," or *boga* "bow"), similarly documents what might have been a tragic story of abduction, mutilation, and captivity if it were not for the object's subsequent retaliation:

hwilum eawunga   eþelfæsten
forðweard brece,   þæt ær frið hæfde (*Brain-Locker*, R.73. 25–6)

(sometimes, [advancing] forward, I openly break into the home-fortress that previously had peace.)

Such weapons acquire not only a voice but also the will and power to attack their own makers.

In the context of weaponry, the issue of human beings creating objects that damage human beings may seem unsurprising and not particularly ironic: of course human beings make weapons, and of course weapons take part in the violence that human beings enact against each other. Yet the riddles do not take this state of affairs for granted;[30] there is no "of course" in these stories of suffering creatures who gain not only value, for example, by performing deeds of glory (*Brain-Locker*, R.73. 11b), but also the power of revenge from the torture of manufacturing. The riddles present these situations for minute inspection, whether we identify the objects or not. Although I have revealed common solutions to these texts, my analysis does not depend upon solving them as weapons, or, indeed, at all, but rather focuses on the turning point, the transformation from victim to perpetrator of violence. In these cases, violence is not glorious but worrying, for violence, it seems, leads inevitably to more violence. Most worrying of all, that violence is not presented as being subject to human control.

---

28 See discussion in chapter 3, above. Cf. also discussion in Neville, "Precarious Insights."
29 See chapter 3, above.
30 Daniel Tiffany, "Lyric Substance: On Riddles, Materialism, and Poetic Obscurity," *Critical Inquiry* 28 (2001): 97.

Retaliation for the violence of manufacturing can also be seen in objects that are (probably) not weapons. *Old Ancestry* (R.83), for example, presents a very dangerous victim of human violence:

> Frod wæs min fromcynn [.....................]
> biden in burgum,   siþþan bæles weard
> [............]   wera lige bewunden,
> fyre gefælsad.   Nu me fah warað
> 5 eorþan broþor,   se me ærest wearð
> gumena to gyrne.   Ic ful gearwe gemon
> hwa min fromcynn   fruman agette
> eall of earde;   ic him yfle ne mot,
> ac ic hæftnyd   hwilum arære
> 10 wide geond wongas.   Hæbbe ic wunda fela,
> middangeardes   mægen unlytel,
> ac ic miþan sceal   monna gehwylcum
> degolfulne dom   dyran cræftes,
> siðfæt minne.   Saga hwæt ic hatte. (*Old Ancestry*, R.83)

(My ancestry was ancient ... [I have] resided in settlements, since the guardian of fire ... men, surrounded by flame, purified by fire. Now the hostile brother of the earth guards me, that one among men who first became a sorrow to me. I remember very well who in the beginning ripped[31] all my ancestry from the earth, [but] I am permitted [to do] him no evil; yet I sometimes raise up slavery throughout the wide fields. I have many wounds [and] a not small power on the earth, but I hide from every man the secret power of my precious strength [and] my journey. Say what I am called.)

Although the former happiness of this creature's natural state is not explicitly narrated, and although the trope of manufacturing is only briefly alluded to in the references to purifying fire, extraction from the earth, and, perhaps, the *wunda* "wounds" of inscription (10b), the present state of antagonism between the riddle-subject (usually identified as *gold* "gold" or *feoh* "money") and a *fah* "hostile" (4b) humanity is clear. In this case, however, the mutilated subject possesses a more subtle power than that of a spear or bow: rather than death, this creature

---

31   Williamson (*Old English Riddles*, 368) accepts Krapp and Dobbie's guess that *agette* refers to some kind of mining operation (374) but see also Pinsker and Ziegler's suggested emendation to *agnette* "appropriated, usurped" (317), which Muir considers attractive (*Exeter Anthology*, 720) but does not adopt (370).

takes its revenge by afflicting its tormenters with *hæftnyd* "slavery" (9a).³² Again, this hostility lies beyond human control.³³

Binder and Scourger (R.27) documents the danger that accompanies the creation of value perhaps most clearly of all:

> Ic eom weorð werum, wide funden,
> brungen of bearwum ond of burghleoþum,
> of denum ond of dunum. Dæges mec wægun
> feþre on lifte, feredon mid liste
> 5 under hrofes hleo. Hæleð mec siþþan
> baþedon in bydene. Nu ic eom bindere
> ond swingere, sona weorpe
> esne to eorþan, hwilum ealdne ceorl.
> Sona þæt onfindeð, se þe mec fehð ongean
> 10 ond wið mægenþisan minre genæsteð,
> þæt he hrycge sceal hrusan secan,
> gif he unrædes ær ne geswiceð.
> Strengo bistolen, strong on spræce,
> mægene binumen – nah his modes geweald,
> 15 fota ne folma. Frige hwæt ic hatte,
> ðe on eorþan swa esnas binde,
> dole æfter dyntum be dæges leohte. (*Binder and Scourger*, R.27)

(I am valued by men, widely found, brought from the groves and from the mountain slopes, from valleys and from hills. By day wings carried me in wagons in the air, with skill under the roof's protection. Afterwards a man bathed me in a barrel. Now I am a binder and scourger; I swiftly throw a slave³⁴ to the earth, sometimes an old freeman. He who reaches out against me and contends against me with violence will swiftly discover that, if he does not first abandon his folly, he must seek the earth on his back, his strength stolen away. Strong in speech but deprived of force, he will not have the power of his mind, or of his feet and hands. Find out what I am called, who thus bind men on the earth, the foolish ones after their blows by the light of day.)

---

32 Cf. *Collectanea Pseudo-Bedae*, no. 150: *Dic quid est aurum? Mancipium mortis.* "Tell me, what is gold? [It is] the price of enslavement to death." For text and translation see *Collectanea Pseudo-Bedae*, ed. and trans. Martha Bayless and Michael Lapidge, Scriptores Latini Hiberniae 14 (Dublin: Dublin Institute for Advanced Studies, 1998), 138–9.
33 For further discussion of this riddle, see Dale, *Natural World*, 123–44.
34 See Katherine Miller for the interpretation of *esne* as "slave" rather than "youth": "The Semantic Field of Slavery in Old English: *Wealh, Esne, Þræl*" (PhD diss., University of Leeds, 2014), 213–20, with discussion of this riddle at 208–9.

Here the trope of manufacturing, with its assertion of value – *Ic eom weorð werum* "I am valued by men" (1) – swiftly becomes a nightmare, for the application of human ingenuity results not in a safely denatured tool or work of art but rather in a rampaging monster.[35] In this case, violence seems to be absent from the manufacturing process itself, since being bathed in a barrel hardly constitutes torture, but nevertheless returns in the interaction between the finished product and its erstwhile creators. Reaching out against the riddle-subject *wið mægenisan* "with violence" (10a) results in defeat and humiliation for free and unfree alike. The text thus demonstrates the levelling effect of the consumption of alcohol, for "all who fall under the influence of mead are its slaves."[36] Yet, without human ingenuity, honey would not be transformed into the *medu* "mead" that binds, scourges, and overcomes both physical and intellectual strength.

Although we could interpret *Wob* (R.23) and *Towering Tree* (R.53) as conveying a kind of moral about the creation of weapons – perhaps something akin to "he who lives by the sword shall die by the sword" (cf. Matthew 26:52) – the same cannot be said about the turning point that we observe in the riddles concerning gold and mead. There is a more profound unease animating these riddles' various applications of the trope of manufacturing than a simple respect for weaponry. Newton's Third Law of Physics states that to every action there is an equal and opposite reaction; in a similarly inevitable way, the violent action that rips ore from the ground in *Old Ancestry* (R.83) both provides the gold that adorns the beautiful *Cristes boc* "Gospel book" of *Famous Name* (R.26) and also enslaves humanity to the deadly sin of greed and the fruitless pursuit of worldly wealth. Human violence may be heroic, productive, and necessary, but it also has worrying side effects.[37]

We do not often hear about these side effects, for anxiety about violence is not especially common in Old English poetry. *The Battle of Maldon*, for example, despite narrating the violent deaths of all its protagonists, apparently approves of its characters' engagement in battle, and thus the poet comments that Offa fulfilled his promise to his lord (i.e., by killing many Vikings) and then *læg ðegnlice ðeodne gehende* "lay

---

35 Cf. Dale's ecotheological reading of this riddle (*Natural World*, 145–65).
36 Miller, "Semantic Field of Slavery," 209.
37 Some of the ideas about *Maldon*, *Judith*, and *Beowulf* in the following discussion have been developed in more detail in Jennifer Neville, "Redeeming Beowulf: The Heroic Idiom as Marker of Quality in Old English Poetry," in *Narration and Hero: Recounting the Deeds of Heroes in Literature and Art of the Early Medieval Period*, ed. Victor Millet and Heike Sahm (Berlin: De Gruyter, 2014), 45–69.

like a thegn close to his lord" (*Maldon* 294): violence leads to a worthy, valued death.[38] Likewise, the terms with which the *Judith*-poet describes the Hebrews' victory over the Assyrians (*Judith* 291b-321a) leave no doubt that such action was meant to receive wholehearted approbation;[39] there is no fear of reprisals, side-effects, or any negative consequences of having *domlice / on ðam folcstede fynd oferwunnen* "gloriously overcome the enemy on the battlefield" (318b-19).

The subtle unease with violence that I have identified in the riddles can, however, be observed in *Beowulf*. The inescapable fact that violence begets violence underlies much of the action in *Beowulf*: just as the necessary and glorious killing of Grendel results in the death of Æschere, so the killing of Hnæf results in the death of Finn. Like the *Maldon*-poet, the *Beowulf*-poet seems to approve of the hero's participation in violent action: the explicit statement that *þæt wæs god cyning* "that was a good king" (2390b) is immediately followed by a brief summary of Beowulf's armed support of Eadgils in his revenge on Onela.[40] Nevertheless, the endless critical argument over whether the poem rejects the hero and his world is not without foundation, for the poem conveys both approbation and sorrow in, for example, the story of Hildeburh, which, in its immediate context, is a story of Danish triumph told during a celebratory feast, even if it impresses most modern readers with its tragedy.[41] This and other embedded narratives suggest an uneasiness about violence, especially the way in which violence may become an ongoing chain that demands further acts of violence.[42] At the same time, however, this uneasiness does not amount to a full-scale rejection of the hero and his world, or, indeed, of violence.[43] As the story of Hrethel's sorrowful death following the loss of his son at his other son's hand

---

38 Cf. Stanley B. Greenfield, "The Authenticating Voice in *Beowulf*," in *Hero and Exile: The Art of Old English Poetry*, ed. George H. Brown (London: Hambledon, 1989), 45.
39 For the characterization of the *Judith*-poet as wholehearted, see Howell Chickering, "Poetic Exuberance in the Old English *Judith*," *SP* 106 (2009): 122 and *passim*.
40 Stanley B. Greenfield, "Beowulf and the Judgement of the Righteous," in *Learning and Literature in Anglo-Saxon England* (Cambridge: Cambridge University Press, 1985), 399. Other scholars argue for different identities of the *god cyning*; see *Klaeber's Beowulf*, 4th ed., ed. R.D. Fulk, Robert E. Bjork, and John D. Niles (Toronto: University of Toronto Press, 2008), 244.
41 For an overview and rejection of the modern obsession with feud, especially in this passage, see Stefan Jurasinski, *Ancient Privileges: Beowulf, Law, and the Making of Germanic Antiquity* (Morgantown: West Virginia University Press, 2006), 79–111.
42 See also the nuanced discussion in David Clark, *Between Medieval Men: Male Friendship and Desire in Early Medieval English Literature* (Oxford: Oxford University Press, 2009), 130–52.
43 Cf. John M. Hill, *The Anglo-Saxon Warrior Ethic: Reconstructing Lordship in Early English Literature* (Gainesville: University Press of Florida, 2000), 15.

shows, the inability to pursue a feud can be equally fatal.[44] Feud, like violence in general, is glorious, necessary, *and* doomed to bring sorrow.

It is this combination of glory, necessity, and doom that I find in the narratives of violence, sympathy, ingenuity, and value that constitute the trope of manufacturing in the Exeter Book riddles. Where other Old English poems, such as *Judith*, *Genesis A*, and *The Battle of Brunanburh*, present the trampling of foes as an enthusiastically embraced route to glory, the superficially trivial world of the riddles reveals a resigned but uneasy meditation on the issue of violence similar to that observed in *Beowulf*: although violence is necessary (whether to create artefacts or to deter violence), it often creates more violence, for neither the strongest king nor the most skilled craftsman can remove the dangerous capacity of the world to "bite back." The pleasure and comfort derived from the successful imposition of human order upon the world can thus be seen to be short-lived. Nevertheless, the riddles, like *Beowulf*, do not advocate pacifism. Despite its deadly side-effects, there is no alternative to or escape from violence.

The Implement Trope: Scrutinizing Social Hierarchy[45]

Among the riddles that are generally interpreted as describing domestic practices, there is a group of thirteen that employ what I call the implement trope, which is a way of describing the interaction between a human operator and an object (often a tool) as a relationship between a lord and a servant.[46] For example, in *Forged by Hammer* (R.91), the implement refers to its owner and user as *min frea* and *min hlaford* "my lord" (6b, 9b) and thus elevates the rather limited turning action of a key to the status of personal service to a rich lord. Similarly, in *One-Footed*

---

44 For a thoughtful discussion of Hrethel's death and its implications for the poem as a whole, see Linda Georgianna, "King Hrethel's Sorrow and the Limits of Heroic Action in *Beowulf*," *Speculum* 62 (1987): 829–50, but see also Jurasinski, *Ancient Privileges*, 113–48 for an important distinction between the "craving" and "duty" for revenge.
45 This section follows the discussion in Jennifer Neville, "The Unexpected Treasures of the 'Implement Trope': Hierarchical Relationships in the Old English Riddles," *RES*, n.s., 62 (2011): 505–19.
46 I derive the term from the discussion in Alger. N. Doane, "Three Old English Implement Riddles: Reconsiderations of Numbers 4, 49, and 73," *MP* 84 (1987): 243–57. The presence or absence of metaphor in any riddle is debatable, but I see the implement trope in *Periodically Busy* (R.4), *Protector* (R.17), *Cursed among Weapons* (R.20), *Downward Nose* (R.21), *Wob* (R.23), *Belly Behind* (R.37), *Guest in the Enclosures* (R.43), *Earth-Fast* (R.49), *One-Footed* (R.58), *Strong Going In/Out* (R.62), *Brain-Locker* (R.73), *Barked, Wavered* (R.87), and *Forged by Hammer* (R.91).

(R.58) the *rad-rod "well-sweep" serves its *mondryhten* "master" (6a) and must obey its *þeoden* "prince" (14a), as any servant should, despite receiving no gifts from its *hlaford* "lord" (13a) in return. In *Strong Going In/Out* (R.62) even the simple *nafu-gar* "auger" or "poker" is *frean unforcuð* "resolute for its lord" (2b), and, as we have already seen, in *Wob* (R.23) the *waldend* "ruler" (6a) of the *boga* "bow" compels its obedience.

Like many tropes, the implement trope is most visible when it is unfamiliar: once a reader or listener has learned to recognize it, it quickly becomes transparent and very easy to dismiss as nothing more than a figure of speech or poetic elaboration of a traditional trope, which does no more than convey a conventional meaning. Thus, for example, having heard that its head is *homere geþruen, / searopila wund, sworfen feole* "forged by a hammer, wounded by artful spikes, [and] scoured by a file" (1b–2), any audience of *Forged by Hammer* (R.91) is unlikely to interpret the "key," "keyhole," or "brooch" as a literal thegn; once the implement trope has been identified, it can be quickly passed over so that a solution to the riddle may be found.[47] However, a continuing focus on the literal meaning of these texts can reveal something arguably more important than solutions: social norms and expectations.[48] In fact, even in the brief examples listed above, it is possible to observe an outline of what is expected of the subordinate member of a hierarchical relationship – not merely a slave, but anyone in a relationship with a superior. As this subset of society includes everyone except, perhaps, the king, these norms apply very widely. Such norms may be considered the foundational principles of a hierarchical society.[49] From these four riddles, for example, it can be observed that a person subject to a superior is expected to dedicate his or her actions to the acquisition and fulfilment of the superior's *modwyn* "heart-joy" and *willum* "wishes" (*Forged by Hammer*, R.91. 7a, 11b); to work loyally even when the expectation of reward is not fulfilled (*One-Footed*, R.58. 12b–14a); to demonstrate courage (*Strong in Going In/Out*, R.62. 2b); and even to

---

47 Cf. Doane's discussion of the necessity to "discount" common conceits when interpreting the implement riddles ("Implement Riddles," 243–4 and 246).
48 Cf. Gerd Althoff, *Family, Friends and Followers: Political and Social Bonds in Early Medieval Europe*, trans. Christopher Carroll (Cambridge: Cambridge University Press, 2004), 105–6.
49 Cf. Stefan Brink's discussion of the Roman and early Germanic *familia* or household, in which all members were subject to the authority of the head of the household and thus legally equivalent to slaves: *Lord and Lady – Bryti and Deigja: Some Historical and Etymological Aspects of Family, Patronage and Slavery in Early Scandinavia and Anglo-Saxon England* (London: Viking Society for Northern Research, University College, London, 2008), 11.

accept the imposition of force as a necessary good (*Wob*, R.23. 15–16a). Such a "person" will hereafter be designated as a "thegn," the most common term in the implement trope riddles, while the superior will be designated as a "lord."

It could, of course, be objected that these are ideals rather than expectations – indeed, that they are impossible ideals, the incongruity of which points to the metaphorical nature of the thegn in question: one does not expect the same level of compliance from a human being as one does from an inanimate object. These are reasonable objections, but the normative quality of these descriptions of thegns remains, for, however ideal, these riddle-subjects are recognizable as thegns. In fact, the model for superior-subordinate relationships posited in the implement trope is identical to that posited for hierarchical relationships more widely. For example, this ideal model can be observed in *The Dream of the Rood*, where the cross, the loyal thegn of Christ, sacrifices itself to inaction in obedience to its Lord's (i.e., Christ's) wishes. Although eventually rewarded with elevation and gems, it initially serves loyally without expectation of reward, demonstrates *ellen micel* "great courage" (60a), and accepts and endures the imposition of force as a necessary good. Nor is this behaviour limited to inanimate objects, for we may also recognize this model in Beowulf's adventure to Denmark. There the hero proclaims that he seeks Grendel without a sword or armour *swa me Higelac sie, / min mondrihten modes bliðe* "so that my lord Higelac might be happy in mind because of me" (435b–6). There are many other desires and obligations operating in this particular case, but with this statement Beowulf situates himself as a thegn, enduring additional danger without expectation of reward merely to prove his courage and thus contribute to his lord's happiness. In contrast, *Genesis B* explores the consequences of not accepting subordination: Satan refuses to gratify his lord's wishes with praise (256b), does not acknowledge the rewards that he has already received (257–8), relies upon subordinates for heroic action instead of demonstrating courage himself (284–9a), and, notoriously, seeks revenge for what he considers to be God's wrongful imposition of force upon him (360b–70).[50] The implement trope thus relies upon an understanding of hierarchical relationships within Old English poetry that operates beyond riddles about useful objects: the

---

50 For discussion of Satan's perversion of the lord-thegn relationship, see, for example, Alvin A. Lee, *The Guest-Hall of Eden: Four Essays on the Design of Old English Poetry* (New Haven, CT: Yale University Press, 1972), 13–22 and Peter J. Lucas, "Loyalty and Obedience in the Old English Genesis and the Interpolation of *Genesis B* into *Genesis A*," *Neophil* 76 (1992): 121–35.

lord-thegn relationship, which has received extensive commentary in many previous discussions.[51]

The implement trope applies the wide-ranging expectations of the service owed by a subordinate to his or her master to the relationship between an inanimate tool and its human operator; this trope thus provides an opportunity to observe the ideals posited for human relationships such as the lord-thegn relationship. Its significance goes further, however, for the implement trope not only reproduces the expectations of hierarchical society depicted in Old English poetry but also disrupts them: the implement trope portrays human beings both as lords of their tools and as thegns of them. That is, the hierarchical relationship between user and implement, lord and thegn, can be reversed. In these cases, instead of a compliant, inanimate object serving its human owner, we see the riddle-object as a lord being served by its human thegn. Thus, in *Belly Behind* (R.37, usually solved as *blæst-belg* "bellows"), the implement is followed or attended (*fylgian*) by a *þegn* "thegn," a *mægenrofa man* "powerful man" who *micel hæfde gefered* "had accomplished much" (2b–3);[52] in *Barked, Wavered* (R.87) the implement (also usually identified as *blæst-belg* "bellows") is similarly attended by a strong, brave *þegn* (2b).

The fact that those human operators can be seen as either masters *or* servants of their tools should give us pause, for the lord-thegn relationship normally admits of no opportunity for role-reversal.[53] Of course, on one level, the variation in the relationship can be seen as nothing more than a trick of perspective: depending on how you look at it, the *blæst-belg* "bellows" in *Barked, Wavered* (R.87) helps its master to achieve his aims, or the blacksmith aids the bellows in its activities. We can also, perhaps, ascribe the apparent inconsistency of relative status in *Periodically Busy* to this change of perspective, for there the riddle-object obeys its *þegne* "servant"

---

51 See, for example, Peter Clemoes, *Interactions of Thought and Language in Old English Poetry* (Cambridge: Cambridge University Press, 1995), 409–37 and Stephen D. White, "Kinship and Lordship in Early Medieval England: The Story of Sigeberht, Cynewulf, and Cyneheard," *Viator* 20 (1989): 1–18; reprinted in *Old English Literature: Critical Essays*, ed. R.M. Liuzza (New Haven, CT: Yale University Press, 2002), 157–81. For discussion of medieval lordship on the continent, see Althoff, *Family, Friends and Followers*, 102–35.
52 I follow Williamson's construal of line 7; see his text and discussion in *Old English Riddles*, 89–90 and 253–4. Krapp and Dobbie present a different reading (see 198–9 and 342), which Muir follows (*Exeter Anthology*, I, 311 and II, 637–8).
53 James Earl expresses this idea starkly in terms derived from psychoanalytical theory in his *Thinking about "Beowulf"* (Stanford, CA: Stanford University Press, 1994), 180–7.

(1b, 9b), which may also be its *hlaford* "lord" (4b).⁵⁴ Similarly, in *Downward Nose* (R.21) the success of the *sulh* "plough" is assured only

>   gif me teala þenaþ
> hindeweardre,   þæt biþ hlaford min. (*Downward Nose* 14b–15)

(if the one who is my lord serves me well from behind.)

In the usual world of the lord-thegn relationship, lords do not serve (either from in front or behind). The incongruous scenarios here may be explained by the peculiar qualities of riddle-texts, but they are nevertheless worthy of exploration.

First of all, it should be noted that the connection between the lord-thegn relationship and the master-tool relationship also occurs in a different context. Alfred's translation of Boethius' *Consolation of Philosophy* includes a much-cited passage, original to the Old English version, which specifies the requirements of successful kingship:

> Þæt bið þonne cyninges andweorc and his tol mid to ricsianne þæt he hæbbe his land fullmannod. He sceal habban gebedmen and fyrdmen and weorcmen. Hwæt þu wast þætte butan þisum tolan nan cyning his cræft ne mæg cyðan.⁵⁵

(These, then, are the king's materials and tools with which to rule: that he should have his land fully peopled. He must have men of prayer, men of war, and men of labour. Indeed, you know that without these tools no king may make known his power.)

---

54 *Periodically Busy* (R.4) has received a large number of solutions, including *belle* "bell," *cweorn-stan* "millstone," *wæter-stoppa* "water bucket," and *penna* "pen." Solving the riddle as *deofol* "devil," Melanie Heyworth proposes a different interpretation of the significance of the fluctuating status apparently described here; see "The Devil's in the Detail: A New Solution to Exeter Book Riddle 4," *Neophil* 91 (2007): 175–96. Solving the riddle as *sulh* "plough," Shannon Ferri Cochran interprets the text more literally and sees no fluctuation, only a separate servant and lord; see "The Plough's the Thing: A New Solution to Old English Riddle 4 of the Exeter Book," *JEGP* 108 (2009): 301–9. Note that both these latter readings deny the presence of the implement trope in this text. For my own attempt at an interpretation, see Jennifer Neville, "Sorting Out the Rings: Astronomical Tropes in *Þragbysig* (R.4)," in *Riddles at Work in the Early Medieval Tradition: Words, Ideas, Interactions*, ed. Megan Cavell and Jennifer Neville, Manchester Medieval Literature and Culture 32 (Manchester: Manchester University Press, 2020), 21–39.
55 *The Old English Boethius: An Edition of the Old English Versions of Boethius's De Consolatione Philosophiae*, ed. Malcolm Godden and Susan Irvine, 2 vols (Oxford: Oxford University Press, 2009), 277.

The earliest mention of the "three orders" of medieval society,[56] this passage is of particular interest for the present discussion because of the one-directional nature of the relationship: the king needs his "tools" to achieve his aims, but there is no corresponding responsibility of the king to the "tools." Although the necessity of kingship is not in question,[57] the obligations here are not imagined to be reciprocal. The services expected of subordinates, which, as we have seen, are substantial, do not entail corresponding duties for their superior.[58]

This is not an accidental omission, for we can see a similar, more telling omission in one of Ælfric's sermons. Although following Paul's argument for the unified body of the church (1 Corinthians 12.12–26),[59] Ælfric develops several nuances within it. For this discussion, the most pertinent development is that he not only substitutes the body parts' hypothetical assertion of independence from the body with the

---

56 Godden and Irvine, 208. The idea is also expressed in Ælfric and Wulfstan's works.

57 Cf. Hill's discussion of a Latin riddle from the *Collectanea Pseudo-Bedae*: the king sits upon the three-legged stool (i.e., the three orders of society), but if the king falls, the stool (i.e., the nation) falls, too. Thomas D. Hill, "A Riddle on the Three Orders in the *Collectanea Pseudo-Bedae*?" *PQ* 80 (2001): 207–8.

58 James W. Earl suggests that early medieval England was "ordered by an ideology which idealized servitude as loyalty"; see "Violence and Non-Violence in Anglo-Saxon England: Ælfric's 'Passion of St. Edmond,'" *PQ* 78 (1999): 126.

59 "The body is a unit, though it is made up of many parts; and though all its parts are many, they form one body. So it is with Christ. For we were all baptized by one Spirit into one body – whether Jews or Greeks, slave or free – and we were all given the one Spirit to drink. Now the body is not made up of one part but of many. If the foot should say, 'Because I am not a hand, I do not belong to the body,' it would not for that reason cease to be part of the body. And if the ear should say, 'Because I am not an eye, I do not belong to the body,' it would not for that reason cease to be part of the body. If the whole body were an eye, where would the sense of hearing be? If the whole body were an ear, where would the sense of smell be? But in fact God has arranged the parts in the body, every one of them, just as he wanted them to be. If they were all one part, where would the body be? As it is, there are many parts, but one body. The eye cannot say to the hand, 'I don't need you!' And the head cannot say to the feet, 'I don't need you!' On the contrary, those parts of the body that seem to be weaker are indispensable, and the parts that we think are less honourable we treat with special honour. And the parts that are unpresentable are treated with special modesty, while our presentable parts need no special treatment. But God has combined the members of the body and has given greater honour to the parts that lacked it, so that there should be no division in the body, but that its parts should have equal concern for each other. If one part suffers, every part suffers with it; if one part is honoured, every part rejoices with it" (NIV).

statement that every body part *serves* the others; he also adds the analogy of a powerful man's reliance upon his servants:

> We magon geseon on urum agenum lichaman hu ælc lim oþrum ðenað; ða fet berað ealne þone lichaman, and þa eagan lædað þa fet, and þa handa gearciað ðone bigleofan. Hraðe lið þæt heafod þæradune, gif þa fet hit ne feriað; and hraðe ealle þa lymu ealle forwurðað, gif þa handa ne doð ðone bigleofan þam muðe. *Swa eac se rica man þe sit on his heahsetle hraðe geswicð he his gebeorscipes gif þa ðeowan geswicað þæra teolunga. Beo se rica gemyndig þæt he sceal ðæra goda þe him god alænde agyldan, gescead hu he ða atuge.* Se bið ðin hand oððe þin fot, se þe ðe þine neoda deð. Se bið ðin eage se þe ðe wisdom tæcð and on rihtum wege ðe gebrincð. Se þe ðe mundað swa swa fæder, he bið swilce he þin heafod sy. Eallswa wel behofað þæt heafod þæra oðra lima, swa swa þa lymu behofiað þæs heafdes.[60]

(We can see in our own bodies how each limb serves the others; the feet carry the entire body, and the eyes lead the feet, and the hands procure food. The head would quickly lie down below if the feet did not carry it, and all the limbs would quickly perish if the hands did not bring food to the mouth. *So also the powerful man who sits on his high seat will quickly be lacking his feast if his servants abandon their work. Let the rich man be mindful that he must give an account of how he used the goods that God lent to him.* He is your hand or foot who gives you your necessities. He is your eye who teaches you wisdom and brings you to the correct path. Similarly, he who protects you like a father is your head. Just as the head needs the other limbs, so do the limbs need the head.)

Although this passage ends with an assertion of the reciprocal relationship between the head and the rest of the body, the analogy of the powerful man's relationship with his servants is strikingly one-sided: the servants *must* do their work, lest their lord suffer, but the lord himself is not obliged to them but rather to God, the ultimate source of all gifts. To put this in another way, the servants are expected to internalize their lord's needs and make them their own, but no such identification is expected of the lord.[61] Presumably the lord *should* provide for the servants

---

60 Ælfric, *Feria III de Dominica oratione*, emphasis added. Text is taken from *Ælfric's Catholic Homilies: The First Series*, ed. by Peter Clemoes, EETS, s.s., 17 (Oxford: Oxford University Press, 1997), 333.
61 Cf. John M. Hill's discussion of the relationship between Beowulf and his retainers in *Anglo-Saxon Warrior Ethic*, 25–7.

who are the immediate source of his own sustenance, but this particular text, at least, leaves that decision to the lord's discretion: providing for subordinates is the prerogative of generosity. Both Ælfric's sermon and Alfred's comment on Boethius recognize the need of the superior for the service of the subordinate, and both warn of the consequences should this service not be rendered. Neither, however, identifies a consequent obligation of the lord to his servants. Such an obligation, it seems, is unthinkable.

In mentioning the unthinkable, my discussion moves into a more specifically Foucauldian idea of discourse, in that I see the trope of hierarchical relationships as *including* what is acceptable and laudable (loyal, courageous service for a lord) and *excluding* what is not (consequent, obligatory service for a servant). As we have seen, the implement trope does represent the usual stringent expectation of loyal service and the same uncompromising internalization of the lord's needs on the part of the servants in its riddling depiction of keys, well-sweeps, augers, and bows (i.e., in *Forged by Hammer*, R.91, *One-Footed*, R.58, *Strong Going In/Out*, R.62, and *Wob*, R.23). In their description of "lords" that serve, however, some riddles present the unthinkable: the idea that hierarchical relationships may be reversible, or, at least, involve reciprocal chains of obligation.[62]

It is worth thinking a bit more about how shocking this idea is. I have always considered the lord-thegn relationship to be a reciprocal one, with the loyalty of the thegn matched by the generosity of the lord, and this is the usual understanding among modern critics.[63] Yet the word "reciprocal" masks the important fact that the obligation in that relationship is one-sided. Thus, for example, in *The Battle of Maldon* we hear Byrhtnoth's identification of his obligation to defend the land of his lord, Æthelred (*Maldon* 51–4a), but we hear no hint that Æthelred endures any returning obligation. Similarly, a large portion of the poem repeatedly rehearses the sense of obligation that Byrhtnoth's own thegns feel to him, but, again, we hear of no corresponding obligation of Byrhtnoth towards his thegns.[64] As in *Beowulf*, we do hear of

---

62 See discussion of *Periodically Busy* (R.4), *Downward Nose* (R.21), *Belly Behind* (R.37), and *Barked, Wavered* (R.87) above.
63 See, for example, the discussion of "reciprocal obligations" in Rolf H. Bremmer Jr, "Old English Heroic Literature," in *Readings in Medieval Texts: Interpreting Old and Middle English Literature*, ed. David F. Johnson and Elaine Treharne (Oxford: Oxford University Press, 2005), 77.
64 Cf. Tolkien's discussion, which sees this lack of consideration as a failing criticized by the poet: J.R.R. Tolkien, "The Homecoming of Beorhtnoth Beorhthelm's Son,"

the lord's past generosity, and it seems natural to see that generosity as an obligation imposed upon the lord. Yet the texts do not, in fact, ever speak that obligation: Beowulf's generosity to his men is given freely, at least on his part. As Ælfric's analogy of the rich man suggests, Beowulf owes (and renders) gratitude to God (*Beowulf* 2794–8), not to his men, not even to Wiglaf, who alone performs his duty as a thegn to serve his lord's needs. We might be inclined to interpret the gifts given to him by his lord after this service as signs of gratitude, but they probably represent further obligation: Beowulf presents his gifts to Wiglaf immediately after commanding him to serve his people and build him a barrow. He does not mention what Wiglaf has just done, much less thank him.

The main point to be made here is that, while generosity is expected from a lord, it is not presented as a duty or obligation; in contrast, the loyalty of the thegn is: *swylc sceolde secg wesan / þegn æt ðearfe* "so must a man be, a thegn in need" (*Beowulf* 2708b–9). The trope of hierarchical relationships thus speaks of the obligation of the subordinate to his or her superior but is silent regarding any corresponding obligation of the superior to the subordinate: *Maldon*'s narrator explicitly approves of the apparently pointless but loyal death of Offa – *he læg ðegenlice ðeodne gehende* "he lay near to his lord, like a thegn" (294) – but leaves modern critics doomed to debate endlessly the import of Byrhtnoth's *ofermod*, an apparently negative term floating without explanatory comment in a sea of approbation.[65]

I have belaboured this point in order to draw attention to the reversals that take place so casually in the riddles, where the requirement to serve well can be shifted without comment onto the lord. Clearly the Riddle-poets were not advocating a social revolution through their depiction of ploughs and bellows, and yet these texts do allow their audiences to think about the lord-thegn relationship in a way that

---

Essays and Studies, n.s., 6 (1953): 14–18. Byrhtnoth does thank Eadward for avenging the death of his kinsman, Wulfmær (*Maldon* 120–1), but this gratitude is particular and thus noteworthy (perhaps Byrhtnoth should have borne the responsibility to avenge Wulfmær, his sister's son, himself?); Byrhtnoth does not thank any of his other men for their brave deeds.

65 In addition to Tolkien's discussion (cited above), see especially the discussion in Helmut Gneuss, "*The Battle of Maldon* 89: Byrhtnoð's *ofermod* Once Again," *SP* 73 (1976): 117–37; Craig R. Davies, "Cultural Historicity in *The Battle of Maldon*," *PQ* 78 (1999): 151–69; Michael Matto, "A War of Containment: The Heroic Image in *The Battle of Maldon*," *SN* 74 (2002): 60–75; and John Halbrooks, "Byrhtnoth's Great-Hearted Mirth, or, Praise and Blame in *The Battle of Maldon*," *PQ* 82 (2003): 235–55.

elsewhere seems unthinkable. A similarly shocking idea lurks within *Bright Warrior* (R.50):

> Wiga is on eorþan   wundrum acenned
> dryhtum to nytte,   of dumbum twam
> torht atyhted,   þone on teon wigeð
> feond his feonde.   Forstrangne oft
> 5 wif hine wrið;   he[66] him wel hereð,
> þeowaþ him geþwære,   gif him þegniað
> mægeð ond mæcgas   mid gemete ryhte,
> fedað hine fægre;   he him fremum stepeð
> life on lissum.   Leanað grimme
> 10 [þam] þe hine wloncne   weorþan læteð. (*Bright Warrior*)

(There is a warrior on the earth born strangely. Useful to men, the noble one is awoken from two dumb ones. A foe bears him in hostility against his foe. Often a woman binds that very strong one. He heeds women and men well, serves them obediently. If they serve him with correct judgement [and] feed him well, he will enrich their life with benefits and joys. He grimly rewards the one who lets him become proud.)

The first three lines of the riddle establish beyond doubt that this is no human warrior, and so the hierarchy of society was unlikely to have been threatened by the power of the *wif* "woman" (5a) to bind this *forstrangne* "very strong" (4b) nobleman, or by the fact that the warrior *þeowaþ* "serves" those who *þegniað* "serve" him (6). It is perfectly clear that this is a metaphor, not a literal description of a hierarchical relationship. Nevertheless, we can observe in this text the same model of the powerful man and his servants that is presented in Ælfric's sermon, and so this text presents an opportunity to see not only *lig* "fire" but also hierarchical relationships in an unexpected and provocative way. In this case, the riddle presents not only the unthinkable ideas of reciprocal duty and reversible roles but also the potentially more revolutionary one of a servant restraining the one who grants benefits and joys. Not only must the servant ration the lord – serve and feed him *mid gemete ryhte* "with correct judgement" (7b) – but he or she must also prevent him from becoming *wlonc* "proud" (10). These lines refer, of course, to the need to prevent a fire from burning out of control, but in the context of a lord-thegn relationship, *wlonc* could refer to a quality proper to the rich and powerful,

---

66 Muir has *be* here – in error, I believe – so I retain *he* as in his facsimile.

indeed, to the defining qualities of the rich and powerful: being rich and powerful.[67] In effect the servant must prevent the lord from being (too much of?) a lord, lest that servant's generosity receive a grim reward.

As I have already acknowledged, these radical statements are framed by more than enough paradoxical markers to ensure that they are not taken literally as a description of real, human servants interacting with a powerful nobleman. At the same time, however, we should not see through the trope too quickly or allow an elegant solution to obliterate the ideas that lead to it, for, in fact, it is possible to see thoughtful sense amongst these laughable, impossible statements. Although King Alfred might not agree, from our position outside the manners and methods of early medieval England, we can observe that it is useful, even necessary, for the *weorcmen* "men of labour" to restrain the elite *fyrdmen* "men of war," lest they become too *wlonc*, too powerful. Just as a fire raging out of control can destroy all in its path, so an elite warrior-class that is not restrained by the prosaic requirements of daily life and obligations to those whom they rule can destroy society.

Scrutiny of the implement trope thus can lead to a reading of *Bright Warrior* (R.50) that is almost allegorical.[68] More than that, however, it can allow us to observe the unthinkable: the labouring classes' power to control the ruling nobility. Such power lies outside early medieval thought and thus cannot be known or named. Nevertheless, through the incongruities created by the implement trope, *Bright Warrior*'s depiction of *lig* "fire" provides an opportunity to see what such power might do. This is not to say that the riddles reveal to us proto-Marxist rebels challenging the hierarchical nature of society. In fact, unlike the trope of manufacturing, the implement trope does not seem to betray any sense of uneasiness about hierarchical relationships. It does, however, allow unexpected perspectives on them. Like the riddles containing the trope of manufacturing, the implement riddles challenge their audiences not only to say *hwæt seo wiht sy* "what the creature might be" (*Word-Spell*, R.67. 16b) but also to observe how value and power are conveyed.

This interest in hierarchical relationships seems to be particular to the Exeter Book collection: the Latin collections that constitute sources and analogues for the Old English riddles do not contain the implement

---

67 For further discussion of pride as a marker of the noble class, see discussion in chapter 6, below.
68 A different allegorical reading for *Torht Wiga* has previously been offered by Marie Nelson; for her interpretation of fire as "anger," see "Four Social Functions of the Exeter Book Riddles," *Neophil* 75 (1991): 448.

trope.[69] In the context of this absence, it is tempting to think that the scrutiny of value and power reflected in the implement trope is a specifically English reflection on hierarchical culture. Whether or not it is native, however, the implement trope is no more reliable than any other trope in the Exeter Book riddles. Recognizing it allows a riddle-solver to discover plausible solutions and interesting insights into the manners and modes of early medieval English culture, but sometimes recognizing it leads to baffling non-solutions, which force a riddlee to think again, not only about a solution, but also about the implement trope itself. This seems to be the case in *Earth-Fast* (R.49).

Deceptive Tropes: When an Implement Is Not an Implement

    Ic wat eardfæstne   anne standan,
    deafne, dumban,   se oft dæges swilgeð
    þurh gopes hond   gifrum lacum.
    Hwilum on þam wicum   se wonna þegn,
5   sweart ond saloneb,   sendeð oþre
    under goman him   golde dyrran,
    þa æþelingas   oft wilniað,
    cyningas ond cwene.   Ic þæt cyn nu gen
    nemnan ne wille,   þe him to nytte swa
10 ond to dugþum doþ   þæt se dumba her,
    eorp unwita,   ær forswilgeð. (*Earth-Fast*, R.49)

(I know about a thing standing alone: fixed to the earth, deaf, [and] dumb. By day it often swallows useful gifts from a servant's hand. The dark thegn, swarthy and black-faced, sometimes sends into[70] the dwellings under its jaws other things dearer than gold – things that princes often desire,

---

69 Apart from a brief reference to the dagger (*Pugio*) defending its lord's life in Enigma 61, the implement trope is absent from Aldhelm's collection, as Amy Clark notes; see "Familiar Distances: Beating the Bounds of Early English Identity" (PhD diss., University of California, Berkeley, 2020), 39. Clark refers to "implement riddles" throughout her discussion, but by this phrase she means riddles about inanimate objects, not riddles deploying the implement trope as I define it here. The implement trope does not appear in the riddle collections of Symphosius, Eusebius, Tatwine, and Boniface.
70 This reading is speculative; one would normally expect the accusative case for this meaning of *on*, but the distinction between accusative of motion and dative of rest "is not always observed": see Bruce Mitchell and Fred C. Robinson, eds, *A Guide to Old English*, 8th ed. (Malden, MA: John Wiley, 2011), 109 (§213). If this reading is not acceptable, I might translate: "Sometimes, among the dwellings, the dark thegn, swarthy and black-faced, sends other things dearer than gold through its jaws."

as well as kings and queens. Even now I do not wish to name that race that makes what this dumb one here, the dark ignorant one, has earlier swallowed so useful and beneficial to them.[71])

Earth-Fast has baffled generations of audiences; Williamson, for example, admits defeat, saying "it seems wisest to list the solution as 'uncertain.'"[72] Many of the solutions that have been offered rely upon an understanding of the implement trope, for two reasons. First, the text presents clear if sometimes unfamiliar language to identify the subservient member of a hierarchical relationship, the thegn: although *gop* (3a) appears nowhere else in Old English, Breeze's argument that it means "servant" seems plausible, especially in conjunction with the word apparently in apposition to it in the next line, *þegn* (4b).[73] Both the *gop* and the *þegn* give something to the other entity in the riddle, which swallows (2b, 11b) and takes the offering under its gums (6a), and it seems likely that the same actor and action are being described in both cases.[74] Second, the text concludes with the language of use and benefit: *Earth-Fast* states that the transformation carried out by the implement through the agency of the servant results in something that is *to nytte* "of use" (9b) and *to dugþum* "of benefit" (10a) to high-ranking people.

Together these ideas lead most modern readers to the solution "oven," which in many ways is not a bad fit. The text describes an object that is fixed to the ground, as an oven might be. That object is deaf and dumb but nevertheless has a mouth. Into that mouth a sooty, black-faced baker places dough, which is transformed into humanity's daily bread, which is more precious than gold. Yet, however smoky early medieval English ovens might have been, there seems to be an excessive emphasis on blackness in this text to represent an oven: the *wonna þegn* "the dark servant" (4b) or baker is both *sweart* "swarthy" and *saloneb* "black-faced" (5a), and the oven itself is *eorp* "dark" (11a), too. Given

---

71 Doane interprets the grammar of this sentence differently and thus translates: "I do not wish to name that kind of thing [*þæt cyn*] which the dumb one, the dark know-nothing [*eorp unwita*], having already swallowed, turns into a useful and beneficial thing for them [*him*, presumably the "princes, kings, and queens," although it could be reflexive]" ("Implement Riddles," 250).
72 Williamson, *Old English Riddles*, 290.
73 Andrew Breeze, "Old English *Gop* 'Servant' in Riddle 49: Old Irish *Gop* 'Snout,'" *Neophil* 79 (1995): 671–3; see also Carole Hough, "Place-Names and the Provenance of Riddle 49," *Neophil* 82 (1998): 617–18.
74 Doane, however, interprets the text as referring to two distinct servants, one human and one not ("Implement Riddles," 249). For further discussion of Doane's argument, see below.

this emphasis on blackness, we might have expected a riddler to draw attention to the contrastingly white (or, at least, light-coloured) product of the oven,[75] but the text does not. Also, however useful and beneficial bread might be, it seems doubtful that the nobility desired it more often than, say, meat or wine – or gold or other treasures.[76]

Sceptical of "oven" (and other previous solutions), Doane proposes that *Earth-Fast* describes a *mylen-pull and troh* "millpond and sluice."[77] The dark, deaf, dumb, immobile thing is the pond; a human operator and a servant-sluice together deliver water into its jaws. Water is essential to survival and thus more precious than gold, but the action of the millpond additionally transforms the water into something useful: a source of power for the mill. Doane thus carefully accounts for all the details of the riddle, and his reading is supported by an attractive pun: the pond swallows *gifrum lacum* (3b), which are probably "useful gifts" but could simultaneously be "greedy waters."[78] Nevertheless, Doane's solution seems not to have found favour with any modern readers, and I myself am not convinced that a pond would be described as being *eardfæst* "fixed to the ground" (1a) or deaf and dumb. A pond *could* be seen in this way, just as a sluice *could* be black. However, while pond water might be quiet, water running through a sluice seems unlikely to be described as *dumb*. Water is indisputably precious. However, once more, princes, kings, and queens seem unlikely to have desired it often, in comparison with the other things that their economic power might procure for them. Finally, I wonder again about the emphasis on blackness. Water may appear dark, but thinking about a sluice as *saloneb* "black-faced" does not result in the "minor rapture" of an "inner click."[79]

Although modern readers have learned to recognize and interpret the implement trope, therefore, and although they see it in operation here, their competence in recognizing this trope has not yet led to fully

---

75 For discussion of the kind of bread that might be produced in such an oven, see Sarah Larratt Keefer, "*Ut in omibus honorificetur Deus*: The *Corsnæd* Ordeal in Anglo-Saxon England," in *The Community, the Family, and the Saint: Patterns of Power in Early Medieval Europe*, ed. Joyce Hill and Mary Swan (Turnhout: Brepols, 1998), 237–64. Cf. also, however, the dissenting views in John D. Niles, "Trial by Ordeal in Anglo-Saxon England: What's the Problem with Barley?" in *Early Medieval Studies in Memory of Patrick Wormald*, ed. Steven Baxter, Catherine Karkov, Janet L. Nelson, and David Pelteret (Farnham: Ashgate, 2009), 369–82.
76 For the early medieval English diet, see Debby Banham, *Food and Drink in Anglo-Saxon England* (Stroud, Gloucestershire: Tempus, 2004).
77 Doane, "Implement Riddles," 251–4.
78 See also Williamson's discussion of this possibility (*Old English Riddles*, 291).
79 Niles, *Old English Enigmatic Poems*, 12.

satisfying solutions. The uncertain fit between the riddle's description and proposed solutions may be because *Earth-Fast*'s apparent use of the implement trope, like the apparent use of the trope of manufacturing in *Lone Dweller* (R.5), is an illusion. In fact, although *Earth-Fast* mentions a servant, the text does not actually describe the relationship that lies at the heart of the implement trope, which, as we have seen, places personal and far-reaching obligations on the servant. Other riddles may provide only the briefest of references to that relationship: *Barked, Wavered* (R.87), for example, merely asserts that the servant in question seems *godlic* "excellent" (4a). *Earth-Fast*, however, narrates the two actions performed by the servant without any reference to pleasure, loyalty, reward, courage, willing acceptance of force, or any other value-laden element of service, despite the usefulness and value of the servant's gifts. Hierarchical relationships in Old English poetry often attract such value-judgements: narrators explicitly express their approval of lords and thegns fulfilling their expected roles.[80] The absence of such approving comments here is useful for drawing attention to the usual collocation of value and service; *Earth-Fast* may reveal as much about hierarchical relationships through what is absent from it as *Forged by Hammer* (R.91) and *Towering Tree* (R.53) do through what is present in them, again, regardless of their solutions. The lack of reference to the usual value-laden elements of service suggests that the relationship in *Earth-Fast* is *not* the usual one between a human being and an implement. The hints of the implement trope thus are a false clue, a pit to trap a riddlee who has already mastered the implement trope.

The same is true of other tropes that have been identified in *Earth-Fast*, for some critics have seen hints of the literacy trope here, too. This trope also appears fairly widely in the Exeter Book collection. Eight riddles are generally accepted as addressing the mystery of writing,[81] and they do so using a recognizable manner or mode that usually includes silent voices, black tracks, benefit, and wonder. *Earth-Fast*'s emphasis on blackness is clear, and that suggestion has led good readers of the riddles, including Tupper and Williamson, to identify the literacy

---

80 For approval of the lord, see, for example, the *Beowulf*-poet's comments on Hrothgar's gift-giving (1027–9); for approval of the thegn, see, for example, the positive epithets awarded to the coastguard and door-warden as they fulfil their appointed duties (229–319, 331b–70): of the latter in particular the narrator notes *cuþe he duguðe þeaw* "he knew custom of noble decorum" (359b).

81 *Famous Name* (R.26), *Hardest and Sharpest* (R.28), *Moth* (R.47), *Abounding in Song* (R.57), *Golden Ring* (R.59), *Mouthless by Sand* (R.60), *Brotherless* (R.88), *Younger Brother* (R.93).

trope in it, even though, as Doane also notes, the evidence for the literacy trope in *Earth-Fast* is actually rather thin: there are no tracks here, no silent voices, and no wisdom. Attempting to solve the riddle as a bookcase demonstrates both the strengths and weaknesses of solutions based on the literacy trope.

First, bookcases (especially full ones) tend to be relatively immobile, so the text's statement that this object is *eardfæst* "fixed to the ground" (1a) makes sense. However, early medieval bookcases were not what modern readers might visualize when thinking about a bookcase. Michael Lapidge suggests that most early medieval books would have been kept in a book-chest – an *arcum* or *booc-hord*.[82] Depending on its size such an item might be portable and thus not fixed to the ground at all. Further, as an inanimate object, a book-chest is *deaf* (2a) and *dumb* (2a, 10b), but, ironically, full of words. Not mentioning the irony of dumb wordfullness seems like a lost opportunity for *Earth-Fast* if it is a riddle about a book-chest. On the other hand, *Earth-Fast*'s reference to swallowing seems to parallel Aldhelm's Enigma 89 (*Arca Libraria* "Library Chest"), in which the book-chest claims that its *viscera* "innards" are full of books, an image that suggests previous ingestion.[83] More support for book-chest can be gleaned from the value ascribed elsewhere to books, which could thus be lauded here as more precious than gold, desired by kings and queens, and both useful (*to nytte* 9b) and beneficial (*to dugþum* 10a).[84] Thus far, then, "bookcase" seems a possible if not fully convincing fit.

The main problem with the *booc-hord*, however, is the way in which the librarian is presented. As already noted, there are three references to the darkness of the thegn that serves the immobile, deaf, and speechless thing, and this thegn is not simply dark-haired but *saloneb* "dark-faced" (5a). A scribe might have ink on his or her hands, but those handling the precious products of the scriptorium have no obvious reason for having dirty faces. As Williamson notes, "dark thegns" in the riddles are invariably low-class, Welsh labourers,[85] not the kind of people entrusted with manuscripts. It is also difficult to see how a book-chest transforms books to make them useful and beneficial, as the last three lines describe; books are always already useful and beneficial, even

---

82 Michael Lapidge, *The Anglo-Saxon Library* (Oxford: Oxford University Press, 2006), 61.
83 For text see *Aenigmata Aldhelmi*, 509.
84 Cf., for example, *Solomon and Saturn II* 238–46 and *Famous Name* (R.26. 27a).
85 Williamson, *Old English Riddles*, 290. See *I Travel on Foot* (R.12. 4a and 8a), *Captives* (R.52. 6a), and *Boundary Paths* (R.72. 11a).

when they are not put away. Similarly, although Shook argues that the dark-faced thegn is the pen who swallows dark ink,[86] neither pens nor the manuscripts on which they write are fixed to the earth, and the idea of writing as "feeding" the "jaws" of a book seems more than strained.

Scrutinizing previous solutions for *Earth-Fast* demonstrates how an experienced riddlee, someone with a knowledge of previous riddles such as Aldhelm's Enigma 89 (*Arca Libraria* "Library Chest") and with a keen understanding of the implement trope and the trope of literacy, may be brought up short by his or her own competence. The frustrated process of trying to solve the riddle thus reveals the tropes themselves rather than making them transparent or automatic passages to the solution, and, as we have seen, it is neither the implement trope nor the trope of literacy that eliminates unsuccessful solutions. Rather, the key clues seem to be a blackness that is not associated with literacy and the attractiveness of the riddle-subject's product to the rich and powerful. What treasure, then, is made by a black-faced servant inside an inanimate, immobile object with an opening?

It may be honey: the only sweetener available in early medieval England and the starting point for mead, a drink for nobles that is both precious and golden. If it is, the speechless mouth with its gaping "gums" belongs to a bee-hive, a silent, deaf thing standing immobile on the earth, and the servant that brings gifts into that mouth is the black-faced honey bee. If this solution is correct, an additional detail in the text falls into place, for, although we might have thought that the reference to day-time activity in line 2b (*dæges*) was simply a useful alliterative filler, bees are famously diurnal (in temperate climates, at least).[87]

The main advantage of this solution is that it specifically addresses the process referred to in the last few lines of the text, as most other solutions do not do so well. Solving *Earth-Fast* as "book-chest," for example, does not explain how the swarthy librarian has made the books "swallowed" by the bookcase so useful, unless what we have here is a very unexpected appreciation of the benefits of cataloguing. Doane's

---

86 Laurence K. Shook, "Riddles Relating to the Anglo-Saxon Scriptorium," in *Essays in Honour of Anton Charles Pegis*, ed. J. Reginald O'Donnell (Toronto: Pontifical Institute of Mediaeval Studies, 1974), 215–36.
87 See, for example, Eric J. Warrant, "Nocturnal Bees," *Current Biology*, 17 (2007): 991. Not only do bees restrict their activity to daytime; they also are most active in the middle of the day. See Romina Rader, Will Edwards, David A. Westcott, Saul A. Cunningham, and Bradley G. Howlett, "Diurnal Effectiveness of Pollination by Bees and Flies in Agricultural *Brassica rapa*: Implications for Ecosystem Resilience," *Basic and Applied Ecology* 14 (2013): 23.

mylen-pull "millpond" does transform flowing water into a reservoir of power to grind grain, but it is difficult to be sure what is meant by the *cyn* "race" that the riddler coyly refuses to name in the last three and a half lines. Strictly speaking the sluice delivers the water into the pond rather than performing the transformation itself, and it would be very strange to be asked to name the race of the sluice-operator, pond-digger, or mill-builder: if the solutions accepted by modern readers are correct, human beings are never found as solutions for the Exeter Book riddles. If *Earth-Fast* is solved as "oven," the race that transforms the dough "swallowed" by the oven should be fire, but I am not aware of anyone solving this riddle as "oven and fire," perhaps because the last few lines of the text seem to be referring to the action mentioned earlier (the baker putting the bread into the oven) rather than to a new actor and event (the heat of the fire transforming the dough into bread).

If we solve *Earth-Fast* as *hyf ond beo* "hive and bee," however, the *cyn* "race" (8b) in question can be identified as the bee, which *doþ* "makes" (10a) the nectar collected from flowers and brought in through the "mouth" of the hive into something precious and useful to the wealthy who often desire it. The earlier emphasis on the servant's blackness is answered by the typical appearance of the *saloneb* "black-faced" honey bee, which, before the introduction of the now familiar black and yellow Italian bees in the 1800s, was purely black.[88] This process might take place in hives kept *on þam wicum* "among (human) settlements" (4a); conversely, it is possible that the servant's "gifts" are sent into tiny dwellings within the hive itself: the cells of the honeycomb.

The case for the hive in *Earth-Fast* is strengthened by comparison with two other riddles from the Exeter Book collection. The first, *Binder and Scourger* (R.27), almost always solved as *medu* "mead,"[89] has been discussed earlier in this chapter; it is important here as a comparator text that we can confidently associate with apiculture. Its concerns are very different from those of *Earth-Fast*, but the two texts share two important clues: the value that the content of the hive holds in human eyes and

---

88 Eve Crane, *The World History of Beekeeping and Honeyhunting* (New York, NY: Routledge, 1999), 13; Friedrich Ruttner, Eric Milner, and John E. Dews, *The Dark European Honey Bee: Apis mellifera mellifera Linnaeus 1758*, 2nd ed. (London: Writers Printshop, 2004), https://books.google.co.uk/books/about/The_Dark_European_Honeybee.html?id=-joPRwmw5scwC&redir_esc=y, 9; Rakesh Kumar Gupta, "Taxonomy and Distribution of Different Honeybee Species," in *Beekeeping for Poverty Alleviation and Livelihood Security*, volume 1: *Technological Aspects of Beekeeping*, ed. Rakesh Kumar Gupta, Wim Reybroeck, Johan W. van Veen, and Anuradha Gupta (Dordrecht: Springer, 2014), 85.
89 See appendix, below.

the bees' daytime activity. Thus *Binder and Scourger* tells us that wings initially carry its subject in the air *dæges* "by day" (3a) and that it is *weorð werum* "valuable to human beings" (1a), despite its power to throw young and old alike on the ground and deprive them of the *modes geweald, / fota ne folma* "control of their mind, feet, and hands" (14b–15a). The second comparator, *Protector* (R.17), has also been discussed earlier in this book.[90] Traditionally solved as a siege engine, a *ballista*,[91] an increasing number of scholars (including myself) now interpret it as a beehive. Again, the two texts differ in focus, but they share four striking parallels. *Protector*, too, refers to its activities as taking place specifically during *dægtidum* "daytimes" (3b). It mentions the passage of unidentified objects (the bees) through a *muþ* "mouth" (11b) which can both *spæte* "spit" (4a) and *swelgan* "swallow" (7b). It emphasizes the value associated with its *wombhord wlitig* "beautiful womb-hoard," which is *wloncum deore* "precious to nobles" (10). Finally, and most notably, *Protector* also identifies blackness as a key characteristic of the "weapons" that fly out of it. Blackness, in fact, sounds an odd note for the traditional solution of *Protector* as a weapon, for there is no obvious reason to describe arrows or spears as *sweart* "black" (7a). Black *beadowæpna* "battle-weapons" flying through the air makes excellent sense in the context of bees, of course, especially the dark bees of northern Europe. This is not to say that there is a bee trope operating in the Exeter Book riddles, but blackness and value do seem to be characteristics that Old English riddlers note about bees.

"Bee-hive" thus seems to be a good solution for *Earth-Fast*, although it does not resolve every issue with the text. Some of these issues can be addressed. For example, *eardfæstne* indicates that the solution should be a masculine noun. This could be a problem for *hyf* "hive," which is a feminine noun, but whether grammatical gender is significant in the riddles is debatable.[92] Regardless, there are other nouns with the correct gender that might serve: **beo-leap* "bee basket," for example, a term proposed as a solution for *Protector*, is the appropriate gender.[93] Similarly, it could be argued that honey is not actually *golde dyrran* "dearer than gold" (6b), but

---

90 See chapter 3, above.
91 See summary in Williamson, *Old English Riddles*, 179–81.
92 Tupper, *Old English Riddles*, asserts that the riddles disregard grammatical gender (181). Elena Afros argues that grammatical gender is manipulated in the riddles to provide false clues; see "Linguistic Ambiguities in Some Exeter Book Riddles," *N&Q* 52 (2005): 431–7. Niles argues strongly and at length that grammatical gender is crucial for confirming solutions (*Old English Enigmatic Poems*, 105–9).
93 See Marijane Osborn, "'Skep' ('B[ie]nenkorb, beoleap') as a Culture-Specific Solution to 'Exeter Book' Riddle 17," *ANQ* 18 (2005): 7–18, and W. Sayers, "Exeter Book Riddle 17 and the L-Rune: British *lester* 'vessel, oat-straw hive'?" *ANQ* 19 (2006): 4–8.

an entry in Alfred's laws suggests that the theft of honey in the past was considered to be more significant that the theft of other goods, equivalent to the theft of gold and horses and lesser only than the theft of human beings.[94] Regardless of the actual monetary value of honey, the strong desire of the noble classes for mead can probably be assumed. Other issues are less easy to resolve. For example, the text indicates that there are two types of things swallowed by the riddle-object: *gifrum lacum* "useful gifts" (3b) and *oþre* "other things" (5b). All other proposed solutions fail to account for the distinction between the two.[95] The hive-solution *can* account for them, but we might reasonably question whether people in early medieval England were aware that bees brought both pollen and nectar back to their hives.[96] A fully satisfying solution to *Earth-Fast* may still await discovery.

In the end, however, I am less interested in defending a particular solution than I am in exploring the way in which tropes are used and abused in *Earth-Fast*. The riddle defies quick and easy resolution because it seems to use familiar riddling tropes pertaining to implements and literacy, but a competent pursuit of those tropes does not lead to an elegant solution. The uncertainty surrounding the tropes thus draws attention to them and makes them visible rather than transparent. To solve this riddle, we must recognize the hints that suggest the implement and literacy tropes, but, more importantly, we must also recognize that these hints cannot simply be read as a code (thegn and lord = tool and user; blackness = inky letters). Confidence in such a methodology leads only to frustration.

Conclusions

The Exeter Book riddles use and re-use riddling tropes, some of which can also be found in Latin riddles as well as in later riddles that represent long-standing oral traditions.[97] The Exeter collection seems to assume an

---

94 *Geo wæs goldðeofe and stodðeofe and beoðeofe, and manig witu maran ðonne oþru; nu sint eal gelic buton manðoefe: CXX scill'* "Previously the punishment for theft of gold, the theft of horses, and the theft of bees, and many [others], was greater than for others; now they are all the same except for the theft of men: 120 shillings." For the text of Alfred's law, see *Die Gesetze der Angelsachsen*, ed. Felix Liebermann, 3 vols (Halle: Niemeyer, 1903–16), 1: 54.
95 Even Doane does not fully address what *oþre* might indicate, although his literal translation suggests it means "to another [feminine singular thing]" (Doane, "Implement Riddles," 250). In this rendering, however, there is no object for the verb *sendeð* (5b).
96 I am grateful to Megan Cavell for this suggestion (personal communication, 7 January 2022).
97 See Dieter Bitterli, *Say What I am Called: The Old English* Riddles *of the Exeter Book and the Anglo-Latin Riddle Tradition*, Toronto Anglo-Saxon Series 2 (Toronto: University

audience that is familiar with these other traditions. Its texts rely upon the audience's competence to allow a kind of short-hand, an economic presentation of familiar metaphors, which can be artfully elaborated to impress those who have seen them before. However, the Exeter collection can also exploit its audience's competence in a different way, one that will lead a well-educated riddlee astray, so that the "short-hand" of the familiar trope prolongs and extends the riddling process rather than abbreviating it, leading not to traditional solutions but rather to frustration and, potentially, new solutions. Because the manuscript does not offer authoritative solutions, it is impossible to know which approach to a recognized trope is required in any particular case. A hopeful riddlee cannot simply assume, for example, that a narrative about a servant and a lord will turn out to be about a human user with an implement. It may do: in *Strong Going In/Out* (R.62), for example, the *unforcuð* "brave" tool serves its wielding *frean* "lord" (2b).[98] Conversely, it may not: in *Earth-Fast* (R.49) the *þegn* "servant" (4b) does not directly serve a human user but rather its own community. In the same way, violence marks the constructive process of the manufacturing trope: in *Famous Name* (R.26), the object's initial suffering leads to an object that conveys a long list of benefits to human beings. Yet that same violence sometimes turns out to be destructive rather than constructive: in *Lone Dweller* (R.5), the object's suffering leads to annihilation rather than the creation of something new.

The fundamental uncertainty about the interpretation of riddling tropes makes these manners or modes a focus of attention in themselves. As a result, even when a trope does lead to an expected, traditional solution, the riddles require audiences to scrutinize the obvious, every day, and taken-for-granted transactions of domestic life. The Exeter Book riddles do not simply

> rely on the basic metaphors of cultural existence, those conventional tropes recognized implicitly by the members which bring together objects or ideas or movements in terms of these culturally recognized similarities.[99]

Rather, these texts ensure that the "culturally recognized similarities," which are "recognized implicitly," receive explicit, focused attention.

---

of Toronto Press, 2009) and Murphy, *Unriddling*, respectively. See also the specific discussion of the "creation" riddle in Erin Sebo, *In Enigmate: The History of a Riddle, 400–1500* (Dublin: Four Courts Press, 2018).

98 For discussion of *Hingonges Strong*, see chapter 6, below.

99 Roger D. Abrahams, "The Literary Study of the Riddle," *Texas Studies in Literature and Language* 14 (1972): 182.

For example, the shockingly casual way in which the relationship between "lords" and "thegns" in the riddles may be reversed not only marks these texts as riddles but also allows unexpected perspectives on the accepted realities of a hierarchical society. Thus, as we have seen, the riddles address weighty issues even when their subject matter appears trivial and mundane. In the following chapter, I shall argue that the riddles require the same scrutiny of the manners and modes governing reproduction and sex.

Chapter Six

The Strange Game of Sex: Asexual Reproduction and Gratuitous Sex

Introduction: Mind the Gap

Certain things go together, naturally and inevitably. *Maxims I*, for example, contains this apparently uncontroversial claim:

> Tu beoð gemæccan;
> sceal wif ond wer in woruld cennan
> bearn mid gebyrdum. (*Maxims I* 23b–5a)

(Two make a match. A woman and a man concieve children through birth.)

Like other ideas in the *Maxims* poems, the truth of these two statements is asserted by the seemingly neutral but rhetorically powerful present-tense verbs *beoð* and *sceal*, through which the text presents its statements as inarguable: this is how the world always is and how the world must be.[1] Yet there is a gap here. The conception of children through birth, should, strictly speaking, be preceded by another act, but *Maxims I* only articulates three out of the four steps of its natural and inevitable process: becoming a couple (*gemæccan*), conception (*cennan*), and

---

[1] Paul Cavill provides a full if ambivalent discussion of the use of these verbs in his *Maxims in Old English Poetry* (Cambridge: Brewer, 1999), 45–50. Cf. the discussion of the truth-claim constituted by the rhetorical use of plain, apparently unrhetorical language in Jennifer Neville, "Making Their Own Sweet Time: The Scribes of Anglo-Saxon Chronicle A," in *The Medieval Chronicle II: Proceedings of the 2nd International Congress on the Medieval Chronicle*, ed. Erik Kooper (Amsterdam: Rodopi, 2002), 168.

birth.[2] The second step in that process, sex,[3] is left unmentioned. Sex may, of course, be understood as part of conception, and thus male genitalia are sometimes described as *þa cennendan limu* "the procreating limbs."[4] However, the verb *cennan* more often refers to the end of the process: not the initiating act of fertilisation but the concluding act of bringing forth a child.[5] In this passage the use of *gebyrdum* makes that focus clear: a woman and a man bring forth children through birth, not through sex. The act that takes place between the pairing up of a man and a woman and the production of children is implied by their juxtaposition (and the editors' semi-colon),[6] and it is unlikely that anyone would argue against the inference that it is the act of sex that leads to the creation of offspring. That causal connection is obvious and natural and so need not be stated, especially in polite company.

That unheeded silence regarding the causal link between sex and reproduction provides an important starting point for my discussion of reproduction and sex in the Exeter Book riddles. Just as our expectation of a link between coupling and offspring obscures the gap in *Maxims I*, so our own imaginings regarding bodily functions can obscure what is actually presented in the riddles often labelled as "obscene," "double entendre," or "sexual."[7] Like the riddles concerning manufacturing and

---

2 See *DOE s.vv. cennan* and *gebyrdum*. The two words are fairly common, with approximately 400 and 110 occurrences respectively.
3 Throughout this discussion I use "sex" to refer to the act of coitus and its attendant activities. For the most part, these texts seem to indicate heterosexual sex, but see also discussion below.
4 See *DOE s.v. cennan*, definition A.2.d (three occurrences).
5 See *DOE s.v. cennan*, definition A1: "to bear or bring forth (a child)" (thirty-five occurrences); cf. definition A2 "to conceive or beget (a child)" (fifteen occurrences). That *cennan* does not inevitably invoke sex is suggested by its collocation with God, the Virgin Mary, and the land as well as with ordinary men and women. For God, see *DOE* definition A.2.c (four occurrences); for the Virgin Mary see A.1.a.i (seven occurrences); for the land see A.4.c (seven occurrences).
6 The connection between the two statements seems uncontroversial, but for discussion of links between individual maxims, see R. MacGregor Dawson, "The Structure of the Old English Gnomic Poems," *JEGP* 61 (1962): 14–22. T.A. Shippey is wary of asserting such links; see *Poems of Wisdom and Learning in Old English* (Cambridge: Brewer, 1976), 13–19. Elaine Tuttle Hansen argues that the maxims poems demand that their readers create links between them; see *The Solomon Complex: Reading Wisdom in Old English Poetry* (Toronto: University of Toronto Press, 1988), 155–77.
7 For discussion of this terminology, see Melane Heyworth, "*Be rihtre æwe*: Legislating and Regulating Marital Morality in Late Anglo-Saxon England" (PhD diss., University of Sydney, 2005), 171; cf. Murphy, *Unriddling*, 181–4.

implements, these texts offer unexpected perspectives on sex if we do not pass through them too quickly. I do not refer here to the much trumpeted earthiness of the double-entendre riddles, which has been discussed at length in previous studies,[8] but rather to a collection of startling characteristics that have not always been fully appreciated by modern readers: the separation that these texts, like *Maxims I*, maintain between reproduction and sex, the limited appearance of pleasure,[9] the emphasis on physical labour, and the association of sex (in almost all cases) with the upper rather than lower classes.[10] Together these characteristics add up to a discussion that is, on the surface, thoroughly improper and unspeakable.

An important point to note from the start is that, if we accept modern interpretations of the riddles, at least, only *one* out of the fifteen riddles that seem to hint at sexual actions actually designates literal sex of any kind. Similarly, while nine of the Exeter Book riddles mention reproduction, *none* of them literally describes the conventional, biological production of offspring.[11] Both the "sex" and the "reproduction" that I discuss here are metaphors for other activities.[12] Just as the potentially subversive presentations of violence and hierarchical reversals discussed in the previous chapter take place safely marked off from reality and so pose no direct challenges to the status quo, so the riddles' unspeakable commentary about sex takes place in a purely metaphorical world. It is not merely metaphor, of course, that allows the unspeakable to be spoken in the riddles; genre is important, too. As Hamnett argued long ago, riddles are recognized as not constituting a threat to

---

8 For example, Edith Whitehurst Williams, "What's So New about the Sexual Revolution? Some Comments on Anglo-Saxon Attitudes towards Sexuality in Women Based on Four Exeter Book Riddles," in *New Readings on Women in Old English Literature*, ed. Helen Damico and Alexandra Hennessey Olsen (Bloomington: Indiana University Press, 1990), 137–45.
9 This is contrary to the assertion of Williams, "What's So New," 139–40.
10 This characteristic has been discussed previously by John William Tanke, "*Wonfeax Wale*: Ideology and Figuration in the Sexual Riddles of the Exeter Book," in *Class and Gender in Early English Literature: Intersections*, ed. Britton J. Harwood and Gillian R. Overing (Bloomington: Indiana University Press, 1994), 23–7 and Ann Harleman Stewart, "Double Entendre in the Old English Riddles," *Lore and Language* 3 (1983): 48–9, but the link between sex and the lower classes is still assumed in recent scholarship. See, for example, Katherine Leah Miller, "The Semantic Field of Slavery in Old English: *Wealh, Esne, Þræl*" (PhD diss., University of Leeds, 2014), 210.
11 I will list and discuss below the fifteen riddles containing "sex" and the nine containing "reproduction."
12 For discussion of metaphor specifically in the sexual riddles, see Murphy, *Unriddling*, 51–2 and 175–219.

order, and they may even reinforce the "definitions and relations which they fictitiously call in question."[13]

Nevertheless, despite the excuse of metaphor, and despite the special exemption from censorship that riddles traditionally enjoy, critics have worried about the presentation of sex in the Exeter Book riddles and felt obliged to explain the existence of the "obscene" riddles in the context of the Christian, perhaps post-Benedictine-reform, religious community that created, consumed, and preserved texts like the Exeter Book.[14] Some of these explanations take the form of elaborate allegorical interpretations;[15] some present readings about censorship that seem to contradict the playful spirit of the riddles themselves.[16] Critics have been right to worry. The sexual content of the riddles should not simply be dismissed as inert, unchallenging, and unthreatening because of its being only metaphorical or safely denuded of risk by the riddle-genre. As I argued in the previous chapter, we should not pass over the surfaces of these riddles too quickly, and so we should not simply read through the riddles' tropes of "reproduction" and "sex" to their safe, "innocent" solutions. The outrageous surfaces presented in the riddles are made visible by the prolonged (indeed, perpetual) absence of authoritative solutions. Because we can never be completely sure what lies behind the surface, we must necessarily look hard at what lies in front, the tropes of "reproduction" and "sex."

The Trope of Reproduction

There are nine riddles in the Exeter Book that mention reproduction, the begetting of offspring. They are:

- *Cursed among Weapons* (R.20, usually solved as *sweord* "sword"),
- *Terrible Laughter* (R.33, *is* "ice" or "iceberg"),
- *Hopeful Garment* (R.35, *byrne* "mail coat"),

---

13 Ian Hamnet, "Ambiguity, Classification and Change: The Function of Riddles," *Man*, n.s., 2 (1967): 389; cf. Tanke, "*Wonfeax Wale*," 29–30.
14 See, for example, Stewart, "Double Entendre," 39. Further examples of this view will be listed in the discussion below.
15 See, for example, Mercedes Salvador, "The Key to the Body: Unlocking Riddles 42–46," in *Naked before God: Uncovering the Body in Anglo-Saxon England*, ed. Benjamin C. Withers and Jonathan Wilcox, Medieval European Studies 3 (Morgantown: West Virginia University Press, 2003), 60–96.
16 An excellent presentation of this position and overview of the scholarship behind it can be found in Tanke, "*Wonfeax Wale*," 27–30. Further examples will be listed below.

- *Belly Behind* (R.37, *blæst-belg* "bellows"),
- *Most Wretched of All* (R.39, solved by some as *mona* "moon," but many other solutions have been proposed; see appendix for full ist),
- *Circle of the Earth* (R.40, a translation of Aldhelm's Enigma 100, [*Creatura* "Creation"]),
- *Bright Warrior* (R.50, *lig* "fire"),
- *In a Corner* (R.54, *cyrn* "churn"),
- and *Mother of Many* (R.84, *wæter* "water").

If these solutions are correct – and most of them have been accepted for many years – none of these riddles literally describes parturition, the biological act of giving birth to offspring. For example, a sword cannot literally father children, water does not literally give birth to ice, and the earth does not literally give birth to the iron from which the mail-coat is made. This limitation to non-literal reproduction seems significant in comparison with Symphosius' depiction of parturition in his *Aenigmata*. While five of Symphosius' riddles use reproduction to refer to non-biological processes just as these Exeter Book riddles do,[17] eight refer to parturition itself, however unusual it might be.[18]

---

17 Aenigmata 6 (*Tegula* "Tile"), 7 (*Fumus* "Smoke"), 48 (*Murra* "Myrrh"), 49 (*Ebur* "Ivory"), and 81 (*Lagena* "Flask"). For texts see *Symphosius, The Aenigmata: An Introduction, Text and Commentary*, ed. T.J. Leary (London: Bloomsbury, 2014). Cf. also Bern 5 (*Mensa* "Table"), 14 (*Oliva* "Olive-Tree"), 19 (*Cera* "Wax"), and 29 (*Speculum* "Mirror"). For texts see *Variae Collectiones Aenigmatum Merovingicae Aetatis*, ed. Fr. Glorie, 2 vols, CCSL 133 and 133A (Turnholt: Brepols, 1968), 2: 547–610.

18 Aenigmata 14 (*Pullus in Ovo* "Chick in Egg"), 15 (*Vipera* "Viper"), 29 (*Phoenix* "Phoenix"), 35 (*Capra* "Nanny Goat"), 36 (*Porcus* "Pig"), 37 (*Mula* "Mule"), 38 (*Tigris* "Tiger"), and 92 (*Mulier quae Geminos Pariebat* "Woman Who Has Given Birth to Twins"). Cf. also Bern 8 (*Ovum* "Egg"). It is interesting to note that the Exeter Book riddle that most closely reflects the "chick and egg" tradition refers to birth only obliquely, at the end of the riddle, rather than making it the focus of wonder; see *Ten Brothers and Sisters* (R.13), usually solved as *tien cicenu* "ten chickens (or chicks)." For discussion, see Dieter Bitterli, *Say What I Am Called: The Old English Riddles of the Exeter Book and the Anglo-Latin Riddle Tradition* (Toronto: University of Toronto Press, 2009), 115–21; but note also the recent argument that this is a riddle about sheep rather than about birds: Rachel Burns, "Spirits and Skins: The *Sceapheord* of Exeter Book Riddle 13 and Holy Labour," *RES* 73 (2022), 429–41. Cf. also *They Gave Me Up for Dead* (R.9), almost always solved as *geac* "cuckoo," which starts with the "born dead" motif common in egg-riddles but leaves it undeveloped in favour of the narrative of the ungrateful stepchild. For discussion of the egg "born dead," see Dieter Bitterli, "The Survival of the Dead Cuckoo: Exeter Book *Riddle 9*," in *Riddles, Knights and Cross-Dressing Saints: Essays on Medieval English Language and Literature*, ed. Thomas Honegger (Bern: Peter Lang, 2004), 95–114.

The Strange Game of Sex 193

Aldhelm's *Aenigmata*, too, refer very frequently to birth.[19] Most of these references are, again, metaphors for non-biological processes. However, while Aldhelm's *Enigmata* "arrogat[e]" the process of birth and elide the female body,[20] they still contain seven references to the birth of biological offspring, albeit unusual forms of it.[21] In contrast, in the Exeter Book riddles, "reproduction" is only a metaphor for other processes. Lees and Overing note this "disappearance of the feminine" specifically in the riddles that are translations or reflexes of Latin riddles and speculate that it might be linked to a decline in women's access to literacy between the seventh century, when Aldhelm began the process, and the tenth century, when the Exeter Book collection was copied.[22] I agree that the change is significant, but, while women may not control the miraculous process of birth in these texts, the feminine does not entirely disappear, and my focus is different. For the present discussion, the key point is that the Exeter Book riddles could have followed their sources and analogues in the Latin riddling tradition and employed a mixture of literal and non-literal births, but they do not. Instead they develop a recognizable trope of reproduction that remains distinct from sex.

One sign of this trope is the verb *cennan* "to conceive, beget," which appears in five of the nine riddles that contain the idea of "reproduction" and in none of those that do not.[23] Along with this

---

19   Lapidge and Rosier note that over a third of them include some reference to the process. *Aldhelm: The Poetic Works*, trans. Michael Lapidge and James L. Rosier, with an appendix by Neil Wright (Cambridge: Brewer, 1985), 64.
20   Clare A. Lees and Gillian R. Overing, *Double Agents: Women and Clerical Culture in Anglo-Saxon England* (Philadelphia: University of Pennsylvania Press, 2001), 56.
21   Aenigmata 17 (*Perna* "Bivalve Mollusc"), 20 (*Apis* "Bee"), 28 (*Minotaurus* "Minotaur"), 47 (*Hirundo* "Swallow"), 82 (*Mustela* "Weasel"), 90 (*Puerpera Geminas Enixa* "Woman Bearing Twins"), and 96 (*Elefans* "Elephant"). For texts see *Aenigmata Aldhelmi*, in *Variae Collectiones Aenigmatum Merovingicae Aetatis*, ed. Fr. Glorie, CCSL 133 (Turnholt: Brepols, 1968), 377–540.
22   Lee and Overing, *Double Agents*, 59. They note, for example, that references to femininity in *Aenigma* 89 (*Arca Libraria* "bookcase") are absent in *Earth-Fast* (R.49). For my interpretation of *Earth-Fast*, see chapter 5, above.
23   *Cennan* is used widely in other Old English texts, both literally and figuratively; see *DOE, s.v. cennan*. Among the riddles, *cennan* appears only in figurative terms in *Hopeful Garment* (R.35. 2b), *Circle of the Earth* (R.40. 44b), *Bright Warrior* (R.50. 1b), and *Mother of Many* (R.84. 1b). Its appearance in *Most Wretched of All* (R.39) might be considered literal, as it refers to *ealra wihta / þara þe æfter gecyndum cenned wære* "all creatures that were born through birth" (14b–15). In context, however, the creature in question (whether it be death, moon, dream, or something else) is probably not literally begotten, and so this instance, too, is probably figurative. *Cennan* does not appear in any of the other riddles of the Exeter Book.

verb, "reproduction" often involves, unsurprisingly, "mothers" and "wombs," and sometimes even a "father" with a "womb."[24] Not all "wombs" pertain to reproduction, however. Some indicate containers, interiority, or even simply corporality without invoking the trope of reproduction. Thus, for example, a *womb* appears in *Protector* (R.17. 10a), which I have discussed in detail in chapter 3, above. Whatever its solution (I am convinced that it is a bee-hive), the riddle-subject is some sort of container for "spears," which enter and leave the *womb* in a way incompatible with the metaphor of childbirth. A *womb* also appears in *Puff-Breasted* (R.81. 11a), which has been widely interpreted as referring to a weathercock, an instrument for determining the direction of the wind; again, for my purposes it is not the solution that is important but rather that the "womb" appears as part of a series of body parts (breast, neck, head, tail, eyes, ears, foot, back, nose, sides, belly) without invoking the trope of reproduction;[25] similarly, in both *Brotherless* (R.88. 30a) and *Younger Brother* (R.93. 30a), the riddle-subject is injured in its *wombe* (30a) without any indication that offspring are involved. *Innaþe* "insides" similarly can be linked with "reproduction," as, for example, in *Hopeful Garment* (R.35. 2a), in which the earth gives birth to iron.[26] More often, however, *innaþ* indicates the interiority of a container with a sense very similar to *innan* "inside, from within."[27] Three of the riddles, *Protector*, *Brotherless*, and *Younger Brother*, emphasize that interiority is the key characteristic of the riddle-subjects by including both *womb* and *innaþ*. That is, these are riddles about containers. The presence of a womb is thus indicative, but it can also point to tropes other than that of reproduction.

---

24 Mothers appear in *Terrible Laughter* (R.33. 9a), *Circle of the Earth* (R.40. 45b), *Mother of Many Races* (R.41. 2a), and *Mother of Many* (R.84. 4a). Wombs appear in *No Escape* (R.3. 48a), *Belly Behind* (R.37. 1b), and *Circle of the Earth* (R.40. 45b). A father (along with a womb) appears in *Belly Behind* (R.37. 8b). Closely related are *Barked, Wavered* (R.87. 1b) and *The Creature Had a Belly* (R.89. 2a); all three contain a *wamb* and probably share the same solution, *blæst-belg* "bellows." The last of these three is too fragmentary to reward much scrutiny, but I shall return to the first two later in this chapter.

25 *Wamb* also appears as one of a series of body parts in *Large Belly* (R.18. 3a), *Man Woman Horse* (R.36.3 b), and *Twelve Hundred Heads* (R.86. 5a).

26 This text is discussed in more detail in chapter 5, above.

27 The *DOE, s.v. innoþ*, presents "womb, uterus" as part of a long list of abdominal organs indicated by this word. See also *DOE s.v. innan*. The word appears in *They Gave Me Up for Dead* (R.9. 3a), *Protector* (R.17. 2b and 9b), *Hardest and Sharpest* (R.28. 7b), *Brotherless* (R.88. 29b), *Belly Behind* (R.37. 6a), and *Younger Brother* (R.93. 17b).

The final characteristic that defines this trope is the subject matter conveyed by it. The trope of reproduction, like its equivalent in Aldhelm's *Ænigmata*, usually pertains to natural processes rather than manufacturing: ice gives birth to water, the earth gives birth to metal, and flint and steel give birth to fire,[28] while man-made implements, discussed in the previous chapter, come into being through tropes of torture rather than birth. Regardless of the presence or absence of particular verbs or concepts, however, and even if we fail to interpret the metaphor and arrive at a satisfactory solution (as with *Most Wretched of All*, R.39, for example), it is still possible to recognize the trope through the idea of paradoxical reproduction, "offspring" that are not literally "born." Another key indication of this trope, then, is wonder. Some riddles, for example, specify that the "birth" is attended by wonders, while others inform us that mothers are born from their own daughters and sons from their own fathers.[29]

This is, then, a rather simple trope. It is of interest mainly because of what it, like *Maxims I*, lacks: reference to sex. On the one hand, this lack might seem surprising, for, although the "reproduction" in these texts refers to non-biological production and thus has nothing literally to do with sexual contact, it would seem reasonable for metaphorical "reproduction" to derive from metaphorical "sex." On the other hand, the absence of an explicit reference to sex might not seem surprising at all, given the general reticence on the subject in the corpus of early medieval English literature.[30] While the absence of even a euphemistic reference to sex is entirely predictable for *Maxims I*, however, its absence in the Exeter Book riddles is worthy of note, for the Exeter Book riddles are notorious for talking about sex. Yet the trope of reproduction in these texts is asexual.

---

28 See *Terrible Laughter* (R.33), *Hopeful Garment* (R.35), and *Bright Warrior* (R.50) respectively.
29 Wonder appears widely in the riddles, but for wonders attached specifically to "reproduction," see *Hopeful Garment* (R.35. 1b) and *Bright Warrior* (R.50. 1b). For the paradoxical generation of parent from offspring, see *Terrible Laughter* (R.33. 9–11) and *Belly Behind* (R.37. 8). For discussions of the role of wonder in the riddles, see, for example, Sharon E. Rhodes, "*Wundor* and *Wrætlic*: The Anatomy of Wonder in the Sex Riddles," in *Riddles at Work in the Early Medieval Tradition: Words, Ideas, Interactions*, ed. Megan Cavell and Jennifer Neville, Manchester Medieval Literature and Culture 32 (Manchester: Manchester University Press, 2020), 40–56 and Peter Ramey, "Crafting Strangeness: Wonder Terminology in the Exeter Book Riddles and the Anglo-Latin Enigmata," *RES* 69 (2018): 201–15.
30 Hugh Magennis, "'No Sex Please, We're Anglo-Saxons'? Attitudes to Sexuality in Old English Prose and Poetry," *LSE*, n.s., 26 (1995): 1–27.

Thinking about Sex

Many riddles in the Exeter Book have been seen to include sexual references, but the total count varies depending upon critical inclination. Here I nominate fifteen, along with commonly accepted solutions, with the usual proviso that these solutions are provided for convenience of identification only:

- *I Travel on Foot* (R.12, *oxa* "ox"),
- *Cursed among Weapons* (R.20, *sweord* "sword"),
- *Useful to Neighbours* (R.25, *cipe* "onion"),
- *Belly Behind* (R.37, *blæst-belg* "bellows"),
- *Two Proud Ones* (R.42, *hana ond hæn* "cock and hen"),
- *Hanging Head* (R.44, *cæg* "key"),
- *Boneless* (R.45, *dah* "dough"),
- *In a Corner* (R.54, *cyrn* "churn"),
- *Head Stuck In* (R.61, *helm* "helmet"),
- *Strong Going In/Out* (R.62, *nafu-gar* "auger"),
- *Shining with Gold* (R.63, *glas-fæt* "glass beaker"),
- *Warrior's Companion* (R.80, *horn* "horn"),
- *Barked, Wavered* (R.87, *blæst-belg* "bellows"),
- *The Creature Had a Belly* (R.89, *blæst-belg*),
- *Forged by Hammer* (R.91, *cæg* "key").

Of these riddles, only one refers to literal, albeit non-human, sex: *Two Proud Ones*. Yet, while the sex in *Two Proud Ones* is literal, the *hwitloc fæmne* "fair-haired maiden" and her companion can be taken as metaphors for a human couple. I will be discussing most of these riddles in more detail below.

Before looking at individual texts, however, it is worth thinking briefly about the broad generalizations that we as modern readers may bring to a discussion of sex. We generally assume that the biological aim of sex is offspring; Christianity (particularly, but not uniquely) associates it with sin;[31] and modern Western society associates it with

---

31 This is, of course, a sweeping generalization, but I refer here to contemporary expectations of early medieval Christian views rather than the history of Christian theology about sex through the centuries. For that history, see, for example, Peter Brown, *The Body and Society: Men, Women, and Sexual Renunciation in Early Christianity* (New York: Columbia University Press, 1988), and Kyle Harper, *From Shame to Sin: The Christian Transformation of Sexual Morality in Late Antiquity* (Cambridge, MA: Harvard University Press, 2013).

pleasure. Scholars working on the sexual riddles of the Exeter Book have thus (unsurprisingly) framed these texts within narratives of reproduction, sin, and pleasure. The most persuasive of these has been the narrative of the sexual riddles functioning as tests of morality for readers and listeners: unwary riddle-solvers are led by these apparently salacious texts to reveal their unreformed desires, which can then be triumphantly corrected by an authority wielding the sanctioned, innocent solution.[32] Such narratives aim to explain the presence of these texts within a manuscript created in a religious community.[33] Previous scholarship has focused on explaining why, given that the topic seems to be forbidden elsewhere, sex is allowed here, in a deluxe manuscript that is a product of the Benedictine Reform period and listed among the legacies made by a bishop in 1072 to his cathedral. The analysis that follows is, of course, indebted to the many excellent discussions that have addressed that provocative and urgent question, but I would like to focus attention instead on the nature of the sex itself, for modern readers' knowledge of Christian attitudes towards sex, along with their knowledge of Freud, may have obscured some of the qualities of

---

32 Influential examples include: Reinhard Gleißner, *Die "zweideutigen" altenglischen Rätsel des Exeter Book in ihrem zeitgenössischen Kontext* (Frankfurt am Main: Peter Lang, 1984), 10–16; Tanke, *"Wonfeax Wale"*; Nina Rulon-Miller, "Sexual Humor and Fettered Desire in Exeter Book Riddle 12," in *Humour in Anglo-Saxon Literature*, ed. Jonathan Wilcox (Cambridge: Brewer, 2000), 99–126; Sarah L. Higley, "The Wanton Hand: Reading and Reaching into Grammars and Bodies in Old English Riddle 12," in *Naked before God: Uncovering the Body in Anglo-Saxon England*, ed. Benjamin C. Withers and Jonathan Wilcox, Medieval European Studies 3 (Morgantown: West Virginia University Press, 2003), 29–59. For reference to Freud's ideas of sexual repression in particular, see, for example *The Old English Riddles of the Exeter Book*, ed. Craig Williamson (Chapel Hill: University of North Carolina Press, 1977), 299; Stewart, "Double Entendre," 49; Tanke, *"Wonfeax Wale"*, 30; Rulon-Miller, "Sexual Humor," 122–4; see also the overview and critique in Peter Robson, "'Feorran broht': Exeter Book Riddle 12 and the Commodification of the Exotic," in *Authority and Subjugation in Writing of Medieval Wales*, ed. Ruth Kennedy and Simon Meecham-Jones (Basingstoke: Palgrave Macmillan, 2008), 76–83. Note, however, John D. Niles' distinction between such "catch" riddles and riddles with "erotic overtones"; see *God's Exiles and English Verse: On the Exeter Anthology of Old English Poetry* (Exeter: University of Exeter Press, 2019), 171–6.
33 Cf. discussion in Glenn Davis, "The Exeter Book Riddles and the Place of Sexual Idiom in Old English Literature," in *Medieval Obscenities*, ed. Nicola McDonald (York: York Medieval Press, 2006), 39–41; Mercedes Salvador, "The Key to the Body: Unlocking Riddles 42–46," in *Naked before God: Uncovering the Body in Anglo-Saxon England*, ed. Benjamin C. Withers and Jonathan Wilcox, Medieval European Studies 3 (Morgantown: West Virginia University Press, 2003), 60–96; Niles, *God's Exiles*, 165–79.

these texts.[34] I argue that Exeter Book riddles present a much stranger and more challenging game than a test for the unwary. As already indicated, reproduction in these texts is disconnected from sex. In addition, as the discussion below will demonstrate, in these riddles sex happens without babies, there is no reference to sin, pleasure is absent more often than not, and the relationship between sex and class contradicts scholarly expectations that persist despite being disproven again and again.

Metaphor

As has already been noted, with only one exception, none of the Exeter Book riddles is literally about sex. Metaphor is thus central to this discussion; what appears in the riddles is "sex," not sex. When I first began thinking about this topic, I felt that this unavoidable fact was unfortunate, as it means that, even here, in one of the very few texts in the corpus of Old English literature that openly mentions sex, there is never any direct comment on it. A brief foray into the world of cognitive linguistics, however, suggests that the presentation of sex in metaphors may convey an important advantage. Proponents of cognitive linguistics argue that metaphors help us to understand and express ideas by correlating the target idea with our lived experience.[35] This means that the surface of a metaphor should match up with our material reality and physical experiences. The theoretical premise can be backed up with common sense, for we do not make metaphors out of things that are unknown to us or to things that do not accurately reflect our own experience. Thus I would not create or use a metaphor based on Somali

---

34 See discussion in Jennifer Neville, "Speaking the Unspeakable: Appetite for Deconstruction in Exeter Book Riddle 12," *ES* 93 (2012): 520–1.

35 The idea of "primary metaphors," that is, metaphors that are associated with concepts that are directly experienced and perceived, is generally attributed to J.E. Grady, "Foundations of Meaning: Primary Metaphors and Primary Scenes" (PhD diss., University of California, Berkeley, 1997). See, for example, George Lakoff and Mark Johnson, *Metaphors We Live By*, 2nd ed. (Chicago: University of Chicago Press, 2003), 245; Vyvyan Evans and Melanie Green, *Cognitive Linguistics: An Introduction* (New York: Routledge, 2006), 305; Paula Lenz Costa Lima, "About Primary Metaphors," *Delta* 22 (2006): 110. For detailed applications of these ideas to metaphor in Old English poetry, see Antonina Harbus, *Cognitive Approaches to Old English Poetry* (Cambridge: Boydell and Brewer, 2012), and Karin Olsen, *Conceptualizing the Enemy in Early Northwest Europe: Metaphors of Conflict and Alterity in Anglo-Saxon, Old Norse, and Early Irish Poetry* (Turnhout: Brepols, 2016).

agricultural techniques, because I know nothing about them, and early medieval English people would not create or use a metaphor based on the operation of a computer, because computers were unknown to them. For the present discussion, what this means is that the sexual activities that are deployed in the Exeter Book riddles as metaphors for washing dishes, kneading dough, picking onions, making butter, unlocking doors, getting dressed, and so on should reflect the lived experience of sex in early medieval England.[36] Counterintuitively, then, the metaphorical nature of "sex" in the riddles may provide a kind of guarantee of accuracy. If the riddles were literally describing sex, we would not be able to take them at face value because of the possibly figurative nature of their language. Because they are describing metaphorical "sex" to characterize other acts, however, their depiction of sex should be an accurate representation of the lived experience of people in early medieval England. This is an exciting prospect, especially given the unexpected qualities that sex has in these texts. Let us turn to those qualities now, keeping the focus as much as possible upon what the sexual surfaces of these metaphorical texts can reveal about the view of sex in early medieval England rather than on the material culture that has supplied the riddles' most widely accepted solutions.

The Trope of Sex

Modern readers have had little difficulty identifying the sexual riddles, even when they do not want to talk about them,[37] and there have been several scholars who have already set out the parameters of what I call the trope of sex in the Exeter Book riddles. Thus Ann Harlemann Stewart identifies a lexicon of erotic double entendre;[38] Julie Coleman lists semantic fields for sexual euphemism;[39] Glenn Davis describes a "sexual

---

36 See, respectively, *I Travel on Foot* (R.12), *Boneless* (R.45), *Useful to Neighbours* (R.25), *In a Corner* (R.54), *Hanging Head* (R.44), and *Head Stuck In* (R.61).
37 See, for example, Frederick Tupper Jr, ed., *The Riddles of the Exeter Book* (London: Ginn, 1910), 96, where he argues for one as opposed to the two "motives" proposed by Prehn in *Wonfeax Wale* but does not say what they are. Thorpe simply declines to translate the sexual riddles; see *Codex Exoniensis: A Collection of Anglo-Saxon Poetry*, ed. and trans. Benjamin Thorpe (London: Society of Antiquaries of London, 1842), 407, where he presents *Useful to Neighbours* (R.25) untranslated alongside facing translations of *Wob* (R.23), *Six Letters* (R.24), and *Famous Name* (R.26).
38 "Double Entendre."
39 "Sexual Euphemism in Old English," *NM* 93 (1992), 93–8.

idiom";[40] and Patrick Murphy finds in these texts "a very recognizable lexicon of dirty riddling": "male tumescence," useful service, "manual stimulation," compounds with *wlanc* "proud," references to foolishness, and the need for concealment,[41] as well as the coy compounds *nathwær* and *nathwæt*.[42] I would add to Murphy's list Coleman's idea of "nearness" or confinement in a tight place.[43] Most of these can be found in *Useful to Neighbours* (R.25), every critic's favourite choice to exemplify the sexual riddles:

> Ic eom wunderlicu wiht,   wifum on hyhte,
> neahbuendum nyt;   nængum sceþþe
> burgsittendra,   nymþe bonan anum.
> Staþol min is steapheah,   stonde ic on bedde,
> 5 neoþan ruh nathwær.   Neþeð hwilum
> ful cyrtenu   ceorles dohtor,
> modwlonc meowle,   þæt heo on mec gripeð,
> ræseð mec on reodne,   reafað min heafod,
> fegeð mec on fæsten.   Feleþ sona
> 10 mines gemotes,   seo þe mec nearwað,
> wif wundenlocc.   Wæt bið þæt eage. (*Useful to Neighbours*)

(I am a wondrous creature, a joy to women, useful to those dwelling nearby. I harm no town-dwellers, except my slayer alone. My foundation is towering high; I stand up in bed, shaggy somewhere or other below. Sometimes a very fair freeman's daughter, a proud-minded maiden, dares

---

40 "Exeter Book Riddles and the Place of Sexual Idiom."
41 Patrick J. Murphy, *Unriddling the Exeter Riddles* (University Park: Pennsylvania State University Press, 2011), 176–7.
42 *Nathwær* and *nathwæt* appear only in the riddles, and in five out of their six occurrences the referent is sexual: see *Useful to Neighbours* (R.25.5a), *Boneless* (R.45.1b), *In a Corner* (R.54.5b), *Head Stuck In* (R.61.9a), and *Strong Going In/Out* (R.62.8a). *Younger Brother* (R.93.27a) provides the exception: there *nathwæt* is used in an apparently non-sexual context. For discussion of these compounds, see Matti Rissanen, "*Nathwæt* in the Exeter Book Riddles," *ANQ* 24 (1986): 116–20.
43 Coleman identifies nearness as a euphemism for sex ("Sexual Euphemism," 96) but provides no textual examples other than *Useful to Neighbours* (R.25), discussed immediately below. *Head Stuck In* (R.61.6b) and *Strong Going In/Out* (R.62.8a) provide support for the double-entendre meaning of "nearness," but it should be noted that "nearness" appears in many riddles without any apparent sexual implication: see, for example, *No Escape* (R.3.1b), *Nose in Confinement* (R.10.1b), *White Neck* (R.15.24b), *Captives* (R.52.3b), *Towering Tree* (R.53.13a), *Clothed in Red* (R.71.4b), *Mother of Many* (R.84.6a), etc.

to grip me, rush upon my red self, ravages my head, fixes me in a confined place. The woman with curly hair[44] who confines me immediately senses the encounter with me. The eye will be wet.)

In order here we find (male) usefulness (*nytt* 2b) and tumescence (*stonde ic on bedde* "I stand up in bed" 4b), *nathwær* "I do not know where" (5a), female pride (*modwlonc* 7a), a female grip (*heo on mec griped* "she grips me" 7b), and what could be considered either penetration or concealment (*feged mec on fæsten* "she fixes me in a confined space" 9a). We might also note the active role taken by the woman,[45] the reference to joy (*hyhte* 1b), and potentially suggestive body parts (the *heafod* "head" 8b, and the wet *eage* "eye" 11b).[46] Despite the irresistible phallic images conjured by this text, most readers accept that it describes a women handling an onion.

As already mentioned, critics often take *Useful to Neighbours* as the model for the sexual riddles in the Exeter Book. It does usefully showcase many of the characteristics found in these riddles, but it is worth noting that, alongside this heterosexual model for sex, there are potentially other models, too. Thus the man urging on the hard, sharp, strong, and bold riddle-object both *æftanweardne* "from behind" (5b) and *nathwær* "I do not know where" (8a) in *Strong Going In/Out* (R.62) is probably

---

44 Like most, my translation assumes that the *wif wundenlocc* is the subject of the verb, but Murphy makes a persuasive argument that it is the victim that is the "woman with curly locks," despite its phallic disguise (*Unriddling*, 232–3). For the translation "curly hair" for *wundenlocc*, see Megan Cavell, "Old English 'Wundenlocc' Hair in Context," *MÆ* 82 (2013): 119–25.
45 This depiction of active, sexual women has received considerable attention in previous discussions. See, for example, Williams, "What's So New," 137–45; Stewart, "Double Entendre," 46–7; Murphy, *Unriddling*, 177.
46 For more detailed discussion, see Murphy, who devotes a whole chapter to this riddle (*Unriddling*, 221–34); in particular, see his discussion of the potential sexual referents for the "eye," which may hint at either the aperture of the penis or the vagina, and the wetness, which may indicate semen or vaginal fluid (229–30); cf. also Rulon-Miller, "Sexual Humor," 110–11 and Stewart, "Double Entendre," 46. Most translators specify that the literal and metaphorical eyes both belong to the woman; see, for example, *The Exeter Book, Part II: Poems IX–XXXII*, ed. and trans. William S. Mackie, EETS, o.s., 194 (London: Humphry Milford and Oxford University Press, 1934), 117; Craig Williamson, trans., *A Feast of Creatures: Anglo-Saxon Riddle-Songs* (Philadelphia: University of Pennsylvania Press, 1982), 83; Michael Alexander, trans., *Old English Riddles from the Exeter Book*, 2nd ed. (London: Anvil Press, 2007), 37; Gerry Murphy, trans., "Call Me Fabulous," in *The Word Exchange: Anglo-Saxon Poems in Translation*, ed. Gregg Delanty and Michael Matto (New York: W. W. Norton, 2011), 163.

using a poker, but he seems to be having rear-entry sex with a partner who could be either male or female. Similarly, it is not clear whether the owner of the *cuþe hol* "familiar hole" (5b) greeted by the stiff, hard thing hanging by a man's thigh in *Hanging Head* (R.44) is male or female. The same ambiguity could attend the conclusion of *Downward Nose* (R.21). The riddle-subject states that it can only carry out its activities

> gif me teala þenaþ
> hindeweardre,   þæt biþ hlaford min. (*Downward Nose* 14b–15)

(if he who is my lord serves me well from behind.)

The preceding lines of the riddle describe the components and activity of ploughing; in this context, it is clear that the text here describes the necessity for a ploughman to direct a plough skilfully. The activity that is hinted at is probably rear-entry sex between a male-female couple, but the possibility of a male-male coupling is only eliminated by the discovery of the solution, the *sulh* "plough," which happens to be a feminine noun. That grammatical gender is suggested by adjective-endings in lines 9a and 15a, but, as Afros has argued, grammatical gender in the riddles may be manipulated.[47] In this case, for example, the adjective-endings might be understood as modifying the (unstated) feminine noun *wiht* "creature," which is the subject of twenty-six of the Exeter Book riddles.[48] The significance of the grammatical gender in 9a and 15a thus remains uncertain and in play until the solution has been found. A less resolvable ambiguity attends upon the activity in the three riddles solved as *blæst-belg* "bellows": *Belly Behind* (R.37), *Barked,*

---

[47] Elena Afros, "Linguistic Ambiguities in Some Exeter Book *Riddles*," *N&Q* 52 (2005): 436. Cf., however, the counterargument in John D. Niles, *Old English Enigmatic Poems and the Play of the Texts* (Turnhout: Brepols, 2006), 105–9 and discussions in Murphy, *Unriddling*, 186 and Corinne Dale, "Freolic, Sellic: An Ecofeminist Reading of Modor Monigra (R.84)," in *Riddles at Work in the Early Medieval Tradition: Words, Ideas, Interactions*, ed. Megan Cavell and Jennifer Neville, Manchester Medieval Literature and Culture 32 (Manchester: Manchester University Press, 2020), 176–92.

[48] See *Large Belly* (R.18), *Cursed among Weapons* (R.20), *Wob* (R.23), *Six Letters* (R.24), *Useful to Neighbours* (R.25), *Air-Vessel* (R.29), *Eager to Go* (R.31), *Grind against Grit* (R.32), *Terrible Laughter* (R.33), *Feeds Cattle* (R.34), *Man Woman Horse* (R.36), *Belly Behind* (R.37), *Greedy for Youth-Mirth* (R.38), *Most Wretched of All* (R.39), *Mother of Many Races* (R.41), *Two Proud Ones* (R.42), *Four Creatures* (R.51), *Turning Wood* (R.56), *Abounding in Song* (R.57), *Word-Spell* (R.67), *Creature Went Away* (R.68), *Sings through Its Sides* (R.70a), *Mother of Many* (R.84), *Twelve Hundred Heads* (R.86), *Barked, Wavered* (R.87), and *The Creature Had a Belly* (R.89).

Wavered (R.87), and the fragmentary *The Creature had a Belly* (R.89). All three describe activities that may be interpreted as the penetration of a male into a female partner, but in fact no partner is mentioned. This means that the activity may be male-female sex, male-male sex, or, indeed, masturbation.[49] *Forged by Hammer* (R.91) creates a different kind of ambiguity. It has traditionally been solved as "key," but an argument has also been made in support of "keyhole."[50] The problem to be addressed by any solution lies in the ambiguous double-entendre surface, which seems simultaneously to present both a metaphorical penis, a thing with a *nebbe* "nose" (8b) that is to *hnitan* "thrust" (4a) and *ascufan*, "shove" (6a), and a metaphorical vagina or anus which *begine þæt me ongean sticað* "swallows what pricks against me" (3) and is *hindan þyrel* "pierced from behind" (5b). A non-sexual solution can resolve that apparently androgynous body – Phyllis Portnoy proposes "brooch" or "buckle" (the Old English word could be *preon*), objects that possess both a receptacle and a piercing part[51] – but until such a solution is found a reader must ponder a sexual act that does not fit the heterosexual norm. The discussion that follows below focuses on heterosexual sex, but the presence of these other models for sexual acts should not be forgotten.

Sex without Reproduction

It seems obvious and natural that heterosexual sex should lead to reproduction in an early medieval context, at least. Of the fifteen sexual riddles in the Exeter Book, however, twelve fail to mention that babies may result from the sexual activity that they describe.[52] *Boneless* (R.45) provides a usefully brief case in point:

---

49 As David Clark has noted, medieval masturbation is a topic that has not received much scholarly attention; see his "Discourses of Masturbation: The (Non)solitary Pleasures of the (Medieval) Text," *Men and Masculinities* 20 (2017): 455.
50 For an overview of the argument through the years, see the appendix, below. For discussion of "key," see, for example, Williamson, *Old English Riddles*, 388–91. For "keyhole," see Williams, "What's So New," 142–4. For a critique of both solutions, see Phyllis Portnoy, "*Laf*-Craft in Five Old English Riddles (K-D 5, 20, 56, 71, 91)," *Neophil* 97 (2013): 570–3.
51 Portnoy, "*Laf*-Craft," 573–6.
52 Chris Bishop argues almost exactly the opposite in his stimulating article, "The Erotic Poetry of the Exeter Book," *Journal of the Australian Early Medieval Association* 1 (2005): 7–26. The discussion that follows strives to support my count.

> Ic on wincle gefrægn   weaxan nathwæt,
> þindan ond þunian,   þecene hebban;
> on þæt banlease   bryd grapode,
> hygewlonc hondum;   hrægle þeahte
> þrindende þing   þeodnes dohtor. (*Boneless*)

(I heard of something – I do not know what – getting bigger in a corner, swelling and thrusting upwards, raising up its covering. A proud-minded woman grabbed that boneless thing with her hands. The prince's daughter covered the swelling thing with her garment.)

The text contains insistent double entendre: it obtrudes with the coy word, *nathwæt* "I do not know what," states three times that the riddle-object grows larger, and describes a proud woman grabbing the riddle-object and putting it under her clothing. In this context, I wonder whether the mention of a "bone" here, even in the negative, is potentially suggestive, too, although there is no evidence for the use of the word "bone" to refer to an erection at this early date.[53] Even if *banleas* "boneless" fails to raise any eyebrows, however, it would take considerable effort to avoid the suggested sexual meaning in this text: what is described seems to be a penis becoming erect so that its presence is visible under its owner's clothing, whereupon a woman seizes it with her hands and puts it under her clothing, presumably, into her own vagina. At the same time, the actions described in the text also correspond equally well to the process of making bread-dough:[54] having left the mixture of leavening, flour, and water to rise

---

53 See *OED* s.v. bone, definition 11. The earliest date for this meaning of "bone" is 1654, but its use is mostly based in North America in the twentieth century. Perhaps related is the entry in the *Online Middle English Dictionary*, s.v. bon, which lists "to put a bone in the hood" as meaning "to cuckold (one's husband)" in approximately 1500. See *The Middle English Dictionary*, ed. Robert E. Lewis, *et al* (Ann Arbor: University of Michigan Press, 1952–2001); online edition in the *Middle English Compendium*, ed. Frances McSparran, *et al* (Ann Arbor: University of Michigan Library, 2000–18): http://quod.lib.umich.edu/m/middle-english-dictionary/ (accessed 15 April 2021). I am grateful to Jane Roberts for alerting me to this example (personal communication, 27 March 2021).

54 It is worth noting that the bread made here is an elite, high status product, not the everyday, unleavened bread consumed in large quantities by early medieval English people. See Debby Banham, *Food and Drink in Anglo-Saxon England* (Stroud: Tempus, 2004), 16–24 and also the discussion by Martha Bayliss and Debby Banham at *The Early Bread Project*, https://earlybread.wordpress.com. The elite status is important; I will return to it later in this chapter.

in a warm corner, the woman returns to find it swollen up, whereupon she grips it with her hands to knead it and distribute the gas released by the fermentation process, covers it with her garment (perhaps an apron?), and leaves it to rise again. This process is what most scholars believe to be the correct, authoritative solution to the riddle.

If it is true that the surface of metaphors provides a reflection of the lived experience of people in early medieval England, what we have here is a description of manual manipulation leading to intercourse, with the female partner taking a dominant, active role. What we do not have is any suggestion that the act leads to babies. It would not require much to add a "bread-baby" as the final conclusion of the woman's encounter with the *banleas* riddle-object, but the text concludes without one.[55] The absence of offspring here is not significant in itself; rather, what is significant is the fact that this absence is characteristic of the sexual riddles in general. When the woman rushes upon the "onion-penis" in *Useful to Neighbours* (R.25) and fixes it in her "tight place," the result is not a baby but the wetness of an eye. The couple copulating openly outdoors in *Two Proud Ones* (R.42) produces no children. The man who introduces his hanging thing into the well-known hole in *Hanging Head* (R.44) does not engender a child; nor does the man sticking his head up into the narrow thing offered by a loyal lady in *Head Stuck In* (R.61); nor does the hard thing that prods and shoves against a hole from behind in *Forged by Hammer* (R.91). *Shining with Gold* (R.63) is fragmentary due to damage in the manuscript, but what remains does not suggest that any offspring is produced by the kissing and fondling enjoyed by the *tillic esne* "good slave" (5a) and the gold adorned "lady" that is the riddle-subject.[56] Other riddles suggest sexual contact that may or may not involve actual coitus; regardless, no children are produced. Thus neither the noble lady who lays her hand on the riddle-subject in *Warrior's Companion* (R.80) nor the Welsh slave apparently masturbating by the fire in *I Travel by Foot* (R.12) bears a child as a result of her activity. I will return to many of these texts later in this chapter. What is important

---

55 The expression "bun in the oven" seems to date from the 20th century; see *OED s.v.* "bun" (definition 2.a, with the earliest listed example from 1951).
56 The difference in status between the members of this couple may be as suggestive of impropriety as the activity itself. For discussion of the term *esne* in the riddles, see Miller, "Semantic Field of Slavery," 203–13, with reference to *Shining with Gold* on 212–13.

for this part of the discussion is that, despite what a modern romance novelist might say,[57] these acts of sex do not lead to babies.

Exceptions to the "Rule"

Twelve out of the fifteen sexual riddles do not mention sex and offspring together, but there are three that do: *Cursed among Weapons* (R.20), *Belly Behind* (R.37), and *In a Corner* (R.54). All three are special cases, exceptions to the generalization that I have sketched out in the previous section. I have already discussed *Cursed among Weapons* at length above in chapter 4, but it is worth looking at one portion of it again in this context.

>   Ic me wenan ne þearf
> þæt me bearn wræce   on bonan feore,
> gif me gromra hwylc   guþe genægeð;
> 20 ne weorþeð sio mægburg   gemicledu
> eaforan minum   þe ic æfter woc,
> nymþe ic hlafordleas   hweorfan mote
> from þam healdende   þe me hringas geaf.
> Me bið forð witod,   gif ic frean hyre,
> 25 guþe fremme,   swa ic gien dyde
> minum þeodne on þonc,   þæt ic þolian sceal
> bearngestreona.   Ic wiþ bryde ne mot
> hæmed habban,   ac me þæs hyhtplegan
> geno wyrneð,   se mec geara on
> 30 bende legde;   forþon ic brucan sceal
> on hagostealde   hæleþa gestreona. (*Cursed among Weapons* 17b–31)

(I need not hope for a son to avenge me on the life of my killer, if some enemy attacks me with war. The family will not be increased with my descendants, those whom I engendered after me, unless I, lordless, am permitted to turn away from the ruler who gave me rings. Henceforth, if I obey my lord [and] perform battle as I hitherto did in gratitude to my lord, it will be ordained that I must do without the begetting of children. I am not permitted to have sex with a woman; rather, the one who years

---

57 See, for example, the discussion of how Stephenie Meyer's *Twilight* novels have adopted the romance trope of sex inevitably followed by pregnancy in Laurie Essig, *Love, Inc.: Dating Apps, the Big White Wedding, and Chasing the Happily Never-after* (Oakland: University of California Press, 2019), 35–8.

ago placed me in bonds refuses me that joyful play. Therefore I must enjoy the treasures of warriors in celibacy.)

Here we certainly do have both sex and offspring, but what is important is that, as in *Maxims I*, the text juxtaposes sex and childbirth but does not acknowledge the causal relationship between those two acts. In fact, *Cursed among Weapons* presents these acts as two distinct events, each with a value that is not dependent on each other. The creation of offspring is not presented as a consequence of sex; rather, it precedes it. Thus the riddle-subject, the "bachelor-sword," laments *first* that it will have no children to avenge its death in war or to continue its family line into the future. Then, in a grammatically independent clause, it laments the prohibition that denies it *hæmed* "sex" (28a). The connection between these two acts is, of course, natural, obvious, and undeniable. Nevertheless, the text does not state it, and the reversal of the causal order means that the gap between sex and offspring for which I have been arguing is not overturned here.

Belly Behind (R.37), the first of three riddles about the *blæst-belg* "bellows," is a text of two halves. The first half, already mentioned above as an example of potentially male-male sex or masturbation, seems to describe a man bringing his penis to a successful ejaculation:

Ic þa wihte geseah – womb wæs on hindan
þriþum aþrunten. Þegn folgade,
mægenrofa man, ond micel hæfde
gefered þæt hit felde, fleah þurh his eage. (*Belly Behind* 1–4)

(I saw the creature: its belly was behind it, swollen with power. Its thegn, a powerful man, attended it and had accomplished much so that what filled it flew [out] through its eye.)

Here we have male tumescence – either the riddle-object (the "penis") or the *womb* "belly" behind it[58] is *þriþum aþrunten* "swollen with power" (2a) – and then the creature's contents ("semen") are expelled from an *eage* "eye" (4b), here most likely the aperture of the "penis" rather than a "vagina." The mention of the thegn, the *mægenrofa man* "powerful man"

---

58 The belly behind a metaphorical "penis" would presumably be a "scrotum." The shared element between *blæst-belg* "bellows" and *herþ-belg* "scrotum" might be part of the game here: a riddle-solver ultimately needs to think about bags rather than bellies.

(3a), who serves the riddle-object superimposes the implement trope on top of the sexual imagery: the riddle-object is both a body part and a tool served by its thegn.[59] The second half of the riddle thus requires its audience to sustain both tropes at once to understand the imagery fully:

Ne swylteð he symle,   þonne syllan sceal
innað þam oþrum,   ac him eft cymeð
bot in bosme,   blæd biþ aræred;
he sunu wyrceð,   bið him sylfa fæder. (*Belly Behind* 5–8)

(He never dies, when he is obliged to give his innards to another one; rather, a remedy comes again to his bosom, [and] his splendour is raised up [again]. He produces a son, who is a father to himself.[60])

With the implement trope in play, we see both the bellows, the tool that expels its contents only for its *blæd* "breath" (7b) to return again to its bosom, and the "penis," which might seem to "die" after expelling its contents but whose *blæd* "glory" is raised up again when it has its next erection.[61]

The key vocabulary in this second half of the text, however, leaves behind the trope of sex and moves incrementally into the trope of reproduction. Thus we have first *innað* (6a), which can refer back to the "belly" introduced in the first half of the riddle and also metaphorically convey the interiority of the bellows.[62] *Bosm* (7a), however, although it can mean "womb" in very special circumstances, normally refers to the chest rather than the abdomen when it is applied to literal bodies;[63] its

---

59   For discussion of the implement trope, see chapter 5, above. The use of the word "tool" to indicate a penis is not attested before 1563 in the *OED* (*s.v.* "tool," definition 2b), but *The Middle English Dictionary* contains a good example of it from a 1425 text (*s.v.* "tol," definition 1d). I am grateful to Jane Roberts for this reference (personal communication, 27 March 2021).
60   Or: "who is himself the father."
61   For these two definitions of *blæd*, see *DOE* definitions 2.1.b and 3.
62   See *DOE s.v. innoð.* For "womb" see definition 6.
63   For the meaning "chest, breast," see *DOE s.v.* bosm, definition 1; for "womb," see definition 1a, where the "breast" of the Virgin Mary is also the site of the incarnation, her womb. The equation of "womb" and "breast" seems to be unique to Mary (cf. also *DOE s.v. breost*, definition 3a). Otherwise the terminology for the thorax and the abdomen seems to be distinct. I have attempted to read this text in the context of Mary and the Incarnation, interpreting the "breath" in the last line as a reference to the Holy Spirit, but I am not convinced that it is appropriate here, both because of the insistently male performance in the first half of the riddle and because of the repetitive nature of the rebirth in the second half.

appearance here, therefore, with the figurative sense of "interiority," continues the movement away from the sexual surface of the riddle towards the target of the metaphor.[64] Most important, of course, is the final line: *he sunu wyrceð, bið him sylfa fæder* "he produces a son, who is father to himself" (8). Here we find the paradoxical reproduction exemplified in *Terrible Laughter* (R.33), in which ice gives birth to her own mother, water. The twist that overturns the sexual surface of the riddle is, in fact, the trope of reproduction. Even here, then, where sex and reproduction are presented side by side, the act of sex remains distinct from the act of reproduction, and there is no causal link between the two.

The final exception, *In a Corner* (R.54), presents a notoriously explicit image of vigorous sex between a *hyse* "young man" (1a) and the "womanchurn" standing in the corner, which I will address in more detail later in this chapter.[65] For this part of the discussion, what is important is its conclusion:

>   Hyre weaxan ongon
> under gyrdelse   þæt oft gode men
> ferðþum freogað   ond mid feo bicgað. (*In a Corner* 10b–12)

(Under her girdle something that good men cherish in their hearts and buy with money began to grow.)

In a Corner juxtaposes its description of the act of sex in its previous lines with what seems to be the inception of pregnancy – the starting point for the children that "good men cherish in their hearts," the natural and obvious result of the sex. In this case, even I would not attempt to deny that the text refers to the causal relationship between the act and the product; although it does not explicitly say "therefore" or "consequently," it is clear that it is the young man's thrusting of the *stiþes nathwæt* "stiff something-or-other" (5b) under the woman's *gyrdels* "girdle" (4b) that has led to something beginning to grow *under gyrdelse* "under her girdle" (11a). This baldly stated connection between sex and pregnancy is, then, an undeniable contravention of my argument that sex and reproduction are not linked in the Exeter Book riddles. The concluding twist of the text in its final half-line, however, is heightened by

---

64   For the sense of interiority, see *DOE s.v. bosm*, definition 4.
65   See also D.K. Smith, "Humor in Hiding: Laughter between the Sheets in the Exeter Book Riddles," in *Humour in Anglo-Saxon England*, ed. Jonathan Wilcox (Cambridge: Brewer, 2000), 79–98.

the statement of that usually unstated causal relationship between sex and offspring. The first eleven and a half lines blatantly describe a thoroughly improper sexual act (the couple are not married; the position is not the sanctioned missionary position;[66] the location is not private), without any break in the logical surface to direct an audience to interpret the text metaphorically. An audience that has any experience of riddles, especially riddles in the early medieval English tradition, will be expecting that break, the cue that will allow the target of the metaphor to be recognized. When the break finally does come, however, it is focused not on the act of sex but on its product, on the "child" that good men not only cherish in their hearts but also buy with money. For the twist to have an impact, two important assumptions about early medieval English culture must be in place: first, fathers loved their children; and, second, men did not normally pay for those children with money. If those assumptions are correct, then *In a Corner* is probably about churning butter.[67] The text conveys that aspect of early medieval English domestic practice, however, with an unforgettably visual metaphor that leads to a punchline whose shock-value is amplified by stating the connection that is usually left unsaid; it is a final ploy to lead an audience to wonder whether this text actually describes sex rather than presenting a metaphor for sex. The pointed use of the causal connection between "sex" and product thus suggests a poet familiar with the usual characteristics of the trope. *In a Corner* really is an exception that proves the rule.

That rule – that the causal relationship between sex and offspring is omitted when sex is used as a metaphor – is a rather strange one, however. Thinking again about riddling metaphors in the context of cognitive linguistics reminds us that the key thing about the metaphor chosen to lead to an ambiguous, unknown target is that the vehicle itself should be unambiguously recognizable. In this case, the sex used as a metaphor to convey other activities should convey the essential core of what early medieval English people thought of as sex. That this essential core does not include the production of offspring is surprising, especially in the context of Christian attitudes towards sex. In a

---

66 Non-missionary sexual positions are eventually classed, alongside bestiality, homosexuality, and masturbation, as sins against nature. See Vern Bullough, *Sexual Variance and History* (New York: Wiley, 1976), 380; James A. Brundage, *Law, Sex, and Christian Society in Medieval Europe* (Chicago: University of Chicago Press, 1987), 161.

67 Most readers have thought so since Moritz Trautman first suggested this solution in 1894. "Die Auflösung der altenglischen Rätsel," *Anglia Beiblatt* 5 (1894): 46–51.

Christian context, sex can only be justified if its purpose is reproduction.[68] Of course, the riddles talk about "sex," not sex, and so there is licence for deviation from a strict, moral position. Nevertheless, in a Christian context, the sexual riddles present a very strange kind of sex, sex that lacks its sole justification and purpose. The official position may be summed up by Ælfric of Eynsham, who says, *Hit byþ swyþe scandlic, þæt eald wif sceole ceorles brucan, þonne heo forwerod byþ and teames ætealdod, ungehealtsumlice, forþan þe gesceafta ne beoþ for nanum oþran þinge asteade butan for bearnteame anum* "It is very shameful for an old woman to enjoy a man unchastely when she is worn out and too old for the begetting of children, because creations are ordained for no other thing but for the begetting of children alone."[69] Worthy of attention here is the word *gesceafta*, which I have tentatively translated as "creations."[70] In context, this word must refer either to experiences of coitus or to the sexual organs. The *Thesaurus of Old English* lists "sex, generation" as possible meanings for *gesceaft*,[71] but neither of those ideas features in dictionary definitions,[72] and Assman does not comment on the word in his edition of the letter, so I conducted my own search of the *DOE* Corpus and found that, while the other 704 instances of *gesceaft* refer to a very wide range of things that God has created (the earth, heavens, angels, humanity, natural laws, etc.), many of which are related to the idea of fruitfulness, only here does the word refer to the act or organs of sex.[73] Ælfric thus seems to be coining his own euphemism here. Whatever the precise meaning of the word, Ælfric's position is clear: sex has

---

68 For an overview of the development of ideas regarding sex from the beginnings of Christian society up to the end of the early medieval period, see Brundage, *Law, Sex, and Christian Society*, 57–175. See also Anthony Davies, "Sexual Behaviour in Later Anglo-Saxon England," in *This Noble Craft: Proceedings of the Xth Research Symposium of the Dutch and Belgian University Teachers of Old and Middle English and Historical Linguistics, Utrecht, 19–20 January 1989*, ed. Erik Kooper (Amsterdam: Rodopi, 1991), 83–105.
69 Ælfric, "Letter to Sigefyrth," in *Angelsächsische Homilien und Heiligenleben*, ed. Bruno Assmann (Kassel: Georg H. Wigand, 1889), 20.
70 I am grateful to Professor Susan Irvine for reminding me that the word appears here in the plural, not the singular: personal communication, 11 June 2016.
71 Jane Roberts and Christian Kay with Lynne Grundy, *A Thesaurus of Old English* (Glasgow: University of Glasgow, 2017), http://oldenglishthesaurus.arts.gla.ac.uk, entry 02.01.03.03 n. I believe that this definition pertains specifically to this citation from Ælfric.
72 See B-T and Clark-Hall *s.v. gesceaft*. The word has not yet been added to the *DOE*.
73 Jane Roberts proposes the translation "sexual acts" (personal communication, 27 March 2021).

no purpose other than the begetting of children. The "sex" that we find in the Exeter Book riddles, then, is truly gratuitous; it is without purpose or justification and thus, from Ælfric's point of view, at least, it is thoroughly *scandlic* "shameful."

Sex without Sin

Children are not the only things missing from the sexual riddles of the Exeter Book, however. The shame of sin is also conspicuously absent. In fact, the language used to describe the act of sex in these texts is usually neutral, as if it has no moral charge at all, and sometimes it is strikingly positive.[74] For example, as I have already mentioned earlier in this chapter and discussed in detail in chapter 4, *Cursed among Weapons* (R.20) refers to sex as *hyhtplegan* "joyful play" (28b).[75] *Head Stuck In* (R.61) presents the wife apparently offering herself for sex with her husband as obeying orders. And the riddle-subject (probably a poker or auger), who is apparently involved in some swift, penetrative sex in *Strong Going In/Out* (R.62), displays the heroic qualities of strength, boldness, and courage as well as rectitude: not only is it *heard* "brave" (1a), *strong* "strong" (1b), *from* "bold" (2a), and *unforcuð* "unafraid" (2b); it also makes a *weg ... ryhtne* "correct way" for itself (3b, 4a).[76] In fact, when they describe their male figures, the sexual riddles provide a prescriptive image of masculinity. These are noble warriors who receive praise in the hall.[77] They are men characterized by physical strength, men who are *mægenrof* "powerful," *mundrof ... micel ... godlic* "strong of hand, big, goodly," and *hror* "vigorous" and *strong* "strong."[78] They are also *hold* "loyal" and expected to perform *ellen* "deeds of courage."[79]

---

74 This positive attitude towards sexuality has been discussed before; see especially Williams, "What's So New," 137–8.

75 *Hyhtplega* appears elsewhere as divine action, in apposition to the sixth of Christ's leaps; see *Christ II* 737a. For discussion and a brief overview of past scholarship on Christ's leaps, see James W. Marchland, "The Leaps of Christ and *The Dream of the Rood*," in *Source of Wisdom: Old English and Early Medieval Latin Studies in Honour of Thomas D. Hill*, ed. Charles D. Wright, Frederick M. Biggs, and Thomas N. Hall (Toronto: University of Toronto Press, 2007), 80–9.

76 See B-T *s.v. riht*: definitions include the physical "straight, erect, direct" and the more abstract "just, equitable, satisfying the requirements of a law, legitimate, proper, fitting, correct, true."

77 See *Cursed among Weapons* (R.20.10b–12) and *Warrior's Companion* (R.80.1 –3a). I shall return to the class implications of this language later in this chapter.

78 See *Belly Behind* (R.37.3a), *Barked, Wavered* (R.87. 3a, 3b, 4a), and *In a Corner* (R.54. 3a, 9b).

79 See *Head Stuck In* (R.61. 4a, 7b).

The one exception to the general atmosphere of neutrality or commendation that attends on the sexual riddles is *I Travel on Foot* (R.12), the notorious riddle about the *wonfeax wale* (8a), the dark-haired, female Welsh slave who (apparently) masturbates by the fire. This figure has received ample attention from scholars, who have thoroughly explored the different ways in which she suffers denigration: she is abjected by her moral status, her servile class, her drunken state, her Welsh race, and her gender.[80] Here I want to focus in particular on her moral status, for her apparently masturbatory activities suggest that she would face harsh penalties when she next visited her confessor: the recommended period of penance for a woman who *sola cum seipsa coitum habet* "has sex alone with herself" in *The Canons of Theodore* is three years, the same length of time as for killing a man in anger.[81] Like Ælfric's authoritative assertion of the necessary link between reproduction and sex, this relatively heavy penitential penalty would seem to support John William Tanke's argument that she is condemned because "her sexual gratification … lies outside the circuit of production and procreation."[82] Yet, as we have seen, *I Travel on Foot* (R.12) is not alone in presenting sex outside the "circuit of production and procreation"; the riddles present us with at least twelve examples of sex without offspring (fourteen if my argument above is accepted), some of which describe prohibited rear-entry positions, masturbation, or male-male sex.[83] None of these other riddles contains the condemnation often attributed to *I Travel on Foot*.

---

80 See especially Tanke, "*Wonfeax Wale*," Higley, "Wanton Hand," Rulon-Miller, "Sexual Humor," Margaret Lindsay Faull, "The Semantic Development of Old English *wealh*," *LSE*, n.s., 8 (1975): 29–30, Robson, "'Feorran broht,'" and Coral Lumbley, "The 'Dark Welsh': Color, Race, and Alterity in the Matter of Medieval Wales," *Literature Compass* 16 (2019): 3–5.

81 See *The Canons of Theodore* 2.13 and 4.7. For text, see *Paenitentiale Umbrense*, ed. Michael D. Elliot, http://individual.utoronto.ca/michaelelliot/manuscripts/texts/transcriptions/pthu.pdf, or *Die Canones Theodori Cantuariensis und ihre Überlieferungsformen*, ed. P. Finsterwalder (Weimar: H. Bölhaus, 1929), 291, 295. For translation see John T. McNeill and Helena M. Gamer, *Medieval Handbooks of Penance: A Translation of the Principal Libri Poenitentiales and Selections from Related Documents* (New York: Columbia University Press, 1938), 185, 187.

82 Tanke, "*Wonfeax Wale*," 37.

83 See discussion above of *Downward Nose* (R.21), *Strong Going In/Out* (R.62), *Hanging Head* (R.44), *Belly Behind* (R.37), *Barked, Wavered* (R.87), and *The Creature Had a Belly* (R.89). For the condemnation of intercourse "from behind, in the manner of dogs" even between married people, see Pierre J. Payer, *Sex and the New Medieval Literature of Confession, 1150–1300* (Toronto: Pontifical Institute of Mediaeval Studies, 2009), 29–30.

In the context of penitential and homiletic sources, it seems inevitable that the *wale* is to be condemned for her proscribed "sexual" activity, and most scholars have read *I Travel on Foot* in precisely these contexts. In the context of the Exeter Book riddles, however, such a view is not only unusual; it is unique: the riddles present sex without any indication of shame. While it is possible to argue that the difference is caused by gender (male sexuality is valued and female sexuality is rejected),[84] I am not convinced that *I Travel on Foot* is actually so unique. Rather, I suggest that the depiction of the sexual act is not as negative as scholars have thought. Leaving aside the first half of the text, which describes the origin of the riddle-subject (usually taken to be the ploughing ox) and three uses for its product (usually ox-hide), I focus here on the fourth use for ox-hide, and the part of the text that has most scandalized previous readers:

> hwilum feorran broht
> wonfeax wale   wegeð ond þyð,
> dol druncmennen   deorcum nihtum,
> 10 wæteð in wætre,   wyrmeð hwilum
> fægre to fyre;   me on fæðme sticaþ
> hygegalan hond,   hwyrfeð geneahhe,
> swifeð me geond sweartne. (*I Travel on Foot*, R.12. 7b–13a)

(Sometimes, brought from far away, a dark-haired Welsh woman, a foolish, drunken slave [or drink-slave[85]] moves, presses, and wets me in water during the dark nights; sometimes she warms me beautifully by the fire. The intoxicated one's hand sticks me in her interior, turns me frequently, sweeps me through that dark thing.)

There is no safe way to translate these lines and probably no accurate way, either: like those before me, I have broken grammatical rules and made unsupported suppositions to present something that looks like a plausible translation.[86] The text raises a flood of questions, starting, of

---

84 Rulon-Miller, "Sexual Humor," 113, but see also discussion later in this chapter.
85 The *hapax legomenon druncmennen* could mean "drink-servant" rather than "drunken slave"; see Tanke, "*Wonfeax Wale*," 42n36, referring to a suggestion in *Die altenglischen Rätsel (Die Rätsel des Exeterbuches)*, ed. Moritz Trautmann (Heidelberg: Carl Winter, 1915), 75. See also, however, the discussion of *hygegal* below.
86 For a full discussion of the pitfalls and delights of the ambiguous language here, see Higley, "Wanton Hand."

course, with the question of what precisely the *wale* is doing; she may be washing dishes with a leather rag or creating a leather bottle, but she *seems* to be masturbating, with something made out of leather.[87] It is not actually necessary to answer this question to solve the riddle; whatever one might think she is doing, she is doing it with ox-hide, and that is all the response that the riddle requires.[88] My question here is different: what precisely is negative in this text? As already mentioned, previous scholars have identified a number of traits that seem designed to attract opprobrium: the *wale*'s ethnicity, gender, her state of being *dol* "foolish" (9a),[89] and her drunkenness. I have argued elsewhere that her state of abjection is not as straightforward as it may seem;[90] here what is important is that, although generations of scholars have expressed shock and disapproval, the *wale*'s behaviour elicits little comment from the poet, and that comment is positive. Whatever she is doing, she does it *fægre* – gently, beautifully, elegantly, courteously, justly, auspiciously, with a happy result.[91] Rather than providing an opportunity to remind readers that unauthorized sexual behaviour leads to damnation, this little interlude simply becomes part of a list of the services that leather does for humanity. Even in *I Travel on Foot*, the least positive of the sexual riddles, sex is not associated with sin.[92]

Truly Gratuitous Sex: Sex without Pleasure

Sex without the justification of offspring is provocative enough – even if it is, ultimately, only "sex." Yet, despite the pleasure that audiences have assumed (and taken) in these texts, the riddles are also notable for another lack: the gratification of sexual gratification. The "sex" that

---

87 See Rulon-Miller, "Sexual Humor" and Higley, "Wanton Hand" for good discussions of both the surface and metaphorical meanings.
88 See Jennifer Neville, "Speaking the Unspeakable: Appetite for Deconstruction in *Exeter Book* Riddle 12," *ES* 93 (2012): 520.
89 Although I do not pursue it here, there may be some ambiguity in this word, since the related word, *dollic*, means "bold" in heroic contexts but "foolish" in homiletic ones; see Roberta Frank, "'Mere' and 'Sund': Two Sea-Changes in *Beowulf*," in *Modes of Interpretation: Essays in Honour of Stanley B. Greenfield*, ed. Phyllis Rugg Brown, Georgia Ronan Crampton, and Fred C. Robinson (Toronto: University of Toronto Press, 1986), 153.
90 Neville, "Speaking the Unspeakable," 523–6.
91 See *DOE s.v. fægre*.
92 I shall return to the possible connection between sex and drunkenness in this riddle later in this chapter.

they present is often for its own sake in a very profound way, for it takes place not only without reference to offspring but also without reference to pleasure. And so sin is not the only thing that is surprisingly absent from *I Travel on Foot* (R.12). Yet not many have noticed; it is a text that seems to make modern readers, at least, go blind, or perhaps, to see what is not there. Thus, for example, Hacikyan discovers in the text a positive relationship of trust and gratitude between the slave and her lord,[93] and Williamson in his translation inserts a man to own the skin thrusting against the Welsh woman.[94] There is no male figure here. Tanke does an excellent job of pointing out the "gratuitous" moves in previous criticism of this text, but even he argues that "the riddle subject serves the pleasure of a woman."[95] That statement may seem uncontroversial in the context of a scene of masturbation, but the text does not actually present the pleasure that most suppose is involved here. Although I have already quoted this text above, it is important to look at it carefully again:

>   ... hwilum feorran broht
> wonfeax wale   wegeð ond þyð,
> dol druncmennen   deorcum nihtum,
> 10 wæteð in wætre,   wyrmeð hwilum
> fægre to fyre;   me on fæðme sticaþ
> hygegalan hond,   hwyrfeð geneahhe,
> swifeð me geond sweartne. (*I Travel on Foot*, R.12. 7b–13a)

(Sometimes, brought from far away, a dark-haired Welsh woman, a foolish, drunken slave moves, presses, and wets me in liquid during the dark nights; sometimes she warms me beautifully by the fire. The hand of the *hygegal* one sticks me in her enclosure, turns me frequently, sweeps me through that dark thing.)

Despite all the suggestive verbs (moving, pressing, wetting warming, sticking, turning, sweeping), and despite the positive outcome suggested by *fægre*, the text does not say that the *wale* derives any pleasure from her activity. Critics and translators have assumed that pleasure is involved, perhaps because of their own expectations of what masturbation

---

93 Agop Hacikyan, *A Linguistic and Literary Analysis of Old English Riddles* (Montreal: Mario Casalini, 1966), 39.
94 Williamson, trans., *Feast of Creatures*, 170.
95 Tanke, "*Wonfeax Wale*," 34; see also his comments on "sexual gratification," 37.

entails,[96] but probably also because of the word that I have not translated above, *hygegal*, which warrants detailed consideration. This word is normally translated as "wanton," "lascivious," or "lustful,"[97] which is a reasonable interpretation of its second element, *gal*, in prose contexts, at least. For example, the adjective *gal* occurs fourteen times, mostly with the meaning "wanton," although it can also mean "frivolous" (in one case) or simply "evil" (in two).[98] The noun *galnes* occurs approximately 175 times, often in glosses to *luxuria* and *libido*; it clearly refers to sexual lust.[99] In the Old English version of Gregory's *Pastoral Care*, those who are *wifgal* "licentious" are to be urged into marriage (but not in such a way that causes the chaste to come into *unryhthæmed* "adultery").[100] The twenty-three appearances of *galscipe* in prose are similarly focused on sexual lust.[101] The nouns *gæls* (two occurrences) and *gælsa* (twenty) occur mainly in prose and most often refer to sexual lust.[102] Among the exceptions, some forms of the word refer to unrestrained playfulness, which may, in fact, simply be a euphemism for lust, given that some of them gloss Aldhelm's references to fertility festivals; others seem to refer to monks with a sense of humour.[103] Despite these additional meanings, the word conveys a clear sexual meaning in most prose texts.

In poetry, however, the meaning of *gal* and its variants becomes generalized and lacks its specific relation to sex. Thus, in addition to the prose occurrences noted above, *gælsa* also occurs twice in poetry with the more generalized meaning of sinful thoughts: in *Juliana*, the devil confesses to the saint that he opposes the efforts of those trying to be good by bringing *monifealde modes gælsan* "an abundance of lust of the

---

96 For the complex relationship between effeminacy, a predilection for masturbation, and giving in to pleasure, see Clark, "Discourses of Masturbation," 462–8. This argument, however, is based on masturbation in men, not women.
97 See discussion in Bogislav von Lindheim, "Traces of Colloquial Speech in OE," *Anglia* 70 (1951): 39–42. His conclusion is accepted by Gleißner, *Die "zweideutigen" altenglischen Rätsel*, 342.
98 See *DOE* s.v. *galnes*.
99 See *DOE* s.v. *gal* (adj).
100 See *King Alfred's West-Saxon Version of Gregory's Pastoral Care*, ed. Henry Sweet, EETS, o.s., 45 and 50 (London: Kegan Paul, 1871), 453, line 30.
101 See *DOE* s.v. *galscipe*. For the single occurrence in poetry, see below.
102 See *DOE* s.v.v. *gæls* and *gælsa*. The latter occurs in poetry with the meaning "lust" in *Judgement Day II* 235; the expected sin associated with sex is explicitly expressed here.
103 For unrestrained playfulness, see *DOE* s.v.v. *gagol* and *gagolisc*. For monks prone to laughter, see s.v. *galsmære* (note the very late date of this text). For glosses on fertility festivals, see s.v. *galfreols*.

mind" (366), a phrase that stands in apposition to the *grimra geþonca, dyrna gedwilda* "grim thoughts, secret doubts" (367b–368a) that the devil brings *þurh gedwolena rim* "through countless errors" (368b); sexual desire may be indicated here, but the plurality suggests a range of sins. Similarly, in *Vainglory*, the wise man refers to the one who does not allow his thoughts to be damaged by *modes gælsan* "the mind's lust" (11b); this may, of course, include sexual desire, but here it occurs in the context of being *druncen to rice* "drunk for power" (12b) and probably drunk with alcohol, too, as the following lines refer to the uproarious noise of men urged on by wine (13–21a).[104] *Gal* appears as a noun only in poetry, and only in two texts. In *Christ III*, *gal* stands in opposition to *god* "good" and thus seems to mean evil in general (1034a). In *Genesis B* the rebel angels fall because of *gal* (327b) and *galscipe* (341a). It seems likely that "arrogance" or "folly" is meant,[105] as I am not aware of any text that suggests that the fall of the angels was caused by sexual desire.[106] *Genesis B*, with its Old Saxon background, is, of course, a special case, but presumably the words would not have been retained in the Old English poem if their meanings were so inextricably linked to sex that their use here created a nonsensical statement about the fall of the rebel angels. Indeed, elsewhere in the Old English *Genesis*, where the influence of Old Saxon meanings is not a factor, *gal* has meanings divorced from sex, too. For example, the dove released from Noah's ark is *rumgal* – perhaps "intoxicated with the relief of escape from incarceration" (1466a), while God states his intention to visit Sodom because of the *gylp ealogal* "boast of those intoxicated with ale" (2410a). Elsewhere, *gal* is combined in compounds with *symbel* "feast" and *win* "wine" to refer to those so engrossed in material life that they forget the spiritual.[107]

---

104 For discussion of the feasting imagery in *Vainglory*, which is not necessarily negative, see Hugh Magennis, *Images of Community in Old English Poetry* (Cambridge: Cambridge University Press, 1996), 98–103.
105 See Lindheim, "Traces of Colloquial Speech," 40–1. *DOE*, s.v. *gal*, notes that the words in *Genesis B* may be semantic loans from Old Saxon, which has cognate adjectives meaning "overbearing, arrogant."
106 *Solomon and Saturn II* has a puzzling reference to Lucifer procreating in a non-approved way (277–278a) but makes no reference to sexual desire; see Daniel Anlezark, "The Fall of the Angels in *Solomon and Saturn II*," in *Apocryphal Texts and Traditions in Anglo-Saxon England*, ed. Kathryn Powell and Donald Scragg (Cambridge: Brewer, 2003), 122–33. The angels thought to be responsible for Noah's flood are, of course, a different story. See Genesis 6:1–4, 1 Enoch: 4, and discussion in Daniel Anlezark, *Water and Fire: The Myth of the Flood in Anglo-Saxon England* (Manchester: Manchester University Press, 2006), 321.
107 For *symbelgal*, see *Judgement Day I* 79a; for *wingal*, see *Seafarer* 29a and *Daniel* 116b.

The possibility that *gal* means "engrossed" – that is, brought completely into the gross, physical body, wholly distracted from higher, spiritual concerns, whether by sexual desire, alcohol, feasting, or even freedom – is important when considering the most relevant comparator for *I Travel on Foot*: *Judith*. In this text, as in the riddle, *gal* is combined with words for "mind" to create unique compounds. Where the *wale* is *hygegal*, the Assyrian general, Holofernes, whom the saint beheads, is *galferhþ* (62a) and *galmod* (256b), words that the *DOE* translates as "lascivious." Holofernes certainly intends to have sex with Judith, and so this translation is undeniably appropriate. However, his thoughts are not only affected by lust; they are also affected by alcohol. Before he is *galferhþ*, he is *medugal* "intoxicated by mead" (26a), and in the course of the poem he is, in fact, more drunk than lustful. The same may be true of the *druncmennen* "drink-server" or "drunken slave" (9a) in *Fotum Ic Fere*. She may be more drunk than lustful, or it may be impossible to separate the two states.[108]

Both proscribed desires are relevant in *I Travel on Foot* but, in translating *hygegal* as "wanton," modern readers have focused exclusively on one. Yet, while the meaning of sexual desire would be almost inevitable in a prose text, the possibility of a more general meaning for *hygegal* is necessary for the double entendre to be sustained through this part of the text. The *wale* must be *both* lustfully masturbating *and* drunkenly washing the dishes. What is important for my argument, however, is that in neither case does pleasure result. However we interpret *hygegal*, the word refers to her state of mind before she uses the leather object rather than the effect of what she is doing with it: *me on fæðme sticaþ / hygegalan hond* "the hand of one whose mind is engrossed sticks me into an enclosure" (11b–12a). It is not that the apparently risqué activity excites her desire; she is already engrossed, whether with drink or with lust. The text withholds not only what she is doing with her hand but also how the act makes her feel. Nevertheless, modern translators and critics are quite certain that she is enjoying herself: Porter, for example, translates *hwyrfeð geneahhe* "turns frequently" (12b) as "[She] loves to twirl me,"[109] while Tanke, as mentioned earlier, builds a very convincing argument that the condemnation of the woman here derives from

---

108 See *DOE* s.v.v. *galian* and *gælslic*: the citations there from the *Liber Scintillarum* and *Rule of Chrodegang* suggest a strong relationship between lechery and drunkenness.
109 *Anglo-Saxon Riddles*, trans. John Porter (Hockwold-cum-Wilton: Anglo-Saxon Books, 1995), 27.

her choice to give herself pleasure.[110] Early medieval English audiences may well have agreed with the assumptions of modern critics, but if so, they, like modern readers, must have read the pleasure into the text, because gratification is not actually depicted here.

The same is true of *Useful to Neighbours* (R.25). As already discussed above, the sexual encounter between the riddle-subject and the *ful cyrtenu ceorles dohtor* "very beautiful freeman's daughter" (6) produces no offspring: the result of *mines gemotes* "the encounter with me" (10a) is a dampened eye (or "eye"), not a child or "child." Equally lacking is pleasure in the act. Although the riddle-subject, whether onion or penis, claims to be *wifum on hyhte* "the joy of women" (1b), the actual act is presented as a violent assault, comparable to that suffered by the subjects of the trope of manufacturing.[111] Recalling *Wob* (R.23) at this point is instructive, for, in the case of both the bow being drawn and the onion being picked, the passive riddle-subject endures torture but nevertheless achieves some kind of revenge; death for the victims of the bow and tears for the plucker of the onion. That is not to argue that *Useful to Neighbours* presents an anxious fear of predatory women,[112] nor to deny the text's essential playfulness,[113] but I do wish to point out that the "sex" presented here, even with its "recognizable lexicon of dirty riddling,"[114] does not, in fact, document any pleasure in the acts of standing firmly, rushing, ravaging, fixing, and afflicting.

The same is true elsewhere, too. Six further riddles are resolutely silent regarding what we might think of as the essential point of gratuitous sex: pleasure. In *Belly Behind* (R.37), the man operating the bellows *micel hæfde / gefered* "had accomplished much" (3b–4a), but his success transpires without any mention of pleasure. In *Hanging Head* (R.44), the wonderful thing hanging by the man's thigh greets and fills its *cupe hol* "familiar hole" (5b), as it had done before, without any mention of enjoyment. In *Boneless* (R.45), when the nobleman's daughter grabs the *dah* "dough" in the corner, neither she nor it report any pleasant sensations. In *Head Stuck In* (R.61), the exchange between the noble woman and her lord, which can be interpreted as a touching scene of marital intimacy,[115]

---

110 Tanke, "*Wonfeax Wale*," 32–9.
111 See chapter 5, above.
112 This is the position, supported by references to discussions by Trautmann, Tupper, Williamson, and Tanke, taken in Rulon-Miller, "Sexual Humor," 111 and notes 56–9.
113 See, for example, Murphy's full discussion in *Unriddling*, 221–34.
114 Murphy, *Unriddling*, 176.
115 Melanie Heyworth, "Perceptions of Marriage in Exeter Book Riddles 20 and 61," *SN* 79 (2007): 179–80.

again transpires without any mention of gratification. In *Strong Going In/ Out* (R.62), the hot, hasty passage of the *nafu-gar* "borer" does not give satisfaction to the *superne secg* "southern man" (9a) or anyone else. And in *Warrior's Companion* (R.80), when the noble lady *mec ... hond on legeð* "lays (her) hand on me" (3b–4), we do not hear how she, or the recipient of her caress, feels.

This is not to say that pleasure is entirely absent. As already discussed at length in chapter 4, for example, the celibate sword in *Cursed among Weapons* (R.20) mourns the *hæmed* "sex" (28a) and *hyhtplegan* "joyful play" (28b) that it cannot have and so *brucan sceal* "must enjoy" (30b) treasure instead. The cock and hen of *Two Proud Ones* (R.42) seem to be enjoying themselves as they *plegan* "play" (2b) their *hæmedlac* "sex-game" (3a), and the hen, especially, has the prospect of receiving her *fyllo* "fill" (5a), of being both physically filled (perhaps by the cock's penis or his semen) and sensually satisfied. The *tillic esne* "good slave" in *In a Corner* (R.54), like the *tillic esne* in *Shining with Gold* (R.63), gets his *willa* "pleasure" (in lines 6a and 7a respectively), by churning butter or drinking from a glass vessel respectively. *The Creature Had a Belly* (R.89) is so fragmentary that it is impossible to make any statement about it with certainty, but it is possible that the activity of the bellows made it *poncade* "feel gratified" (8b).[116] Finally, in *Forged by Hammer* (R.91), the *frea* "lord" partakes of his *mod wyn* "mind-joy" (7a) in the middle of the night *willum sinum* "for his own pleasures" (11b),[117] whether through the action of a key, keyhole, buckle, or brooch.[118] While pleasure is clearly present in this last case, "sex" may not be. As Portnoy observes, some readers have taken this as a "straight" text, without double entendre,[119] and, although I agree that sticking, swallowing, and shoving from behind in the middle of the night are suggestive, I am not entirely sure that a sexual act is represented here. Even if we give *Forged by Hammer* and the fragmentary *The Creature Had a Belly* the benefit of the doubt, however, we find references to pleasure in only six out of the fifteen sexual riddles. It is worth noting as well that two of those instances derive from an assumption that the "play" in *Cursed among Weapons* and *Two Proud Ones* actually connotes pleasure; *plegan* might simply mean "to move rapidly" or "to busy oneself," meanings

---

116 See B-T, definition III.
117 *Wyn* is conveyed by a runic letter in the manuscript.
118 See discussion, above, and the summary of solutions in the appendix, below.
119 Portnoy, "Laf-Craft," 570. Portnoy herself strongly supports a sexual reading (570–3).

which contribute very well to double entendre but do not necessarily include the idea of pleasure.[120]

The modern, critical assumption seems to be that pleasure is simply an essential component of sex and so need not be mentioned by the Old English text to be understood – or, at least, that seems to be the underlying explanation for the addition of pleasure to discussions and translations of these texts.[121] Again, this may be an assumption shared with early medieval English audiences. However, the fact that more than half of the sexual riddles fail to mention pleasure raises another possibility: that pleasure, like offspring, is *not* essential to convey the idea of sex. What is essential, then?

Hard Work

A writer who wished to convey the idea of sex in a way that could not possibly be misunderstood – for the sake of creating a clever, double-entendre metaphor, for example – might adopt the strategy taken in *Cursed among Weapons* and *Two Proud Ones* and simply use the word *hæmed* "sex" (at R.20. 28b and R.42. 3a, respectively). Most Old English riddlers wishing to play this game, however, opt for descriptions of work: hard, physical labour. This fact has, of course, been noted before, but previous scholarship has focused mostly on the representation of women's hands. Thus Anthony Davies argues that "hands" constitute part of the sexual idiom of Old English poetry,[122] and, as mentioned earlier, Murphy includes "manual stimulation," particularly by women, as part of his "lexicon of dirty riddling."[123] These references to women's hands in sexual contexts are worth noting, but they occur in only four riddles,[124] and there are too many other hands, doing too many other things, to isolate them as a reliable sign of sexual innuendo. Hands are not signs of sex; they are signs of labour and power.

---

120 See Clark Hall, *s.v. plegan*. Cf. B-T, *s.v. plega* "quick movement."
121 See, for example, Williams, "What's So New," 143–4, Williamson, *Feast of Creatures*, 150, and the discussion of *Fotum Ic Fere*, above.
122 "Sexual Behaviour," 44–54.
123 Murphy, *Unriddling*, 177: "To be sure, the grip of a proud woman is explosively suggestive in these riddles." I shall turn to pride later in this chapter.
124 See *I Travel on Foot* (R.12. 12a), *Boneless* (R.45. 4a), *Head Stuck In* (R.61. 3a), *Warrior's Companion* R.80. 4b. It also is worth noting the woman gripping the riddle-subject in *Useful to Neighbours* (R.25. 7b); hands are certainly implied here, even if they are not explicitly mentioned.

In the context of Old English poetry in general, hands represent power, control, and responsibility. For example, the idea of fighting until unable to hold weapons runs like a refrain through *The Battle of Maldon*.[125] In *Genesis A*, Satan's expectations are defeated as soon as God lifts up his hands (50b, 62a); Cain's personal responsibility for the murder of his brother, like Lamech's for the murder of Cain, is emphasized by repeated references to hands (983a, 1010b, 1094b, 1096a); the doomed attempt to build the Tower of Babel takes place with the insufficient power of men's hands (1678a); the inhabitants of Sodom take Lot into their evil hands (2485b, 2486a); and Abraham is commanded to kill his son with his own hands (2907a). In *Genesis B*, Satan's conflict with God begins with his claim to be able to create the same wonders with his hands (279b); God's retaliation results in Satan losing *handa geweald* "control of his hands" (368b; cf. 380a, 388b); and God replaces Satan by establishing his new *handgesceaft* "handiwork" with his hands (455a, 463b, 494a, 628a, 702b, 748a). Hands appear significantly and frequently in *Beowulf*, too.[126] Not only are the hero's exploits often explicitly associated with his hands (540a, 558b, 2137b, 2502a), but the defeat of Grendel is literally the removal of his hand (983b, 986a, 2099a), the death of Æschere is conveyed as the stillness of his gift-granting hand (1343b–4),[127] and Hrothgar acquires the giants' sword hilt, just as Beowulf later acquires his uncle's kingdom, when it is given into his hand (1678b, 2208a).

This equation of hands with power may underlie the limitation of the possession of hands to men rather than women; even after taking into account their lower numbers, women in Old English poetry seem to wield hands only in exceptional circumstances. Thus, in the Old English *Genesis B*, Eve's wielding of hands is part of her assertion of authority over Adam: Adam initially resists the offer to take the fruit from the

---

125 See lines 14–15a, 83, 167–8a, and 235b–7a. Explicit references to hands also appear in lines 4a, 7a, 21a, 108a, 141b, 150a. For discussion, see, for example Stephen J. Harris, "Oaths in *The Battle of Maldon*," in *The Hero Recovered: Essays on Medieval Heroism in Honor of George Clark*, ed. Robin Waugh and James Weldon (Kalamazoo, MI: Medieval Institute, 2010), 85–109.
126 See especially discussion in David D. Day, "Hands across the Hall: The Legalities of Beowulf's Fight with Grendel," *JEGP* 98 (1999): 313–24 and Larry J. Swain, "Of Hands, Halls, and Heroes: Grendel's Hand, Hroþgar's Power, and the Problem of *Stapol* in *Beowulf*," *Anglia* 134 (2016): 260–84.
127 There is some debate over the ownership of the hand here, but the connection between power and hands remains regardless. See discussion in J.J. Anderson, "The 'cuþe Folme' in *Beowulf*, Line 1303a," *Neophil* 67 (1983): 127.

false messenger into his hand (518b), but Eve's successful persuasion of him is marked by the transfer of the fruit into and out of her hands (545a, 636a, 678a), and Adam describes his transgression as an acceptance of fruit from Eve into his hand (883a). Beowulf acknowledges the exceptional power of Grendel's mother in his report to Hygelac by summing up the battle that almost cost him his life with the statement that *þær unc hwile wæs hand gemæne* "there for a while it was hand-to-hand for the two of us" (*Beowulf* 2137b). Judith gives the severed head of Holofernes into the hands of her maidservant (*Judith* 130b) and later announces to the Hebrews that God has given them victory through her hand (*Judith* 198b). Other than these three cases, I have been unable to find any references to women's hands outside the Exeter Book riddles. Even Wealhtheow, when she asserts her authority over the men in Heorot (*Beowulf* 1162b–1232a), is depicted without reference to her hands.

As scholars have noted, women *do* have hands in the sexual riddles – four women, at least – and their hands turn up in situations that seem to describe sexual activity. They are not the only hands in the riddles, however. Men's hands participate in (apparently) sexual activities when they embrace and press on the riddle-subject in *Shining with Gold* (R.63. 6a) and heave up a man's clothing in *In a Corner* (R.54. 4a); the latter activity also takes place in *Hanging Head* (R.44. 5a), although the word "hand" does not actually appear. Yet there are other hands in the riddles, too, whose activities do not necessarily suggest sexual activity. In *Flame-Busy* (R.30. 5b) men and women both pass the riddle-subject (probably a cup) from hand to hand to be kissed.[128] In *Earth-Fast* (R.49. 3a) the riddle-object (perhaps a bee-hive)[129] is seen to receive gifts from the hand of its servant. In *Mouthless by Sand* (R.60. 10b–17) the riddle-subject reflects with awe on the ability of the craftsman's hand to transform it into something that can speak without being heard on the mead-bench. In *Twelve Hundred Heads* (R.86. 5b), two hands are reassuringly normal components of the monstrous, multi-headed creature that invades the assembly of the wise. And in *Cursed among Weapons* (R.20) hands appear not when procreation and sex are being discussed (17b–31) but rather when the woman claps her hands in a gesture of grief or anger (34a).[130]

---

128 Kissing may be considered sensual, but passing an object amongst a group of men and women does not suggest any sexual act of which I am aware.
129 See discussion in chapter 5, above.
130 For discussion of this gesture, see chapter 4, above. Cf. also Tauno F. Mustanoja, "The Unnamed Woman's Song of Mourning over Beowulf and the Tradition of Ritual Lamentation," *NM* 68 (1967), 1–27; Heyworth, "Perceptions of Marriage," 177.

As these examples show, hands are not an inevitable marker of double entendre in Old English poetry or even in the Exeter Book riddles.

What makes hands suggestive in the riddles is their connection to work, for, although not all work represents sex, almost all sex is depicted as work. *In a Corner* (R.54), whose ending with its unusual reference to offspring as the product of sex was discussed above, provides a good model of work being used as an apparent euphemism for sex:

>   Hyse cwom gangan,   þær he hie wisse
>   stondan in wincsele,   stop feorran to,
>   hror hægstealdmon,   hof his agen
>   hrægl hondum up,   hrand[131] under gyrdels
> 5 hyre stondendre   stiþes nathwæt,
>   worhte his willan;   wagedan buta.
>   Þegn onnette,   wæs þragum nyt
>   tillic esne,   teorode hwæþre
>   æt stunda gehwam   strong ær þon hio,
> 10 werig þæs weorces.   Hyre weaxan ongon
>   under gyrdelse   þæt oft gode men
>   ferðþum freogað   ond mid feo bicgað. (*In a Corner*)

(A young man came walking to where he knew she was standing in a corner. The vigorous bachelor marched there from afar. He lifted up his own garment with his hands and thrust something stiff under her girdle as she stood there and worked his pleasure. Both of them shook. The man hastened, and for awhile the good servant was useful, but, although he was previously stronger than she, he always grew tired, weary from his work. Under her girdle something that good men cherish in their hearts and buy with money began to grow.)

The text ensures that its audience knows that double entendre is intended, for, even if *nathwæt* were not there, sticking something "stiff" (5b) under a woman's clothing would make it difficult *not* to think about coitus. Lines 3 through 10a then belabour the labour: the servant, characterized as *hror* "strong, vigorous" (3a) and initially *strong ... þon*

---

131 Muir retains the manuscript reading, *rand* (*Exeter Anthology*, 323), but here I follow Williamson's emendation (*Old English Riddles*, 100), which is also accepted by Krapp and Dobbie (207) and *The Old English and Anglo-Latin Riddle Tradition*, ed. and trans. Andy Orchard, Dumbarton Oaks Medieval Library, 69 (Cambridge, MA: Harvard University Press, 2021), 372.

hio "stronger than she" (9b), heaves, thrusts, works, shakes, hastens, and is useful until worn out from his exertion. There are no hands in this part of the text, but there is repeated movement (*wagedan* 6b) and work (*worhte, weorc* 6a, 10a).

A similar pattern can be observed in *Strong Going In/Out*, R.62, which has been mentioned previously in this chapter to illustrate a possible reference to male-male intercourse, proscriptive masculinity, and the absence of gratification, but not yet quoted in full.

> Ic eom heard ond scearp, ingonges strong,
> forðsiþes from, frean unforcuð,
> wade under wambe ond me weg sylfa
> ryhtne geryme. Rinc bið on ofeste,
> 5 se mec on þyð æftanweardne,
> hæleð mid hrægle; hwilum ut tyhð
> of hole hatne, hwilum eft fereð[132]
> on nearo nathwær; nydeþ swiþe
> suþerne secg. Saga hwæt ic hatte. (*Strong Going In/Out*)

(I am hard and sharp, strong in going in,[133] bold in going forth, unafraid for [the sake of] my lord; I proceed under a belly and open up for myself a straight road. The man who thrusts me on from behind,[134] the warrior with the garment, is in haste. Sometimes he draws me out, hot from the

---

132 I follow Muir here, who accepts the emendation of the MS from *fareð* to *fereð*; this emendation is also adopted by Mackie (*Exeter Book*, 202–3), Williamson (*Old English Riddles*, 104), and Orchard (*Old English and Anglo-Latin Riddle Tradition*, 382). In contrast, ASPR's influential edition retains *fareð*, which leads to a different reading: "sometimes the southern man travels again into a narrow place somewhere, forces strongly." In my reading, the riddle-subject is forced into the narrow space rather than its attendant travelling into it.

133 I like the idea of back-and-forth motion suggested by the opposition between *ingong* "going in" and *forðsiþ* "going forth." Following Muir, I retain the manuscript reading here, but most editors emend to *hingong* to supply alliteration in this line. If the emendation is accepted, both *hingong* "going hence, departure, death" and *forðsiþ* "journey, departure, death" may be taken as references to coitus as death. See discussion in Muir, *Exeter Anthology*, 2: 706. I am grateful to Jane Roberts for alerting me to this matter (personal communication, 27 March 2021). I suspect we are meant to keep both possibilities in mind until a solution is reached and thus represent both in my title: *Strong Going In/Out*. See also E.G. Stanley, "Exeter Book *Riddles*, II: The Significant but Often Misleading Opening Word," *N&Q* 64 (2017): 361.

134 During an informal presentation at King's College London (5 July 2018), Erik Wade suggested "in the backside" as a translation for *æftanweardne*, and the hint of a rear-entry sexual position is probably part of the game of this text.

hole; sometimes again the southern man carries [and] strongly forces [me] into a tight spot somewhere or other. Say what I am called.)

The riddle's double-entendre meaning may be suggested in the very first line by the subject's claim to be *heard and scearp* "hard and sharp" (1a); it is confirmed in the penultimate line by the activity taking place *on nearo nathwær* "in a tight space somewhere or other" (8a); and the (to us) opaque reference to a *suþerne secg* "southern man" in the final line might also be suggestive.[135] In between the sexual act is represented by labour: vigorous movement (*hingonges strong* and *forðsiþes from* 1b, 2a), haste (*ofeste* 4b), thrusting (*þyð* 5a), and forcing (*nydeþ swiþe* 8b), alongside a series of verbs for movement and exertion (*wade* "proceed" 3a, *ryme* "open up" 4a, and *fereð* "carries" 7b). There is no woman here, and there are no hands, but there certainly is hard work.

That hard work may also be observed in riddles already discussed in this chapter. Thus all three riddles meditating on the *blast-belg* "bellows," despite lacking explicit references to hands, include the language of labour. In *Belly Behind* (R.37), for example, the *mægenrofa man ... micel hæfde / gefered* "powerful man had accomplished much" (3b–4a), while in *Barked, Wavered* (R.87) the man who is *mægenstrong ond mundrof* "powerful and strong of hand" (3a) briskly grips the object (*grap on sona* 4b) to achieve his objective, and among the fragments left of *The Creature Had a Belly* (R.89) is the verb *worhte* "worked" (7b). As discussed earlier, there is some doubt over whether *Forged by Hammer* (R.91) does indeed convey a double entendre, but, if it does, the riddle-subject's claims to *hnitan...hearde* "thrust hard" (4a–5a) and *forð ascufan* "shove forth" (6a) are important supports of its suggestive qualities, despite, once again, the absence of hands. Even *Two Proud Ones* (R.42), which explicitly refers to the cock and hen's *hæmedlac* "sex-game" (3a) and naturally

---

135 It is also possible to interpret *suþerne secg* as "southern sword" and see it as referring to the riddle-subject itself: "sometimes again he carries (and) strongly forces (me), a southern sword, into a tight spot somewhere or other." As we do not know the implication of "southern," it is difficult to choose between these two possibilities. See discussions in Tupper, *Riddles*, 203; Williamson, *Old English Riddles*, 323; and Muir, *Exeter Anthology*, 2: 707. While in current slang it is possible to link "southern" to the genitals "down below," medieval thinkers placed west, not south, at the bottom of maps and so were unlikely to make that connection; see Gleißner, *Die "zweideutigen" altenglischen Rätsel*, 387–92. It has been argued, however, that there is an ancient correlation between southern regions and libido; see Jacky Bolding, "The Sexual Riddles of the *Exeter Book*" (MA diss., Simon Fraser University, 1992), 40.

lacks reference to hands, notes that effort must be expended so that *þæs weorces speow* "the work succeeds" (4b).

Class and Gendered Pride: Men

As the preceding discussion has demonstrated, the double-entendre riddles of the Exeter Book pose ongoing challenges to modern readers' expectations of the representation of sex. In this section, I turn to another expectation that, despite being demolished more than thirty years ago, still lingers on: the collocation of class and sexuality. Although certainly not the first to make the connection, Frederick Tupper may stand as an example of an excellent scholar who nevertheless suffers a peculiar form of blindness when reading the double-entendre riddles. Thus in his 1910 edition he categorizes the double-entendre riddles as "folk riddles" (as opposed to literary riddles) and notes that these texts feature predominantly lower-class characters.[136] This is untrue. As Stewart notes in 1983, only four of the fifteen class-specific terms in these texts refer to the lower classes,[137] and, as Tanke notes in 1994, the fact that Stewart found that number surprising is telling.[138] The correlation between "coarseness," low class, and sexuality has momentum; modern scholars either re-inscribe it or rediscover that the riddles do not support it. In hope of forestalling those expectations in future scholarship, I shall lay out the evidence once again, looking first at men and then at women.

Strong Going In/Out (R.62), quoted in full a few pages ago, presents a hard thing being shoved in haste into a hole. The act is presented to look like penetrative sex, but the description also suits a man using a poker, gimlet, or auger. What is important for this part of the discussion is the value-laden language used to describe the riddle-subject and its attendant. I mentioned this language earlier in this chapter as an example of prescriptive masculinity; here the class implications of that prescriptive masculinity should be noted, for neither subject nor attendant is described in language consonant with anything other than the elite warrior class. Thus the penis-poker is *heard* "hard" but also "hardy" or "bold" (1a), *strong* "strong" (1b), *from* "bold" or "strong"

---

136 Tupper, *Riddles*, 203.
137 Stewart, "Double Entendre," 48–9.
138 Tanke, "*Wonfeax Wale*," 24.

(2a), and *unforcuð* "unafraid" (2b), while its *frea* "lord" (2b), who is in *ofeste* "haste," is a *rinc* (4b), *hæleð* (6a), and *secg* (9a), all terms that may simply mean "a man," but only in the context of the noble elite, with the result that all three also carry the idea of "warrior" or "hero."[139] The adjectives and nouns here are all words that could be used to describe Beowulf or Byrhtnoth. In fact, all but one appear in *Beowulf*, and all but two appear in *The Battle of Maldon*.[140] The state of mind of this man engaging in apparently sexual acts is not presented as base or lowly. It is heroic.

Strong Going In/Out is not an isolated case of heroism. In *Head Stuck In* (R.61), the man putting on his helmet or byrnie in a way that suggests he is having sex with his wife is said to need sufficient *ellen* "courage" to complete the act (7b). In *Belly Behind* (R.37), the man operating the bellows is *mægenrofa* "powerful" (3a). *In a Corner* (R.54), the young man working with his churn is *hror* "brave" (3a). His class is initially ambiguous: *hyse* (1a) and *þegn* (7a) may indicate a youth who serves regardless of his nobility, but *esne* (8a), while perhaps sharing the same connotations of youth, is more certainly associated with non-noble class.[141] While this last example provides an important reminder that heroic action may also be performed by members of the lower classes, the language of heroism is usually associated with the military elite,[142] and, overall, as Stewart has already noted, the class of the men participating in what seem to be explicit, sexual acts is generally high. Although there are a few *esne* "slaves" among them,[143] and although

---

139 See *DOE* s.v. *hæleð, heard, from, frea*; see B-T s.v. *strong, unforcuð, rinc, secg*. For discussion of how the meanings of such words can be inflected by context, see Dennis Cronan, "Poetic Meanings in the OE Poetic Vocabulary," *ES* 84 (2003): 397–425.
140 *Beowulf* lacks *unforcuð*. *Maldon* lacks *strong* and *from*.
141 See *DOE* s.v.v. *hyse, þegn*, and *esne*, and note the argument for the centrality of the meaning "slave" for *esne* in Miller, 224–8.
142 See discussion in chapter 2, above.
143 In addition to the one already mentioned in *In a Corner* 8a, see *Hanging Head* (R.44. 4a) and *Shining with Gold* (R.63. 5a). Note that *esne* also appears in three other Exeter Book riddles that do not associate slaves with sex: *Peace-Horses* (R.22. 13b), which refers to slaves pulling a barge; *Binder and Scourger* (R.27. 8a), in which the intoxicating power of mead affects old and young, enslaved and free alike; and *Guest in the Enclosures* (R.43. 5a, 8b, and 16a), in which the "slave" represents the body serving the soul. For further analysis of *esne* in the riddles, see Miller, "Semantic Field of Slavery," 203–13. While Miller asserts that that "lewd and unseemly behaviour also fits with the pattern of the depiction of slaves in the riddles" (210), I dispute that connection between sexuality and class.

some terms may convey subordination, especially because of youth,[144] other men participating in "sex" are simply men,[145] and many are specifically noble men, distinguished by terms such as *frea* "lord,"[146] *hlaford* "lord,"[147] *þeoden* "lord,"[148] *eorl* "earl/warrior,"[149] *gode men* "good men,"[150] and *rinc* "man/warrior."[151] Collectively they constitute a *dryht* "body of retainers"[152] and *burhsittendra* "fortress dwellers,"[153] both terms that may indicate a community composed of all classes but may also retain a sense of the noble war-band.

In this context let us look briefly at *A Man Sat at Wine* (R.46):

Wer sæt æt wine   mid his wifum twam
ond his twegen suno   ond his twa dohtor,
swase gesweostor,   ond hyra suno twegen,
freolico frumbearn;   fæder wæs þær inne
5   þara æþelinga   æghwæðres mid,
eam ond nefa.   Ealra wæron fife
eorla ond idesa   insittendra. (*A Man Sat at Wine*, R.46)

(A man sat at wine with his two wives, two sons, two daughters – dear sisters – and their two sons – noble first-borns. The father of each of those

---

144 *Þegn* "thegn," for example, which appears in *Belly Behind* (R.37 .2b) and *In a Corner* (R.54. 7a), means one who serves, but it may also be a term for a fighting man. See H.R. Loyn, "Gesiths and Thegns in Anglo-Saxon England from the Seventh to the Tenth Century," *English Historical Review* 70 (1955): 540–9; he concludes that "the term thegn [emerges in the tenth century] as the normal means of describing a noble engaged on the business of helping to govern the realm" (549). Loyn notes that *þegn* may connote youth (544); *In a Corner* may convey youth rather than servile class with its terms *hyse* "young man/warrior" (1a) and *hægsteadmon* "bachelor/warrior" (3a); see definitions in *DOE*. Cf. also *hagosteadle* "bachelorhood," a state associated explicitly with the world of the military elite rather than the servile class in *Cursed among Weapons* (R.20. 31a).
145 The terms are *wer, secg,* and *guma,* which appear in *Hanging Head* (R.44. 1b), *Strong Going In/Out* (R.62. 9a), and *Shining with Gold* (R.63. 1a and 3b). For definitions of these terms, see B-T s.v.v. *wer* and *secg,* and *DOE* s.v. *guma*. B-T notes that *secg* is restricted to poetry, and so it may additionally convey a sense of nobility.
146 *Hanging Head* (R.44. 2a), *Head Stuck In* (R.61. 3b), and *Strong Going In/Out* (R.62. 2b).
147 *Forged by Hammer* (R.91. 9b).
148 *Boneless* (R.45. 5b).
149 *A Man Sat at Wine* (R.46. 7a) and *Warrior's Companion* (R.80. 5a).
150 *In a Corner* (R.54. 11b).
151 *Strong Going In/Out* (R.62. 4b) and *Shining with Gold* (R.63. 15a).
152 *I Travel on Foot* (R.12. 15b). For discussion of this word's range of meanings, see Neville, "Speaking the Unspeakable," 525.
153 *Useful to Neighbours* (R.25. 3a).

princes was there, the uncle and nephew. In all there were five noblemen and ladies sitting there.)

The impossible sum at the conclusion of the riddle can only be achieved through incest, and so the solution accepted by almost all readers is Lot and his family – a domestic arrangement created in despair following the destruction of Sodom and Gomorrah (Genesis 19:31–8), with two women who are simultaneously Lot's daughters and his wives, and two sons who are simultaneously Lot's sons and his grandsons, as well as simultaneously brothers and cousins to each other. The situation is both extreme and Biblical, and so it is unlikely that any confessor would seek to calculate the time of penance required of the individuals involved[154] or feel a need to warn others against following such an example.[155] It may be that this unique situation, involving the nephew of the great patriarch Abraham himself, is all that is necessary to explain the positive language here, but it is worth noting that these *eorla ond idesa* "noblemen and ladies" (7a), these *freolico frumbearn* "noble firstborn" (4a) and *æþelinga[s]* "princes" (5a), are by no means out of place among the other riddles in the collection that seem openly to present sexual activity.

The body of evidence presented here is small, but it is sufficient to refute the perennial tendency to link sexual behaviour with the servile classes: sex is not something that only slaves do, even only metaphorically. The class of men focused upon in the sexual riddles is, for the most part, precisely the same class of men focused upon in Old English poetry in general, and, as already mentioned, directly comparable to the courageous men living up to demanding standards of noble behaviour in *Beowulf* and *The Battle of Maldon*. Yet, as Glenn Davis has noted, scholars tend to isolate the double-entendre riddles and see them as distinct from other Old English texts,[156] and thus interpret that familiar, heroic language in startlingly different ways. For example, Rulon-Miller interprets the heroic language in these texts not as an identifier of the familiar noble elite but as evidence of "impotence anxiety."[157] Although

---

154 Based on *The Canons of Theodore*, it would presumably be fifteen years. See 2.16 and 17.
155 The risk of people misunderstanding the standards of behaviour presented in the Book of Genesis, however, is precisely Ælfric's explanation of his reluctance to translate it. See his *Prefatio Genesis Anglice* in *The Old English Heptateuch and Ælfric's Libellus de Veteri Testamento et Novi*, Volume 1: *Introduction and Text*, ed. Richard Marsden, EETS OS 330 (Oxford: Oxford University Press, 2009), 3–4.
156 "Exeter Book Riddles and the Place of Sexual Idiom," 39–40.
157 Rulon-Miller, "Sexual Humor," 112.

I value her readings highly, I do not see anxiety here. Just as there is no language of shame in these riddles, so also there is no language of anxiety: the heroically hasty man urging on his strong, hard thing in *Strong Going In/Out* expresses no worry about not being man enough for the job, just as Byrhtnoth's men express no fear of failure when they urge each other to avenge their lord on the Vikings in *The Battle of Maldon*, even though, in the latter case at least, failure is inevitable. The ethic of unflinching advance, whatever the odds, remains in place, and so, both on the battlefield and in the *wincle* "corner," noble, strong men are expected to step up to perform deeds of *ellen* "courage."[158]

Class and Gendered Pride: Women

Things are, of course, different for women, as previous scholarship has repeatedly shown. Despite some differences in detail, for example, Rulon-Miller advances more or less the same position that I have been developing here about noble masculinity when she argues that the double-entendre riddles condone male sexuality, even the masturbation apparently presented in *Belly Behind* (R.37), in strong contrast with female sexuality, which she argues is rejected and feared.[159] Like the association between the sexuality and the coarse lower classes, this condemnation of women's sexuality seems assured and inevitable; it is certainly a position that Ælfric would support.[160] As is so often the case, however, looking closely at the language used in the sexual riddles makes that condemnation less certain. Thus if we return to *Boneless* (R.45) and look carefully at the woman instead of the swelling, thrusting thing that she is handling, we see that she is a *þeodnes dohtor* "prince's daughter" (5b); even the bread that she is preparing is high class, since the rising process at the heart of the riddle is a characteristic of the leavened bread enjoyed only by the wealthy, perhaps only on special occasions.[161] Other women in double-entendre riddles may not

---

158 For the "corner" as a place for "sex," see *Boneless* (R.45. 1a) and *In a Corner* (R.54. 2a). For "sex" as a deed of courage, see *Head Stuck In* (R.61. 7b).
159 Rulon-Miller, "Sexual Humor," 113.
160 See discussion in Catherine Cubitt, "Virginity and Misogyny in Tenth- and Eleventh-Century England," *Gender and History* 12 (2000): 1–32.
161 See Debby Banham and Martha Bayless, "The Early English Bread Project," http://earlybread.wordpress.com. We might question whether a noble woman would be involved in such manual labour, but the etymology of the word "lady" (*hlæf* "loaf" + *dige* "kneader") links the female head of a household with breadmaking, in theory, at least. See *OED*, s.v. lady.

hold such a lofty rank, but they are certainly respectable: they include the *bryd* "wife" forbidden to the noble warrior in *Cursed among Weapons* (R.20. 27b) and the *ful cyrtenu ceorles dohtor* "very beautiful freeman's daughter" in *Useful to Neighbours* (R.25. 6). In *Head Stuck In* (R.61), the *ides* "lady" (2a) presenting the receptacle to be filled with something rough is *freolicu* "noble" (1b). In *Shining with Gold* (R.63) the metaphorical "lady" (probably a cup), who is kissed and fondled, is *glæd mid golde* "shining with gold" (3a), like a queen.[162] In *Warrior's Companion* (R.80) a *cwen* "queen" (3b), a *hwitloccedu...eorles dohtor* "fair-haired earl's daughter" (4a, 5a), lays her hand on the riddle-subject, *þeah hio æþelu sy* "although she is noble" (5b). This last comment suggests that a noble woman would not normally indulge in such (apparently) amorous caresses, at least in public, but, as the examples listed here have shown, she is not alone. With the exception of the *wonfeax wale* "dark-haired slave" in *I Travel on Foot* (R.12), all the women participating in the action of the double-entendre riddles are free, not servile, and, as I have argued above, their activities seem blameless and shameless. Thus, even for women, these texts do not connect sexual behaviour with low class.

This focus on members of the upper classes is true even when the "people" involved are actually chickens.

>Ic seah wyhte   wrætlice twa
>undearnunga   ute plegan
>hæmedlaces;   hwitloc anfeng
>wlanc under wædum,   gif þæs weorces speow,
>5 fæmne fyllo ...[163]
>15   Nu is undyrne
>werum æt wine   hu þa wihte mid us,
>heanmode twa,   hatne sindon. (*Two Proud Ones*, R.42.1–5a and 15b–17)

---

162 Cf. the description of Wealhtheow as *goldhroden* (*Beowulf* 614a) and, for example, discussion in Nathan A. Breen, "The King's Closest Counselor: The Legal Basis of Wealhtheow's Comments to Hrothgar, *Beowulf* 1169–87," *The Heroic Age* 14 (2010): https://www.heroicage.org/issues/14/breen.php.

163 For the sake of brevity, I omit lines 5b to 15a, which contain the runic clues to the solution and other issues full of interest but not relevant here. For discussion of these lines, see, for example, Seth Lerer, "The Riddle and the Book: Exeter Book Riddle 42 in Its Contexts," *Papers on Language and Literature*, 25 (1989): 3–18; Niles, *Old English Enigmatic Poems*, 257; Victoria Symons, *Runes and Roman Letters in Anglo-Saxon Manuscripts* (Berlin: Walter de Gruyter, 2016), 52–6 (§2.1.2).

(I saw two amazing creatures playing openly outside in the sport of sex. The woman, proud and bright-haired, received her fill under her garments, if the work was successful ... Now for men at wine it is obvious how those two *heanmode* creatures are called among us.)

The hen receiving the attentions of a cock here is presented as a *fæmne* "young woman" (5a)[164] who is *hwitloc* "fair-haired" (3b). Although modern readers run the risk of imposing later views upon the text, it is possible that her hair colour connotes nobility as well as race and attractiveness;[165] the *cwen* in *Warrior's Companion* (R.80) is also *hwitloccedu* "fair-haired" (4a). That attribute may suggest that this "woman," like the women discussed above, signifies a member of the nobility. There are, however, two important adjectives that require further scrutiny, since they have led to interpretations different from those offered in this chapter: *wlanc* (4a) and *heanmode* (17a).

I shall address the latter first. The conclusion of the riddle tells us that we should already know the names of the riddle-subjects: it is *undyrne* "obvious" (15b) how the *heanmode twa* are called. At first glance, it seems plausible to interpret *heanmode* literally as "low minded"; the riddle-subjects, with their indulgence in open sexual practice, can be seen as base, unenlightened, coarse, and unrefined. Past translators have thus rendered *heanmode* as "shameless,"[166] "vulgar-minded,"[167] "low-down,"[168] and "feather-brained,"[169] all meanings that ascribe negative attributes to the riddle subjects. If this interpretation is correct, then *Heanmode Twa* contradicts my earlier statement that the riddles ascribe no shame to sex. However, as Bitterli has noted, instances of this rare word elsewhere mean "sad" or "humble," not "shameless."[170] Being

---

164 *Fæmne* seems to connote not a particular class but rather youth and sometimes virginity, although the latter is probably not relevant in this case; see *DOE*.
165 See Rulon-Miller, "Sexual Humor," 104; Bitterli, *Say What I Am Called*, 123; Neville, "Speaking the Unspeakable," 523.
166 See, for example, Porter, *Anglo-Saxon Riddles*, 73 and Alexander, *Old English Riddles*, 49.
167 See, for example, *Anglo-Saxon Poetry*, trans. S.A.J. Bradley (London: J.M. Dent and Sons, 1982), 378.
168 See, for example, *The Complete Old English Poems*, trans. Craig Williamson, with an introduction by Tom Shippey (Philadelphia: University of Pennsylvania Press, 2017), 545 (originally published in *A Feast of Creatures: Anglo-Saxon Riddle-Songs*, trans. Craig Williamson [Philadelphia: University of Pennsylvania Press, 1982], 102).
169 See, for example, *The Exeter Book Riddles*, trans. Kevin Crossley-Holland, rev. ed. (London: Enitharmon, 2008), 45.
170 Bitterli, *Say What I Am Called*, 123n28. Bitterli notes that both *heanmod* "sad" or "humble" and *heahmod* "proud, haughty" occur only in the Exeter Book, the former in *Guthlac B* 1379a and *Juliana* 390a, the latter in *The Phoenix* 112b and *Vainglory* 54a. The contexts in these four cases are unambiguous.

"focused on sordid, corrupt, or disreputable concerns" is a meaning that has been attached to "low-minded" only since 1602; before that time, to be low-minded was to have "a modest or humble character."[171] Such a description contradicts the earlier description of at least one of the riddle-subjects as *wlanc* "proud" (4a), and so Bitterli's interpretation of *heanmode* as "haughty" seems inescapable.[172]

Heanmode "haughty" throws *wlanc* (4a) into high relief, and a significant amount of previous attention has been devoted to this term. Murphy includes "compounds with *wlanc*" as part of his "lexicon of dirty riddling,"[173] and, fifty years earlier, Von Lindheim argued that the word had a colloquial meaning now to be found only in the riddles:

> While in one [of the four instances in which *wlonc* appears in the riddles] the translation "proud, haughty" is at least very doubtful, it is out of the question in the three others. Here the meaning "lustful, lascivious, desirous for sexual intercourse" is clearly demanded by the context.[174]

I previously was fully convinced by this argument that "pride" was a euphemism for lust, part of a discourse of sex in the Exeter Book riddles, and I thought that I had confirmed its exclusive, gendered nature by my search of the corpus of Old English poetry, which revealed that women are never described as proud in verse outside the double-entendre riddles.[175] Now, however, I believe that that conclusion misrepresents the texts, and that the context that generates a meaning for *wlanc* is not sex, as Lindheim assumes, but nobility. Michael von Rüden's full-length study of the word provides ample evidence to show that Old English poets use *wlanc* not only in a wide range of contexts (wealth,

---

171 See *OED, s.v.* "low-minded." The quotation provided for 1602 is a bit ambiguous, but the difference between the 1549 meaning and the 1744 meaning is clear. Cf also the 1579 quotation *s.v.* "low-mindedness," which equates the term with "Meekmyndednes."
172 Bitterli thus emends the text to *heahmode*, following Grein and Pinsker and Ziegler (*Say What I Am Called*, 123n28), but, other than to avoid the confusion of modern readers, there is no need to emend the text, since it is not unusual for the second "h" of *heah* to disappear. See *A Guide to Old English*, ed. Bruce Mitchell and Fred C. Robinson, 8th ed. (Malden, MA: John Wiley, 2011), §72; for an example, see the *heanne weall* "lofty wall" in *Judith* 161a.
173 Murphy, *Unriddling*, 176–7.
174 Lindheim, "Traces of Colloquial Speech," 34.
175 In fact I was wrong about that, too: as the discussion below indicates, women are described as proud in a riddle that lacks double entendre, albeit only in a mixed group of men and women (see *Flame-Busy* (R.30. 6).

decoration, audacity, presumption, nobility, beauty, sex) but also with deliberate ambiguity.[176] In my preceding discussion, I have shown that the women involved in (apparently) sexual acts in the double-entendre riddles, with the one exception of the *wonfeax wale*, belong to the ranks of the free, and some are specifically designated as royalty. They are appropriate companions for the heroic noblemen who populate the double-entendre riddles. I suggest, therefore, that their pride is primarily an aspect of their class, not a euphemism for lust.

Support for this assertion can be found in riddles that refer to pride as the defining characteristic of the nobility outside the double-entendre context. In *I Travel on Foot* (R.12), for example, before we come to the Welsh slave and the nocturnal activities that have already been discussed in detail above, a floor-covering or shoes made from ox hide is trodden upon by a *felawlonc* "very proud" (7a) woman. Lindheim suggests that the following "leeringly obscene" description of the *wale* lends support to a sexual meaning for *felawlonc*, but walking on shoes or a rug or mat does not obviously lend itself to double entendre. Rather, the image of a noble lady is appropriate in the context of the immediately preceding *deorum ... / beorne* "brave man" (5–6a) who drinks from what seems to be a leather drinking bottle,[177] and readers or listeners see her, initially at least, in the company of the upper class, not in the context of the double entendre that follows. Further support for the absence of leering obscenity can be found in other riddles. In *Weapon-Warrior* (R.14), for example, the horn *rincas laðige / wlonce to wine* "summons proud men to wine" (16b–17a). In *Protector* (R.17) the contents of the bee-hive are *wloncum deore* "precious to proud ones" (10b). In *Flame-Busy* (R.30) *weras and wif wlonce* "proud men and women" (6) kiss something, perhaps a cup or a crucifix.[178]

---

176 Michael von Rüden, *Wlanc und Derivate im Alt-und Mittelenglischen: Eine wortgeschichtliche Studie* (Frankfurt: Peter Lang, 1978), 107–75. Note especially 147–75, where he discusses uncertain cases, some of which leave a reader unable even to decide whether the usage is positive or negative ("Mitunter ist die Bedeutung von wlanc so wenig auszumachen, dass sich nicht einmal entscheiden laßt, ob das Wort negativ oder positiv gebraucht wird," 157). He specifically rejects Lindheim's reading of *wlanc* on 143.

177 Pirkko Koppinen solves *I Travel on Foot* not as ox but wood, which would supply equally appropriate images of wooden floorboards and turned cups at this point. See "Breaking the Mould: Solving Riddle 12 as *Wudu* 'Wood,'" in *Trees and Timber in the Anglo-Saxon World*, ed. Michael D.J. Bintley and Michael G. Shapland (Oxford: Oxford University Press, 2014), 158–76.

178 For discussion of whether *wlonce* might have a sexual meaning in this case, see Gleißner, *Die "zweideutigen" altenglischen Rätsel*, 351–2.

In *Golden Ring* (R.59) the communion cup is turned in *wloncra folmum* "the hands of proud ones" (18b). No one, as far as I am aware, has attempted to read sexual meanings into these references to proud men and women, even though these texts provide key comparators for the meaning of the word *wlanc* in the double-entendre riddles. Again, as Davis has noted before, scholars tend to "sequester" the double-entendre riddles from the rest of the riddle collection and from the corpus of Old English poetry.[179]

Doing so risks misreading them. The idea of "pride" is important in other contexts, and it has a wide range of associations. Hugh Magennis, for example, provides a thoughtful analysis of a feast in the Old Saxon *Heliand*, in which Herod is *uuinu giuulenkid* "made proud (or arrogant) with wine" (2747).[180] In other accounts Herod is presented negatively, but in this case Magennis argues that Herod is presented as a good king whose judgement has been impaired by drinking, in a situation that brings to mind the Assyrians in *Judith*, who come *wlance to wingedrince* "proud to the wine-drinking" (16a), and Holofernes' ill-fated decision to have an assassin brought to his bed after becoming *medugal* "intoxicated by mead" (26a).[181] Alcohol leads to an exaggerated sense of one's self-importance, and such inflated pride comes before a fall. Yet pride is not always negative, as Magennis has argued in another study: the *wlance wigsmiþas* (72a) in *The Battle of Brunanburh* and the *wlanc* (325a) tribe of Bethulians returning after their victory over the Assyrians are justly proud of their achievements.[182] Likewise, Beowulf is justly *goldwlanc* "gold-proud" (*Beowulf* 1881a) when he boards his ship with the gifts he has earned from Hrothgar. As Dennis Cronan notes, while *wlenco* usually carries a pejorative sense ("arrogance"), in a poetic context it may mean "a great-spirited courage which could lead one to daring undertakings for the good of others or to reckless endeavours that produce unnecessary risk,"[183] and *Beowulf* contains a full range of positive and negative examples of this kind of courage.[184]

---

179 Davis, "Exeter Book Riddles and the Place of Sexual Idiom," 39–41.
180 Hugh Magennis, *Anglo-Saxon Appetites: Food and Drink and their Consumption in Old English and Related Literature* (Dublin: Four Courts, 1999), 118–19. His quotation from *The Heliand* is taken from *Heliand und Genesis*, ed. Otto Behaghel, 9th ed., rev. Burkhard Taeger (Tübingen: Max Niemeyer, 1984).
181 See also my discussion of *gal* and its compounds above.
182 See *Images of Community*, 100 and 158.
183 "Poetic Words, Conservatism and the Dating of Old English Poetry," *ASE* 33 (2004): 34. See also Cronan., "Poetic Meanings," 400.
184 For example, Wulfgar, Hrothgar's messenger, is first introduced as *wlonc* (331b) and later commended as being well known for his *wig ond wisdom* "war-craft and

The point, again, is that both positive and negative aspects of pride are characteristics ascribed to nobility. The expected stereotype may be found stated succinctly and explicitly in *Maxims I*:

Þrym sceal mid wlenco,   þriste mid cenum,
sceolun bu recene   beadwe fremman. (*Maxims I* 60–1)

(Power must be with pride, daring among bold ones, both must promptly commit to battle.)

As I noted at the beginning of this chapter, the use of *sceal* here is important. Although I have translated it as "must," it may be more accurate and even more telling to follow Cavill's suggestion and interpret the auxiliary verb as indicating not what is required but rather what is characteristically true.[185] The members of the elite military class, the nobility, characteristically have power (*þrym*), and with their status comes not only an expectation of heroic action (that is, prompt commitment to battle) but also *wlenco* "pride."

In the Exeter Book riddles, the "pride" of the women is the equivalent of the "bravery" of the men: not a euphemism for lust but another marker to identify the noble class of the people engaged in these (apparently) sexual acts. That pride may be positive or negative, but, whether seen as dangerous arrogance or the proper quality of those belonging to the elite, it is a key marker of class. Previous scholars have interpreted "proud women" as a marker of double entendre, but, if they are, they are suggestive only indirectly. Pride is a key signifier not of lustfulness but of the noble classes. And those noble classes are here associated with engagement in (apparently) sexual practices, much more frequently than humble farmers and their wives or even more humble slaves.

---

wisdom" (350a). Wulfgar himself approves of Beowulf because he assumes that the visitor has come to fight Grendel because of *wlenco* "pride" (338a) rather than exile. The formidable Ongentheow retreats when he hears that Hygelac, *wlonces wigcræft* "proud in his war-craft" (2953a), is approaching. Conversely, Unferth accuses Beowulf of *wlence* "reckless pride" (508a), and Hygelac *for wlenco wean ahsode* "looked for woe out of pride" (1206a). When the trait is applied to monsters, its import is probably negative, but it may also carry a sense of awe-inspiring power: Grendel is remembered as *æse wlanc* "proud of his carrion" (1332a), and the dragon is remembered as *maðmæhta wlonc* "proud of its treasures" (2833b).

185 Cavill, *Maxims*, 45–50.

Conclusions

What does the association between the nobility and sexual activity mean? Ultimately, of course, we cannot know, and perhaps there is no need to look for a deep significance: we could ascribe the association between sex and nobility simply to the pursuit of humorous incongruity.[186] Yet the question may still be useful, if only to remind ourselves of the dangers of drawing what seem to be logical conclusions. For example, on a literal level, we might theorize that the issue of succession is a legitimate concern for the noble classes: heirs must be produced for a dynasty to persist. As we have seen, however, sex in these riddles does not lead to the production of offspring. In the same way, we might conclude that the riddles express a subversive egalitarianism, with the aim of showing that the upper classes are no better than the rest of the society, that they are human, "just like us." I fear, however, that to find egalitarianism in these texts is to impose an anachronistic wishful thinking on them. Such a reading might be attractive to modern readers, but it will not do for the members of the church, often from the upper classes themselves,[187] who were certainly the editors and mostly likely the authors and audiences of these texts.[188]

Another line of thinking, occasionally mentioned by scholars but rarely fully explored, is the Bakhtinian idea of the carnivalesque.[189] Based on a reading of a sixteenth-century text, this, too, is anachronistic, but it offers some very tempting lines of thought. As D.K. Smith notes, we can read the riddles as a place where the body is turned upside down, where what is supressed becomes openly desired, and where

---

186 For an overview of incongruity theory and its relevance to the Exeter Book riddles, see Jonathan Wilcox, "Humour and the *Exeter Book* Riddles: Incongruity in *Feþegeorn* (R.31)," in *Riddles at Work in the Early Medieval Tradition: Words, Ideas, Interactions*, ed. Megan Cavell and Jennifer Neville, Manchester Medieval Literature and Culture 32 (Manchester: Manchester University Press, 2020), 128–45.

187 Their leaders, at least, had relatives among the highest levels of society; as Thornbury notes, "Abbots and bishops with kinship ties to royalty and aristocracy were the norm, rather than the exception, in Anglo-Saxon England." Emily V. Thornbury, *Becoming a Poet in Anglo-Saxon England* (Cambridge: Cambridge University Press, 2014), 154.

188 For the learned context of these texts, see, for example, Mercedes Salvador-Bello, *Isidorean Perceptions of Order: The Exeter Book Riddles and Medieval Latin Enigmata* (Morgantown: West Virginia University Press, 2015) and Bitterli, *Say What I Am Called*.

189 Mikhail Bakhtin, *Rabelais and His World*, trans. Hélène Iswolsky (1965; Cambridge, MA: MIT Press, 1968).

high becomes low.[190] On the surface that statement provides a good explanation for the riddles' presentation of sexual activity among the noble classes, but, as this chapter has demonstrated, it is not the whole story, either. While one could argue that the riddles provide a special place where the low becomes high (that is, sex is presented as heroic activity), it is not true to say that the high becomes low: (apparently) sexual activity does not degrade the prince's daughter in *In a Corner* (R.54) or the obedient lady and her loyal lord in *Head Stuck In* (R.61).

The carnivalesque possibility of inversion, however, recalls the inversions made possible by the implement trope, which I discussed in chapter 5. As I noted there, Exeter Book riddles such as *Bright Warrior* (R.50) do not call for rebellion or the reorganization of society when they describe lords serving their thegns, but they do require their audiences to become aware of the discourse of the heroic idiom, with its familiar, undisputed ethics and values, as a construct that can be scrutinized and even parodied rather than simply an expression of truth. In the same way, I do not believe that the sexual riddles discussed in this chapter seek to puncture, censure, or reject the upper classes when they describe the noble elite earnestly labouring in *hæmedlaces* "the play of sex" (*Two Proud Ones*, R.42. 3a).[191] This is not satire or, at least, I do not think so. If it were satire, I would expect to find a clear connection between the sexual behaviour indulged in by the noble classes and the degradation of sin, but that, like many of the things we might expect, does not actually appear in the texts. We can, of course, read censure and deflation into them, as many scholars have. Yet the fact that scholars can look at the same text and draw wildly contradictory conclusions, even when they agree on solutions to the riddle itself, suggests to me that the humorous incongruity here is meant to focus our attention on how we arrive at those conclusions rather than the conclusions themselves. Even in our present, sexually permissive society, the sexual riddles startle us out of expected thinking patterns, while scholars have been baffled by their presence and have laboured mightily to explain it, as I mentioned at the beginning of this chapter.

---

190 Smith, "Humor in Hiding," 89–90. For the ideas underlying this analysis, see Peter Stallybrass and Allon White, *The Politics and Poetics of Transgression* (Ithaca, NY: Cornell University Press, 1986).

191 For a useful discussion of the way in which early Middle English texts might use deprecation and deflation even when no clear moral lesson is being drawn, see Ben Parsons, "'The Werste Lay That Euer Harper Sange with Harp': The Forms of Early Middle English Satire," *Comitatus* 39 (2008): 113–36.

That labour is the point, the reason, the explanation for the presence of these outrageous texts in the Exeter Book, and so perhaps the emphasis on labour within the texts themselves is not coincidental. As this chapter has demonstrated, the sexual imagery within these texts is remarkable not merely for its presence but also for its confounding of expectations: this is sex without reproduction, sex without sin, sex with only occasional references to pleasure, sex practised by the noble classes. We cannot know what early medieval English readers and listeners would have finally concluded about these texts, but they could not fail to be confounded by what they discovered. Many riddles revel in incongruity that makes us look at the world again, but these ones stop their audiences (then and now) in their tracks. The world that we thought we knew is not quite what we thought. It demands our attention. And it demands a response.

Every riddle forces its audience to respond,[192] even if it does not conclude with the challenge to *saga hwæt ic hatte* "say what I am called," but in the sexual riddles the challenge is urgent: the unspeakable has been spoken; what will we say in response? Previous scholars have talked about the shame of incorrect answers, but for this discussion I am more interested in what the fear of shame drives us to do. What it drives us to do is to labour: to read more carefully, to excavate the imagery, to be suspicious of assumptions, to revisit familiar tropes, to go back and start again (and again and again). When we do that labour, we not only see homely, familiar objects like churns and keys in a new light; we also discover the underlying assumptions that make up cultural discourses of value and power. However trivial and light-hearted they may seem to be, the sexual riddles force their audiences to evaluate their ways of evaluating things.

Finally, it is worth remembering, once again, that all this interpretive work is only possible because there are no solutions in the manuscript, and also that some of the work is created by the competence of an audience composed of people who are too clever by half and know how riddles work. A riddle-solver who has successfully negotiated the double entendre of *Useful to Neighbours* (R.25) to arrive at "onion" rather than "penis" is quite likely to assume that *Two Proud Ones* (R.42) is

---

192 For discussion of the riddles' "culture of responsiveness," see Patricia Dailey, "Riddles, Wonder and Responsiveness in Anglo-Saxon Literature," in *The Cambridge History of Early Medieval English Literature*, ed. Clare Lees (Cambridge: Cambridge University Press, 2012), 451–72.

describing not sex but "sex." Such a reader might thus attempt to interpret the "woman" and her lover as some kind of object, such as a key and keyhole. *Two Proud Ones*, however, plays a double bluff: it looks like a sexual joke, but it is no joke at all; it is, actually, sex. Responding to the sexual riddles, then, requires us not only to read "the basic metaphors of cultural existence" which are "recognized implicitly"[193] but also to pay direct, explicit attention to what we think we know.

---

[193] Roger D. Abrahams, "The Literary Study of the Riddle," *Texas Studies in Literature and Language* 14 (1972): 182.

Chapter Seven

Not Concluding but Continuing

When I think about the riddles of the Exeter Book, I imagine a group of people sitting around a table, drinking beer, and talking animatedly:

Cum, cunna!
"Go on, have a go!"

Hit is teors.
"It's a penis."

Beo eornest.
"Be serious."

Hit is horn.
"It's a horn."

Nis is seo andsweru unnyt. Ne tosæleþ. Ac hwæt cweðest þu, Leoba?
"That's not a bad guess. It works. But what do you say, Leoba?"

Seo andsweru is horn, ac þu cnawest þæt þæt giedd ne mæneð þæt soðlice. Hit is dol swefn ymb ealdum wisum – ymb life swa swa hit no wære, spell þæt we gelifdon in geardagum.
"Horn is the answer, but you know that the text doesn't truly mean that. It's a foolish vision about the old ways – about life as it never was, a fairy tale that we believed in past times."

Þæt mæg riht wesan, ac horn is to eaðfynde. Soðlice, hit is haliges rodes laf.

"That may be right, but horn is too obvious. Really, it's a relic of the true cross."

Hwæt, þæt is tilu andsweru. Ælfred, canst þu cweðan sum oþer þing?
"Hey, that's a good answer! Alfred, can you come up with anything else?"

And so on. Of course, we have no way of knowing how the poems assembled at the end of the Exeter Book were received by early medieval English audiences. Nonetheless, hundreds of years later, this is exactly how modern readers of the Exeter Book have responded to the riddles: these texts have inspired an ongoing process of interpretation, an unending series of proposals, debates, and counter-proposals, although not, admittedly, in one room, around one table, at one time (but probably, on some occasions, with beer). Although I cannot be certain, I assume that these texts exercised a similarly provocative effect on their original audiences, that they both frustrated and fascinated them, and that the absence of authoritative answers prompted multiple, competing solutions. The possibility of multiple solutions is the motivation for, not the consequence of, having no solutions in the manuscript.

Thus, over the course of this book I have discussed seven different solutions for *Lone Dweller* (R.5): in addition to the traditional solution, *scield* "shield," I have considered *onheaw* "chopping block" (for wood), **mete-bord* "cutting board" (for food), *hwet-stan* "whetstone," *scyld* "guilt," *gewyrged gast* "damned soul," and *tabula* "writing tablets." I have argued that some of these (*scield*, *onheaw*, and *scyld*) fail the test set by *Most Wretched of All* (R.39), which reminds us that

> Soð is æghwylc
> þara þe ymb þas wiht   wordum becneð. (25b–26)

(Everything that is made known in words [here] about this creature is true.)

Despite the confidence that most modern readers feel about *scield* as *Lone Dweller*'s solution, some of the text's clues seem to be only partially true, while the last words of the text, *dagum ond nihtum* "by day and night" (14b), seem to me to be a final twist to disqualify what would otherwise have been a logical and obvious answer to the problem set by the text. The victim of swords that cannot be cured by a doctor is obviously a shield, except for the fact that shields are not characteristically used both night and day. Neither are chopping blocks, since chopping wood in the dark is too dangerous to be profitable. Cutting boards, whetstones, and writing tablets, however, can be used indoors, using fire- or candle-light for nocturnal activities, and so they are better solutions. Yet even these solutions do not preclude the possibility of a moral, allegorical reading of the text: suffering wounds by day and night could be a narrative of temptation, guilt, and damnation, leading to the solution *fæge sawol* ("damned soul").[1]

Yet even seven solutions, every one with strengths and supporters, leave a lingering sense of queerness in this fourteen-line text, an emotional charge that shows that the riddling tactic of disidentification cannot easily be explained away. Even if, despite my best efforts, the view that *Lone Dweller* describes a shield continues to convince the majority of readers, the image of the suffering veteran – the surface that should be discarded, "empty and of no importance"[2] once the riddle is solved – remains. The "third term" created by the riddle still demands our attention; it "resists the binary of identification and counteridentification" and "the oppressive and normalizing discourse of dominant ideology":[3] we cannot read this text and still believe that courage in battle always leads to glory. That lingering queerness has led me to yet another way of dealing with blades by night. Although I have no expectation that many readers will choose it as their preferred way of solving *Lone Dweller*, I offer it as a testament to the games that Exeter Book riddles play with tropes and intertextuality, as support for the argument that the game is best enjoyed by one who has played this kind of game before,[4] as an example of riddling queerness, and as a closing plea for allowing the riddles to retain their disidentifications rather than insisting on the move from counteridentification to identification, from perplexity to solution.

Here is *Lone Dweller* (R.5) one more time:

Ic eom anhaga   iserne wund,
bille gebennad,   beadoweorca sæd,
ecgum werig.   Oft ic wig seo,

---

1 For discussion of these solutions, see chapter 4 above.
2 Annikki Kaivola-Bregenhøj, *Riddles: Perspectives on the Use, Function and Change in a Folklore Genre*, trans. Susan Sinisalo (Helsinki: Finnish Literature Society, 2001), 19. Cf. Northrop Frye: puzzles are "to be solved and annihilated." *Anatomy of Criticism: Four Essays* (Princeton: Princeton University Press, 1957), 88.
3 José Esteban Muñoz, "'The White to Be Angry': Vaginal Davis's Terrorist Drag," *Social Text* 52–3 (1997), 83.
4 Patrick Murphy, *Unriddling the Exeter Riddles* (University Park: Pennsylvania State University Press, 2011), 11; Winfried Rudolf, "Riddling and Reading: Iconicity and Logographs in Exeter Book Riddles 23 and 45," *Anglia* 130 (2012): 500.

frecne feohtan. Frofre ne wene,
5 þæt mec geoc cyme   guðgewinnes,
ær ic mid ældum   eal forwurðe,
ac mec hnossiað   homera lafe,
heardecg heoroscearp,   ondweorc smiþa,
bitað in burgum;   ic abidan sceal
10 laþran gemotes.   Næfre læcecynn
on folcstede   findan meahte,
þara þe mid wyrtum   wunde gehælde,
ac me ecga dolg   eacen weorðað
þurh deaðslege   dagum ond nihtum. (*Lone Dweller*, R.5)

(I am a lone dweller, wounded by iron, injured by blade, sated with battle-work, weary of swords. I often see a dangerous battle fought. I do not expect comfort – that rescue from war-struggle will come to me before I entirely perish among men [*or* in flames]. Instead, the leavings of hammers, the handiwork of smiths, hard-edged and battle sharp, will bite me within the fortifications. I must await a more unpleasant meeting. In the settlement I could never find [one of] the race of doctors, [one of those] who might heal [my] wounds with herbs. Instead day and night the scars from swords become greater with [every] deadly stroke.)

The text displays the poet's mastery of the appositive style[5] with a proliferation of terms for sword: *iserne* "iron [sword]" (1b), *bille* "blade" (2a), *ecg* "edge" (3a and 13a), *homera lafe* "leavings of hammers" (8b). Swords are important here. The insistence on swords draws attention to this key thing that needs to be interpreted, whether literally or metaphorically. Previous solutions have taken these "swords" as swords or as other types of edged tools: axes, knives, writing styli. I have also suggested seeing them as allegorical weapons of the devil. A riddlee who has successfully solved *Cursed among Weapons* (R.20), however, with its story of the celibate sword unable to father children with a bride, will also be familiar with figuring swords as phalluses, and, of course, there are plenty of other texts that make that connection, too.[6] If the swords are phalluses, however, what is their victim?

---

5   I adopt this term from Fred C. Robinson, *Beowulf and the Appositive Style* (Knoxville: University of Tennessee Press, 1985).
6   The connection is built into the lexis: to be male is to be "weaponed" (equipped with a penis). See, for example, Bosworth-Toller s.v.v. *wæpnedbearn* "male child," *wæpnedcild* "male child," *wæpnedcynn* "the male sex," *wæpnedhad* "the male sex," *wæpnedhand* "the male line," *wæpnedmann* "a male." Although some of these males may also carry literal weapons, even a plant can be a *wæpnedmann*.

It is a vagina.[7] At first glance, such an act of interpretation is unsupportable, but it makes surprisingly good sense out of *Lone Dweller*'s narrative. The *anhaga* "lone-dweller" (1a), the singular vagina between a woman's legs, having been repeatedly penetrated by penises, is *werig* "tired" (3a) of the *beadoweorca* "battle-works" (2b) of sex but knows that it can expect no *geoc* "rescue" (5a) from this *guðgewinn* "battle-struggle" (5b) until after death (6b). The men's penises (glorified by multiple, appositive epithets that stress their dangerous power) *bitað* "bite" (9a) the vagina; that is, like swords, they strike and penetrate it. They characteristically do this indoors, or, at least, within the *burgum* "fortifications" (9a).[8] As a result of this *wig* "war" (3b), the vagina expects a *laþran gemotes* "more unpleasant meeting" (10a) between itself and the emerging head of the child during childbirth in the future. Indeed, there are medical charms aimed at ensuring the safe passage of the infant through that opening,[9] and there is archaeological evidence to show that the "encounter" could be much *laþran* "worse"; it could be

---

7 It is possible to read this text as a story of male-male sexual behaviour, too, and solve the riddle as *arsgang* "anus," but I have not yet been able to find a good interpretation of the *laþran gemotes* "more unpleasant meeting" (10a) in such a scenario. For an explicit reference to an anus in a riddling text, see the logogriphic riddle attributed to Bede: *Littera queque culum facit ut videat velut oc[u]llus* "And which letter makes it so that an anus sees like an eye?" The solution is "O," because, as the gloss helpfully spells out, adding *o* to *culus* creates the word *oculus* "eye." For the text of the Latin riddle, alongside its explanatory gloss, see Frederick Tupper Jr, "Riddles of the Bede Tradition: The "Flores" of Pseudo-Bede," Modern Philology 2 (1904–5): 569; see also the more recent edition and translation in *The Old English and Anglo-Latin Riddle Tradition*, ed. Andy Orchard, Dumbarton Oaks Medieval Library 69 (Cambridge, MA: Harvard University Press, 2021), 98–9.
8 Note *Two Proud Ones* (R.42), where the incongruity of having sex outdoors is part of what signals the non-human status of the cock and hen. For discussion of this text see chapter 6, above.
9 See *Lacnunga* item 162, which includes an incantation against late, difficult, and lame births, and the *Old English Herbarium* CIV 2, a recipe and ritual to speed up a birth. For texts see *Anglo-Saxon Remedies, Charms and Prayers from British Library MS Harley 585: The Lacnunga*, ed. Edward Pettit, 2 vols (Lampeter: Edwin Mellen Press, 2001) and *The Old English Herbarium and Medicina de Quadrupedibus*, ed. H.J. Vriend, EETS 286 (London: Oxford University Press, 1984). For discussion of these texts see Marilyn Deegan, "Pregnancy and Childbirth in the Anglo-Saxon Medical Texts: A Preliminary Survey," in Medicine in Early Medieval England, ed. Marilyn Deegan and D.G. Scragg (Manchester: Centre for Anglo-Saxon Studies, University of Manchester, 1987), 20; L.M.C. Weston, "Women's Magic: The Old English Metrical Childbirth Charms," Modern Philology 92 (1995): 288; Audrey L. Meaney, "Extra-Medical Elements in Anglo-Saxon Medicine," Social History of Medicine 24 (2011): 54.

fatal.[10] On the other hand, no *læc* "doctor" (10b) should cause the *wund* "wound" (12b) of the vaginal opening to close up. And, finally, the act of sex may take place both *dagum ond nihtum* "day and night" (14b), perhaps especially the latter.

I am not aware of any other early medieval English text that presents the vagina as a suffering wound, yet there are analogues for it, albeit distanced in time and space. Even before the wound in Christ's side wound became a place where one could be born again,[11] the vagina as a wound appears in 13th century French fabliaux. For example, in *La Saineresse*, the wife concludes her revenge on her husband's arrogance by openly telling him how the "lady"-doctor (the *saineresse*, who is in fact male) repeatedly beat her "wound" to cure her gout,[12] and in *La Maignien qui foti la dame*, a tinker summoned to assist a woman, who fell trying to get into the bath, attends to her "wound."[13] In both cases, of course, there is no actual wound, only the vigorously assailed vaginal opening. The idea seems to be an old one; discussions of its appearance assume that it is a long-standing folklore motif.[14] The motif persists in later stories, too; for example, in his sixteenth-century satire, *The Life of Gargantua and of Pantagruel*, Rabelais relates a story of a lion exhorting a fox to treat an old woman's "wound" with his tail.[15]

---

10 Deegan, 17–18; Duncan Sayer and Sam D. Dickinson, "Reconsidering Obstetric Death and Female Fertility in Anglo-Saxon England," *World Archaeology* 45 (2013): 285–97.

11 See the discussion in Vibeke Olson, "Penetrating the Void: Picturing the Wound in Christ's Side as a Performative Space," in *Wounds and Wound Repair in Medieval Culture*, ed. Larissa Tracey and Kelly DeVries (Leiden: Brill, 2015), 313–39.

12 For text of *La Saineresse*, see *Recueil Général et complet des fabliaux des XIIIe et XIVe siècles imprimés ou inédits*, ed. Anatole de Montaiglon and Gaston Raynaud, 6 vols (Paris: Librairie des bibliophiles, 1872–1890), 1:289–93 (http://gallica.bnf.fr/ark:/12148/bpt6k209379m).

13 For text of *La Maignien qui foti la dame*, see *Recueil Général*, 5:179–83 (https://gallica.bnf.fr/ark:/12148/bpt6k209383p/f185.item).

14 Malcolm Jones, "Folklore Motifs in Late Medieval Art III: Erotic Animal Imagery," *Folklore* 102 (1991): 217n120. For an earlier dating for the fabliau, see discussion in Peter Dronke, "The Rise of the Medieval Fabliau: Latin and Vernacular Evidence," *Romanische Forschungen*, 85 (1973): 275–97, where he suggests that these ribald stories were probably not an innovation even in the tenth century (287).

15 See book 2, chapter 15 in *Les Cinq Livres de Rabelais, Volume 1: Gargantua, Pantagruel*, ed. Roger Delbiausse (Paris: Éditions Magnard, 1965), 195–6; for translation see François Rabelais, *Gargantua and Pantagruel*, trans. M.A. Screech (London: Penguin, 2006), 83. For "tail" as penis in Latin, see J.N. Adams, *The Latin Sexual Vocabulary* (London: Duckworth, 1982), 35–7; see also the comparison to Old French words in Ellen L. Friedrich, "When a Rose Is Not a Rose: Homoerotic Emblems in the *Roman de la Rose*," in *Gender Transgressions: Crossing the Normative Barrier in Old French Literature*, ed. Karen J. Taylor (London: Routledge, 1998), 29.

There are strong arguments against this interpretation of *Lone Dweller*. The text presents none of the cues that would lead us to the trope of sex: *nathwæt* does not make an appearance; no proud woman represents her class; no reference is made to male usefulness or tumescence; and there is neither constriction nor confinement, neither "play" nor "work." If any of the tropes explored in this book is here, it is the trope of manufacturing, with its invocation of torture, and yet *Lone Dweller* lacks the justification of a product even if it seems to describe the same violent processes that lead to artifice in, for example, *Cursed among Weapons* (R.20) or *Forged by Hammer* (R.91).[16] The fact that understanding traditional tropes fails to lead to a solution is important. Even if we accept the traditional solution *scield* "shield" for *Lone Dweller*, the riddle works by subverting our expectation of the trope of manufacturing. The story of the shield, which could have been a story of craft that leads to a useful and beautiful object, ends up being a story of destruction that leads to oblivion. The same subversion takes place if *Lone Dweller* is a story of a chopping block, a cutting board, a whetstone, or writing tablets. Indeed, this text is full of surprises. It confronts us with four unusual things: a sympathetic vision of a defeated warrior;[17] an absence of triumphalist glory in battle; a rare reference to a doctor;[18] and torture without art or artifice. Although I suspect that no early medieval English riddlee would have shouted out "vagina" in response to this text, *Lone Dweller* might present a disidentified vagina as yet another one of its surprises.

It is useful to consider why finding a vagina here would be so surprising. The relationship between penises and vaginas is, of course, as familiar as that between swords and shields. The radical nature of

---

16 See discussion in chapter 5, above.
17 Edward B. Irving Jr, "Heroic Experience in the Old English Riddles," in *Old English Shorter Poems: Basic Readings*, ed. Katherine O'Brien O'Keeffe (New York: Garland, 1994), 199–212. Elsewhere defeated warriors are presented as contemptible or glorious; see, for example, the Egyptians in *Exodus* and Byrhtnoth's loyal retainers in *The Battle of Maldon*, respectively.
18 Leaving aside references to Christ as healer (*A Prayer* 6b, *The Lord's Prayer II* 62b, *Judgement Day II* 46a and 66b), Christ's spiritual *læcedom* "medicine" (*Judgement Day II* 81a, *Christ III* 1572b, *Christ and Satan* 588b), the Pater Noster's role as *lamena læce* "doctor of the lame" (*Solomon and Saturn I* 77a), and the ironic comment that the violently aggressive runic letter R will not be a *læce god* "good doctor" for evil spirits (*Solomon and Saturn I* 102b), I can find only one reference to a human doctor in Old English poetry (*Lef mon læces behofað* "a weak man needs a doctor" [*Maxims I* 45a]), and even that comes in the immediate context of God's mercy. Physical as opposed to spiritual *læcedom* "medicine" is rare in verse, too, appearing only in the *Charm for the Water-Elf Disease* (3a), where it appears in the context of a recipe designed to alleviate physical symptoms.

this argument, then, is less the possibility of a sexual subject than *Lone Dweller*'s tone and perspective on it. There are few other texts in Old English that talk about sex in this way: not with the humour that characterizes the texts discussed in the previous chapter but rather with sorrow and sympathy for a female victim – texts that tell a story of swords and shields rather than swords and scabbards, of violent opposition between the sexes rather than the congruence and natural fit alluded to in the *efenlang* "equally long" recipient of the key in *Hanging Head* (R.44. 7a).[19] And yet that story does exist in other Old English poems, even if it is not explicitly narrated. We might think of *Judith*, which presents a scenario that *could* have paralleled the one I have imagined in *Lone Dweller*, if divine intervention had not transformed it so that the woman turned a literal sword against her would-be attacker before he could wield his metaphorical one. We might think of *Wulf and Eadwacer*, which hints at sexual approaches that are *lað* "hated" even while they bring *wyn* "pleasure" (*Wulf and Eadwacer* 12). We might think of Beadohild, whose sorrow for the death of her brother is outweighed by the awareness of her unwanted pregnancy, and presumably, the unwanted sex that preceded it (*Deor* 8–11a). Only in *Lone Dweller*, however, can we find (perhaps) a reflection on a woman's experience of her everyday sexual life, rather than the acute experience of rape.

What is *soð* here? Perhaps this unique reference to the vagina as wound is only a discardable surface. Perhaps it is not there at all. Yet, as we have seen, *Lone Dweller* is not the only Exeter Book riddle with such a unique perspective, such a queer offering. *Fight against Wave* (R.16, the anchor or anchorite), for example, presents passivity as heroism;[20] *Bright Warrior* (R.50, the fire) presents the lower classes as needing to control the pride of their rulers to preserve stability and peace;[21] and *Cursed among Weapons* (R.20, the sword) refers to sex as joyous play.[22] Even if only in passing, these are texts that allow us to think the unthinkable.

---

19 Megan Cavell reminded me that *vagina* is the Latin word for "scabbard" and that the relationship between sword and scabbard could be imagined as being more penetrative and less congruent than I have presented it here (personal communication, 7 January 2022). I have not sought to propose "scabbard" as a solution for *Lone Dweller* because I am not certain that the insertion of a sword would characteristically cause damage to it, but the connection is tempting.
20 See discussion in chapter 4, above.
21 See discussion in chapter 5, above.
22 See discussion in chapter 6, above.

To think the unthinkable, however, we need to be stopped in our tracks long enough to notice the "third term" and to linger in its queerness. The "normalizing discourse of dominant ideology" will always tempt us with its apparent rightness and the elegance of its "inner click," but, luckily, the creator of the Exeter Book left us without shortcuts to arrive there. Please linger. And go on, have another go.

Appendix: The Argument over Solutions

The list below aims to represent the argument that has been stimulated by the Exeter Book riddles over more than 150 years, up to the end of 2021. As E.G. Stanley argues, "'[s]olution' is too firm a concept for texts by riddlers who played with their contemporaries, as with us a thousand years later";[1] what I present here is not a collection of final solutions but the ebb and flow of consensus over time. I thus list not only the first proposal of a solution, the most popular solution, or my favourite solution, but also the significant discussions that supported and developed each solution over time. This list is indebted to past lists, such as those by Trautmann, Fry, and Niles,[2] as well as the solutions listed in past editions and translations of the collection.[3] In addition

---

1 "Exeter Book *Riddles*, II: The Significant but Often Misleading Opening Word," *N&Q* 64 (2017): 365.
2 Moritz Trautmann, "Zu den Lösungen der Rätsel des Exeterbuchs," *Beiblatt zur Anglia Mitteilungen* 25 (1914), 273–9; Donald K. Fry, "Exeter Book Riddle Solutions," *Old English Newsletter* 15 (1981), 22–33; John D. Niles, *Old English Enigmatic Poems and the Play of the Texts* (Turnhout: Brepols, 2006), 141–8. I have also consulted online lists, including those by Aaron K. Hostetter (https://oldenglishpoetry.camden.rutgers .edu/exeter-book-riddles-solutions/) and Megan Cavell (the riddleages.com).
3 The main editions consulted include: *The Riddles of the Exeter Book*, ed. Frederick Tupper Jr (London: Ginn, 1910); *Die altenglischen Rätsel (Die Rätsel des Exeterbuchs)*, ed. Moritz Trautmann (Heidelberg: Carl Winter, 1915); *The Exeter Book, Part II: Poems IX–XXXII*, ed. and trans. W.S. Mackie, EETS , o.s., 194 (London: Humphry Milford and Oxford University Press, 1934); *The Exeter Book*, ed. George Philip Krapp and Elliott van Kirk Dobbie, ASPR 3 (London: Routledge and Kegan Paul, 1936); *The Old English Riddles of the Exeter Book*, ed. Craig Williamson (Chapel Hill: University of North Carolina Press, 1977); *Die altenglischen Rätsel des Exeterbuchs: Text mit deutscher Übersetzung und Kommentar*, ed. and trans. Hans Pinsker and Waltraud Ziegler, Anglistische Forschungen (Heidelberg: Carl Winter, 1985); *The Exeter Anthology of OE Poetry: An Edition of Exeter Dean and Chapter MS 3501*, ed. Bernard

to the solutions accepted in lists, I add further entries from critical discussions, translations of individual texts, and influential textbooks. A rough sense of a solution's popularity can be gained by the number of scholars listed after it. I have not attempted to count every vote of acceptance for each solution; I usually do not note a critical discussion of a riddle, for example, unless it contains an argument for a solution, whether to propose a new solution or develop a pre-existing one. For some riddles there are very few entries, with a large majority of scholars being confident that the riddle has been solved; for some there is a long list of past choices, with scholars reluctantly committing themselves to doubtful guesses; for others a solution that was persuasive at one time is eventually abandoned in favour of another. Looking at the accumulation of entries listed next to each riddle can be as illuminating as the entries themselves.

Niles persuasively argues that riddles should be answered in their own language,[4] so I provide Old English (and occasionally Latin) solutions here followed by translations into modern English (even if the original proposer of the solution did not supply it in the original language). Many of these Old English solutions derive from Niles' own list.[5] Old English solutions marked with a star (*) have been coined by modern scholars, sometimes myself. If no Old English solution is provided, I have been unable to find or create a plausible coinage (e.g., for "cross-bow," an object that may not have existed in the early medieval period, or "phallus," whose meaning relies on Freudian concepts not known in the period).

Solutions are listed in the order in which they were first proposed. I include here only the last name and date of each vote; full references can be found in the bibliography.

J. Muir, 2nd rev. ed., 2 vols (Exeter: University of Exeter Press, 2000); *The Old English and Anglo-Latin Riddle Tradition*, ed. and trans. Andy Orchard, Dumbarton Oaks Medieval Library 69 (Harvard: Harvard University Press, 2021). Translations consulted include *Anglo-Saxon Riddles*, trans. John Porter (Hockwold-cum-Wilton: Anglo-Saxon Books, 1995); *Old English Riddles from the Exeter Book*, trans. Michael Alexander, 2nd ed. (London: Anvil Press, 2007); *The Exeter Book Riddles*, trans. Kevin Crossley-Holland, rev. ed. (London: Enitharmon, 2008).

4 Niles, *Old English Enigmatic Poems*, 101–40.
5 Niles, *Old English Enigmatic Poems*, 141–8.

The Argument over Solutions 255

ASPR Number	Riddle Title	Solutions
1	*Glorious I Thunder*	*storm* "storm" (Dietrich 1859b, Prehn 1883, Brooke 1892, E. Erlemann 1903, Brandl 1908b, Tupper 1910, Wood 1912, Wyatt 1912, Trautmann 1915, Sedgefield 1922, Mackie 1934, Krapp and Dobbie 1936, Baum 1963, Hacikyan 1966, Conlee 1968, Pinsker 1981b, Porter 1995, Williams 1999, Alexander 2007, Crossley-Holland 2008, Bitterli 2009, Liuzza 2014, Salvador-Bello 2015, Cavell 2020) *wind* "wind" (Wyatt 1912, Mackie 1934, Young 1942, Liuzza 2014, Salvador-Bello 2015, Cavell 2020) *lig* "fire" (Shook 1946) *lyft* "atmosphere" (Erhardt-Siebold 1949a) "power of nature" (Campbell 1975) "apocalyptic storm" (Foley 1976) *God* "God" (Foley 1976, Salvador-Bello 2015) *here* "raiding party" (Jember 1976)[6] *fierd* "army" (Mitchell 1982)
2	*Under Waves' Pressure*	*ancor* "anchor" (Grein 1857–8, Jember 1976) *storm* "storm", "storm at sea" (Dietrich 1859b, Prehn 1883, Brooke 1892, Cook and Tinker 1902, E. Erlemann 1903, Brandl 1908b, Tupper 1910, Wood 1912, Wyatt 1912, Trautmann 1915, Mackie 1934, Krapp and Dobbie 1936, Baum 1963, Hacikyan 1966, Pinsker 1981, Porter 1995, Alexander 2007, Crossley-Holland 2008, Bitterli 2009, Cavell 2020) *sælicu eorðstyren* "submarine earthquake" (Brandl 1908b, Tupper 1910, Mackie 1934, Crossley-Holland 2008, Salvador-Bello 2015) *wind* "wind" (Wyatt 1912, Mackie 1934, Kennedy 1943, Salvador-Bello 2015, Cavell 2020) *lyft* "atmosphere" (Erhardt-Siebold 1949a) "power of nature" (Campbell 1975) "apocalyptic storm" (Foley 1976) *Crist* "Christ" (Foley 1976) *God* "God" (Salvador-Bello 2015)

(*Continued*)

---

6 Jember's proposals are not solutions in the usual sense, but I have included them as they have often been viewed as such, even if they have not often been taken very seriously. For explanation of his approach, see Gregory K. Jember, "A Generative Method for the Study of Anglo-Saxon Riddles," *Studies in Medieval Culture* 11 (1977): 33–9.

ASPR Number	Riddle Title	Solutions
3	No Escape	*yst* "hurricane" (Grein 1857–8, Sedgefield 1922) *storm* "storm (at sea)" (Dietrich 1859b, Prehn 1883, Brooke 1892, Cook and Tinker 1902, Brandl 1908b, Tupper 1910, Wood 1912, Wyatt 1912, Trautmann 1915, Krapp and Dobbie 1936, Baum 1963, Hacikyan 1966, Pinsker 1981, Irving 1994, Porter 1995, Crossley-Holland 2008, Bitterli 2009, Salvador-Bello 2015, Cavell 2020) *wind* "wind" (Wyatt 1912, Kennedy 1943, Lapidge 1994, Niles 2006, Salvador-Bello 2015, Cavell 2016b, Cavell 2020, Paz 2020) *eorþbeofung* "earthquake" [lines 1–16], *stormsæ* "storm at sea" [lines 17–36], *oferweder* "thunderstorm" [lines 37–67] (Mackie 1934, Alexander 2007) *lyft* "atmosphere" (Erhardt-Siebold 1949a) "apocalyptic storm" (Foley 1976) *rod* "cross" (Foley 1976) "revenant" (Jember 1976) *gæst* "spirit" (Jember 1976) "supernatural force" (Jember 1976) God "God" (Salvador-Bello 2015)
1–3 as one riddle	Glorious Servant	*storm* "storm" (E. Erlemann 1903, Wyatt 1912, Trautmann 1914, Trautmann 1915, Schneider 1975, E. Williams 1975, Pinsker and Ziegler 1985, Irving 1994, Niles 2006, Salvador-Bello 2015, Williamson 2017, Hostetter 2018, Paz 2020) *wind* "wind" (Mackie 1934, Williamson 1977, Williamson 1982, Muir 1994, Niles 2006, Cavell 2016b, Williamson 2017, Paz 2020) *lyft* "atmosphere" (Erhardt-Siebold 1949a) "power of nature" (Campbell 1975) "apocalyptic storm" (Foley 1976) *pneuma* "cosmic wind" (Lapidge 1994) God "God" (Ireland 1991, Niles 2006, Williamson 2017) *Godes wind* "wind of God" (Orchard 2021)
2–3 as one riddle	Ocean's Bottom	*sunne* "sun" (Coneybeare 1826) *sæ-storm* "sea-storm" (Wyatt 1912) *wind* "wind" (Kennedy 1943) *storm* "storm" (Conlee 1968) *lyft* "atmosphere" (Conlee 1968)

(*Continued*)

ASPR Number	Riddle Title	Solutions
4	Periodically Busy	*belle* "bell" (Dietrich 1859b, Grein 1861–4, Tupper 1910, Krapp and Dobbie 1936, Baum 1963, Shook 1974, Williamson 1977, Crossley-Holland 1978, Porter 1995, Crossley-Holland 2008, Murphy 2011, Cavell 2016b, Hostetter 2018, Cavell 2020, Orchard 2021) *cweorn-stan* "millstone" (Dietrich 1865, Prehn 1883, Wood 1912, Williamson 1977) *þerscel* "flail" (Brandl 1908b, Trautmann 1915,[7] Mackie 1934, Hartley 1979, Pinsker and Ziegler 1985, Bitterli 2009) *licwiglung* "necromancy" (Bradley 1911) *loc* "lock" (Holthausen 1917) **hand-mylen* "handmill" (Holthausen 1920, Erhardt-Siebold 1946a) *clipur* "bell's clapper" (Conlee 1968) *feðer or penna* "pen" (Shook 1974) "phallus" (Jember 1976) *stoppa* "bucket (of freezing water)" (Stewart 1981, Cavell 2016b, Cavell 2020) *stoppa on racentum in wæterpytte* "bucket on chain in a well" (Doane 1987) *weard-hund* "guard-dog" (Brown 1991, Tigges 1991) *wæter-stoppa* "water bucket" (Niles 2006) *deofol* "devil" (Heyworth 2007a) *sulh-team* "plough-team" (Cochran 2009, Cavell 2016b, Cavell 2020) *sweord* "sword" (Dale 2017) *geat* "city gate" (Breeze 2020a) *sunne* "sun" (Neville 2020)
5	Lone Dweller	*scield* "shield" (Müller 1835, Dietrich 1859b, Prehn 1883, Brooke 1892, Tupper 1910, Wood 1912, Wyatt 1912, Holthausen 1919, Mackie 1934, Krapp and Dobbie 1936, Baum 1963, Hacikyan 1966, Conlee 1968, Hamer 1970, Schneider 1975, Williamson 1977, Crossley-Holland 1978, Williamson 1982, Muir 1994, Porter 1995, Riedinger 2003, Niles 2006, Alexander 2007, Murphy 2011, Crossley-Holland 2008, Bitterli 2009, Portnoy 2013, Salvador-Bello 2015, Paz 2017, Williamson 2017, Hostetter 2018, Cavell 2020, Olsen 2020) *onheaw* "chopping block (for wood)" (Trautmann 1894,[8] Brandl 1908b, Trautmann 1914, Trautmann 1915, Trautmann 1919, Pinsker and Ziegler 1985)

(Continued)

---

[7] Moritz Trautmann claims to have proposed this solution first in 1887 in an unpublished lecture; see *Die altenglischen Rätsel*, 68.

[8] Moritz Trautmann claims to have proposed this solution first in 1887 in an unpublished lecture; see *Die altenglischen Rätsel*, 69.

ASPR Number	Riddle Title	Solutions
		scyld "guilt" (Jember 1976, Cavell 2020)
		onheaw "chopping block (for food)" (Tigges 1994, Stanley 1995, Riedinger 2003, Bitterli 2009, Cavell et al. 2020)
		hwet-stan "whetstone" (Sayers 1996)
		*mete-bord "chopping board" (for food) (Neville 2007; see also discussion in chapter 4, above)
		haga "hedge" (Massey and DeGruy 2015)
		bord "board (chopping board/shield)" (Murphy 2011, Orchard 2021)
		anfilt "anvil" (Jane Roberts, personal communication, 2019; see chapter 4, above)
		gast "soul" (see chapter 4, above)
		tabula "writing tablets" (see chapter 4, above)
		cwið "vagina" (see chapter 7, above)
6	I Burn the Living	*sunne* or *sigel* "sun" (Dietrich 1859b, Prehn 1883, Tupper 1910, Wood 1912, Wyatt 1912, Trautmann 1914, Trautmann 1915, Mackie 1934, Krapp and Dobbie 1936, Baum 1963, Hacikyan 1966, Conlee 1968, Schneider 1975, Williamson 1977, Crossley-Holland 1978, Williamson 1982, Pinsker and Ziegler 1985, Muir 1994, Porter 1995, Niles 2006, Crossley-Holland 2008, Bitterli 2009, Hill 2011, Murphy 2011, Salvador-Bello 2015, Neville 2016, Williamson 2017, Hostetter 2018, Cavell 2020, Orchard 2021; see also discussion in chapter 3, above)
		scyld ond ingeðoht "guilt and conscience" (Jember 1976)
7	Travelling Spirit	*swan* "swan" (Dietrich 1859b, Cook and Tinker 1902, Brandl 1908b, Tupper 1910, Wood 1912, Wyatt 1912, Trautmann 1914, Trautmann 1915, Mackie 1934, Krapp and Dobbie 1936, Baum 1963, Hacikyan 1966, Conlee 1968, Hamer 1970, Cassidy and Ringler 1971, Schneider 1975, Williamson 1977, Crossley-Holland 1978, Pinsker and Ziegler 1985, Mitchell and Robinson 1986, Muir 1994, Porter 1995, Niles 2006, Alexander 2007, Crossley-Holland 2008, McCully 2008, Bitterli 2009, Murphy 2011, Liuzza 2014, Salvador-Bello 2015, Orchard 2016, Paz 2017, Stanley 2017b, Williamson 2017, Hostetter 2018, Cavell et al. 2020, Orchard 2021)
		sawol "soul" (Jember 1976)
		swan "whistling swan" (Williamson 1982)
		swan "mute swan" (Kitson 1994)

(Continued)

The Argument over Solutions 259

ASPR Number	Riddle Title	Solutions
8	Old Evening Poet	*nihtegale* "nightingale" (Dietrich 1859b, Brooke 1892, Wood 1912, Wyatt 1912, Trautmann 1914, Trautmann 1915, Baum 1963, Hacikyan 1966, Cassidy and Ringler 1971, Williamson 1977, Williamson 1982, Porter 1995, D. Hill 1999, Salvador-Bello 1999, Niles 2006, Bitterli 2009, Salvador-Bello 2015, Orchard 2016, Stanley 2017b, Williamson 2017, Hostetter 2018, Cavell 2020, Orchard 2021) *pipe* "pipe" (Dietrich 1859b, Padelford 1899, Cavell 2020) *cuscote* "woodpigeon" (Dietrich 1865, Prehn 1883) *belle* "bell" (Trautmann 1894, Padelford 1899, Holthausen 1899, Brandl 1908b, Swaen 1941–2) *higera* "jay" (Tupper 1910, Mackie 1934, Krapp and Dobbie 1936, Kennedy 1943, Baum 1963, Hacikyan 1966, D. Hill 1999, Alexander 2007, Crossley-Holland 2008) *ceahhe* "jackdaw," "chough" (Mackie 1933, Mackie 1934, Baum 1963, Alexander 2007) *ðrostle* "thrush" (Young 1942) "celebrant singing vespers" (Conlee 1968) *stærling* "starling" (Crossley-Holland 1978, D. Hill 1999) *frogga* "frog" (Cassidy and Ringler 1971, Jember 1976) *wepende bearn* "crying baby" (Jember 1976) *sawol* "soul" (Jember 1976) *deofol* "devil (as buffoon)" (Jember 1977) *hwistle* "flute" (Pinsker and Ziegler 1985, Cavell 2020) **sang-fugel* "songbird" (Muir 1994)
9	They Gave Me Up for Dead	*geac* "cuckoo" (Dietrich 1859b, Prehn 1883, Brandl 1908b, Wood 1912, Tupper 1910, Trautmann 1914, Trautmann 1915, Wyatt 1912, Mackie 1934, Krapp and Dobbie 1936, Baum 1963, Hacikyan 1966, Conlee 1968, Hamer 1970, Schneider 1975, Williamson 1977, Crossley-Holland 1978, Williamson 1982, Pinsker and Ziegler 1985, Mitchell and Robinson 1986, Muir 1994, Porter 1995, Bitterli 2004, Niles 2006, Neville 2007, Alexander 2007, Crossley-Holland 2008, McCully 2008, Bitterli 2009, Murphy 2011, Salvador-Bello 2015, Williamson 2017, Hostetter 2018, Cavell 2020, Orchard 2021) *eacnung ond gebyrd* "conception and birth" (Jember 1976) "revenant" (Jember 1976) *sawol* "soul" (Jember 1976) *fostorling* "fosterling" (Neville 2007) *sinnig geþanc* "sinful thought" [allegorically] (Neville 2007)

(Continued)

ASPR Number	Riddle Title	Solutions
10	*Nose in Confinement*	*scip-furh* "ocean furrow/ship-wake" (Dietrich 1859b, Prehn 1883) *byrnete* "barnacle goose" (Brooke 1892, Tupper 1903b, Tupper 1906, Tupper 1910, Wood 1912, Wyatt 1912, Trautmann 1912, Trautmann 1914, Trautmann 1915, Mackie 1934, Krapp and Dobbie 1936, Swaen 1945b, White 1945, Baum 1963, Hacikyan 1966, Conlee 1968, Williamson 1977, Crossley-Holland 1978, Williamson 1982, Pinsker and Ziegler 1985, Kitson 1994, Muir 1994, Porter 1995, Williams 2000, Niles 2006, Alexander 2007, Crossley-Holland 2008, McCully 2008, Bitterli 2009, Murphy 2011, Salvador-Bello 2015, Williamson 2017, Hostetter 2018, Cavell 2020, Orchard 2021) *wapul* "bubble" (Trautmann 1894) *collon-crog* "waterlily" (Holthausen 1905) *ancor* "anchor" (Trautmann 1905a, Trautmann 1905b) *alchimi* "alchemy" (Jember 1976) *fulwiht* "baptism" (Jember 1976, Williams 2000)
11	*Dark-Stained*	*niht* "night" (Dietrich 1859b, Prehn 1883, Tupper 1906, Brandl 1908b, Tupper 1910, Löwenthal 1914, Swaen 1945a, Gleißner 1984) *win* "wine" or *drync* "drink" (Trautmann 1894, Trautmann 1905a, Klaeber 1906, Brandl 1908b, Wood 1912, Wyatt 1912, Trautmann 1914, Trautmann 1915, Holthausen 1920, Mackie 1934, Krapp and Dobbie 1936, Conlee 1968, Baum 1963, Hacikyan 1966, Hamer 1970, Crossley-Holland 1978, Gleißner 1984, Muir 1994, Porter 1995, Biggam 1998, Alexander 2007, Crossley-Holland 2008, McCully 2008, Bitterli 2009, Stanley 2014, Salvador-Bello 2015, Hostetter 2018, Cavell 2020, Orchard 2021) *gold* "gold" (Walz 1896, Brandl 1908) "phallus" (Jember 1976) *winfæt* "cup or beaker of wine/spirits" (Williamson 1977, Williamson 1982, Gleißner 1984, Pinsker and Ziegler 1985, Orton 2015, Williamson 2017, Cavell 2020) *win ond winfæt* "wine and wine cup" (Niles 2006)

(*Continued*)

ASPR Number	Riddle Title	Solutions
12	*I Travel on Foot*	*leðer* "leather" (Dietrich 1859b, Tupper 1910, Trautmann 1914, Trautmann 1915, Krapp and Dobbie 1936, Baum 1963, Hacikyan 1966, Conlee 1968, Hamer 1970, Jember 1976, Crossley-Holland 1978, Niles 2006, Alexander 2007, Crossley-Holland 2008, Murphy 2011, Hostetter 2018, Cavell 2020) *hyd* "hide" or "skin" (Prehn 1883, Wyatt 1912, Sedgefield 1922, Jember 1976) *oxan-hyd* "oxhide" (Tupper 1910, Wood 1912, Mackie 1934, Hacikyan 1966, Williamson 2017, Cavell 2020) *oxa* "ox" (Williamson 1977, Williamson 1982, Pinsker and Ziegler 1985, Muir 1994, Porter 1995, Davis 2006, Bitterli 2009, Neville 2012, Laird 2013, Orton 2015, Salvador-Bello 2015, Cavell 2016b, Williamson 2017, Cavell 2020, Orchard 2021) *eofor* "wild boar (made into leather)" (Gleißner 1984) *oxa ond oxan-hyd* "ox and ox-hide" (Niles 2006, Paz 2017, Niles 2019) *cealf* "bull calf" (Murphy 2011) *wudu* "wood" (Koppinen 2013)
13	Ten Brothers and Sisters	"butterfly aurelia" (i.e. chrysalis) (Wright 1842, Klipstein 1849, Cavell 2020) "cicada aurelia" (i.e. chrysalis) (Klipstein 1849) *leafwyrm* "caterpillar" (Grein 1857–58, Grein 1865a) *stæf-ræw* "alphabet", "22 letters" (Dietrich 1859b, Prehn 1883, Cavell 2020) *moðða* "moth" (Grein 1865, Cavell 2020) *fingras ond glofe* "fingers and glove" (Tupper 1903b, Tupper 1906, Tupper 1910, Cavell 2020) *tien cicenu* "ten chickens/chicks" (Trautmann 1894, Trautmann 1912, Wyatt 1912, Löwenthal 1914, Trautmann 1914, Trautmann 1915, Mackie 1934, Krapp and Dobbie 1936, Erhardt-Siebold 1950a, Baum 1963, Hacikyan 1966, Jember 1976, Williamson 1977, Crossley-Holland 1978, Williamson 1982, Muir 1994, Porter 1995, Niles 2006, Crossley-Holland 2008, Bitterli 2009, Murphy 2011, Salvador-Bello 2015, Williamson 2017, Hostetter 2018, Cavell 2020, Orchard 2021) *tien worhanan* "ten pheasants" (Wyatt 1912, Cavell 2020) *twelf cicenu* "twelve chicks" (Pinsker and Ziegler 1985)

(Continued)

ASPR Number	Riddle Title	Solutions
		"hatchling chicks" (i.e. *ova et pulli* "eggs and chickens", *hana ond hæn* "male chicken and female chicken", or another similar answer with six consonants and four vowels) (Murphy 2011) *cealf* "calf" (Linden Currie via Ammon 2013) *sceapheord* "flock of sheep" (Burns, 2022)
14	Weapon-Warrior	*horn* "(ox or bull) horn" (Dietrich 1859b, Prehn 1883, Padelford 1899, Cook and Tinker 1902, Brandl 1908b, Tupper 1910, Wyatt 1912, Trautmann 1914, Trautmann 1915, Mackie 1934, Krapp and Dobbie 1936, Swaen 1941b, Baum 1963, Hacikyan 1966, Conlee 1968, Hamer 1970, Schneider 1975, Jember 1976, Williamson 1977, Crossley-Holland 1978, Williamson 1982, Pinsker and Ziegler 1985, Mitchell and Robinson 1986, Muir 1994, Porter 1995, Alexander 2007, Crossley-Holland 2008, Bitterli 2009, Cavell 2014, Liuzza 2014, Orton 2015, Paz 2017, Stanley 2017b, Williamson 2017, Hostetter 2018, S. Breeze 2019, Cavell 2020, Orchard 2021; see also chapter 2 above) *oxa ond ox-horn* "ox and ox-horn" (Niles 2006) "aurochs" (Salvador-Bello 2015)
15	White Neck	*brocc* "badger" (Dietrich 1859b, Prehn 1883, Brooke 1892, Tupper 1910, Wood 1912, Wyatt 1912, Trautmann 1914, Trautmann 1915, Sedgefield 1922, Mackie 1934, Swaen 1941a, Baum 1963, Hacikyan 1966, Crossley-Holland 1978, Porter 1995, Tigges 1994, Alexander 2007, Crossley-Holland 2008, Hostetter 2018, Cavell 2020) *il* or *igil* "porcupine" (Walz 1896, Brandl 1908b, Holthausen 1907, Mackie 1934, Bitterli 2002, Bitterli 2009, Cavell 2017d, Cavell 2020) *il* or *igil* "hedgehog" (Holthausen 1907, Brett 1927, Cavell 2017d, Cavell 2020, Orchard 2021) *fox* "fox" (Brett 1927, Young 1944, Williamson 1977, Williamson 1982, Pinsker and Ziegler 1985, Muir 1994, Tigges 1994, Porter 1995) *weosule* "weasel" (Young 1944, Cavell 2020) *fyxe* "vixen" (Young 1944, Salvador-Bello 2015, Williamson 2017, Hostetter 2018, Cavell 2020) *wer* "man" (Jember 1976) *fox ond hund* "fox and hound" (Niles 2006)

(*Continued*)

The Argument over Solutions   263

ASPR Number	Riddle Title	Solutions
16	*Fight against Wave*	*ancor* "anchor" (Dietrich 1859b, Prehn 1883, Brandl 1908b, Tupper 1910, Wood 1912, Wyatt 1912, Trautmann 1914, Trautman 1915, Mackie 1934, Krapp and Dobbie 1936, Baum 1963, Hacikyan 1966, Conlee 1968, Jember 1976, Schneider 1975,Williamson 1977, Crossley-Holland 1978, Williamson 1982, Pinsker and Ziegler 1985, Irving 1994, Muir 1994, Porter 1995, Niles 2006, Alexander 2007, Crossley-Holland 2008, Bitterli 2009, Murphy 2011, Salvador-Bello 2015, Williamson 2017, Hostetter 2018, Cavell 2020, Orchard 2021) *gast* "soul" (Jember 1988) *lic-hama* "body" (see chapter 4 above) *ancra* "anchorite" (Orchard 2021) *ancor* "anchor/anchorite" (see chapter 4 above)
17	*Protector*	*ballista* "ballista" (Dietrich 1859b, Tupper 1906, Tupper 1910, Wood 1912, Trautmann 1915, Mackie 1934, Krapp and Dobbie 1936, Baum 1963, Hacikyan 1966, Conlee 1968, Crossley-Holland 1978, Porter 1995, Crossley-Holland 2008, Cavell 2020) *boga* "bow" (Grein 1861–4) *burg* "fortress" (Lange via Dietrich 1865, Wyatt 1912, Conlee 1968, Cavell 2020) *ofen* "oven" (Trautmann 1894, Trautmann 1905, Trautmann 1914, Trautmann 1915) *catapulta* "catapult" (Trautmann 1914, Trautmann 1915) *tun* "town" (Baum 1963) *smið首* "smelting furnace" (Pinsker 1973) *blæchorn* "inkwell" (Shook 1974) "phallus" (Jember 1976) *beona hyf* / **beo-hyf* "bee-hive" (Bierbaumer and Wannagat 1981, Pinsker and Ziegler 1985, Tigges 1991, Sorrell 2005, Bitterli 2009, Williamson 2017, Hostetter 2018) *cnearr* "viking ship" (Hosler 2001) *cocer* "quiver" (Wilcox 1990, Niles 2006, Stanley 2017a, Williamson 2017, Cavell 2020, Orchard 2021) **beo-leap* "bee-basket" / **beo-skep* "bee-skep" / **beo-lester* "bee-basket" (Osborn 2005, Niles 2006, Osborn 2006, Sayers 2006, Williamson 2017, Cavell 2020; see also discussion in chapter 3, above) *leo ond beo* "Samson's lion and bees" (Murphy 2007, Murphy 2011, Sebo 2019) *anfilt* "anvil" (Jane Roberts, personal communication, 2018; see chapter 4 above)

(Continued)

ASPR Number	Riddle Title	Solutions
18	Large Belly	*leðer-flaxe* "leather bottle" (Dietrich 1859b, Prehn 1883, Wyatt 1912, Trautmann 1914, Mackie 1934, Krapp and Dobbie 1936, Hacikyan 1966, Schneider 1975, Cavell 2020) *cist* "cask" (Wood 1912, Trautmann 1915, Cavell 2020) *blæc-horn* "inkhorn" (Shook 1974, Cavell 2020) "phallus" (Jember 1976, Cavell 2020) *crog* or *win-crog* "wine-jug, amphora" (Wood 1912, Williamson 1977, Williamson 1982, Porter 1995, Niles 2006, Hostetter 2018, Williamson 2017, Cavell 2020, Orchard 2021) **win-cyll* "wineskin" (Alexander 2007)
19	Bright-Headed	*eored-man ond hafoc* "horseman and hawk" [with various interpretations of the individual runes] (Thorpe 1842, Klipstein 1849, Ettmüller 1850, Grein 1857–8, Tupper 1903b, Tupper 1910, Wood 1912, Trautmann 1915, Mackie 1934, Krapp and Dobbie 1936, Hacikyan 1966, Conlee 1968, Porter 1995, Crossley-Holland 2008 Hostetter 2018, Cavell 2020) *hafocung* "falconry" (Hicketier 1888, Erhardt-Siebold 1948, Cavell 2020) *gewritere ond gewrit* "scribe and writing" (Eliason 1952, Conlee 1968, Shook 1974, Cavell 2020) *huntoð* "hunting" (Baum 1963, Hacikyan 1966) *scip* "ship" (Williamson 1977, Williamson 1982, Pinsker and Ziegler 1985, Muir 1994, Bitterli 2009, Murphy 2011, Orton 2015, Cavell 2020) *snac(c)* "war-ship" (Griffith 1992, Niles 2006, Williamson 2017, Niles 2019, Simms 2016, Orchard 2021) "the riddler" (mock riddle) (Wilcox 1996) *stafas* "letters" (Symons 2013, Symons 2016) *fyr-torr* "lighthouse" (see chapter 2, above) *sunne* "sun" (see chapter 2, above)
20	Cursed among Weapons	*sweord* "sword" (Dietrich 1859b, Prehn 1883, Brooke 1892, Tupper 1910, Wood 1912, Wyatt 1912, Holthausen 1920, Mackie 1934, Krapp and Dobbie 1936, Davidson 1962, Baum 1963, Hacikyan 1966, Pinsker 1973, Williamson 1977, Crossley-Holland 1978, Williamson 1982, Gleißner 1984, Irving 1994, Muir 1994, Tigges 1994, Porter 1995, Heyworth 2007b, Crossley-Holland 2008, Murphy 2011, Salvador-Bello 2011, Portnoy 2013, Orton 2015, Paz 2017, Williamson 2017, Hostetter 2018, Cavell 2020, Olsen 2020; see also discussion in chapters 2 and 4 above)

(*Continued*)

ASPR Number	Riddle Title	Solutions
		wealhhafoc "falcon" (Trautmann 1894, Trautmann 1914, Trautmann 1915, Trautmann 1919, Swaen 1919, Pinsker and Ziegler 1985, Tigges 1994, Bitterli 2009, Cavell 2020) *hafoc* "hawk" (Trautmann 1915, Davidson 1962, Tigges 1994) *heoruswealwe* "sword-swallow, hawk" (Shook 1965, Conlee 1968, Nelson 1982) "phallus" (Kay 1968, Pinsker 1973, Jember 1976, Cavell 2020) "testosterone" (Irving 1994) *sawol* "soul" [allegorically] (Tigges 1994) *munuc* "monk" [allegorically] (Tigges 1994) *wæpen* "sword/penis" (Wehlau 1997, Tanke 2000, Niles 2006, Murphy 2011, Cavell 2016b) *secg* "sword/man" (Orchard 2021)
21	Downward Nose	*sulh* "plow" (Thorpe 1842, Dietrich 1859b, Brandl 1908b, Tupper 1910, Wood 1912, Wyatt 1912, Trautmann 1914, Trautmann 1915, Mackie 1934, Krapp and Dobbie 1936, Colgrave 1937, Baum 1963, Hacikyan 1966, Conlee 1968, Hamer 1970, Schneider 1975, Williamson 1977, Crossley-Holland 1978, Williamson 1982, Pinsker and Ziegler 1985, Muir 1994, Porter 1995, Hill 2000b, Niles 2006, Alexander 2007, Crossley-Holland 2008, Bitterli 2009, Murphy 2011, Neville 2013, Cavell 2016b, Williamson 2017, Hostetter 2018, Cavell 2020, Orchard 2021) "phallus"(Jember 1976)
22	Peace-Horses	*Geolmonað* "month of December" (Dietrich 1859b, Wood 1912, Sedgefield 1922, Mackie 1934, Hacikyan 1966, Crossley-Holland 1978, Porter 1995, Crossley-Holland 2008) *monað* "month" (Dietrich 1859b, Prehn 1883, Tupper 1903b, Tupper 1906, Tupper 1910, Wyatt 1912, Cavell 2020) *bricg* "bridge" (Trautmann 1914, Trautmann 1915, Cavell 2020) *Carles wæn* "Ursa major" or "wagon of stars" (Blakeley 1958, Williamson 1977, Osborn 1980, Williamson 1982, Muir 1994, Porter 1995, Tigges 1994, Murphy 2006, Niles 2006, Bitterli 2009, Salvador-Bello 2015, Murphy 2011, Neville 2016, Williamson 2017, Hostetter 2018, Cavell 2020, Orchard 2021) *niwe gear* "new year" (Baum 1963, Cavell 2020) **fær-rihte* "rite of passage" (Jember 1976) *is-bricg* "ice bridge" (Pinsker and Ziegler 1985)

(Continued)

ASPR Number	Riddle Title	Solutions
23	Wob	*boga* "bow" (Dietrich 1859b, Prehn 1883, Cook and Tinker 1902, Brandl 1908b, Tupper 1910, Wood 1912, Wyatt 1912, Trautmann 1914, Mackie 1934, Krapp and Dobbie 1936, Brown 1940, Erhardt-Siebold 1950b, Baum 1963, Hacikyan 1966, Conlee 1968, Schneider 1975, Williamson 1977, Crossley-Holland 1978, Stewart 1979, Williamson 1982, Pinsker and Ziegler 1985, Mitchell and Robinson 1986, Irving 1994, Muir 1994, Porter 1995, Niles 2006, Crossley-Holland 2008, Bitterli 2009, Murphy 2011, Rudolf 2012, Cavell 2016b, Williamson 2017, Hostetter 2018, Stanley 2017b, Cavell 2020, Orchard 2021; see also discussion in chapters 2 and 5 above) "cross-bow" (Trautmann 1915) "phallus"(Jember 1976)
24	Six Letters	*higoræ* "jay" (Dietrich 1859b, Müller 1861, Brandl 1908b, Tupper 1910, Trautmann 1914, Trautmann 1915, Mackie 1934, Krapp and Dobbie 1936, Baum 1963, Conlee 1968, Jember 1976, Schneider 1975, Williamson 1977, Crossley-Holland 1978, Pinsker and Ziegler 1985, Muir 1994, Porter 1995, Crossley-Holland 2008, Bitterli 2009, Symons 2013, Salvador-Bello 2015, Symons 2016, Williamson 2017, Hostetter 2018, Cavell 2020, Orchard 2021) *higoræ* "magpie" (Dietrich 1859b, Wyatt 1912, Mackie 1934, Baum 1963, Hacikyan 1966, Conlee 1968, Williamson 1982, Muir 1994, Niles 2006, Crossley-Holland 2008, Paz 2017, Murphy 2011, Williamson 2017, Cavell 2020, Orchard 2021) *higoræ* "woodpecker" (Whitman 1898, Cavell 2020) *leasere* "mime" (Sonke 1907)
25	Useful to Neighbours	*hænep* "hemp" (Bouterwek 1854, Lange via Dietrich 1865, Tupper 1903b, Wood 1912) *cipe* "onion" (Dietrich 1859b, Tupper 1903b, Tupper 1906, Tupper 1910, Wood 1912, Wyatt 1912, Trautmann 1914, Trautmann 1915, Mackie 1934, Krapp and Dobbie 1936, Swaen 1946, Baum 1963, Hacikyan 1966, Conlee 1968, Williamson 1977, Crossley-Holland 1978, Williamson 1982, Gleißner 1984, Pinsker and Ziegler 1985, Muir 1994, Porter 1995, Smith 2000, Niles 2006, Alexander 2007, Crossley-Holland 2008, Bitterli 2009, Murphy 2011, Symons 2013, Orton 2015, Salvador-Bello 2015, Symons 2016, Paz 2017, Williamson 2017, Hostetter 2018, Cavell 2020, Fay 2020, Orchard 2021)

(Continued)

ASPR Number	Riddle Title	Solutions
		cipe-leac "garlic" (Dietrich 1859b)
		leac "leak" (Dietrich 1859b, Wood 1912, Mackie 1934, Cavell 2020)
		heope "rose hip" (Trautmann 1894, Trautmann 1905a)
		senep "mustard" (Walz 1896, Wood 1912, Cavell 2020)
		"phallus" (Jember 1976, Cavell 2020)
		teors "penis" (Bolding 1992)
26	Famous Name	*boc* "book" (Müller 1835, Dietrich 1859b, Prehn 1883, Tupper 1906, Brandl 1908b, Tupper 1910, Wood 1912, Wyatt 1912, Trautmann 1914, Trautmann 1915, Krapp and Dobbie 1936, Baum 1963, Hacikyan 1966, Schneider 1975, Crossley-Holland 1978, Williamson 1982, Murphy 2011, Williamson 2017, Hostetter 2018, Brooks 2020, Cavell 2020, Orchard 2021)
		biblioðece "Bible" (Grein 1857–8, Dietrich 1859b, Cook and Tinker 1902, Wyatt 1912, Trautmann 1915, Mackie 1934, Baum 1963, Conlee 1968, Hamer 1970, Cassidy and Ringler 1971, Shook 1974, Jember 1976, Williamson 1977, Williamson 1982, Porter 1995, Marsden 1998, Bitterli 2009, Holsinger 2009, Liuzza 2014, Orton 2015, Williamson 2017, Hostetter 2018, Brooks 2020, Cavell 2020)
		hyd "hide" (Trautmann 1915)
		halig gewrit "religious book, holy scriptures" (Shook 1974, Pinsker and Ziegler 1985, Lester 1991, Muir 1994, Crossley-Holland 2008, Williamson 2017)
		Cristes boc "Gospel Book" (Niles 2006, Alexander 2007, Salvador-Bello 2015, Paz 2017, Williamson 2017, Brooks 2020, Cavell 2020; see also discussion in chapter 5, above)
27	Binder and Scourger	*swipu* "whip, scourge" (Dietrich 1859b, Cavell 2020)
		medu "mead" (Lange via Dietrich 1865, Prehn 1883, Cook and Tinker 1902, Brandl 1908b, Tupper 1910, Wood 1912, Wyatt 1912, Trautmann 1914, Trautmann 1915, Mackie 1934, Krapp and Dobbie 1936, Baum 1963, Hacikyan 1966, Conlee 1968, Schneider 1975, Williamson 1977, Crossley-Holland 1978, Williamson 1982, Pinsker and Ziegler 1985, Mitchell and Robinson 1986, Muir 1994, Porter 1995, Teele 2004, Alexander 2007, Crossley-Holland 2008, Bitterli 2009, Murphy 2011, Price 2015, Salvador-Bello 2015, Cavell 2016b, Dale 2017, Price 2017, Williamson 2017, Hostetter 2018, Cavell 2020, Orchard 2021)

(Continued)

ASPR Number	Riddle Title	Solutions
		slæp "sleep" (Jember 1976, Cavell 2020)
		mele-deaw ond medu "mead and its source" (Niles 2006)
28	Hardest and Sharpest	*beow* "barley," "John Barleycorn" (Wright 1842, Klipstein 1849, Brooke 1892, Brandl 1908b, Wood 1912, Wyatt 1912, Mackie 1934, Hacikyan 1966, Cassidy and Ringler 1971, Crossley-Holland 1978, Alexander 2007, Crossley-Holland 2008, Salvador-Bello 2015, Cavell 2020)
		hearpe "harp" (Trautmann 1894, Padelford 1899, Brandl 1908b, Trautmann 1914, Trautmann 1915, Kock 1918, Krapp and Dobbie 1936, Porter 1995, Cavell 2020)
		*win-ceac "wine cask" (Dietrich 1859b, Prehn 1883, Brandl 1908b, Cavell 2020)
		beor "beer" (Tupper 1910, Conlee 1968, Niles 2006, Hostetter 2018, Cavell 2020)
		ealu "ale" (Tupper 1910, Conlee 1968, Crossley-Holland 2008, Hostetter 2018, Cavell 2020)
		"stringed instrument" (Mackie 1933, Cavell 2020)
		*fenyce-hearpe "tortoise lyre" (Shook 1958, Nelson 1974, Cavell 2020)
		mealt-gewring "malt liquor" (Baum 1963)
		beorg "barrow" (Jember 1976, Cavell 2020)
		sawle costnung "trial of soul" (Jember 1976, Cavell 2020)
		iw-horn "yew horn" (Williamson 1977, Cavell 2020)
		hringmæled sweord "damascened sword" (Göbel and Göbel 1978, Cavell 2020)
		wifmann "woman" (Stewart 1979)
		cine or *boc-fell* "parchment" (Ziegler 1982, Pinsker and Ziegler 1985, Cavell 2016b, Orchard 2021)
		bere ond ealu "ale and its source" (Niles 2006)
		biblioðece "bible codex" (Bitterli 2009, Cavell 2016b, Cavell 2020)
		"musical instrument" (Williamson 2017)
		medu "mead" (Cavell 2020)
29	Air-Vessel	*mona ond sunne* "moon and sun" (Dietrich 1859b, Prehn 1883, Brooke 1892, Tupper 1906, Tupper 1910, Wood 1912, Wyatt 1912, Mackie 1934, Krapp and Dobbie 1936, Bone 1943, Baum 1963, Hacikyan 1966, Conlee 1968, Whitman 1969, Cassidy and Ringler 1971, Joyce 1973, Jember 1976, Williamson 1977, Crossley-Holland 1978, Williamson 1982, Muir 1994, Porter 1995, Niles 2006, Alexander 2007, Crossley-Holland 2008, Bitterli 2009, Murphy 2011, Salvador-Bello 2015,

(Continued)

The Argument over Solutions 269

ASPR Number	Riddle Title	Solutions
		Neville 2016, Stanley 2017b, Williamson 2017, Bitterli 2019a, Cavell 2020, Orchard 2021) *swealwe ond spearwa* "swallow and sparrow" (Trautmann 1894, Cavell 2020) *wolcen ond wind* "cloud and wind" (Walz 1896, Cavell 2020) *fugel ond wind* "bird and wind" (Trautmann 1905a, Trautmann 1914, Trautmann 1915, Cavell 2020) *Venus opboren* "Venus carried off" (Pinsker and Ziegler 1985)
30a	Flame-Busy A	*regn* "rainwater" (Dietrich 1859b, Prehn 1883, Brandl 1908b) *corn-æcer* "cornfield" (Trautmann 1894[9], Brandl 1908b) *beam* "wood" or *treow* "tree" (Blackburn 1900, Tupper 1906, Brandl 1908b, Tupper 1910, Wood 1912, Löwenthal 1914, Trautmann 1914, Trautmann 1915, Mackie 1934, Krapp and Dobbie 1936, Williamson 1977, Crossley-Holland 1978, Williamson 1982, Mitchell and Robinson 1986, Muir 1994, Porter 1995, Niles 2006, Alexander 2007, Crossley-Holland 2008, Koppinen 2014, Salvador-Bello 2015, Murphy 2011, Paz 2017, Williamson 2017, Stanley 2017b, Hostetter 2018, Cavell 2020, Orchard 2021) *osculatorium* (religious object to be kissed) (H. Schrör via Trautmann 1905) *rod* "cross" (Trautmann 1915, Baum 1963, Conlee 1968, Talentino 1981, Cavell 2020) "birch as Maypole and Numinosum" (Schneider 1975) *snaw* "snow, snowflake" (Pinsker 1973, Pinsker and Ziegler 1985, Cavell 2020) "phallus" (Jember 1976) *Lyra* "the constellation of the harp" (Morgan and McAllister 1993) *ora* "ore" (Koppinen 2020)
30b	Flame-Busy B	[Most solve as for *Flame-busy A*, above] *Cygnus* "the constellation of the cross" (Morgan and McAllister 1993)

(*Continued*)

---

9 Moritz Trautmann claims to have proposed this solution first in 1887 in an unpublished lecture; see *Die altenglischen Rätsel*, 94.

ASPR Number	Riddle Title	Solutions
31	Eager to Go	*blæst-pipe "bagpipe" (Dietrich 1859b, Padelford 1899, Tupper 1910, Wyatt 1912, Wood 1914, Mackie 1934, Krapp and Dobbie 1936, Baum 1963, Hacikyan 1966, Conlee 1968, Jember 1976, Williamson 1977, Crossley-Holland 1978, Williamson 1982, Pinsker and Ziegler 1985, Muir 1994, Porter 1995, Niles 2006, Crossley-Holland 2008, Bitterli 2009, Williamson 2017, Hostetter 2018, S. Breeze 2019, Brooks 2020, Cavell 2020, Wilcox 2020) fiðele "fiddle" (Trautmann 1894, Brandl 1908b, Trautmann 1914) "musical instrument" (Trautmann 1915, Cavell 2020) "organistrum, hurdy-gurdy" (Holthausen 1919) organa "organ" (Holthausen 1940) hearpe "harp" or "lyre" (Jember 1976, Osborn 1976) feðer ond fingras "quill-pen and fingers" (Fry 1992, Cavell 2020) "cithara" (Musgrave 2002) "psaltery" (plucked by a quill) (Orchard 2021)
32	Grind against Grit	wægen "wagon" (Conybeare 1826, Cavell 2020) cweorn-stan "millstone" (Bouterwek 1854, Grein 1861–4, Cavell 2020) scip "ship" (Dietrich 1859b, Prehn 1883, Brandl 1908b, Tupper 1910, Wyatt 1912, Wood 1914, Trautmann 1914, Trautmann 1915, Mackie 1934, Krapp and Dobbie 1936, Baum 1963, Hacikyan 1966, Conlee 1968, Jember 1976, Williamson 1977, Crossley-Holland 1978, Williamson 1982, Fiocco 1984–7, Muir 1994, Porter 1995, Salvador-Bello 2015, Crossley-Holland 2008, Orton 2015, Williamson 2017, Hostetter 2018, Cavell 2020) hweol "wheel" (Wyatt 1912, Sedgefield 1922, Hacikyan 1966, Bitterli 2009, Cavell 2020) bearwe "hand- or wheel-barrow" (Pinsker and Ziegler 1985, Cavell 2020) ceap-scip "merchant ship" (Niles 2006, Orchard 2021)
33	Terrible Laughter	is "ice-floe" (i.e. sea-ice) (Brooke 1892, Dietrich 1859b, Prehn 1883, Wyatt 1912, Trautmann 1914, Trautmann 1915, Schneider 1975, Pinsker and Ziegler 1985, Muir 1994, Niles 2006, Bitterli 2009, Williamson 2017, Cavell 2020, Orchard 2021)

(Continued)

The Argument over Solutions 271

ASPR Number	Riddle Title	Solutions
		is-beorg "iceberg" (Tupper 1910, Wyatt 1912, Wood 1914, Mackie 1934, Krapp and Dobbie 1936, Baum 1963, Hacikyan 1966, Conlee 1968, Williamson 1977, Crossley-Holland 1978, Williamson 1982, Porter 1995, Riedinger 2003, Alexander 2007, Crossley-Holland 2008, Mize 2015, Orton 2015, Salvador-Bello 2015, Cavell 2016b, Williamson 2017, Hostetter 2018, Dale 2019, Cavell 2020)
		is "ice" (Brandl 1908b, Wyatt 1912, Mackie 1934, Alexander 2007, Murphy 2011, Williamson 2017, Cavell 2020, Orchard 2021; see also discussion in chapter 3, above)
		"archetypal feminine" (Jember 1976)
		feogað "hatred" [allegorically] (Nelson 1991)
		wæter "water" (Klein, Klein, and Delehanty 2014)
		storm "storm" (Klein, Klein, and Delehanty 2014)
34	Feeds Cattle	*raca* "rake" (Dietrich 1859b, Prehn 1883, Tupper 1910, Trautmann 1912, Wyatt 1912, Trautmann 1914, Wood 1914, Trautmann 1915, Mackie 1934, Krapp and Dobbie 1936, Baum 1963, Hacikyan 1966, Conlee 1968, Hamer 1970, Schneider 1975, Williamson 1977, Crossley-Holland 1978, Williamson 1982, Pinsker and Ziegler 1985, Muir 1994, Porter 1995, Salvador-Bello 2015, Niles 2006, Alexander 2007, Crossley-Holland 2008, Bitterli 2009, Murphy 2011, Stanley 2017b, Williamson 2017, Hostetter 2018, Cavell 2020, Orchard 2021)
		beo "bee" (Trautmann 1894, Brandl 1908b)
		"spiritual harrowing" [anagogically] (Nelson 1974)
		hergung on helle "harrowing of hell" (Jember 1976)
		"phallus" (Jember 1976)
		bocera "scholar" (Dale 2015)
35	Hopeful Garment	*byrne* or *lorica* "mail coat" (Dietrich 1859a, Dietrich 1859b, Prehn 1883, Brandl 1908b, Tupper 1910, Wyatt 1912, Trautmann 1914, Wood 1914, Trautmann 1915, Sedgefield 1922, Mackie 1934, Krapp and Dobbie 1936, Erhardt-Siebold 1949b, Baum 1963, Hacikyan 1966, Conlee 1968, Schneider 1975, Jember 1976, Williamson 1977, Crossley-Holland 1978, Williamson 1982, Pinsker and Ziegler 1985, Muir 1994, Porter 1995, Klein 1997, Hyer 1998, Riedinger 2003, Niles 2006, Alexander 2007, Crossley-Holland 2008, Bitterli 2009, Murphy 2011, Weber 2012, Pantaleoni 2013, Cavell 2016b, Williamson 2017, Hostetter 2018, Cavell 2020, Orchard 2021)

(*Continued*)

ASPR Number	Riddle Title	Solutions
36	Man Woman Horse	*sugu ond fif fearas* "sow and five piglets" or *gefearh-sugu* "pregnant sow" (Dietrich 1859b, Prehn 1883, Heusler 1901, Brandl 1908b, Wood 1914, Cavell 2020) *mann, wifmann, hors* "man woman horse" [i.e. the items given in the text are the solution] (Trautmann 1894, Holthausen 1907, Trautmann 1914, Trautmann 1915, Hacikyan 1966, Cavell 2020) *porcus* "pig/dolphin" (Tupper 1903b) *bat* "boat" or *scip* "ship" with passengers (*mann, wifmann, hors, hund* "man, woman, horse, dog") (Tupper 1910, Löwenthal 1914, Mackie 1934, Krapp and Dobbie 1936, Eliason 1952, Williamson 1977, Crossley-Holland 1978, Williamson 1982, Muir 1994, Porter 1995, Crossley-Holland 2008, Bitterli 2009, Orton 2015, Williamson 2017, Hostetter 2018, Cavell 2020, Orchard 2021) *dopenede huntung* "waterfowl hunt" (Erhardt-Siebold 1948, Cavell 2020) *hors eacen ond twa wif eacenu* "pregnant horse, two pregnant women" (Eliason 1952, Cavell 2020) *huntoð* "hunting" (Baum 1963, Hacikyan 1966, Cavell 2020) *hired unstille* "family on the go" (i.e. man and woman carrying dog and bird on horse and on a ship) (Niles 2006)
36.1–7 as separate riddle	Six Heads	*mann wifmann hors* "man woman horse" (Trautmann 1894, Trautmann 1915) *hors eacen ond twa wif eacenu* "pregnant horse with two pregnant women" (Eliason 1952) *scip* "ship" (Conlee 1968, Pinsker and Ziegler 1985)
36.8–13 as separate riddle	Travel Flood-Ways	*scip* "ship" (Trautmann 1894, Trautmann 1915, Eliason 1952, Conlee 1968, Pinsker and Ziegler 1985)
37	Belly Behind	*wægen* "wagon" (Dietrich 1859b, Cavell 2020) *blæst-belg* "bellows" (Dietrich 1865, Prehn 1883, Tupper 1910, Wyatt 1912, Wood 1914, Trautmann 1914, Trautmann 1915, Mackie 1934, Krapp and Dobbie 1936, Baum 1963, Hacikyan 1966, Conlee 1968, Williamson 1977, Crossley-Holland 1978, Williamson 1982, Gleißner 1984, Pinsker and Ziegler 1985, Muir 1994, Porter 1995, Hill 2000a, Niles 2006, Alexander 2007, Crossley-Holland 2008, Bitterli 2009, Murphy 2011, Salvador-Bello 2011, Orton 2015, Salvador-Bello 2015, Williamson 2017, Hostetter 2018, Cavell 2020, Rhodes 2020, Orchard 2021) "phallus" (Jember 1976)

(*Continued*)

ASPR Number	Riddle Title	Solutions
38	Greedy for Youth-Mirth	hryðer or bulluc "bullock, bull calf" or oxa "ox" (Dietrich 1859b, Prehn 1883, Brandl 1908b, Tupper 1910, Wyatt 1912, Trautmann 1914, Trautmann 1915, Wood 1914, Mackie 1934, Krapp and Dobbie 1936, Baum 1963, Hacikyan 1966, Conlee 1968, Schneider 1975, Williamson 1977, Crossley-Holland 1978, Williamson 1982, Pinsker and Ziegler 1985, Mitchell and Robinson 1986, Muir 1994, Porter 1995, Niles 2006, Alexander 2007, Crossley-Holland 2008, Bitterli 2009, Murphy 2011, Cavell 2015a, Cavell 2016b, Orton 2015, Salvador-Bello 2015, Stanley 2017b, Williamson 2017, Hostetter 2018, Cavell 2020, Orchard 2021) wer "man" (Jember 1976)
39	Most Wretched of All	dæg "day" (Dietrich 1859b, Wyatt 1912, Sedgefield 1922, Mackie 1934, Baum 1963, Hacikyan 1966, Porter 1995, Crossley-Holland 2008, Cavell 2020) tid "time" (Trautmann 1894, Brandl 1908, Trautmann 1912, Löwenthal 1914, Trautmann 1914, Trautmann 1915, Crossley-Holland 2008, Cavell 2020) mona "moon" (Tupper 1910, Mackie 1934, Jember 1987b, Cavell 2020) deað "death" (as a creature) (Erhardt-Siebold 1946b, Baum 1963, Conlee 1968, Barley 1974, Nelson 1974, Jember 1976, Tigges 1994, Cavell 2020, Orchard 2021) wyrd "fate" (Conlee 1968) wolcen "cloud" (Kennedy 1975, Meyvaert 1976, Pinsker and Ziegler 1985, Salvador-Bello 2015, Cavell 2020) "revenant" (Jember 1976) word, to gesecgenne "speech" (Williamson 1977, Porter 1995, DiNapoli 2015, Cavell 2020) swefn or somnium "dream" (Greenfield 1980, Pinsker and Ziegler 1985, Stanley 1991, Muir 1994, Harbus 1998, Niles 2006, Bitterli 2009, Murphy 2011, Cavell 2020) cometa "comet" (Wilson 1991, Cavell 2020) treow "faith" (Dennis 1995, Cavell 2020) niht ond dæg "night and day" (Hostetter 2018)
40	Circle of the Earth	gesceaft / creatura "creation" (Dietrich 1859a, Dietrich 1859b, Prehn 1883, Tupper 1910, Wyatt 1912, Trautmann 1914, Trautmann 1915, Wood 1914, Mackie 1934, Krapp and Dobbie 1936, Baum 1963, Hacikyan 1966, Conlee 1968, Schneider 1975, Jember 1976, Williamson 1977,

(Continued)

274 Appendix

ASPR Number	Riddle Title	Solutions
		Crossley-Holland 1978, O'Brien O'Keeffe 1980, O'Brien O'Keeffe 1985, Williamson 1982, Muir 1994, Porter 1995, Niles 2006, Crossley-Holland 2008, Bitterli 2009, Murphy 2011, Sebo 2014, Orton 2015, Salvador-Bello 2015, Cavell 2016b, Williamson 2017, Cavell 2020, Orchard 2021)
		natura "nature" (Mackie 1934, Williamson 2017, Hostetter 2018)
		lagu "water" (Pinsker and Ziegler 1985)
40–41 as one riddle	Circle Renewed	*gesceaft* or *creatura* "creation" (Konick 1939)
41	Mother of Many Races	*eorðe* "earth" (Dietrich 1859b, Mackie 1934, Crossley-Holland 2008)
		fyr "fire" (Trautmann 1894, Trautmann 1914, Trautmann 1915, Crossley-Holland 2008)
		wisdom "wisdom" (Tupper 1903b, Wood 1914, Crossley-Holland 2008, Cavell 2020)
		wæter "water" (Tupper 1910, Mackie 1934, Williamson 1977, Williamson 1982, Muir 1994, Porter 1995, Niles 2006, Crossley-Holland 2008, Bitterli 2009, Orton 2015, Price 2015, Williamson 2017, Cavell 2020, Orchard 2021)
		beorm "barm" (yeast starter) (Moser 2017)
		gewrit "writing" (Hostetter 2018)
42	Two Proud Ones	*hana ond hæn* "cock and hen" (Dietrich 1859b, Brandl 1908b, Tupper 1910, Wyatt 1912, Trautmann 1914, Trautmann 1915, Wood 1914, Mackie 1934, Krapp and Dobbie 1936, Baum 1963, Hacikyan 1966, Conlee 1968, Schneider 1975, Jember 1976, Williamson 1977, Crossley-Holland 1978, Williamson 1982, Gleißner 1984, Pinsker and Ziegler 1985, Lerer 1989, Muir 1994, Porter 1995, Salvador-Bello 2003, Niles 2006, Alexander 2007, Crossley-Holland 2008, Bitterli 2009, Murphy 2011, Salvador-Bello 2011, Symons 2013, Neville 2015, Salvador-Bello 2015, Symons 2016, Williamson 2017, Hostetter 2018, Cavell 2020, Orchard 2021)
43	Guest in Enclosures	*gæst ond lic-hama* "soul and body" (Dietrich 1859b, Prehn 1883, Tupper 1910, Wyatt 1912, Trautmann 1914, Trautmann 1915, Wood 1914, Mackie 1934, Krapp and Dobbie 1936, Baum 1963, Hacikyan 1966, Conlee 1968, Jember 1976, Williamson 1977, Crossley-Holland 1978, Williamson 1982, Pinsker and Ziegler 1985, Muir 1994, Porter 1995, Salvador-Bello 2003, Niles

(Continued)

The Argument over Solutions 275

ASPR Number	Riddle Title	Solutions
		2006, Alexander 2007, Crossley-Holland 2008, Bitterli 2009, Neville 2009, Murphy 2011, Liuzza 2014, Paz 2015, Salvador-Bello 2015, Williamson 2017, Hostetter 2018, Cavell 2020, Orchard 2021) *lic-hama ond mod* "body and mind" (Wyatt 1912) *gast, lif, erd* "spirit, life, earth" (Schneider 1975) *engel* "guardian angel" (Breeze 2018, Breeze 2020)
44	Hanging Head	**seax-sceað* "dagger sheath" (Dietrich 1859b, Tupper 1903b, Tupper 1910, Krapp and Dobbie 1936, Cavell 2020) *cæg* "key" (Dietrich 1859b, Trautmann 1894, Walz 1896, Tupper 1903b, Tupper 1906, Trautmann 1905, Tupper 1910, Wyatt 1912, Trautmann 1914, Trautmann 1915, Mackie 1934, Krapp and Dobbie 1936, Swaen 1946, Baum 1963, Hacikyan 1966, Conlee 1968, Cassidy and Ringler 1971, Williamson 1977, Crossley-Holland 1978, Williamson 1982, Pinsker and Ziegler 1985, Muir 1994, Porter 1995, Smith 2000, Risden 2001a, Salvador-Bello 2003, Davis 2006, Alexander 2007, Crossley-Holland 2008, Bitterli 2009, Murphy 2011, Liuzza 2014, Cavell 2015b, Orton 2015, Salvador-Bello 2015, Stanley 2017b, Williamson 2017, Hostetter 2018, Rhodes 2020, Ferhatović 2021, Orchard 2021) "phallus" (Jember 1976, Ferhatović 2021, Cavell 2020) *feþer* 'quill' or *hreod* "reed" (Gleißner 1984) *teors* "penis" (Bolding 1992, Davis 2006, Liuzza 2014) *cæg ond cluster* "key and lock" (Niles 2006, Paz 2017, Cavell 2020)
45	Boneless	*beo* "bee" (Dietrich 1859b) *tunge* "tongue" (Dietrich 1859b) *dah* "dough"[10] (Herzfeld 1890, Holthausen 1894, Tupper 1903b, Trautmann 1905, Tupper 1910, Wyatt 1912, Trautmann 1914, Trautmann 1915, Mackie 1934, Krapp and Dobbie 1936, Swaen 1946, Baum 1963, Hacikyan 1966, Conlee 1968, Williamson 1977, Crossley-Holland 1978, Williamson 1982, Gleißner 1984, Pinsker and

(Continued)

---

10 Moritz Trautmann claims to have proposed this solution first in 1887 in an unpublished lecture; see *Die altenglischen Rätsel*, 107.

ASPR Number	Riddle Title	Solutions
		Ziegler 1985, Muir 1994, Porter 1995, Hill 2002, Salvador-Bello 2003, Davis 2006, Niles 2006, Alexander 2007, Crossley-Holland 2008, Murphy 2011, Salvador-Bello 2011, Rudolf 2012, Cavell 2015c, Salvador-Bello 2015, Williamson 2017, Hostetter 2018, Cavell 2020, Fay 2020, Rhodes 2020, Orchard 2021) "phallus" (Jember 1976, Rudolph 2012) *teors* "penis" (Bolding 1985, Davis 2006, Fay 2020) *Ishmael unboren* "Ishmael unborn" (Rudolph 2012) *Crist unboren* "Christ unborn" (Rudolph 2012) *dah ond ofen* "dough and oven" (Salvador-Bello 2015)
46	A Man Sat at Wine	*Adam, Eue, ond cneoris* "Adam, Eve, and family" (Conybeare 1826, Wood 1914) *Loð ond his tuddor* "Lot and his offspring" (Wright 1842, Klipstein 1849, Tupper 1903b, Brandl 1908b, Tupper 1910, Wyatt 1912, Trautmann 1914, Trautmann 1915, Mackie 1934, Krapp and Dobbie 1936, Baum 1963, Hacikyan 1966, Conlee 1968, Schneider 1975, Jember 1976, Williamson 1977, Crossley-Holland 1978, Williamson 1982, Gleißner 1984, Pinsker and Ziegler 1985, Mitchell and Robinson 1986, Muir 1994, Porter 1995, Niles 2006, Crossley-Holland 2008, Bitterli 2009, Murphy 2011, Salvador-Bello 2011, Cavell 2015d, Salvador-Bello 2015, Stanley 2017b, Williamson 2017, Hostetter 2018, Cavell 2020, Orchard 2021)
47	Moth	*boc-moðǒe "bookmoth or bookworm" (Grein 1857–58, Dietrich 1859b, Prehn 1883, Brandl 1908b, Tupper 1910, Wyatt 1912, Trautmann 1914, Wood 1914, Trautmann 1915, Mackie 1934, Krapp and Dobbie 1936, Bone 1943, Baum 1963, Hacikyan 1966, Conlee 1968, Hamer 1970, Cassidy and Ringler 1971, Robinson 1975, Schneider 1975, Stewart 1975, Russom 1977, Williamson 1977, Crossley-Holland 1978, Stewart 1979, Williamson 1982, Pinsker and Ziegler 1985, Mitchell and Robison 1986, Muir 1994, Porter 1995, Scattergood 1999, Alexander 2007, Crossley-Holland 2008, Bitterli 2009, Murphy 2011, Liuzza 2014, Salvador-Bello 2015, Paz 2017, Williamson 2017, Hostetter 2018, Foys 2018, Cavell 2020, Orchard 2021) *deofol* "demon" (Jember 1976) *gewrit* "writing (on vellum)" (Jacobs 1988) *maþa ond sealm-boc* "maggot and psalter" (Niles 2006, Williamson 2017, Cavell 2020) *moðǒe* "clothes-moth" (Stanley 2017b)

(Continued)

The Argument over Solutions 277

ASPR Number	Riddle Title	Solutions
48	Ring without Tongue	*chrismal* "chrismal" (container for consecrated oil) (Dietrich 1859b, Dietrich 1865) *pyxis* "pyx" or "monstrance" (container for eucharistic bread) (Dietrich 1859b, Dietrich 1865, Prehn 1883, Crossley-Holland 2008) *husel-disc* "paten" (plate for eucharistic bread) (Tupper 1910, Trautmann 1914, Mackie 1934, Conlee 1968, Williamson 1977, Crossley-Holland 1978, Muir 1994, Niles 2006, Crossley-Holland 2008, Salvador-Bello 2015, Orchard 2016, Cavell 2017c, Williamson 2017, Cavell 2020, Orchard 2021) *calic* "chalice" (cup for eucharistic wine) (Wyatt 1912, Wood 1914, Mackie 1934, Baum 1963, Hacikyan 1966, Conlee 1968, Williamson 1977, Crossley-Holland 1978, Williamson 1982, Muir 1994, Porter 1995, Crossley-Holland 2008, Bitterli 2009, Murphy 2011, Ramey 2013, Orton 2015, Salvador-Bello 2015, Brooks 2016, Orchard 2016, zk. Williams 2017, Williamson 2017, Foys 2018, Hostetter 2018, Cavell 2020) *belle* "bell" (Jember 1976, Jember 1977) "sacramental vessel" (Jember 1976, Cavell 2020) "inscription ring on chalice" (Pinsker and Ziegler 1985) "illuminated holy book" (Anderson 1983) *hring* "finger ring" (Okasha 1993, Orton 2009)
49	Earth-Fast	**hafoc-cist* "falcon cage" (Dietrich 1859b, Cavell 2020) *boc-fodder* "bookcase or chest" (Dietrich 1865, Prehn 1883, Tupper 1906, Tupper 1910, Wood 1914, Mackie 1934, Conlee 1968, Crossley-Holland 1978, Pinsker and Ziegler 1985, Porter 1995, Crossley-Holland 2008, Bitterli 2009, Salvador-Bello 2015, Williamson 2017, Hostetter 2018, Cavell 2020) *ofen* "oven" or *bæc-ofen* "baking oven" (Trautmann 1894,[11] Trautmann 1905a, Trautmann 1914, Trautmann 1915, Baum 1963, Williamson 1982, Williamson 2017, Cavell 2020, Orchard 2021) *boc* "book" (Swaen 1946, Williamson 1977) *penn ond atrum* "pen and ink" (Shook 1974, Cavell 2020)

(*Continued*)

---

11 Moritz Trautmann claims to have proposed this solution first in 1887 in an unpublished lecture; see "Zu den Lösungen der Rätsel des Exeterbuchs," *Beiblatt zur Anglia Mitteilungen* 25 (1914): 274.

ASPR Number	Riddle Title	Solutions
		hlæw "barrow" (Jember 1976, Cavell 2020)
		*lac-weafod "sacrificial altar" (Jember 1976, Cavell 2020)
		mylen-pull and troh "millpond and sluice" (Doane 1987, Cavell 2020)
		half ond ofen "bread and oven" (Niles 2006)
		hyf ond beo "hive and bee" (Neville 2015, Cavell 2020; see chapter 5 above)
50	Bright Warrior	*hund* "dog" (Dietrich 1859b, Prehn 1883, Cavell 2020)
		lig or *fyr* "fire"[12] (Herzfeld 1890, Trautmann 1894, Heusler 1901, Tupper 1910, Wyatt 1912, Trautmann 1914, Wood 1914, Trautmann 1915, Mackie 1934, Baum 1963, Hacikyan 1966, Conlee 1968, Williamson 1977, Crossley-Holland 1978, Williamson 1982, Pinsker and Ziegler 1985, Mitchell and Robinson 1986, Muir 1994, Porter 1995, Hill 2000a, Niles 2006, Alexander 2007, Crossley-Holland 2008, Bitterli 2009, Salvador-Bello 2015, Cavell 2016a, Stanley 2017b, Williamson 2017, Hostetter 2018, Cavell 2020, Orchard 2021; see also discussion in chapter 5, above)
		"phallus" (Jember 1976)
		*nydfyr "need-fire" (purifying fire kindled by boring) (Schneider 1975)
		ierre "anger" [allegorically] (Nelson 1991, Cavell 2020)
		ealdorduguð "aristocracy" [allegorically] (Neville 2011)
51	Four Creatures	*draca* "dragon" (Dietrich 1859b, Prehn 1883, Brooke 1892)
		hors and wægn "horse and wagon" (Trautmann 1894)
		feþer ond fingras "pen and fingers" or *hand writende* "hand writing" (Trautmann 1905a, Tupper 1906, Tupper 1910, Trautmann 1914, Wood 1914, Trautmann 1915, Mackie 1934, Hacikyan 1966, Conlee 1968, Shook 1974, Williamson 1977, Crossley-Holland 1978, Williamson 1982, Pinsker and Ziegler 1985, Mitchell and Robinson 1986, Muir 1994, Porter 1995, Niles 2006, Alexander 2007, Crossley-Holland 2008, McCully 2008, Murphy 2011,

(Continued)

---

12 Moritz Trautmann claims to have proposed this solution first in 1887 in an unpublished lecture; see *Die altenglischen Rätsel*, 109.

ASPR Number	Riddle Title	Solutions
51		Symons 2013, Neville 2014, Salvador-Bello 2015, Symons 2016, Mize 2017, Paz 2017, Williamson 2017, Hostetter 2018, Cavell 2020, Stanton 2020, Orchard 2021; see also discussion in chapter 4, above) *writingfeþer* "quill pen" (Trautmann 1905a, Tupper 1906, Wyatt 1912, Baum 1963, Bitterli 2009) *alchimi* "alchemy" (Jember 1976) *bocere writende Cristes boc* "scribe writing the Gospels" (Gwara and Bolt 2007) *sacerd mæssiende* "priest performing mass" (Gwara and Bolt 2007)
52	Captives	*twa stoppa* "two buckets" or *wiell-stoppa* "well buckets" (Dietrich 1859b, Grein 1865a, Prehn 1883, Tupper 1903b, Wyatt 1912, Baum 1963, Porter 1995, Murphy 2011, Brady 2014, Brady 2016, Cavell 2020) *besma* "broom" (Trautmann 1894, Cavell 2020) *þerscel* "flail" (Trautmann 1895,[13] Tupper 1906, Tupper 1910, Trautmann 1914, Wood 1914, Trautmann 1915, Mackie 1934, Krapp and Dobbie 1936, Baum 1963, Hacikyan 1966, Williamson 1977; Crossley-Holland 1978, Williamson 1982, Pinsker and Ziegler 1985, Muir 1994, Niles 2006, Alexander 2007, Crossley-Holland 2008, Bitterli 2009, Hill 2011, Murphy 2011, Brady 2014, Salvador-Bello 2015, Brady 2016, Cavell 2016b, Williamson 2017, Hostetter 2018, Cavell 2020, Orchard 2021) *geoc oxena* "yoke of oxen" (Walz 1896, Brady 2014, Cavell 2020) **gelom-wæge* "loom weights" (see chapter 4 above)
53	Towering Tree	*ramm* "battering ram" (Dietrich 1859b, Prehn 1883, Brooke 1892, Tupper 1910, Wyatt 1912, Wood 1914, Trautmann 1915, Mackie 1934, Krapp and Dobbie 1936, Baum 1963, Hacikyan 1966, Conlee 1968, Foley 1977, Williamson 1977, Crossley-Holland 1978, Williamson 1982, Pinsker and Ziegler 1985, Irving 1994, Muir 1994, Porter 1995, Alexander 2007, Crossley-Holland 2008, Bitterli 2009, Salvador-Bello 2015, Stanley 2017b, Williamson 2017, Hostetter 2018, Cavell 2020)

(Continued)

---

13 Moritz Trautmann claims to have proposed this solution first in 1887 in an unpublished lecture; see *Die altenglischen Rätsel*, 110.

Appendix

ASPR Number	Riddle Title	Solutions
		gar "spear" (Trautmann 1894, Brandl 1908b, Tupper 1910, Trautmann 1914)
		"phallus" (Jember 1976)
		rod "cross" (Whitman 1977, Cavell 2020)
		gealga "gallows" (Wilcox 1990, Orchard 2021)
		gealg-treow "gallows/cross" (Niles 2006, Cavell 2020)
		boga "bow" (Neville 2013)
		flan "arrow" (Neville 2013)
		þerscel "flail" (Neville 2013; see also discussion in chapters 2 and 3 above)
		turnus "pole-lathe" (Neville 2013; see also chapter 3 above)
		boc ond feðer "book and quill-pen" (Aiello 2020)
54	In a Corner	*bæcere-cnapa and ofen* "baker's boy and oven" (Dietrich 1859b, Cavell 2020)
		cyrn "(butter) churn" (Trautmann 1894, Tupper 1910, Wyatt 1912, Trautmann 1914, Trautmann 1915, Mackie 1934, Baum 1963, Hacikyan 1966, Foley 1977, Williamson 1977, Crossley-Holland 1978, Williamson 1982, Gleißner 1984, Muir 1994, Porter 1995, Smith 2000, Hill 2001, Alexander 2007, Bitterli 2009, Murphy 2011, Salvador-Bello 2015, Stanley 2017b, Williamson 2017, Hostetter 2018, Cavell 2020, Rhodes 2020, Orchard 2021)
		hæmedlac "intercourse" (Jember 1976, Bolding 1992)
		"phallus" (Jember 1976)
		þegn cyrnende buteran "servant churning butter" (Conlee 1968, Pinsker and Ziegler 1985)
		cyrn ond butere "churn and butter" (Niles 2006)
55	Wolf-Head-Tree	*scyld* "shield" (Dietrich 1859b, Cavell 2020)
		sceað "scabbard" (Dietrich 1865, Brooke 1892, Wyatt 1912, Löwenthal 1914, Wood 1914, Mackie 1934, Hacikyan 1966, Cavell 2020)
		hearpe "harp" (Trautmann 1894, Trautmann 1914, Trautmann 1915, Cavell 2020)
		rod "cross" (Jordan 1903, Tupper 1910, Holthausen 1912, Mackie 1934, Baum 1963, Conlee 1968, Foley 1977, Pinsker and Ziegler 1985, Mitchell and Robinson 1986, Tristram 1986, Bitterli 2009, Salvador-Bello 2015, Hostetter 2018, Cavell 2020)
		gealga "gallows" (Jordan 1903, Liebermann 1905, Cavell 2020)

(Continued)

The Argument over Solutions 281

ASPR Number	Riddle Title	Solutions
		"sword-rack" (Liebermann 1905, Brandl 1908b, Holthausen 1919, Krapp and Dobbie 1936, Crossley-Holland 1978, Muir 1994, Porter 1995, Crossley-Holland 2008, Cavell 2020) *sweord-arc "sword-box" (Sedgefield 1922, Williamson 1977, Cavell 2020) "tetraktys" (Jember 1976) scrin "reliquary" (Fanger 1985–6, Machan and Peterson 1987) *meadu-byden and bledu "mead-barrel and drinking bowl" (Taylor 1995) *wæpen-hengen "weapon rack" (Niles 2006, Murphy 2011, Williamson 2017, Cavell 2020, Orchard 2021)
56	Turning Wood	web ond web-beam "cloth and loom" (Dietrich 1859b, Prehn 1883, Tupper 1910, Wood 1914, Mackie 1934, Krapp and Dobbie 1936, Erhardt-Siebold 1949b, Baum 1963, Hacikyan 1966, Conlee 1968, Williamson 1977, Crossley-Holland 1978, Whitman 1982, Williamson 1982, Owen-Crocker 1986, Muir 1994, Porter 1995, Hyer 1998, Hyer 2004, Owen-Crocker 2004, Niles 2006, Crossley-Holland 2008, Cavell 2011, Portnoy 2013, Salvador-Bello 2015, Cavell 2016b, Frederick 2016, Williamson 2017, Hostetter 2018, J. Roberts 2019, Cavell 2020, Cavell 2021c) turnus "pole-lathe" (Lange via Dietrich 1865, Pinsker and Ziegler 1985, Bitterli 2009, Cavell 2020; see also chapter 3, above) þerscel "flail" (Wyatt 1912, Trautmann 1914, Trautmann 1915) cwealm "execution" (Jember 1976) *rid-rod "pole-lathe" (Orchard 2021)
57	Abounding in Song	gnættas "gnats" (Dietrich 1859b, Sweet 1908, Wyatt 1912, Wood 1914, Mackie 1934, Baum 1963, Porter 1995, Cavell 2020) swealwan "swallows" (Dietrich 1859b, Tupper 1906, Tupper 1910, Trautmann 1914, Mackie 1934, Baum 1963, Hacikyan 1966, Conlee 1968, Williamson 1977, Williamson 1982, Muir 1994, Porter 1995, Riedinger 2003, Alexander 2007, Bitterli 2009, Salvador-Bello 2015, Warren 2017, Williamson 2017, Cavell 2020) stærlingas "starlings" (Dietrich 1865, Prehn 1883, Löwenthal 1914, Cavell 2020)

(Continued)

ASPR Number	Riddle Title	Solutions
		stæðswealwan "martins" (Brooke 1892, Crossley-Holland 1978, Crossley-Holland 2008, Cavell 2020) **hagol-stanas* "hailstones" (Trautmann 1894, Heusler 1901, Brandl 1908b, Cavell 2020) **regn-dropan* "raindrops" (Trautmann 1895, Cavell 2020) *beon* "bees" (Blackburn 1900, Garvin 1966, Cavell 2020) **storm-wolcnu* "stormclouds" (Trautmann 1905a, Cavell 2020) *micga* "midges" (Wyatt 1912, Cavell 2020) "swifts" (Trautmann 1915, Meaney 1996, Warren 2017, Cavell 2020) *ceo* "jackdaw" (Brett 1927, Krapp and Dobbie 1936, Erhardt-Siebold 1947a, Baum 1963, Cassidy and Ringler 1971) *crawan* "crows" (Holthausen 1927, Krapp and Dobbie 1936, Pinsker and Ziegler 1985, Niles 2006, Cavell 2020) **ca* "jackdaw" (Erhardt-Siebold 1947a, Cavell 2020) *stafas* "musical notes, neumes" (Shook 1974, Orchard 2016, Hostetter 2018, Cavell 2020, Orchard 2021) *awyrgde gastas* "damned souls" (Jember 1976, Pulsiano and Wolf 1991, Meaney 1996, Cavell 2020) *deoflu* "demons" (Jember 1977, Cavell 2020) *swealwe/swelgan/swelgend* "swallow/to swallow/whirlpool" (Welsh 1990) *bocstafas* "letters" (Murphy 2005, Murphy 2011, Symons 2013, Symons 2016, Cavell 2020, Orchard 2021)
58	One-Footed	**rad-burna* "riding-well", "draw-well", "well with a well-sweep" (Dietrich 1859b, Prehn 1883, Tupper 1910, Wyatt 1912, Mackie 1934, Baum 1963, Hacikyan 1966, Conlee 1968, Schneider 1975, Jember 1976, Pinsker and Ziegler 1985) **rad-pytt* "riding-well" (Grein 1865) *rod* "pole, well-sweep" (Holthausen 1894, Wood 1914, Krapp and Dobbie 1936, Muir 1994, Bitterli 2009) **rad-rod* "riding-well" (Trautmann 1914, Trautmann 1915)

(Continued)

The Argument over Solutions 283

ASPR Number	Riddle Title	Solutions
		rad-lim "well-sweep" (Blakeley 1958) "phallus" (Jember 1976) *rad-rod* "well-sweep" or "well-beam" (Williamson 1977, Crossley-Holland 1978, Williamson 1982, Porter 1995, Crossley-Holland 2008, Symons 2013, Salvador-Bello 2015, Symons 2016, Stanley 2017b, Hostetter 2018,) ᚱᚱᚫᛗ *rad-rod* "well-sweep"(spelled out in runic letters) (Niles 2006, Murphy 2011, Symons 2017a, Williamson 2017, Niles 2019, Cavell 2020, Orchard 2021; see also discussion in chapter 3, above) *rid-rod* "pole-lathe" (Orchard 2021)
59	Golden Ring	*calic* "chalice" or *husel-fæt* "communion cup" (Dietrich 1865, Tupper 1910, Wyatt 1912, Wood 1914, Mackie 1934, Baum 1963, Hacikyan 1966, Conlee 1968, Schneider 1975, Jember 1976, Williamson 1977, Crossley-Holland 1978, Williamson 1982, Muir 1994, Porter 1995, Niles 2006, Crossley-Holland 2008, Bitterli 2009, Ramey 2013, Salvador-Bello 2015, Brooks 2016, Orchard 2016, Roscoe 2017, Williamson 2017, Cavell 2020, Orchard 2021) "inscription ring on chalice" (Pinsker and Ziegler 1985) *hring* "finger ring" (Okasha 1993) *husel-disc* "paten" (Conlee 1968, Orchard 2016) *Cristes reord* "Christ's voice" (Hayes 2008) *hring* "ring" (sign-language gesture, shape of chalice, sound of bell) (Foys 2014) *rosarium* "rosary" (Hostetter 2018)
60	Mouthless by Sand	*hreod* "reed pipe or flute" (Dietrich 1859b, Prehn 1883, Brooke 1892, Padelford 1899, Porter 1995) *hreod-writ* "reed pen" (Müller 1861, Tupper 1910, Trautmann 1912, Trautmann 1914, Trautmann 1915, Mackie 1934, Leslie 1959, Baum 1963, Leslie 1968, Whitman 1971, Williamson 1977, Porter 1995, Crossley-Holland 2008, Bitterli 2009, Murphy 2011, Hostetter 2018, Cavell 2020) *run-stæf* "rune staff" (Strobl 1887, Trautmann 1894, Baum 1963, Williamson 1977, Muir 1994, Porter 1995, Cavell 2020) "letter beam cut from an old jetty stump" (Morley 1888)

(*Continued*)

ASPR Number	Riddle Title	Solutions
		hreod "reed" (plant, pipe, and pen) (Wyatt 1912, Mackie 1934, Hacikyan 1966, Hamer 1970, Crossley-Holland 1978, Niles 2006, Alexander 2007, Ramey 2013, Orchard 2016, Paz 2017, Roscoe 2017, Williamson 2017, Brooks 2020, Stanton 2020, Orchard 2021)
		waroð "kelp weed" (inscribed with runes) (Colgrave and Griffiths 1936, Baum 1963)
		"revenant" (Jember 1976)
		gæst "spirit" (Jember 1976)
		"inscribed rock near high water mark" (Kirby 2001)
		sond "message" (Stanley 2017a)
60 as part of *Husband's Message*		(Blackburn 1900, Wood 1914, Elliott 1955, Kaske 1967, Conlee 1968, Goldsmith 1975, Pinsker and Ziegler 1985)
61	Head Stuck In	*cyrtel* "kirtle" or "shirt" (Dietrich 1859b, Tupper 1910, Wood 1914, Mackie 1934, Swaen 1946, Baum 1963, Conlee 1968, Williamson 1977, Crossley-Holland 1978, Gleißner 1984, Muir 1994, Niles 2006, Crossley-Holland 2008, Murphy 2011, Williamson 2017, Hostetter 2018, Cavell 2020, Orchard 2021)
		byrne "mailshirt" (Trautmann 1914, Trautmann 1915)
		helm "helmet" (Wyatt 1912, Wood 1914, Mackie 1934, Krapp and Dobbie 1936, Hacikyan 1966, Conlee 1968, Osborn 1976, Williamson 1977, Crossley-Holland 1978, Williamson 1982, Muir 1994, Porter 1995, Alexander 2007, Heyworth 2007b, Crossley-Holland 2008, Murphy 2011, Salvador-Bello 2015, Williamson 2017, Cavell 2020)
		cwið "vagina" (Jember 1976, Osborn 1976, Crossley-Holland 1978, Gleißner 1984)
		hæmed "intercourse" (Bolding 1992)
		hod "hood" (Pinsker and Ziegler 1985)
		syrica for þære nihtware "night-shirt" (Stanley 2017b)
62	Strong Going In/Out[14]	*nafu-gar* or *bor* "gimlet, borer, auger" (wood-working tool) (Dietrich 1859b, Wyatt 1912, Baum 1963, Hacikyan 1966, Conlee 1968, Williamson 1977, Williamson 1982, Muir 1994, Niles 2006, Murphy 2011, Salvador-Bello 2015, Williamson 2017, Cavell 2020, Ferhatović 2021)

(Continued)

---

14 For discussion of the word *hingong*, see chapter 5, above.

ASPR Number	Riddle Title	Solutions
		fot ond scoh "foot and shoe" (Dietrich 1859b)
		fyr-gierd "fire-rod" or "poker" (Tupper 1910, Mackie 1934, Krapp and Dobbie 1936, Swaen 1942, Baum 1963, Conlee 1968, Pinsker and Ziegler 1985, Porter 1995, Bitterli 2009, Murphy 2011, Salvador-Bello 2015, Symons 2017b, Hostetter 2018, Cavell 2020, Ferhatović 2021)
		mearc-isern, hoc, ond tinder "branding iron, hook, and tinder" (Holthausen 1912, Löwenthal 1914)
		biernende flan "burning arrow" (Trautmann 1914, Trautmann 1915)
		ofnes raca "oven rake" (Swaen 1942)
		"phallus" (Jember 1976, Crossley-Holland 1978, Cavell 2020, Ferhatović 2021)
		"tool for tapping a smelting oven" (Gleißner 1984)
		teors "penis" (Bolding 1992, Crossley-Holland 2008)
		spura "spur" (Bitterli 2019b, Orchard 2021)
63	Shining with Gold	*glas-fæt* "glass beaker" or *bune* "cup" (Dietrich 1859b, Prehn 1883, Tupper 1910, Wyatt 1912, Mackie 1934, Baum 1963, Hacikyan 1966, Conlee 1968, Williamson 1977, Crossley-Holland 1978, Williamson 1982, Gleißner 1984, Pinsker and Ziegler 1985, Muir 1994, Porter 1995, Niles 2006, Crossley-Holland 2008, Murphy 2011, Orton 2015, Salvador-Bello 2015, Cavell 2017a, Stanley 2017b, Williamson 2017, Hostetter 2018, Cavell 2020, Orchard 2021)
		hwistle "flute" (Trautmann 1894, Cavell 2020)
		flaxe "flask or can" (Trautmann 1914, Trautmann 1915, Cavell 2020)
64	Joy and Ice	*pea *beah-swifeda* "ring-tailed peacock" (Dietrich 1859b)
		aspide-uf "snake-eating bird" (Grein 1865a)
		wicg, beorn, hafoc, þegn, falca, ea, spear-hafuc "horse, man, hawk, servant, falcon, water, sparrow-hawk", etc. [with various interpretations of the individual runes – i.e. the runes simply spell out the solution] (Hicketier 1888, Trautmann 1894, Tupper 1910, Wyatt 1912, Trautmann 1914, Wood 1914, Trautmann 1915, Mackie 1934, Conlee 1968, Porter 1995)
		hafocung "falconry" (Erhardt-Siebold 1948, Cavell 2020)

(Continued)

ASPR Number	Riddle Title	Solutions
		gewritere ond gewrit "scribe and writing" (Eliason 1952, Conlee 1968, Shook 1974, Symons 2017c, Cavell 2020)
		huntoð "hunting" (Baum 1963, Hacikyan 1966, Cavell 2020)
		hunta "hunter" (Porter 1995)
		scip "ship" (Williamson 1977, Williamson 1982, Pinsker and Ziegler 1985, Muir 1994, Bitterli 2009, Orton 2015, Salvador-Bello 2015, Williamson 2017, Cavell 2020, Orchard 2021)
		brim-hengest "sea-horse, ship" (Niles 2006)
		stafas "letters" (Symons 2013, Symons 2016, Cavell 2020)
		eoredman ridende "nobleman riding" (Hostetter 2018)
65	I Was Alive	*cipe* "onion" (Dietrich 1859b, Prehn 1883, Tupper 1910, Wyatt 1912, Wood 1914, Trautmann 1915, Mackie 1934, Baum 1963, Hacikyan 1966, Conlee 1968, Schneider 1975, Williamson 1977, Crossley-Holland 1978, Williamson 1982, Pinsker and Ziegler 1985, Muir 1994, Porter 1995, Niles 2006, Alexander 2007, Crossley-Holland 2008, Bitterli 2009, Murphy 2011, Orton 2015, Salvador-Bello 2015, Stanley 2017b, Williamson 2017, Hostetter 2018, Cavell 2020, Orchard 2021)
		"chive" (Trautmann 1914, Trautmann 1915, Cavell 2020)
		cipe "leek" (Trautmann 1894, Wood 1914, Trautmann 1915, Cavell 2020)
		"phallus" (Jember 1976)
		"revenant" (Jember 1976)
		gæst "spirit" (Jember 1976)
66	Bigger than the Earth	*godes æht* "God's power" (Conybeare 1826, Wood 1914)
		gesceaft, creatura "creation" (Dietrich 1859b, Tupper 1910, Wyatt 1912, Trautmann 1914, Trautmann 1915, Baum 1963, Hacikyan 1966, Conlee 1968, Jember 1976, Williamson 1977, Crossley-Holland 1978, Williamson 1982, Muir 1994, Porter 1995, Niles 2006, Crossley-Holland 2008, Sebo 2014, Orton 2015, Salvador-Bello 2015, Sebo 2017, Williamson 2017, Sebo 2018, Cavell 2020, Orchard 2021)
		natura "nature" (Mackie 1933, Mackie 1934, Alexander 2007, Williamson 2017, Hostetter 2018)
		wæter "water" (Pinsker and Ziegler 1985, Bitterli 2009)
		god "God" (Niles 2006, Cavell 2020)

(Continued)

The Argument over Solutions   287

ASPR Number	Riddle Title	Solutions
67	Word-Spell	biblioðece "Bible" (Trautmann 1894, Trautman 1905, Tupper 1910, Trautmann 1914, Trautmann 1915, Mackie 1933, Mackie 1934, Hacikyan 1966, Conlee 1968, Schneider 1975, Williamson 1977, Crossley-Holland 1978, Williamson 1982, Muir 1994, Pinsker and Ziegler 1985, Porter 1995, Crossley-Holland 2008, Ramey 2013, Orton 2015, Roscoe 2017, Williamson 2017, Hostetter 2018, Cavell 2020) boc "book" (Conlee 1968, Williamson 1982, Bitterli 2009) Cristes boc "Gospel book" (Pinsker and Ziegler 1985, Salvador-Bello 2015, Orchard 2021) rod "cross" (Mackie 1933, Mackie 1934) Word "the Word" (Hayes 2008)
68	Creature Went Away	[fragment of separate, unfinished riddle] (Thorpe 1842, Trautmann 1905, Trautmann 1914, Tupper 1910, Krapp and Dobbie 1936, Conlee 1968, Crossley-Holland 1978, Crossley-Holland 2008)
69	Wonder on the Way	is "ice" (Trautmann 1905, Tupper 1910, Trautmann 1915, Krapp and Dobbie 1936, Conlee 1968, Crossley-Holland 1978, Porter 1995, Niles 2006, Crossley-Holland 2008, Orton 2015, Bitterli 2019c) is-mere "frozen pond" (Niles 2006) gicel "icicle" (Murphy 2011) "River Thames at sunset" (A. Roberts 2013) meolc "milk" (A. Roberts 2013)
68–9 as one riddle	Water Turned to Bone	winter "winter" (Grein 1857–8, Wood 1912) is "ice" (Dietrich 1859b, Trautmann 1915, Mackie 1934, Porter 1995, Niles 2006, Alexander 2007, Salvador-Bello 2015, Cavell 2017b, Stanley 2017b, Hostetter 2018, Cavell 2020, Orchard 2021) "petrification" (Wyatt 1912) "Christ walking on the sea" (Eliason 1949) *is-beorg "iceberg" (Williamson 1977, Williamson 1982, Muir 1994, Salvador-Bello 2015, Williamson 2017, Cavell 2020) iernende wæter "running water" (Baum 1963) is-mere "frozen pond" (Niles 2006, Cavell 2020) gicel "icicle" (Cavell 2020)

(*Continued*)

ASPR Number	Riddle Title	Solutions
70	Cunningly Made	*sceap-hyrdes pipe* "shawm or shepherd's pipe" (Dietrich 1859b, Padelford 1899, Tupper 1910, Wyatt 1912, Mackie 1934, Baum 1963, Hacikyan 1966, Crossley-Holland 1978, Porter 1995, Alexander 2007, Crossley-Holland 2008, Hostetter 2018, Cavell 2020) **ryge-hwistle* "rye flute" (Trautmann 1894, Cavell 2020) *heorpe* "lyre or harp" (Trautmann 1914, Trautmann 1915, Krapp and Dobbie 1936, Hacikyan 1966, Crossley-Holland 1978, Crossley-Holland 2008) "hurdygurdy" (Holthausen 1919) *organa* "organistrum" (Holthausen 1919, Cavell 2020) *hrisel* "shuttle" (Erhardt-Siebold 1949b, Cavell 2020) *hearpe* "harp/grain-dryer"[15] (Schneider 1975)
70a (1–4)	Sings through Its Sides	*hearpe* "lyre or harp" (Pope 1974, Williamson 1977, Williamson 1982, Muir 1994, Salvador-Bello 2015, S. Breeze 2019, Cavell 2020, Williamson 2017) *belle* "bell" (Pinsker and Ziegler 1985, Cavell 2020, Orchard 2021) *nosu* "nose" (Stévanovitch 1995) *cyricean belle* "church bell" (Niles 2006) *twyfyldu pipe* "double flute" (Moser 2016)
70b (5–6)	Tall and Beautiful	*fyr-torr* or *beacen-stan* "light-house" (Pope 1974, Williamson 1977, Williamson 1982, Pinsker and Ziegler 1985, Muir 1994, Salvador-Bello 2015, Williamson 2017, Cavell 2020, Orchard 2021) *candel* "candle" (Niles 2006, Cavell 2020, Williamson 2017)
71	Clothed in Red	*glæs* "cupping glass" (Dietrich 1859b, Prehn 1883, Cavell 2020) *hand-seax* "dagger" (suggested but rejected by Dietrich 1859b, Tupper 1910, Holthausen 1919, Mackie 1934, Cavell 2020)

(*Continued*)

---

15 While "harp" can denote a sieve (see *OED s.v.* harp, definition 5), Schneider refers to a different agricultural implement: a cereal drying rack. For a history of the structure, see Klaus Zwerger, *Cereal Drying Racks: Culture and Typology of Wood Buildings in Europe and East Asia*, trans. Julian Reisenberger (2011; Berlin: Walter de Gruyter, 2020). Photos of some simple examples can be found on 8, 11, and 13.

The Argument over Solutions 289

ASPR Number	Riddle Title	Solutions
		sweord "sword" (suggested but rejected by Dietrich 1859b, Tupper 1910, Wood 1914, Holthausen 1919, Mackie 1934, Davidson 1962, Williamson 1977, Williamson 1982, Pinsker and Ziegler 1985, Muir 1994, Porter 1995, Niles 2006, Portnoy 2013, Orton 2015, Williamson 2017, Cavell 2020; see also discussion in chapter 2, above)
		isen helm "iron helmet" (Trautmann 1894, Cavell 2020)
		isen "iron (ore)" (Wyatt 1912, Alexander 2007, Crossley-Holland 2008, Cavell 2020)
		isen scield "iron shield" (Trautmann 1914, Cavell 2020)
		brasen scield "bronze shield" (Trautmann 1915, Cavell 2020)
		gar "lance" or "spear" (Hacikyan 1966)
		wæpen "weapon" (Conlee 1968)
		"revenant" (Jember 1976)
		hilte "hilt" (of sword) (Portnoy 2013, Cavell 2020)
		þegn "retainer" (Portnoy 2013, Cavell 2020)
		secg "sword/man/sedge" (Orchard 2021)
72	Boundary-Paths	*eax ond hweolas* "axle and wheels" (Dietrich 1859b, Prehn 1883)
		oxa "(plough) ox" (Grein 1861–4, Brooke 1892, Trautmann 1894,[16] Tupper 1910, Wyatt 1912, Trautmann 1914, Wood 1914, Trautmann 1915, Mackie 1934, Baum 1963, Hacikyan 1966, Conlee 1968, Williamson 1977, Crossley-Holland 1978, Williamson 1982, Pinsker and Ziegler 1985, Muir 1994, Porter 1995, Niles 2006, Alexander 2007, Crossley-Holland 2008, Bitterli 2009, Brady 2014, Orton 2015, Cavell 2016b, Stanton 2017, Williamson 2017, Cavell 2020, Orchard 2021)
		ðeow "slave" (Jember 1976)
		cealf "(bull) calf" (Murphy 2011, Hostetter 2018)
		cu "cow" (Cavell 2020)
		hriðer "heifer" (Cavell 2020)
73	Brain-Locker	*gar* "lance" (Dietrich 1859b, Prehn 1883, Tupper 1910, Wyatt 1912, Krapp and Dobbie 1936, Baum 1963, Conlee 1968, Williamson 1982, Williamson 2017)

(*Continued*)

---

16 Moritz Trautmann claims to have proposed this solution first in 1887 in an unpublished lecture; see "Zu den Lösungen der Rätsel," 274.

ASPR Number	Riddle Title	Solutions
		gar "spear" (Brooke 1892, Brandl 1908b, Tupper 1910, Wyatt 1912, Wood 1914, Mackie 1934, Krapp and Dobbie 1936, Baum 1963, Conlee 1968, Williamson 1977, Williamson 1982, Muir 1994, Porter 1995, Niles 2006, Alexander 2007, Crossley-Holland 2008, Bitterli 2009, Symons 2017d, Williamson 2017, Hostetter 2018, Cavell 2020, Orchard 2021; see also discussion in chapter 2, above) *ramm* "battering ram" (Trautmann 1914, Trautmann 1915, Trautmann 1919, Krapp and Dobbie 1936) *beam* "beam" (Conlee 1968) *rod* "cross" (Whitman 1977, Cavell 2020) "revenant" (Jember 1976) *gæst* "spirit" (Jember 1976) *hreod* "pen" (Whitman 1982) *boga ond *blæse-flan* "bow and incendiary arrow" (Pinsker and Ziegler 1985) *boga* "bow" (Doane 1987, Cavell 2020)
74	Grey-Haired Queen	*wasescite* "cuttlefish" (Dietrich 1859b, Prehn 1883, Dietrich 1865, Walz 1896, Cavell 2020) *sunne* "sun" (Müller 1861, McCarthy 1993) *wæter* "water" (Trautmann 1894, Trautmann 1905, Trautmann 1912, Trautmann 1914, Trautmann 1915, Baum 1963, Klein, Klein, and Delehanty 2014, Klein 2015a, Paz 2017, Hostetter 2018, Cavell 2020) *meremenn* "siren" (Tupper 1903b, Tupper 1906, Tupper 1910, Krapp and Dobbie 1936, Baum 1963, Hacikyan 1966, Jember 1976, Crossley-Holland 1978, Crossley-Holland 2008, Cavell 2020) *hyna* "hyena" (Löwenthal 1914) *swan* "swan" (Holthausen 1925, Salvador-Bello 1998) "metempsychosis" (Erhardt-Siebold 1946c) *sawol* "soul" (Erhardt-Siebold 1952) *regn* "rain" (Baum 1963) *feðer* "quill pen" (Conlee 1968, Cavell 2020) *gewrit* "writing" (Whitman 1968) **brim-earn* "sea eagle" or "diving bird" (Kiernan 1975b) *scipes heafod* "ship's figurehead" (Williamson 1977, Porter 1995, Cavell 2020)

(Continued)

ASPR Number	Riddle Title	Solutions
		anlicnes "reflection" or *sceadu* "shadow" (Morgan 1991) *ylfetu* "whooper swan" (Kitson 1994) *byrnete* "barnacle goose" (Donoghue 1998, Mitchell and Robinson 1986) *ac* "boat made of oak" (Niles 1998) *halig gast* "holy spirit" (Klein 1999) *mona* "moon" (Hosler 2001) *ac ond bat* "boat made of oak" (Niles 2006, Murphy 2011, Cavell 2020) *ac* [runic letter] "oak, boat" (Griffith 2008, Orchard 2021) *snaw* "snow" (Alexander 2007) **mere-fugol* "water bird" (Bitterli 2009) *storm* "thunderstorm" (Klein, Klein, and Delehanty 2014) *scead* "[through word-play] shade/crown of the head/shadow/understanding" (Stanley 2017b) *scip* "ship" (Williamson 2017)
75	Swift on a Track	*hund* "(hunting) dog" (Thorpe 1842, Grein 1857–8, Tupper 1910, Trautmann 1915, Mackie 1934, Baum 1963, Hacikyan 1966, Porter 1995, Crossley-Holland 2008, Bitterli 2009, Bitterli 2019c, Cavell 2020) *hælend* "saviour" (Mackie 1933, Mackie 1934, Baum 1963, Hacikyan 1966, Cavell 2020) *hand* "hand" (Conlee 1968) *grom* "groom, boy, or servant" (Reisner 1970)
75–6 as one riddle	Swift and Sitting	**eolh-hunta* "elk-hunter" (Eliason 1952) *hland* "piss" or "peeing" (Williamson 1977, Williamson 1982, Gleißner 1984, Muir 1994, Salvador-Bello 2011, Salvador-Bello 2015, Williamson 2017, Hostetter 2018, Cavell 2020) *hund ond hind* "hound and hind" (Niles 2006, Murphy 2011, Cavell 2020) *ac* "oak" (Orchard 2021)
76	Woman Sitting Alone	*hænn* "hen" (Wyatt 1912, Mackie 1934, Baum 1963, Conlee 1968, Crossley-Holland 1978, Lees 2007, Crossley-Holland 2008, Bitterli 2019c) *hind* "hind, female deer" (Dewa 1995, Bitterli 2019c) *sceawere* "mirror" (Alexander 2007) *ened* "duck" (Bitterli 2019b) *fyxe* "vixen" (Bitterli 2019b) *ræge* "roe doe" (Bitterli 2019c)

(Continued)

ASPR Number	Riddle Title	Solutions
76–77 as one riddle	Footless Woman	*ostre* "oyster" (Dietrich 1859b)
77	Footless	*ostre* "oyster" (Dietrich 1859b, Prehn 1883, Tupper 1910, Wyatt 1912, Trautmann 1914, Wood 1914, Trautmann 1915, Mackie 1934, Krapp and Dobbie 1936, Baum 1963, Hacikyan 1966, Conlee 1968, Schneider 1975, Jember 1976, Williamson 1977, Williamson 1982, Crossley-Holland 1978, Pinsker and Ziegler 1985, Porter 1995, Salvador-Bello 2004, Niles 2006, Alexander 2007, Crossley-Holland 2008, Bitterli 2009, Salvador-Bello 2015, Williamson 2017, Cavell 2018a, Stanley 2017b, Hostetter 2018, Cavell 2020, Orchard 2021) *mægpblæd* "female genitals" (Jember 1976) *facg* or *floc* "flatfish" (Preston 2011)
78	Cunning Thing in Waves	*wæter-deor* "water animal" (Holthausen 1901, Bitterli 2009, Cavell 2020) *ostre* "oyster" (Tupper 1910, Trautmann 1915, Mackie 1934, Hacikyan 1966, Crossley-Holland 1978, Alexander 2007, Crossley-Holland 2008, Cavell 2020) *lamprede* "lamprey" (Williamson 1977, Williamson 1982, Porter 1995, Cavell 2020) *crabba* "crab" (Salvador-Bello 2004, Niles 2006, Salvador-Bello 2015, Cavell 2018b, Cavell 2020, Orchard 2021)
79	Noble's Possession and Desire	*rice* "power" (Muir 1994) "phallus" (Jember 1976) *wæpen* "weapon/penis" (Bitterli 2019c)
79–80 as one riddle	Noble's Shoulder-Companion	*horn* "horn" (Williamson 1977, Williamson 1982, Niles 2006, Salvador-Bello 2015, Orchard 2021, Williamson 2017, Cavell 2020)
80	Warrior's Companion	*hafoc* "hunting falcon or hawk" (Dietrich 1859b, Prehn 1883, Brooke 1892, Cook and Tinker 1902, Cavell 2020) *horn* "horn" (Müller 1861, Herzfeld 1890, Trautmann 1905a, Tupper 1906, Tupper 1910, Trautmann 1914, Wood 1914, Trautmann 1915, Mackie 1934, Swaen 1941b, Baum 1963, Hacikyan 1966, Conlee 1968, Crossley-Holland 1978, Pinsker and Ziegler 1985, Muir 1994, Porter 1995, Alexander 2007, Crossley-Holland 2008, Bitterli 2009, Orton 2015, Williamson 2017, Hostetter 2018, S. Breeze 2019, Cavell 2020) *gar* "spear" (Trautmann 1894, Walz 1896, Cavell 2020)

(Continued)

The Argument over Solutions 293

ASPR Number	Riddle Title	Solutions
		sweord "sword" (Trautmann 1894, Walz 1896, Davidson 1962, Cavell 2020) *sceað* "scabbard" (Davidson 1962, Cavell 2020) "phallus" (Jember 1976) *rod* "cross" (see chapter 3 above)
81	Puff-Breasted	*scip* "ship" (Dietrich 1859b, Conlee 1968, Cavell 2020) *grim-helm* "visored helmet", "visor" (Lange via Dietrich 1865, Brooke 1892, Wood 1914, Cavell 2020) *weder-coc "weathercock" or "weathervane" (Trautmann 1894, Tupper 1910, Wyatt 1912, Trautmann 1914, Trautmann 1915, Mackie 1934, Krapp and Dobbie 1936, Baum 1963, Hacikyan 1966, Williamson 1977, Crossley-Holland 1978, Williamson 1982, Pinsker and Ziegler 1985, Muir 1994, Porter 1995, Niles 2006, Alexander 2007, Crossley-Holland 2008, Bitterli 2009, Salvador-Bello 2015, Williamson 2017, Hostetter 2018, Kendall 2018, Cavell 2020, Orchard 2021) *wer* "man" (Jember 1976)
82	Swallows Grit	*crabba* "crab" (Holthausen 1919, Bitterli 2009, Cavell 2020, Orchard 2021) *egðe* "harrow" (Williamson 1977, Williamson 1982, Muir 1994, Porter 1995, Williamson 2017, Cavell 2020)
83	Old Ancestry	*ora* "ore" (Dietrich 1859b, Prehn 1883, Tupper 1910, Wyatt 1912, Krapp and Dobbie 1936, Hacikyan 1966, Conlee 1968, Nelson 1974, Crossley-Holland 1978, Porter 1995, Nelson 2000, Niles 2006, Crossley-Holland 2008, Murphy 2011, Klein 2015b, Dale 2017, Hostetter 2018, Cavell 2020) *feoh* "money" or "coins" (Trautmann 1894, Wyatt 1912, Trautmann 1914, Wood 1914, Trautmann 1915, Pinsker and Ziegler 1985, Cavell 2020) *bloma* "metal" (Wyatt 1912, Mackie 1934, Baum 1963, Klein 2015b, Hostetter 2018, Cavell 2020) *gold* "gold" (Mackie 1934, Williamson 1977, Williamson 1982, Muir 1994, Porter 1995, Klein 2015b, Williamson 2017, Cavell 2020, Orchard 2021) "revenant" (Jember 1976, Cavell 2020) *gæst* "spirit" (Jember 1976, Cavell 2020)

(*Continued*)

ASPR Number	Riddle Title	Solutions
84	Mother of Many	*wæter* "water" (Dietrich 1859b, Prehn 1883, Tupper 1910, Brandl 1908b, Wyatt 1912, Trautmann 1914, Wood 1914, Trautmann 1915, Mackie 1934, Krapp and Dobbie 1936, Baum 1963, Hacikyan 1966, Conlee 1968, Schneider 1975, E. Williams 1975, Jember 1976, Williamson 1977, Crossley-Holland 1978, Williamson 1982, Pinsker and Ziegler 1985, Muir 1994, Porter 1995, Niles 2006, Crossley-Holland 2008, Bitterli 2009, Orton 2015, Dale 2017, Stanley 2017b, Williamson 2017, Hostetter 2018, Whaley 2019, Dale 2020, Cavell 2020, Oberman 2020, Orchard 2021)
85	My Hall Is Not Silent	*fisc ond flod* "fish and river" (Dietrich 1859b, Prehn 1883, Holthausen 1894, Tupper 1903b, Brandl 1908b, Tupper 1910, Wyatt 1912, Trautmann 1914, Wood 1914, Trautmann 1915, Mackie 1934, Krapp and Dobbie 1936, Baum 1963, Hacikyan 1966, Conlee 1968, Schneider 1975, Williamson 1977, Crossley-Holland 1978, Williamson 1982, Pinsker and Ziegler 1985, Mitchell and Robinson 1986, Muir 1994, Porter 1995, Niles 2006, Alexander 2007, Crossley-Holland 2008, McCully 2008, Bitterli 2009, Murphy 2011, Paz 2017, Williamson 2017, Hostetter 2018, Cavell 2019a, Cavell 2020, Harlow 2020, Orchard 2021) *lic ond sawol* "body and soul" (Jember 1976, Cavell 2020, Orchard 2021) *husel on lichama* "housel in body" (Harlow 2020)
86	Twelve Hundred Heads	*organa* "organ" (Dietrich 1859b, Padelford 1899) *an-eagede gar-leac monger* "one-eyed garlic seller" (Müller 1861, Dietrich 1865, Prehn 1883, Tupper 1910, Wyatt 1912, Wood 1914, Trautmann 1915, Mackie 1934, Krapp and Dobbie 1936, Baum 1963, Hacikyan 1966, Conlee 1968, Williamson 1977, Crossley-Holland 1978, Williamson 1982, Pinsker and Ziegler 1985, Mitchell and Robinson 1986, Muir 1994, Porter 1995, Niles 2006, Alexander 2007, Crossley-Holland 2008, Bitterli 2009, Murphy 2011, Liuzza 2014, Stanley 2017b, Williamson 2017, Hostetter 2018, Cavell 2019b, Cavell 2020, Orchard 2021) *an-eaged cipe monger* "one-eyed onion seller" (Wyatt 1912, McCully 2008) "the riddler" (mock riddle) (Wilcox 1996)

(Continued)

The Argument over Solutions 295

ASPR Number	Riddle Title	Solutions
87	Barked, Wavered	*cyf ond *cyf-wyrhta* "cask and cooper" (Grein 1857–8, Dietrich 1859b, Wood 1914) *blæst-belg* "bellows" (Müller 1861, Trautmann 1894, Tupper 1910, Wyatt 1912, Trautmann 1914, Trautmann 1915, Mackie 1934, Krapp and Dobbie 1936, Baum 1963, Hacikyan 1966, Conlee 1968, Williamson 1977, Crossley-Holland 1978, Williamson 1982, Pinsker and Ziegler 1985, Muir 1994, Porter 1995, D. Hill 2000a, Niles 2006, Alexander 2007, Crossley-Holland 2008, Bitterli 2009, Murphy 2011, Orton 2015, Salvador-Bello 2015, Stanley 2017b, Williamson 2017, Hostetter 2018, Cavell 2020, Orchard 2021) "phallus" (Jember 1976)
88	Brotherless	*heortes hornas* "stag-horns" (one made into an inkhorn and one placed on a building) (Dietrich 1859b, Prehn 1883) *heortes hornas* "stag-horns" (one placed on each gable of a building) (Heyne 1864, Brooke 1892, Wood 1914) *heortes hornas* "stag-horns" (as handles for weapons) (Brooke 1892) *blæc-horn* "antler inkhorn" (Brandl 1908b, Tupper 1910, Trautmann 1914, Trautmann 1915, Wyatt 1912, Mackie 1934, Krapp and Dobbie 1936, Swaen 1941b, Baum 1963, Hacikyan 1966, Conlee 1968, Williamson 1977, Crossley-Holland 1978, Williamson 1982, Pinsker and Ziegler 1985, Muir 1994, Porter 1995, Williams 2000, Niles 2006, Crossley-Holland 2008, Bitterli 2009, Murphy 2011, Salvador-Bello 2015, Williamson 2017, Hostetter 2018, Cavell 2020, Orchard 2021; see also discussion in chapter 3, above) *lic ond sawol* "body and soul" (Jember 1976, Cavell 2020)
89	The Creature Had a Belly	*hydig fæt* "leather bottle" (Tupper 1910, Mackie 1934, Cavell 2021a) *blæst-belg* "bellows" (Tupper 1910, Cavell 2020, Cavell 2021a, Orchard 2021) "phallus" (Jember 1976) [unsolved] (Oberman 2020)

(*Continued*)

ASPR Number	Riddle Title	Solutions
90	Wolf	*lupus* "wolf" (Dietrich 1859b, Dietrich 1865)
		hacod "pike" (Dietrich 1859b)
		eowo-humele "hops" (Dietrich 1859b)
		bærs "perch" (Dietrich 1865)
		Cynewulf "Cynewulf [the poet]" (Dietrich 1865, Hicketier 1888, E. Erlemann 1903, F. Erlemann 1905, Brandl 1908b)
		agnus Dei "lamb of God" (Morley 1888, Tupper 1910, Wood 1914, Mackie 1934, Hacikyan 1966, Conlee 1968, Cavell 2020, Orchard 2021)
		Wulfstanes cierrednes "Wulfstan's conversion" (Bradley 1911)
		wulflys ond web-beam "web and loom" (Williamson 1977, Cavell 2020)
		Augustinus ond Tertullianus "Augustine and Tertullian" (Davis and Schlueter 1989, Muir 1994)
		candel-treow "candelabra" (Anderson 1992, Cavell 2020)
		wulfes gelicnes on ea-stream mid hacode ond sunne "wolf reflected in river with pike and sun" (E. Williams 2000)
		[not a riddle but a school drill] (Salvador-Bello 2018)
91	Forged by Hammer	*cæg ond loc* "key and bar" (Dietrich 1859b)
		cæg "key" (Prehn 1883, Tupper 1910, Wyatt 1912, Trautmann 1914, Wood 1914, Trautmann 1915, Mackie 1934, Krapp and Dobbie 1936, Baum 1963, Hacikyan 1966, Conlee 1968, Schneider 1975, Williamson 1977, Crossley-Holland 1978, Gleißner 1984, Williamson 1982, Pinsker and Ziegler 1985, Muir 1994, Porter 1995, Niles 2006, Alexander 2007, Crossley-Holland 2008, Bitterli 2009, Portnoy 2013, Orton 2015, Stanley 2017b, Williamson 2017, Hostetter 2018, Cavell 2020, Orchard 2021)
		rip-isern "sickle" (Trautmann 1894[17])
		*cæg-ðyrel "keyhole" (E. Williams 1975, Portnoy 2005, Portnoy 2013, Cavell 2020)
		laf "survivor, treasure" (Portnoy 2005, Portnoy 2013)
		preon "brooch" or "buckle" (Portnoy 2013)
		"phallus" (Jember 1976)

(Continued)

---

[17] Moritz Trautmann claims to have proposed this solution first in 1887 in an unpublished lecture; see "Zu den Lösungen der Rätsel," 274.

ASPR Number	Riddle Title	Solutions
92	Brown Ones' Boast	*boc* "beech (tree and book)" (Trautmann 1894, Tupper 1910, Wyatt 1912, Holthausen 1919, Trautmann 1919, Mackie 1934, Baum 1963, Hacikyan 1966, Conlee 1968, Williamson 1977, Crossley-Holland 1978, Williamson 1982, Muir 1994, Porter 1995, Niles 2006, Alexander 2007, Crossley-Holland 2008, Williamson 2017, Cavell 2020, Orchard 2021) *æsc* "ash" (Holthausen 1907, Cavell 2020) *boc-scyld* "beechwood shield" (Trautmann 1914, Trautmann 1915, Cavell 2020, Oberman 2020) *boc-ramm* "beech battering ram" (Trautmann 1919, Cavell 2020) **eohboga ond *eohflan* "yew-bow and yew-arrow" (Schneider 1975) *gar* "spear" (Bitterli 2009) *wudu* "wood, the covers of a book" (Hostetter 2018) *ac* "oak" (Cavell 2020, Kendall 2020)
93	Younger Brother	*heortes hornas* "stag-horns (placed on gables of a building and used as an inkhorn)" (Dietrich 1859b, Prehn 1883) *heortes hornas* "stag-horns (placed on gables of a building and used as handles for weapons)" (Brooke 1892) *blæc-horn* "antler inkhorn" (Tupper 1910, Wyatt 1912, Trautmann 1914, Wood 1914, Trautmann 1915, Mackie 1934, Krapp and Dobbie 1936, Swaen 1941b, Baum 1963, Hacikyan 1966, Conlee 1968, Jember 1976, Williamson 1977, Crossley-Holland 1978, Williamson 1982, Pinsker and Ziegler 1985, Muir 1994, Porter 1995, Williams 2000, Niles 2006, Alexander 2007, Crossley-Holland 2008, Bitterli 2009, Murphy 2011, Salvador-Bello 2015, Williamson 2017, Hostetter 2018, Cavell 2020, Cavell 2021b, Orchard 2021)
94	Higher than Heaven	*gesceaft or creatura* "creation" (Tupper 1910, Trautmann 1914, Trautmann 1915, Mackie 1933, Krapp and Dobbie 1936, Hacikyan 1966, Jember 1976, Williamson 1977, Crossley-Holland 1978, Williamson 1982, Muir 1994, Porter 1995, Niles 2006, Sebo 2014, Salvador-Bello 2015, Williamson 2017, Sebo 2018, Cavell 2020, Orchard 2021, Sebo 2021) *natura* "nature" (Mackie 1933, Mackie 1934

(Continued)

ASPR Number	Riddle Title	Solutions
95	*Hide My Track*	*Cynewulf* "Cynewulf [the poet]" (Dietrich 1859b)
		wæðende scop "wandering singer" (Dietrich 1859b, Prehn 1883, Hicketier 1888, Nuck 1888, Brooke 1892, Wyatt 1912, Baum 1963, Hacikyan 1966, Cavell 2020)
		rædels or *giedd* "riddle" (Trautmann 1883, Trautmann 1884, Trautmann 1905a, Brandl 1908b, Bradley 1911, Wyatt 1912, Baum 1963, Borysławski 2004, Liuzza 2014, Hostetter 2018, Cavell 2020, Roscoe 2021)
		Godes word "word of God" (Morley 1888)
		mon "moon" (Tupper 1906, Tupper 1910, Wood 1914, Mackie 1934, Baum 1963, Hacikyan 1966, Jember 1976, Niles 2006, Liuzza 2014, Cavell 2020)
		sawol "soul" or *gæst* "spirit" (Trautmann 1912, Trautmann 1914, Trautmann 1915)
		ðoht "thought" (Holthausen 1925)
		feðer "quill pen" (Erhardt-Siebold 1947b, Conlee 1968, Salvador-Bello 2015, Cavell 2020)
		cwene "prostitute" (Kiernan 1975a, Cavell 2020)
		boc "book" (Williamson 1977, Göbel 1980, Muir 1994, Porter 1995, Bitterli 2009, Clarke 2009, Murphy 2011, Liuzza 2014, Williamson 2017, Cavell 2020, Orchard 2021)
		swefn "dream" (Williamson 1982)
		rædels-boc "riddle book [colophon]" (Pinsker and Ziegler 1985, Cavell 2020)
		halige gewritu "Holy Scriptures" or "religious codex" (Korhammer 2003, Ramey 2013)
		sunne "sun" (Bitterli 2019a)
		wissung in wisdome "instruction in wisdom" (Breeze 2020)

Bibliography

Primary Sources

Ælfric of Eynsham. *Ælfric's Colloquy*. Ed. G.N. Garmonsway. Rev. ed. Exeter: University of Exeter Press, 1991.
- *Ælfric's Catholic Homilies, The Second Series: Text*. Ed. Malcolm Godden. EETS, s.s., 5. London: Oxford University Press, 1979.
- *Ælfric's Catholic Homilies: The First Series*. Ed. Peter Clemoes. EETS, s.s., 17. Oxford: Oxford University Press, 1997.
- *The Old English Heptateuch and Ælfric's Libellus de Veteri Testamento et Novi, Volume One: Introduction and Text*. Ed. Richard Marsden. EETS, o.s., 330. Oxford: Oxford University Press, 2008.
Aldhelm. *The Riddles of Aldhelm*. Ed. James Hall Pitman. Yale Studies in English 67. New Haven: Yale University Press, 1925.
- *Aenigmata Aldhelmi*, in *Variae Collectiones Aenigmatum Merovingicae Aetatis*. Ed. Fr. Glorie, 377–540. CCSL 133. Turnhout: Brepols, 1968.
Alfred. *King Alfred's West-Saxon Version of Gregory's Pastoral Care*. Ed. Henry Sweet. EETS, o.s., 45 and 50. London: Kegan Paul, 1871.
Anlezark, Daniel, ed. *The Old English Dialogues of Solomon and Saturn*. Woodbridge: Brewer, 2009.
Assmann, Bruno, ed. *Die Handschrift von Exeter, Metra des Boetius, Salomo und Saturn, Die Psalmen*. 2nd ed. Bibliothek der angelsächsischen Poesie 3. Leipzig: G.H. Wigand, 1898.
Augustine. *Saint Augustin: Sermon on the Mount, Harmony of the Gospels, Homilies on the Gospels*. Ed. Philip Schaff. Trans. William Findlay, S.D.F. Salmond, and R.G. MacMullen. Select Library of the Nicene and Post-Nicene Fathers 6. New York: Christian Literature, 1888.
Bately, Janet M., ed. *The Anglo-Saxon Chronicle*. Vol. 3, *MS A*. Cambridge: Brewer, 1986.

Bayless, Martha, and Michael Lapidge, eds. and trans. *Collectanea Pseudo-Bedae*. Scriptores Latini Hiberniae 14. Dublin: Dublin Institute for Advanced Studies, 1998.

Bede. *Bede's Ecclesiastical History of the English People*. Ed. Bertram Colgrave and R.A.B. Mynors. Rev. ed. Oxford: Clarendon, 1991.

Behaghel, Otto, ed. *Heliand und Genesis*. 9th ed. Rev. Burkhard Taeger. Altdeutsche Textbibliothek 4. Tübingen: Max Niemeyer, 1984.

Bible. *Biblia sacra iuxta vulgatam versionem*. 5th ed. Ed. Robert Weber and Roger Gryson. Stuttgart: Deutsche Bibelgesellschaft, 2007.

Bible. *The Holy Bible: New International Version*. London: Hodder and Stoughton, 1973.

Boethius. *The Old English Boethius: An Edition of the Old English Versions of Boethius's De Consolatione Philosophiae*. Ed. Malcolm Godden and Susan Irvine. 2 vols. Oxford: Oxford University Press, 2009.

Boniface. *Aenigmata Bonifatii*. In *Variae Collectiones Aenigmatum Merovingicae Aetatis*. Ed. Fr. Glorie, 273–343. CCSL 133. Turnhout: Brepols, 1968.

Bruster, Douglas, and Eric Rasmussen, eds. *Everyman and Mankind*. London: Methuen, 2009.

Cassidy, F.G., and Richard N. Ringler, eds. *Bright's Old English Grammar and Reader*. 3rd ed. New York: Holt, Reinhart, and Winston, 1971.

Cassiodorus. *Cassiodori Senatoris Institutiones*. Ed. R.A.B. Mynors. Oxford: Clarendon Press, 1937; repr. 1963.

Chambers, Raymond W., Max Förster, and Robin Flower, eds. *The Exeter Book of Old English Poetry*. With introductory chapters by R.W. Chambers, Max Förster, and Robin Flower. London: Percy Lund, 1933.

Chickering, Howell D., ed. and trans. *Beowulf: A Dual-Language Edition*. Garden City, NY: Anchor Press/Doubleday, 1977.

Conybeare, John Josias, ed. *Illustrations of Anglo-Saxon Poetry*. London: Harding and Lepard, 1826.

Dobbie, Elliott Van Kirk, ed. *The Anglo-Saxon Minor Poems*. ASPR 6. New York: Columbia University Press, 1942.

– ed. *Beowulf and Judith*. ASPR 4. New York: Columbia University Press, 1953.

Ettmüller, Ludwig, ed. *Engla and Seaxna Scôpas and Bôceras: Anglosaxonum Poëtae atque Scriptores Prosaici*. Bibliothek der Gersammten Deutschen National-Literatur von der Aeltesten bis auf die Neuere Zeit 28. London: Williams and Norgate, 1850.

Eusebius. *Aenigmata Eusebii*. In *Variae Collectiones Aenigmatum Merovingicae Aetatis*, ed. Fr. Glorie, 211–71. CCSL 133. Turnhout: Brepols, 1968.

Fulk, R.D., Robert E. Bjork, and John D. Niles, eds. *Klaeber's Beowulf*. 4th ed. Toronto: University of Toronto Press, 2008.

Glorie, Fr, ed. ["The Bern Riddles"]. *Aenigmata Tullii seu Aenigmata quaestionum artis rhetoricae (Aenigmata "Bernensia")*. In *Variae Collectiones Aenigmatum*

Merovingicae Aetatis (Pars Altera), 547–610. CCSL 133A. Turnhout: Brepols, 1968.
– ed. ["The Lorsch Riddles"]. In *Variae Collectiones Aenigmatum Merovingicae Aetatis*, 347–58. CCSL 133. Turnhout: Brepols, 1968.
Grein, C.W.M, ed. *Bibliothek der angelsächsischen Poesie*. 2 vols. Göttingen: Georg H. Wigand, 1857–8.
Hamer, Richard, ed. and trans. *A Choice of Anglo-Saxon Verse*. London: Faber, 1970.
Krapp, George Philip, ed. *The Junius Manuscript*. ASPR 1. New York: Columbia University Press, 1931.
– ed. *The Vercelli Book*. ASPR 2. New York: Columbia University Press, 1932.
– ed. *The Paris Psalter and the Meters of Boethius*. ASPR 5. New York: Columbia University Press, 1932.
Krapp, George Philip, and Elliott Van Kirk Dobbie, eds. *The Exeter Book*. ASPR 3. New York: Columbia University Press, 1936.
Liebermann, Felix, ed. *Die Gesetze der Angelsachsen*. 3 vols. Halle: Niemeyer, 1903–16.
Macrae-Gibson, O.D., ed. and trans. *The Old English Riming Poem*. Cambridge: Brewer, 1983.
Mackie, William S., ed. and trans. *The Exeter Book, Part II: Poems IX-XXXII*. EETS, o.s., 194. London: Humphry Milford and Oxford University Press, 1934.
Marsden, Richard. *The Cambridge Old English Reader*. 2nd ed. Cambridge: Cambridge University Press, 2015.
Mitchell, Bruce, and Fred C. Robinson, eds. *Beowulf: An Edition with Relevant Shorter Texts*. Oxford: Blackwell, 1998.
– eds. *A Guide to Old English*. 8th ed. Maldon, MA: John Wiley, 2011. [riddles were added to the 4th edition in 1986]
Montaiglon, Anatole de, and Gaston Raynaud, eds. *Recueil Général et complet des fabliaux des XIIIe et XIVe siècles imprimés ou inédits*. 6 vols. Paris: Librairie des bibliophiles, 1872–90. https://gallica.bnf.fr/ark:/12148/bpt6k209379m.
Muir, Bernard J.– *The Exeter Anthology of OE Poetry: An Edition of Exeter Dean and Chapter MS 3501*. 2 vols. Exeter: University of Exeter Press, 1994.
– ed. *The Exeter Anthology of OE Poetry: An Edition of Exeter Dean and Chapter MS 3501*. 2nd rev. ed. 2 vols. Exeter: University of Exeter Press, 2000.
Müller, Ludvig Christian, ed. *Collectanea Anglo-Saxonica*. Copenhagen: Hauniae, 1835.
Norman, H.W., ed. *The Anglo-Saxon Version of the Hexameron of St. Basil, or, Be Godes Six Daga Weorcum and the Saxon Remains of St. Basil's Admonitio ad filium spiritualem*. 2nd ed. London: J.R. Smith, 1849.
North, Richard, and Michael D.J. Bintley, eds. *Andreas: An Edition*. Liverpool: Liverpool University Press, 2016.
Pettit, Edward, ed. *Anglo-Saxon Remedies, Charms and Prayers from British Library MS Harley 585: The Lacnunga*. 2 vols. Lampeter: Edwin Mellen Press, 2001.

O'Neill, Patrick P., ed. and trans. *Old English Psalms*. Dumbarton Oaks Medieval Library 42. Cambridge, MA: Harvard University Press, 2016.

Orchard, Andy, ed. and trans. *The Old English and Anglo-Latin Riddle Tradition*. Dumbarton Oaks Medieval Library 69. Cambridge, MA: Harvard University Press, 2021.

Pinsker, Hans, and Waltraud Ziegler, eds and trans. *Die altenglischen Rätsel des Exeterbuchs: Text mit deutscher Übersetzung und Kommentar*. Anglistische Forschungen 183. Heidelberg, Germany: Carl Winter, 1985.

Pope, Alexander. *Alexander Pope: Selected Poetry*. Ed. Pat Rogers. Oxford: Oxford University Press, 1996.

Rabelais, François. *Les Cinq Livres de Rabelais*. Vol. 1, *Gargantua, Pantagruel*. Edited by Roger Delbiausse. Paris: Éditions Magnard, 1965.

Sedgefield, W.J., ed. *An Anglo-Saxon Verse Book*. Manchester: Manchester University Press, 1922.

Sisam, Kenneth, ed. "An Old English Translation of a Letter from Wynfrith to Eadburga (a.d. 716–17) in Cotton MS Otho C." In *Studies in the History of Old English Literature*, 199–224. Oxford: Clarendon, 1953.

Sweet, Henry. *An Anglo-Saxon Reader in Prose and Verse*. 1st ed. Oxford: Clarendon, 1876.

Symphosius. *Aenigmata Symphosii*. In *Variae Collectiones Aenigmatum Merovingicae Aetatis (Pars Altera)*. Ed. Fr. Glorie, 620–723. CCSL 133A. Turnhout: Brepols, 1968.

– *Aenigmata Symposii: La Fondazione dell'Enigmistica come Genere Poetico*. Ed. Manuela Bergamin. Per Verba: Testi Mediolatini con Traduzione 22. Florence: Edizioni del Galluzzo per la Fondazione Ezio Franceschini, 2005.

– *Symphosius, The Aenigmata: An Introduction, Text and Commentary*. Ed. T.J. Leary. London: Bloomsbury, 2014.

Tatwine. *Aenigmata Tatvini*. In *Variae Collectiones Aenigmatum Merovingicae Aetatis*. Ed. Fr. Glorie, 167–208. CCSL 133. Turnhout: Brepols, 1968.

Theodore. *Die Canones Theodori Cantuariensis und ihre Überlieferungsformen*. Ed. P. Finsterwalder. Weimar: H. Bölhaus, 1929.

– *Paenitentiale Umbrense*. Ed. Michael D. Elliot. http://individual.utoronto.ca/michaelelliot/manuscripts/texts/transcriptions/pthu.pdf.

Thorpe, Benjamin, ed. *Codex Exoniensis: A Collection of Anglo-Saxon Poetry*. London: Society of Antiquaries of London, 1842.

Trautmann, Moritz, ed. *Die altenglischen Rätsel*. Heidelberg: Carl Winter, 1915.

Tupper, Frederick, Jr, ed. *The Riddles of the Exeter Book*. London: Ginn, 1910.

Vriend, H.J. de, ed. *The Old English Herbarium and Medicina de Quadrupedibus*. EETS 286. London: Oxford University Press, 1984.

Whitelock, Dorothy, ed. and trans. *Anglo-Saxon Wills*. Cambridge: Cambridge University Press, 1930.

Whitman, F.H., ed. *Old English Riddles*. Canadian Federation for the Humanities Monograph Series 3. Ottawa: Canadian Federation for the Humanities, 1982.

Williamson, Craig, ed. *The Old English Riddles of the Exeter Book*. Chapel Hill: University of North Carolina Press, 1977.
Wrenn, C.L., and W.F. Bolton, eds. *Beowulf with the Finnsburg Fragment*. 5th ed. Exeter: University of Exeter Press, 1996.
Wyatt, A.J., ed. *Old English Riddles*. London: D.C. Heath, 1912.

Secondary Sources

Abbeyhorn England. "Sources of Horn." https://www.abbeyhorn.co.uk/index/sources-of-horn_41.htm.
Abrahams, Roger D. "The Literary Study of the Riddle." *Texas Studies in Literature and Language* 14 (1972): 177–97.
Abrams, M.H., ed. *The Norton Anthology of English Literature*. 7th ed. 2 vols. New York: W.W. Norton, 2000.
Adams, J.N. *The Latin Sexual Vocabulary*. London: Duckworth, 1982.
Adams, Sharif. "How to Turn a Wooden Bowl on a Pole Lathe." https://youtu.be/aKU-2ZUE8lA.
Aertsen, Henk, and Rolf H. Bremmer, Jr, eds. *Companion to Old English Poetry*. Amsterdam: VU University Press, 1994.
Afros, Elena. "*Sindrum Begrunden* in Exeter Book *Riddle 26*: The Enigmatic Dative Case." *N&Q* 51 (2004), 7–9.
– "Linguistic Ambiguities in Some Exeter Book Riddles." *N&Q* 52 (2005): 431–37.
Aiello, Matthew. "Books in Battle: The Violent Poetics of Misdirection in Old English *Riddle 53*." *RES* 71 (2020): 207–28.
Alexander, Michael, trans. *Old English Riddles from the Exeter Book*. 2nd ed. London: Anvil, 2007.
Althoff, Gerd. *Family, Friends and Followers: Political and Social Bonds in Early Medieval Europe*. Translated by Christopher Carroll. Cambridge: Cambridge University Press, 2004.
Ammon, Matthias. "Commentary for Exeter Riddle 13." *The Riddle Ages* (blog), 8 October 2013. https://theriddleages.com/riddles/post/commentary-for-exeter-riddle-13/
Amodio, Mark C., and Katherine O'Brien O'Keeffe, eds. *Unlocking the Wordhord: Anglo-Saxon Studies in Memory of Edward B. Irving Jr*. Toronto: University of Toronto Press, 2003.
Anderson, James E. "*Deor, Wulf and Eadwacer,* and *The Soul's Address*: How and Where the Old English Exeter Book Riddles Begin." In *The Old English Elegies: New Essays in Criticism and Research*, ed. Martin Green, 204–30. Rutherford, NJ: Fairleigh Dickinson University Press; London: Associated University Presses, 1983.
– "Two Spliced Riddles of the Exeter Book." *In Geardagum* 5 (1983): 57–76.
– "Exeter Latin Riddle 90: A Liturgical Vision." *Viator* 23 (1992): 73–93.

Anderson, J.J. "The 'Cuþe Folme' in *Beowulf*, Line 1303a." *Neophil* 67 (1983): 126–30.
Anlezark, Daniel. "The Fall of the Angels in *Solomon and Saturn* II." In *Apocryphal Texts and Traditions in Anglo-Saxon England*. Ed. Kathryn Powell and Donald G. Scragg, 122–33. Cambridge: Brewer, 2003.
– *Water and Fire: The Myth of the Flood in Anglo-Saxon England*. Manchester: Manchester University Press, 2006.
Appleton, Helen, and Francis Leneghan. "The Psalms in Anglo-Saxon and Anglo-Norman England." *ES* 98 (2017): 1–4.
Baker, Peter S. *Honour, Exchange, and Violence in Beowulf*. Anglo-Saxon Studies 20. Cambridge: Brewer, 2013.
Baker, Peter S., and Nicholas Howe, eds. *Words and Works: Studies in Medieval English Language and Literature in Honour of Fred C. Robinson*. Toronto: University of Toronto Press, 1998.
Bakhtin, Mikhail. *Rabelais and His World*. Trans. Hélène Iswolsky. Bloomington: Cambridge, MA: MIT Press, 1968.
Baldick, Chris. *The Concise Oxford Dictionary of Literary Terms*. Oxford: Oxford University Press, 1990.
Bammesberger, Alfred. "*Maxims II*, Line 10a: *Soð bið swicolost*, and the Meaning of Old English *Soð*." *N&Q* 67 (2020): 166–8.
Banham, Debby. "Anglo-Saxon Attitudes: In Search of the Origins of English Racism." *European Review of History* 1 (1994): 143–56.
– *Food and Drink in Anglo-Saxon England*. Stroud, Gloucestershire: Tempus, 2004.
Banham, Debby, and Rosamond Faith. *Anglo-Saxon Farms and Farming*. Oxford: Oxford University Press, 2014.
Banham, Debby, and Christine Voth. "The Diagnosis and Treatment of Wounds in the Old English Medical Collections: Anglo-Saxon Surgery?" In *Wounds and Wound Repair in Medieval Culture*. Ed. Larissa Tracey and Kelly DeVries, 153–74. Leiden: Brill, 2015.
Barley, Nigel F. "Old English Colour Classification: Where do Matters Stand?" *ASE* 3 (1974): 15–28.
– "Structural Aspects of the Anglo-Saxon Riddle." *Semiotica* 10 (1974): 143–75.
Battles, Paul. "'Contending Throng' Scenes and the *Comitatus* Ideal in Old English Poetry, With Special Attention to *The Battle of Maldon* 122a." *SN* 83 (2011): 41–53.
Baum, Paull F., trans. *Anglo-Saxon Riddles of the Exeter Book*. Durham, NC: Duke University Press, 1963.
Baxter, Steven, Catherine Karkov, Janet L. Nelson, and David Pelteret, eds. *Early Medieval Studies in Memory of Patrick Wormald*. Farnham: Ashgate, 2009.
Bayliss, Martha, and Debby Banham. *The Early Bread Project* (blog). https://earlybread.wordpress.com.

Beaston, Lawrence. "The Ruin and the Brevity of Human Life." *Neophil* 95 (2011): 477–89.
Beckers, Hartmut, and Hans Schwarz, eds. *Gedenkschrift für Jost Trier*. Cologne: Böhlau, 1975.
Beechy, Tiffany. "Wisdom and the Poetics of Laughter in the Old English Dialogues of Solomon and Saturn." *JEGP* 116 (2017): 131–55.
Belanoff, Pat. "The Fall(?) of the Old English Female Poetic Image." *PMLA* 104 (1989): 822–31.
Ben-Amos, Dan. "Solutions to Riddles." *Journal of American Folklore* 89 (1976): 249–54.
Benson, Larry Dean, and Siegfried Wenzel, eds. *The Wisdom of Poetry: Essays in Early English Literature in Honor of Morton W. Bloomfield*. Kalamazoo: Medieval Institute Publications, Western Michigan University, 1982.
Bessinger, Jess B., Jr, and Robert P. Creed, eds. *Franciplegius: Medieval and Linguistic Studies in Honor of Francis Peabody Magoun, Jr*. New York: Allen and Unwin, 1965.
Bessinger, Jess B., Jr, and Stanley J. Kahrl, eds. *Essential Articles for the Study of Old English Poetry*. Hamden, CT: Archon, 1968.
Best, Stephen, and Sharon Marcus. "Surface Reading: An Introduction." *Representations* 108 (2009): 1–21.
Bierbaumer, Peter, and Elke Wannagat. "Ein neuer Lösungsvorschlag für ein altenglisches Rätsel (Krapp-Dobbie 17)." *Anglia* 99 (1981): 379–82.
Biggam, C.P. *Blue in Old English: An Interdisciplinary Semantic Study*. Costerus n.s. 110. Amsterdam: Rodopi, 1997.
– *Grey in Old English: An Interdisciplinary Semantic Study*. London: Runetree, 1998.
Bintley, Michael D.J. *Settlements and Strongholds: Texts and Landscapes in Early Medieval England*. Studies in the Early Middle Ages 45. Turnhout: Brepols, 2020.
Bintley, Michael D.J., Martin Locker, Victoria Symons, and Mary Wellesley, eds. *Stasis in the Medieval West? Questioning Change and Continuity*. New York: Palgrave Macmillan, 2017.
Bintley, Michael D.J. and Michael G. Shapland, eds. *Trees and Timber in the Anglo-Saxon World*. Oxford: Oxford University Press, 2013.
Bird, Christy. "Formulaic Jokes in Interaction: The Prosody of Riddle Openings." *Pragmatics and Cognition* 19 (2011): 268–90.
Bishop, Chris. "The Erotic Poetry of the Exeter Book." *Journal of the Australian Early Medieval Association* 1 (2005): 7–26.
Bitterli, Dieter. "Exeter Book Riddle 15: Some Points for the Porcupine." *Anglia* 120 (2002): 461–87.
– "The Survival of the Dead Cuckoo: Exeter Book *Riddle 9*." In *Riddles, Knights and Cross-dressing Saints: Essays on Medieval English Language and Literature*. Ed. Thomas Honegger, 95–114. Variations 5. Bern: Peter Lang, 2004.

- *Say What I Am Called: The Old English Riddles of the Exeter Book and the Anglo-Latin Riddle Tradition.* Toronto Anglo-Saxon Series 2. Toronto: University of Toronto Press, 2009.
- "Alkuin und die angelsächsische Rätseldichtung." In *Alkuin von York und die geistige Grundlegung Europas: Akten der Tagung vom 30. September bis zum 2. Oktober 2004 in der Stiftsbibliothek St Gallen.* Ed. Ernst Tremp and Karl Schmuki, 161–8. Monasterium Sancti Galli 5. St Gallen: Verlag am Klosterhof, 2010.
- "Exeter Book Riddle 95: 'The Sun,' a New Solution." *Anglia* 137 (2019): 612–38.
- "Spur, a New Solution to Exeter Book *Riddle 62*." *N&Q* 66 (2019): 343–7.
- "The One-Liners among the Exeter Book *Riddles*." *Neophil* 103 (2019): 419–34.

Blackburn, F.A. "The Husband's Message and the Accompanying Riddles of the Exeter Book." *Journal of Germanic Philology* 3 (1900): 1–13.

Blakeley, L. "Riddles 22 and 58 of the Exeter Book." *RES* 9 (1958): 241–52.

Blauner, D.G. "The Early Literary Riddle." *Folklore* 78 (1967): 49–58.

Bloomfield, M.W. "The Notion of Wisdom." In *The Role of the Poet in Early Societies.* Ed. M.W. Bloomfield and C.W. Dunn, 106–19. Cambridge: Brewer, 1989.

- "Wisdom Genres and Types of Literature." In *The Role of the Poet in Early Societies.* Ed. M.W. Bloomfield and C.W. Dunn, 120–49. Cambridge: Brewer, 1989.

Bloomfield, M.W., and C.W. Dunn, eds. *The Role of the Poet in Early Societies.* Cambridge: Brewer, 1989.

Blud, Victoria. *The Unspeakable, Gender and Sexuality in Medieval Literature, 1000–1400.* Cambridge: Brewer, 2017.

Böckmann, Paul, ed. *Stil- und Form-probleme in der Literatur.* Heidelberg: Carl Winter, 1959.

Bolding, Jacky. "The Sexual Riddles of the *Exeter Book*." MA diss., Simon Fraser University, 1992.

Bollard, J.K. "The Cotton Maxims." *Neophil* 57 (1973): 179–87.

Bolton, W.F. *Alcuin and Beowulf: An Eighth-Century View.* London: Edward Arnold, 1979.

Bone, Gavin. *Anglo-Saxon Poetry: An Essay with Specimen Translations in Verse.* Oxford: Clarendon, 1943.

Borysławski, Rafał. "The Elements of Anglo-Saxon Wisdom Poetry in the Exeter Book Riddles." *Studia Anglica Posnaniensia* 38 (2002): 35–49.

- *The Old English Riddles and the Riddlic Elements of Old English Poetry.* Studies in English Medieval Language and Literature 9. Frankfurt: Peter Lang, 2004.

Bosworth, Joseph, and T. Northcote Toller, *An Anglo-Saxon Dictionary.* Rev. and enlarged addenda by A. Campbell. 3 vols. 1972; Oxford: Clarendon Press, 1898–1921.

Boutewek, Karl Wilhelm. *Cædmon's des Angelsachsen biblische Dichtungen.* 2 vols. Gütersloh: C. Bertelsmann, 1854.

Bradley, Henry. "Two Riddles of the Exeter Book." *MLR* 6 (1911): 433–40.

Brady, Lindy. "The 'Dark Welsh' as Slaves and Slave Traders in Exeter Book Riddles 52 and 72." *ES* 95 (2014): 235–55.
- "Commentary for Exeter Riddle 52." *The Riddle Ages* (blog), 8 June 2016. https://theriddleages.com/riddles/post/commentary-for-exeter-riddle-52/.
Brandl, Alois. *Geschichte der altenglischen Literatur*. Strassburg: Karl J. Trübner, 1908.
Breen, Nathan A. "The King's Closest Counselor: The Legal Basis of Wealhtheow's Comments to Hrothgar, *Beowulf* 1169–87." *The Heroic Age* 14 (2010): https://www.heroicage.org/issues/14/breen.php.
Breeze, Andrew. "Old English *Gop* 'Servant' in Riddle 49: Old Irish *Gop* 'Snout.'" *Neophil* 79 (1995): 671–3.
- "The Exeter Book's Riddle 43 and Guardian Angels." *Devon and Cornwall N&Q* 42 (2018): 44–9.
- "Exeter Book Riddles 4 and 43: City Gate and Guardian Angel." *Devon and Cornwall N&Q* 42 (2020): 213–18.
- "Exeter Book Riddle 95 and Instruction in Wisdom." *Devon and Cornwall N&Q* 42 (2020): 238–41.
Breeze, Steven. "Greeting the Lyre: Instrumental Interrelationships in the Anglo-Saxon Cultural Imagination." *Quaestio Insularis* 19 (2019): 92–125.
Bremmer, Rolf H. Jr. "Old English Heroic Literature." In *Readings in Medieval Texts: Interpreting Old and Middle English Literature*. Ed. David F. Johnson and Elaine Treharne, 75–90. Oxford: Oxford University Press, 2005.
Brett, Cyril. "Notes on Old and Middle English." *MLR* 22 (1927): 257–64.
Brink, Stefan. *Lord and Lady – Bryti and Deigja: Some Historical and Etymological Aspects of Family, Patronage and Slavery in Early Scandinavia and Anglo-Saxon England*. Dorthea Coke Memorial Lecture in Northern Studies. London: Viking Society for Northern Research, University College, London, 2008.
Brogyanyi, Bela, and Thomas Krömmelbein, eds. *Germanic Dialects: Linguistic and Philological Investigations*. Current Issues in Linguistic Theory 38; Amsterdam Studies in the Theory and History of Linguistic Science 4. Amsterdam: John Benjamins, 1986.
Brooke, Stopford A. *The History of Early English Literature*. New York: Macmillan, 1892.
Brooks, Francesca. "Sight, Sound and the Perception of the Anglo-Saxon Liturgy in Exeter Book Riddles 48 and 59." In *Sensory Perception in the Medieval West*. Ed. Simon Thomson and Michael Bintley, 141–58. Utrecht Studies in Medieval Literacy 34. Turnhout: Brepols, 2016.
- "The Crafting of Sound in the Riddles of the *Exeter Book*." In *Riddles at Work in the Early Medieval Tradition: Words, Ideas, Interactions*. Ed. Megan Cavell and Jennifer Neville, 76–91. Manchester Medieval Literature and Culture 32. Manchester: Manchester University Press, 2020.
Brown, Carleton. "*Poculum Mortis* in Old English." *Speculum* 15 (1940): 389–99.

Brown, Peter. *The Body and Society: Men, Women, and Sexual Renunciation in Early Christianity*. New York: Columbia University Press, 1988.
Brown, Phyllis Rugg, Georgia Ronan Crampton, and Fred C. Robinson, eds. *Modes of Interpretation in Old English Literature: Essays in Honour of Stanley B. Greenfield*. Toronto: University of Toronto Press, 1986.
Brown, Ray. "The Exeter Book's Riddle 2: A Better Solution." *English Language Notes* 29 (1991): 1–4.
Buckley, Thomas, and Alma Gottlieb, eds. *Blood Magic: The Anthropology of Menstruation*. Berkeley: University of California Press, 1988.
Burke, Kenneth. *A Grammar of Motives*. Appendix D, 503–17. New York: Prentice Hall, 1945.
Burns, Rachel. "Spirits and Skins: The *Sceapheord* of Exeter Book Riddle 13 as a Celebration of Holy Labour." *RES* 73 (2022): 429–41.
Butler, Judith. *Bodies That Matter: On the Discursive Limits of "Sex."* New York: Routledge, 1993.
Caie, Graham, and Michael D.C. Drout, eds. *Transitional States: Change, Tradition, and Memory in Medieval Literature and Culture*. Medieval and Renaissance Texts and Studies 530. Tempe: Arizona Center for Medieval and Renaissance Studies, 2018.
Calder, Daniel G. "Figurative Language and its Contexts in *Andreas*: A Study in Medieval Expressionism." In *Modes of Interpretation in Old English Literature: Essays in Honour of Stanley B. Greenfield*. Ed. Phyllis Rugg Brown, Georgia Ronan Crampton, and Fred C. Robinson, 115–36. Toronto: University of Toronto Press, 1986.
Campbell, Alistair. *Old English Grammar*. Oxford: Clarendon, 1959; repr. 1983.
Campbell, Jackson J. "A Certain Power." *Neophil* 59 (1975): 128–38.
Casiday, Augustine. "St Aldhelm's Bees (*De uirginitate prosa* cc. IV–VI): Some Observations on a Literary Tradition." *ASE* 33 (2004): 1–22.
Cavell, Megan. "Looming Danger and Dangerous Looms: Violence and Weaving in Exeter Book Riddle 56." *LSE*, n.s., 42 (2011): 29–42.
– "Sounding the Horn in Exeter Book Riddle 14." *Explicator* 72 (2014): 324–7.
– "Commentary for Exeter Riddle 38." *The Riddle Ages* (blog), 4 May 2015a. https://theriddleages.com/riddles/post/commentary-for-exeter-riddle-38/.
– "Commentary for Exeter Riddle 44." *The Riddle Ages* (blog), 21 September 2015b. https://theriddleages.com/riddles/post/commentary-for-exeter-riddle-44/.
– "Commentary for Exeter Riddle 45." *The Riddle Ages* (blog), 7 October 2015c. https://theriddleages.com/riddles/post/commentary-for-exeter-riddle-45/.
– "Commentary for Exeter Riddle 46." *The Riddle Ages* (blog), 21 October 2015d. https://theriddleages.com/riddles/post/commentary-for-exeter-riddle-46/.
– "Commentary for Exeter Riddle 50." *The Riddle Ages* (blog), 10 March 2016a. https://theriddleages.com/riddles/post/commentary-for-exeter-riddle-50/.

– *Weaving Words and Binding Bodies: The Poetics of Human Experience in Old English Literature*. Toronto: University of Toronto Press, 2016b.
– "Commentary for Exeter Riddle 63." *The Riddle Ages* (blog), 7 June 2017a. https://theriddleages.com/riddles/post/commentary-for-exeter-riddle-63/.
– "Commentary for Exeter Riddle 68 and 69." *The Riddle Ages* (blog), 23 October 2017b. https://theriddleages.com/riddles/post/commentary-for-exeter-riddles-68-and-69/.
– "Powerful Patens in the Anglo-Saxon Medical Tradition and Exeter Book Riddle 48." *Neophil* 101 (2017c): 129–38.
– "The *Igil* and Exeter Book *Riddle 15*." *N&Q* 64 (2017d): 206–10.
– "Commentary for Exeter Riddle 77." *The Riddle Ages* (blog), 17 May 2018a. https://theriddleages.com/riddles/post/commentary-for-exeter-riddle-77/.
– "Commentary for Exeter Riddle 78." *The Riddle Ages* (blog), 6 June 2018b. https://theriddleages.com/riddles/post/commentary-for-exeter-riddle-78/.
– "Commentary for Exeter Riddle 85." *The Riddle Ages* (blog), 18 July 2019a. https://theriddleages.com/riddles/post/commentary-for-exeter-riddle-85/.
– "Commentary for Exeter Riddle 86." *The Riddle Ages* (blog), 7 October 2019b. https://theriddleages.com/riddles/post/commentary-for-exeter-riddle-86/.
–, ed. *The Riddle Ages: Early Medieval Riddles, Translations and Commentaries* (blog). With Matthias Ammon, Neville Mogford, Jennifer Neville, Alexandra Reider, and Victoria Symons. Redeveloped 2020. https://theriddleages.com
– "Commentary for Exeter Riddle 89." *The Riddle Ages* (blog), 24 February 2021a. https://theriddleages.com/riddles/post/commentary-for-exeter-riddle-89/.
– "Commentary for Exeter Riddle 93." *The Riddle Ages* (blog), 12 January 2021b. https://theriddleages.com/riddles/post/commentary-for-exeter-riddle-93/
– "Seeing Red: Visuality, Violence, and the Making of Textiles in Early Medieval Enigmatic Poetry." *Medieval Feminist Forum* 57 (2021): 17–48.
Cavell, Megan, and Jennifer Neville, eds. *Riddles at Work in the Early Medieval Tradition: Words, Ideas, Interactions*. Manchester Medieval Literature and Culture 32. Manchester: Manchester University Press, 2020.
Cavill, Paul. *Maxims in Old English Poetry*. Cambridge: Brewer, 1999.
Certeau, Michel de. *The Practice of Everyday Life*. Translated by Steven Rendall. Berkeley: University of California Press, 1984.
Chamberlain, Daniel F., and J. Edward Chamberlain, eds. *Or Words to That Effect: Orality and the Writing of Literary History*. Comparative History of Literatures in European Languages 28. Amsterdam: John Benjamins, 2016.
Chance, Jane. "The Structural Unity of *Beowulf*: The Problem of Grendel's Mother." In *New Readings on Women in Old English Literature*. Ed. Helen Damico and Alexandra Hennessey Olsen, 248–61. Bloomington: Indiana University Press, 1990.
Chickering, Howell. "Poetic Exuberance in the Old English *Judith*." *SP* 106 (2009): 119–36.

Clark, Amy W. "Familiar Distances: Beating the Bounds of Early English Identity." PhD diss., University of California, Berkeley, 2020.

Clark, David. "Relaunching the Hero: The Case of Scyld and Beowulf Re-opened." *Neophil* 90 (2006): 621–42.

– *Between Medieval Men: Male Friendship and Desire in Early Medieval English Literature*. Oxford: Oxford University Press, 2009.

– "Discourses of Masturbation: The (Non)solitary Pleasures of the (Medieval) Text." *Men and Masculinities* 20 (2017): 453–81.

Clark, David, and Nicholas Perkins, eds. *Anglo-Saxon Culture and the Modern Imagination*. Medievalism 1. Cambridge: Brewer, 2010.

Clark, George. "The Battle of Maldon: A Heroic Poem." *Speculum* 43 (1968): 52–71.

Clark, Willene B., and Meradith T. McMunn, eds. *Beasts and Birds of the Middle Ages: The Bestiary and its Legacy*. Philadelphia: University of Pennsylvania Press, 1989.

Clarke, Catherine A.M. "Old English Poetry." In *The Blackwell Companion to the Bible in English Literature*. Ed. Rebecca Lemon, Emma Mason, Jonathan Roberts, and Christopher Rowland. 61–75. Maldon, MA: Wiley-Blackwell, 2009.

Clark Hall, J.R. *A Concise Anglo-Saxon Dictionary*. 4th ed. Supplement by Herbert T. Merritt. Medieval Academy Reprints for Teaching 14. 1894; Toronto: University of Toronto Press, 1960.

Clemoes, Peter. "'Symbolic' Language in Old English Poetry." In *Modes of Interpretation in Old English Literature: Essays in Honour of Stanley B. Greenfield*. Ed. Phyllis Rugg Brown, Georgia Ronan Crampton, and Fred C. Robinson, 3–14. Toronto: University of Toronto Press, 1986.

– *Interactions of Thought and Language in Old English Poetry*. Cambridge Studies in Anglo-Saxon England 12. Cambridge: Cambridge University Press, 1995.

Clover, Carol J. "The Germanic Context of the Unferþ Episode." *Speculum* 55 (1980): 444–68.

Coatsworth, Elizabeth. "The Robed Christ in Pre-conquest Sculptures of the Crucifixion." *ASE* 29 (2000): 153–76.

Cobley, Paul, ed. *The Routledge Companion to Semiotics and Linguistics*. New York: Routledge, 2001.

Cochran, Shannon Ferri. "The Plough's the Thing: A New Solution to Old English Riddle 4 of the Exeter Book." *JEGP* 108 (2009): 301–9.

Coleman, Julie. "Sexual Euphemism in Old English." *NM* 93 (1992): 93–8.

Coles, J.M., S.V.E. Heal, and B.J. Orme. "The Use and Character of Wood in Prehistoric Britain and Ireland." *Proceedings of the Prehistoric Society* 44 (1978): 1–45.

Colgrave, B. "Some Notes on Riddle 21." *MLR* 32 (1937): 281–3.

Colgrave, B., and B.M. Griffiths, "A Suggested Solution of Riddle 61." *MLR* 31 (1936): 545–7.

Coneybeare, John J. *Illustrations of Anglo-Saxon Poetry*. London: Harding and Lepard, 1826.

Conlee, John Wayne. "Artistry in the Riddles of the *Exeter Book*." PhD diss., Urbana, IL, 1968.

Conner, Patrick W. *Anglo-Saxon Exeter: A Tenth-Century Cultural History*. Studies in Anglo-Saxon History 4. Woodbridge: Boydell, 1993.

Cook, Albert S., and Chauncey B. Tinker, eds. *Select Translations from Old English Poetry*. London: Ginn, 1902.

Cook, Brian. "The Ruin: An Old English Mnemonic?" *Neophil* 105 (2021): 123–36.

Cook, Eleanor. *Enigmas and Riddles in Literature*. Cambridge: Cambridge University Press, 2006.

Corazza, Vittoria Dolcetti, and Renato Gendre, eds. *Antichità germaniche I Parte, I Seminario avanzato in filologia germanica*. Bibliotheca Germanica, Studi e Testi 10. Alessandria: Edizioni dell'Orso, 2001.

Couch, Christopher L. "From under Mountains to beyond Stars: The Process of Riddling in Leofric's *The Exeter Book* and *The Hobbit*." *Mythlore* 14 (1987): 9–13, 55.

Crane, Eve. *The World History of Beekeeping and Honeyhunting*. New York: Routledge, 1999.

Cronan, Dennis. "Poetic Meanings in the Old English Poetic Vocabulary." *ES* 84 (2003): 397–425.

– "Poetic Words, Conservatism and the Dating of Old English Poetry." *ASE* 33 (2004): 23–50.

Crossley-Holland, Kevin, trans. *The Exeter Riddle Book*. London: Folio Society, 1978.

– trans. *The Exeter Book Riddles*. Rev. ed. London: Enitharmon, 2008.

Cubitt, Catherine. "Review Article: The Tenth-Century Benedictine Reform in England." *Early Medieval Europe* 6 (1997): 77–94.

– "Virginity and Misogyny in Tenth- and Eleventh-Century England." *Gender and History* 12 (2000): 1–32.

Culler, Jonathan. *Structuralist Poetics: Structuralism, Linguistics and the Study of Literature*. London: Routledge and Kegan Paul, 1975.

– *The Pursuit of Signs: Semiotics, Literature, Deconstruction*. London: Routledge and Kegan Paul, 1981.

Dailey, Patricia. "Riddles, Wonder and Responsiveness in Anglo-Saxon Literature." In *The Cambridge History of Early Medieval English Literature*. Ed. Clare Lees, 451–72. Cambridge: Cambridge University Press, 2012.

Dalbey, Marcia A. "The Good Shepherd and the Soldier of God: Old English Homilies on St. Martin of Tours." *NM* 85 (1984): 422–34.

Dale, Corinne. "Commentary on Riddle 34." *The Riddle Ages* (blog), 2 February 2015. https://theriddleages.com/riddles/post/commentary-for-exeter-riddle-34/

– "A New Solution to Exeter Book Riddle 4." *N&Q* 64 (2017): 1–3.

– *The Natural World in the Exeter Book Riddles*. Nature and Environment in the Middle Ages 1. Woodbridge: Brewer, 2017.

- "(Re)viewing the Warrior Woman: Reading the Old English 'Iceberg' Riddle from an Ecofeminist Perspective." *Neophil* 103 (2019): 435–49.
- "*Freolic, Sellic*: An Ecofeminist Reading of *Modor Monigra* (R.84)." In *Riddles at Work in the Early Medieval Tradition: Words, Ideas, Interactions*. Ed. Megan Cavell and Jennifer Neville, 176–92. Manchester Medieval Literature and Culture 32. Manchester: Manchester University Press, 2020.

Damico, Helen. *Beowulf's Wealhtheow and the Valkyrie Tradition*. Madison: University of Wisconsin Press, 1984.

Damico, Helen, and Alexandra Hennessey Olsen, eds. *New Readings on Women in Old English Literature*. Bloomington: Indiana University Press, 1990.

Damico, Helen, and John Leyerle, eds. *Heroic Poetry in the Anglo-Saxon Period: Studies in Honor of Jess B. Bessinger Jr*. Studies in Medieval Culture 32. Kalamazoo, MI: Medieval Institute, 1993.

Davidson, Hilda Ellis. *The Sword in Anglo-Saxon England: Its Archaeology and Literature*. Corrected reprint. Woodbridge, Suffolk: Boydell, 1962; repr. 1994.

Davies, Anthony. "Sexual Behaviour in Later Anglo-Saxon England." In *This Noble Craft: Proceedings of the Xth Research Symposium of the Dutch and Belgian University Teachers of Old and Middle English and Historical Linguistics, Utrecht, 19–20 January 1989*. Ed. Erik Kooper, 83–105. Costerus, n.s., 80. Amsterdam: Rodopi, 1991.

Davies, Craig R. "Cultural Historicity in *The Battle of Maldon*." *PQ* 78 (1999): 151–69.

Davies, Joshua. *Visions and Ruins: Cultural Memory and the Untimely Middle Ages*. Manchester Medieval Literature and Culture 19. Manchester: Manchester University Press, 2018.

Davies, N.B., R.M. Kilner, and D.G. Noble. "Nestling Cuckoos, *Cuculus canorus*, Exploit Hosts with Begging Calls That Mimic a Brood." *Proceedings: Biological Sciences* 265 (22 Apr 1998): 673–8.

Davis, Adam. "Agon and Gnomon: Forms and Functions of the Anglo-Saxon Riddles." In *De Gustibus: Essays for Alain Renoir* Ed. John Miles Foley, 110–50. New York: Garland, 1992.

Davis, Glenn. "The Exeter Book Riddles and the Place of Sexual Idiom in Old English Literature." In *Medieval Obscenities*. Ed. Nicola McDonald, 39–54. York: York Medieval Press, 2006.

Davis, Patricia, and Mary Schlueter. "The Latin Riddle of the Exeter Book." *Archiv* 226 (1989): 92–9.

Dawson, R. MacGregor. "The Structure of the Old English Gnomic Poems." *JEGP* 61 (1962): 14–22.

Day, David D. "Hands across the Hall: The Legalities of Beowulf's Fight with Grendel." *JEGP* 98 (1999): 313–24.

De Boe, Guy, and Frans Verhaeghe, eds. *Urbanism in Medieval Europe, Proceedings of an International Conference of Medieval and Later Archaeology, 1st–4th October 1997*. 11 vols. Zellik, Belgium: Instituut voor het Archeologisch Patrimonium, 1997.

Deegan, Marilyn. "Pregnancy and Childbirth in the Anglo-Saxon Medical Texts: A Preliminary Survey." In *Medicine in Early Medieval England*. Ed. Marilyn Deegan and Donald G. Scragg, 17–26. Manchester: Centre for Anglo-Saxon Studies, University of Manchester, 1987.

Deegan, Marilyn, and Donald G. Scragg, eds. *Medicine in Early Medieval England*. Manchester: Centre for Anglo-Saxon Studies, University of Manchester, 1987.

Dekker, Kees, Karin Olsen and Tette Hofstra, eds. *The World of Travellers: Exploration and Imagination*. Germania Latina 6. Leuven: Peeters, 2009.

Delanty, Gregg, and Michael Matto, eds. *The Word Exchange: Anglo-Saxon Poems in Translation*. Foreword by Seamus Heaney. New York: W.W. Norton, 2011.

Dennis, Caroline. "Exeter Book Riddle 39: Creature Faith." *Medieval Perspectives* 10 (1995): 77–85.

Denno, Jerry. "Oppression and Voice in Anglo-Saxon Riddle Poems." *CEA Critic* 70 (2007): 35–47.

Derolez, R.L.M. "'– And That Difficult Word, *Garsecg*' (Gummere)." *MLQ* 7 (1946): 445–52.

Dewa, Roberta. "The Runic Riddles of the Exeter Book: Language Games and Anglo-Saxon Scholarship." *Nottingham Medieval Studies* 39 (1995): 26–36.

Diamond, Robert E. "Heroic Diction in *The Dream of the Rood*." In *Studies in Honor of John Wilcox*. Ed. A. Dayle Wallace and Woodburn O. Ross, 3–7. Detroit, MI: Wayne State University Press, 1958.

Dictionary of Old English: A to H Online. Ed. Angus Cameron, Ashley Crandell Amos, Antonette diPaolo Healey, et al. Toronto: Dictionary of Old English Project, 2016.

DiNapoli, Robert. "Response to Riddle 39." *The Riddle Ages* (blog), 10 June 2015. https://theriddleages.com/riddles/post/response-to-exeter-riddle-39/.

Discenza, Nicole Guenther. *Inhabited Spaces: Anglo-Saxon Constructions of Place*. Toronto: University of Toronto Press, 2017.

Dienhart, J.M. "A Linguistic Look at Riddles." *Journal of Pragmatics* 31 (1999): 95–126.

Dietrich, Franz. *Commentatio de Kynewulfi Poetae Aetate: Aenigmatum Fragmento e Codice Lugdunensi*. Marburg: N.G. Elwert, 1859.

– "Die Räthsel des Exeterbuchs: Würdigung, Lösung und Herstellung." *Zeitschrift für deutsches Alterthum* 11 (1859): 448–90.

– "Die Räthsel des Exeterbuchs: Verfasser, Weitere Lösungen." *Zeitschrift für deutsches Alterthum* 12 (1865): 232–52.

Doane, Alger N. "Three Old English Implement Riddles: Reconsiderations of Numbers 4, 49, and 73." *MP* 84 (1987): 243–57.

Dockray-Miller, Mary. "Beowulf's Tears of Fatherhood." *Exemplaria* 10 (1998): 1–28.

Donoghue, Daniel. "An *Anser* for Exeter Book Riddle 74." In *Words and Works: Studies in Medieval English Language and Literature in Honour of Fred C. Robinson*. Ed. Peter S. Baker and Nicholas Howe, 45–58. Toronto: University of Toronto Press, 1998.

Doubleday, James F. "The Allegory of the Soul as Fortress in Old English Poetry." *Anglia* 88 (1970): 503–8.
Draper, Simon. "The Significance of Old English *Burh* in Anglo-Saxon England." *Anglo-Saxon Studies in Archaeology and History* 15 (2008): 240–53.
Dronke, Peter. "The Rise of the Medieval Fabliau: Latin and Vernacular Evidence." *Romanische Forschungen* 85 (1973): 275–97.
Dungey, Kevin R. "Faith in the Darkness: Allegorical Theory and Aldhelm's Obscurity." In *Allegoresis: The Craft of Allegory in Medieval Literature*. Ed. J. Stephen Russell, 3–26. New York: Garland, 1988.
Eaglestone, Robert, ed. *Reading the Lord of the Rings: New Writings on Tolkien's Classic*. London: Continuum, 2005.
Earl, James W. *Thinking about "Beowulf."* Stanford, CA: Stanford University Press, 1994.
– "Violence and Non-Violence in Anglo-Saxon England: Ælfric's 'Passion of St. Edmond.'" *PQ* 78 (1999): 125–49.
Eco, Umberto. *A Theory of Semiotics*. Bloomington: Indiana University Press, 1976.
– *The Role of the Reader: Explorations in the Semiotics of Texts*. Midland Book 318. Bloomington: Indiana University Press, 1979; repr. 1984.
Ekirch, A. Roger. *At Day's Close: A History of Nighttime*. London: Weidenfeld and Nicolson, 2005.
Elias, Michael. "The Mimetic Praxis of Riddles and TV Quizzes." Paper given at the "Violence, Mimesis and the Subject of Responsibility" conference at Loyola University Chicago, 1 June 1995. https://www.girard.nl/texts_online/e/Elias_Michael_4.pdf.
– "Neck Riddles in Mimetic Theory." *Contagion* 2 (1995): 189–202.
Eliason, Norman E. "Riddle 68 of the *Exeter Book*." In *Philologica: The Malone Anniversary Studies*. Ed. Thomas Austin Kirby and Henry Bosley Woolf, 18–19. Baltimore: Johns Hopkins Press, 1949.
– "Four Old English Cryptographic Riddles." *SP* 49 (1952): 553–65.
Elliott, R.W.V. "The Runes in *The Husband's Message*." *JEGP* 54 (1955): 1–8.
Enright, Michael J. *Lady with a Mead Cup: Ritual, Prophecy and Lordship in the European Warband from La Tène to the Viking Age*. Dublin: Four Courts Press, 1996.
– "The Warband Context of the Unferth Episode." *Speculum* 73 (1998): 297–337.
Erhardt-Siebold, Erika von. *Die lateinischen Rätsel der Angelsachsen: Ein Beitrag zur Kulturgeschichte Altenglands*. Anglistische Forschungen 61. Heidelberg: Carl Winters, 1925.
– "Old English Riddle No. 4: Handmill." *PMLA* 61 (1946): 620–3.
– "Old English Riddle No. 39: Creature Death." *PMLA* 61 (1946): 910–15.
– "The Anglo-Saxon Riddle 74 and Empedokles' Fragment 117." *MÆ* 15 (1946): 48–54.

- "Old English Riddle No. 57: OE *Cā 'Jackdaw.'" *PMLA* 62 (1947): 1–8.
- "Old English Riddle No. 95." *MLN* 62 (1947): 558–9.
- "The Old English Hunt Riddles." *PMLA* 63 (1948): 3–6.
- "The Old English Storm Riddles." *PMLA* 64 (1949): 884–8.
- "The Old English Loom Riddles." In *Philologica: The Malone Anniversary Studies*. Ed. Thomas Austin Kirby and Henry Bosley Woolf, 9–17. Baltimore: Johns Hopkins Press, 1949.
- "Old English Riddle 13." *MLN* 65 (1950): 93–6.
- "Old English Riddle 23: Bow, OE *Boga*." *MLN* 65 (1950): 97–100.
- "Note on Anglo-Saxon Riddle 74." *MÆ* 21 (1952): 36–7.

Erlemann, Edmund. "Zu den altenglischen Rätseln." *Archiv* 111 (1903): 49–63.

Erlemann, Fritz. "Zum 90. angelsächsischen Rätsel." *Archiv* 115 (1905): 391–2.

Essig, Laurie. *Love, Inc.: Dating Apps, the Big White Wedding, and Chasing the Happily Neverafter*. Oakland: University of California Press, 2019.

Evans, Angela Care. *The Sutton Hoo Ship Burial*. Rev. ed. London: British Museum, 1994.

Evans, David. "Riddling and the Structure of Context." *Journal of American Folklore* 89 (1976): 166–88.

Fanger, Claire. "A Suggestion for a Solution to Exeter Book Riddle 55." *Scintilla* 2–3 (1985–6): 19–28.

Farrell, Robert T. ed. *Bede and Anglo-Saxon England: Papers in Honour of the 1300th Anniversary of the Birth of Bede*. BAR 46. Oxford: BAR, 1978.

Faull, Margaret Lindsay. "The Semantic Development of Old English *wealh*." *LSE*, n.s., 8 (1975): 20–44.

Fay, Jacqueline. "Becoming an Onion: The Extra-Human Nature of Genital Difference in the Old English Riddling and Medical Traditions." *ES* 101 (2020): 60–78.

Fell, Christine. "Runes and Riddles in Anglo-Saxon England." In *"Lastworda Betst": Essays in Memory of Christine E. Fell with Her Unpublished Writings*. Ed. Carole Hough and Kathryn A. Lowe, 264–77. Donington: Shaun Tyas, 2002.

Ferguson, Margaret W. "Saint Augustine's Region Of Unlikeness: The Crossing of Exile and Language." *The Georgia Review* 29 (1975): 842–64.

Ferhatović, Denis. "Detachable Penises and Holes in Knowledge: Reading Exeter Riddles 44 and 62 alongside *Le Fevre de Creil* [*The Blacksmith of Creil*] and Jean Bodel's *Le Sohait des Vez* [*The Dream of Cocks*]." *Exemplaria* 33 (2021): 1–18.

Fern, Chris. "The Archaeological Evidence for Equestrianism in Early Anglo-Saxon England, c.450–700." In *Just Skin and Bones? New Perspectives on Human-Animal Relations in the Historical Past*. Ed. Aleksander Pluskowski, 43–71. BAR International Series 1410. Oxford: Archaeopress, 2005.

Finch, Chauncey E. "The Bern Riddles in Codex Vat. Reg. Lat. 1553." *Transactions and Proceedings of the American Philological Association* 92 (1961): 145–55.

Fiocco, Teresa. "Il viaggio della nave nell'enigma 32 dell'Exeter Book." *Blue Guitar* 7–8 (1984–7): 80–9.
Foley, John Miles. "'Riddle I' of the Exeter Book: The Apocalyptical Storm." *NM* 77 (1976): 347–57.
– "Riddles 53, 54, and 55: An Archetypal Symphony in Three Movements." *Studies in Medieval Culture* 10 (1977): 25–31.
– "How Genres Leak in Traditional Verse." In *Unlocking the Wordhord: Anglo-Saxon Studies in Memory of Edward B. Irving Jr.* Ed. Mark C. Amodio and Katherine O'Brien O'Keeffe, 76–108. Toronto: University of Toronto Press, 2003.
Foley, John Miles, J. Chris Womack, and Whitney A. Womack, eds. *De Gustibus: Essays for Alain Renoir*. Albert Bates Lord Studies in Oral Tradition 11. New York: Garland, 1992.
Förster, Max. "General Description of the Manuscript." In *The Exeter Book of Old English Poetry*. Ed. Raymond W. Chambers, Max Förster, and Robin Flower, 55–67. London: Bradford, Percy Hund, Humphries for the Dean and Chapter of Exeter Cathedral, 1933.
– *Zur Geschichte des Reliquienkultes in Altengland*. Sitzungsberichte der Bayerischen Akademie der Wissenschaften, Philosophisch-historische. Abteilung 8. Munich: Verlag der Bayerischen Akademie der Wissenschaften, 1943.
Fowler, Peter. *Farming in the First Millennium AD: British Agriculture between Julius Caesar and William the Conqueror*. Cambridge: Cambridge University Press, 2002.
Foys, Martin. "A Sensual Philology for Anglo-Saxon England." *Postmedieval* 5 (2014): 456–72.
– "The Undoing of Exeter Book Riddle 47: 'Bookmoth.'" In *Transitional States: Change, Tradition and Memory in Medieval Literature and Culture*. Ed. Graham Caie and Michael D.C. Drout, 101–30. Medieval and Renaissance Texts and Studies 530. Tempe: Arizona Center for Medieval and Renaissance Studies, 2018.
Fox, Cyril, and Bruce Dickins, eds. *The Early Cultures of North-West Europe: H.M. Chadwick Memorial Studies*. Cambridge: Cambridge University Press, 1950.
Frank, Roberta. "'Mere' and 'Sund': Two Sea-Changes in Beowulf." In *Modes of Interpretation: Essays in Honour of Stanley B. Greenfield*. Ed. Phyllis Rugg Brown, Georgia Ronan Crampton, and Fred C. Robinson, 153–72. Toronto: University of Toronto Press, 1986.
– "The Incomparable Wryness of Old English Poetry." In *Inside Old English: Essays in Honour of Bruce Mitchell*. Ed. John Walmsley, 59–73. Oxford: Blackwell, 2006.
Frantzen, Allen. *The Literature of Penance in Anglo-Saxon England*. New Brunswick, NJ: Rutgers University Press, 1983.

Foucault, Michel. *The Archaeology of Knowledge and the Discourse on Language.* Translated by A.M. Sheridan Smith. New York: Pantheon, 1969; repr. 1972.

Frederick, Jill. "At Cross Purposes: Six Riddles in the *Exeter Book.*" In *Cross and Culture in Anglo-Saxon England: Studies in Honor of George Hardin Brown.* Ed. Karen Louise Jolly, Catherine E. Karkov, and Sarah Larratt Keefer, 49–76. Medieval European Studies 9; Sancta Crux/Halig Rod 1; Cross and Culture in Anglo-Saxon England 1. Morgantown: West Virginia University Press, 2008.

– "Ships and the Sea in the Exeter Book Riddles." In *The Anglo-Saxons: The World through Their Eyes.* Ed. Gale R. Owen-Crocker and Brian W. Schneider, 79–86. BAR British Series 595. Oxford: Archaeopress, 2014.

– "The Weft of War in the Exeter Book Riddles." In *Textiles, Text, Intertext: Essays in Honour of Gale R. Owen-Crocker.* Ed. Maren Clegg Hyer and Jill Frederick, 130–52. Woodbridge: Boydell, 2016.

Friedrich, Ellen L. "When a Rose Is Not a Rose: Homoerotic Emblems in the *Roman de la Rose.*" In *Gender Transgressions: Crossing the Normative Barrier in Old French Literature.* Ed. Karen J. Taylor, 21–44. London: Routledge, 1998.

Fry, Donald K. "Exeter Book Riddle Solutions." *Old English Newsletter* 15 (1981): 22–33.

– "Exeter Riddle 31: Feather-Pen." In *De Gustibus: Essays for Alain Renoir.* Ed. John Miles Foley, J. Chris Womack, and Whitney A. Womack, 234–59. Albert Bates Lord Studies in Oral Tradition 11. New York: Garland, 1992.

Frye, Northrop. *Anatomy of Criticism: Four Essays.* Princeton, NJ: Princeton University Press, 1957.

Gadamer, Hans Georg. "Rhetoric, Hermeneutics, and the Critique of Ideology: Metacritical Comments on Truth and Method." In *The Hermeneutics Reader: Texts of the German Tradition from the Enlightenment to the Present.* Ed. Kurt Mueller-Vollmer, 274–92. New York: Continuum, 1985.

Gameson, Richard. "The Origin of the Exeter Book of Old English Poetry." *ASE* 25 (1996): 135–85.

– *The Scribe Speaks? Colophons in Early English Manuscripts.* H.M. Chadwick Memorial Lectures 12. Cambridge: Department of Anglo-Saxon, Norse and Celtic, 2001.

Garvin, Katharine. "Nemnað hy sylfe: A Note on Riddle 57, Exeter Book." *Classica et Mediaevalia* 27 (1966): 294–5.

Gates, Jay Paul. "The *Fulmannod* Society: Social Valuing of the (Male) Legal Subject." In *Castration and Culture in the Middle Ages.* Ed. Larissa Tracy, 131–48. Woodbridge: Boydell and Brewer, 2013.

Geldof, M.R. "'And Describe the Shapes of the Dead': Making Sense of the Archaeology of Armed Violence." In *Wounds and Wound Repair in Medieval Culture.* Ed. Larissa Tracy and Kelly DeVries, 57–80. Leiden: Brill, 2015.

Georges, Robert A., and Alan Dundes. "Towards a Structural Definition of the Riddle." *Journal of American Folklore* 76 (1963): 111–18.

Georgianna, Linda. "King Hrethel's Sorrow and the Limits of Heroic Action in *Beowulf*." *Speculum* 62 (1987): 829–50.
Gleißner, Reinhard. *Die "zweideutigen" altenglischen Rätsel des Exeter Book in ihrem zeitgenössischen Kontext.* Sprache und Literatur 23. Frankfurt am Main: Peter Lang, 1984.
Gneuss, Helmut. "*The Battle of Maldon* 89: Byrhtnoð's *ofermod* Once Again." *SP* 73 (1976): 117–37.
Göbel, Helga. *Studien zu den altenglischen Schriftwesenrätseln.* Epistemata: Literaturwissenschaft 7. Würzburg: Königshausen and Neumann, 1980.
Göbel, Helga, and Rüdiger Göbel. "The Solution of an Old English Riddle." *SN* 50 (1978): 185–91.
Goldsmith, Margaret E. "The Christian Perspective in *Beowulf*." In *An Anthology of Beowulf Criticism*. Ed. Lewis E. Nicholson, 373–86. Notre Dame, IL: University of Notre Dame Press, 1963.
– "The Enigmas of *The Husband's Message*." In *Anglo-Saxon Poetry: Essays in Appreciation for John C. McGalliard*. Edited by Lewis E. Nicholson and Dolores Warwick Frese, 242–63. Notre Dame: University of Notre Dame Press, 1975.
Goodburn, Damian M. "Some Unfamiliar Aspects of Early Woodworking Revealed by Recent Rescue Excavations in London." In *Proceedings of the 4th ICOM Group on Wet Organic Archaeological Materials Conference*. Ed Per Hoffmann, 143–55. Bremerhaven, Germany: ICOM International Committee for Conservation Working Group on Wet Archaeological Materials, 1991.
– "London's Early Medieval Timber Buildings: Little Known Traditions of Construction." In *Urbanism in Medieval Europe, Proceedings of an International Conference of Medieval and Later Archaeology, 1st–4th October 1997*. 11 vols. Ed. Guy De Boe and Frans Verhaeghe, 1:249–57. Zellik, Belgium: Instituut voor het Archeologisch Patrimonium, 1997.
Green, D.H. *The Carolingian Lord: Semantic Studies on Four Old High German Words: Balder, Frô, Truhtin, Hêrro.* Cambridge: Cambridge University Press, 1965.
Green, Martin, ed. *The Old English Elegies: New Essays in Criticism and Research.* Rutherford, NJ: Fairleigh Dickinson University Press; London: Associated University Presses, 1983.
Greenfield, Stanley B. "The Formulaic Expression of the Theme of 'Exile' in Anglo-Saxon Poetry." *Speculum* 30 (1955): 200–6.
– "Old English Riddle 39 Clear and Visible." *Anglia* 98 (1980): 95–100.
– "Beowulf and the Judgement of the Righteous." In *Learning and Literature in Anglo-Saxon England: Studies Presented to Peter Clemoes on the Occasion of his Sixty-Fifth Birthday*. Ed. Michael Lapidge and Helmut Gneuss, 393–407. Cambridge: Cambridge University Press, 1985.
– *Hero and Exile: The Art of Old English Poetry.* Ed. George H. Brown. London: Hambledon, 1989.

Greenfield, Stanley B., and Daniel G. Calder. *A New Critical History of Old English Literature*. New York: New York University Press, 1986.

Grein, C.W.M. "Kleine Mittheilungen." *Germania* 10 (1865): 305–10.

– "Zur Textkritik der angelsächsischen Dichter." *Germania* 10 (1865): 416–29.

Griffith, Mark S. "Poetic Language and the Paris Psalter: The Decay of the Old English Tradition." *ASE* 20 (1991): 167–86.

– "Riddle 19 of the *Exeter Book*: SNAC, an Old English Acronym." *Notes and Queries* 39 (1992): 15–16.

– "Exeter Book *Riddle 74 AC* 'Oak' and *Bat* 'Boat.'" *N&Q* 55 (2008): 393–6.

Gruber, Loren C., Meredith Crellin Gruber, and Gregory K. Jember, eds. *Essays on Old, Middle, Modern English and Old Icelandic in Honour of Raymond P. Tripp, Jr.* Lewiston, NY: Edwin Mellen, 2000.

Guerra, Javier Pérez, ed. *AEDEAN: Select Papers in Language, Literature, and Culture: Proceedings of the 17th International Conference*. Vigo: Universidad de Vigo, 2000.

Gupta, Rakesh Kumar, Wim Reybroeck, Johan W. van Veen, and Anuradha Gupta, eds. *Beekeeping for Poverty Alleviation and Livelihood Security*. Volume I: *Technological Aspects of Beekeeping*. Dordrecht: Springer, 2014.

– "Taxonomy and Distribution of Different Honeybee Species." In *Beekeeping for Poverty Alleviation and Livelihood Security. Volume I: Technological Aspects of Beekeeping*. Ed. Rakesh Kumar Gupta, W. Reybroeck, Johan W. van Veen, and Anuradha Gupta, 63–103. Dordrecht: Springer, 2014.

Gwara, Scott, and Barbara L. Bolt. "A 'Double Solution' for Exeter Book Riddle 51, 'Pen and Three Fingers.'" *N&Q* 54 (2007): 16–19.

Hacikyan, Agop. *A Linguistic and Literary Analysis of Old English Riddles*. Montreal: Mario Casalini, 1966.

Halbrooks, John. "Byrhtnoth's Great-Hearted Mirth, or, Praise and Blame in *The Battle of Maldon*." *PQ* 82 (2003): 235–55.

Hall, Alaric. *Elves in Anglo-Saxon England: Matters of Belief, Health, Gender and Identity*. Anglo-Saxon Studies 8. Cambridge: Boydell, 2007.

Hall, J. R. Clark. *A Concise Anglo-Saxon Dictionary*. 4th ed. With a supplement by Herbert T. Merritt. Medieval Academy Reprints for Teaching 14. Toronto: University of Toronto Press, 1960.

Hall, Thomas N., ed., with the assistance of Thomas D. Hill and Charles D. Wright. *Via Crucis: Essays on Early Medieval Sources and Ideas in Memory of J.E. Cross*. Medieval European Studies 1. Morgantown: West Virginia University Press, 2002.

Halsall, Guy. *Warfare and Society in the Barbarian West, 450–900*. London: Routledge, 2003.

Hamnet, Ian. "Ambiguity, Classification and Change: The Function of Riddles." *Man*, n.s., 2 (1967): 379–92.

Hansen, Elaine Tuttle. *The Solomon Complex: Reading Wisdom in Old English Poetry*. Toronto: University of Toronto Press, 1988.
Harbus, Antonina. "*Exeter Book Riddle 39* Reconsidered." *SN* 70 (1998): 139–48.
Hardy, James. "Popular History of the Cuckoo." *The Folk-Lore Record* 2 (1879): 47–91.
Härke, Heinrich. "Early Anglo–Saxon Social Structure." In *The Anglo-Saxons from the Migration Period to the Eighth Century: An Ethnographic Perspective*. Ed. John Hines, 125–60. Studies in Historical Archaeoethnology 2. Woodbridge: Boydell, 1997.
Harlow, Lucy. "Housel and *Hyhtplega*: The Play of the Eucharist in the *Exeter Book*." *Neophil* 104 (2020): 119–29.
Harper, Kyle. *From Shame to Sin: The Christian Transformation of Sexual Morality in Late Antiquity*. Cambridge, MA: Harvard University Press, 2013.
Harris, Stephen J. "Oaths in *The Battle of Maldon*." In *The Hero Recovered: Essays on Medieval Heroism in Honor of George Clark*. Ed. Robin Waugh and James Weldon, 85–109. Kalamzoo, MI: Medieval Institute, 2010.
Hartley, Dorothy. *Lost Country Life*. New York: Pantheon Books, 1979.
Harwood, Britton J., and Gillian R. Overing, eds. *Class and Gender in Early English Literature: Intersections*. Bloomington: Indiana University Press, 1994.
Hasan-Rokem, Galit, and David Shulman, eds. *Untying the Knot: On Riddles and Other Enigmatic Modes*. Oxford: Oxford University Press, 1996.
Hawkes, Sonia Chadwick, ed. *Weapons and Warfare in Anglo-Saxon England*. Oxford University Committee for Archaeology Monograph 21. Oxford: Oxford University Committee for Archaeology, 1989.
Hayes, Mary. "The Talking Dead: Resounding Voices in Old English Riddles." *Exemplaria* 20 (2008): 123–42.
Head, Pauline. *Representation and Design: Tracing a Hermeneutics of Old English Poetry*. Albany: State University of New York Press, 1997.
Herbison, Ivan. "Generic Adaptation in *Andreas*." In *Essays on Anglo-Saxon and Related Themes in Memory of Lynne Grundy*. Ed. Jane Roberts and Janet Nelson, 181–211. King's College London Medieval Studies 17. London: King's College London, Centre for Late Antique and Medieval Studies, 2000).
– "Heroism and Comic Subversion in the Old English *Judith*." *ES* 91 (2010): 1–25.
Hermann, John P. *Allegories of War: Language and Violence in Old English Poetry*. Ann Arbor: University of Michigan Press, 1989.
Herzfeld, Georg. *Die Räthsel des Exeterbuches und ihr Verfasser*. Acta Germanica 2. Berlin: Mayer and Müller, 1890.
Heyne, Moritz. *Über die Lage und Construction der Halle Heorot im angelsächsischen Beovulfliede*. Paderborn: Ferdinand Schoningh, 1864.
Heyworth, Melanie. "*Be rihtre æwe*: Legislating and Regulating Marital Morality in Late Anglo-Saxon England." PhD diss., University of Sydney, 2005.

- "The Devil's in the Detail: A New Solution to Exeter Book Riddle 4." *Neophil* 91 (2007): 175–96.
- "Perceptions of Marriage in *Exeter Book Riddles 20* and *61*." *SN* 79 (2007): 171–84.

Heusler, Andreas. "Die altnordischen Rätsel." *Zeitschrift des Vereins für Volkskunde* 11 (1901): 117–49.

Hicketier, F. "Fünf Rätsel des Exeterbuches." *Anglia* 10 (1888): 564–600.

Higham, N.J. *An English Empire: Bede and the Early Saxon Kings*. Manchester: Manchester University Press, 1995.

Higley, Sarah Lynn. "The Mouthful of the Giants: Words and Space in Indo-European Revelation Discourse." In *De Gustibus: Essays for Alain Renoir*. Ed. John Miles Foley, J. Chris Womack, and Whitney A. Womack, 266–303. Albert Bates Lord Studies in Oral Tradition 11. New York: Garland, 1992.

- "The Wanton Hand: Reading and Reaching into Grammars and Bodies in Old English Riddle 12." In *Naked before God: Uncovering the Body in Anglo-Saxon England*. Ed. Benjamin C. Withers and Jonathan Wilcox, 29–59. Medieval European Studies 3. Morgantown: West Virginia University Press, 2003.

Hill, David. "Riddle 8: A Problem of Identification or a Problem of Translation." *Medieval Life* 11 (1999): 22–3.

- "Anglo-Saxon Mechanics. 1. *blæstbel(i)g* – the Bellows; 2. *ston mid stel* – the Strikealight." *Medieval Life* 13 (2000): 9–13.
- "*Sulh*: The Anglo-Saxon Plough c. 1000 A.D." *Landscape History* 22 (2000): 5–19.
- "*Cyrn*: The Anglo-Saxon Butter Churn." *Medieval Life* 15 (2001): 19–20.
- "Prelude: Agriculture through the Year." In *The Material Culture of Daily Living in the Anglo-Saxon World*. Ed. Maren Clegg Hyer and Gale R. Owen-Crocker, 9–22. Exeter: University of Exeter Press, 2011.

Hill, John M. *The Anglo-Saxon Warrior Ethic: Reconstructing Lordship in Early English Literature*. Gainesville: University Press of Florida, 2000.

- ."The Sacrificial Synecdoche of Hands, Heads, and Arms in Anglo-Saxon Heroic Story." In *Naked before God: Uncovering the Body in Anglo-Saxon England*. Ed. Benjamin C. Withers and Jonathan Wilcox, 116–37. Medieval European Studies 3. Morgantown: West Virginia University Press, 2003.

Hill, Joyce. "The Soldier of Christ in Old English Prose and Poetry." *LSE*, n.s., 12 (1981): 57–80.

- "The Exeter Book and Lambeth Palace Library MS 149: A Reconsideration." *ANQ* 24 (1986): 112–16.
- "'Þæt wæs geomuru ides!' A Female Stereotype Examined." In *New Readings on Women in Old English Literature*. Ed. Helen Damico and Alexandra Hennessey Olsen, 235–47. Bloomington: Indiana University Press, 1990.

Hill, Joyce, and Mary Swan, eds. *The Community, the Family, and the Saint: Patterns of Power in Early Medieval Europe*. International Medieval Research 4. Turnhout: Brepols, 1998.

Hill, Thomas D. "A Riddle on the Three Orders in the *Collectanea Pseudo-Bedae*?" *PQ* 80 (2001): 205–12.
– "The Old English Dough Riddle and the Power of Women's Magic: The Traditional Context of Exeter Book Riddle 45." In *Via Crucis: Essays on Early Medieval Sources and Ideas in Memory of J.E. Cross*. Ed. Thomas N. Hall, with the assistance of Thomas D. Hill, and Charles D. Wright, 50–60. Medieval European Studies 1. Morgantown: West Virginia University Press, 2002.
– "Killer and Healer: Late Classical Analogues for the Old English Sun Riddle." *PQ* 90 (2011): 387–94.
Hines, John, ed. *The Anglo-Saxons from the Migration Period to the Eighth Century: An Ethnographic Perspective*. Studies in Historical Archaeoethnology 2. Woodbridge: Boydell, 1997.
Historic England. "Waterlogged Wood: Guidelines on the Recording, Sampling, Conservation and Curation of Waterlogged Wood." 1 April 2010. https://content.historicengland.org.uk/images-books/publications/waterlogged-wood/waterlogged-wood.pdf/
Hoffman, David S. "Enigma, Paradox, Parable: Western Traditions of Teaching through Riddles." *Parabola* 25 (2000): 14–21.
Hoffmann, Per, ed. *Proceedings of the 4th ICOM Group on Wet Organic Archaeological Materials Conference*. Bremerhaven, Germany: ICOM International Committee for Conservation Working Group on Wet Archaeological Materials, 1991.
Holo, Joshua. "Genizah Letter from Rhodes Evidently concerning the Byzantine Reconquest of Crete." *Journal of Near Eastern Studies* 59 (2000): 1–12.
Holsinger, Bruce. "Of Pigs and Parchment: Medieval Studies and the Coming of the Animal." *PMLA* 124 (2009): 616–23.
Holthausen, Ferdinand. Review of "Komposition und Quellen des Exeterbuches" by August Prehn. *Anglia* 7 (1884): Anzeiger, 120–9.
– "Beiträge zur Eklärung und Textkritik altenglischer Dichtungen." *Indogermanische Forschungen* 4 (1894): 379–88.
– "Review of Grein's *Bibliothek der angelsächsischen Poesie* (1897)." *Anglia Beiblatt* 9 (1899): 353–8.
– "Zu alt- und mittelenglischen Dichtungen. XV." *Anglia* 24 (1901): 264–7.
– "Zur altenglischen Literatur." *Anglia Beiblatt* 16 (1905): 227–31.
– "Zur Textkritik altenglischer Dichtungen." *Englische Studien* 37 (1907): 198–211.
– "Zu den altenglischen Rätseln." *Anglia* 35 (1912): 165–77.
– "Zu altenglischen Denkmälern." *Englische Studien* 51 (1917): 180–8.
– "Zu den altenglischen Rätseln." *Anglia Beiblatt* 30 (1919): 50–5.
– "Zu altenglischen Dichtungen." *Anglia* 44 (1920): 346–56.
– "Anglosaxonica Minora." *Anglia Beiblatt* 36 (1925): 219–20.
– "Ein altenglisches Rätsel." *Germanisch-romanische Monatsschrift* 15 (1927): 453–4.
– "Zu altenglischen Dichtungen." *Englische Studien* 74 (1940): 324–8.
Honegger, Thomas, ed. *Riddles, Knights and Cross-Dressing Saints: Essays on Medieval English Language and Literature*. Variations 5. Bern: Peter Lang, 2004.

Hook, Derek. "Discourse, Knowledge, Materiality, History: Foucault and Discourse Analysis." *Theory and Psychology* 11 (2001): 521–47.

Horner, Shari. "'Why Do You Speak So Much Foolishness?' Gender, Humor, and Discourse in Ælfric's Lives of Saints." In *Humour in Anglo-Saxon Literature*. Ed. Jonathan Wilcox, 127–36. Cambridge: Brewer, 2000.

– *The Discourse of Enclosure: Representing Women in Old English Literature*. Albany: State University of New York Press, 2001.

Hosler, John Donald. "Two Historical Riddles of the Old English *Exeter Book*." MA diss., Iowa State University, 2001.

Hostetter, Aaron K. "Exeter Book Riddles Solutions" (last updated 8 January 2018). Part of *The Old English Poetry Project*. https://oldenglishpoetry.camden.rutgers.edu/exeter-book-riddles-solutions/.

Hough, Carole. "Place-Names and the Provenance of Riddle 49." *Neophil* 82 (1998): 617–18.

Hough, Carole, and Kathryn A. Lowe, eds. *"Lastworda Betst": Essays in Memory of Christine E. Fell with Her Unpublished Writings*. Donington: Shaun Tyas, 2002.

Howard, Elizabeth. "Modes of Being in Anglo-Saxon Riddles." *In Geardagum* 25 (2005): 61–77.

Howe, Nicholas. "Aldhelm's *Enigmata* and Isidorian Etymology." *ASE* 14 (1985): 37–59.

– *Migration and Mythmaking in Anglo-Saxon England*. New Haven: Yale University Press, 1989.

Hume, Kathryn. "The Concept of the Hall in Old English Poetry." *ASE* 3 (1974): 63–74.

Hyer, Maren Clegg. "Textiles and Textile Imagery in Old English Literature." PhD diss., University of Toronto, 1998.

– "Textiles and Textile Imagery in the Exeter Book." *Medieval Clothing and Textiles* 1 (2004): 29–39.

Hyer, Maren Clegg, and Jill Frederick, eds. *Textiles, Text, Intertext: Essays in Honour of Gale R. Owen-Crocker*. Woodbridge: Boydell, 2016.

Hyer, Maren Clegg, and Gale Owen-Crocker. "Woven Works: Making and Using Textiles." In *The Material Culture of Daily Living in the Anglo-Saxon World*. Ed. Maren Clegg Hyer and Gale R. Owen-Crocker, 157–84. Exeter: University of Exeter Press, 2011.

Hyer, Maren Clegg, and Gale Owen-Crocker, eds. *The Material Culture of Daily Living in the Anglo-Saxon World*. Exeter: University of Exeter Press, 2011.

Igarashi, Michelle. "A Contextual Study of the *Exeter Book* Riddles." PhD diss., New York Stony Brook, 1999.

– "Riddles." In *A Companion to Old and Middle English Literature*. Ed. Laura Cooner Lambdin and Robert Thomas Lambdin, 336–51. Westport, CT: Greenwood Press, 2002.

Ireland, Colin A. "Some Analogues of the O.E. *Seafarer* from Hiberno-Latin Sources." *NM* 92 (1991): 1–14.
Irvine, Martin. *The Making of Textual Culture: "Grammatica" and Literary Theory, 350–1100*. Cambridge: Cambridge University Press, 1994.
Irving, Edward B., Jr. "A Reading of *Andreas*: The Poem as Poem." *ASE* 12 (1983): 215–37.
– "The Nature of Christianity in *Beowulf*." *ASE* 13 (1984): 7–21.
– *Rereading Beowulf*. Philadelphia: University of Pennsylvania Press, 1989.
– "Heroic Experience in the Old English Riddles." In *Old English Shorter Poems: Basic Readings*. Ed. Katherine O'Brien O'Keeffe, 199–212. New York: Garland, 1994.
Itnyre, Cathy Jorgensen, ed. *Medieval Family Roles: A Book of Essays*. Garland Medieval Casebooks 15. New York: Garland, 1996.
– "The Emotional Universe of Medieval Icelandic Fathers and Sons." In *Medieval Family Roles: A Book of Essays*. Ed. Cathy Jorgensen Itnyre, 173–96. Garland Medieval Casebooks 15. New York: Garland, 1996.
Jacobs, Nicolas. "The Old English Book-Moth Riddle Reconsidered." *N&Q* n.s. 35 (1988): 290–92.
Jember, Gregory K. "An Interpretive Translation of the Exeter Riddles." PhD diss., University of Denver, 1975.
–, trans. *The Old English Riddles: A New Translation*. Denver, CO: Society for New Language Study, 1976.
– "A Generative Method for the Study of Anglo-Saxon Riddles." *Studies in Medieval Culture* 11 (1977): 33–9.
– "Prolegomena to a Study of the Old English Riddles." *Journal of Faculty of Liberal Arts* 19 (1987): 155–78.
– "Some Hints on Ambiguity and Meaning in Riddle 39." *Hiroshima Studies in English Language and Literature* 31 (1987): 26–37.
– "Literal and Metaphorical: Clues to Reading the Old English Riddles." *Studies in English Literature* n.v. (English and Japanese Issues) (1988): 47–56.
Johnson, David F., and Elaine Treharne, eds. *Readings in Medieval Texts: Interpreting Old and Middle English Literature*. Oxford: Oxford University Press, 2005.
Jolly, Karen Louise, Catherine E. Karkov, and Sarah Larratt Keefer, eds. *Cross and Culture in Anglo-Saxon England: Studies in Honor of George Hardin Brown*. Medieval European Studies 9; Sancta Crux/Halig Rod 1; Cross and Culture in Anglo-Saxon England 1. Morgantown: West Virginia University Press, 2008.
Jones, Malcolm. "Folklore Motifs in Late Medieval Art III: Erotic Animal Imagery." *Folklore* 102 (1991): 192–219.
Jordan, Richard. *Die altenglischen Säugertiernamen*. Anglistische Forschungen 12. Heidelberg: Carl Winter, 1903

Jorgensen, Alice. "The Exeter Book Riddles and the Unmaking of the World." Paper given to the Leeds International Medieval Congress, 9 July 2008.

Joyce, John J. "Natural Process in Exeter Book Riddle #29: 'Sun and Moon.'" *Annuale Mediaevale* 14 (1973): 5–8.

Jurasinski, Stefan. *Ancient Privileges: Beowulf, Law, and the Making of Germanic Antiquity*. Medieval European Studies 6. Morgantown: West Virginia University Press, 2006.

Kaivola-Bregenhøj, Annikki. *Riddles: Perspectives on the Use, Function and Change in a Folklore Genre*. Translated by Susan Sinisalo. Studia Fennica Folkloristica 10. Helsinki: Finnish Literary Society, 2001.

– "Sexual Riddles: The Test of the Listener." In *Myth and Mentality: Studies in Folklore and Popular Thought*. Ed. Anna-Leena Siikala, 301–17. Helsinki, Finland: Finnish Literature Society, 2002.

Karkov, Catherine E., and George Hardin Brown, eds. *Anglo-Saxon Styles*. Albany: State University of New York Press, 2003.

Kaske, Robert E. "A Poem of the Cross in the Exeter Book: 'Riddle 60' and 'The Husband's Message.'" *Traditio* 23 (1967): 47–71.

Kay, Donald. "Riddle 20: A Revaluation." *Tennessee Studies in Literature* 13 (1968): 133–9.

Keefer, Sarah Larratt. "*Ut in omibus honorificetur Deus*: The *Corsnæd* Ordeal in Anglo-Saxon England." In *The Community, the Family, and the Saint: Patterns of Power in Early Medieval Europe*. Ed. Joyce Hill and Mary Swan, 237–64. International Medieval Research 4. Turnhout: Brepols, 1998.

Keller, May Lansfield. *The Anglo-Saxon Weapon Names, Treated Archaeologically and Etymologically*. Anglistische Forschungen 15. Heidelberg: Winter, 1906.

Kendall, Judy. "Commentary for Exeter Riddle 65." *The Riddle Ages* (blog), 17 August 2017. https://theriddleages.com/riddles/post/commentary-for-exeter-riddle-65/.

– "Commentary for Exeter Riddle 81." *The Riddle Ages* (blog), 1 October 2018. https://theriddleages.com/riddles/post/commentary-for-exeter-riddle-81/.

– "Commentary for Exeter Riddle 92." *The Riddle Ages* (blog), 3 December 2020. https://theriddleages.com/riddles/post/commentary-for-exeter-riddle-92/.

Kennedy, C.W. *The Earliest English Poetry: A Critical Survey of the Poetry Written before the Norman Conquest with Illustrative Examples*. London: Oxford University Press, 1943.

Kennedy, Christopher B. "Old English Riddle No. 39." *English Language Notes* 13 (1975): 81–5.

Kennedy, Ruth, and Simon Meecham-Jones, eds. *Authority and Subjugation in Writing of Medieval Wales*. Basingstoke: Palgrave Macmillan, 2008.

Kiernan, Kevin S. "*Cwene*: The Old Profession of Exeter Riddle 95." *MP* 72 (1975): 384–9.

– "The Mysteries of the Sea-Eagle in Exeter Riddle 74." *PQ* 54 (1975): 518–22.

Kirby, Ian J. "The Exeter Book, Riddle 60." *N&Q* 48 (2001): 219–20.
Kirby, Thomas Austin, and Henry Bosley Woolf, eds. *Philologica: The Malone Anniversary Studies*. Baltimore: Johns Hopkins Press, 1949.
Kitson, Peter. "Swans and Geese in Old English Riddles." *Anglo-Saxon Studies in Archaeology and History* 7 (1994): 79–84.
Klaeber, Frederick. "Wanderer 44; Rätsel XII 3 f.." *Anglia Beiblatt* 17 (1906): 300–1.
Klein, Stacy S., William Schipper, and Shannon Lewis-Simpson, eds. *The Maritime World of the Anglo-Saxons*. Medieval and Renaissance Texts and Studies 448; Essays in Anglo-Saxon Studies 5. Tempe: Arizona Centre for Medieval and Renaissance Studies, 2014.
Klein, Thomas. "The Old English Translation of Aldhelm's Riddle *Lorica*." *RES*, n.s., 48 (1997): 345–9.
– "A New Solution to Riddle 74." Paper given at the International Congress on Medieval Studies (Kalamazoo, MI) on 8 May 1999.
– "Of Water and the Spirit: Metaphorical Focus in Exeter Book Riddle 74." *RES*, n.s., 66 (2015): 1–19.
– "The Metaphorical Cloak of Exeter Riddle 83, 'Ore/Gold/Metal'." *ANQ* 28 (2015): 11–14.
Klein, Thomas, William F. Klein, and David Delehanty. "Resolving Exter Book Riddles 74 and 33: Stormy Allomorphs of Water." *Quidditas* 35 (2014): 29–48.
Klipstein, Louis F. *Analecta Anglo-Saxonica: Selections in Prose and Verse from the Anglo-Saxon Literature, with an Introductory Ethnological Essay, and Notes, Critical and Explanatory*. 2 vols. New York: G.P. Putnam, 1849.
Kock, Ernst Albin. *Jubilee Jaunts and Jottings: 250 Contributions to the Interpretation and Prosody of Old West Teutonic Alliterative Poetry*. Lunds Universitets Årsskrift, n.s., 1, 14, no. 26. Lund: Gleerup, 1918.
Konick, Marcus. "Exeter Book Riddle 41 as a Continuation of Riddle 40." *MLN* 54 (1939): 259–62.
Kooper, Erik, ed. *This Noble Craft: Proceedings of the Xth Research Symposium of the Dutch and Belgian University Teachers of Old and Middle English and Historical Linguistics, Utrecht, 19–20 January 1989*. Costerus, n.s., 80. Amsterdam: Rodopi, 1991.
– ed. *The Medieval Chronicle II: Proceedings of the 2nd International Congress on the Medieval Chronicle*. Costerus, n.s., 144. Amsterdam: Rodopi, 2002.
Koppinen, Pirkko Anneli. "*Swa þa Stafas Becnaþ*: Ciphers of the Heroic Idiom in the Exeter Book Riddles, *Beowulf*, *Judith*, and *Andreas*." PhD diss., Royal Holloway, University of London, 2009.
– "Breaking the Mould: Solving the Old English Riddle 12 as *Wudu* 'Wood'." In *Trees and Timber in the Anglo-Saxon World*. Ed. Michael D.J. Bintley and Michael G. Shapland, 158–74. Oxford: Oxford University Press, 2013.

- "Commentary for Exeter Riddles 30a and b." *The Riddle Ages* (blog), 21 October 2014. https://theriddleages.com/riddles/post/commentary-for-exeter-riddle-30a-and-b/.
Korhammer, Michael. "The Last of the Exeter Book Riddles." In *Bookmarks from the Past: Studies in Early English Language and Literature in Honour of Helmut Gneuss*. Ed. Lucia Kornexl and Ursula Lenker, 69–80. Münchener Universitätsschriften 30. Frankfurt am Main: Peter Lang, 2003.
Kornexl, Lucia, and Ursula Lenker, eds. *Bookmarks from the Past: Studies in Early English Language and Literature in Honour of Helmut Gneuss*. Münchener Universitätsschriften 30. Frankfurt am Main: Peter Lang, 2003.
Korninger, Siegfried, ed. *A Yearbook of Studies in English Language and Literature*. Vienna: Braumüller, 1981.
Kossick, S.G. "Gnomic Verse and Old English Riddles." *Unisa English Studies* 24 (1986): 1–6.
Kries, Susanne. "*Fela í rúnum eða í skáldskap*: Anglo-Saxon and Scandinavian Approaches to Riddles and Poetic Disguises." In *Riddles, Knights and Cross-Dressing Saints: Essays on Medieval English Language and Literature*. Ed. Thomas Honegger, 139–64. Variations 5. Bern: Peter Lang, 2004.
Lakoff, George and Mark Johnson. *Metaphors We Live By*. With a new afterword. Chicago: University of Chicago Press, 1980; repr. 2003.
Lambdin, Laura Cooner, and Robert Thomas Lambdin, eds. *A Companion to Old and Middle English Literature*. Westport, CN: Greenwood, 2002.
Lapidge, Michael. "Stoic Cosmology and the Source of the First Old English Riddle." *Anglia* 112 (1994): 1–25.
- *The Anglo-Saxon Library*. Oxford: Oxford University Press, 2006.
Lapidge, Michael, and James L. Rosier, trans. *Aldhelm: The Poetic Works*. With an appendix by Neil Wright. Cambridge: Brewer, 1985.
Lagnum, Virginia. "'The Wounded Surgeon': Devotion, Compassion and Metaphor in Medieval England." In *Wounds and Wound Repair in Medieval Culture*. Ed. Larissa Tracy and Kelly DeVries, 269–90. Leiden: Brill, 2015.
Laing, Gregory L. "Exeter Book Riddle 17: A Possible Solution." Paper given at the International Congress on Medieval Studies, 6 May 2006.
Laird, Cameron. "Commentary for Exeter Riddle 12." *The Riddle Ages* (blog), 7 September 2013. https://theriddleages.com/riddles/post/commentary-for-exeter-riddle-12/
Laszlo, Renate. *Das erste Rätsel des Exeterbuches*. Marburg: Tectum, 1988.
- *Köcherfliege und Seidenraupe in den altenglischen Rätseln*. Marburg: Tectum, 1997.
- *Die Sonne bringt es an den Tag: Ein altenglisches Rätsel des siebten Jahrhunderts und seine Lösung*. Marburg: Tectum, 1998.
- *Ewig ist der Schöpfer: Cædmons Schöpfunghymnus im Codex Exoniensis*. Marburg: Tectum, 2000.

- *Germanische Rätseltradition: Die Zeit, der Fisch im Fluss und andere Rätsel*. Marburg: Tectum, 2001.
- *Germanische Rätsel in der Literatur des Mittelalters*. Marburg: Tectum, 2003.

Lee, Alvin A. *The Guest-Hall of Eden: Four Essays on the Design of Old English Poetry*. New Haven: Yale University Press, 1972.

Lees, Clare A. "Nonsense Verse?" Paper presented at the Doggerel: Disesteemed Verse in the Middle Ages Conference (Birkbeck College, London) on 10 March 2007.

- "Basil Bunting, Briggflatts, Lindisfarne, and Anglo-Saxon Interlace." In *Anglo-Saxon Culture and the Modern Imagination*. Ed. David Clark and Nicholas Perkins, 111–28. Medievalism 1. Cambridge: Brewer, 2010.
- , ed. *The Cambridge History of Early Medieval English Literature*. Cambridge: Cambridge University Press, 2012.

Lees, Clare A., and Gillian R. Overing. *Double Agents: Women and Clerical Culture in Anglo-Saxon England*. Philadelphia: University of Pennsylvania Press, 2001.

Leisi, Ernst. "Gold und Manneswert im *Beowulf*." *Anglia* 71 (1952–3): 259–73.

Lendinara, Patrizia. "Aspetti della società germanica negli enigmi del Codice Exoniense." In *Antichità germaniche I Parte, I Seminario avanzato in filologia germanica*. Ed. Vittoria Dolcetti Corazza and Renato Gendre, 3–41. Bibliotheca Germanica, Studi e Testi 10. Alessandria: Edizioni dell'Orso, 2001.

Le Lievre, Kerrie. "'I Will Play No Games with You': Riddlery, Narrative and Ethics in the Riddle-Master's Game." *Journal of the Fantastic in the Arts* 16 (2005): 233–45.

Lemon, Lee T., and Marion J. Reis, trans. *Russian Formalist Criticism: Four Essays*. Lincoln: University of Nebraska Press, 1965.

Leo, Heinrich. *Quae de se ipso Cynevulfus (sive Cenevulfus, sive Coenevulfus) Poeta Anglosaxonicus Tradiderit*. Halis: Formis Hendeliis, 1857.

Lerer, Seth. "The Riddle and the Book: Exeter Book Riddle 42 in its Contexts." *Papers on Language and Literature* 25 (1989): 3–18.

Lerner, L.D. "Colour Words in Anglo-Saxon." *Modern Language Review* 46 (1951): 246–9.

Leslie, Roy F. "Analysis of Stylistic Devices and Effects in Anglo-Saxon Literature." In *Stil- und Form-probleme in der Literatur*. Ed. Paul Böckmann. Heidelberg: Carl Winter, 1959. Repr. in *Old English Literature: Twenty-two Analytical Essays*. Ed. Martin Stevens and Jerome Mandel, 73–81. Lincoln: University of Nebraska Press 1968.

- "The Integrity of Riddle 60." *JEGP* 67 (1968): 451–7.

Lester, G.A. "*Sindrum Begrunden* in Exeter Book Riddle No. 26." *N&Q* 236 (1991): 13–15.

Levin, Daniel T., ed. *Thinking and Seeing: Visual Metacognition in Adults and Children*. Cambridge, MA: MIT Press, 2004.

License, Tom. "Evidence of Recluses in Eleventh-Century England." *ASE* 36 (2007): 221–34.
– *Hermits and Recluses in English Society 950–1200*. Oxford: Oxford University Press, 2011.
Liebermann, F. "Das angelsächsische Rätsel 56: 'Galgen' als Waffenständer." *Archiv für das Studium der neueren Sprachen und Literaturen* 114 (1905): 163–4.
Lindheim, Bogislav von. "Traces of Colloquial Speech in OE." *Anglia* 70 (1951): 22–42.
Liuzza, Roy Michael. "The Texts of the Old English Riddle 30." *JEPG* 87 (1988): 1–15.
–, ed. *Old English Literature: Critical Essays*. New Haven, CT: Yale University Press, 2002.
–, ed. *The Poems of MS Junius 11: Basic Readings*. New York: Routledge, 2002.
–, ed. and trans. *Old English Poetry: An Anthology*. Peterborough, ON: Broadview, 2014.
Louviot, Elise. *Direct Speech in Beowulf and Other Old English Poems*. Cambridge: Brewer, 2016.
Löwenthal, Fritz. *Studien zum germanischen Rätsel*. Heidelberg: Carl Winter, 1914.
Loyn, H.R. "Gesiths and Thegns in Anglo-Saxon England from the Seventh to the Tenth Century." *English Historical Review* 70 (1955): 529–49.
Lucas, Peter J. "Loyalty and Obedience in the Old English *Genesis* and the Interpolation of *Genesis B* into *Genesis A*." *Neophil* 76 (1992): 121–35.
Lumbley, Coral. "The 'Dark Welsh': Color, Race, and Alterity in the Matter of Medieval Wales." *Literature Compass* 16, no. 9–10 (2019): 1–19.
Luo, Shu-han. 'Tender Beginnings in the *Exeter Book* Riddles.' In *Childhood and Adolescence in Anglo-Saxon Literary Culture*. Ed. by Susan Irvine and Winfried Rudolph, 71–94. Toronto: University of Toronto Press, 2018.
Machan, Tim William, and Robyn G. Peterson. "The Crux of Riddle 53." *English Language Notes* 24.3 (1987): 7–14.
Mackie, William S. "Notes on the Text of the 'Exeter Book.'" *MLR* 28 (1933): 75–8.
Magennis, Hugh. "The Cup as Symbol and Metaphor in Old English Literature." *Speculum* 60 (1985): 517–36.
– "'No Sex Please, We're Anglo-Saxons?' Attitudes to Sexuality in Old English Prose and Poetry." *LSE*, n.s., 26 (1995): 1–27.
– *Images of Community in Old English Poetry*. Cambridge Studies in Anglo-Saxon England 18. Cambridge: Cambridge University Press, 1996.
– *Anglo-Saxon Appetites: Food and Drink and Their Consumption in Old English and Related Literature*. Dublin: Four Courts, 1999.
– "A Funny Thing Happened on the Way to Heaven: Humorous Incongruity in Old English Saints' Lives." In *Humour in Anglo-Saxon Literature*. Ed. Jonathan Wilcox, 137–57. Cambridge: Brewer, 2000.

Manley, J. "The Archer and the Army in the Late Saxon Period." *Anglo-Saxon Studies in Archaeology and History* 4 (1985): 223–35.

Mapping Metaphor with the Historical Thesaurus, University of Glasgow. https://mappingmetaphor.arts.gla.ac.uk/

Maranda, Elli Köngäs. "Structure des énigmes." *L'Homme* 9 (1969): 5–48.

– "Riddles and Riddling: An Introduction." *Journal of American Folklore* 89 (1976): 127–37.

Marino, Matthew. "The Literariness of the *Exeter Book Riddles*." *NM* 79 (1978): 258–65.

Marsden, Richard. "'Ask What I Am Called': The Anglo-Saxons and Their Bibles." In *The Bible as Book: The Manuscript Tradition*. Ed. John L. Sharpe III and Kimberly Van Kampen, 145–76. New Castle, DE: Oak Knoll, 1998.

Massey, Jeff, and Karma DeGruy. "Riddling Meaning from Old English -*haga* Compounds." *SP* 112 (2015): 24–38.

Matto, Michael. "A War of Containment: The Heroic Image in *The Battle of Maldon*." *SN* 74 (2002): 60–75.

McCarthy, Marcella. "A Solution to Riddle 72 in the Exeter Book." *RES*, n.s., 44 (1993): 204–10.

McCully, Chris, trans. *Old English Poems and Riddles*. Manchester: Carcanet, 2008.

McDonald, Nicola, ed. *Medieval Obscenities*. York: York Medieval Press, 2006.

McFadden, Brian. "Raiding, Reform, and Reaction: Wondrous Creatures in the Exeter Book Riddles." *Texas Studies in Literature and Language* 50 (2008): 329–51.

McGrail, Seàn. *Ancient Boats in North-West Europe: The Archaeology of Water Transport to AD 1500*. London: Routledge, 1987.

McNeill, John T. and Helena M. Gamer, trans. *Medieval Handbooks of Penance: A Translation of the Principal Libri Poenitentiales and Selections from Related Documents*. Records of Civilization: Sources and Studies 29. New York: Columbia University Press, 1938.

Mead, William E. "Color in Old English Poetry." *PMLA* 14 (1899): 169–206.

Meaney, Audrey L. "Exeter Book Riddle 57 (55): A Double Solution?." *ASE* 25 (1996): 187–200.

– "Birds on the Stream of Consciousness: Riddles 7 to 10 of the Exeter Book." In *Medieval Animals*. Ed. Aleks Pluskowski. Special Issue of *Archaeological Review from Cambridge* 18 (2002): 120–52.

– "Extra-Medical Elements in Anglo-Saxon Medicine." *Social History of Medicine* 24 (2011): 41–56.

Merrell, Floyd. "Charles Saunders Peirce's Concept of the Sign." In *The Routledge Companion to Semiotics and Linguistics*. Ed. Paul Cobley, 28–39. London: Routledge, 2001.

Meyvaert, Paul. "The Solution to Old English Riddle 39." *Speculum* 51 (1976): 195–201.

Miller, Katherine. "The Semantic Field of Slavery in Old English: *Wealh, Esne, Þræl*." PhD diss., University of Leeds, 2014.

Millet, Victor, and Heike Sahm, eds. *Narration and Hero: Recounting the Deeds of Heroes in Literature and Art of the Early Medieval Period*, Ergänzungsbände zum Reallexikon der Germanischen Altertumskunde 87. Berlin: De Gruyter, 2014.

Missuno, Filip. "Glowing Paradoxes and Glimmers of Doom: A Re-evaluation of the Meaning of Old English *fāh* in Poetic Contexts." *Neophil* 99 (2015): 125–42.

Mitchell, Bruce. *Old English Syntax*, 2 vols (Oxford: Clarendon, 1985)

– "Linguistic Facts and the Interpretation of Old English Poetry." In *On Old English: Selected Papers*, 152–71. Oxford: Basil Blackwell, 1988.

Mitchell, Stephen A. "Ambiguity and Germanic Imagery of OE Riddle 1: 'Army.'" *SN* 54 (1982): 39–52.

Mize, Britt. "Commentary for Exeter Riddle 33." *The Riddle Ages* (blog), 22 January 2015. https://theriddleages.com/riddles/post/commentary-for-exeter-riddle-33/

– "Commentary for Exeter Riddle 51." *The Riddle Ages* (blog), 5 January 2017. https://theriddleages.com/riddles/post/commentary-for-exeter-riddle-51/

– "Enigmatic Knowing and the Vercelli Book." In *Riddles at Work in the Early Medieval Tradition: Words, Ideas, Interactions*. Ed. Megan Cavell and Jennifer Neville, 247–64. Manchester Medieval Literature and Culture 32. Manchester: Manchester University Press, 2020.

Moffat, Douglas. "Anglo-Saxon Scribes and Old English Verse." *Speculum* 67 (1992): 805–27.

Morgan, Gwendolyn. "Duality in *Piers Plowman* and the Anglo-Saxon Riddles (A Response to Arthur Versluis)." *Connotations* 1 (1991): 168–72.

– "Dualism and Mirror Imagery in Anglo-Saxon Riddles." *Journal of the Fantastic in the Arts* 5 (1992): 74–85.

Morgan, Gwendolyn, and Brian McAllister. "Reading Riddles 30A and 30B as Two Poems." *In Geardagum* 14 (1993): 67–77.

Morley, Henry. *From Caedmon to the Conquest*. English Writers: An Attempt towards a History of English Literature 2. London: Cassell, 1888.

Morris, Carol A. *Craft, Industry and Everyday Life: Wood and Woodworking in Anglo-Scandinavian and Medieval York*. The Archaeology of York: The Small Finds 17. York: Council for British Archaeology for the York Archaeological Trust, 2000.

– "Anglo-Saxon Lathe-Turning: Tools, Techniques, Products." Paper given at the Woodlands, Trees, and Timber in the Anglo-Saxon World conference, 14 November 2009.

Moser, Luisa Maria. "A New Solution for the Exeter Book Riddle Number 70 – A Double Flute." *N&Q* 63 (2016): 2–4.

- "A New Solution to the Exeter Book Riddle 41 – Barm, a Dough-Starter." *N&Q* 64 (2017): 210–12.
Müller, Eduard. *Ueber die angelsächsischen Räthsel des Exeterbuches*. Cöthen: P. Schettler, 1861.
Mueller-Vollmer, Kurt, ed. *The Hermeneutics Reader: Texts of the German Tradition from the Enlightenment to the Present*. New York: Continuum, 1985.
Muir, Bernard J. "Issues for Editors of Anglo-Saxon Poetry in Manuscript Form." In *Inside Old English: Essays in Honour of Bruce Mitchell*. Ed. John Walmsley, 181–202. Oxford: Blackwell, 2006.
Muñoz, José Esteban. "'The White to Be Angry': Vaginal Davis's Terrorist Drag." *Social Text* 52/53 (1997): 80–103.
- *Disidentifications: Queers of Color and the Performance of Politics*. Cultural Studies of the Americas 2. Minneapolis: University of Minnesota Press, 1999.
Murphy, Patrick J. "*Bocstafas*: A Literal Reading of Exeter Book Riddle 57." *PQ* 84 (2005): 139–60.
- "The Riders of the Celestial Wain in Exeter Book *Riddle 22*." *N&Q* 53 (2006): 401–7.
- "*Leo ond beo*: Exeter Book Riddle 17 as Samson's Lion." *ES* 88 (2007): 371–87.
- *Unriddling the Exeter Riddles*. University Park: Pennsylvania State University Press, 2011.
Musgrave, Elaine K. "Cithara as the Solution to Riddle 31 of the Exeter Book." *Pacific Coast Philology* 37 (2002): 69–84.
Mustanoja, Tauno F. "The Unnamed Woman's Song of Mourning over Beowulf and the Tradition of Ritual Lamentation." *NM* 68 (1967): 1–27.
Needham, Walter. *A Book of Country Things*. Recorded by Barrows Mussey. Brattleboro, VT: Stephen Greene, 1965.
Neidorf, Leonard. "Unferth's Ambiguity and the Trivialization of Germanic Legend." *Neophil* 101 (2017): 439–54.
- "*Maxims II*, Line 10: Truth and Textual Criticism." *SN* 91 (2019): 241–8.
- "On *Beowulf* and the *Nibelungenlied*: Counselors, Queens, and Characterization." *Neohelicon* 47 (2020): 655–72.
Neidorf, Leonard, Rafael J. Pascual, and Tom Shippey, eds. *Old English Philology: Studies in Honour of R. D. Fulk*. Anglo-Saxon Studies 31. Cambridge: Brewer, 2016.
Nelson, Marie. "The Rhetoric of the Exeter Book Riddles." *Speculum* 49 (1974): 421–40.
- "The Paradox of Silent Speech in the Exeter Book Riddles." *Neophil* 62 (1978): 609–15.
- "Old English Riddle 18 (20): A Description of Ambivalence." *Neophil* 66 (1982): 291–300.
- "Plus Animate: Two Possible Transformations of Riddles by Symphosius." *Germanic Notes* 18 (1987): 46–8.

- "Four Social Functions of the Exeter Book Riddles." *Neophil* 75 (1991): 445–50.
- "Tolkien's 'Orthanc' and Exeter Book Riddle 83: An Ecological Connection." *Germanic Notes and Reviews* 31 (2000): 18–24.

Neville, Jennifer. *Representations of the Natural World in Old English Poetry*. Cambridge Studies in Anglo-Saxon England 27. Cambridge: Cambridge University Press, 1999.

- "Making Their Own Sweet Time: The Scribes of Anglo-Saxon Chronicle A." In *The MedievalChronicle II: Proceedings of the 2nd International Congress on the Medieval Chronicle*. Ed. Erik Kooper, 166–77. Costerus, n.s., 144. Amsterdam: Rodopi, 2002.
- "Women." In *Reading the Lord of the Rings: New Writings on Tolkien's Classic*. Ed. Robert Eaglestone, 101–10. London: Continuum, 2005.
- "Hrothgar's Horses: Feral or Thoroughbred?" *ASE* 35 (2006): 131–57.
- "Fostering the Cuckoo: Exeter Book Riddle 9." *RES*, n.s., 58 (2007): 431–46.
- "Pondering the Soul's Journey in *Exeter Book* Riddle 43." In *The World of Travellers: Exploration and Imagination*. Ed. Kees Dekker, Karen E. Olsen, and Tette Hofstra, 147–62. Germania Latina 7. Leuven: Peeters, 2009.
- "The Unexpected Treasures of the 'Implement Trope': Hierarchical Relationships in the Old English Riddles." *RES*, n.s., 62 (2011): 505–19.
- "Joyous Play and Bitter Tears: The *Riddles* and the Elegies." In *Beowulf and Other Stories: A New Introduction to Old English, Old Icelandic and Anglo-Norman Literatures*. Ed. Richard North and Joe Allard, 130–59. Harlow: Pearson, 2007.
- "Speaking the Unspeakable: Appetite for Deconstruction in *Exeter Book* Riddle 12." *ES* 93 (2012): 519–28.
- "The Exeter Book Riddles' Precarious Insights into Wooden Artefacts." In *Trees and Timber in the Anglo-Saxon World*. Ed. Michael D.J. Bintley and Michael G. Shapland, 122–43. Oxford: Oxford University Press, 2013.
- "Redeeming Beowulf: The Heroic Idiom as Marker of Quality in Old English Poetry." In *Narration and Hero: Recounting the Deeds of Heroes in Literature and Art of the Early Medieval Period*. Ed. Victor Millet and Heike Sahm, 45–69. Ergänzungsbände zum Reallexikon der Germanischen Altertumskunde 87. Berlin: De Gruyter, 2014.
- "Enigmatic Discourses in Riddle 49 (and Another New Solution)." Paper presented at the International Medieval Congress (Leeds) on 9 July 2015.
- "Commentary for Exeter Riddle 42." *The Riddle Ages* (blog), 24 September 2015. https://theriddleages.com/riddles/post/commentary-for-exeter-riddle-42/
- "Space for Uncertainty: The Movement of Celestial Bodies in the Exeter Book Riddles." In *Heavenly Discourses*. Proceedings of the Heavenly Discourses: Myth, Astronomy and Culture Conference held in Bristol, UK 14–16 October 2011. Ed. Nicholas Campion, 47–56. Ceredigion: Sophia Centre Press, 2016.

- "A Modest Proposal: Titles for the *Exeter Book Riddles*." *MÆ* 88 (2019): 116–23.
- "Sorting Out the Rings: Astronomical Tropes in *Þragbysig* (R.4)." In *Riddles at Work in the Early Medieval Tradition: Words, Ideas, Interactions*. Ed. Megan Cavell and Jennifer Neville, 21–39. Manchester Medieval Literature and Culture 32. Manchester: Manchester University Press, 2020.

Newman, Barbara. *Medieval Crossover: Reading the Secular against the Sacred*. Notre Dame, IN: University of Notre Dame Press, 2013.

Nicholson, Lewis E., ed. *An Anthology of Beowulf Criticism*. Notre Dame, IN: University of Notre Dame Press, 1963.

Nicholson, Lewis E., and Dolores Warwick Frese, eds. *Anglo-Saxon Poetry: Essays in Appreciation for John C. McGalliard*. Notre Dame, IN: University of Notre Dame Press, 1975.

Niles, John D. "Exeter Book Riddle 74 and the Play of the Text." *ASE* 27 (1998): 169–207.
- "Byrhtnoth's Laughter and the Poetics of Gesture." In *Humour in Anglo-Saxon Literature*. Ed. Jonathan Wilcox, 11–32. Cambridge: Brewer, 2000.
- *Old English Enigmatic Poems and the Play of the Texts*. Turnhout: Brepols, 2006.
- "Trial by Ordeal in Anglo-Saxon England: What's the Problem with Barley?" In *Early Medieval Studies in Memory of Patrick Wormald*. Ed. Steven Baxter, Catherine Karkov, Janet L. Nelson, and David Pelteret, 369–82. Aldershot: Ashgate, 2009.
- *God's Exiles and English Verse: On the Exeter Anthology of Old English Poetry*. Exeter: University of Exeter Press, 2019.

Norris, Robin. "Sad Men in *Beowulf*." In *Dating Beowulf: Studies in Intimacy*. Ed. Daniel C. Remein and Erica Weaver, 210–26. Manchester Medieval Literature and Culture 30. Manchester: Manchester University Press, 2020.

North, Richard, and Joe Allard, eds. *Beowulf and Other Stories: A New Introduction to Old English, Old Icelandic and Anglo-Norman Literatures*. Harlow: Pearson, 2007.

Nuck, R. "Zu Trautmanns Deutung des ersten und neunundachtzigsten Rätsels." *Anglia* 10 (1888): 390–4.

Oberman, Miller Wolf. "*Dyre Cræft*: New Translations of Exeter Riddle Fragments *Modor Monigra* (R.84), *Se Wiht Wombe Hæfde* (R.89), and *Brunra Beot* (R.92), Accompanied by Notes on Process." In *Riddles at Work in the Early Medieval Tradition: Words, Ideas, Interactions*. Ed. Megan Cavell and Jennifer Neville, 277–87. Manchester Medieval Literature and Culture 32. Manchester: Manchester University Press, 2020.

O'Donnell, J. Reginald, ed. *Essays in Honour of Anton Charles Pegis*. Toronto: Pontifical Institute of Mediaeval Studies, 1974.

Ogura, Michiko, and Hans Sauer, eds. *Aspects of Medieval English Language and Literature*. Studies in English Medieval Language and Literature 55. Bern: Peter Lang, 2019.

Okasha, Elisabeth. "Old English *Hring* in Riddles 48 and 59." *MÆ* 62 (1993): 61–9.
O'Keeffe, Katherine O'Brien. "Exeter Riddle 40: The Art of an Old English Translator." *Proceedings of the Patristic, Mediaeval, and Renaissance Conference* 5 (1983 for 1980): 107–17.
– "The Text of Aldhelm's Enigma no. c in Oxford, Bodleian Library, Rawlinson C.697 and Exeter Riddle 40." *ASE* 14 (1985): 61–73.
– *Old English Shorter Poems: Basic Readings*. Basic Readings in Anglo-Saxon England 3; Garland Reference Library of the Humanities 1432. New York: Garland, 1994.
O'Keeffe, Katherine O'Brien, and Andy Orchard, eds. *Latin Learning and English Lore: Studies in Anglo-Saxon Literature for Michael Lapidge*. 2 vols. Toronto: University of Toronto Press, 2005.
Olsen, Karin E. "Warriors and Their Battle Gear: Conceptual Blending in *Anhaga* (R.5) and *Wæpnum Awyrged* (R.20)." In *Riddles at Work in the Early Medieval Tradition: Words, Ideas, Interactions*. Ed. Megan Cavell and Jennifer Neville, 111–27. Manchester Medieval Literature and Culture 32. Manchester: Manchester University Press, 2020.
Olson, Vibeke. "Penetrating the Void: Picturing the Wound in Christ's Side as a Performative Space." In *Wounds and Wound Repair in Medieval Culture*. Ed. Larissa Tracey and Kelly DeVries, 313–39. Explorations in Medieval Culture 1. Leiden: Brill, 2015.
Orchard, Andy. "Conspicuous Heroism: Abraham, Prudentius, and the Old English Verse *Genesis*." In *The Poems of MS Junius 11: Basic Readings*. Ed. R. M. Liuzza, 119–36. New York: Routledge, 2002.
– "Enigma Variations: The Anglo-Saxon Riddle-Tradition." In *Latin Learning and English Lore: Studies in Anglo-Saxon Literature for Michael Lapidge*. 2 vols. Ed. Katherine O'Brien O'Keeffe and Andy Orchard, 1:284–304. Toronto: University of Toronto Press, 2005.
– "Performing Writing and Singing Silence in the Anglo-Saxon Riddle-Tradition." In *Or Words to That Effect: Orality and the Writing of Literary History*. Ed. Daniel F. Chamberlain and J. Edward Chamberlain, 73–91. Comparative History of Literatures in European Languages 28. Amsterdam: John Benjamins, 2016.
– "The Originality of *Andreas*." In *Old English Philology: Studies in Honour of R.D. Fulk*. Ed. Leonard Neidorf, Rafael J. Pascual, and Tom Shippey, 331–52. Anglo-Saxon Studies 31. Cambridge: Brewer, 2016.
Orford, Ben, and Lois Orford. "How to Turn a Bowl on the Pole Lathe with Ben Orford," five part series on YouTube.
Oring, Elliott. *Jokes and Their Relations*. Lexington: University Press of Kentucky, 1992.
Orton, Peter. "The Technique of Object-Personification in *The Dream of the Rood* and a Comparison with the Old English Riddles." *LSE*, n.s., 11 (1980): 1–18.

- "The Speaker in *The Husband's Message.*" *LSE*, n.s., 12 (1981): 43–56.
- "Burning Idols, Burning Bridges: Bede, Conversion and *Beowulf.*" *LSE*, n.s., 36 (2005): 5–46.
- "Old English Riddles and Cognitive Linguistics." Paper given to the London Old and Middle English Research Seminar, 20 June 2009.
- "The Exeter Book *Riddles*: Authorship and Transmission." *ASE* 44 (2015): 131–62.

Osborn, Marijane. "From the Old English, the Exeter Book, #31 and #61: Two Anglo-Saxon Riddles." *Hyperion* 13–14 (1976): 74.
- "Old English Ing and His Wain." *NM* 81 (1980): 388–89.
- "'Skep' (*Beinenkorb*, **beoleap*) as a Culture-Specific Solution to *Exeter Book* Riddle 17." *ANQ* 18 (2005): 8–18.
- "Anglo-Saxon Tame Bees: Some Evidence for Beekeeping from Riddles and Charms." *NM* 107 (2006): 271–83.
- "Vixen as Hero: Solving Exeter Book Riddle 15." In *The Hero Recovered: Essays on Medieval Heroism in Honor of George Clark*. Ed. Robin Waugh and James Weldon, 173–87. Kalamazoo, MI: Medieval Institute, 2010.

Overing, Gillian R. *Language, Sign, and Gender in Beowulf*. Carbondale: Southern Illinois University Press, 1990.

Oxford English Dictionary Online. 3rd ed. Oxford: Oxford University Press, 2013. www.oed.com

Owen-Crocker, Gale R. *Dress in Anglo-Saxon England*. Revised ed. Cambridge: Brewer, 2004.
- "'Seldom ... Does the Deadly Spear Rest for Long': Weapons and Armour." In *The Material Culture of Daily Living in the Anglo-Saxon World*. Ed. Maren Clegg Hyer and Gale R. Owen-Crocker, 201–30. Exeter: Exeter University Press, 2011.

Owen-Crocker, Gale R., Elizabeth Coatsworth, and Maria Hayward, eds. *Encyclopedia of Medieval Dress and Textiles of the British Isles, c. 450–1450*. Leiden: Brill, 2012.

Owen-Crocker, Gale R., and B.W. Schneider, eds. *The Anglo-Saxons: The World through Their Eyes*, BAR British Series 595. Oxford: Archaeopress, 2014.

Padelford, Frederick Morgan. *Old English Musical Terms*. Bonner Beiträge zur Anglistik 4. Bonn: P. Hanstein, 1899.

Page, R.I. *An Introduction to English Runes*. 2nd ed. Woodbridge: Boydell, 1999.

Pantaleoni, Federico. "Aldhelm's *Lorica*, the *Leiden Riddle*, and *Riddle* 33 of the Exeter Book." In *In principio fuit interpres*. Ed. Alessandra Petrina, 163–73. The Medieval Translator/Traduire au Moyen Age 15. Turnhout: Brepols, 2013.

Parkes, M.B., and Andrew G. Watson, eds. *Medieval Scribes, Manuscripts and Libraries: Essays Presented to N. R. Ker*. London: Scolar, 1978.

Parsons, Ben. "'The Werste Lay That Euer Harper Sange with Harp': The Forms of Early Middle English Satire." *Comitatus* 39 (2008): 113–36.

Payer, Pierre J. *Sex and the New Medieval Literature of Confession, 1150–1300*. Studies and Texts 163; Medieval Law and Theology 1. Toronto: Pontifical Institute of Mediaeval Studies, 2009.

Paz, James. "Commentary for Exeter Riddle 43." *The Riddle Ages* (blog), 17 August 2015. https://theriddleages.com/riddles/post/commentary-for-exeter-riddle-43/.

– "Commentary for Exeter Riddle 74" (19 December 2017), *The Riddle Ages* (blog), https://theriddleages.com/riddles/post/commentary-for-exeter-riddle-74/.

– *Nonhuman Voices in Anglo-Saxon Literature and Material Culture*. Manchester Medieval Literature and Culture. Manchester: Manchester University Press, 2017.

– "Mind, Mood, and Meteorology in *Þrymful Þeow* (R.1–3)." In *Riddles at Work in the Early Medieval Tradition: Words, Ideas, Interactions*. Ed. Megan Cavell and Jennifer Neville, 193–209. Manchester Medieval Literature and Culture 32. Manchester: Manchester University Press, 2020.

Pelteret, David A.E. *Slavery in Early Mediaeval England from the Reign of Alfred until the Twelfth Century*. Woodbridge: Boydell, 1995.

Pepicello, W.J., and Thomas A. Green. *The Language of Riddles: New Perspectives*. Columbus: Ohio State University Press, 1984.

Persson, K. "*Scip* : A Proposed Solution to Exeter Book Riddle 95." In *The Maritime World of the Anglo-Saxons*. Ed. Stacy S. Klein, William Schipper, and Shannon Lewis-Simpson, 227–46. Medieval and Renaissance Texts and Studies 448; Essays in Anglo-Saxon Studies 5. Tempe: Arizona Centre for Medieval and Renaissance Studies, 2014.

Petrina, Alessandra, ed. *In principio fuit interpres*. The Medieval Translator/Traduire au Moyen Age 15. Turnhout: Brepols, 2013.

Petty, Christina. "Warp Weighted Looms: Then and Now: Anglo-Saxon and Viking Archaeological Evidence and Modern Practitioners." PhD diss., University of Manchester, 2014.

Pfeffer, Wendy. "Spring, Love, Birdsong: The Nightingale in Two Cultures." In *Beasts and Birds of the Middle Ages: The Bestiary and its Legacy*. Ed. Willene B. Clark and Meradith T. McMunn, 88–95. Philadelphia: University of Pennsylvania Press, 1989.

Pinsker, Hans. "Neue Deutungen für zwei altenglische Rätsel (Krapp-Dobbie 17 und 30)." *Anglia* 91 (1973): 11–17.

– "Ein verschollenes altenglisches Ratsel?" In *A Yearbook of Studies in English Language and Literature*. Ed. Siegfried Korninger, 53–59. Weiner Beiträge zur englischen Philologie 78. Vienna: Braumuller, 1981.

- "Bemerkungen zum ae. Sturmrätsel." *Arbeiten aus Anglistik und Amerikanistik* 6 (1981): 221–6.
Pluskowski, Aleksander, ed. *Just Skin and Bones? New Perspectives on Human-Animal Relations in the Historical Past.* BAR International Series 1410. Oxford: Archaeopress, 2005.
Pope, John C. "An Unsuspected Lacuna in the Exeter Book: Divorce Proceedings for an Ill-Matched Couple in the Old English Riddles." *Speculum* 49 (1974): 615–22.
- "Palaeography and Poetry: Some Solved and Unsolved Problems of the Exeter Book." In *Medieval Scribes, Manuscripts and Libraries: Essays Presented to N.R. Ker.* Ed. M.B. Parkes and Andrew G. Watson, 25–65. London: Scolar, 1978.
Porter, John, trans. *Anglo-Saxon Riddles.* Hockwold-cum-Wilton: Anglo-Saxon Books, 1995.
Portnoy, Phyllis. *The Remnant: Essays on a Theme in Old English Verse.* London: Runetree, 2005.
- "*Laf*-Craft in Five Old English Riddles (K-D 5, 20, 56, 71, 91)." *Neophil* 97 (2013): 555–79.
Powell, Kathryn, and Donald G. Scragg, eds. *Apocryphal Texts and Traditions in Anglo-Saxon England.* Cambridge: Brewer, 2003.
Prehn, August. *Komposition und Quellen der Rätsel des Exeterbuches.* Neuphilologische Studien 3. Paderborn: Schöningh, 1883.
Preston, Todd. "An Alternative Solution to Exeter Book Riddle 77." *Viator* 42 (2011): 25–34.
Price, Helen. "Commentary for Exeter Riddle 41." *The Riddle Ages* (blog), 21 July 2015. https://theriddleages.com/riddles/post/commentary-for-exeter-riddle-41/.
- "A Hive of Activity: Realigning the Figure of the Bee in the Mead-Making Network of *Exeter Book* Riddle 27." *Postmedieval* 8 (2017): doi:10.1057/pmed.2015.1.
Pulsiano, Phillip, and Kirsten Wolf, "*Exeter Book* Riddle 57: Those Damned Souls, Again." *Germanic Notes* 22 (1991): 2–5.
Rader, Romina, Will Edwards, David A. Westcott, Saul A. Cunningham, and Bradley G. Howlett. "Diurnal Effectiveness of Pollination by Bees and Flies in Agricultural *Brassica rapa*: Implications for Ecosystem Resilience." *Basic and Applied Ecology* 14 (2013): 20–7.
Ramey, Peter. "Writing Speaks: Oral Poetics and Writing Technology in the Exeter Book Riddles." *PQ* 92 (2013): 335–56.
- "Crafting Strangeness: Wonder Terminology in the Exeter Book Riddles and the Anglo-Latin Enigmata." *RES* 69 (2018): 201–15.
Remein, Daniel C., and Erica Weaver, eds. *Dating Beowulf: Studies in Intimacy.* Manchester Medieval Literature and Culture 30. Manchester: Manchester University Press, 2020.

Renoir, Alain. "A Reading Context for the Wife's Lament." In *Anglo-Saxon Poetry: Essays in Appreciation for John C. McGalliard*. Ed. Lewis E. Nicholson and Dolores Warwick Frese, 224–41. Notre Dame, IN: Notre Dame University Press, 1975.

Reisner, Thomas A. "Riddle 75 (Exeter Book)." *Explicator* 28 (1970): 146–7.

Revard, Carter. "Beads, Wampum, Money, Words – and Old English Riddles." *American Indian Culture and Research Journal* 23 (1999): 177–89.

– "Some Riddles in Old English Alliterative Verse." *Florilegium* 18 (2001): 1–9.

Reynolds, Andrew J. *Anglo-Saxon Deviant Burial Customs*. Oxford: Oxford University Press, 2009.

Rhodes, Sharon E. "*Wundor* and *Wrætlic*: The Anatomy of Wonder in the Sex Riddles." In *Riddles at Work in the Early Medieval Tradition: Words, Ideas, Interactions*. Ed. Megan Cavell and Jennifer Neville, 40–56. Manchester Medieval Literature and Culture 32. Manchester: Manchester University Press, 2020.

Riedinger, Anita R. "The Formulaic Relationship between *Beowulf* and *Andreas*." In *Heroic Poetry in the Anglo-Saxon Period: Studies in Honor of Jess B. Bessinger Jr.*. Ed. Helen Damico and John Leyerle, 283–312. Studies in Medieval Culture 32. Kalamazoo, MI: Medieval Institute, 1993.

– "The Formulaic Style in the Old English Riddles." *SN* 75 (2003): 30–43.

Risden, Edward L. "Heroic Humor in *Beowulf*." In *Humour in Anglo-Saxon Literature*. Ed. Jonathan Wilcox, 71–8. Cambridge: Brewer, 2000.

– "Script-Based Semantic Theory of Humor and the Old English Riddles." *Publications of the Medieval Association of the Midwest* 8 (2001): 61–70.

– "Some Thematic Implications of Humor in Anglo-Saxon Poetry." *In Geardagum* 22 (2001): 77–90.

Rissanen, Matti. "Nathwæt in the Exeter Book Riddles." *ANQ* 24 (1986): 116–20.

Roberts, Adam. *The Riddles of the Hobbit*. Basingstoke: Palgrave Macmillan, 2013.

Roberts, Jane. "Some Thoughts about the Old English WEAVING and SPINNING Terms." In *Aspects of Medieval English Language and Literature*. Ed. Michiko Ogura and Hans Sauer, 259–72. Studies in English Medieval Language and Literature 55. Bern: Peter Lang, 2019.

Roberts, Jane, Christian Kay, with Lynne Grundy, eds. *A Thesaurus of Old English*. 2 vols. King's College London Medieval Studies 11. London: King's College London, Centre for Late Antique and Medieval Studies, 1995. As of 2017 online at http://oldenglishthesaurus.arts.gla.ac.uk.

Roberts, Jane, and Janet Nelson, eds. *Essays on Anglo-Saxon and Related Themes in Memory of Lynne Grundy*. London: King's College London, 2000.

Robinson, Fred C. "Artful Ambiguities in the Old English 'Book Moth' Riddle." In *Anglo-Saxon Poetry: Essays in Appreciation for John C. McGalliard*.

Ed. Lewis E. Nicholson and Dolores W. Frese, 355–62. Notre Dame: University of Notre Dame Press, 1975.
- "Understanding an Old English Wisdom Verse: Maxims II, lines 10ff." In *The Wisdom of Poetry: Essays in Early English Literature in Honor of Morton W. Bloomfield*. Ed. Larry Dean Benson and Siegfried Wenzel, 1–11, 261–4. Kalamazoo: Medieval Institute Publications, Western Michigan University, 1982.
- *Beowulf and the Appositive Style*. Knoxville: University of Tennessee Press, 1985.

Robson, Peter. "'Feorran broht:' Exeter Book Riddle 12 and the Commodification of the Exotic." In *Authority and Subjugation in Writing of Medieval Wales*. Ed. Ruth Kennedy and Simon Meecham-Jones, 71–84. Basingstoke: Palgrave Macmillan, 2008.

Rodrigues, Louis J. *Anglo-Saxon Verse Runes*. Felinfach: Llanerch, 1992.

Roscoe, Brett. "Commentary for Exeter Riddle 59." *The Riddle Ages* (blog), 27 February 2017. https://theriddleages.com/riddles/post/commentary-for-exeter-riddle-59/.
- "Commentary for Exeter Riddle 60." *The Riddle Ages* (blog), 24 April 2017. https://theriddleages.com/riddles/post/commentary-for-exeter-riddle-60/.
- "Commentary for Exeter Riddle 67." *The Riddle Ages* (blog), 9 October 2017. https://theriddleages.com/riddles/post/commentary-for-exeter-riddle-67/.
- "Commentary for Exeter Riddle 95." *The Riddle Ages* (blog), 18 February 2021. https://theriddleages.com/riddles/post/commentary-for-exeter-riddle-95/.

Rowe, Elizabeth Ashman. "Irony in the Old English and Old Norse Interrogative Situation." *Neophil* 73 (1989): 477–9.

Rüden, Michael von. *Wlanc und Derivate im Alt- und Mittelenglischen: Eine wortgeschichtliche Studie*. Europäische Hochschulschriften 15; Angelsächsische Sprache und Literatur 61. Frankfurt: Peter Lang, 1978.

Rudolf, Winfried. "Riddling and Reading: Iconicity and Logogriphs in Exeter Book Riddles 23 and 45." *Anglia* 130 (2012): 499–525.

Rulon-Miller, Nina. "Sexual Humor and Fettered Desire in Exeter Book Riddle 12." In *Humour in Anglo-Saxon Literature*. Ed. Jonathan Wilcox, 99–126. Cambridge: Brewer, 2000.

Russell, J. Stephen, ed. *Allegoresis: The Craft of Allegory in Medieval Literature*. New York: Garland, 1988.

Russom, Geoffrey. "Exeter Riddle 47: A Moth Laid Waste to Fame." *PQ* 56 (1977): 129–36.

Ruttner, Friedrich, Eric Milner, and John E. Dews, eds. *The Dark European Honey Bee: Apis mellifera mellifera Linnaeus 1758*. 2nd ed. London: Writers Printshop, 2004.

Salvador-Bello, Mercedes. "The Bird Riddles of the Exeter Book." MA diss., University of Seville, 1994.
- "Direct and Indirect Clues: Exeter Riddle no 74 Reconsidered." *NM* 99 (1998): 17–29.

- "The Evening Singer of Riddle 8 (K-D)." *Spanish Society for Medieval English Language and Literature (SELIM)* 9 (1999): 57–68.
- "Word-Play in the Old English Riddles of the Exeter Book." In *AEDEAN: Select Papers in Language, Literature, and Culture: Proceedings of the 17th International Conference*. Ed. Javier Pérez Guerra, 359–62. Vigo: Universidad de Vigo, 2000.
- "A Case of Editorial Hypercorrection in Exeter Riddle 35 (8b)." *ANQ* 14 (2001): 5–11.
- "The Key to the Body: Unlocking Riddles 42–46." In *Naked before God: Uncovering the Body in Anglo-Saxon England*. Ed. Benjamin C. Withers and Jonathan Wilcox, 60–96. Medieval European Studies 3. Morgantown: West Virginia University Press, 2003.
- "The Oyster and the Crab: A Riddle Duo (nos. 77 and 78) in the Exeter Book." *Modern Philology* 101 (2004): 400–19.
- "The Sexual Riddle Type in Aldhelm's Enigmata, the Exeter Book, and Early Medieval Latin." *PQ* 90 (2011): 357–85.
- *Isidorean Perceptions of Order: The Exeter Book Riddles and Medieval Latin Enigmata*. Medieval European Studies 17. Morgantown: West Virginia University Press, 2015.
- "Exeter Book Riddle 90 under a New Light: A School Drill in Hisperic Robes." *Neophil* 102 (2018): 107–23.

Sayer, Duncan, and Sam D. Dickinson, "Reconsidering Obstetric Death and Female Fertility in Anglo-Saxon England." *World Archaeology* 45 (2013): 285–97.

Sayers, William. "Exeter Book Riddle No. 5: Whetstone?" *NM* 97 (1996): 387–92.
- "Exeter Book Riddle 17 and the L-Rune: British **lester* 'vessel, oat-straw hive?'" *ANQ* 19 (2006): 4–8.

Scarry, Elaine. *The Body in Pain: The Making and Unmaking of the World*. Oxford: Oxford University Press, 1985.

Scattergood, John. "Eating the Book: Riddle 47 and Memory." In *Text and Gloss: Studies in Insular Learning and Literature Presented to Joseph Donovan Pheifer*. Ed. Helen Conrad O'Briain, Anne Marie D'Arcy, and John Scattergood, 119–27. Dublin: Four Courts Press, 1999.

Schaefer, Ursula. "From an Aesthetic Point of View: Receptional Aspects of Old English Poetry." In *De Gustibus: Essays for Alain Renoir*. Ed. John Miles Foley, J. Chris Womack, and Whitney A. Womack, 494–541. Albert Bates Lord Studies in Oral Tradition 11. New York: Garland, 1992.

Schlauch, Margaret. "*The Dream of the Rood* as Prosopopoeia." In *Essential Articles for the Study of Old English Poetry*. Ed. Jess B. Bessinger Jr. and Stanley J. Kahrl, 428–41. Hamden, CT: Archon, 1968.

Schneider, Karl. "Zu vier ae. Rätseln." In *Gedenkschrift für Jost Trier*. Ed. Hartmut Beckers and Hans Schwarz, 330–54. Köln: Böhlau, 1975.

Scragg, Donald G. and Paul E. Szarmach, eds. *The Editing of Old English.* Cambridge: Brewer, 1994.
Screech, M.A. trans. *Rabelais: Gargantua and Pantagruel.* London: Penguin, 2006.
Sebo, Erin. "The Creation Riddle and Anglo-Saxon Cosmology." In *The Anglo-Saxons: The World through Their Eyes.* Ed. Gale R. Owen-Crocker and Brian W. Schneider, 149–56. BAR British Series 595. Oxford: Archaeopress, 2014.
– "Commentary for Exeter Riddle 66." *The Riddle Ages* (blog), 26 September 2017. https://theriddleages.com/riddles/post/commentary-for-exeter-riddle-66/.
– *In Enigmate: The History of a Riddle, 400–1500.* Dublin Studies in Medieval and Renaissance Literature 8. Dublin: Four Courts Press, 2018.
– "The (Non-)Reception of Samson's Riddle in Anglo-Saxon England." *ANQ,* 32 (2019): 205–8
– "Commentary for Exeter Riddle 94." *The Riddle Ages* (blog), 9 June 2021. https://theriddleages.com/riddles/post/commentary-for-exeter-riddle-94/.
Shane, Adolph. *Archery Tackle: How to Make It and How to Use It.* Azle, TX: Bois d'Arc Press, 1936; repr. 1990.
Sharpe, John L., III, and Kimberly Van Kampen, eds. *The Bible as Book: The Manuscript Tradition.* New Castle, DE: Oak Knoll, 1998.
Shippey, T.A. *Poems of Wisdom and Learning in Old English.* Cambridge: Brewer, 1976.
– "Boar and Badger: An Old English Heroic Antithesis?" *LSE,* n.s., 16 (1985): 220–39.
– "'Grim Wordplay': Folly and Wisdom in Anglo-Saxon Humor." In *Humour in Anglo-Saxon Literature.* Ed. Jonathan Wilcox, 33–48. Cambridge: Brewer, 2000.
Shklovsky, Victor. "Art as Technique." In *Russian Formalist Criticism: Four Essays.* Trans. Lee T. Lemon and Marion J. Reis, 3–24. Lincoln: University of Nebraska Press, 1965.
Shook, Laurence. K. "Old English Riddle I: Fire." *Mediaeval Studies* 8 (1946): 316–18.
– "Old English Riddle 28 – *Testudo* (Tortoise-Lyre)." *Mediaeval Studies* 20 (1958): 93–7.
– "Old English Riddle No. 20: *Heoruswealwe.*" In *Franciplegius: Medieval and Linguistic Studies in Honor of Francis Peabody Magoun Jr.* Ed. Jess B. Bessinger Jr. and Robert P. Creed, 194–204. New York: Allen and Unwin, 1965.
– "Riddles Relating to the Anglo-Saxon Scriptorium." In *Essays in Honour of Anton Charles Pegis.* Ed. J. Reginald O'Donnell, 215–36. Toronto: Pontifical Institute of Mediaeval Studies, 1974.
Siikala, Anna-Leena, ed. *Myth and Mentality: Studies in Folklore and Popular Thought.* Helsinki, Finland: Finnish Literature Society, 2002.
Silvestre, Juan Camilo Conde. "The Semiotics of Allegory in Early Medieval Hermeneutics and the Interpretation of *The Seafarer.*" *Atlantis* 16 (1994): 71–90.

Simms, Douglas P.A. "Exeter Book Riddle 19: Its Runes and Transmission." *N&Q* 63 (2016): 351–54.
Sisam, Kenneth. *Studies in the History of Old English Literature*. Oxford: Clarendon, 1953.
Smith, D.K. "Humor in Hiding: Laughter between the Sheets in the Exeter Book Riddles." In *Humour in Anglo-Saxon England*. Ed. Jonathan Wilcox, 79–98. Cambridge: Brewer, 2000.
Smith, Julia M.H. "Gender and Ideology in the Early Middle Ages." *Studies in Church History* 34 (1998): 51–73.
Smith, Scott Thompson. "Faith and Forfeiture in the Old English *Genesis A*." *Modern Philology* 111 (2014): 593–615.
Smithers, G.V. "The Meaning of *The Seafarer* and *The Wanderer* (cont)." *MÆ* 28 (1959): 1–22.
Sonke, Emma. "Zu dem 25 Rätsel des Exeterbuches." *Englische Studien*, 37 (1907): 313–18.
Soper, Harriet. "Reading the Exeter Book Riddles as Life-Writing." *RES* 68 (2017): 841–65.
Sorrell, Paul. "Oaks, Ships, Riddles and the Old English *Rune Poem*." *ASE* 19 (1990): 103–16.
– "A Bee in My Bonnet: Solving Riddle 17 of the Exeter Book." In *New Windows on a Woman's World: Essays for Jocelyn Harris*. 2 vols. Ed. Colin Gibson and Lisa Marr, 2.544–53. Otago Studies in English 9. Dunedin, NZ: Department of English, University of Otago, 2005.
Spamer, James B. "The Old English Bee Charm: An Explication." *Journal of Indo-European Studies* 6 (1978): 279–91.
Spitzer, Leo. *Linguistics and Literary History: Essays in Stylistics*. Princeton, NJ: Princeton University Press, 1948.
Stallybrass, Peter, and Allon White. *The Politics and Poetics of Transgression*. Ithaca, NY: Cornell University Press, 1986.
Stanley, E.G. "Stanley B. Greenfield's Solution of Riddle (ASPR) 39: 'Dream.'" *N&Q* 38 (1991): 148–9.
– "Heroic Aspects of the Exeter Book Riddles." In *Prosody and Poetics in the Early Middle Ages: Essays in Honour of C.B. Hieatt*. Ed. M.J. Toswell, 197–218. Toronto: University of Toronto Press, 1995.
– "Exeter Book *Riddle 11*: 'Alcohol' and Its Effects." *N&Q* 61 (2014): 182–5.
– "The Gnomes of Cotton MS Tiberius B.I." *N&Q* 62 (2015): 190–9.
– "Exeter Book *Riddles*, I: *Riddles 60* and *17*." *N&Q* 64 (2017): 213–17.
– "Exeter Book *Riddles*, II: The Significant but Often Misleading Opening Word." *N&Q* 64 (2017): 355–65.
Stanton, Robert. "Commentary for Exeter Riddle 72." *The Riddle Ages* (blog), 19 December 2017. https://theriddleages.com/riddles/post/commentary-for-exeter-riddle-72/

- "Sound, Voice, and Articulation in the Exeter Book Riddles." In *Riddles at Work in the Early Medieval Tradition: Words, Ideas, Interactions*. Ed. Megan Cavell and Jennifer Neville, 92–106. Manchester Medieval Literature and Culture 32. Manchester: Manchester University Press, 2020.
Stévanovitch, Collette. "Exeter Book *Riddle 70A*: Nose?" *N&Q* 42 (1995): 8–10.
Stevens, Martin, and Jerome Mandel, eds. *Old English Literature: Twenty-Two Analytical Essays*. Lincoln: University of Nebraska Press 1968.
Stewart, Ann Harleman. "Old English Riddle 47 as Stylistic Parody." *Papers on Language and Literature* 11 (1975): 227–41.
- "Kenning and Riddle in Old English." *Papers on Language and Literature* 15 (1979): 115–36.
- "The Solution to Old English Riddle 4." *SP* 78 (1981): 52–61.
- "Double Entendre in the Old English Riddles." *Lore and Language* 3 (1983): 39–52.
- "Inference in Socio-Historical Linguistics: The Example of Old English Word-Play." *Folia Linguistica Historica* 6 (1985): 63–85.
Strobl, Joseph. "Zur Spruchdichtung bei den Angelsachsen." *Zeitschrift für deutsches Altertum* 31 (1887): 54–64.
Strohm, Paul. *Theory and the Premodern Text*. Minneapolis: University of Minnesota Press, 2000.
Sutherland, A.C. "The Paradoxes in the Riddles of the Anglo-Saxons." PhD diss., Cambridge, 1983.
Swaen, A.E.H. "Het 18e Oudengelsche Raadsel." *Neophil* 4 (1919): 258–62.
- "Riddle XIII (XVI)." *Neophil* 26 (1941): 228–31.
- "The Anglo-Saxon Horn Riddles." *Neophil* 26 (1941): 298–302.
- "Riddle 9 (6, 8)." *SN* 14 (1941–1942): 67–70.
- "Riddle 63 (60, 62)." *Neophil* 27 (1942): 220.
- "Riddle 9 (12)." *Neophil* 30 (1945): 126.
- "Riddle 8 (10, 11)." *Neophil* 30 (1945): 126–7.
- "Notes on Anglo-Saxon Riddles." *Neophil* 31 (1946): 145–8.
Swain, Larry J. "Of Hands, Halls, and Heroes: Grendel's Hand, Hrothgar's Power, and the Problem of *Stapol* in *Beowulf*." *Anglia* 134 (2016): 260–84.
Swanton, Michael J. *The Spearheads of the Anglo-Saxon Settlements*. Leeds: Royal Archaeological Institute, 1973.
Symons, Victoria. "Runes and Roman Letters in the Writing of Old English Manuscripts." PhD diss., University College London, 2013.
- "Doing Things with Words: Language and Perception in Old English Riddles and Charms." In *Sensory Perception in the Medieval West*. Ed. Simon Thomson and Michael Bintley, 123–40. Utrecht Studies in Medieval Literacy 34. Turnhout: Brepols, 2016.
- *Runes and Roman Letters in Anglo-Saxon Manuscripts*. Ergänzungsbände zum Reallexikon der Germanischen Altertumskunde 99. Berlin: Walter de Gruyter, 2016.

- "Commentary for Exeter Riddle 58." *The Riddle Ages* (blog), 6 February 2017. https://theriddleages.com/riddles/post/commentary-for-exeter-riddle-58/.
- "Commentary for Exeter Riddle 62." *The Riddle Ages* (blog), 22 May 2017. https://theriddleages.com/riddles/post/commentary-for-exeter-riddle-62/.
- "Commentary for Exeter Riddle 64." *The Riddle Ages* (blog), 4 August 2017. https://theriddleages.com/riddles/post/commentary-for-exeter-riddle-64/.
- "Commentary for Exeter Riddle 73." *The Riddle Ages* (blog), 11 December 2017. https://theriddleages.com/riddles/post/commentary-for-exeter-riddle-73/.

Talentino, Arnold. "Riddle 30: The Vehicle of the Cross." *Neophil* 65 (1981): 129–36.

Tanke, John William. "Riddles of Subjectivity in Old English Poetry." PhD diss., Cornell University, 1993.
- "*Wonfeax Wale*: Ideology and Figuration in the Sexual Riddles of the Exeter Book." In *Class and Gender in Early English Literature: Intersections*. Ed. Britton J. Harwood and Gillian R. Overing, 21–42. Bloomington: Indiana University Press, 1994.
- "The Bachelor-Warrior of Exeter Book Riddle 20." *PQ* 79 (2000): 409–27.
- "Beowulf, Gold-Luck, and God's Will." *SP* 99 (2002): 356–79.

Taylor, Archer. *The Literary Riddle before 1600*. Berkeley: University of California Press, 1948; repr. Westport, CT: Greenwood, 1976.
- "The Varieties of Riddles." In *Philologica: The Malone Anniversary Studies*. Ed. Thomas Austin Kirby and Henry Bosley Woolf, 1–8. Baltimore, MD: Johns Hopkins, 1949.
- *English Riddles from Oral Tradition*. Berkeley: University of California Press, 1951.

Taylor, Karen J., ed. *Gender Transgressions: Crossing the Normative Barrier in Old French Literature*. London: Routledge, 1998.

Taylor, Keith P. "Mazers, Mead, and the Wolf's-head Tree: A Reconsideration of Old English *Riddle 55*." *JEGP* 94 (1995): 497–512.

Teele, Elinor. "The Heroic Tradition in the Old English Riddles." PhD diss., University of Cambridge, 2004.

Tenner, Edward. *Why Things Bite Back: Technology and the Revenge of Unintended Consequences*. New York: Knopf, 1996.

Thornbury, Emily V. *Becoming a Poet in Anglo-Saxon England*. Cambridge Studies in Medieval Literature 88. Cambridge: Cambridge University Press, 2014.

Tiffany, Daniel. "Lyric Substance: On Riddles, Materialism, and Poetic Obscurity." *Critical Inquiry* 28 (2001): 72–98.

Tigges, Wim. "Signs and Solutions: A Semiotic Approach to the Exeter Book Riddles." In *This Noble Craft: Proceedings of the Xth Research Symposium of the Dutch and Belgian University Teachers of Old and Middle English and Historical Linguistics, Utrecht, 19–20 January 1989*. Ed. Erik Kooper, 59–82. Costerus, n.s., 80. Amsterdam: Rodopi, 1991.

- "Snakes and Ladders: Ambiguity and Coherence in The Exeter Book Riddles and Maxims." In *Companion to Old English Poetry*. Ed. Henk Aertsen and Rolf H. Bremmer, 95–118. Amsterdam: VU University Press, 1994.
Tolkien, J.R.R. *The Hobbit*. 5th ed. 1937; London: HarperCollins, 1995.
- "The Homecoming of Beorhtnoth Beorhthelm's Son." *Essays and Studies*, n.s., 6 (1953): 1–18.
- *The Lord of the Rings*. 1955; London: HarperCollins, 1991.
Toller, T.N. *An Anglo-Saxon Dictionary Based on the MS Collections of the Late Joseph Bosworth*. Revised and enlarged addenda by A. Campbell. 3 vols. Oxford: Clarendon Press, 1898–1921; repr. 1972.
Tongson, Karen. "Queer Fundamentalism." *Social Text* 32 (2014): 117–23.
Toswell, M.J., ed. *Prosody and Poetics in the Early Middle Ages: Essays in Honour of C.B. Hieatt*. Toronto: University of Toronto Press, 1995.
Tracy, Larissa, ed. *Castration and Culture in the Middle Ages*. Woodbridge: Brewer, 2013.
Tracy, Larissa, and Kelly DeVries, eds. *Wounds and Wound Repair in Medieval Culture*. Explorations in Medieval Culture 1. Leiden: Brill, 2015.
Trautmann, Moritz. "Cynewulf und die Rätsel." *Anglia* 6 (1883): 158–69.
- "Zum 89. Rätsel." *Anglia* 7 (1884): Anzeiger, 210–11.
- "Die Auflösung der altenglischen Rätsel." *Anglia Beiblatt* 5 (1894): 46–51.
- "Zu den alt-englischen Rätseln." *Anglia* 17 (1895): 396–400.
- "Alte und neue Antworten auf altenglische Rätsel." *Bonner Beitrage zur Anglistik* 19 (1905): 167–215.
- "Die Auflösung des 11ten (9ten) Rätsels." *Bonner Beiträge zur Anglistik* 17 (1905): 142.
- "Zum Streit um die Altenglischen Rätsel." *Anglia* 36 (1912): 127–33.
- "Zu den Lösungen der Rätsel des Exeterbuchs." *Beiblatt zur Anglia Mitteilungen* 25 (1914): 273–9.
- "Zu meiner Ausgabe der altenglischen Rätsel." *Anglia* 42 (1918): 125–41.
- "Weiteres zu den altenglischen Rätseln und Metrisches." *Anglia* 43 (1919): 245–60.
Tremp, Ernst, and Karl Schmuki, eds. *Alkuin von York und die geistige Grundlegung Europas: Akten der Tagung vom 30. September bis zum 2. Oktober 2004 in der Stiftsbibliothek St Gallen*. Monasterium Sancti Galli 5. St Gallen: Verlag am Klosterhof, 2010.
Trilling, Renée Rebecca. "Beyond Abjection: The Problem with Grendel's Mother Again." *Parergon* 24 (2007): 1–20.
Tripp, Raymond P., Jr. "Humor, Wordplay, and Semantic Resonance in *Beowulf*." In *Humour in Anglo-Saxon Literature*. Ed. Jonathan Wilcox, 49–69. Cambridge: Brewer, 2000.
Tristram, Hildegard L.C. "In Support of Tupper's Solution of the Exeter Book Riddle (Krapp-Dobbie) 55." In *Germanic Dialects: Linguistic and Philological*

Investigations. Ed. Bela Brogyanyi and Thomas Krömmelbein, 585–98. Current Issues in Linguistic Theory 38; Amsterdam Studies in the Theory and History of Linguistic Science 4. Amsterdam: John Benjamins, 1986.

Tupper, Frederick, Jr. "The Comparative Study of Riddles." *MLN* 18 (1903): 1–8.

– "Originals and Analogues of the Exeter Book Riddles." *MLN* 18 (1903): 97–106.

– "Riddles of the Bede Tradition. The 'Flores' of Pseudo-Bede." *MP* 2 (1904–5): 561–72.

– "Solutions of the Exeter Book Riddles." *MLN* 21 (1906): 97–105.

Tyler, Elizabeth M. *Old English Poetics: The Aesthetics of the Familiar in Anglo-Saxon England*. Cambridge: Boydell and Brewer, 2006.

Walker-Pelkey, Faye. "'Frige hwæt ic hatte': *The Wife's Lament* as Riddle." *Papers on Language and Literature* 28 (1992): 242–66.

Wallace, A. Dayle, and Woodburn O. Ross, eds. *Studies in Honor of John Wilcox*. Detroit, MI: Wayne State University Press, 1958.

Walmsley, John, ed. *Inside Old English: Essays in Honour of Bruce Mitchell*. Oxford: Blackwell, 2006.

Walz, John A. "Notes on the Anglo-Saxon Riddles." *Harvard Studies and Notes in Philology and Literature* 5 (1896): 261–8.

Warrant, Eric J. "Nocturnal Bees." *Current Biology* 17 (2007): 991–2.

Warren, Michael J. "Commentary for Exeter Riddle 57." *The Riddle Ages* (blog), 24 January 2017. https://theriddleages.com/riddles/post/commentary-for-exeter-riddle-57.

– *Birds in Medieval English Poetry: Metaphors, Realities, Transformations*. Nature and Environment in the Middle Ages. Cambridge: Brewer, 2018.

Watten, Barrett. *A Constructivist Moment: From Material Text to Cultural Poetics*. Middletown, CT: Wesleyan University Press; London: Eurospan, 2003.

Waugh, Robin, and James Weldon, eds. *The Hero Recovered: Essays on Medieval Heroism in Honor of George Clark*. Kalamazoo, MI: Medieval Institute, 2010.

Weaver, Erica. "Premodern and Postcritical: Medieval Enigmata and the Hermeneutic Style." *New Literary History* 50 (2019): 43–64.

Weber, Benjamin. "The Isidorian Context of Aldhelm's 'Lorica' and Exeter Riddle 35." *Neophil* 96 (2012): 457–66.

Webster, Leslie. *Anglo-Saxon Art: A New History*. London: British Museum, 2012.

Wehlau, Ruth. *"The Riddle of Creation": Metaphor Structures in Old English Poetry*. New York: Peter Lang, 1997.

Wells, Richard. "The Old English Riddles and their Ornithological Content." *Lore and Language* 2 (1978): 57–67.

Welsh, Andrew. *The Roots of Lyric: Primitive Poetry and Modern Poetics*. Princeton, NJ: Princeton University Press, 1978.

- "Swallows Name Themselves: Exeter Book Riddle 55." *ANQ* 3 (1990): 90–3.
Wenham, S.J. "Anatomical Interpretations of Anglo-Saxon Weapon Injuries." In *Weapons and Warfare in Anglo-Saxon England*. Ed. Sonia Chadwick Hawkes, 123–39. Oxford University Committee for Archaeology 21. Oxford: Oxford University Committee for Archaeology, 1989.
Weston, Lisa M. C. "Women's Magic: The Old English Metrical Childbirth Charms." *Modern Philology* 92 (1995): 279–93.
- "Guthlac Betwixt and Between: Literacy, Cross-Temporal Affiliation, and an Anglo-Saxon Anchorite." *The Journal of Medieval Religious Cultures* 42 (2016): 1–27.
Whaley, Beth. "Commentary for Exeter Riddle 84." *The Riddle Ages* (blog), 20 June 2019. https://theriddleages.com/riddles/post/commentary-for-exeter-riddle-84/.
White, Beatrice. "Whale-Hunting, The Barnacle Goose, and the Date of the 'Ancrene Riwle': Three Notes on Old and Middle English." *Modern Language Review* 40 (1945): 205–7.
White, Stephen D. "Kinship and Lordship in Early Medieval England: The Story of Sigeberht, Cynewulf, and Cyneheard." *Viator* 20 (1989): 1–18. Reprinted in *Old English Literature: Critical Essays*. Ed. R.M. Liuzza, 157–81. New Haven: Yale University Press, 2002.
Whitman, Charles Huntingdon. "The Birds of Old English Literature." *Journal of Germanic Philology* 2 (1898): 149–98.
Whitman, F.H. "OE Riddle 74." *ELN* 6 (1968): 1–5.
- "The Christian Background to Two Riddle Motifs." *SN* 41 (1969): 93–8.
- "Medieval Riddling: Factors Underlying Its Development." *NM* 71 (1970): 177–85.
- "Riddle 60 and Its Source." *PQ* 50 (1971): 108–15.
- "Significant Motifs in Riddle 53." *MÆ* 46 (1977): 1–11.
- "Aenigmata Tatwini." *NM* 88 (1987): 8–17.
Wilcox, Jonathan. "New Solutions to the Old English Riddles: Riddles 17 and 53." *PQ* 69 (1990): 393–408.
- "Mock-Riddles in Old English: Exeter Riddles 86 and 19." *SP* 93 (1996): 180–7.
- ed. *Humour in Anglo-Saxon Literature*. Cambridge: Brewer, 2000.
- "Eating People Is Wrong: Funny Style in *Andreas* and its Analogues." In *Anglo-Saxon Styles*. Ed. Catherine E. Karkov and George Hardin Brown, 201–22. Albany: State University of New York Press, 2003.
- "Humour and the *Exeter Book* Riddles: Incongruity in *Feþegeorn* (R.31)." In *Riddles at Work in the Early Medieval Tradition: Words, Ideas, Interactions*. Ed. Megan Cavell and Jennifer Neville, 128–45. Manchester Medieval Literature and Culture 32. Manchester: Manchester University Press, 2020.
Williams, Edith Whitehurst. "The Relation between Pagan Survivals and Diction in Two Old English Riddles." *PQ* 54 (1975), 664–70.

- "Annals of the Poor: Folk Life in Old English Riddles." *Medieval Perspectives* 3 (1988), 67–82.
- "What's So New about the Sexual Revolution? Some Comments on Anglo-Saxon Attitudes towards Sexuality in Women Based on Four Exeter Book Riddles." In *New Readings on Women in Old English Literature*. Ed. Helen Damico and Alexandra Hennessey Olsen, 137–45. Bloomington: Indiana University Press, 1990.
- "Hwa mec raere?...Hwa mec staeðþe? The Quest for Certainty in the Old English Storm Riddle." *Medieval Perspectives* 14 (1999): 255–72.
- "An Insight of Form: New Genres in Four Exeter Book Riddles." In *Essays on Old, Middle, Modern English and Old Icelandic in Honor of Raymond P. Tripp, Jr*. Ed. Loren C. Gruber, Meredith Crellin Gruber, and Gregory K. Jember, 231–61. Lewiston, NY: Edwin Mellen, 2000.

Williams, Kyle Joseph. "The Worm and the Chalice: Eucharistic Imagery and the Unity of Exeter Riddles 47 and 48." *Modern Philology* 114 (2017): 482–502.

Williamson, Craig, trans. *A Feast of Creatures: Anglo-Saxon Riddle-Songs*. Philadelphia: University of Pennsylvania Press, 1982.

–, trans. *The Complete Old English Poems*. With an introduction by Tom Shippey. Philadelphia: University of Pennsylvania Press, 2017.

Williamson, Paul. *Medieval Ivory Carvings: Early Christian to Romanesque*. London: Victoria and Albert Museum, 2010.

Williamson, Roland, and Ben Levick. "Woodworking." *Regia Anglorum* (2009), https://regia.org/research/life/woodwork.htm.

Wilson, Anna. "Fan Fiction and Premodern Literature: Methods and Definitions." *Transformative Works and Cultures*, 36 (2021), https://journal.transformativeworks.org/index.php/twc/article/view/2037.

Wilson, David M. "Anglo-Saxon Rural Economy: A Survey of the Archaeological Evidence and a Suggestion." *Archaeological History Review* 10 (1962): 65–79.

Wilson, John. "Old English Riddle No. 39: 'Comet.'" *N&Q* 236 (1991): 442–3.

Winer, Gerald A., and Jane E. Cottrell. "The Odd Belief That Rays Exit the Eye during Vision." In *Thinking and Seeing: Visual Metacognition in Adults and Children*. Ed. Daniel T. Levin, 97–119. Cambridge, MA: MIT Press, 2004.

Withers, Benjamin C., and Jonathan Wilcox, eds. *Naked before God: Uncovering the Body in Anglo-Saxon England*. Medieval European Studies 3. Morgantown: West Virginia University Press, 2003.

Wogan-Browne, Jocelyn. "The Hero in Christian Reception: Ælfric and Heroic Poetry." In *Old English Literature: Critical Essays*. Ed. R.M. Liuzza, 215–35. New Haven and London: Yale University Press, 2002.

Wolf, Carol Jean. "Christ as Hero in *The Dream of the Rood*." *NM* 71 (1970): 202–10.

Wood, G.A. "The Anglo-Saxon Riddles." *Aberystwyth Studies* 1 (1912): 9–62.
– "The Anglo-Saxon Riddles (continued)." *Aberystwyth Studies* 2 (1914): 1–41.
Woosnam-Savage, Robert C., and Kelly DeVries. "Battle Trauma in Medieval Warfare: Wounds, Weapons and Armour." In *Wounds and Wound Repair in Medieval Culture*. Ed. Larissa Tracy and Kelly DeVries, 27–56. Leiden: Brill, 2015.
Wormald, Patrick. "Bede, *Beowulf*, and the Conversion of the Anglo-Saxon Aristocracy." In *Bede and Anglo-Saxon England: Papers in Honour of the 1300th Anniversary of the Birth of Bede*. Ed. Robert T. Farrell, 32–95. BAR 46. Oxford: BAR, 1978.
Wright, Thomas. *Biographia Britannica Literaria; or Biography of Literary Characters of Great Britain and Ireland, Arranged in Chronological Order: Anglo-Saxon Period*. London: John W. Parker, 1842.
Wright, Thomas, and R.P. Wülcker. *Anglo-Saxon and Old English Vocabularies*. 2 vols. 2nd ed. London: Trübner, 1884.
Young, Jean I. "Riddle 8 of the Exeter Book." *RES* 18 (1942): 308–12.
– "Riddle 15 of the *Exeter Book*." *RES* 29 (1944): 304–6.
– "*Glaed waes ic gliwum*: Ungloomy Aspects of Old English Poetry." In *The Early Cultures of North-West Europe: H.M. Chadwick Memorial Studies*. Ed. Cyril Fox and Bruce Dickins, 273–87. Cambridge: Cambridge University Press, 1950.
Zahavi, Amotz. "Parasitism and Nest Predation in Parasitic Cuckoos." *The American Naturalist* 113 (1979): 157–9.
Zehnder, Ursula. "Hypermetrical Verse Patterns in the *Riddles* of the Exeter Book." *N&Q* 47 (2000): 405–9.
Ziegler, Waltraud. "Ein neuer Losungsversuch für das altenglische Rätsel Nr. 28." *Arbeiten aus Anglistik und Amerikanistik* 7 (1982): 185–90.
Zimmermann, Gunhild. *The Four Old English Poetic Manuscripts: Texts, Contexts, and Historical Background*. Anglistische Forschungen 230. Heidelberg: Universitätsverlag C. Winter, 1995.
Zwerger, Klaus. *Cereal Drying Racks: Culture and Typology of Wood Buildings in Europe and East Asia*. Translated by Julian Reisenberger. 2011; Berlin: Walter de Gruyter, 2020.

Index of Solutions

Adam, Eve, and family: *A Man Sat at Wine* (R.46)
alchemy: *Nose in Confinement* (R.10), *Four Creatures* (R.51)
ale: *Hardest and Sharpest* (R.28)
ale, and its source: *Hardest and Sharpest* (R.28)
alphabet: *Ten Brothers and Sisters* (R.13)
altar, sacrificial: *Earth-Fast* (R.49)
amphora: *Large Belly* (R.18)
anchor: *Under Waves' Pressure* (R.2), *Nose in Confinement* (R.10), *Fight against Wave* (R.16)
anchor/anchorite: *Fight Against Wave* (R.16)
anchorite: *Fight Against Wave* (R.16)
angel, guardian: *Guest in Enclosures* (R.43)
anger: *Bright Warrior* (R.50)
animal, water: *Cunning Thing in Waves* (R.78)
antler: *Brotherless* (R.88), *Younger Brother* (R.93)
anvil: *Lone Dweller* (R.5)
archetypal feminine: *Terrible Laughter* (R.33)
aristocracy: *Bright Warrior* (R.50)
army: *Glorious I Thunder* (R.1)

arrow: *Towering Tree* (R.53)
arrow, burning: *Strong Going In/Out* (R.62)
arrow, incendiary, and bow: *Brain-Locker* (R.73)
ash tree: *Brown One's Boast* (R.92)
atmosphere: *Glorious I Thunder* (R.1), *Under Waves' Pressure* (R.2), *No Escape* (R.3), *Glorious Servant* (R.1–3), *Ocean's Bottom* (R.2–3)
auger: *Strong Going In/Out* (R.62)
Augustine and Tertullian: *Wolf* (R.90)
aurelia, butterfly: *Ten Brothers and Sisters* (R.13)
aurelia, cicada: *Ten Brothers and Sisters* (R.13)
aurochs: *Weapon-Warrior* (R.14)
axle and wheels: *Boundary Paths* (R.72)

badger: *White Neck* (R.15)
bagpipe: *Eager to Go* (R.31)
baker's boy and oven: *In a Corner* (R.54)
ballista: *Protector* (R.17)
baptism: *Nose in Confinement* (R.10)
barley: *Hardest and Sharpest* (R.28)
barm (yeast starter): *Mother of Many Races* (R.41)

352   Index of Solutions

barnacle goose: *Nose in Confinement* (R.10), *Grey-Haired Queen* (R.74)
barrow: *Hardest and Sharpest* (R.28), *Earth-Fast* (R.49)
beaker of wine/spirits: *Dark-Stained* (R.11)
beaker, glass: *Shining with Gold* (R.63)
beam: *Brain-Locker* (R.73)
bee: *Feeds Cattle* (R.34), *Boneless* (R.45)
bee-basket: *Protector* (R.17)
beech tree: *Brown One's Boast* (R.92)
bee-hive: *Protector* (R.17)
beer: *Hardest and Sharpest* (R.28)
bees: *Abounding in Song* (R.57)
bell: *Periodically Busy* (R.4), *Old Evening Poet* (R.8), *Ring without Tongue* (R.48), *Sings through Its Sides* (R.70a)
bell, church: *Sings through Its Sides* (R.70a)
bell's clapper: *Periodically Busy* (R.4)
bellows: *Belly Behind* (R.37), *Barked, Wavered* (R.87), *The Creature Had a Belly* (R.89)
bible: *Famous Name* (R.26), *Word-Spell* (R.67)
bible codex: *Hardest and Sharpest* (R.28)
birch (as Maypole and Numinosum): *Flame-Busy A* (R.30)
bird and wind: *Air-Vessel* (R.29)
bird, diving: *Grey-Haired Queen* (R.74)
bird, snake-eating: *Joy and Ice* (R.64)
bird, water: *Grey-Haired Queen* (R.74)
boar, wild (made into leather): *I Travel on Foot* (R.12)
board: *Lone Dweller* (R.5)
boat: *Man Woman Horse* (R.36), *Grey-Haired Queen* (R.74)

boat, made of oak: *Grey-Haired Queen* (R.74)
body: *Fight Against Wave* (R.16)
body and mind: *Guest in Enclosures* (R.43)
body and soul: *Guest in Enclosures* (R.43), *My Hall Is Not Silent* (R.85), *Brotherless* (R.88)
book: *Famous Name* (R.26), *Earth-Fast* (R.49), *Word-Spell* (R.67), *Brown One's Boast* (R.92), *Hide My Track* (R.95)
book and quill-pen: *Towering Tree* (R.53)
book, covers of: *Brown One's Boast* (R.92)
book, Gospel: *Famous Name* (R.26), *Word-Spell* (R.67)
book, religious: *Famous Name* (R.26), *Hide My Track* (R.95)
book, riddle: *Hide My Track* (R.95)
bookcase: *Earth-Fast* (R.49)
bookchest: *Earth-Fast* (R.49)
bookmoth: *Moth* (R.47)
bookworm: *Moth* (R.47)
borer: *Strong Going In/Out* (R.62)
bottle, leather: *Large Belly* (R.18), *The Creature Had a Belly* (R.89)
bow: *Protector* (R.17), *Wob* (R.23), *Towering Tree* (R.53), *Brain-Locker* (R.73)
bow and incendiary arrow: *Brain-Locker* (R.73)
bow, yew, and yew-arrow: *Brown One's Boast* (R.92)
boy: *Swift on a Track* (R.75)
branding iron, hook, and tinder: *Strong Going In/Out* (R.62)
bread and oven: *Earth-Fast* (R.49)
bridge: *Peace-Horses* (R.22)
brooch: *Forged by Hammer* (R.91)
broom: *Captives* (R.52)

Index of Solutions   353

bubble: *Nose in Confinement* (R.10)
bucket of freezing water: *Periodically Busy* (R.4)
bucket on chain in a well: *Periodically Busy* (R.4)
bucket, water: *Periodically Busy* (R.4)
buckets, two: *Captives* (R.52)
buckets, well: *Captives* (R.52)
buckle: *Forged by Hammer* (R.91)
bullock: *Greedy for Youth-Mirth* (R.38)

cage, falcon: *Earth-Fast* (R.49)
calf: *Ten Brothers and Sisters* (R.13)
calf, bull: *I Travel on Foot* (R.12), *Greedy for Youth-Mirth* (R.38), *Boundary Paths* (R.72)
can: *Shining with Gold* (R.63)
candelabra: *Wolf* (R.90)
candle: *Tall and Beautiful* (R.70b)
cask: *Large Belly* (R.18)
cask and cooper: *Barked, Wavered* (R.87)
caterpillar: *Ten Brothers and Sisters* (R.13)
celebrant singing vespers: *Old Evening Poet* (R.8)
chalice: *Ring without Tongue* (R.48), *Golden Ring* (R.59)
chalice, inscription ring on: *Golden Ring* (R.59)
chickens/chicks, ten: *Ten Brothers and Sisters* (R.13)
chicks, hatchling: *Ten Brothers and Sisters* (R.13)
chicks, twelve: *Ten Brothers and Sisters* (R.13)
chive: *I Was Alive* (R.65)
chopping block for food: *Lone Dweller* (R.5)
chopping block for wood: *Lone Dweller* (R.5)
chopping board for food: *Lone Dweller* (R.5)

chough: *Old Evening Poet* (R.8)
chrismal: *Ring without Tongue* (R.48)
Christ: *Under Waves' Pressure* (R.2)
Christ unborn: *Boneless* (R.45)
Christ walking on the sea: *Water Turned to Bone* (R.68–9)
Christ's voice: *Golden Ring* (R.59)
chrysalis: *Ten Brothers and Sisters* (R.13)
churn and butter: *In a Corner* (R.54)
churn, butter: *In a Corner* (R.54)
cithara: *Eager to Go* (R.31)
city gate: *Periodically Busy* (R.4)
cloth and loom: *Turning Wood* (R.56)
clothes-moth: *Moth* (R.47)
cloud: *Most Wretched of All* (R.39)
cock and hen: *Two Proud Ones* (R.42)
codex, religious: *Hide My Track* (R.95)
coins: *Old Ancestry* (R.83)
comet: *Most Wretched of All* (R.39)
conception and birth: *They Gave Me up for Dead* (R.9)
conversion of Wulfstan: *Wolf* (R.90)
cornfield: *Flame-Busy A* (R.30)
cow: *Boundary Paths* (R.72)
crab: *Cunning Thing in Waves* (R.78), *Swallows Grit* (R.82)
creation: *Circle of the Earth* (R.40), *Circle Renewed* (R.40-41), *Bigger than the Earth* (R.66), *Higher than Heaven* (R.94)
cross: *No Escape* (R.3), *Flame-Busy A* (R.30), *Towering Tree* (R.53), *Wolf-Head-Tree* (R.55), *Word-Spell* (R.67), *Brain-Locker* (R.73), *Warrior's Companion* (R.80)
cross-bow: *Wob* (R.23)
crown of the head: *Grey-Haired Queen* (R.74)
crows: *Abounding in Song* (R.57)
crying baby: *Old Evening Poet* (R.8)
cuckoo: *They Gave Me up for Dead* (R.9)

354   Index of Solutions

cup: *Shining with Gold* (R.63)
cup of wine/spirits: *Dark-Stained* (R.11)
cuttlefish: *Grey-Haired Queen* (R.74)
Cygnus (the constellation): *Flame-Busy B* (R.30b)
Cynewulf (the poet): *Wolf* (R.90), *Hide My Track* (R.95)

dagger: *Clothed in Red* (R.71)
dagger sheath: *Hanging Head* (R.44)
day: *Most Wretched of All* (R.39)
death (as a creature): *Most Wretched of All* (R.39)
deer, female: *Woman Sitting Alone* (R.76)
demon: *Moth* (R.47)
demons: *Abounding in Song* (R.57)
devil: *Periodically Busy* (R.4), *Old Evening Poet* (R.8)
doe, roe: *Woman Sitting Alone* (R.76)
dog: *Bright Warrior* (R.50)
dog, guard: *Periodically Busy* (R.4)
dog, hunting: *Swift on a Track* (R.75)
dolphin: *Man Woman Horse* (R.36)
dough: *Boneless* (R.45)
dough and oven: *Boneless* (R.45)
dragon: *Four Creatures* (R.51)
draw-well: *One-Footed* (R.58)
dream: *Most Wretched of All* (R.39), *Hide My Track* (R.95)
duck: *Woman Sitting Alone* (R.76)

eagle, sea: *Grey-Haired Queen* (R.74)
earth: *Mother of Many Races* (R.41)
earthquake: *No Escape* (R.3)
earthquake, submarine: *Under Waves' Pressure* (R.2)
execution: *Turning Wood* (R.56)

faith: *Most Wretched of All* (R.39)
falcon: *Cursed among Weapons* (R.20)

falcon, hunting: *Warrior's Companion* (R.80)
falconry: *Bright-Headed* (R.19), *Joy and Ice* (R.64)
family on the go: *Man Woman Horse* (R.36)
fate: *Most Wretched of All* (R.39)
fiddle: *Eager to Go* (R.31)
figurehead, ship's: *Grey-Haired Queen* (R.74)
fingers and glove: *Ten Brothers and Sisters* (R.13)
fire: *Glorious I Thunder* (R.1), *Mother of Many Races* (R.41), *Bright Warrior* (R.50)
fire-rod: *Strong Going In/Out* (R.62)
fish and river: *My Hall Is Not Silent* (R.85)
fish, flat: *Footless* (R.77)
flail: *Periodically Busy* (R.4), *Captives* (R.52), *Towering Tree* (R.53), *Turning Wood* (R.56)
flask: *Shining with Gold* (R.63)
flatfish: *Footless* (R.77)
flute: *Old Evening Poet* (R.8), *Shining with Gold* (R.63)
flute, double: *Sings through Its Sides* (R.70a)
flute, rye: *Cunningly Made* (R.70)
foot and shoe: *Strong Going In/Out* (R.62)
force, supernatural: *No Escape* (R.3)
fortress: *Protector* (R.17)
fosterling: *They Gave Me up for Dead* (R.9)
fox: *White Neck* (R.15)
fox and hound: *White Neck* (R.15)
frog: *Old Evening Poet* (R.8)
furnace, smelting: *Protector* (R.17)

gallows: *Towering Tree* (R.53), *Wolf-Head-Tree* (R.55)

Index of Solutions   355

gallows/cross: *Towering Tree* (R.53)
garlic: *Useful to Neighbours* (R.25)
genitals, female: *Footless* (R.77)
gimlet: *Strong Going In/Out* (R.62)
glass, cupping: *Clothed in Red* (R.71)
gnats: *Abounding in Song* (R.57)
God: *Glorious I Thunder* (R.1), *Under Waves' Pressure* (R.2), *No Escape* (R.3), *Glorious Servant* (R.1–3), *Bigger than the Earth* (R.66)
God's power: *Bigger than the Earth* (R.66)
gold: *Dark-Stained* (R.11), *Old Ancestry* (R.83)
goose, barnacle: *Nose in Confinement* (R.10), *Grey-Haired Queen* (R.74)
groom: *Swift on a Track* (R.75)
guilt: *Lone Dweller* (R.5)
guilt and conscience: *I Burn the Living* (R.6)

hailstones: *Abounding in Song* (R.57)
hand: *Swift on a Track* (R.75)
hand-barrow: *Grind against Grit* (R.32)
handmill: *Periodically Busy* (R.4)
harp: *Hardest and Sharpest* (R.28), *Eager to Go* (R.31), *Wolf-Head-Tree* (R.55), *Cunningly Made* (R.70), *Sings through Its Sides* (R.70a)
harp (grain dryer): *Cunningly Made* (R.70)
harrow: *Swallows Grit* (R.82)
harrowing of hell: *Feeds Cattle* (R.34)
harrowing, spiritual: *Feeds Cattle* (R.34)
hatred: *Terrible Laughter* (R.33)
hawk: *Cursed among Weapons* (R.20), *Warrior's Companion* (R.80)
hedge: *Lone Dweller* (R.5)
hedgehog: *White Neck* (R.15)
heifer: *Boundary Paths* (R.72)

helmet: *A Head Stuck In* (R.61)
helmet, iron: *Clothed in Red* (R.71)
helmet, visored: *Puff-Breasted* (R.81)
hemp: *Useful to Neighbours* (R.25)
hen: *Woman Sitting Alone* (R.76)
hen and cock: *Two Proud Ones* (R.42)
hide: *I Travel on Foot* (R.12), *Famous Name* (R.26)
hide, ox: *I Travel on Foot* (R.12)
hilt: *Clothed in Red* (R.71)
hind (female deer): *Woman Sitting Alone* (R.76)
hive and bee: *Earth-Fast* (R.49)
holy book, illuminated: *Ring without Tongue* (R.48)
hood: *A Head Stuck In* (R.61)
hops: *Wolf* (R.90)
horn: *Weapon-Warrior* (R.14), *Noble's Shoulder Companion* (R.79–80), *Warrior's Companion* (R.80)
horn, yew: *Hardest and Sharpest* (R.28)
horn, stag: *Brotherless* (R.88), *Younger Brother* (R.93)
horse and wagon: *Four Creatures* (R.51)
horse, man, hawk, servant, falcon, water, sparrow-hawk: *Joy and Ice* (R.64)
horseman and hawk: *Bright-Headed* (R.19)
hound and hind: *Swift and Sitting* (R.75-76)
housel in body: *My Hall Is Not Silent* (R.85)
hunt, waterfowl: *Man Woman Horse* (R.36)
hunter: *Joy and Ice* (R.64)
hunter, elk: *Swift and Sitting* (R.75-76)
hunting: *Bright-Headed* (R.19), *Joy and Ice* (R.64)

356 Index of Solutions

hurdy gurdy: *Eager to Go* (R.31), *Cunningly Made* (R.70)
hurricane: *No Escape* (R.3)
hyena: *Grey-Haired Queen* (R.74)

ice: *Water Turned to Bone* (R.68–9), *Wonder on the Way* (R.69)
ice bridge: *Peace-Horses* (R.22)
iceberg: *Terrible Laughter* (R.33), *Water Turned to Bone* (R.68–9)
ice-floe: *Terrible Laughter* (R.33)
icicle: *Wonder on the Way* (R.69), *Water Turned to Bone* (R.68–9)
inkhorn: *Large Belly* (R.18)
inkhorn, antler: *Brotherless* (R.88), *Younger Brother* (R.93)
inkwell: *Protector* (R.17)
instrument, musical: *Hardest and Sharpest* (R.28), *Eager to Go* (R.31)
instrument, stringed: *Hardest and Sharpest* (R.28)
intercourse: *In a Corner* (R.54), *A Head Stuck In* (R.61)
iron: *Clothed in Red* (R.71)
Ishmael unborn: *Boneless* (R.45)

jackdaw: *Old Evening Poet* (R.8), *Abounding in Song* (R.57)
jay: *Old Evening Poet* (R.8), *Six Letters* (R.24)
John Barleycorn: *Hardest and Sharpest* (R.28)

kelp weed (inscribed with runes): *Mouthless by Sand* (R.60)
key: *Hanging Head* (R.44), *Forged by Hammer* (R.91)
key and bar: *Forged by Hammer* (R.91)
key and lock: *Hanging Head* (R.44)
keyhole: *Forged by Hammer* (R.91)
kirtle: *A Head Stuck In* (R.61)

lamb of God: *Wolf* (R.90)
lamprey: *Cunning Thing in Waves* (R.78)
lance: *Clothed in Red* (R.71), *Brain-Locker* (R.73)
leather: *I Travel on Foot* (R.12)
leather bottle: *Large Belly* (R.18)
leek: *Useful to Neighbours* (R.25), *I Was Alive* (R.65)
letter beam cut from an old jetty stump: *Mouthless by Sand* (R.60)
letters: *Bright-Headed* (R.19), *Abounding in Song* (R.57), *Joy and Ice* (R.64)
letters, twenty-two: *Ten Brothers and Sisters* (R.13)
lighthouse: *Bright-Headed* (R.19), *Tall and Beautiful* (R.70b)
lock: *Periodically Busy* (R.4)
loom and cloth: *Turning Wood* (R.56)
loom and web: *Wolf* (R.90)
loom weights: *Captives* (R.52)
Lot and his offspring: *A Man Sat at Wine* (R.46)
Lyra (the constellation): *Flame-Busy A* (R.30a)
lyre: *Eager to Go* (R.31), *Cunningly Made* (R.70), *Sings through Its Sides* (R.70a)
lyre, tortoise: *Hardest and Sharpest* (R.28)

maggot and psalter: *Moth* (R.47)
magpie: *Six Letters* (R.24)
mail coat/shirt: *Hopeful Garment* (R.35), *A Head Stuck In* (R.61)
malt liquor: *Hardest and Sharpest* (R.28)
man: *White Neck* (R.15), *Greedy for Youth-Mirth* (R.38), *Clothed in Red* (R.71), *Puff-Breasted* (R.81)
man/sword (*secg*): *Cursed among Weapons* (R.20)

Index of Solutions 357

man woman horse: *Man Woman Horse* (R.36), *Six Heads* (R.36.1–7)
martins: *Abounding in Song* (R.57)
mead: *Binder and Scourger* (R.27), *Hardest and Sharpest* (R.28)
mead and its source: *Binder and Scourger* (R.27)
mead-barrel and drinking bowl: *Wolf-Head-Tree* (R.55)
message: *Mouthless by Sand* (R.60)
metal: *Old Ancestry* (R.83)
metempsychosis: *Grey-Haired Queen* (R.74)
midges: *Abounding in Song* (R.57)
milk: *Wonder on the Way* (R.69)
millpond and sluice: *Earth-Fast* (R.49)
millstone: *Periodically Busy* (R.4), *Grind against Grit* (R.32)
mime: *Six Letters* (R.24)
mind and body: *Guest in Enclosures* (R.43)
mirror: *Woman Sitting Alone* (R.76)
money: *Old Ancestry* (R.83)
monk: *Cursed among Weapons* (R.20)
monstrance (container for eucharistic bread): *Ring without Tongue* (R.48)
month: *Peace-Horses* (R.22)
month of December: *Peace-Horses* (R.22)
moon: *Most Wretched of All* (R.39), *Grey-Haired Queen* (R.74), *Hide My Track* (R.95)
moon and sun: *Air-Vessel* (R.29)
moth: *Ten Brothers and Sisters* (R.13)
musical notes: *Abounding in Song* (R.57)
mustard: *Useful to Neighbours* (R.25)

nature: *Circle of the Earth* (R.40), *Bigger than the Earth* (R.66), *Higher than Heaven* (R.94)

necromancy: *Periodically Busy* (R.4)
need-fire (purifying fire kindled by boring): *Bright Warrior* (R.50)
neumes: *Abounding in Song* (R.57)
new year: *Peace-Horses* (R.22)
night: *Dark-Stained* (R.11)
night and day: *Most Wretched of All* (R.39)
nightingale: *Old Evening Poet* (R.8)
night-shirt: *A Head Stuck In* (R.61)
nobleman riding: *Joy and Ice* (R.64)
nose: *Sings through Its Sides* (R.70a)

oak: *Grey-Haired Queen* (R.74), *Swift and Sitting* (R.75–6)
ocean furrow: *Nose in Confinement* (R.10)
one-eyed garlic seller: *Twelve Hundred Heads* (R.86)
one-eyed onion seller: *Twelve Hundred Heads* (R.86)
onion: *Useful to Neighbours* (R.25), *I Was Alive* (R.65)
ore: *Flame-Busy A* (R.30), *Old Ancestry* (R.83)
organ: *Eager to Go* (R.31), *Twelve Hundred Heads* (R.86)
organistrum: *Eager to Go* (R.31), *Cunningly Made* (R.70)
osculatorium (religious object to be kissed): *Flame-Busy A* (R.30)
oven: *Protector* (R.17), *Earth-Fast* (R.49)
ox: *I Travel on Foot* (R.12), *Greedy for Youth-Mirth* (R.38), *Boundary Paths* (R.72)
ox and ox-hide: *I Travel on Foot* (R.12)
ox and ox-horn: *Weapon-Warrior* (R.14)
oxen, yoke of: *Captives* (R.52)
oyster: *Footless Woman* (R.76–7), *Footless* (R.77), *Cunning Thing in Waves* (R.78)

358   Index of Solutions

parchment: *Hardest and Sharpest* (R.28)
party, raiding: *Glorious I Thunder* (R.1)
paten: *Ring without Tongue* (R.48), *Golden Ring* (R.59)
peacock, ring-tailed: *Joy and Ice* (R.64)
pen: *Periodically Busy* (R.4), *Brain-Locker* (R.73)
pen and fingers: *Four Creatures* (R.51)
pen and ink: *Earth-Fast* (R.49)
penis: *Useful to Neighbours* (R.25), *Hanging Head* (R.44), *Boneless* (R.45), *Strong Going In/Out* (R.62), *Noble's Possession and Desire* (R.79)
penis/sword (*wæpen*): *Cursed among Weapons* (R.20)
perch: *Wolf* (R.90)
petrification: *Water Turned to Bone* (R.68–9)
phallus: *Periodically Busy* (R.4), *Dark-Stained* (R.11), *Protector* (R.17), *Large Belly* (R.18), *Cursed among Weapons* (R.20), *Wob* (R.23), *Useful to Neighbours* (R.25), *Flame-Busy A* (R.30), *Feeds Cattle* (R.34), *Belly Behind* (R.37), *Hanging Head* (R.44), *Boneless* (R.45), *Bright Warrior* (R.50), *Towering Tree* (R.53), *In a Corner* (R.54), *One-Footed* (R.58), *Strong Going In/Out* (R.62), *I Was Alive* (R.65), *Noble's Possession and Desire* (R.79), *Warrior's Companion* (R.80), *Barked, Wavered* (R.87), *The Creature Had a Belly* (R.89), *Forged by Hammer* (R.91)
pheasants, ten: *Ten Brothers and Sisters* (R.13)
pig: *Man Woman Horse* (R.36)
pike: *Wolf* (R.90)
pipe: *Old Evening Poet* (R.8)

pipe, shepherd's: *Cunningly Made* (R.70)
piss: *Swift and Sitting* (R.75-76)
plough-team: *Periodically Busy* (R.4)
plow: *Downward Nose* (R.21)
poker: *Strong Going In/Out* (R.62)
pole-lathe: *Towering Tree* (R.53), *Turning Wood* (R.56), *One-Footed* (R.58)
pond, frozen: *Wonder on the Way* (R.69), *Water Turned to Bone* (R.68–9)
porcupine: *White Neck* (R.15)
power: *Noble's Possession and Desire* (R.79)
power of nature: *Glorious I Thunder* (R.1), *Under Waves' Pressure* (R.2), *Glorious Servant* (R.1–3)
pregnant horse, two pregnant women: *Man Woman Horse* (R.36), *Six Heads* (R.36.1–7)
priest performing mass: *Four Creatures* (R.51)
prostitute: *Hide My Track* (R.95)
psaltery (plucked by a quill): *Eager to Go* (R.31)
pyx: *Ring without Tongue* (R.48)

quill: *Hanging Head* (R.44)
quill-pen: *Four Creatures* (R.51), *Grey-Haired Queen* (R.74), *Hide My Track* (R.95)
quill-pen and book: *Towering Tree* (R.53)
quill-pen and fingers: *Eager to Go* (R.31)
quiver: *Protector* (R.17)

rain: *Grey-Haired Queen* (R.74)
raindrops: *Abounding in Song* (R.57)
rake: *Feeds Cattle* (R.34)
rake, oven: *Strong Going In/Out* (R.62)

ram, battering: *Towering Tree* (R.53), *Brain-Locker* (R.73)
ram, battering, made of beech: *Brown One's Boast* (R.92)
reed: *Hanging Head* (R.44)
reed (plant, pipe, and pen): *Mouthless by Sand* (R.60)
reed flute: *Mouthless by Sand* (R.60)
reed pen: *Mouthless by Sand* (R.60)
reed pipe: *Mouthless by Sand* (R.60)
reflection: *Grey-Haired Queen* (R.74)
reliquary: *Wolf-Head-Tree* (R.55)
retainer: *Clothed in Red* (R.71)
revenant: *No Escape* (R.3), *They Gave Me up for Dead* (R.9), *Most Wretched of All* (R.39), *Mouthless by Sand* (R.60), *I Was Alive* (R.65), *Clothed in Red* (R.71), *Brain-Locker* (R.73), *Old Ancestry* (R.83)
riddle: *Hide My Track* (R.95)
riddler, the: *Bright-Headed* (R.19), *Twelve Hundred Heads* (R.86)
riding-well: *One-Footed* (R.58)
ring (shape of chalice): *Golden Ring* (R.59)
ring (sign-language gesture): *Golden Ring* (R.59)
ring (sound of bell): *Golden Ring* (R.59)
ring, finger: *Ring without Tongue* (R.48), *Golden Ring* (R.59)
rite of passage: *Peace-Horses* (R.22)
River Thames at sunset: *Wonder on the Way* (R.69)
rock, inscribed near high water mark: *Mouthless by Sand* (R.60)
roe doe : *Woman Sitting Alone* (R.76)
rosarium: *Golden Ring* (R.59)
rose hip: *Useful to Neighbours* (R.25)
rune staff: *Mouthless by Sand* (R.60)

sacramental vessel: *Ring without Tongue* (R.48)

Samon's lion and bees: *Protector* (R.17)
saviour: *Swift on a Track* (R.75)
scabbard: *Wolf-Head-Tree* (R.55), *Warrior's Companion* (R.80)
scholar: *Feeds Cattle* (R.34)
scourge: *Binder and Scourger* (R.27)
scribe and writing: *Bright-Headed* (R.19), *Joy and Ice* (R.64)
scribe writing the Gospels: *Four Creatures* (R.51)
scriptures, holy: *Famous Name* (R.26), *Hide My Track* (R.95)
sea-horse (ship): *Joy and Ice* (R.64)
sea-ice: *Terrible Laughter* (R.33)
sedge: *Clothed in Red* (R.71)
servant: *Swift on a Track* (R.75)
servant churning butter: *In a Corner* (R.54)
shade: *Grey-Haired Queen* (R.74)
shadow: *Grey-Haired Queen* (R.74)
shawm: *Cunningly Made* (R.70)
sheep, flock of: *Ten Brothers and Sisters* (R.13)
shepherd's pipe: *Cunningly Made* (R.70)
shield: *Lone Dweller* (R.5), *Wolf-Head-Tree* (R.55)
shield, beechwood: *Brown One's Boast* (R.92)
shield, bronze: *Clothed in Red* (R.71)
shield, iron: *Clothed in Red* (R.71)
ship: *Bright-Headed* (R.19), *Grind against Grit* (R.32), *Joy and Ice* (R.64), *Grey-Haired Queen* (R.74), *Puff-Breasted* (R.81)
ship, merchant: *Grind against Grit* (R.32)
ship, war: *Bright-Headed* (R.19)
ship, with passengers: *Man Woman Horse* (R.36), *Six Heads* (R.36.1–7), *Travel Flood-Ways* (R.36.8–13)

360 Index of Solutions

ship-wake: *Nose in Confinement* (R.10)
shirt: *A Head Stuck In* (R.61)
shuttle: *Cunningly Made* (R.70)
sickle: *Forged by Hammer* (R.91)
sinful thought: *They Gave Me up for Dead* (R.9)
singer, wandering: *Hide My Track* (R.95)
siren: *Grey-Haired Queen* (R.74)
skin: *I Travel on Foot* (R.12), *Famous Name* (R.26)
slave: *Boundary Paths* (R.72)
sleep: *Binder and Scourger* (R.27)
smelting furnace: *Protector* (R.17)
snow/snowflake: *Flame-Busy A* (R.30), *Grey-Haired Queen* (R.74)
songbird: *Old Evening Poet* (R.8)
soul: *Lone Dweller* (R.5), *Travelling Spirit* (R.7), *Old Evening Poet* (R.8), *They Gave Me up for Dead* (R.9), *Fight against Wave* (R.16), *Cursed among Weapons* (R.20), *Grey-Haired Queen* (R.74), *Hide My Track* (R.95)
soul and body: *Guest in Enclosures* (R.43), *My Hall Is Not Silent* (R.85), *Brotherless* (R.88)
souls, damned: *Abounding in Song* (R.57)
sow and five piglets: *Man Woman Horse* (R.36)
sparrow and swallow: *Air-Vessel* (R.29)
spear: *Towering Tree* (R.53), *Clothed in Red* (R.71), *Brain-Locker* (R.73), *Warrior's Companion* (R.80), *Brown One's Boast* (R.92)
speech: *Most Wretched of All* (R.39)
spirit: *No Escape* (R.3), *Mouthless by Sand* (R.60), *I Was Alive* (R.65), *Brain-Locker* (R.73), *Old Ancestry* (R.83)

spirit, holy: *Grey-Haired Queen* (R.74)
spirit, life, earth: *Guest in Enclosures* (R.43)
spur: *Strong Going In/Out* (R.62)
starling: *Old Evening Poet* (R.8)
starlings: *Abounding in Song* (R.57)
storm: *Glorious I Thunder* (R.1), *Under Waves' Pressure* (R.2), *No Escape* (R.3), *Glorious Servant* (R.1–3), *Ocean's Bottom* (R.2–3), *Terrible Laughter* (R.33)
storm, apocalyptic: *Glorious I Thunder* (R.1), *Under Waves' Pressure* (R.2), *No Escape* (R.3), *Glorious Servant* (R.1–3)
storm, sea: *Ocean's Bottom* (R.2-3)
storm, thunder: *Grey-Haired Queen* (R.74)
stormclouds: *Abounding in Song* (R.57)
sun: *Ocean's Bottom* (R.2-3), *Periodically Busy* (R.4), *I Burn the Living* (R.6), *Bright-Headed* (R.19), *Grey-Haired Queen* (R.74), *Hide My Track* (R.95)
survivor (*laf*): *Forged by Hammer* (R.91)
swallow: *Abounding in Song* (R.57)
swallow and sparrow: *Air-Vessel* (R.29)
swallow, to (the verb): *Abounding in Song* (R.57)
swallows: *Abounding in Song* (R.57)
swan: *Travelling Spirit* (R.7), *Grey-Haired Queen* (R.74)
swan, mute: *Travelling Spirit* (R.7)
swan, whistling: *Travelling Spirit* (R.7)
swan, whooper: *Grey-Haired Queen* (R.74)
swifts: *Abounding in Song* (R.57)
sword: *Periodically Busy* (R.4), *Cursed among Weapons* (R.20), *Clothed in Red* (R.71), *Warrior's Companion* (R.80)

Index of Solutions   361

sword, damascened: *Hardest and Sharpest* (R.28)
sword/man (*secg*): *Cursed among Weapons* (R.20)
sword/penis (*wæpen*): *Cursed among Weapons* (R.20)
sword-box: *Wolf-Head-Tree* (R.55)
sword-rack: *Wolf-Head-Tree* (R.55)
sword-swallow (hawk): *Cursed among Weapons* (R.20)

testosterone: *Cursed among Weapons* (R.20)
tetraktys: *Wolf-Head-Tree* (R.55)
thegn: *Clothed in Red* (R.71)
thought: *Hide My Track* (R.95)
thrush: *Old Evening Poet* (R.8)
time: *Most Wretched of All* (R.39)
tongue: *Boneless* (R.45)
tool for tapping a smelting oven: *Strong Going In/Out* (R.62)
town: *Protector* (R.17)
treasure (*laf*): *Forged by Hammer* (R.91)
tree: *Flame-Busy A* (R.30)
tree, ash: *Brown One's Boast* (R.92)
tree, beech: *Brown One's Boast* (R.92)
trial of soul: *Hardest and Sharpest* (R.28)

understanding: *Grey-Haired Queen* (R.74)
Ursa major (constellation): *Peace-Horses* (R.22)

vagina: *Lone Dweller* (R.5), *A Head Stuck In* (R.61)
Venus carried off: *Air-Vessel* (R.29)
Viking ship: *Protector* (R.17)
vixen: *White Neck* (R.15), *Woman Sitting Alone* (R.76)

wagon: *Grind against Grit* (R.32), *Belly Behind* (R.37)

wagon of stars: *Peace-Horses* (R.22)
wandering singer: *Hide My Track* (R.95)
war-ship: *Bright-Headed* (R.19)
water: *Terrible Laughter* (R.33), *Circle of the Earth* (R.40), *Mother of Many Races* (R.41), *Bigger than the Earth* (R.66), *Grey-Haired Queen* (R.74), *Mother of Many* (R.84)
water, rain: *Flame-Busy A* (R.30)
water, running: *Water Turned to Bone* (R.68–9)
water animal: *Cunning Thing in Waves* (R.78)
waterlily: *Nose in Confinement* (R.10)
weapon: *Clothed in Red* (R.71), *Noble's Possession and Desire* (R.79)
weapon rack: *Wolf-Head-Tree* (R.55)
weasel: *White Neck* (R.15)
weathercock: *Puff-Breasted* (R.81)
weathervane: *Puff-Breasted* (R.81)
web and loom: *Wolf* (R.90)
well with a well-sweep: *One-Footed* (R.58)
well-beam: *One-Footed* (R.58)
well-sweep: *One-Footed* (R.58)
wheel: *Grind against Grit* (R.32)
wheel-barrow: *Grind against Grit* (R.32)
wheels and axle: *Boundary Paths* (R.72)
whetstone: *Lone Dweller* (R.5)
whip: *Binder and Scourger* (R.27)
whirlpool: *Abounding in Song* (R.57)
wind: *Glorious I Thunder* (R.1), *Under Waves' Pressure* (R.2), *No Escape* (R.3), *Glorious Servant* (R.1–3), *Ocean's Bottom* (R.2–3)
wind of God: *Glorious Servant* (R.1–3)
wind, cosmic: *Glorious Servant* (R.1–3)
wine: *Dark-Stained* (R.11)
wine and wine cup: *Dark-Stained* (R.11)

wine cask: *Hardest and Sharpest* (R.28)
wine-jug: *Large Belly* (R.18)
wineskin: *Large Belly* (R.18)
winter: *Water Turned to Bone* (R.68–9)
wisdom: *Mother of Many Races* (R.41)
wisdom, instruction in: *Hide My Track* (R.95)
wolf: *Wolf* (R.90)
wolf, reflected in river with pike and sun: *Wolf* (R.90)
woman: *Hardest and Sharpest* (R.28)
wood: *I Travel on Foot* (R.12), *Flame-Busy A* (R.30), *Brown One's Boast* (R.92)

woodpecker: *Six Letters* (R.24)
woodpigeon: *Old Evening Poet* (R.8)
word: *Most Wretched of All* (R.39)
word of God: *Hide My Track* (R.95)
Word, the: *Word-Spell* (R.67)
writing: *Mother of Many Races* (R.41), *Grey-Haired Queen* (R.74)
writing (on vellum): *Moth* (R.47)
writing tablets: *Lone Dweller* (R.5)
Wulfstan's conversion: *Wolf* (R.90)

yeast starter (barm): *Mother of Many Races* (R.41)

Index

Abraham, 107, 223, 231
Ælfric of Eynsham, 5, 88, 97, 114, 135, 171–5, 211–12, 231, 232
Ælfric's *Colloquium*, 136
Æschere, 131, 165, 223
alcohol, 86, 127, 164, 218, 219, 237. *See also* ale; beer; mead; wine
Aldhelm, 5, 10, 11, 17, 36, 51, 53, 86, 100, 102, 145, 146, 147, 157, 177, 181, 182, 192, 193, 217; Enigma 17: *Perna* "Bivalve Mollusc," 193; Enigma 20: *Apis* "Bee," 193; Enigma 28: *Minotaurus* "Minotaur," 193; Enigma 47: *Hirundo* "Swallow," 193; Enigma 82: *Mustela* "Weasel," 193; Enigma 90: *Purpera Geminas Enixa* "Woman Bearing Twins," 193; Enigma 96: *Elefans* "Elephant," 193
ale, 218
Alfred the Great, King, 5, 24, 88, 170, 173, 176, 185, 217, 244
allegory, vii, 10, 24, 77–8, 102, 103, 110–17, 129, 147, 148, 176, 191, 245, 246
alliteration, 46, 49, 94, 99, 133, 182, 226
anachronism, 25, 114, 119, 149, 239
anchor, 109–16, 128, 148, 250
anchorite, 113–14, 148, 250
Andreas, 31, 40, 49, 50, 76–8, 92, 115, 131, 142

Andrew (the apostle), 77, 79
angel, 32, 211, 218
Anglo-Latin riddles, vii, 5, 10, 11, 36, 128, 185, 192–3, 247
Anglo-Saxon Chronicle, 31, 140
anthropomorphism, 90, 95, 126, 130
antler, 71, 82, 83, 127, 139
anus, 203, 226, 247
anvil, 144, 147, 149
aporia, 105, 108, 113, 116, 122, 126
apposition, 55, 178, 212, 218
archaeology, 49, 54, 67, 75, 110, 137, 138, 139, 144, 145, 150, 151, 247, 248
Aristotle, 92
arm, 50, 67, 110, 130, 131
armour, 168. *See also* byrnie; helmet; mail-coat; shield
army, 47, 50, 53, 84
arrow, 36, 47, 54–5, 64, 66, 75, 78, 79, 93, 96, 152, 184
artifice, 249
Assyrians, 165, 219, 237
auger, 167, 173, 196, 212, 228
axe, 143, 246

bachelor, 207, 230
back, 82, 130, 194
backside, in the, 226
bacteria, 93

364 Index

badger, 70, 93
bag, 207. *See also* scrotum
Baggins, Bilbo, 9
Bakhtin, Mikhail, 239
ballista, 95, 96, 97, 184
barrel, 164
barrow, 174
bath, 164, 248
Bath, 28
battle (literal), 19, 43, 45, 62, 82, 120, 123, 125, 130, 138–40, 157, 160, 161, 164–5, 224, 232
battle (metaphorical), 38, 65–6, 68, 70, 71, 76–8, 79, 103, 109–10, 116, 129, 130–1, 142–7, 148, 157, 247
Battle of Brunanburh, The, 140, 166, 237
Battle of Maldon, The, 25, 28, 31, 40, 42, 57, 65, 97, 106, 116, 134, 139, 142, 145, 159, 164, 165, 173, 174, 223, 229, 231, 232, 249
battlefield, 77, 140, 157, 165, 232
battle-standard, 149
Beadohild, 250
beaker, glass, 86, 94, 196
beauty, xv, 19, 24, 96, 101, 153, 155, 159, 160, 164, 184, 215, 220, 233, 236
Bede, 134, 135
Bede, Pseudo-, 247
beehive, 20, 62, 99, 100–3, 182, 183–5, 194, 224, 236
bee-keeper, 100
beer, 86, 243, 244
bellows, 150, 169, 174, 192, 196, 202, 207–8, 220, 221, 229
belly, 36, 93, 94, 100, 194, 207, 208
Benedictine Reform, 5, 148, 191, 197
benefit, 55, 145, 154, 159, 175, 178, 180, 182, 186
Beowulf, 28, 29, 30, 31, 32, 34, 40, 41, 42, 43, 48, 49, 50, 55, 76, 82, 85, 87, 90, 92, 94, 96, 98, 106, 126, 127, 131, 132, 134, 139, 140, 141, 144, 145, 148, 164, 165, 166, 168, 172, 173, 174, 180, 223, 224, 229, 231, 233, 237, 238,
Beowulf, 28, 30, 31, 40, 41, 43, 49, 50, 140, 165, 168, 172, 174, 223, 224, 229, 237, 238
Bern Riddles, The, 10, 11, 192; Enigma 5: *Mensa* "Table," 192; Enigma 8: *Ovum* "Egg," 192; Enigma 14: *Oliva* "Olive-Tree," 192; Enigma 19: *Cera* "Wax," 192; Enigma 29: *Speculum*, "Mirror," 192
Bestiary, The, 148
Bible, The, 148; 1 Corinthians, 171; Ephesians, 77; Genesis, 218, 231; Hebrews, 111; Luke, 114; Matthew, 112, 147, 164; Psalms, 116, 117, 121
bird, 50, 114, 192. *See also* chicken; cock; cuckoo; dove; hawk; hen; falcon; sea-bird
birth, 20, 188–9, 192–5, 207, 208, 209, 247
bishop, 87, 90, 197, 239
Blythburgh tablet, 145, 146
body, 46, 55, 94, 103, 105, 111, 112–14, 131, 143, 159, 171–2, 193, 194, 201, 203, 208, 219, 229, 239. *See also* arm; back; backside; belly; bone; bosom; brain; breast; chest; ear; eye; eyebrow; finger; foot; hand; innards; mouth; neck; nose; penis; scrotum; shoulder; sides; tail; vagina; womb
Boethius, 134
bone, 5, 88, 146, 204
Boniface, 11, 177
book, 5–6, 19, 131, 181–2. *See also* Gospel Book
bookcase (bookchest), 181, 182
borer, 221
bosom, 85, 86, 88, 208

Index 365

bottle, leather, 215, 236
bow, 18, 24, 35, 36, 46–8, 54, 61, 75, 93, 96, 160, 161, 162, 167, 173, 220
bowl, 67, 74, 75, 104
brain, 16, 46, 47
bread, 105, 178, 179, 183, 204, 205, 232
breast, 194, 208
British Library Cotton Tiberius B.i, 6
brooch, 167, 203, 221
broom, 73, 135
brother, 22, 80, 81, 82, 127, 223, 231, 250
buckle, 92, 203, 221
burial, 68, 87, 139
butter, 105, 199, 210, 221
Byrhtnoth, 28, 42, 65, 106, 173, 174, 229, 232, 249
byrnie, 156, 229. *See also* mail-coat

Cain, 223
Cambridge, Corpus Christi College, MS 383, 22
camouflage, 18, 60, 61–76, 79, 86, 101, 104, 108, 109, 128
Canons of Theodore, 106, 213, 231
captive, 133–5, 137
caress, 221, 233
carnivalesque, 239–40
celibacy, 15, 124, 207, 221, 246
censorship, 191
charm, 100, 247, 249
chest (part of the body), 208
chicken, 233
child, 51, 123, 124, 125, 126, 145, 188, 189, 192, 205, 207, 209, 210, 211, 212, 220, 246, 247
chopping block, 141, 142–4, 147, 149, 244, 249
Christ, 6, 77, 79, 87, 88, 92, 104, 107, 112, 129, 131, 147, 168, 171, 212, 248, 249
Christ and Satan, 24, 144, 249
Christ I, 24, 34, 41, 112

Christ II, vii, 34, 46, 49, 96, 111, 112
Christ III, 34, 218, 249
Christianity, 6, 76, 79, 88, 90, 106, 107, 113, 115, 116, 122, 123, 151, 191, 196, 197, 210, 211
churn, 150, 192, 196, 209, 210, 221, 229, 241
clapping, 125, 224
class, 20, 85, 134, 176, 181, 185, 190, 198, 212, 213, 228–30, 231–2, 232–8, 239–41, 249, 250
cock, 196, 221, 227, 234, 247
code, viii, 11, 17, 18, 23–6, 38–43, 44–8, 48–51, 52–8, 132, 185
cognitive linguistics, 12, 198, 210
coitus, 20, 189, 205, 211, 225, 226
Collectanea Pseudo-Bedae, 163, 171
colour, 87, 97, 98, 119, 179, 234
comitatus, 25, 84
community, 99, 123, 186, 191, 197, 230. *See also* religious community
companion, 26, 30, 54, 56, 62, 73, 75, 84, 87, 133–7, 196, 236
compound, 34, 94, 135, 141, 200, 218, 219, 235, 237
confinement, 200, 249
container, 82, 85, 86, 87, 94, 97, 194
corpse, 66
counteridentification, 14, 15, 104, 245
courage, 39, 42, 45, 53, 63, 83, 128, 130, 142, 167, 168, 173, 212, 229, 231, 232, 237, 245
craftsman, 154, 166, 224
craftsmanship, 27, 155
creation, 19, 74, 79, 80, 152, 155, 160, 164, 186, 192, 211
cross, 87, 88, 104, 115, 168, 244
cross-bow, 254
crucifix, 87, 236
crucifixion, 92
cuckoo, 22, 192, 194
cup, 36, 67, 74, 75, 224, 233, 236–7

cupping glass, 42
cutting board, 144, 147, 149, 244–5, 249
Cynewulf (the poet), vii, 146
Cyprian, *De Mortalitate*, 111

dagger, 42, 177
damage. *See* injury, manuscript damage, wound
Danes, 43, 132, 140, 165
darkness, 16, 52, 56, 74, 82, 87, 88, 94, 96–9, 108, 125, 128, 143
daughter, 69, 195, 220, 231, 232, 233, 240
day (as opposed to night), 54, 55, 94, 99, 140, 143, 144, 146, 147, 182, 184, 244, 245, 248
De Certeau, Michel, 151–2
De consolatione Philosophiae, 134
death, 36, 42, 43, 55, 77, 104, 106, 112, 121, 123, 145, 147, 160, 164–5, 174, 207, 220, 223, 226, 248
defamiliarisation, 115
demon, 111, 112, 113, 129
Deor, 132, 250
desire (non-sexual), 124, 152, 156, 168, 179, 181, 183, 185, 219, 239
desire (sexual), 85, 150, 197, 217, 218, 219, 227, 235, 236, 238, 239
devil, 4, 40, 112, 116, 129, 130, 146, 147, 170, 217, 218, 246. *See also* Satan
discourse, 12, 14–15, 19, 25, 119–20, 121, 123, 126, 145, 148, 149, 173, 235, 240, 241, 245, 251
disguise, 18, 33, 38, 60, 61–2, 76–83, 83–8, 89–103, 104, 108, 115, 117–18, 126, 131, 132, 134, 140, 159, 201
dish, 199, 215, 219
disidentification, 14, 245
doctor, 140, 147, 244, 248, 249
door, 94, 199
door-warden, 180
double bluff, 242

double entendre, 85, 155–6, 189–90, 199–201, 203, 204, 219, 221–2, 225, 227, 228, 232–7, 238, 241
dough, 178, 183, 196, 199, 204, 220
dove, 218
dragon, 90, 238
Dream of the Rood, The, 27, 53, 87, 104, 107, 115, 168
dressing (act of getting dressed), 199
drink, 28, 29, 32, 36, 66, 68, 85, 86, 87, 88, 121, 182, 214, 219, 221, 236, 237, 243
drunkenness, 86, 132, 213, 214, 215, 218, 219, 237
duty, 166, 171, 174, 175, 180

ear, 73, 119, 171, 194
earth, 20, 34, 85, 92, 106, 112, 123, 143, 147, 155, 156, 162, 182, 192, 194, 195, 211
earthquake, 116
earwig, 31
ecotheology, 164
effeminacy, 217
ejaculation, 207
elegy, 107, 128
Elene, 31, 40, 49, 92, 97, 144, 146
elf-shot, 93
emendation, 6–7, 46–7, 48, 51, 82, 83, 89, 110, 121, 133, 162, 225, 226, 235
enclosure, 90, 91, 139, 219
erection. *See* tumescence
ethnicity, 134, 135, 215
euphemism, 195, 199, 200, 211, 217, 225, 235, 236, 238
Eusebius, 10, 11, 177
Eve, 224
everyday, 5, 151, 152, 250
Exeter Dean and Chapter Manuscript 3501 (the Exeter Book), vii, 5–7, 9–10, 13, 16, 18, 20, 25, 33, 34, 35, 36, 40, 44, 46, 47–8,

Index   367

50–1, 52, 53, 59, 60, 75, 80–1, 82, 89, 103, 106, 110, 124–5, 126, 129, 133, 145, 151, 186, 191, 197, 205, 221, 225, 226, 241, 244, 251

Exeter Book Riddles:
Riddle 1: *Glorious I Thunder*, 86, 142
Riddle 2: *Under Waves' Pressure*, 142
Riddle 3: *No Escape*, 70, 142, 160, 194, 200
Riddle 4: *Periodically Busy*, 4, 16, 22, 72, 166, 169, 170, 173
Riddle 5: *Lone Dweller*, 19, 80, 107, 108, 138–49, 158–60, 180, 186, 244–50
Riddle 6: *I Burn the Living*, 62, 78, 79, 80, 92, 139
Riddle 9: *They Gave Me Up for Dead*, 22, 192, 194
Riddle 10: *Nose in Confinement*, 200
Riddle 11: *Dark-Stained*, 21, 111, 149
Riddle 12: *I Travel on Foot*, 16, 137, 155, 181, 196, 205, 213–15, 216, 219, 222, 230, 233, 236
Riddle 13: *Ten Brothers and Sisters*, 51, 19–2
Riddle 14: *Weapon-Warrior*, 24, 26–34, 35, 36, 49, 78, 85, 86, 92, 106, 116, 118, 120, 236
Riddle 15: *White Neck*, 70, 93, 200
Riddle 16: *Fight against Wave*, 19, 109, 110, 112–17, 117, 122, 128, 129, 148, 149, 250
Riddle 17: *Protector*, 18, 62, 89–103, 140, 166, 184, 194
Riddle 18: *Large Belly*, 94, 194, 202
Riddle 19: *Bright-Headed*, 11, 48–51, 52, 59, 90
Riddle 20: *Cursed among Weapons*, 15, 18, 19, 24, 37–8, 52, 59, 61, 92, 117–26, 137, 166, 191, 196, 202, 206–7, 212, 221–2, 224, 230, 233, 246, 249, 250
Riddle 21: *Downward Nose*, 86, 141, 151, 166, 170, 173, 202, 213

Riddle 22: *Peace-Horses*, 31, 49, 70, 229
Riddle 23: *Wob*, 18, 24, 35–8, 47, 54, 59, 61, 79, 93, 160, 164, 166, 167, 168, 173, 199, 202
Riddle 24: *Six Letters*, 11, 199, 202
Riddle 25: *Useful to Neighbours*, 150, 196, 199, 200–1, 202, 205, 220, 222, 230, 233, 241
Riddle 26: *Famous Name*, 19, 92, 154–5, 164, 180, 181, 186, 199
Riddle 27: *Binder and Scourger*, 19, 86, 163–4, 183–4, 229
Riddle 28: *Hardest and Sharpest*, 16, 154–5, 180, 194
Riddle 29: *Air-Vessel*, 51, 71, 202
Riddle 30: *Flame-Busy*, 87, 224, 235, 236
Riddle 31: *Eager to Go*, 202
Riddle 32: *Grind against Grit*, 49, 51, 202
Riddle 33: *Terrible Laughter*, 18, 62, 69–71, 160, 191, 194, 195, 202, 209
Riddle 34: *Feeds Cattle*, 51, 141, 202
Riddle 35: *Hopeful Garment*, 24, 156–8, 191, 193, 194, 195
Riddle 36: *Man Woman Horse*, 49, 51, 105, 194, 202
Riddle 37: *Belly Behind*, 51, 166, 169, 173, 192, 194, 195, 196, 202, 206, 207–8, 212, 213, 220, 227, 229, 230, 232
Riddle 38: *Greedy for Youth-Mirth*, 51, 105, 202
Riddle 39: *Most Wretched of All*, 16, 192, 193, 195, 202, 244
Riddle 40: *Circle of the Earth*, 92, 192, 193, 194
Riddle 41: *Mother of Many Races*, 194, 202
Riddle 42: *Two Proud Ones*, 11, 51, 196, 202, 205, 221, 222, 227, 233, 240–2, 247

Riddle 43: *Guest in the Enclosures*, 103, 113, 166, 229
Riddle 44: *Hanging Head*, 150, 196, 199, 202, 205, 213, 220, 224, 229, 230, 250
Riddle 45: *Boneless*, 141, 196, 199, 200, 203, 204, 220, 222, 230, 232
Riddle 46: *A Man Sat at Wine*, 90, 105, 230–1
Riddle 47: *Moth*, 180
Riddle 49: *Earth-Fast*, 20, 133, 166, 177–85, 186, 193, 224
Riddle 50: *Bright Warrior*, 20, 175–6, 192, 193, 195, 240, 250
Riddle 51: *Four Creatures*, 19, 51, 83, 108, 126–33, 141, 145, 146, 202
Riddle 52: *Captives*, 15, 19, 72, 133–7, 145, 181, 200
Riddle 53: *Towering Tree*, 18, 24, 27, 52–8, 59, 60, 71–5, 87, 89, 95, 103, 104, 116, 127, 133, 152, 161, 164, 180, 200
Riddle 54: *In a Corner*, 141, 150, 192, 196, 199, 200, 206, 209, 210, 212, 221, 224, 225–6, 229, 230, 232, 240
Riddle 56: *Turning Wood*, 18, 62, 63–8, 69, 71, 79, 103, 152, 157, 202
Riddle 57: *Abounding in Song*, 92, 180, 202
Riddle 58: *One-Footed*, 18, 62, 63–4, 72, 79, 130, 166–7, 173
Riddle 59: *Golden Ring*, 105, 180, 237
Riddle 60: *Mouthless by Sand*, 153, 180, 224
Riddle 61: *Head Stuck In*, 196, 199, 200, 205, 212, 220, 222, 229, 230, 232, 233, 240
Riddle 62: *Strong Going In/Out*, 166, 167, 173, 186, 196, 200, 201, 212, 213, 221, 226–7, 228–9, 230, 232
Riddle 63: *Shining with Gold*, 86, 94, 196, 205, 221, 224, 229, 230, 233

Riddle 64: *Joy and Ice*, 11, 49, 90
Riddle 67: *Word-Spell*, 176, 202
Riddle 68: *Creature Went Away*, 202
Riddle 69: *Wonder on the Way*, 4
Riddle 70: *Sings through Its Sides*, 202
Riddle 71: *Clothed in Red*, 24, 38–43, 45, 48, 52, 59, 60, 89, 200
Riddle 72: *Boundary Paths*, 181
Riddle 73: *Brain-Locker*, 24, 44–8, 52, 54, 89, 95, 161, 166
Riddle 80: *Warrior's Companion*, 24, 30–1, 49, 62, 83–8, 92, 196, 212, 221, 222, 230, 233, 234
Riddle 81: *Puff-Breasted*, 194
Riddle 83: *Old Ancestry*, 162–3, 164
Riddle 84: *Mother of Many*, 192, 193, 200, 202
Riddle 86: *Twelve Hundred Heads*, 90, 142, 194, 202, 224
Riddle 87: *Barked, Wavered*, 166, 169, 173, 180, 194, 196, 202–3, 212, 213, 227
Riddle 88: *Brotherless*, 80–3, 89, 127, 133, 134, 139, 180, 194
Riddle 89: *The Creature Had a Belly*, 194, 196, 202, 203, 213, 221, 227
Riddle 91: *Forged by Hammer*, 152, 155, 158, 166–7, 173, 180, 196, 203, 205, 221, 227, 230, 249
Riddle 93: *Younger Brother*, 22, 71, 83, 180, 194, 200
Riddle 95: *Hide My Track*, 90
Exhortation to Christian Living, 144
exile, vii, 32, 34, 80, 82, 112, 134, 238
Exodus, 40, 112, 143, 249
expectation, 8–9, 11, 13, 15, 17, 20, 25, 37, 51, 115, 134, 158, 159, 167–9, 173, 189, 196, 198, 216, 228, 238, 241, 249
extramission, 51
eye, 51, 63, 104, 171, 172, 183, 194, 201, 205, 207, 220, 247
eyebrow, 204

fabliaux, 248
falcon, 85
family, 90, 105, 231
farmer, 238
father, 42, 192, 194, 195, 209, 210, 230, 246
feast, 30, 140, 165, 218, 219, 237
femininity, 41, 111, 184, 185, 193, 202
fermentation, 205
feud, 32, 34, 86, 165, 166
finger, 40, 88, 128, 129, 130
Finn, 165
Finnish riddles, 10
Finnsburg, 43
fire, 20, 38–9, 40, 140, 141, 143, 144, 162, 175–6, 183, 192, 195, 205, 213, 245, 250
flail, 4, 72–5, 95, 103, 104, 127, 135–6
flint, 195
flock, 91, 129
folklore riddles, 5, 10, 14
food, 145, 244
foot, 63, 67, 68, 163, 172, 184, 194
foot-treadle, 74
forest, 81
forge, 95, 96
formula, 11, 143–4
formula, closing, 33, 37, 78
formula, opening, 51, 78, 134
fortification, 46, 47, 53, 139, 140
fortress, 46, 47, 78, 95, 96, 114, 230
Foucault, 119, 148, 149, 173
fox, 70, 93, 248
freeman, 220, 233
Freud, Sigmund, 197, 254

gal, 217–19, 237
gallows, 55–8, 75, 104, 127
game, viii, 8, 20, 21, 33, 47, 59, 96, 108, 122, 156, 198, 207, 221, 222, 226, 227, 245
Gargantua and Pantagruel, 248

garlic-seller. 90
garment, 66
gender, 41, 134, 213, 214, 215, 228–32, 232–8
gender, grammatical, 47, 184, 202
generosity, 23, 107, 119, 173–4, 176
Genesis A, 28, 32, 40, 49, 87, 97, 107, 166, 218, 223
Genesis B, 32, 168, 218, 223
genre, 3, 5, 7, 8, 13, 14, 28, 59, 78, 90, 190, 191
giant, 223
gift, 32, 39, 40, 42, 84, 123, 167, 172, 174, 179, 180, 182, 183, 185, 223, 224, 237
Gifts of Men, 31
God, 28, 34, 80, 90, 107, 116, 129, 131, 154, 168, 172, 174, 189, 211, 218, 223, 224, 249
gold, 28, 31, 39–42, 49, 61, 97, 121, 124, 129, 162, 163, 164, 178, 179, 181, 182, 184, 185, 205, 233, 237
gospel, 77
Gospel book, 154, 159, 164
grain, 72, 73, 183
Grendel, 32, 165, 168, 238
Grendel's mother, 28, 41, 224
grove, 85, 86, 88
guilt, 146–7, 244, 245
Guthlac, 113
Guthlac, vii, 34, 49, 144, 234

hair, 16, 85, 181, 196, 201, 213, 233, 234
hall, 27, 32, 37, 40, 64, 66, 67, 84, 85, 86, 94, 121, 123, 134, 135, 140, 212
hand, 77, 85, 102, 110, 112, 129, 131, 153, 165, 171, 172, 181, 184, 204, 205, 212, 219, 221, 222, 223–8, 233, 237
handle, 73, 127, 135, 136
hapax legomena, 34, 53, 89, 94, 214
hawk, 50, 85, 90, 117, 121

head, 49, 50, 54–6, 64, 73, 74, 82, 140, 155, 161, 167, 171, 172, 194, 201, 205, 219, 224, 247
healing. *See* medicine
heanmode, 234–5
Hebrews, 165, 224
hedgehog, 70, 93
Heliand, The, 237
hell, 55, 57, 113, 147
helmet, 40, 42, 77, 92, 196, 229
hen, 196, 221, 227, 234, 247
herb, 144, 145, 147
herd, 91, 93, 99
heroic idiom, 12, 17–19, 23–60, 61–104, 106–10, 115–22, 126, 128–33, 134–5, 137, 140, 145, 148–9, 157, 240
hierarchy, 15, 19, 20, 100, 152, 166–9, 174–7, 178–80, 187, 190
Higelac, 30, 31, 168, 224, 238
Hildeburh, 43, 165
hill, 86
hilt, 223
Hnæf, 165
hoard, 29, 53–7, 59, 72–3, 74, 91, 93, 94, 96, 99, 111, 155, 161, 184
Holofernes, 219, 224, 237
homeland, 109, 113, 115
Homiletic Fragment I, 102, 144
homily, 135, 147, 172, 214, 215
honey, 99–102, 164, 182, 183, 184–5
horn, 24, 26–9, 31–4, 61–2, 82, 85–7, 88, 196, 236, 243–4
horse, 26, 28, 30–2, 48–51, 70, 71, 84, 85, 88, 90, 98, 185
Hrethel, 42, 165, 166
Hrothgar, 30, 32, 40, 41, 42, 43, 49, 127, 140, 223, 237
humour, 14, 56, 57, 101, 106, 127, 128, 131, 132, 141, 145, 217, 239–40, 250
hunting, 50, 90
husband, 125, 204, 212, 248
Husband's Message, The, 49

Hygd, 30, 41
hygegal, 214, 216–20

ice, 18, 20, 62, 69–70, 71, 112, 160, 191, 192, 195, 209
identification (as opposed to disidentification), 14–16, 104, 245
ideology, 14–15, 20, 23, 25, 137, 151, 169–74, 245, 251
implement trope, viii, 12, 19–20, 64, 66, 84, 93, 100, 118, 152, 166–77, 178–80, 182–3, 185, 186, 208, 240
inaction, 115–17, 168. *See also* stasis
incongruity, 3, 57, 61, 64, 78, 82, 92, 94, 96–7, 113, 128, 130–2, 134–5, 137, 139–44, 146, 153, 168, 170, 176, 239, 240, 241, 247
index (i.e., type of sign), 10, 27, 84, 86
indoors, 65, 68, 103, 121, 136, 144, 245, 247
ingenuity, 4, 8, 19, 152–4, 160, 164, 166
injury, 36, 45, 93, 121, 138, 140, 144, 145, 159, 161, 194, 218, 250
inkhorn, 62
innards, 82, 94, 156, 181, 194, 208
inner click, 13, 20, 47, 53, 58, 89, 99, 103, 110, 114, 179, 251
insect, 31
iron, 143, 145, 192, 194. *See also* metal
irony, 19, 29, 64, 105–8, 126–33, 134, 137, 139–43, 145, 161, 181, 249
Isidore, 36

jewellery, 92
joke, vii, 19, 51, 127, 132, 133, 141–2, 150, 242
Judith, 40, 41, 96, 142, 165, 166, 219, 224, 235, 237, 250
Judith, 219, 224, 250
Juliana, 40, 78, 90, 111, 114, 217, 234, Juliana, 217

kenning, 31, 34, 49, 117,
key, 150, 155, 166, 167, 173, 196, 203, 221, 241, 242, 250
keyhole, 167, 203, 221, 242, 250
king, 77, 84, 85, 87, 88, 90, 119, 121, 127, 165, 166, 167, 170–1, 176, 178, 179, 181, 223. *See also* lord
kissing, 29, 33, 86, 205, 224, 233, 236

labour, 65, 67, 129, 146, 153, 154, 160, 176, 190, 222–4, 225, 227, 232, 241
lady. *See* noble woman
Lamech, 223
laughter, 42, 70, 142, 160, 176, 217
laws, 31, 54, 55, 114, 121, 150, 164, 165, 185, 210, 211, 212
leather, 155, 215, 219, 236
Leoba, 243
librarian, 181, 182
lighthouse, 51
lion, 102, 248
literacy, 10, 20, 83, 128, 180–1, 182, 185, 193. *See also* writing
litotes, 42, 106
loom, 18, 62, 65, 66, 68, 136–7, 156, 157. *See also* weaving
loom-weights, 136–7
lord, viii, 20, 24, 39, 40, 42, 43, 47, 64, 66, 67, 71, 78, 84, 87, 90, 93, 94, 100, 101, 106, 107, 109, 115, 118, 123, 124, 126, 130, 155, 164–5, 166–76, 177, 180, 185, 186, 187, 216, 220, 221, 229, 230, 232, 240,
lord-thegn relationship, viii, 20, 24, 84, 100, 118, 123, 164–5, 166–76, 177, 180, 186, 187
Lord's Prayer II, 144, 249
Lorsch Riddles, 10, 11
Lot, 90, 223, 231

loyalty, 24, 28, 32, 62, 82, 83, 84, 106, 109, 118, 119, 122, 123, 128, 137, 167, 168, 171, 173, 174, 180, 212
lyric, 80, 82

maiden, 196
Maignien qui foti la dame, La, 248
mail-coat, 24, 38, 40, 157, 191, 192
man, 29, 42, 50, 53, 54, 55, 80, 100, 117, 119, 132, 134, 157, 160, 169, 174, 175, 188–9, 201, 205, 207, 209, 211, 213, 216, 218, 220, 221, 225, 227, 228–32, 236, 249. *See also* bachelor; brother; father; king; lord; noble man; servant; slave; southern man; thegn; warrior; youth (male)
Mankind, 112
manufacturing, 12, 19, 20, 27, 38, 59, 65, 73, 83, 152–9, 160–4, 166, 176, 180, 186, 189, 195, 220, 249
manuscript. *See* British Library Cotton Tiberius B.i; Cambridge, Corpus Christi College, MS 383; Exeter Dean and Chapter Manuscript 3501
manuscript damage, 9, 22, 25, 38, 39, 48, 53, 59, 80, 81, 82, 89, 126, 205
marriage, 43, 125, 126, 217, 220
Martyrology, The, 31
masculinity, 41, 47, 60, 110, 111, 122, 184, 212, 226, 228, 232
master, 167, 169, 170. *See also* lord
masturbation, 203, 205, 207, 210, 213, 215, 216, 217, 219, 232
material culture, 53, 58, 75, 78, 83, 89, 102, 118, 150, 199
Matthew (the apostle), 77, 78
maxim, 7, 27, 81, 189, 238
Maxims I, 41, 188–90, 195, 207, 238, 249
Maxims II, 6–8, 13, 97

mead, 19, 86, 101, 164, 182, 183, 185, 219, 229, 237
mead hall. *See* hall
meat, 179
medicine, 79, 93, 140, 145, 147, 244, 247, 248, 249
metal, 20, 38, 39, 65, 66, 74, 88, 92, 98, 146, 152, 195. *See also* gold; iron
metaphor, 12, 18, 29, 33, 36, 38, 40, 46, 50, 51, 55, 59, 62, 66, 70–1, 78, 79, 83, 89, 91–6, 99, 101, 111, 112, 114, 115, 117, 118, 126, 130, 132, 146, 147, 148, 159, 166, 168, 175, 186, 190–1, 193–5, 196, 198–9, 201, 203, 205, 207, 208, 209, 210, 215, 222, 233, 242, 246, 250
Meters of Boethius, 49, 143, 170, 173
metonymy, 5, 24, 42, 139
microcosm, 26, 32, 33
miles Christi, 129, 131
milk, 5
mill, 4, 179
millpond, 179, 183
millstone, 4, 170
mind, 102, 147, 218, 219, 221, 229, 234–5
mining, 162
misogyny, 137, 232
mock heroic, 126–37, 142–8
mock riddle, 51
mode. *See* trope
monasticism, 10, 15, 34
monk, 113, 117, 148, 217
monster, 15, 40, 82, 164, 238
moon, 71, 192, 193
moral regulation, 34, 85, 196–7, 211–12, 213
mother, 28, 41, 69, 194, 195, 209, 224
mountain, 86
mourning, 41, 42, 83, 125, 221, 224
mouth, 86, 94, 95, 102, 172, 178, 182, 183, 184
music, 29–30, 85, 86

narrowness. *See* nearness
nathwær, 200, 201, 227
nathwæt, 200
nearness, 54, 55, 65, 67, 68, 73, 74, 119, 120, 146, 200, 227
neck, 45, 47, 130, 194
nectar, 86, 183, 185
Newton, Isaac, 164
night, 16, 81, 140, 143–4, 146, 147, 221, 244, 245, 248
Noah's ark, 218
nobility, 20, 84, 85, 87, 119, 137, 176, 179, 180, 185, 229, 230, 231, 234, 235, 236, 238, 239, 240, 241
noble equipment, 28, 91, 92
noble man, 15, 31, 85, 101, 114, 122, 134, 135, 137, 175, 176, 182, 184, 212, 220, 229–30, 231, 232, 232, 236
noble woman, 28, 31–2, 41, 43, 84, 85, 88, 101, 136, 182, 184, 205, 220, 221, 231, 232, 233, 234, 236, 240, 248, 249
noise. *See* sound
nose, 96, 194, 203

obligation, 27, 28, 57, 168, 171, 173–4, 176, 180
ofermod, 106, 174
Offa, 164, 174
offspring, 20, 123, 189, 190, 191, 192, 193, 194, 195, 205, 206–7, 210, 213, 215, 216, 220, 222, 225, 239
Onela, 165
Ongentheow, 238
onion, 151, 196, 199, 201, 205, 220, 241
ore, 164
ornamentation, 24, 28, 30, 38, 43, 49, 74, 87, 92, 96, 104, 125, 129
outdoors, 205, 247
oven, 95, 96, 178–9, 183, 205
ox, 135, 136, 155, 196, 214, 236
ox-herd, 136
ox-hide, 215, 236

Index 373

pacifism, 27, 166
pain, 74, 94, 97, 127, 139, 152, 155, 161. *See also* suffering; torture
paradox, 3, 15, 19, 69, 70, 105, 110, 112, 116, 122, 139, 159, 176, 195, 209
Paris Psalter, The, 96, 97, 116, 144
parturition. *See* birth
Pater Noster, 129, 249
pathos, 152
pen, quill-pen, 4, 96, 103, 128, 129, 132, 133, 170, 182
penance, 88, 106, 122, 147, 213, 214, 231
penis, 117, 201, 203, 204, 205, 207, 208, 220, 221, 228, 241, 243, 246, 247, 248, 249
phallus, 4, 117, 246, 254. *See also* penis
physician. *See* doctor
Physics, Third Law of, 164
play, 17, 20, 59, 60, 86, 88, 107, 108, 124, 141, 191, 202, 208, 212, 217, 220, 221, 222, 240, 242, 245, 249, 250, 253
pleasure, 20, 29, 30, 32, 84, 124, 126, 153, 166, 180, 190, 197, 198, 215–17, 219–22, 241, 250
plough, 151, 170, 174, 202
ploughing, 136, 145, 202, 214
ploughman, 136, 202
ploughshare, 74
plough-team, 4
poetic diction, 24, 25, 33, 34, 42, 50, 53, 59, 62, 71, 76–8, 79, 94, 116, 135, 144, 148, 229, 237
pole-lathe, 18, 62, 66–8, 74–5, 103, 104
pollen, 185
Pope, Alexander, 131, 142
porcupine, 70, 93
prayer, 34, 88, 106, 112, 113
Prayer, A, 144, 249
Prefatio Genesis Anglice, 231
pregnancy, 206, 209, 247, 250

pride, 20, 49, 96, 149, 176, 201, 222, 228–32, 232–8, 250
procreation, 189, 207
prosopopoeia, 24, 152
prostitute, 90
pun. *See* wordplay

queen, 41, 85, 86, 178, 179, 181, 233
queer theory, 14–16, 245
queerness, 13, 16, 19, 68, 245, 250, 251
quill-pen. *See* pen
quiver, 94, 95, 96, 97

Rabelais, François, 239, 248
racism, 85, 135, 137, 213, 234
ram, battering, 24, 44, 47, 52, 53, 54, 55, 58, 59, 75, 95, 103, 104, 161
rank, 85, 178, 233, 236
Rape of the Lock, The, 131, 142
reciprocity, 20, 171, 172, 173, 175
relic, 88, 92, 243
religious community, 34, 148, 191, 197
reliquary, 88
reproduction, 12, 20, 187, 188–95, 197, 198, 203, 208, 209, 211, 213, 241
revenge, 19, 106, 120, 123, 160, 161, 163, 165, 166, 168, 174, 207, 220, 232, 248
riddle, definition of, 8
Riming Poem, The, 30, 31, 32, 49, 86
ring, 40, 41, 42, 43
Ruin, The, 28–9, 86, 92
Rune Poem, The, 30, 31, 49
runic letter, vii, viii, 9, 11, 25, 48–51, 53, 59, 64, 80, 99, 110, 147, 221, 233, 249

Saineresse, La, 248
saint, 76, 88, 90, 92, 217, 219
Samson, 102
Satan, 168, 223. *See also* devil
scabbard, 38, 85, 250

scribe, vii, 6, 7, 9, 10, 19, 21, 36, 44, 47, 50, 52, 53, 84, 99, 129–33, 181
scriptorium, 117, 128, 133, 146, 181
scrotum, 207
sea, 28, 31, 40, 51, 71, 109, 110, 112, 114, 174
sea-bird, 114, 147
Seafarer, The, vii, 32, 86, 111, 112, 114, 147, 218
sea-horse, 31, 49, 50, 51
season, 6, 82, 88, 100
Seasons for Fasting, 31
seed, 145
semen, 201, 207, 221
semiotics, 27, 39, 59, 112
sermon, 147, 171, 173, 175
servant, viii, 20, 62, 118, 166, 167, 169, 170, 172, 173, 175, 176, 178, 179, 180, 182, 183, 186, 214, 224, 225. *See also* slave; thegn
service, 28, 64, 123, 166, 169, 171, 173–4, 180, 200, 215
sex, 15, 16, 20, 108, 124, 126, 150, 187, 188–242, 246, 247–8, 249–50
shame, 20, 211–12, 214, 232, 233, 234, 241
shepherd, 91
shield, 42, 77, 107, 110, 139–43, 144, 146, 147, 149, 244, 245, 249, 250
shield-wall, 70
shininess, 97–8
ship, 31, 40, 48–51, 61, 70, 92, 111, 160, 237
shoes, 236
shoulder, 45, 130
sides, 45, 194
siege engine, 95, 184
silver, 31, 87, 124
sin, 104, 121, 122, 147, 164, 196, 197, 198, 210, 212–13, 215, 216, 217, 240, 241
slave, 15, 134–6, 137, 163, 167, 205, 213, 214, 216, 219, 221, 229, 233, 236

slavery, 163, 167, 190
sluice, 179, 183
soð, viii, 6–7, 22, 24, 244, 250
Sodom and Gomorrah, 218, 223, 231
soldier. *See* warrior
Solomon and Saturn I, 31, 40, 129–30, 249
Solomon and Saturn II, 181, 218
son, 42, 123, 165, 174, 195, 209, 223, 231
sorrow, 32, 43, 83, 86, 165, 166, 250
soul, 46, 103, 110–13, 114, 143, 147, 149, 160, 229, 244, 245
sound, 32, 127, 157, 218
southern man, 221, 226, 227
spear, 24, 40, 44, 46, 47–8, 50, 54, 55, 65, 75, 85, 93–100, 101, 103, 140, 148, 161, 162, 184, 194
speech, 95, 105, 167, 181, 182
Springmount Bog Tablets, 146
stag, 71, 82
stasis, 115–16, 122, 149
steel, 195
stone, 40, 112, 113, 114, 116, 136, 144. *See also* millstone; whetstone
stylus, 145
suffering, 19, 21, 43, 59, 82, 130, 144, 146, 152, 153, 158–9, 160, 161, 169, 172, 186, 213, 220, 245, 248
sun, 4, 45, 51, 62, 71, 78–80, 140, 144
Sutton Hoo, 68, 87, 92
swarm, 100–1
swelling. *See* tumescence
sword, 4, 15, 18, 19, 24, 27, 28, 37–8, 40–3, 61, 70, 74, 85, 92, 98, 110, 117–22, 125–6, 139–40, 142, 143, 144, 146, 148, 157, 164, 168, 191, 192, 196, 207, 221, 223, 227, 244, 246, 247, 249–50
sympathy, 19, 83, 139, 152, 153, 154, 155, 166, 250
Symphosius, 10, 11, 111, 115, 142, 177, 192; Enigma 6: *Tegula* "Tile,"

192; Enigma 7: *Fumus* "Smoke,"
192; Enigma 14: *Pullus in Ovo*
"Chick in Egg," 192; Enigma
15: *Vipera* "Viper," 192; Enigma
19: *Cera* "Wax," 192; Enigma 29:
Phoenix "Phoenix," 192; Enigma
35: *Capra* "Nanny Goat," 192;
Enigma 36: *Porcus* "Pig," 192;
Enigma 37: *Mula* "Mule," 192;
Enigma 38: *Tigris* "Tiger," 192;
Enigma 48: *Murra* "Myrrh," 192;
Enigma 49: *Ebur* "Ivory," 192;
Enigma 81: *Lagena* "Flask," 192;
Enigma 92: *Mulier quae Geminos Pariebat*, 192
synecdoche, 24, 114, 131

tail, 64, 102, 110, 112, 114, 194, 248
Taplow, 87
Tatwine, 10, 11, 177
tears, 40, 41, 42, 60, 220
thegn, 23, 24, 40, 42, 43, 80, 84, 118, 122, 165, 167, 168–70, 173–5, 178, 180, 181–2, 185, 187, 207–8, 230, 240
thief, 55–8, 114, 127
thing (as defined by Thing Theory), 13–14, 18, 19, 36, 40, 51, 63, 93, 104, 151, 160, 203, 205, 228, 232
Thing-theory, 13, 14, 15, 151
third term, 15, 104, 245, 251
threshing, 72, 73, 136
tongue, 64, 86, 88, 129
tool, viii, 20, 54, 62, 66, 67, 72, 82, 104, 145, 157, 158, 159, 164, 166, 169–71, 185, 186, 208, 246
torture, 62, 73, 104, 160, 161, 164, 195, 220, 249
Tower of Babel, 223
tracks, 7, 21, 79, 82, 83, 108, 128, 129, 180, 181, 241, 251
trade, 31, 134

travel, 28, 31, 32, 50, 51, 95, 136, 226
treasure, 18, 28, 29, 30, 31, 32, 37, 38, 43, 49, 70, 73, 90, 91–2, 94–6, 99, 101, 102, 111, 114, 118–19, 121, 122, 123, 124, 125, 129, 179, 182, 221
tree, 27, 44, 46, 53, 54, 55, 57, 59, 65, 66, 67, 68, 74, 79, 86, 88, 152
trope, 12, 14, 24, 84, 151, 152–4, 156, 159, 164, 166, 176, 177, 179–80, 187, 220
truth, viii, 3, 6–8, 13, 22, 23, 85, 103, 146, 149, 188, 240
tumescence, 200, 201, 204, 207, 208, 232, 249

Unferth, 132, 238
Ursa Major, 70
usefulness, 64, 144, 153, 168, 176, 178, 179, 180, 181, 182, 183, 185, 200, 201, 226, 249
utopia, 32, 33, 85

vagina, 201, 203, 204, 207, 247–50
Vainglory, 34, 218, 234
valley, 86
value, 19, 33, 42–3, 78, 82, 83, 104, 106–8, 118–24, 126, 127–9, 130, 133, 137, 140, 145, 148–9, 151, 153–5, 158, 159, 160, 161, 163–6, 176–7, 180–1, 183–5, 207, 214, 228, 240, 241
vengeance. *See* revenge
veteran, 139, 245
vice, 106, 116
victim, 19, 55, 66, 79, 139, 154, 161, 162, 201, 220, 244, 246, 250
Vikings, 42, 65, 164, 232
violence, 19, 42, 71, 118–22, 125, 130, 146, 152–3, 158–9, 160–6, 186, 190, 220, 249, 250
Virgin Mary, 41, 189, 208
virtue, 92, 106, 112, 114, 115, 119, 122

virus, 93
Vision of the Monk of Wenlock, The, 113
voice, 14, 19, 55, 86, 90, 95, 105, 125, 159, 161, 180, 181

Waldere, 28, 40, 43
Wanderer, The, vii, 32, 34, 40, 80, 82, 90, 111
warrior, 48, 50, 53–6, 58, 59, 74, 79, 138, 139, 148
washing up, 199, 215, 219
water, 5, 20, 62, 64, 69, 74, 75, 79, 111, 128, 135, 179, 183, 192, 195, 204, 209. *See also* sea
Wealhtheow, 31, 41, 224, 233
wealth, 28, 30, 31, 35, 164, 183, 232, 235
weapon, 93, 97, 98, 100, 184. *See also* arrow; axe; bow; sword; dart; spear
weasel, 70, 93
weaving, 62, 65, 68, 71, 136–7, 156–7, 158
weeping. *See* tears
Weland, 43
well, 62, 64, 135, 136
well-beam or well-sweep, 18, 61, 62, 64, 128, 167, 173
Welsh, 16, 134, 135, 136, 137, 181, 205, 213, 216, 236
whetstone, 144, 147, 149, 244–5, 249
wife, 85, 102, 212, 229, 233, 248
Wiglaf, 174
wind, 6, 50, 110, 111, 113, 114, 194
wine, 28, 29, 86, 149, 179, 218, 236, 237
wine-jug, 94
winter, 6, 100

wisdom, 17, 82, 101, 112, 181, 218, 224, 237–8
wisdom literature, 79
wlanc, 31, 200, 234–7, 238. *See also* pride
woman, 16, 28, 31, 41, 43, 84, 85, 123–5, 126, 134, 175, 188–9, 201, 204–5, 209, 211, 213, 216, 219, 220, 222, 224, 225, 227, 232, 233, 234, 236, 242, 247, 248, 249, 250. *See also* daughter; maiden; mother; noble woman; servant; slave; wife; youth (female)
womb, 94, 95, 184, 194, 207, 208
wonder, 5, 14, 104, 105, 145, 153, 180, 192, 195, 220, 223
wood, 44, 45, 46, 53, 54, 55, 56, 65, 66–7, 68, 71, 72, 73, 74, 75, 86, 87, 104, 140, 141, 143, 146, 151, 152, 236, 244
wood-turning, 66–8, 74–5, 104. *See also* pole-lathe
word-play, 36, 91, 99, 113, 179
work, x, 5, 13, 20, 36, 48, 51, 52, 56, 62, 66, 67, 75, 86, 101, 104, 131, 143, 144, 145, 148–9, 151, 157, 164, 167, 171, 172, 197, 222–8, 229, 241, 247, 249
wound, 65, 68, 157
writing, 19, 51, 52, 83, 128–31, 141, 145–6, 180–1, 182
writing stylus, 145–6, 246
writing tablet, 145–6, 149, 244, 245, 249
Wulf and Eadwacer, 132, 250

youth (female), 234
youth (male), 80, 163, 229–30

www.ingramcontent.com/pod-product-compliance
Ingram Content Group UK Ltd.
Pitfield, Milton Keynes, MK11 3LW, UK
UKHW042156260125
454147UK00002B/9/J